D1557554

MICHAEL BAKUNIN

MICHAEL BAKUNIN

Roots of Apocalypse

Arthur P. Mendel

PRAEGER

PRAEGER SPECIAL STUDIES • PRAEGER SCIENTIFIC

Library of Congress Cataloging in Publication Data

Mendel, Arthur P.
    Michael Bakunin: roots of apocalypse.

    Bibliography: p.
    Includes index.
    1. Bakunin, Mikhail Aleksandrovich, 1814–1876.
2. Anarchism and anarchists—Soviet Union—Biography
I.Title.
HX915.B3M45   335′.83′0924 [B]   81-5168
ISBN 0-03-059218-6   AACR2

Published in 1981 by Praeger Publishers
CBS Educational and Professional Publishing
A Division of CBS, Inc.
521 Fifth Avenue, New York, New York 10175 U.S.A.

23456789 052 98765432

Printed in the United States of America

For Sara and our children, Ruth, Aaron,
Matthew, Joanna, and Aliza

CONTENTS

"Do not think that I have come to bring peace on earth; I have not come to bring peace, but a sword. For I have come to set a man against his father, and a daughter against her mother, and a daughter-in-law against her mother-in-law; and man's foes will be those of his own household...."

(Matthew 10:34-36)

So it will be at the close of the age. The angels will come out and separate the evil from the righteous, and throw them into the furnace of fire; there men will weep and gnash their teeth.

(Matthew 13:49-50)

And when you hear of wars and rumors of wars, do not be alarmed; this must take place, but the end is not yet. For nation will rise against nation, and kingdom against kingdom; there will be earthquakes in various places, there will be famines; this is but the beginning of the sufferings.

(Mark 13:7-8)

And brother will deliver up brother to death, and the father his child, and children will rise against parents and have them put to death; and you will be hated by all for my name's sake. But he who endures to the end will be saved.

(Mark 13:12-13)

He is clad in a robe dipped in blood, and the name by which he is called is The Word of God. And the armies of heaven, arrayed in fine linen, white and pure, followed him on white horses. From his mouth issues a sharp sword with which to smite the nations, and he will rule them with a rod of iron; he will tread the wine press of the fury of the wrath of God the Almighty. On his robe and on his thigh he has a name inscribed, King of kings and Lord of lords.

Then I saw an angel standing in the sun, and with a loud voice he called to all the birds that fly in mid-heaven, "Come, gather for the great supper of God, to eat the flesh of kings, and flesh of captains, the flesh of mighty men, the flesh of horses and their riders, and the flesh of all men, both free and slave, both small and great." And I saw the beast and the kings of the earth with their armies gathered to make war against him who sits upon the horse and against his army. And the beast was captured, and with it the false prophet who in its presence had worked the signs by which he deceived those who had received the mark of the beast and those who worshiped its image. These two were thrown alive into the lake of fire that burns with brimstone. And the rest were slain by the sword of him who sits upon the horse, the sword that issues from his mouth; and all the birds were gorged with their flesh.

(Revelations 13:21)

Keshab (with a smile): "Describe to us, sir, in how many ways Kali, the Divine Mother, sports in the world."

Sri Ramakrishna (also with a smile): "Oh, She plays in different ways.... She is the Dispenser of boons and the Dispeller of fear. People worship Raksa Kali, the Protectress, in times of epidemic, famine, earthquake, drought, and flood. Smasana Kali is the embodiment of the power of destruction. She resides in the cremation ground, surrounded by corpses, jackals, and terrible female spirits. From Her mouth flows a stream of blood, from Her neck hangs a garland of human heads, and around Her waist is a girdle made of human hands. After the destruction of the universe, at the end of a great cycle, the Divine Mother garners the seeds for the next creation.

(H. Zimmer, *Philosophies of India,* pp. 565-66)

INTRODUCTION

I began this book because I thought that the only full biography of Michael Bakunin available in English, E.H. Carr's, did not take seriously enough Bakunin's contribution to freedom. I finished the book convinced that neither the Carr biography nor other works on Bakunin take seriously enough his *threat* to freedom. While I continued to share a widespread admiration for Bakunin's eloquent defense of individual and communal liberty and his prophetic critique of state socialism, it became increasingly obvious to me that there was another side to Bakunin's life and work that favored rigid authoritarianism as vigorously as his familiar theories and pronouncements favor limitless freedom, that, in fact, the "freedom" itself was, dialectically, an integral part of the authoritarianism. It also became apparent that the reasons for this radical contradiction lay within the man himself and that his anarchist, antinomian freedom was born not of the heroic strength and courage it seems to reflect, but rather of weakness, fear, and flight.

Besides changing my mind about Bakunin's "freedom," I changed my view of his violence. I saw, first of all, that there was vastly more of it in what he wrote than is usually supposed. But I also saw that, as in the case of his "freedom," there was another side, one that was surprisingly nonviolent. Here, too, the reasons for the ambivalence were to be found within Bakunin himself.

As the biography unfolds the darker sides of Bakunin's political heritage will become increasingly apparent. Their disclosure, however, has not been the main focus of this study. Its aims are, first, to show the relationship between those darker sides and the utopian vision, between Bakunin's violence and authoritarianism, on the one hand, and, on the other, his celebrated defense of freedom,

1

peace, and justice; and, second, to search for the roots of both the vision and the violence in Bakunin's personal life and character. It is a principal conclusion of the study, and a major theme throughout it, that virtually everything Bakunin said and did finds its explanation in Bakunin himself rather than in the reality outside, the social and political world towards which he directed his theories and actions and from which he drew his repertoire of themes and concepts.

Since one main concern has been, therefore, to understand the man and the ways his character informed and directed his words and deeds, I have drawn heavily on what I believe to be the most relevant and useful psychological theories. Even were it not my desire to know this relationship between Bakunin the man and Bakunin the revolutionary anarchist, his extraordinarily candid and revealing letters, volume after volume of them, cry out for such psychological analysis, as excerpts from them will show. Why, after all, resist an approach that is so obviously called for by such revelations? Still, I am only too aware of the distress and even anger that the application of psychological (and especially psychoanalytic) theory to historical themes arouses in many scholars, not to mention the fury it is bound to provoke in Bakunin admirers who will consider it an act of insolent desecration. Yet, the alternative is to abandon the hope of understanding the man and the personal source of his ideas and either to pretend that the extraordinary and aberrational traits of his life and thought are not there, which is to betray the man, or to acknowledge their presence but discount them as quaint eccentricities and leave them unexplained, which is to betray the historian's obligation to attempt, at least, to explain. Many studies of Bakunin do, in fact, mention at least some of his unusual psychosexual traits— his impotence, his incestual attraction to his sister Tatiana, his marriage in which the children were fathered by a close friend and follower. But no attempt has been made either to follow up these hints into a more thorough analysis of his personality or, more crucial, to work out in detail the connection between these traits of character and Bakunin's theories and actions.

Because of the widespread doubts about or clear hostility towards "psychohistory," the evidence must be ample, even excessive. To provide it, I have included more examples from Bakunin's works, more quotations for each of the various points and themes argued, than would otherwise be necessary or, stylistically, desirable. There is also another reason for what might seem a redundancy of citations. It would be absurd to base psychological interpretation on one or a few remarks, however "suggestive" they might seem. Besides their "fit" in the general psychological portrait, what makes the statements I have quoted psychologically relevant are their repeated usage, the repeated similarities of contexts in which they are used, their mutual reenforcement, and their echoes in his actions. I have, therefore, taken care throughout to give a number of examples for each of the principal features of the portrait. However, they will be presented bit by bit, slowly gathering as Bakunin's life and thought develop. The evidence to demonstrate and the examples to illustrate this interpretation, in other words, will be cumulative, and it is hoped that judgment of its validity will be postponed until all the evidence is in.

One final question about the use of psychology in the study should be raised. It is often asked, so what? What does it prove? What, for instance, does the source or genesis of ideas have to say about their "validity"? With respect to the question of "validity," we will have more than enough occasion to see how well Bakunin's theories stood the test of reality. In one sense, though, these are strange criticisms and challenges coming, as they usually do, from academics, for whom explanation and understanding are, generally, the proper and adequate goals of inquiry. A work showing, for example, the social-economic background of Bakunin's thought and action or one tracing the intellectual or philosophical influences behind them would not likely provoke this kind of response. Why does psychological explanation do so? It is, I think, because explanation of an intellectual's motivations, especially unconscious motivations, seems demeaning in ways that other explanations, even economic reductivism, do not, and demeaning not only to the particular intellectual studied, but, implicitly, to other intellectuals as well, including the "objective" academic. However, it is precisely because of these broader implications regarding some intellectuals, especially among the "intelligentsia," that, I believe, this approach offers something of value in addition to explanation: by disclosing the deeper motivations and self-deceptions underlying Bakunin s theory and practice one may hope to prompt a "shock of recognition" in those who share Bakunin's political aims and inclinations, especially with respect to violence and authoritarianism.

Presumptuous as this intention may seem, it will no doubt seem less so than the claim implicit in the religiously-tinged title and chapter headings. While I knew that Bakunin was sympathetic in his youth to a kind of romantic, mystical evangelism, I did not realize how passionately intense that religious dedication was, how much he saw himself walking in the footsteps of Jesus, and how great a role this messianic megalomania played in his later revolutionary career. Bakunin provides, therefore, one more example to illustrate the important but often repressed truth that maximalist, cataclysmically violent revolutionary strategies of the kind that he, Lenin, and numerous other visionary zealots have proclaimed are barely disguised versions of the Christian Apocalypse. More will be said of this at several points in the study and in the concluding chapter.

It is doubtful that this book could have been written without the generous support of the National Endowment for the Humanities, the American Council of Learned Societies, and, at the University of Michigan, the Rackham School of Graduate Studies and the Center for Russian and East European Studies. To all of them, I want to express my gratitude for their material help and for the confidence it reflected. I would also like to thank Professor Nicholas Riasanovsky, of the University of California, Berkeley, and Professor Richard Pipes of Harvard University, both of whom read parts of an early draft of the manuscript and offered useful criticisms and suggestions. On a number of occasions, I discussed the psychoanalytic aspects of my interpretation with Dr. Howard Shevrin and Dr. Jeffrey Urist, both in the department of psychiatry of the University of Michigan. Dr. Urist also read the concluding chapter, "Narcissus and Oedipus." I am most grateful to them for their thoughtful comments. Finally, to my wife, Sara, who read and reread the chapters, convinced me to rephrase, rethink, reorganize, cut this out and that down, and in dozens of other ways improved the force and flow of the argument, I owe a very special thank you.

1.   ESTRANGEMENT

"The Russians are not Frenchmen. They love their fatherland. They revere their Tsar. His will is their law. Among them there is not one who would hesitate to sacrifice his most valued possessions, cherished interests and even his own life for [the Tsar's] good and for the welfare of his fatherland."[1] Whatever other faults Michael Bakunin's parents saw in their son, a 17 year old cadet when he wrote this, a lack of patriotism was not one of them. He had left home for artillery school three years before, in 1828, as a fervent young nationalist, announcing excitedly in his first brief note home that "the siege of Silistra is on again,"[2] that the Russians had renewed their attack on the Turkish fortress. He ended his military career six years later no less dedicated to his country and its government, still "sustained" by the conviction that he "must be useful to [his] fatherland," "that to fulfill one's obligation is the sacred duty of a man and citizen."[3]

Among the authors he read during his first year at the school and recommended to his sisters were M. N. Agoskin, N. O. Grech, and F. V. Bulgarin, the first, a chauvinistic historical novelist, the latter two, Russia's most illustrious reactionary publicists of the period.[4] Of the Pushkin poems he read at the time, the only one he wrote home about was one concerning, as he interpreted it, an irreconcilable conflict between Europe and the Slavs, led by Russia, and denouncing Lafayette—"a big windbag"—for supporting the Poles in their rebellion against Russia. It was a "wonderful poem," he said, "full of fire and genuine patriotism."[5] As to those who denounced Russia's harsh repression of the Polish rising, such criticism, he wrote during his last months of military service, was based on "abstract principles" and not on real facts. Knowing the facts as he did, he went on, "I not only excuse the measures but consider them necessary."[6] Whether because of these sentiments or as a cause for them, M. N. Muraviev, the general in charge of the repression and a relative of the Bakunins, took the young Bakunin into his confidence, showed him documents concerning the Polish opposition, and permitted him to eavesdrop in his office while he harassed and humiliated Polish landlords.[7] There is nothing surprising, therefore, in the "inexpressible rapture" Bakunin later recalls he had felt when Tsar Nicholas I visited Bakunin's school, in the "tremulous reverence" with which, he said, he along with his comrades had gazed at the Tsar, or in his envy of those to whom the Tsar spoke "even a single word."[8]

There is nothing unusual, in fact, about any of these statements or sentiments: they are just what one would have expected of someone from Bakunin's class and background, a family of high officials and landed gentry that traced its noble lineage back to the seventeenth century. Also, he was merely reflecting his time, the first years of Nicholas I's nationalistic and marital reign. Most of all, though, he was echoing the feelings and judgments of his father, Alexander Michailovich Bakunin. By all accounts, Alexander Michailovich was a paragon of cultural refinement, social and material success, and responsible community service, whose achievements included a Ph.D. from Padua University (along with a three-volume dissertation), years of service for the Russian legations in Turin and Florence, a smooth ascent through the bureaucratic ranks, and the composition of several histories and numerous poems. A strong sense of duty appears to have been his salient trait. He had wanted to remain abroad longer but had yielded to his mother's wish that he return to help his ailing father run Premukhino, an estate and serf village of some 500 "souls" that his father had recently purchased. The manor house was relatively small, unpretentious, and sparsely furnished, but the estate was beautifully situated, set among the low hills and dense forests along the shores of the Osuga, a narrow meandering river that flows, by way of the Tvertsa, into the Volga, passing Moscow some 150 miles to the southeast. Besides helping to manage Premukhino, Alexander Michailovich also took a government post in the capital, to supplement the family income and to fulfill another of the many established obligations incumbent on his class. Less ambitious than his powerful and volatile father, however, he was satisfied with a relatively modest position and readily agreed when his parents asked him to retire, leave the capital, and devote himself completely to Premukhino.

He adored the countryside, "away from the urban dust," as he said in a lengthy poem he wrote about the estate, and he gave himself unstintingly to its enhancement. To judge from his children's descriptions of their life at Premukhino, and from impressions made on visitors to it, Alexander Michailovich succeeded superbly in making of Premukhino a scenic and cultural showcase and, for himself, an idyllic sanctuary for the country gentleman, tending to his parks and gardens, enjoying his library and his music, and dutifully meeting the responsibilities of the estate, the local (Tver) community, and, especially, his large family. About a decade after his return to Russia, Alexander married Varvara Muraviev, the daughter of one of Russia's most prominent families, or rather, of two such families, since her mother had married into the Poltoratsky clan after her first husband, Varvara's father, died. At the time Alexander married Varvara, she was less than half his age (18, while he was 40), so much younger that Alexander admitted considering her more like one of the children than their mother. The children came soon and in rapid succession, 11 in 14 years. First, there were two girls, Liubov (1811) and Varvara (1812), then the first son, Michael (1814), followed by two more daughters, Tatiana (1815) and Alexandra (1816), then five sons in a row, Nicholas (1818), Ilya (1819), Paul (1820), Alexander (1821), Alexei (1823), and finally, a daughter, Sophia (1824), who died of dysentary when she was two.[9]

We will see presently something of the substance and style of the pastoral, "romantic" life on Premukhino, so important for understanding several essential traits in Bakunin's character, but first we should consider more fully those aspects of the period, and of Alexander Michailovich's part in it, that fostered Bakunin's early conservatism. While it is an oversimplification to make the War of 1812, the Napoleonic invasion of Russia, a sharp dividing line between a prewar "liberal" period and a postwar "reactionary" period in the reign of Alexander I (1801-25), there is enough substance in that division to make it relevant here. It is true—and one of the reasons for muting the division—that even during his "liberal" years in the first decade of the century, Tsar Alexander's "liberalism" was largely rhetorical and had no appreciable effect on either of the two pillars of the system, autocracy and serfdom. But it is also true that he encouraged the spread of that liberal rhetoric and the ideas and hopes associated with it in a variety of ways—establishing new educational institutions, encouraging the translation of Western publications and travel to the West, making impressively liberal-sounding declarations that spoke of "constitutions," choosing prominent liberals as his closest advisors, supporting the introduction of constitutional systems abroad, and so forth. One result of this was to arouse in others, in the young noblemen particularly, a desire to see these ideas given the practical implementation that the Tsar himself obviously feared, his fine speeches notwithstanding.

Alexander Michailovich was one such young nobleman. His years abroad, at Padua University and in the foreign service, had coincided with the reign of Catherine the Great, the most famous of all Russian "enlightened despots" and the one most effective in importing and propagating ideas that radically challenged the foundations of Russian Tsarist and gentry society. While in the West, Alexander Michailovich is said not only to have witnessed the French Revolution, but, according to the memoirs of one of his sons, even to have participated in the siege of the Bastille. Until about the time of the War of 1812 he apparently continued to express liberal sentiments and undertake liberal enterprises. He tried to introduce a "constitution" for his serfs, who would have no part in it; he served for three years, until 1808, as the elected marshall of the local nobility; and he took the liberal side in local political discussions, supporting the constitutional against the autocratic principle in debates with N. M. Karamzin, the famous conservative historian and advisor to Tsar Alexander.

Although the Tsar's lip-service liberalism had significantly weakened ever since the conflict with Napoleon had begun, from about 1808, it was the impact of the 1812 war that finally ended it as far as Russia was concerned, except for an occasional statement of liberal intentions that now fooled no one other than, perhaps, the Tsar himself.[10] Deep economic troubles resulting from the war, the necessity of strengthening and tightening the army in order to maintain the new international stature that victory over Napoleon had given Russia, a new wave (from the West) of social and political conservative theory, an accompanying revival of religious mysticism piously sponsored by the Tsar in place of his earlief Enlightenment creed—these and other influences created conditions that were hardly encouraging for the young noblemen who had been lead, in part by the Tsar himself, to expect major reforms from above and who now considered such reforms more urgently needed than ever. The successful war against Napoleon, followed by a lengthy eyewitness experience in the West that many young noble officers gained while chasing Napoleon across Europe, then occupying France, only intensified their resentment at Russia's backwardness and their desire to modernize Russia by one means or another.

Soon after they returned home, these young officers began gathering to discuss the reforms needed and to plan ways of bringing them about. The more they planned, the worse conditions seemed to get. The war had been costly, and the nobility had suffered rising prices, reduced and sometimes skipped payments for their service, and forced loans. Also, reenforcing the army meant a more rigorous discipline for these gentry officers who had traditionally regarded military service as a brief interlude for adventure, bravado, and gorgeous uniforms. In their eyes, drills and discipline belonged in Prussia, not Russia. And with Tsar Alexander now believing that Truth lay with the spiritually devout rather than with the rationally enlightened, what could one hope for from that quarter?

By the early 1820s, the rebels had made their plans. They all agreed that serfdom must end, but they differed on politics: the moderates in the North aimed at a constitutional monarchy, while the militants in the South called for regicide, a republic, and the "temporary" dictatorship of a revolutionary directory. Alexander Michailovich was apparently aware of at least some of these preparations. His marriage to Varvara Muraviev on the eve of the war had closely related him to a family, the Muravievs, that played a central role in the formation of the conspiratorial cells, and Alexander Michailovich himself may well have been a member of one of the more moderate factions, the Union of Welfare. Although the evidence, largely destroyed by the Bakunin family during the investigations that followed the insurrection, leaves this uncertain, one source claims that Alexander, then in his 50s, had helped turn some of the young officers against extremist goals and tactics and that it was in his own Premukhino study that these moderates had worked out their program.

According to this account, he had urged the young men to resist the temptations of Western ideas and above all to avoid tampering with Tsarist autocracy. Only an autocrat, he was now convinced, could hold together the vast and disparate Russian Empire, for the state had still a long way to go in its task of transforming this polyglot people, with its multiplicity of religions, customs, and laws, into an integrated political whole. It was one thing, he said, to adopt democratic government in small, rich, densely populated, temperate lands where the majority of the population was educated. It was quite another matter to do so in Russia, where, in addition to uncongenial geographic conditions, the people had not yet even learned to respect the law, much less abide by the rules and procedures that a constitutional government would establish. Moreover, the dissidents must keep in mind that Russia was surrounded by enemies ready to take advantage of the weakness that would inevitably come from any attempt to change the system. To convince themselves of this, he added, they need only recall the fate of those other Slavic states that did weaken central monarchic rule. The way to advance popular welfare, he concluded, was not to conspire against the government, but to teach the people a love of work, sobriety, honesty, discipline, and cleanliness.

As it turned out, Alexander Michailovich need not have worried about the dangers to Russia from the rebellious young officers: the "Decembrist rising," such as it was, ended in complete fiasco. Taking advantage of the fact that Tsar Alexander I had kept secret the name of his chosen successor (his younger brother Nicholas), about 3,000 young officers took to the Senate Square in St. Petersburg hoping to win support from others of their class, especially from some inside the government, and to put Nicholas' older brother, Constantine, on the throne in the strange belief that Constantine would establish a constitutional monarchy. But no significant support was forthcoming, neither from within the government (the Senate had already accepted Nicholas) nor from outside, from their own gentry class (why, indeed, should serf owners support a party calling for an end to serfdom?). The rebels were left stranded, defenseless, and were easily crushed. Many of them were killed during the rising; five were hanged and dozens exiled after it; and instead of an era of liberalism that the rebels had hoped to bring their country, Russia now faced 30 years of oppression under a frightened and vengeful Nicholas I.

Recalling the family's ties with the Muravievs and Alexander Michailovich's own liberal reputation and associations with the Decembrists, one can well imagine the fear that must have swept the Bakunin household after the rising and during the subsequent years of intensive investigation, trials, and heavy sentences. Michael Bakunin was 11 years old at the time of the insurrection, and, therefore, some three years of repression, fear, and zealous family caution had gone by when, as we saw, he went off to military school in 1828, as ardently patriotic and as safely conservative as his father had prudently become.

If the young Bakunin's patriotism was reassuring to his parents, however, there was little else in the flood of letters he sent home from military school to bring them joy. Letter after letter brimmed over with anguish, loneliness, and complaints, leading his parents, as we will see below, to doubt increasingly that their son had the character to turn noble sentiments into responsible action. From the start, he loathed everything about his life away from Premukhino, the "filth" and "stench" of St. Petersburg[11] and, especially, what he considered the moral depravity of the barracks, "the dark, filthy, and vile side of life" they had taught him and that he contrasted with "the pure and virginal" life he had known before at Premukhino.[12] His response was withdrawal: "I kept completely apart from most of our young people, my comrades, where wine, cards and other occupations, which modesty does not permit me to name, were just about the only way they passed the time and the only subjects of conversation."[13] Withdrawal, in turn, brought loneliness, deepening with the years and more bitterly lamented as time went on, as we see in the following excerpts from his letters:

> Oh, dear sisters, how I would like to see you!...How I want to squeeze you in my embrace....When will we see each other again? I await that moment with such impatience. I love you so. Still two years—how unpleasant those words sound. (March 2, 1830)

> I begin to think about the length of our separation. It seems to me to stretch out so long. What wouldn't I do if only I could shorten the time! I would give half of my life for the chance of being in Premukhino if only for a minute, to embrace you and assure you of the full depth of

my friendship. How I envy my brothers for their enjoying, all the time, the presence of our parents, and you, dear sisters. What a child I was when I was happy at the thought of the trip to St. Petersburg! I would willingly agree to give up forever the chance of seeing any capital in the world if only I had the chance of spending my entire life among people dear to my heart, having no other aim than to please them and to strive to guess their slightest wish. Oh, when will I see you again, dearest sisters? Only then will you see how fervently I love you. (spring 1831)

How I want to see Premukhino. What happiness I feel just to think of it! Only now can I truly feel how unhappy one can be when separated from everything one loves. (September 20, 1831)

You write, dear mother, that only a year remains before I will have the joy of seeing you, and you say that—it's not long. What do you mean, not long! To me this year seems longer than the three whole years I have spent away from dear Premukhino. (February 6, 1832)

You give me hope, dear parents, that you may come here in the fall. Oh, if that will only be! For it has already been four years that I have been separated from you and my sisters. You can imagine how great is my impatience. Just the thought that I will not see you earlier than a year from now leads me to despair. What then will it be if even after a year we cannot see each other? (February 10, 1833)

And so I am again buried in this wretched Petersburg life, where everyone thinks and lives for himself. I am overwhelmed by profound sadness....There is not a single person to whom I can open my heart, with whom I could share my grief, from whom I might expect some small solace....You live together, your sorrows are not felt so oppressively. You share with each other. But I, here, am alone, completely alone. (September 1833)

I am here in an alien land, with people whose ways of thought and feeling are completely different from mine, people who are cold and who lack any trace of education. (June 28, 1834)

Stuck in this miserable hole...among people who virtually walk on all fours, I keep entirely apart from everyone....I live in a desert and can share my thoughts, impressions, feelings with no one. (July 11, 1834)

Finding nothing attractive in my fellow soldiers and their occupations cards and vodka—I keep completely apart from them, and so I am alone

here, entirely alone! Eternal silence, eternal sorrow, eternal anguish—
these are the comrades of my seclusion! And should the raptures of
pure joy flash and for a moment illuminate the darkness that reigns in
my soul, I must repress it in my bosom. No one will listen to me!...
[sic] I am alone. (October 4, 1834)[14]

The letters over these five years tell one and the same story: Bakunin was
utterly and woefully out of place in the army, whether in the barracks or in the
field. In part, his distress, often despair, was due to ordinary homesickness and
the "petty details of military service and discipline"[15] that are the common
complaints of many others in like circumstances. In part, it may have been because he felt that, as he wrote his parents, "there is not in me that heroism, that
courage that leads one to seek danger."[16] But most of all his loneliness and long
suffering seem to have been the result of his being temperamentally so completely
ill-suited to the "dark, filthy, and vile" barrack's life that weighed so heavily on
him. The tones that make up the portrait of this "violent" anarchist as a young
man, in other words, are soft pastels. This is the first essential trait of character
we must keep in mind as we see his complex personality unfold.[17]

In this connection, surely one of the most remarkable aspects of Bakunin's
correspondence, not only during these military years, but also in the five years
that followed (down to his departure from Russia), is the extent and, especially,
the character of his relationship with young ladies, mainly his sisters and cousins.
In the space he allots to them, these relationships take second place only to his
endless introspection into his own shifting moods and sensibilities. But more
significant than the attention he gives them is the nature of those relationships,
for in them he seems himself to be one of the adolescent girls, acting as a go-
between, smoothing or sparking misunderstandings, gossiping about this or that
with effervescent delight.[18] On the rare occasions that men enter the scene, they
are quickly engulfed by the same dense romantic atmosphere: he is overjoyed,
for example, at the thought of a visit to Premukhino by his cousin Peter Poltoratsky, for "when he is there a certain slight spirit of secrecy prevails!...the
strolls alone, the constant friendly exchanges, secretly murmured, the eternal
whispering...."[19]

We are not surprised after this to find how hypersensitive he was, how vulnerable to slights, how quick to take offense. Visiting friends, the Lvovs, he
thought they were cold to him. A bitter letter followed to his sister Varvara
(whom "I adore more than is usual to love a sister")[20] bemoaning the loss of
"illusions with which a too trusting heart tries to surround itself," the loss of
friendship that "like a soap bubble becomes ever more lovely as it grows larger
then suddenly bursts, leaving behind only a moist spray." "How stupid I was!"

he went on, "As though anything in life is stable and secure! As though I did not know that there was only one reality—death!"[21] He wrote this May twentieth. On June tenth his sisters learned that he and the Lvovs "are again the very best of friends," that he is again their daily visitor, and that he had been entirely mistaken in his doubts about their feelings toward him.[22] On another occasion, "incomparable Varinka" was critical of him for showing her letters to a friend of his. He was crushed again. It was clear now that "my thoughts, my hopes, were an empty chimera, that this tender friendship, this priceless gift of heaven, does not exist for me, poor unfortunate that I am, since I cannot even find it in the person of my sister, a sister whom I worship...."[23] Shortly afterwards, he is euphoric again, fully reconciled with Varvara (for "whom else can I trust if not you?")[24] and thrilled with news that his family will soon visit St. Petersburg: "Ah, let that heavenly moment come sooner, when we will come together again, never more to separate."[25]

Central as these romantic strains are in the character of young Bakunin, they were no more unique at the time than was his dedicated patriotism. For Russia in those decades, at least the Russia of Bakunin's class, abounded with little nests of romantic young gentlefolk who read together, yearned together, cherished together the nuances of each other's letters or dissected the hidden meanings of the latest novel, philosophical treatise or religious trace, merged their spirits in communal celebration of the shifting tones and contours of the countryside, and, with a special dedication, sought together in all they read, saw, thought, and felt the signs of their own glorious or woeful destinies. This effusive Romanticism, usually in its cruder form of maudlin sentimentalism, had been the prevailing temper and style among the educated class at least as far back as the last decade of the eighteenth century, when Russians wept inconsolably over the works of Richardson, Sterne, Thomson, Young, Ossian, and other English sentimental novelists.[26] The translator of Richardson's *Pamela* probably spoke for most other Russian readers when he said in his introduction that he had suffered deeply the plight of the heroine and "with the most tender compassion had wept continually over her unhappiness." Richardson was everywhere. Pushkin had copies in English of his three novels and made him the favorite of his own heroine Tatiana and her mother. Two years after *Pamela* was translated, we find *A Russian Pamela, or The History of Maria, A Virtuous Peasant Girl*. Both the character and the thought of the most illustrious Russian heroine of the day, Karamzin's *Poor Liza*, is a composite of Pamela and Richardson's other leading lady, Clarissa. The very titles of the best-loved works indicate the source and focus of the appeal: Thomson's *The Seasons*, Young's *Night Thoughts*, Sterne's *Sentimental Journey*, Karamzin's *Poor Liza*, Galinowski's *Hours of Pensiveness*, Klushin's *Unhappiness*, and so on. Of all the prominent English novelists of the period, only Fielding found few imitators: his robust optimists and dashing rogues left too little room for melancholy, too few opportunities for a good cry.

In both the English originals and their Russian copies, the themes are few and familiar: a reverent adoration of nature and the simple rural life; the deification of ideal, ineffable, abstract beauty; the pleasure of grief, of "sweet sadness"; a penchant for presentiment, usually painful or morose; a yearning for pure love and "friendship" unsullied by carnal lust; and a compassion—usually intellectual and passive—for the downtrodden poor folk. Thus, when we find Bakunin arguing with a young cousin about the "definition of love, enthusiasm, feeling and sensitivity, which we distinguished very clearly from cloying sentimentalism,"[27] watching as his "soul, tearing itself free of the mortal barriers that constrain it, pours itself over the entire universe, encompassing all in nature, the whole world," or listening as "every object, each plant and flower speaks to me in the language of love,"[28] we are encountering the mood of the age as much as we are aspects of Bakunin's own personality.

Nor was Michael the only Bakunin to immerse himself so fully in that heady mood. Romanticism was the soul of Premukhino, and Michael's father, a devotee of Rousseau, took the lead in stimulating and maintaining it. Two weeks after his own mother's death (and four months after Michael's birth), Alexander Michailovich vowed that he would raise his children in a totally different manner than the one in which he himself had been raised. Whereas his mother had been severe and domineering with her children ("the slightest opposition or disagreement intensely irritated her"), he would be gentle and permissive with his own children. He would not let himself be "offended by their disagreement" and would guide them "by tenderness, affection, and indulgence,...through advice, example and reason, and not by parental authority." Also, while discouraging idleness and encouraging the children's participation in the estate when they would come of age, he would see that "as far as possible, they live joyfully and pleasantly."[29] To make sure that his Rousseauean views guided the education of the children, he himself assumed some of the tutorship, teaching them what he knew of natural science, geography, and history, often during long walks in the fields. "You are fused with the very best memories of our childhood," Bakunin later said of his father, going on in this letter to provide us with an exceptional fine portrait of their relationship and of the Premukhino milieu that encompassed it:

> You rarely scolded us and, I believe, never once punished us, but the thought that you would find out about something wrong we had done, the thought that you would be angry at us, struck terror in us. I also recall with what love, with what indulgence and ardent attention you

listened to our childish chatter. I remember how happy we were when we brought you a butterfly we had caught or a flower that we had not seen before. I will never forget those evening strolls to the dusty factory or to Kostiushino, where you would tell us one or another historical anecdote or story, where you had us search for a rare plant—and how proud and happy was the one who would find it. And I recall also one moonlit night, when the sky was bright and sown with stars. We went to Mytnitskii grove and you, together with sister Varinka, told us about the sun, the moon, the clouds, thunder, lightening and so on. I remember one summer day when I had done well with my studies and you were pleased with me and helped me build a bridge to our little island.... Yes, dear father, memories about you and the love for you, about the Premukhino house, the garden and all its surroundings, about the love of nature and the pleasures of nature, and about our childhood—all this is merged in one, all this comprises our inalienable treasure and the best period of our family life.[30]

Music, art, foreign languages, and religion rounded out this gentle and relaxed manoral education. Michael had violin lessons, the girls took piano, harp, and mandolin, and several of the children developed impressive skill at drawing, as Michael was later to show in his talented self-portraits. Languages—mainly French and German, some Italian, and a little English—came both naturally, from usage around the house, and from tutors. The household religion, finally, as befit the Romantic era, favored strong emotion, showed an intense evangelic pietism, and made a deep and abiding impression on Bakunin, as we see in another remembrance of times past that Bakunin sent his father:

Lent came and we fasted with you. That holy week was something ineffable, glorious for us. The sacred glory, etched in your face, the black frames of the icons, the sad and somber service, the late night vespers. After vespers, we went into the parlor, which was not yet lit. Varinka sat at the piano and began playing chords, and you talked to us about suffering, about the divine sanctity of the Savior. Then, when there was light, we read the Gospels together. Wednesday came, and we went to confession together, and after confession we gathered in the evening for dinner. Everything was so quiet, so holy, so glorious. We did not understand it then, but we felt that something grand was happening. You, mother, sisters, we all were in one room, with no outsider, no one to disturb this sacred harmony by his unwanted presence. Then, on Thursday, we took communion, and afterwards came the washing of the icons, the 12 evangels, Good Friday and Christ's shroud, the dyeing of the artificial marble eggs, midnight resurrection service on Saturday, when we walked together after Christ's shroud, then Easter Sunday Matins, waiting for the sunrise, the return of spring—Oh, all this has fused, indissolubly fused with our lives. These events seem insignificant, but they penetrated deeply into our soul; they left unforgettable impressions.[31]

And it was all done in consort; they were always together: studying and reading together, playing together in the meadows, by the pond or sawmill, or on a tiny island in the Osuga, singing French songs together on their moonlight walks in the countryside or while gathered around the piano in the evening. Music, poetry, art, and endless intimate conversations about nuances of private sentiment or timeless philosophical or spiritual truths, and all cradled in the tranquil rhythm and beauty of nature and rooted fast in the security of an allembracing family love—such was Premukhino for the Bakunin children.

Now, whatever else one might say about this pastoral education, it was hardly the best preparation for a rigidly disciplinary military school in the reign of Nicholas I. No wonder Michael suffered the shock of contrast so deeply and longed so fervently to be back home. Rarely, it seems, and for only brief periods, did joy break into these otherwise dismal years away from Premukhino. One such period began at the end of 1832 when Michael became infatuated with his 16 year old cousin, Maria. The two were constantly together, at evening gatherings, church services, and concerts. They read together, talked about the family at Premukhino, "since that's my favorite subject," and argued about the familiar Romantic themes.[32] The following January (1833) life brightened still more. He became an officer candidate and, if not entirely free, was now at least able to live away from the loathsome barracks. But in early March paradise was lost again. Maria and her mother left for a six month stay in Moscow. On leaving she gave him a bracelet to remember her by, and he kissed her hand. "Varinka! Dear Varinka! I kissed her hand!...Now I was truly happy! Tears came to my eyes." Their carriage pulled away. "I ran behind it. I even overtook it and ran ahead, but since my strength was exhausted, I had to fall behind....Her image was lost to my eyes, and Petersburg, for me, was empty."[33]

In the months that followed Maria's departure, Michael was again lonely and depressed. He tried to fill the void with another stream of passionate letters to Premukhino, which had slackened markedly while Maria had been in town. To make matters worse, he just then had a bitter quarrel with relatives, the Nilov family, who had provided him an apartment after he had left the barracks. The cause of the quarrel was his aunt's interference in his private life. She had received a letter from Maria's aunt complaining that Michael had spent too much time alone with the young lady, and to make sure that this breach of propriety did not occur again, Michael's aunt forbade him to leave the house without permission. She had also learned a little later that Michael, having squandered his allowance, was heavily in debt, and she had felt it her duty to so inform his parents. "Having just obtained external independence and freedom, I could not see why, for what reason I should sacrifice them," he later said, recalling the quarrel and referring here to his recent liberation from the cadet barracks. So he moved out of his "despotic" aunt's home, leaving St. Petersburg soon afterwards to join his company on maneuvers that summer (1833).[34] But there was light ahead for him, or so he had good reason to expect: in September, after maneuvers, he was able to return to Premukhino on furlough. The hope that had sustained him for those past five hard years was realized. He was home again.

It was not, however, the Premukhino he had yearned for and cherished in memory. Neither the embraces that had welcomed him nor his attempts after the visit to refurbish the tarnished fantasy could hide the fact, which he later acknowledged, that this brief stay home irreparably damaged his idyllic image of Premukhino and, even more, his trust in his parents. The cause of the disillusionment was a continuing bitter quarrel between him and his parents over the intended marriage of his sister, Liubov.[35] Rooting himself firmly in what he called his rights as eldest brother, he accused his parents of trying to force Liubov into what he considered a loveless marriage. The conflict went on throughout the furlough, climaxing in a particularly stormy scene the final evening. Both the powerful effect this crisis had on him and some of the deeper reasons for his intense response are evident in a review of the events that he wrote some four and one-half years later. As he saw it, the marriage would be a grotesque sacrifice of a "girl brought up in virginal purity," a "pure and saintly soul whom until that time no unclean attraction had dared touch," to a man "who will with hellish lust take off of her, one after another, the covers of sacred modesty, who will little by little exhaust and befoul by his vile breath this heavenly flower, this wonderful, sacred, divine creation!" Why had his parents raised a young girl in purity, he asked, if they intended later to

> fling her into the abyss of despair, to prepare her for that terrible, re-
> pulsive moment in which all her happiness must be destroyed, all her
> dreams, all her hopes, all her faith, that moment in which she must see
> corrupt reality in all its repulsiveness, in which she must say goodby to
> love and, contrary to all that is sacred, all that is fine and inspiring for
> her, submit to this hellish, dreadful duty and come to know that life
> is not given for bliss but for eternal lament and eternal despair!...Oh,
> how terrible this is, terrible. Better never to have been born than to
> suffer such a terrible fate.[36]

More will be said later about this impassioned defense of Liubov's "virginal purity," extraordinarily intense in any case, but especially so considering again how long a time had elapsed, some four and one-half years, since this quarrel over a marriage that, in fact, never did take place.

Back in St. Petersburg, he found "this wretched Petersburg life" as lonely and miserable as he had left it before going on maneuvers and, then, on the disillusioning furlough. How long he remained "overwhelmed by profound sadness" after his return is difficult to say, for there is a break in his correspondence for several months. By the end of the year, however, his mood had improved. He had found a new family to replace the Nilovs, the Lvovs, and, now, his own Premukhino family, that of N. N. Muraviev, an uncle on his mother's side and one of his father's closest friends. A man of about 60 at the time, Muraviev had just gone into retirement after an illustrious career that had included the governorship of a province, the rank of Senator, and the position of State Secretary. As one might imagine, he was a man of deeply conservative convictions and had been on best terms with Count A. A. Arakcheev, a pillar of the Nicholas I regime.

Judging by the correspondence between Michael, his father, and Muraviev, it seems that Michael regarded his uncle as a kind of second father, one who praised and encouraged him as his own father did not. The Muravievs' many daughters—seven of them were still at home—added to the family's appeal: they were all so "charming, attractive, especially the second daughter, well educated, modest, little given to social affairs, leading a restrained life, kind to the highest degree, abundantly talented, in a word, entirely like you. So, my dear friends," he continued, lest his sisters be jealous, "you need not be angry if I love them very much (not all the same), since loving them, I love you in them, for they are like you in all details." Maria, too, was back in town, but "she has changed immensely, and I no longer even recognize her. I won't say another word about her."[37]

The light and cheerful mood did not last long. Sometime in January 1834 a blow more severe than any he had yet received turned his spirits downwards again into a descent that was to continue throughout the year, bringing him to the point of near-suicidal despair at the end of the year and de facto desertion early the next year (1835). The trouble began when he went out in improper uniform one day and met the general in command of the artillery school. The general reproached him in' a manner that Michael considered insulting. Michael's response was taken as insolence and, as punishment, he was expelled from school and transferred to an artillery brigade quartered in the western provinces, first in Minsk and then, that fall, in Grodnenskii.[38] While insolence may have precipitated the expulsion, the official statement noted that Michael and another officer were being expelled because of "inadequate achievement and constant lack of attention throughout the entire course of studies."[39] (Bakunin himself told his father in a later review of these years that "during the three years at military school I did just about nothing at all and worked only the last month of the year in order to pass the examinations.")[40]

His father was furious, especially since he learned of Michael's expulsion not from Michael himself but from N. N. Muraviev and then suffered the added humiliation of reading about it in the papers. Striking at what he considered the heart of the matter, he warned his son in a cold and angry letter that he would have to make his own way in life, that he had better not count either on his influential relatives or on the family wealth. He should realize that his father was no N. N. Muraviev, that while Muraviev received a state pension over and above his handsome estate incomes, he himself was making high payments on far more modest and mortgaged holdings. And Michael should also bear in mind that his part of these holdings was but one in ten. Still, there was hope if only he mended his ways: "if it is impossible to bring back the past you can at least make amends for your misdeeds by constant fulfillment in the future of your familial and service obligations. So renounce your idleness and write us everything that concerns you, without concealment, right away and in detail."[41]

For the rest of that year (1834) Michael remained in the provinces, in his "desert" with those people who "walked on all fours."[42] As so often before, he again sought relief through long, woeful letters home deploring the tedium of routine military obligations, "the rote study, the inspections, the guard and officer-of-the-day duties...the heat, the cold, the fatigue, the hunger, the thirst, and all the other unpleasantness inextricably tied to military service."[43] But worst of all, as we have seen from earlier quotations, was the isolation and the loneliness, "the eternal silence, eternal sorrow, eternal anguish."[44] He urged his parents repeatedly to use their influence to get him transferred nearer home. "Maybe we will succeed in having you moved," his father replied. "But if not, don't be despondent. Go on with your studies and ardently carry out, I beg you, your responsibilities, no matter how trivial they might seem to you."[45] He even tried to make himself ill in the hope of winning reprieve.[46] By the year's end he was including in letters to his sisters long excerpts from a Moldavian author's morbid reflections on death and its appeal.[47]

Such were the circumstances of Bakunin's life during his years in the military (1829–34) from ages 15 through 20. But what is essential for our understanding of the man is not so much to know the conditions he faced or even to know that, in a general way, he thoroughly disliked and resented them, but rather to know what he did about those conditions and that discontent. What actions did he take and what traits of character did this long and oppressive experience, so radically different from his Premukhino childhood, foster in him? The crucial year, as we will see, was 1834, the year following his bitter disappointment with Premukhino (in connection with the quarrels over Liubov's intended marriage) and his humiliating expulsion from officers' training school. But to appreciate the reasons for the direction he took that year—a direction he was to follow for the rest of his life—we must first see his earlier responses to the continuing unhappiness and sense of deprivation. Through most of these years away from home, his response is that of a timid, withdrawn boy who avoids his more raucous and rebellious peers, tries to keep out of trouble, except for imprudent borrowing, and fears admitting failures and reprimands, keeping his expulsion from his parents, for example.[48] He was not at all, in other words, a strident young rebel. When a group of cadets accused an officer of confiscating money from one of them for his personal use and were punished for the effrontery of such an accusation, Michael assured his parents that he was not among the accusers. He did take pride, however, in not informing on the guilty ones when pressed to do so: "I preferred to be unjustly punished rather than commit such a vile act."[49] In another such incident, the cadets were grumbling about rudeness and injustice on the part of some officers, and one of the officers threatened reprisals. Michael, in his account of the episode, then said aloud, "Oho" and was arrested on the spot. He excused himself, however, and, for reasons left unclear in the letter, was neither among the five cadets punished as leaders nor the three-quarters of the rest whose leaves were cancelled.[50] The following spring, he was confined to quarters for two weeks. He was afraid to tell his parents, who found out about it from relatives in St. Petersburg. When they confronted him with their knowledge of his confinement, he confessed that his commander had caught him in a lie he had thought up in order to avoid "severe punishment" for some "misfortune," and he vowed never to keep anything from them again no matter what trouble he got into or punishment he might suffer for it.[51]

Contrition, excuses, and promises were his usual response to his parents' irritation and reproaches, those that came down on him, for example, when he lied about his final grades one year, telling them he had done well when he had in fact done badly. Explanations and vows were especially needed when the issue of his already well-formed penchant for borrowing came up:

> Feeling myself guilty before you, I wanted personally to open my heart to you, to ask in person for your forgiveness....I am guilty of much, of very much before you, my dear parents. I have done much that is stupid, and with sincere repentance, and a firm intention of correcting my ways, I ask you to forgive me....From this moment I want, without fail, to remake myself, to make of myself a sensible, upright person, but I feel that this will be difficult and almost impossible without your

blessing and your advice....I will check carefully with you not only all my actions, but even my slightest feelings, my slightest thought, each evening writing them down in my journal, which I will begin now sending to you each week. I will keep nothing from you, since I will see in you not severe judges, but people who wish only my happiness.

Following this preamble, and getting to the real issue, his debts, the penitent traced his fall to bad influences. "Entering school with the sincere intention of getting an education, I was drawn away from study by one of my fellow students (whose disgraceful escapades do not permit me to mention his name)...." One thing led to another, and before he knew it, Bakunin had dropped serious study and assumed higher and higher debts, which he itemized in detail here not "in order for you to pay them, no I am too well aware of your financial situation for such a thought even to enter my head," but simply to unburden himself, as he said, of the guilt of concealment. He assured them that he had now learned his lesson, had suffered much for his misbehavior, and was determined now, with their help, "to change myself completely."[52]

Concealment and promises to reform were a small price to pay for preserving his ties with his family in Premukhino: they were, at least during most of those military years, his only solace throughout a heavy ordeal. In this sense, one might say that he lived much of those years less in the oppressive reality that in fact engulfed him, than at home, through imagination, in Premukhino, "that blessed and sacred world...where we taught each other to understand and to love, where we spent our childhood so happily, where, under the influence of our splendid parents, our first feelings, thoughts, and knowledge took form."[53] Recalling in fantasy those earlier, happier years of childhood became his most effective response to his troubles, his most reliable means of escaping the miseries that harrassed him. The emergence of a highly active and vivid imagination in the service of this consoling nostalgia was, in fact, one of the most enduring consequences of these difficult years. He was himself fully aware of how much his loneliness was eased "thanks to the gift of imagination, which I possess to a sufficiently high degree."[54] "I am happy only when alone, when I neither see nor hear anyone, when, immersed by the full force of my soul in Premukhino, I turn over in my imagination the most trivial occurrences of my life among you.... Alone, I am always with you. I refurbish in my memory the wonderful moments of life at Premukhino.....Dear friends, carried among you by the force of my imagination, it seemed as though I were pressing you to my heart, kissing you, hearing your voices."[55]

Here, too, as in the case of Bakunin's patriotism and his gentle romanticism, there is nothing uncommon about this dependence on memories of childhood to help one forget the anguish of a trying adolescence. But the familiarity of the process does not lessen its importance in Bakunin's life, the importance that "imagination" now begins to have for him because of its dependable talent for reawakening memories of an idyllic childhood as a defense against an intolerably harsh adult reality. At this point in his life, Bakunin's use of imagination for comfort and escape is, as is his romanticism, characteristic of his age, in both senses of the word. The question will be, as it will be with his romanticism, whether or not he continues to depend on imagination in this way: will he outgrow the escapism and come to accept the constraints of reality or will fantasy become a habitual vehicle for flight into other imagined Premukhinos?

The inward voyage, begun through imagination in response to the painful contrast of the "pure and virginal" with the "dark, filthy, and vile" was given a powerful added impetus by Bakunin's expulsion from officers' school and transfer to what he considered a desolate alien wasteland. But now, however, in 1834, he could not so easily find relief in his enchanted memory of Premukhino. That fantasy had failed him. The fierce conflicts with his parents at the end of 1833 had destroyed the cherished illusion that had helped him bear the many hardships of those past five years. He must find another sanctuary. In his search, he turned first to the favored refuge of so many before and after who found reality, for whatever reason, unbearable. Insightfully realizing the significance of this discovery in his life, he rightfully called it an "intellectual revolution":

> I never felt myself particularly suited for life in society. I felt stupid, awkward, inarticulate. I used to think that this was merely because of my inexperience....I did everything in my power to overcome this. I immersed myself in society; I ran around this way and that, and what did I find? A terrible emptiness. The pleasures and distractions that delighted others seemed to me trivial. Dances, balls—these, the pinnacle of pleasure for our youth, the highest ideal they can imagine, bored me to death. I at once felt out of place and just as trivial as they were. I had to reject all this, and I did so, joyfully, enthusiastically, and vowed never to return. But, then, I had to find something else: the vacuum that overwhelmed me had to be filled. I locked myself within myself. I studied myself, and, in the end, I found within myself something to fill the emptiness....At last I made a decision, and as soon as I did, a warmth so sweet poured through my heart. I threw myself into my study; I threw myself passionately into it.[56]...I feel as though I am being reborn; I feel that I am watching myself being fed and nurtured. Until now I have lived only an external life. I want now to build for myself an inner existence....No, my dear friends, there is true happiness on earth, but it is not external happiness, the product of circumstances and dependent entirely on superficialities.[57]

Here, within himself, was a refuge that could be trusted as the Nilovs, the Lvovs, Maria, and, most recently, even his own revered Premukhino could not. For the rest of his life it would be for him an inexhaustible source of solace and approval, and he would strengthen and enrich this inner sanctuary and come to love it. "I am fed up with society," he wrote later that year, in June. "I do not find in it that which my soul seeks, that which even I cannot yet well define."[58]

The specific focus of his "study," as he turned inwards, away from "external happiness" and the society he was "fed up with," points to the next stage in this evolution. His plan, he said, was to begin "the study of nature," a "profound probing of nature's secrets" as revealed at the time in Schelling's *Naturphiloso-phie*. He had been reading the Russian Schellingites at least since June 1833, when he was enraptured by the Schellingesque poetry of Venevitinov.[59] In the months following his "intellectual revolution" of early 1834, he moved more deeply into Schelling's nature philosophy with the help of a young artillery officer, Dr. Krasnopolsky, who had studied philosophy at Moscow University and had brought his enthusiasm for Idealism with him into the service. Bakunin read Oken, a particularly influential German philosopher for the Russians, Galitch and Vellansky, two leading Russian popularizers of German Idealism with whom Krasnopolsky was in correspondence, and "other writers of the German school."[60] But Schelling was only one facet of his new-found inner world of study and thought. In October of that year, 1834, he listed his fields of interest in a letter home—geography, travelogues "to the five corners of the world," physics, Russian grammar, politics, and history, by way of "'De l'histoire de la restauration et des causes, qui ont amene la chute des Bourbons, par un homme d'Etat' (M-r de Capegifus)." From a letter to his father two months later, we learn that, in addition to reading philosophy, he is translating something German into Russian, studying Polish, physics, and mathematics (his "practical studies"), and copying excerpts from books on history and statistics.[61]

Were we to consider only such thoughts and sentiments as those reviewed thus far—the Romanticism, the timidity, the withdrawal inward and into nature and study—we might easily image the young Bakunin maturing into, say, a sentimental poet or Idealistic philosopher, of which that Romantic era in particular could boast so many, a detached, gentle misanthrope, dismayed by conventional society, and keeping quietly to himself to refine and nurture cherished sensibilities. But then, of course, he would not be Michael Bakunin. There was another side. The soft pastels were already starkly offset by explosive reds and even some black.

It is, perhaps, a touch of these darker hues that he is revealing when he tells his sisters that Maria "was frightened by the expression on my face when I listened to [Beethoven's] music. It seemed that I was ready to destroy the entire world."[62] However, when that was written, in March 1833, such remarks were rare. Significantly, they become increasingly more frequent and emphatic through the next year, following, that is, his loss of "trust" in his parents after the conflict over Liubov's planned marriage, the consequent disillusionment with Premukhino, and his expulsion from school. In other words, *the more he withdrew inwards, "locked" himself inside himself, the more aggressive his rhetoric of self-assertion became.* "I am still young," he wrote his parents in December 1834, his last month in service. "Passions, intensified through constraint, rage within me; emotional forces seethe and demand nourishment, but all this remains inactive, limited only to dreams, which themselves cannot fill the emptiness of my heart....Everything in me demands action, movement, but all my activity is completely restricted to working for the future...basing my work on reminiscences of the past."[63] At the end of his military career, as we have seen, he was still committed to fulfilling "the sacred duty of a man and citizen" by being "useful to my fatherland." More than anything else he was already determined never to become "a futile, meaningless link in the chain of humanity."[64]

Thus, if flight inwards was Bakunin's main response to the distress he had suffered over these years, and especially from the fall of 1833 through the seeming exile of 1834, a rhetoric of power, ambition, anger, and defiance began that year, 1834, to emerge as companion response. When, for example, he heard rumors that rather than be reassigned to a camp near home, he was to be sent to another distant province, he wrote to his parents:

> Let God's will be done! There is nothing one can do to escape it! But I will not again be depressed by it. I will stand firm against the persecution of implacable fate! The greater the travail, the greater the service, and the better the chance of strengthening one's character! Man is born for eternal struggle against the impediments that he constantly meets on his life's path.[65]

Similarly, he wrote to some childhood friends and manoral neighbors:

> I am not happy here. Oh far from it! I have become ten times more gloomy than when you saw me in Premukhino. But I will not submit. On the contrary, I get pleasure from the blows of fate. I laugh at them. "Spit at them"–that's my principle, and this principle, offensive to public opinion, has caused me quite a lot of trouble, but, in spite of all that, I spit on [them] and will always spit, if only for the sake of standing steadfast....Habit is a great thing. I am becoming more and more indifferent to the blows of fate. Let it beat away. I'm not frightened

anymore! It has already caused me all the pain that it's able to cause, having taken from me all the illusions of youth. I am no longer suscepti- ble to its attacks. I have come to take the attitude of an observer, and I follow with cold curiousity all the devices it uses to try and crush me. I pity it, because it will not attain it's aim. Let it try![66]

It would be the wrong question to ask which is the "real" Michael Bakunin, the lonely, acutely sensitive, shy, and withdrawn boy or the fiercely aggressive- sounding young man determined to "stand firm against the persecution of implacable fate!" Both sides were then and would remain genuine: were either lacking, he would not have been Michael Bakunin. However, it is already appar- ent, and, again, would remain so throughout his life, that of the two sets of colors, the soft pastels are primary. Man may be "born for eternal struggle against impediments," "however," he adds in the above letter to his parents about the rumored transfer, and without even a period to break the thought, "in spite of all these truths it will be very, very difficult for me to give up the thought of serving at Tver and spending every moment with you."[67] It might well be that "passions...rage within," and he is no doubt entirely earnest in his determina- tion to make his mark and to serve honorably his country and his family, laughing at the slings of outrageous fortune along the way. However, taken as a whole, his·correspondence throughout that crucial year (1834) reveals the same fearful, endlessly introspective romantic rhapsodist that he had been earlier, filling letter after letter with detailed accounts of precious episodes that took place at the homes of relatives and friends, taking great delight in the endless gossip, the innocent romantic intrigues, and the constant interchange of confidences and advice. In the letter to his father in which he speaks of reining in his ardent na- ture, he recounted at length the advice and rebuke he had written a cousin for prematurely, in Michael's view, declaring his love for one Maria Fedorovna Moiarkina. Since Michael had discussed this in a postscript, he added: "P.S. They say that in a woman's letter the main purpose of the letter must be looked for in the Post-Scriptum."[68]

One other aspect of these defiant pronouncements of 1834 should be noted, for we will see a great deal more of it in the years to come: the feeling of power is gained not primarily through actually opposing "fate," but through being its stoic victim, being "indifferent to the blows of fate," getting "pleasure" from the blows of fate," assuming the posture of a detached "observer" watching as fate tries to "crush" him. One can see here already what will become one of Bakunin's characteristic ways of merging the two opposing poles that define his life and thought—withdrawal and power: *it is precisely by seeing himself as a long-suffering victim that he here enjoys a sense of power.*

But why was that sense of power so necessary for him in the first place? What accounts for the aggressive and increasingly violent side of the persistent dualism? With regard to the gentler side, the sources, or at least some of them, seem obvious: the popularity of Romantic writers and the corresponding encouragement of Romantic sensibilities, the elder Bakunin's apparent indulgence and permissiveness, the pastoral setting, the evangelic pietism that pervaded Premukhino, and, most influential of all, the fact that Michael's early years were spent in an almost exclusively feminine milieu, with two sisters slightly older and two sisters slightly younger, forming a young girls' circle distinctly apart from the five boys that came later. In the following chapter, we will see a number of other young Russian romantic Idealists, most of whom display much the same lyrically gentle temperament that we have seen in Bakunin. In their case, however, that side stands alone, unopposed by a side of personality in which explosive passions "rage" and "emotional forces seethe," the side that will lead Bakunin some nine years after these defiant declarations of 1834 to call for "a storm of destruction," "the restless and ruthless annihilation of every positively existing thing," "the complete annihilation of the present political and social world."[69]

One part, or level, of an explanation for Bakunin's need at least *to appear* powerful (and, towards that end, violent) should be apparent from his background and situation. He had been subject to a radically ambivalent set of values. On the one hand, there were all the romantic, permissive, emotionally indulgent experiences of that idyllic Premukhino childhood. On the other hand, there were the traditional values of courage and responsible service instilled in all young noblemen, especially in the reign of Nicholas I, and endlessly reaffirmed through five years of military training; the particular demands on him as the eldest son of an already aged father and the obligations for maintaining a family of three yet-unmarried sisters and five brothers;[70] and, finally, the awesome model of his own father, who, as we have seen, constantly reminded Michael, by word and example, of the many onerous obligations that awaited him.

The contradiction helped form Bakunin's task for life: he must find some way to hold on to the pleasures of childhood indulgence and the personality they had helped to form while meeting the demands, or at least appearing to meet the demands, of responsible, honorable, powerful manhood. In his first test, his military training, he had utterly failed. His response to the failure was his strategy of *withdrawing aggressively*, turning inwards into the inner refuge where he had preserved the pleasures of childhood, the echoes and symbolic recreations of his "pure and virginal" Premukhino, while at the same time adopting a pose and rhetoric that made withdrawal seem motivated by strength not meekness, aggressiveness not passivity, virile manliness not childish fear and flight. In short, he must be both child and man, a child safe and at ease in his "inner existence," where he could "watch" himself "being fed and nurtured," and a man, powerful enough to avoid being just another "futile, meaningless link in the chain of humanity." And the more insistent he was on remaining a child, the more emphatic and aggressive he must be in demonstrating his powerful manliness. In this context the reds and blacks are camouflage.[71]

While this explanation—Bakunin's ambivalent, contradictory upbringing—takes us some distance towards understanding the important place of violence in Bakunin's later life, it does not take us far enough. Indeed, it not only raises more questions than it asks, but it raises the most important questions. If Premukhino childhood ambiguities are to blame, why then did the other sons, especially the next eldest, Nicholas, turn out so different from Michael? Such value inconsistencies, in any case, were common among the upper class in Russia in that period of cultural change. In fact, a swift, cruel shift from indulgence to discipline in adolescence is far too familiar an experience in general, one too easily managed by others, to explain Bakunin's failure ever, psychologically, to leave his Premukhino childhood. Why did he in particular fail to make the transition? More important, why, unable to meet the demands of a military career did he not accept the fact and simply carry out his intention, as he wrote home at the end of 1834, "to retire from service and devote myself to serious study and civilian service."[72] As intelligent, ambitious, enterprising, and well-connected as he was, moreover, he could even have satisfied the contradictory demands implied in withdrawal-with-honor by doing what he told his parents at another time he planned to do, become a professor of history, law, or philosophy. Why was he unable even to begin a serious pursuit of such a career? Why did even the thought of entering a conventional career lead him to contemplate suicide?[73] Why did he prefer to remain forever dependent on support from others rather than use his remarkable talents to support himself? Why did he extend his revulsion towards the army to encompass all of society and why did this total rejection of society continue so long, his entire lifetime? Why, above all—the essential question—could his need for some display of manly power be satisfied only by apocalyptically violent and destructive visions and pronouncements?

What, in short, drove Bakunin so fiercely and relentlessly throughout his life from one extreme statement, theory, program, and action to another? What was the source of his "ineradicable desire," in the words of a recent biographer, "to create a revolution anywhere, at any time, or, more accurately, to 'revolt,' regardless of historical circumstances or potential sacrifices and without bothering about the proper organization of forces or the readiness of the people for new forms of life…?"[74] The point is that there is simply too much violence, too much force welling up from within and continuing too long—a lifetime—for it to be explained as merely a superficial attempt to conceal meekness, failure, and, in general, a temperament ill-suited to the challenge of circumstance. The social and familial conditions described above do not provide adequate explanation. We must look elsewhere for the causes of those extremes in character and behavior that more than anything else identify Bakunin in history. We must look more deeply into the man himself if we are to account for the violence, the failures, the "passions, intensified through constraint" that "rage," the "emotional forces" that "seethe." Because of the grave and persistent psychosexual and ego aberrations in Bakunin's life, the body of theory that I believe best equipped to guide this inquiry is the psychoanalytic. I have focused on four aspects of this theme: (1) Bakunin's impotence[75] and revulsion towards sexuality and anything "animal," as he called it; (2) the sources, mainly oedipal, that I believe were responsible for those disorders; (3) the deeper pathological narcissism, the malformation of the self, that was in part the cause of the oedipal failure and was, in turn, further exacerbated and decisively altered by that failure; and (4) the direct and indirect influences these oedipal and preoedipal, narcissistic roots had on Bakunin's thoughts and actions, and particularly on his violent visions and programs.[76]

There is another problem, or level of explanation, that one might pursue in this connection: a search for the ultimate causes, the specific traumatic events or situations responsible for the oedipal and narcissistic pathologies in the first place. Other than indicate some circumstances in Bakunin's early life conducive to this outcome, I say nothing about this, because the evidence is lacking. Some will argue that it is only here, at this most deeply concealed level, that one can properly speak of psychological cause and that all the rest—the oedipal and narcissistic aberrations, the resulting abnormal sexuality, and the peculiarities of thought and action reflecting those disturbances—are only "symptoms." If, in other words, there are those who will be distressed with any psychological explanation,[77] others will feel that the explanation does not go far enough.

Although most of the evidence relevant to these issues will be forthcoming, gradually, in succeeding chapters, there are a few suggestive hints in the period covered so far. With reference to Bakunin's revulsion toward sexuality, for example, while it may have been common for young romantics of the time to honor Platonic over carnal love, for Bakunin to describe his love for Maria as "divine pleasure granted one through the contemplation of a fine soul," statements such as the following surely indicate something deeper and more personally his own:

> It only needs some kind of sensual thought to penetrate my heart for
> my blood to quicken, my feelings to dull and my soul to be cast again
> into black gloom, anguish, suffering, self-laceration, and, when strength

is exhausted, silence. I collapse into a dreadful, numb despair. All of
nature then seems lifeless to me, dead. Everything appears to me as
through a stifling, bitter fog, gloomy, bent under the heavy hand of
a fierce and pitiless fate....[78]

Similarly, while it may have been quite within the Romantic vein for Bakunin
to have felt such loathing for those "occupations which modesty does not permit" him to name, for the "dark, filthy, and vile" side of barracks life (in contrast to the "pure and virginal"), we should keep in mind that he offered that
description and comparison in December 1837, when he was 23 years old. And,
surely, much more than commonplace Platonism comes through in his intense
reaction to Liubov's intended marriage, in the words and phrases he uses to express his revulsion at the sexual prospects facing Liubov. And that, too, was
written when he was 23. The extraordinary importance of that crisis in his life
is apparent not only from the fact that he returned to it with such passion over
four years later, but also from the attention he gave to it in a letter that he had
written as a survey of his entire life down to December 1837. The first five or so
pages of the letter (as printed) cover the years down to the time of the crisis, the
fall furlough of 1833. Then, with the exception of one page, the rest of the
letter, some 15 pages, is entirely devoted to the Liubov affair and to Bakunin's
related thoughts about sex and "purity," which he bolsters with dozens of
lengthy quotations from Scriptures in defense of chastity. The letter simply
breaks off while still on the subject, with nothing at all said about the next four
and one-half years.[79]

No less important for our understanding of Bakunin than these revelations
of his inner psychosexual turmoil is the talent he displays for projecting and
generalizing it, a practice that will soon become habitual with him. Even now,
in his youth, we see this process well underway. Beginning a letter written home
in October 1834 with another declaration of his determination to "rein in my
ardent nature and those passions that might lead me away from the true road"
and comparing his vow to that of "the apostle Paul" for whom as well "the spirit
is strong, but the flesh is weak!," Bakunin went on to project his war against the
"dark, filthy, and vile" onto the plane of universal history:

The soul, as a reflection of the divine, as pure flame, which burns only
with what is lofty and fine, can have no evil inclination, but advances
steadily to its fulfillment! The body has its own tendencies, its own
demands, its own inclinations which are dependent on its material
existence and which are quite incompatible with our lofty destiny! The
struggle between these two elements, which form man, fills the pages of
humanity's historical life. The victory of one or the other decides its

fate, the happiness or unhappiness, the bloom or ruin of a people, and the same for the individual man.[80]

These few examples, which will be richly reenforced in succeeding chapters, relate to Bakunin's abhorrence of anything sexual or "animal," as he will soon begin to call it. Part of the reason for that abhorrence, I will argue, was oedipal: sex meant incest to him and had, therefore, to be completely avoided by such strategies as impotence and the adoption of ideas and whole philosophies extolling "purity." Several conditions relevant to this oedipal theme (and also, in part, to the deeper, narcissistic, preoedipal cause) have also been noted above: the intensely emotional and, one would suspect, subtly erotic relationships nurtured in that romantic period of strong and explicit feeling, especially considering the almost exclusively feminine milieu in which Michael found himself the only male; the relative youth of his mother, making her closer in age to Michael than she was to her husband; the strange infrequency, verging on complete omission, of references to his mother in his numerous letters home during his six years away, compared with his constant and warmly affectionate references to and about his father; and the fact that Bakunin's retreat inwards came so soon, just a few months, after the Liubov crisis in which he experienced such profound disgust at the thought of the sexual experiences awaiting his sister. The Liubov crisis is the first instance of a process that we will see occurring repeatedly in Bakunin's life—a merger in his mind between his sisters and himself (in this case identifying himself with the repulsive fate threatening Liubov) and between his sisters and his mother (displacing incestual attractions from mother to sisters and, therefore, making anything sexual involving his sisters all the more abhorrent to him). Among the evidence we will see later in support of the oedipal side of this interpretation (and the bulk of that evidence is still to come) are: Bakunin's incestual love for his sister Tatiana; his bitter "hatred" towards his mother, which he reveals when he does begin to express his feelings towards her and which he justifies by accusing her of sensuality (seduction); his persistent efforts to break up marriages or to keep them from taking place; and a variety of statements and actions throughout his life that mirror an underlying oedipal disturbance with striking clarity, especially those involving his attitudes toward conventional male social and familial roles and towards "power."

With respect, more specifically, to the narcissistic pattern thus far, perhaps the most revealing of Bakunin's adolescent experiences is the relationship between the Liubov conflict of late 1833 and Bakunin's escape inwards, when he spurned the "empty" outer world, "locked" himself narcissistically within himself, and there found relief as "a warmth so sweet poured" through him and as he felt himself "being reborn...being fed and nurtured." Those phrases and the overall general feelings they express are remarkably precise reflections of the primitive processes involved in the early stages of narcissistic development. While Freud never developed a complete theory of narcissism, perhaps because he did not consider that disorder amenable to psychoanalytic treatment, he did distinguish between two types of narcissism, the second of which describing a child's return into himself after having failed, for whatever reason, to establish rapport with the world outside. We have already seen throughout this chapter, and will see further as this study progresses, how central that pattern of withdrawal was in Bakunin's life. Besides focusing attention on the child's withdrawal of emotional investment (cathexis) from the outer world and reinvesting it back into himself, more recent theories of narcissism have emphasized the critical importance of the preoedipal child-mother psychological merger in what the child experiences as a subjective unity, a "dual unity" or "symbiotic couple," an infantile union and identification with the idealized, all-good image of the one by whom the child is "fed and nurtured." In normal maturation, the child emerges from that union as an autonomous, self-aware individual, clearly distinguishing between himself and the no less autonomous, individual objects in the outside world. In pathological narcissism, however, the child, in effect, remains locked within that idealized maternal world and permanently estranged from an external world that forever appears to the child as both inextricably connected and inflexibly hostile to him.[81] Echoes of this process as well will come through again and again as we watch Bakunin's life unfold.

Finally, and an essential theme in this interpretation of Bakunin's motivations, there is the decisive relationship between the two sets of dynamics, oedipal and narcissistic. While this will become clearer as the study advances, we can see already one expression of that relationship in the association between the Liubov conflict of 1833 and Bakunin's subsequent retreat inwards to be "fed and nurtured" from within. What we see here, I believe, is a retreat from a revived oedipal crisis back into an undemanding, consoling, preoedipal narcissistic "dual unity."[82] If that was indeed the process involved, then I would suggest further that his behavior in 1833–34 was a reenactment of a much earlier experience and one that was critical in determining Bakunin's later personality and politics: his regression more deeply into the preoedipal, narcissistic "symbiotic couple" after the initial oedipal failure. More will be said later about this interaction and its effects on Bakunin's thought and deeds. In general, it is the relationship between these two patterns, oedipal and narcissistic, that will be presented as the ultimate source of Bakunin's millennial aims and destructive means, the roots of his apocalypse.[83]

2.

SANCTUARY

At the end of 1834 Bakunin got his chance to escape the ordeal that had driven him to despair. He was chosen to go to Tver, near Premukhino, to get horses for his regiment. Once there, he was determined to remain, come what may. He had had enough. His parents pleaded with him to go back, fearing his arrest and forced return, but he was adamant. Month after month he malingered, claiming illness, while his father, drawing on the good offices of high-ranking relatives and friends, worked strenuously to save him and the family from the disgrace of dishonorable discharge or worse.[1]

Notwithstanding worries over the government's response to his de facto desertion, the year 1835 was a happy year for Bakunin, a year of emotional ascent, contrasting sharply with the previous years of deepening gloom. He was showered with all that he had missed so long—the gentle ease of the countryside, many old and new friendships with young men and women who fully shared his luxuriantly Romantic sentiments, and, best of all, an abundance of recognition and admiration that had been almost totally denied him since he had left home seven years earlier. One discordant note rudely jarred the harmony, however: his parents took no part in the chorus of praise. On the contrary, they regarded those who praised him and the reasons for the praise with growing anxiety, animosity, and disgust. As the year progressed, the doubts about their eldest son's character and future that had taken root during his dismal army career became firmly fixed.

While serving in the provinces Bakunin had little but his own inner world, his memories, and his grandiose ambitions to ease the pain he suffered both from his surroundings and from his parents' criticisms. He had been alone and could share his feelings with no one. Now back home, free of the barracks, everything was different. He was at once drawn into a variety of intimate circles of closely kindred spirits—his own sisters, the Beyer sisters (long-time neighbors and friends of the Bakunins) and the extraordinary "Stankevich circle." Natalie Beyer had for some years been a member of this most famous of all Russian circles and in love with its leader, Nicholas Stankevich.[2] At first Stankevich had reciprocated her affections, but by then, the beginning of 1835, his feelings had cooled and relations were strained. Still, he and his friends continued to visit regularly the Moscow apartment where the Beyer family spent the winter and provided one of the many salons for young Moscow intellectuals. It was at one of these evening gatherings that Bakunin, on a brief visit to Moscow with his family in March, met Stankevich and "spent half the night" talking with him and other members of his circle.[3]

It is difficult now, if not impossible, to know just what sort of person Stankevich really was. His contemporaries idealized him into a demigod of goodness and wisdom, and his principal biographers virtually elevated him to sainthood. "I have never loved anyone as I loved that man, whom I have never met. What purity! What tenderness!" Tolstoy exclaimed after reading one of these hagiographic accounts.[4] He "stretched out a hand to me and showed me the true path," Ivan Turgenev wrote.[5] "In him I have lost the better half of myself," the eminent historian Granovsky said when Stankevich died of consumption at the age of 27.[6]

Wistfully gentle, selfless, graceful and gracious, devoted to the life of the mind and spirit, to art, music, nature, love and friendship, taller than most, with a sloping forehead, dark eyes, long curly black hair down to his shoulders, and with a foreboding of early death hovering over him—he was the archetypical Romantic, a personification of Schiller's *Schöne Seele*, the beautiful soul towards which all noble youth aspired. Although on occasion lighthearted, and often surprisingly practical, he was, on the whole, a sad, brooding, melancholy soul, more enraptured by darkness and pain than by light and joy. "I would like to go to Eger to take a look at the room where Wallenstein was killed. I love that epoch, and I do, it appears, because of Schiller's tragedies," Stankevich wrote to Y. M. Neverov, a circle intimate.[7] His own poems, correspondingly, extoll the renunciation of life's joys, the rejection of "The Angel of Pleasure" for the sake of some higher love, dedication, destiny. Of the "Two Paths" and "Two Ways of Life" (titles of poems) it was for him the path of sorrow rather than of happiness "which alone speaks truth."[8]

His biography is fairly standard for the period: noble and wealthy parents owning thousands of serfs; a special school for the sons of the nobility at the age of 12; Moscow University five years later, in 1830, where he studied literature, philosophy, and—his dissertation field—history; and dilettantish excursions into poetry and music. After graduating in 1834 he received the customary sinecure, "honorary inspector of schools," which, however, in no way disturbed his scholarly and aesthetic pursuits and which he abandoned three years later in order to go to Berlin and enrich his knowledge of Hegel at the source. In the spring of 1840 his illness, which had been with him throughout his university years, rapidly worsened, and in June he died quietly in a town north of Genoa on his way to Lake Como, where his doctors had advised him to spend the winter.

He left little of intellectual or artistic value: a few mediocre poems, a Schillerian tragic drama, an unctious short story, some journal essays, and a collection of historically invaluable letters. But it was in his person, not in his productions, that he proved of great and lasting importance, for he managed to gather around himself and influence men who were soon to become some of the most prominent leaders of Russian thought and literature. Belinsky, Turgenev, Bakunin, Granovsky, Katkov, Aksakov, Kolstov—these are the most illustrious of a larger list of those who, at various times after 1831 (Stankevich's second year at the university), met in his apartment to read poetry, listen to music, and discuss art, literature, religion, and philosophy. It was an aesthetic brotherhood where the form of rapport, the cult of intimate friendship, blended perfectly with the intellectual content—almost exclusively Romantic literature, Idealistic philosophy, and evangelic religious works.

Scholars writing on the period quite reasonably attribute the prominence and remarkable intellectual influence of Stankevich and his circle of detached philosophical Idealists to the bleak repression that followed the Decembrist rising of 1825, and that was further intensified by Nicholas I in the wake of the 1830 revolutions in Poland and France. Terrified and, in his view, betrayed by the young noblemen who had risen against his throne, Nicholas was determined not only to punish the malefactors, but to stifle in advance any recurrence of such audacious opposition. In one office after another, he replaced the unreliable nobility by career military men. A report to the Tsar in 1832, by one Count S. S. Uvarov—soon to become minister of education—set the tone of the regime by urging a curriculum inspired by "the authentically Russian conservative principles of Orthodoxy, Autocracy and Nationality" and directed toward increasing "as far as possible, the number of 'intellectual dams.'" One might have thought that enough dams were already in place since the new education law of 1828, revising the laws of 1803, had lengthened the high school program, dropped the more humanistic subjects, increased control of university affairs by state officials, appointed school inspectors to watch over student behavior, required students to wear uniforms and take courses in theology, church history, and church law, abolished university courts, and filled professorial positions (a discretionary power now given to the minister of education) with properly conservative instructors. Moreover, to strengthen the dams further, overlapping networks of censors had been established involving virtually every administrative office in the government, the department of horse breeding included. At the top, overseeing everything, stood the fearsome and ubiquitous "secret police," the notorious Third Section organized in 1826. Constant surveillance and controls, ever increasing and tightening centralization, universal fear, suspicion, secrecy, distrust and obsessive precaution—such were the hallmarks of political and, to a considerable extent, social life under Nicholas.

"Western" liberal thought and expression of the kind that had prevailed during much of the preceding reign now went underground, taking refuge in the few secret organizations, mainly centered in and around Moscow University, that had the temerity to survive. By 1831–32, however, these daring heirs of the Decembrist tradition had been apprehended and exiled. Even those, like Alexander Herzen and his friend Nicholas Ogarev, who had confined their liberal sentiments to salon discussions and private correspondence had been arrested for sedition by 1835, the year that Bakunin decided he had had his fill of the military. However, it is hardly likely that Bakunin would have been drawn to the Herzen circle or into any other political opposition group even had they still been on the Moscow scene at the time. Whatever Bakunin was to become, young Michael Bakunin was politically conservative if not simply apolitical. One need only compare the statements quoted in the beginning of Chapter 1 with the views of Herzen and his friends to see how wide a gap separated them. Not only had members of the Herzen circle seen themselves as dedicated followers of the Decembrists, prepared to devote their lives to continuing the political struggle against Tsarism, but several of them, Herzen included, had already advanced beyond constitutional liberalism to a form of St. Simonian socialism. Although Bakunin and the Herzen group were approximately the same age—all born about the time of the 1812 war—there is not a hint in Bakunin's voluminous correspondence in these years to suggest anything like that. With Stankevich and his friends, on the contrary, there are echoes everywhere, and one can easily understand why Bakunin would have felt very much at home among them and their poetry, their love of nature, their devotion to Romantic sensibility, and their study of abstract German philosophy. It was precisely toward these preferences and involvements, we should keep in mind, that Bakunin's reading of Venevitinov, his "intellectual revolution," his work on German Idealism with Krasnopolsky, and most of his other experiences had been taking him during those last years of his military career.

"Come on over, please, and we'll chat about the immortality of the soul and all the rest," Stankevich wrote to Neverov, cofounder of the circle and his closest friend, at least until Bakunin arrived.[9] "And all the rest" meant not political, social, or economic concerns, but a poetry reading by Stankevich or by the peasant poet Kolstov, a discussion of Goethe, Hoffman, or Schiller, or, more likely than anything else, some more Schelling—Schelling above all. No other intellectual influence can compare with German Idealism—Schelling, Fichte, Hegel—in its lasting impact on Bakunin's ideas and actions. What German Idealism did for Bakunin was to legitimize to his satisfaction all his purely subjective intuitions, all his intellectual projections, all the products of his richly fertile imagination. Although this process of legitimation was to be further strengthened and sanctified as Bakunin moved from Schelling through Fichte and, especially, to Hegel, we can already see in this Schelling period, roughly 1834–35, the foundations being laid for that extraordinary self-assurance that later allowed Bakunin to deduce, with only an occasional glance at the real world, long, detailed, complex analysis and surveys of social, economic, political, cultural, and historical conditions, interactions, and developments. To review some main themes of this philosophy (in its Russian form), however archaic, arcane, or turgid it might at times seem to readers today, is essential, therefore, for our understanding of Bakunin's later mode and substance of thought: the following survey concerns, in other words, not just a passing, juvenile phase in Bakunin's formative years, but the permanent base and frame of his entire life and thought.

The first and principal contribution of German Idealism, beginning with Schelling, in helping define the pattern and direction of Bakunin's intellectual and political evolution, was to show Bakunin how to meet the basic problem discussed earlier, how to preserve the gratification of an indulgent childhood while at the same time seeming to fulfill the requirements of an honorable manhood. His temperament and its psychological sources had already led him to reject society and to "lock" himself within his own inner world and its "warmth so sweet." But could he go on doing that after he left the army? He was already 21 years old. His father, well into his 60s by then, looked to him as the eldest son for help and, as we will see, expected him at least to begin preparations for another career, now that a military future was closed to him. Moreover, how could he go on ensconced in his consoling and delightful inner refuge when at the same time he felt those "passions...rage," those "emotional forces seethe" within him, when he was determined not to be "a futile, meaningless link in the chain of humanity," when he shared his father's belief that "to fulfill one's obligation is the sacred duty of a man and citizen"?

German Idealism provided Bakunin with the first of a series of highly effective systems he was to use as means of reconciling those contradictory needs. It did so by dignifying, indeed glorifying, Romantic withdrawal: to leave society and its conventional pleasures, aims, and interests and devote oneself instead to the world within was not to escape fearfully from reality, but to advance boldly into Reality. The ordinary Romantic aesthete might have reason to feel guilty for so lavishly and exclusively indulging his sensibilities in philosophy, poetry, music, and nature while others took care of his mundane physical needs. The Idealist, however, was convinced that he was as far removed as possible from egoistical self-indulgence. On the contrary, he was engaged in an arduous self-denying ascent towards Truth, thereby fulfilling his sacred calling and charting the way for other, weaker spirits to follow. What had been at first a fragile personal refuge from a repugnant external world thus became, thanks to philosophy, the fortress sanctuary of the "warrior for holy truth," as Bakunin would soon present himself.[10] He regretted, of course, that his parents and others, failing to understand what he was doing, criticized him for what they considered immaturity, egoism, laziness, and thoughtless irresponsibility. But he would stoically bear their reproaches, strong in the knowledge that the path he had chosen—or rather, for which he had been chosen—was infinitely more honorable, noble, and sacred than the trivial Philistine careers his father urged on him.

Besides transmuting the inner refuge of a fearful boy into the proud bastion of a fearless warrior, German Idealism taught Bakunin that the imagination that had helped him bear those lonely army years by conjuring up visions of his Premukhino childhood was capable of far grander miracles: imagination in the form of introspective, speculative philosophy was the vehicle for reaching Absolute Knowledge of Objective Reality. Indeed, Idealism taught him—and he never forgot the lesson—that there was no other path to authentic Truth except the path that lay within his own subjective intuitions. Professor D. M. Vellansky, the doyen of Russian Schellingites (a "voice in the wilderness," in hiw own words, until the Decembrist debacle made Schellingesque withdrawal fashionable) insisted that "true knowledge consists of ideas, not sense data," that "experience and observation deal with the transient and limited forms of things, but do not touch their limitless and eternal essence."[11] What Vellansky taught in St. Petersburg, Professor Davydov echoed in Moscow, arguing that since "everything perceptible must be known through the Spirit, and since this is only possible if the laws of the knowing Spirit conform to the laws of phenomenal existence, it is clear that the forms of knowledge are in accord with the forms of being and that they may be reciprocally explained."[12] Or, as Prince V. F. Odoevsky, one of Vellansky's most productive students, put it, "rational being...reflects the essence itself of the Absolute."[13] D. F. Venevitinov, a student of another of Russia's leading Schellingite popularizers, M. G. Pavlov, and apparently the first to introduce Bakunin to Schelling's world-view,[14] concisely summarized the Idealists' argument in his prediction that "all knowledge will be founded on one science alone, that of a knowledge of the self."[15]

What was promised as the fruit of speculative philosophy, moreover, was not knowledge of one or another aspect of reality, but the total knowledge of all Being, both in its constituent parts and in all their complex interrelations. "We believed," Odoevsky later recalled, "in the possibility of an absolute theory by means of which one would be able to arrange all the phenomena of nature....At the time, all of nature, all of human life, seemed very clear to us, and we rather looked down on the physicists and chemists...who rooted about in 'vulgar matter'."[16] Similarly, Stankevich set as his goal the attainment of "complete unity in the universe of my knowledge. I wish to give myself an account of each phenomenon. I wish to see the connection of each phenomenon with the life of the whole world, its necessity, its role in the development of the one idea."[17]

The world for the Idealist, a world accessible to man not through empirical observation but through deductive speculation, was an all-inclusive and elegantly integrated whole in which everything was rationally, neatly, harmoniously inter-connected, symbiotically intertwined. Trusting entirely to "rational" intuition and using empirical facts and events only as illustrations of the intuited "idea," Vellansky and Galitch of the University of St. Petersburg and, later and more influentially, Pavlov and Davydov at Moscow University created fascinating portraits of the universe, describing with meticulous precision the kaleidoscopic relationships that mutually linked everything with everything else, each phenom-enon reflecting all others. Biology, art, physics, poetry, morality, history, min-erology, cosmology—nothing was omitted. Phenomena from one realm of Being wonderfully mirrored counterparts in others. Each order of existence (inorganic, organic, spiritual), so they argued, had its corresponding spiritual principle (Truth, Beauty, Goodness) and its corresponding human faculty for apprehend-ing it (thought, sensibility, will). An awesome symphony of echoes played on endlessly for man's illumination and enjoyment. What poets had thought to be mere metaphors and images were transmuted through the alchemy of Schelling's Idealism into objective, scientific facts. "The flower corresponds to a circle, and the fruit, to an ellipse. The living hyperbole (which is the circle in its contrasting value) is our organ of smell. The living oval (which corresponds to the ellipse) is our organ of taste. For this reason, the flower pleases our scent, and the fruit, our taste."[18]

As another example, there is a characteristic essay by D. V. Venevitinov in which he relates the four phases of the day (morning, afternoon, evening, night) to the four phases of human life, both individual life and the life of mankind. In the morning of life, the individual and mankind vainly strive toward the inaccessible. During noontime they come to accept necessity and the limits of their own power, as a result of struggling to conquer nature. These combative passions wane towards evening. At night, there is silence and peace. All this, it must be kept in mind, was not intended as Romantic, poetic metaphor, but rather as natural science, as descriptions of objective, "Absolute" Reality.

Besides being indebted to German Idealism for his conviction that he could intuit the general outlines and details of reality, past, present, and future, Bakunin owed to it something no less fateful, for himself and for the world: his belief that since he could predict the general course of future reality, he had been chosen to lead others into it. While this gift of leadership was to come to him mainly through Fichte's influence, as we will see later, it is already implicit in this earlier Schelling phase, both in Schelling's aesthetics, which contained for many of his Russian adepts, like Stankevich, his most attractive message, and in his organic and dialectical theories of growth.

It was in man's "aesthetic development," Odoevsky wrote, that "the life of the future is symbolically and prophetically prefigured . . . a life which will provide that wholeness which existed in Adam before the fall."[19] Consequently, by nature of their crafts, by their involvement in this realm of perfect forms and harmonious unities, great painters, poets, and musicians provided mankind with models for the ideal social life of justice and peace. At root, aesthetics and ethics were engaged in the same concerns and pursuits—proportion, balance, harmony. "Sculpture, Painting, and Music" became, in an essay by Venevitinov bearing that title, goddesses who inspired in humanity the ideal of turning dead matter into living forms (sculpture), expressed the harmony of the infinite (painting), and raised man into a higher, ineffable world (music).[20] "Man possesses a *moral sentiment* which is the principle of his action and which consists of a need for harmony and sympathy," Davydov wrote. And as a need for harmony fostered moral sentiment, the latter, in turn, inspired a sense of society and of one's responsibility to it: "happiness is only the need of a *harmony of sentiments.* Happiness for the man of virtue consists, therefore, in the welfare of all and each."[21] If, as Odoevsky said, reflecting one side of the credo, "Science must become poetic," it was also true, he went on, reflecting the other, that "the poet is always a moral man."[22]

While Schelling's aesthetics provided the harmonious ideal for society to strive towards, his organic and dialectical theories of growth in nature implied the means of realizing that ideal. Beginning with the classical idea of the "seed" being the "form" containing (potentially, ideally) all that later evolves from it, Pavlov went on to describe this evolution as dialectical, a sequence of resolutions reconciling opposing forces or attributes. (Matter, for instance, was a synthesis of light, which was the centrifugal force, and weight, which was the opposing centripital force.)[23] In an essay called *The Dialogue between Plato and Anaxagorus*, Venevitinov, especially well-endowed with the Idealists' ear for echoes, skillfully transferred the Idealist's dialectic from nature to man and society. Outlining a theme that Bakunin was later to use repeatedly, he described the individual's life as well as the career of humanity as a three-stage dialectic. In the first period the individual lived in complete harmony with nature. But it was a childish, innocent harmony: the youngster was neither aware of the harmony nor of himself. In his progress towards self-awareness, which consumed most of his life, the individual exchanged this innocent harmony for an existence filled with struggle and pain, since only by testing his capacities through work and conflict could the individual acquire self-consciousness. Finally, near life's end the lost harmony was regained, but it was now an infinitely more sublime and joyful harmony, for the individual was now fully aware of himself, of the world, and of the beatific bonds that joined them. It was the same with humanity as a whole: a golden age of unconscious harmony, first sacrificed for the sake of achieving self-awareness, then regained, but on a higher level because consciously enjoyed. In both cases, that of the individual and of mankind as a whole, struggle and suffering were as inevitable as they were beneficial, for without them there would be neither self-awareness—the quintessential attribute of man's soul and the world's—nor the attainment of the ultimate goal, paradise regained. Venevitinov could already see hints of that final realization and fulfillment. "Believe me, Anaxagorus, believe me, it will come again, this era of happiness of which mortals dream....What does it matter how long it will be? We will no longer be alive, but this thought consoles me: my spirit is proud to have foreseen and perhaps to have brought this future nearer."[24]

Here, in brief, was the world of thought and feeling inhabited by Stankevich and his friends when the young Bakunin, still in uniform, met them in 1835. Shortly before his first meeting with Stankevich, several changes had taken place in the circle that eased Bakunin's entry. Following Stankevich's lead, the circle had recently shifted its interests in the direction that Bakunin had also just begun to follow. Throughout most of his university years, Stankevich's first love had been art and literature rather than philosophy: of the two main influences on him, Schiller and Schelling, it had been the former, with his "beautiful soul" and aesthetic humanism, that had most fascinated him. Then, in the fall of 1834, at the same time, that is, that Bakunin was beginning his study of German philosophy under Dr. Krasnopolsky's guidance, Stankevich had turned his attention to Schelling, in part to prepare himself for the M. A. degree examinations he planned to take in the spring (1835). Stankevich's serious study of philosophy undermined somewhat his relationship with Neverov, who until then had been his closest friend, but who had no wish to abandon pleasantly dilettantish discussions on art and literature for more rigorous philosophical analysis. Bakunin's succession to Neverov as the favored friend was also encouraged by some romantic maneuvers then underway in the circle. When, as we have seen, Stankevich's feelings for Natalie Beyer cooled, she reacted, perhaps to demonstrate the nobility of her own "beautiful soul," by trying to spark a romance between Stankevich and Bakunin's sister, Liubov. Probably to her chagrin, it worked, for Stankevich at once fell in love with Liubov.

In mid-April (1835), about a month after their meeting, Bakunin sent Stankevich a note inviting him to visit Premukhino. In his reply, which he wrote within the week, Stankevich shows that he was as pleased to welcome Bakunin into the circle as Bakunin was to join. "Besides the very natural wish to be with someone whose thoughts you share completely," Stankevich said that he sought friends like Bakunin because "they sustain my activity, keep me energetic."[25] As for Bakunin's invitation to visit Premukhino, however, Stankevich said only that he hoped to be able to come sometime. He would wait, he said in a later letter, until A. P. Efremov (a member of the Stankevich circle who had already visited Premukhino that summer) would be able to go with him. At the end of September, Bakunin again invited him and Efremov, this time to join the family in celebration of the elder Bakunin's nameday.[26] The invitation was made "so kindly and delicately," Stankevich wrote the Beyer sisters, that "it would have been impolite not to go."[27] The visit was a great success and resulted in "a very close friendship," Stankevich told the Beyers. For days on end he and Bakunin sat together in Bakunin's room smoking their pipes and fervently planning for the future. What "a pure and noble soul" Bakunin was,[28] "so much intelligence, feeling, honesty," Stankevich told Neverov and the Beyers.[29] "My friend! I think I know you well," he wrote Bakunin two weeks after the visit. "You are formed for some noble work, you understand things so easily, believe so much in the worth of man that one cannot doubt your destiny."[30]

Besides gaining for Bakunin a privileged place in Stankevich's esteem, the brief visit to Premukhino seems to have had a powerful and positive effect on Stankevich. On the eve of his and Efremov's departure for Premukhino, during a short delay due to Efremov's poor health, Stankevich wrote Bakunin a quiet, mellow, rather depressed letter in which he spoke of his need of sympathetic friends "to save me from deadly boredom."[31] In a letter sent immediately after his return to Moscow, however, he wrote that the time he had spent with Bakunin had "decided my fate," that he was now "resolved in my plans," and that he would "not deviate from them a single step. I will not anticipate even the slightest difficulty. I will regard my work as the only possible pleasure for me, as my life."[32] Bakunin's path and his own were one, he told the Beyers after the visit. "We have the same ideas, the same doubts, the same needs," he wrote Bakunin a little later.[33]

The first step in their mutual plans was to study together. They would begin with Kant, under Stankevich's guidance. This in no way meant their abandonment of Schelling, however, for time and again in the correspondence following the visit, Stankevich reasserted his allegiance to Schelling's world view. "Schelling forms already so much a part of my life," he said, "that no general idea enters my head other than in relationship to his system." Nevertheless, he now argued, Kant's "dry critique is a preparation for Schelling's poetry"; it provided a "foundation for Schelling's system."[34]

But it was rough going: Stankevich clearly preferred the "poetry" of Schelling to Kant's "dry critique." He doggedly stuck to it, however. Though he complained in letter after letter about Kant's tedious concepts and complex arguments and about the constant, fierce headaches they gave him, Stankevich continued to give seven hours a day to Kant and would have given more but for his doctor's insistence that he limit himself and that he spend at least a couple of hours daily on afternoon walks. Nor could he study in the evenings, for he found it utterly impossible to sleep after Kant. "My headache returns often, and I sleep poorly. Dry formulas, incomprehensible during the day, abandoned in irritation, come back to me in delirium. If even a slight headache comes again, I'm going to throw Kant to the devil, or else I'll destroy myself once and for all."[35] It was especially Kant's discussion of the categories, a "mess of boiled kasha," that infuriated Stankevich. "What tormenting concepts! You read it, reread it, break your skull on it, but nothing, you get nowhere. You throw it down, take a walk, your head bursting, tortured by despair and hurt pride, you see that all your dreams, all your passionate vows, must perish."[36]

Since this was his own reaction to Kant, he understandably assumed that Bakunin, who had himself acknowledged his inadequate background in philosophy, would soon "hurl [Kant's] book into some corner out of frustration," convinced that "German philosophy was nonsense."[37] So he spurred Bakunin on, advised him repeatedly to be patient, to go slowly and methodically, to read regularly, but not at night. He sent him his only copy of Kant's *Critique of Pure Reason*, spent much time preparing outlines of Kant's arguments for Bakunin, answered his questions along the way ("Is reason a consequence of organization? Of course. All nature is organization....There is nothing in this offensive to reason and nothing anti-religious"),[38] and loaned him copies of various secondary sources and commentaries to guide him through the labyrinth.

But this correspondence course that Stankevich provided Bakunin involved more than Kant and philosophy. Bakunin must also study mathematics, two or three hours a day,[39] Stankevich insisted, and history as well. He was particularly emphatic about history: by studying history "We will not lose human feeling in the abstract absolute, but carry the ideal into life and give life to the ideal."[40] "For God's sake, don't forget history. Without it knowledge will be too dry and dead. We must join the unity of the idea with the diversity of the facts—this is the ideal of knowledge: then it becomes poetry....Study history so that you can give a clear account of the origins and development of each society and its influence on others."[41]

It is important for what is to follow to keep in mind this historical, temporal, "realistic" facet of German Idealism, at least as it was interpreted by its Russian adherents. As we have seen, German Idealism pointed in two directions: while most of these young Russian Idealists would have agreed with Neverov that "Art is becoming a divinity" and that man must live with art "if he is not to sink to the level of the beast,"[42] they were also attentive to its social message, implicit and expressed, as discussed above.[43] If Stankevich could ask Bakunin to "persuade me that we are not of this world, though it lures us, that our happiness lies entirely in the universal,"[44] he also urged him, as we saw, to study history and the "facts." Displaying one facet of the dualism, one young Idealist at the time wrote: "I search for consolation in Schelling and Plato. How happy I am to find them after having spent much time among the shadow-show....I swear to you that had these divine geniuses not recalled me to my celestial fatherland, I would have been in the end completely brutalized by the atmosphere that surrounds me...."[45] There was probably no one in the Stankevich circle, and least of all Bakunin at the time, who would have felt otherwise. Still, there were also probably none who would have taken issue with Stankevich's intention to remain in that "brutalizing" atmosphere in order "to show people their worth and their destiny"[46] or who would have disagreed with his belief that "human action...by the first act of will begins a new creation. History is a second nature created by man."[47]

In all these discussions and through all this correspondence with Stankevich and his friends that year (1835) Bakunin heard resonant and encouraging echoes of what he had been telling himself at least as far back as his "intellectual revolution" in January 1834. Disclosing from the outset his remarkable gifts—as thinker, writer, and inspirational leader—Bakunin quickly moved ahead of the others in the circle, including even Stankevich, both in his ability to master the volumes they were reading and in his relentless zeal to draw others into the new faith. His enthusiasm is understandable, for the doctrines met all his needs at the time: legitimation of his retreat inwards permitted him to remain safely detached, "locked" within himself, "fed and nurtured"; while the designation of the artist, poet, and philosopher as society's custodians of harmony, justice, and peace who were called upon to lead mankind through its dialectical ascent, assured him that the retreat inwards in no way doomed him to the life of "a futile, meaningless link in the chain of humanity." What was especially gratifying was that both sides, child and man, were served by the same act—preaching to others the need of withdrawing from society and devoting themselves to the inner life, the only true way since it was the only way to the Truth.

Counselling Natalie Beyer, who was distressed by Stankevich's change of heart towards her, Bakunin urged her that April (1835) to attempt a "moral rebirth" by becoming "absorbed in contemplation of your soul." "You must try to know its nature," he went on, "by studying all its facets....You speak of inner life, but you have never known its sweetness, because all your thoughts and feelings are tied to external things. And precisely here is the reason for your depression and despair. For the person living an inner life always has in his own heart a friend, a friend who lavishly recompenses him for all that he suffers."[48] She must depend always and only on this "friend" within and take care "never to sacrifice your inner life to the whims of other people."[49] This was the message that he liberally dispersed to his friends and relatives that year. Only within one's own trustworthy inner world could one find happiness and fulfillment. "Everything external depends on fate, only our inner world is entirely dependent on us....Heaven is within us, and we must live within ourselves....The heaven we have within ourselves is eternal....The main thing is not to subordinate one's spiritual life to external circumstances. Hopes founded on the outside world— that is the main reason for our spiritual and moral ruin....I continue to tell myself that concentration within oneself, estrangement from any kind of aspiration in the external world, that this is what remains for us to do."[50]

While "concentration within oneself" was his first concern, it was clearly, even now, not his last. For if one side of him experienced "estrangement from any kind of aspiration in the external world," the other side felt the pull of the "divine hand that had inscribed in my heart these sacred words, encompassing my whole being: 'He shall not live for himself.'" "To be capable of sacrificing everything for this sacred aim," he went on in this letter to the Beyers, "this is my only ambition."[51] The only unhappiness, he told A. P. Efremov, the member of the Stankevich circle to whom he felt closest, was to "lose the desire, the aspiration, and the strength for action and to lack an aim. Then a man not only could, but even should shoot himself. We are still only preparing ourselves for action....One thing only; we must try to eliminate as completely as possible the influence of the outside world."[52]

Although Bakunin was the newest member of the circle, his role seems to have been to emphasize this missionary, activist side of its philosophical Idealism. He stressed repeatedly that he and his friends must fulfill their high calling, and towards that end they must above all get rid of "the stifling swaddling clothes of our eighteenth century," especially its "scepticism towards anything lofty."[53] It was this scepticism that had made them "all weak, all Hamlets... shallow, futile people, incapable of great deeds."[54] He, for one, was determined to overcome that weakness, and he called upon them to join him. "No, my friends, the future is within us; we have the strength....We will not stop. Then will the great deeds be fruitful, our conscience clean....There is nothing for us to fear. We ask nothing. Everything depends on us....You say that one cannot always do what one chooses to do. Nonsense. One can do whatever he has strength enough to want to do. Strength of will, my friend—that is everything."[55] So, "March forward without looking back, Hurrah!" he urged Efremov,[56] raising the militant martial pitch still higher (at the very time his father was trying to save him from dishonor for deserting the army). The passions that "rage" and emotional forces that "seethe" were, thus, already flowing freely into the messianic channel that was to be their main outlet for the rest of his life. "We will not pass through this temporal world in vain," he assured Efremov. "Our passage will not be fruitless: we will revive the dead, lift the fallen."[57] Even now, he could see ahead to a "better world, a fuller, more harmonious life."[58]

Bakunin had found in the Stankevich circle both a new family, one that would appreciate him as his parents did not, and the beginnings at least of a company of elite missionaries chosen, as he felt he had been, to save mankind from its sundry corruptions. He had been drawn to Efremov, for example, as he told him that July, 1835, because he had seen in him "that burning emotion, that thirst for action, for a better, more poetic life, a thirst for the welfare of our fatherland, of all humanity, which I had already long since (and almost in vain) set as the object of what I looked for in people...."[59] And now that they had met, he felt that, "I am no longer alone, my hopes are not mere smoke, but sacred, inspired dreams, not vapid sounds, but substance, sublime substance, *given to only a very few on earth,* substance obligated to become our steadfast, constant guide in the career of action."[60] "Under the conditions of our social life," he similarly wrote Neverov in October, "such friendship is necessary if one is not to lose completely a faith in the lofty destiny of man....This is why one inevitably seeks out the company of people with whom one might live a genuine life."[61] By the year's end these friendships had become indispensable for Bakunin. "Withdraw your friendship," he wrote Efremov in November, "and I think [my future] will fall and never be raised again...we must never part...that would be my death sentence."[62]

The above reference to this group as a circle of missionaries is entirely appropriate, for in Bakunin's eyes the work they were destined to do was indeed God's work. Not only did he proudly, explicitly, and repeatedly proclaim the religious devotion he had imbibed at Premukhino, but this devotion and its expression were to become increasingly stronger as the years went on, down to *and including* his entry into the revolutionary movement in 1842. When he spoke of the "divine hand" having inscribed a sacred calling on his heart, he was drawing upon a well-defined theistic world view that encompassed and fused for him all spheres of nature, man, and society. One quotation will have to do as illustration, although it should be stressed that over the next six or so years his letters and articles are filled with comparable thoughts and sentiments:

> God, having reflected himself in nature then created animal life and breathed into it the divine spark, a particle of the transcendent idea that is so well reflected in the harmony of the universe. And this animal was transformed into man, for whom God became the end and nature the means. What really is Humanity? God imprisoned in matter. Its life is the striving toward freedom, toward unity with the aim. The expression of its life is love, this fundamental element of the eternal. It comprises individual parts, related as kin but separated one from the other through the force of matter, torn from its transcendent origin. Here is the source of the sympathy of one man for another, of man for the human specie, of man for the perfectability of humanity. All of them join hands to overthrow the yoke of matter. United they are strong, for the more numerous they are, the more powerful is the idea and the nearer is man to God.[63]

We see in this remarkably gnostic statement the same projection that was evident in Bakunin's elevation of his own inner struggle with "sensual thought" onto the level of a universal contest between the desires of the "body" and those of the "soul."[64] Rejection of "matter" and everything "sensual" represents one side of Bakunin's strategy. The other is apparent in his association between "freedom" and "unity with the aim," his belief that the purpose of human life is to end the present deplorable situation in which "individual parts, related as kin" are "separated one from the other through the force of matter, torn from [their] transcendent origin." Everything that exists, he said elsewhere, reflects "the eternal aspiration of a part towards the whole," "the aspiration towards wholeness."[65] The essential thought (Freudian dream-thought) latent in these combined oedipal and narcissistic projections is the yearning of the "part" for reunion with the "whole," "its transcendent origin," and the conviction that it is "matter" (everything "animal," sexual) that keeps them apart. Only by eliminating "matter," "body," "sensual thought," can the "part" be joined again to the "whole." Only in preoedipal innocence, free of all sexual-incestual "matter" can this child return to the fantasy paradise of infancy—his "transcendent origin"—that he had discovered in his "inner existence." Impotence and asexuality are, thus, not only oedipal defenses but also the price for remaining in the preoedipal "dual unity," for being "fed and nurtured" with the "warmth so sweet," for being among "the first born of a new mother,"[66] as he characterized for Efremov the happy prospects awaiting them in the "better world." So all mankind must "join hands to overthrow the yoke of matter," or as he described his task to Efremov, to "revive the dead, lift the fallen."[67]

In sum, humanity must join to destroy the "forces of matter" that symbolized grave oedipal dangers and at the same time kept Bakunin from returning, narcissistically, to his "transcendent origin," that separated this particular "part" from the "whole" to which he aspired. By sanctioning his retreat into an "inner existence" and by providing him an inner "friend who lavishly recompenses him for all that he suffers" (the same friend who "fed and nurtured" him), Schelling's Idealism helped him to achieve within himself the desired union, or reunion. But that inner merger with the maternal friend had to be accompanied by the most strenuous and vigilant efforts to purge the union of everything even remotely sexual, every trace of "body," of "matter." Otherwise, the "symbiotic couple" would itself become the incestual couple that the retreat inwards was meant to avoid.[68] Such purification rites were futile. Even in earliest childhood the "symbiotic couple" had already lost its preoedipal innocence simply as a result of having been pathologically preserved and strengthened after the oedipal failure and having been used as compensation for that failure. Now, again, in adolescence the same pattern was repeated. Fleeing inwards to be "fed and nurtured" by the maternal "friend" and her "warmth so sweet" as a way of escaping the sexual-incestual dangers that now, in the barracks and at home, so fiercely threatened him, he unavoidably further transformed the already corrupted "symbiotic couple" into an incestual union, requiring still more zealous purification, which in turn sunk him still more deeply into the infantile union, and so on around the circle.

Considering the urgency of the need, it is no wonder, therefore, that Bakunin was so insistent in his assault on the sexual, animal, and material world, that he defined his purpose and that of his fellow Idealists as helping in "the continual and progressive process of God's triumph over matter."[69] "We will be happy . . . our suffering will come to an end," he assured Efremov, "only when we can say, 'what I want, God wants'."[70] And what "God" and "I" both wanted was the "triumph over matter," since only thereby might the "I" and "God" be joined and the "suffering" ended. "Every person has two 'I's'," he told Efremov in November, "one of them is weak, not fully human, sensual, vacillating; the other is identical with the aim and is universally human, infallible, steadfast, lofty and rigorously serves [the aim]."[71] When he told Efremov, as he was telling everyone else that year, that they all must depend only on the "inner world" and have nothing to do with the "external world," he added that the hardest period in a "spiritual life, a life of self-sacrifice" was at the beginning "when one often experiences periods of sensual passions." The way to fight such passions was to exert "all possible force of will, as much as possible concentrate on oneself," and regard "these moments of despondency as moments of sickness that will pass." However, "if force of character cannot tear one free of this state, then one should not surrender to it, but should rather forget oneself in something outside, even sleep if possible."[72]

He might well have been an abbot counselling his novices. He, himself, he told the Beyers earlier that year, 1835, had already passed through the stage of personal love between man and woman: he had already "experienced to the fullest that divine pleasure granted one through the contemplation of a fine soul, a soul that could understand me, a soul by whom I was loved." But, "those wonderful days are over":

> You see, my dear friends, for me that love no longer exists; henceforth its sweetness will remain unknown to me. Henceforth I must strengthen the love for mankind, the hope in its progress and friendship. But is this not really a splendid fate? Is it not really finer than love for a woman? For such love is merely a double egoism. But to live for one's brothers, to show them the way to truth, to tear from nature its secrets in order to reveal them to mankind, to overwhelm matter and habit by the force of one's ideas—is this not really a splendid future.[73]

Nor should Natalie Beyer, therefore, blame Stankevich for offering her only "brotherly love," since he, too, had already loved once and was now ascending beyond it to a loftier love. To love more than once, in fact, proved that it was only the "senses" that loved and not the soul, and Bakunin could only "despise" such a person, not consider him "a man."[74] He realized, he told the Beyers, that all this made him seem "cold" to others, but he had faith that in time they would see in him "a soul that because of continuing circumstances and impediments must concentrate on itself and shackle outbursts of activity, a soul forced to be silent in order to be able to speak more meaningfully, to appear cold in order to be able to preserve and make use of his passion."[75]

Not that Bakunin lacked passion for others or remained silent about it. His letters to Efremov, for instance, reveal both the need and the capacity for strong emotional relationships, albeit more with men than women. "Give me your hand and we will travel together the lonely trail to our aim. . . . And so let us live together, fuse our souls into one. . . . Give me your hand and we will not fail." Expressing his eagerness for the moment when he would receive his official discharge, leave Premukhino, and join Efremov in Moscow, he wrote Efremov near the end of the year: "I would be yours entirely: the service would no longer keep my heart apart from you."

> My friend, I am frank with you because I know you, because I love you more than you can imagine. We will be frank with each other. We will not let any external and meaningless relationship constrain or influence our friendship. We will place ourselves in a relationship that is so mutual that I will be as you, and you as me. It will then be easier to fulfill our deeds, easier to pass through the vales, disappointments, distress, and sacrifices. . . . Give me your hand, friend, for an eternal union. We were born for each other. Our friendship is written in the book of fate.[76]

Somewhat later, it will be time to speculate again about the psychological roots of Bakunin's fateful messianism, why, for instance, he associated "great deeds" with "our conscience clean" or why, when prophecying to Efremov the coming of the "better world," he went on to speak of himself and Efremov as "the first born of a new mother." But whatever the source of his nascent messianic message, there is no doubt that he was already demonstrating remarkable success in preaching it. We have seen how great an impact his zealous dedication had made on Stankevich. That hardly compares, however, to the influence he had on his own sisters and on their friends, the Beyer sisters, all of whom adored him. It was to Bakunin rather than to other members of the circle that the Beyer sisters turned for help and guidance in a seemingly endless stream of crises that plagued their relationship with their widowed mother and brother. Judging from their first letter about him, they were especially attracted by his extravagant, precipitous, explosive nature, although perhaps as well by his smart uniform and epaulets, which he continued to wear that year.[77] He was still a child, Natalie Beyer wrote on the last day of his March visit to Moscow, but one that had best not be restrained by lead strings or he would break both them and his head as well. Continuing the letter the next day, following another evening with Bakunin, Stankevich, and their friends, she changed her mind about his being a child and urged his sisters to stop thinking of him as one. His ideas and his principles were just and true, she said. He was obviously one of those people who had the force of character and the passion of soul to do great things in life. But, she went on, this same force and passion could also do him great harm, especially since they had been so long repressed. Describing her general response to him, she wrote his sisters that "it was chaos, a flood of feelings, of ideas, that shook me completely. I tried a thousand times to pull my thoughts together, to follow all these things into their depth, but each time I lost myself in the labyrinths. Oh, it is because Michael's heart and mind are the kind of labyrinth in which one does not easily find guide lines, and the sparks that flash out from time to time (for his heart and mind are filled with flame) similarly catch in your heart and mind without your noticing it."

Although she insisted she was not in love with him, she conceded that Bakunin was the kind of man "for whom a woman would want passionately to sacrifice everything" and that there were moments when she had wanted "to buy, were this possible, at the cost of the most terrible suffering, the force needed for his rebirth or through my own self-destruction to bring forth some new woman who could be his guardian angel."[78] Over the next few years, as we will see below, Bakunin was to turn such adoration into the base and bonds of his first "commune," the model of all the many others that were to follow.

Meanwhile, his parents could only stand by in utter dismay. Although his father assured him that he had nothing against serious study and, in fact, had "often advised you to study in order to obtain the sound knowledge you lacked," he could not see any value at all in his son spending hours on end "with your pipe over what you call philosophical discussion, but which was really only shallow, idle talk." Michael had time enough for that, but not, his father added with obvious chagrin, for reading to him the books and newspaper that, now nearly blind, he could no longer read to himself. What bothered his father most, even more than his son's attempt "to play Diogenes," was Michael's "wish to rule the family." As to Michael's plans for the future, "I will neither say anything nor advise you. You have never listened to my advice. Follow your own fancy, and do what you want." However, "I ask you, if you value my contentment, do not enlighten [your brothers and sisters] with your counsel and leave to me at least their moral direction.... I am not forbidding you to follow your path, but I ardently beseech you at least not to lead Nicholas and the younger brothers astray."[79]

While the son went right on reading and talking philosophy, preparing himself to "revive the dead, lift the fallen," the father worked strenuously through that year both to save his son from a dishonorable discharge and to find him a position that would allow him to begin some career. In July (1835) Bakunin wrote Stankevich that he had been offered a job with his uncle, then governor of Tver Province, and that he intended to accept it. Stankevich replied in late September, congratulating Bakunin on the new position that he had "so willingly chosen" and predicting that his "love of activity will be well fed in it."[80] Even before Bakunin had received Stankevich's letter, however, Bakunin had written the Beyers in August that his plans were to go to Moscow that fall and audit courses, that, in other words, he had no intention of taking such a "hectic, fussy, bureaucratic job,"[81] as he was later to refer to the offer. If we are to believe what he told his father some years later, there was far more emotion involved in his rejection of a job than these letters to Stankevich and the Beyers would indicate. "I could not stand firm against your wishes, and so I agreed. But you do not know how very much that agreement cost me. You do not know the depression, the despair that overwhelmed my soul. I could not bear this deprivation, and for an entire week after my agreement, I drank until really drunk from morning until night. Thoughts of suicide flashed incessantly before me, and if I had not then gone to Moscow, my state might well have come to a very bad end."[82]

At the end of October, Bakunin went with his family to Tver for the usual round of balls, parties, and housecalls, mainly for the benefit of his unmarried sisters. He was deeply depressed and angered by the social whirl. What had all this to do with the universal and the eternal? He locked himself in his room, adamantly refused to accompany his sisters to the parties, and urged them to resist at all costs the sorry fate of their sister Varvara, who, in his eyes, had foolishly married and was now suffering deeply because of it.[83] By November he had made up his mind to leave, first to St. Petersburg, which, he told Efremov, he now thought about day and night, and then to Berlin.[84] He would leave, he said, just as soon as his official discharge was in hand, and he would leave, moreover, with his parents approval: his family "finally understands that I cannot search for happiness along the common road of wealth, high society, and rank..."[85]

He left sometime in January, not to St. Petersburg, but to Moscow, without money, position, prospects, or even a place to live, secure only in his determination to remain absolutely free to live the life he chose. He would not submit, he wrote his sister Varvara after leaving, to the "wretched conditions of social existence."[86] He left, he told Tatiana, in order "to shake off the yoke of hated obligations which, unilluminated by feeling, were merely ignominious chains, unworthy of a man in the true sense of that word.... I had to decide either to become a man consistent with my own ideas or to sacrifice everything for my family, live through its happiness, its love, its future. They did not understand me. They tried to turn me into a social hero, a prim and proper person, the likes of Sologub [Tatiana's current suitor] and so I left, for I was unfit for anything and could do nothing for a family that did not respect me."[87] "My freedom is not for sale, no more than is my human dignity," he told Tatiana, and he closed a letter to his sisters sent ten days later with the same sentiment: "I can no longer live in the family. It is impossible. I need my personal freedom."[88]

Of all the letters he wrote to justify his flight from Premukhino, the most important to him, judging from the length, tone, and contents, was the one he wrote his father:

So we have parted forever. We are no longer condemned to see each other. We have died to each other. But I cannot leave you without expressing for the last time my love, my gratitude, and my profound sadness at our being thus separated, not merely externally, by physical distance, but internally, by our different ways of thought and feelings, and, still more painful, by your indifference to me....In my soul no other feelings for you remain now but love and gratitude, gratitude for what you did for us during our childhood. You were our teacher. You awakened in us a sense of the good, a sense of the fine, a love of nature, and the love which still now tightly and inseparably binds us all, sisters and brothers. Without you we would probably have been dull and empty, but you ignited in our hearts the sacred spark of love for truth, developed in us a feeling of proud dignity and freedom. You did this because you loved us, and we were devoted to you with all our souls.

Afterwards, when we were no longer children, you kept apart from us, as though you were frightened by your own work.... But love for you during our childhood set down such deep roots in our hearts that nothing, no injustice or insult could destroy it. . . .Our convictions are so different and the path I have chosen so foreign and unpleasant to you that I will not disturb you by useless talk about my life and plans. My situation is often difficult. I am often despondent and discouraged; but I would be lying were I to tell you that I even slightly regretted my decision. I followed my convictions, apart from which I can understand neither life nor human dignity, and I now have the right to hope that I will remain true to myself, since I have already experienced many difficulties and obstacles which have not changed either my feelings or my thoughts. But I would be happy if you finally were able to accept the fact, now that we are parting forever and are speaking to each other for the last time, that I do not pursue some egotistical goal and that it is not pleasure that I seek on my hard and lonely road.[89]

His father's reply, parts of which were quoted above in reference to the tensions between them that year,[90] infuriated him, and he reacted vehemently, not directly to his father, but through a letter to Varvara and Tatiana. In it, he attacked everything he felt his father stood for, but which he himself considered simply crass hypocrisy—the countless trivial courtesies of "polite society," the alleged love for the fatherland that, in fact, comprised "only dead phrases rote-memorized from Karamzin and lacking any real meaning," the love of family that was, in fact, only "habit and duties," a concern for knowledge that reflected nothing but a desire for fame, and a love of God that for these hypocrites meant only the fear of hell and the desire for paradise. Why should he sacrifice himself and his freedom for all these—as he quoted his father's letter—"proprieties that all well-bred people observe and without which no society can possibly exist?" "What do I care about its existence?" he said, "let it fall apart—I would not take a step to support it!...Am I to blame that I cannot prune down my soul to the conditions of custom, propriety, and obligation?" Once and for all he had had enough of all these "duties," these "cold formulas and rules."[91]

The bitter exchange may seem at first just another instance of the oldest of all confrontations, sons against fathers. Yet, even superficially, this is actually the reverse of the conventional plot. Usually, the story told is one of sons competing with fathers for power and possession, while in Bakunin's case what is at issue is the son's adamant *refusal to assume the power and possession offered to him.* Now, this, too, is hardly rare: it is all too familiar for sons to delay moving on from the childhood in which others responsibly take care of them into a maturity in which they must assume the responsibility of caring for themselves and for others. To forego this maturation, however, usually means to forego as well the sense of power and honor that customarily go with the fulfillment of responsible roles. While some are willing to pay that price, many are not and try somehow to have it both ways. This, I have suggested, was—at one level—precisely Bakunin's need and task; how to preserve the carefree freedom of childhood while enjoying as well the feeling of honor and power. I believe, further, that it was Bakunin's great talent for composing theories, programs, and strategies for having it both ways that accounts for his enormous appeal to others facing the same need and task, mainly the youth of successive privileged classes.

To "blame" Bakunin for this would be to misunderstand the character or underestimate the force of the motivations that set this task before him. His parents were understandably and, from their perspective, rightfully disappointed and angry at the way their son was behaving. They expected him to assume the conventional responsibilities, and they needed his help. He chose instead to follow his own will and whim wherever they lead him. Yet, could he do otherwise? If one appreciates the strength of the inner barriers keeping him from accepting that "fussy" job, for example, forcing him to drink himself into oblivion and even to consider suicide "incessantly" rather than accept it, one can agree with him when he says that he was not to blame for his inability to "prune down" his soul "to the conditions of custom, propriety, and obligation."

The substance and source of the barriers are clearly apparent in the psychological associations that had already become firmly rooted in Bakunin by that time (1835). There was, first, the association of foes, the enemy camp. As we have seen and will see repeated through the following chapters, Bakunin fused in his mind two sets of antagonists; those centered around the "sensual," "animal" world, all that was "dark, filthy, and vile," and those located in the world of social "custom, propriety, and obligation." Both together formed the alien "external world," the world of matter, and Bakunin easily shifts back and forth between the two sets, using them interchangeably in his attacks. Opposed to them was the good alliance of God, the inner world, the "friend" within, all that was "pure and virginal," the realms of spirit, idea, true (i.e. non-physical) love, poetry, and absolute freedom. It was already, and would remain, in other words, a starkly gnostic conflict, a war between the *Civitas Dei* and *Civitas Diabol;* and its purpose was and would remain always twofold: "God's triumph over matter," the oedipal repression of everything "sensual," and the reunion of the "part" with the "whole," the narcissistic regression inwards into the "transcendent origin."

With respect to the narcissistic factor in Bakunin's rejection of society, it is obvious why regression inwards, reunion with the inner "friend", should imply "freedom" from society. But why should his oedipally rooted rejection of sexuality have the same effect? Why did he fuse sexuality and society such that rejecting the first he had to go on to reject the second? This is perhaps the most important question raised thus far, since it concerns the traits and themes by which Bakunin is most often identified—his unqualified "freedom" from society and his violently maximalistic assault against it. There were several points of linkage that I believe joined Bakunin's rejection of sexuality with his rejection of society, transmuting (displacing) the fear and hatred aroused by one into a life-long war to destroy the other. The first and most obvious linkage occurred during those difficult years in the army, when "society" meant the barracks with its (for him) vile corruptions that "modesty" would not let him even mention. The exceptionally acute loneliness and alienation he felt after being first expelled and then sent out to the provinces reenforced this estrangement and helped lead, it will be recalled, to his "intellectual revolution" out of society and into his newly discovered "inner existence."

The second link involves the prominent place that marriages played in the life of Premukhino. Both the general character of manoral family life and the particular fact that the Bakunin family had four young ladies to marry off made sex and society virtually synonymous for the Bakunins at the time. We have seen how Bakunin responded to the planned marriage of Liubov. The same fate not only awaited his other sisters, but himself as well. To follow his father's foot-steps and meet the social expectations of his class meant first of all to be fruitful and multiply. Everything that we have seen so far, everything that Bakunin has said and done, shows that that kind of life, the life his father represented so completely and so successfully, could not be his. It is significant that he decided to leave Premukhino soon after the Tver ball (one of those dances and balls that had taught him that he was "not suited for life in society") at which his sisters had been displayed to prospective suitors.

Both of the above associations between sex and society assume Bakunin's hostility toward sex as such, quite apart from the origins of the hostility. The third link more specifically concerns some of the roots of that rejection. It is related to Bakunin's bizarrely excessive reaction to the "fussy" job his father had arranged for him (his week of drunkenness and thoughts of suicide) and to the fact that Bakunin was to persist all his life in this avoidance of any conven-tional employment, preferring to fall deeply and repeatedly into debt. It is also related to Bakunin's most familiar political theories and declarations, those con-nected with his denunciation of "power" and with his "anarchism." Neither the innocuous sinecure, of the kind that even Stankevich was able to handle, nor the assumption of responsibilities on Premukhino was acceptable to Bakunin, because, I believe, they represented steps on the way to becoming like his father, assum-ing his father's power, role, and possessions, replacing his old and near-blind father and managing Premukhino in actual consort with his mother. Society was unacceptable to Bakunin, in other words, not only because it so thoroughly involved sexuality, but also because it comprised and depended on positions of responsibility and power that he dare not assume because of the associations they held for him in the oedipal drama. Beginning with this rejection of social and familial responsibility because of these associations, Bakunin was to extend this rejection to all explicit power and authority. To accept authority, responsibility, power would continue to mean to him his replacement of his father, the inheritance of his father's *total* role and, on the level of psychosexual dread, the symbolic risk of the prohibited union and the terrible punishments it entailed. Power meant father; and father implied mother. He must struggle or at least seem to struggle to destroy the rival, father-authority; but he must never replace him.

These oedipal motivations and associations, together with those resulting from Bakunin's pathological narcissism and consequent withdrawal inwards, best explain, I believe, the extraordinary intensity and lifelong persistence of his rejection of any manner of responsibility or power. Throughout the later chapters of the book we will see the many ingenious ways by which Bakunin tried to reconcile this uncompromising avoidance of power with an equally compelling need *to appear* powerful in order (among other purposes) to conceal the reasons for that avoidance as well as the impotence that was itself a strategy for the avoidance. We will see him in last minute flights from opportunities to have the power that his rhetoric seemed to demand. We will see him involved repeatedly in insurrections that fail too often and at times too absurdly for the failures to have been unintended or unexpected. We will see especially the contradictions between, on the one hand, his defense of freedom, his anarchism, and his rightly famous attacks on authoritarian organizations and, on the other, his constant, obsessive planning for tightly centralized, rigorously authoritarian parties—that are always, however, secret or "invisible."

Over the next few years, this bond between sex and society was to become ever tighter, as Bakunin continued his attacks against all things "animal" and his insistence that his followers transcend their lower instincts and join him in his spiritual pilgrimage. It should already be evident, however, that "freedom" from society's "custom, propriety, and obligation" meant for Bakunin in these early years first and foremost freedom from the threat of sexuality and everything related to it. The other side of this freedom "from" (to recall again the other side of the constant dualism) was the freedom "to" that he had discovered through his "intellectual revolution," the freedom to live narcissistically apart with his "friend" in an inner world where pleasure and reality were one, where impotence became omnipotence, and where "great deeds" might be accomplished with "our conscience clean."

3. THE FICHTEAN MISSIONARY: FIRST CRUSADE

Rather than "parting forever," as he had written his father, Bakunin remained away only a few months, until May 1836, when he returned home for the summer. But in these four months he came into his own for the first time in his life. He tested his capacity for freedom and flourished in it. Lacking money or residence, he lived with Stankevich,[1] who had just returned to Moscow from the year-end holidays on his estate. For the first three months Bakunin was entirely free to do as he chose and spent most of the time on philosophy, history, and desultory reading in Romantic belles lettres—Goethe, Schiller, and Hoffman. For some source of income, he began in April to tutor a boy preparing for the university entrance examinations.[2] Evenings were usually spent with the Beyer family, although there were occasional visits elsewhere, such as a dinner party where Bakunin and the illustrious Peter Chaadaev, according to Bakunin, joined in criticizing conventional views on children's responsibilities to their parents.[3]

It was all, except for the short period—a month—of tutoring, exactly what he had wanted. He could live as he chose and do what he wanted to do, whenever, wherever, and to whatever extent it pleased him, unconstrained by anyone or anything. He could read at leisure without feeling the weight of irritation his apparent indolence had caused his parents, and he could then freely share his thoughts and feelings, assured of the most sympathetic and admiring listeners. "My life has begun here; here all the capacities of my spirit have unfolded; here I have begun to breathe freely."[4] "I am now following my own path, in my own sphere. I love everything now, am satisfied with everything, and ask nothing of the external world...."[5] At last he was free "of the stagnant, lifeless crowd."[6]

One reason for his euphoria, besides this heady liberation, and certainly the most significant event for him during these months, was his encounter with Fichte's philosophy. So impressed was he by Fichte, that he spent much of this period translating two of the popular lectures Fichte had delivered at the University of Jena in 1793, "The Way towards the Blessed Life" and "The Vocation of the Scholar."[7] To appreciate the significance of Bakunin's great attraction to Fichte, it would be useful to compare it with Stankevich's response to Fichte about the same time. Whereas Bakunin had spent only two or three months[8] with Kant's "mess of boiled kasha," the "dry critique" that Stankevich considered a necessary "preparation for Schelling's poetry," Stankevich had struggled on until sleepless nights, relentless headaches, and his doctor's orders forced him to stop. Given the Romantic and Idealistic traits of character they shared, one might have expected Stankevich to follow Bakunin's example and turn next to Fichte. Instead, Stankevich found Fichte intolerable, because Fichte was much too subjective: In Fichte everything, the "entire world," became "a modification of thought," and the result was an "oppressive state of complete uncertainty, complete doubt."[9]

For Bakunin, on the contrary, Fichte's radical subjectivism was one of his most alluring appeals. As did Schelling and all Idealism, Fichte first of all, in effect, assured Bakunin that he was right in abandoning, in Fichte's words, the "vain, miserable, and unblessed external world," the "Apparent Life," and concerning himself only with the "True Life" that "loves the One, unchangeable, and eternal...what we mean by the name God."[10] In addition, and more specifically his own contribution, Fichte's words entirely supported Bakunin's decision to heed only his own inner voice and will. Each man, Fichte wrote, "exists not in order that something else might be, but just and only in order that *he himself* should be." "Man must constantly be at one with himself. He must never contradict his own self....He should determine himself and never allow himself to be determined by anything foreign to himself. He should be what he is because he wills to be so and ought to be so."[11] Bakunin, in other words, was right; his parents and society were wrong.

Fichte also went further than Schelling in celebrating the meaning and marvels of Thought. Since "True Life and its blessedness consists in a union with the unchangeable and eternal" and since "the eternal can be approached only through Thought" (which "alone is the eye to which God can become visible"), it followed logically that "the substantial form of True Life is Thought," that "in the mind—in the self-supporting life of Thought—life itself subsists, that beyond the mind there is no true existence." Truth and happiness, therefore, would come only with "the return of mind to the eternal," which could only result from "the concentration of mind, its indwelling in itself." Here, indeed, was a philosophy of total solipsism made to order for this young narcissist.

"Consciousness of Being is the only possible form and mode of existence of Being....Thus, the actual life of knowledge is, at bottom, the essential Being of the Absolute itself....Hence, Consciousness is the true world-creator."[12]

If, however, Fichte had only served, as he does here, the "pastel" side, the fearful boy seeking refuge in his "inner world," it is unlikely that Bakunin would have taken to him so enthusiastically. What was irresistible about Fichte was the fact that he promised the timid youth not only a tranquil sanctuary, but also a hero's destiny. For who should lead mankind if not those who already lived the True Life and were, therefore, able to guide a lost and desperate humanity into it, "to make humanity in deed what it is in its original intention—the express image, copy, and revelation of the inward and essential divine nature"? Such was the task of "some favoured and inspired men" who find themselves "on a higher standpoint from which to survey the world," the "religious men, sages, heroes and poets." To belong to this select and sacred company was to be "the teacher of the human race," "the guide of humanity," "morally the best man of the age," one of "the priests of truth."[13] Since, finally, "divine existence, in its essence, is nothing else than pure Thought," and Thought the only "eye to which God can become visible," these "priests of truth" were nothing less than God's chosen executors of His sacred purpose.

Having eagerly assimilated these Truths, Bakunin was more certain than ever of his divine destiny, for he could hardly doubt that everything about himself and his relationship to the "True Life" and "Apparent Life" made him one of these favored and inspired "priests of truth." Through the remainder of 1836, both in Moscow and then after May in Premukhino, he zealously pursued his Fichtean mission with which, moreover, he had now become publicly identified after the appearance of one of his Fichtean translations in *Telescope,*[14] an influential periodical under the direction at the time of the Stankevich group. The message he preached represented, essentially, a further elaboration and intensification of the ideas and attitudes he had adopted the previous, Schelling, year. The core was still the gnostic war between the divine and the "animal." There was "only one genuine duty," he told the Beyer sisters in his struggle to win them away from the influence of their mother and her conventional values, "and that is to help love, God, with all the strength of our will against egoism, against that which is animal."[15] They must all "cleanse," "purge" their souls of the "heap of customs, petty weaknesses, wretched vanity, consecrated by society but repudiated by God...since their source is egoism, since they arise from the material, animal 'I',"[16] he said, showing once more how closely the "animal" and the "social" were joined for him.

"Two lives" live within us, he told them, one "divine" and the other "artificial," comprised of all the hateful "dogmas," "obligations," and "rules."[17]

Having himself, he said, fallen for a time from the "lofty and sublime sphere of divine love" and having been, consequently, "defiled by lethal contact with our animal nature,"[18] he repeatedly warned his disciples against the evils of sensuality:

> I respect and love only the human, and my heart is deaf to everything beneath man's dignity, beneath his divine source and destiny, in a word, everything that is animal....Sensuality replaced feeling, and you wanted to find in this sensuality your entire life....Strength belongs only to pure and lofty sentiments: weakness and flabbiness are the necessary properties of sensuality. Sensuality is strong, but it is strong only with animal strength; it is powerless for what is elevated and splendid. If it had prevailed over you for even a while longer, it would have forever expelled you from divine and moral life and entirely immersed you forever in the mire of animal existence....From then on, the most debased, the most vulgar instincts would have been your lot; for once adopting sensuality, you would have renounced humanity, its sublime heritage, the one and only source of authentic bliss....What is proper to man are his moral and divine, not his physical and animal tendencies.... The flame of sensuality is not a moral flame, not love: it is entirely a material flame, animal, hostile to every feeling. It will devour whatever it dominates. It hates everything human and is able to love only what is animal....Thus, man himself represents the eternal struggle of the beastly and the divine. The beastly will be destroyed and man will become God. And all humanity, all individual beings will merge into a single person, into love, into God....[19]

He could understand, he wrote Varvara, the feeling of personal love between two people, "even though I have not experienced this in my own life," but why was it necessary? Why could a man not be content simply to "share joy, hope, and grief with his friend"?[20] In any case, he himself "wanted nothing from the external world, not even the love of a woman, since within me lives the love of God."[21] In another letter, he asked why the Beyers could not be satisfied with friendship from someone like himself who is "submerged in metaphysical speculations" and "who cannot and must not form any external ties": Was there no "possibility of a purely moral relationship between man and woman"?[22]

Liberated from the "mire of animal existence" and all the social obligations connected with it he could now live "purely an internal life." "I do not leave my 'I'. I am entirely immersed in my 'I', and only this 'I' binds me to God, and only God binds me to other people. My entire religion, all my responsibilities consist in my 'I'. I have no external religion or external responsibilities."[23] Or, as he described his mood to Alexandra Beyer, "I am able to love and feel strong only in my own sphere. I am insignificant everyplace else. I am paralyzed by everything else," everything that is beneath man's "divine source and destiny, in a word, everything that is animal."[24] And just as he opposed everything "animal" because it "paralyzed him," so must he rise in protest "when duty paralyzes the action of the mind and heart,"[25] when convention "exhausts one's soul, deprives it of all its strength, all its energy." He refused to tolerate such paralysis and exhaustion because, as he said continuing that last sentence, "I want to be strong."[26]

Thus, by rising above everything animal and everything associated with obligation (sex and society), Bakunin would escape being "paralyzed" and become "strong," a real "man," as he often put it.[27] But that was only the beginning of the boon: freed of "duty" and "animal tendencies" he could attain to the heights of God Himself, as we see in the following and succeeding examples of Bakunin's narcissistic megalomania:

> How great I feel myself at this moment! I feel myself a man! My purpose is God. Vast storms and thunder shake the earth; but I do not fear you, I despise you, because I am a man! My proud and inflexible will tranquilly passes through your shocks in order to achieve my high destiny. I am a man. I will be God....I suffer because I am a man and want to be God. I am tranquil because I know my powers, because I see myself standing on the road that will continually bring me nearer to God....One must purify one's soul in order to become God, for that is man's aim....Thus, man represents the eternal struggle of the animal and the divine. The animal will be destroyed, and man will become God....Love is God. Passion is man. Changing passion to love—this is man's task.[28]

Here again we see the close interaction of narcissistic and oedipal dynamics. The messianic identification with God simultaneously bolsters the weak ego (narcissism) and provides a cloak of grandiose power to disguise the impotence (oedipal). God is for Bakunin at this time both the nurturing all-good mother of the preoedipal "dual unity" and the emulated omnipotent father-rival of the oedipal crisis. While the surface is pure megalomania, generated both by the oedipal Promethean pose and by narcissistic omnipotence, the concealed truth underneath is just the opposite of power and self-assurance: impotence, fear, and flight lie hidden beneath the oedipal power pose, and a pathologically underdeveloped, weak ego beneath the narcissistic omnipotence. Notwithstanding all the bombast, it is the hidden weakness that comes through most emphatically, both to demonstrate withdrawal in the oedipal crisis and to regain entry back into the infantile, narcissistic "symbiotic couple." It is only by repressing authentic selfhood and manhood, avoiding sexual and social power and responsibility and regressing back into an infantile maternal reunion, that Bakunin can feel "strong," a real "man." Genuine paralysis is transfigured into its opposite, the sole escape from "paralysis," to recall Bakunin's terms. Impotence is his only path to power. Radical paradox, in which words mean their opposite, is, thus, already the hallmark of Bakunin's rhetoric as it will later become the core of his political dialectics.

Had it been enough for him to "cleanse" his soul "in order to become God," had the "eternal struggle of the beastly and the divine" been confined to the arena of his own "inner existence," had, in other words, he left the world alone, his life would have been entirely other than it was and, most likely, few today would have heard of him. But that was out of the question. For a variety of reasons, some of which we have seen earlier, he must at least appear powerful, and in carrying out his lofty calling as one of the chosen "priests of Truth,"[29] he attained even grander heights of megalomania than he had reached in those foregoing claims to becoming God:

> And it is this God, this absolute love, that is bliss. Alexandra, I am called to be its priest, its instrument before you. Forget, Alexandra, that you are speaking to a young man you know, forget my person and look upon me as the being called upon to save you, to open before you the doors of truth. Pour your heart entirely into mine, do not be held back by false shame. I speak with you in the name of God, who wants to have you among his children. He will speak to you through my lips. My soul at this moment is expansive enough to encompass your whole soul. Tell all, dear friend, I can understand you, I feel all your feelings, and I will return them to you purer; I will return to you that purity which you, so you believe, lost, but which, in fact, is only hidden in the depths of your soul: it will emerge again more lustrous than ever.... Dear friends, move more quickly along the path that I will show you, that God will show you through my lips, and you will be happy, your bliss will be immortal, infinite.... Oh my God! Have I not yet and forever blessed you for having allowed me to read the hearts of these friends so dear to my heart? Have I not yet blessed you for having predestined me for this splendid mission of leading to you such fine souls, so clearly created for you, although they have temporarily gone astray thinking that they were serving you?[30]

It is no wonder, considering such declarations as these, that Bakunin at times came near thinking himself another Jesus. Referring to his own spiritual ascent, he held out to the Beyer sisters the promised joy of taking their "share of a man becoming God" and urged them to draw strength from his soul, for he, too, was "a servant of God" called upon to guide lost spirits such as theirs. If this guidance caused constant troubles at home, his own and the Beyers, he had the example of Jesus to justify him, for had Jesus not also said, Bakunin quoted, "'leave everything, father and mother, follow me, for I am the truth'"? True, Bakunin conceded, only Jesus had been able to destroy entirely the "animal" in himself, whereas Bakunin realized that all he could do was "govern it, cleanse it." Still, once internally cleansed and governed, he, too, could say: "I feel God within me....My soul is all love....I sense paradise within me." It was Jesus' suffering and martyrdom that seemed most to attract him, however: "Look at Christ, my friends, who suffered so much, who did not even know the joy of being fully understood by those around him, and yet he was happy, for he was the son of God, for his life was suffused with divinity, filled with self-denial, for he did everything for mankind and found all his satisfaction, his pleasure in the dissolution of his material I and in the salvation of all mankind."[31]

The suffering savior, victim as victor. Here, indeed, was the ideal symbol for merging the two sides that Bakunin had to reconcile—the pure, innocent child and the would-be powerful leader. We have earlier seen hints of Bakunin's stoic and heroic suffering as his preferred way of experiencing honor and power. Now, in this year of his Fichtean mission, he seems virtually obsessed with suffering, "the most sublime manifestation of the divinity of man," returning to the theme again and again. As to the objective substance, the causes of the oppression he incessantly laments, they are nowhere evident in his letters. Everything now seemed to favor him—health, talent, opportunities, friends, recognition, and even his parents' apparent willingness to let him live his own life. Where in the following examples, drawn at random from countless others, is there even a suggestion of some specific, real constraint or deprivation?

> Whoever has not suffered cannot really love; for suffering is an act of liberation of man from all external expectations, from attachment to instinctual, unconscious pleasures....The man who does not suffer does not live. Suffering alone can bring one to an awareness of life, and if happiness means complete awareness of life, then suffering is also a necessary condition for happiness....He who has not suffered cannot love and cannot be happy....Yes, we will suffer, my dear friends, but we will find our happiness in our suffering. Happiness consists only in transcendence, and transcendence is only found in the strength to suffer without complaint and to act without cessation....The worse things go for me, the stronger I will be....You see that it is quite bleak, with abysses on all sides, and raging storms above, but I am firm and courageous. I will fear nothing. I will enter on this path with the thought of God in my soul and with love in my heart....To love truth, sacrifice

everything for it, suffer for it, even die for its greater glory if need be, and to have the chance to express one's feelings, one's sorrow—here is real happiness, the only happiness worthy of man. Yes, my dear friends, heed this thought: true happiness consists in suffering, joined with an awareness of man's dignity and strength. I have searched so much, suffered so much, in order to find the true path that it is impossible that I will not find it....I am happy, because I am suffering for truth; for truth constitutes all my dignity, all my religion, all my being.[32]

It is central to the argument of this study to appreciate the intensity of this "suffering" and to understand its character and cause, for, as we will see later, this idealization of "suffering" was directly related to Bakunin's apocalyptic revolutionary violence. What this early cult of suffering shows, first of all, is that years before Bakunin developed any interest in politics at all, much less opposition politics, he celebrated suffering as a good in and of itself, as virtually (in both meanings of the word) synonymous with love, happiness, awareness, truth, religion, and manly strength. Suffering is here not an oppressive burden to be overthrown in order to attain happiness; suffering *is* happiness. It is not an unfortunately necessary means to some good end; it is the good end itself, or, at least, a necessary companion or even component of that good end. It is to be sought, not avoided; intensified, not minimized. At this period in his life, the glorification of suffering concerned only Bakunin himself and his few disciples. Later, it will become the prism through which he will view the suffering masses and the measure by which he will determine the best means for their liberation.

Why, then, keeping this later significance in mind, does Bakunin suffer so? There is obviously nothing yet involving compassion for the suffering "people"— that lies some distance in the future. As for himself, the only "objective" cause of suffering is the ongoing conflict with his parents over his rejecting their way of life. Now, that pain was surely real and perhaps severe but hardly enough by itself to prompt the intensity of feeling or, especially, the idealization of suffering these quotations reflect. For an answer, we must look again not at any cause coming from outside, but rather for one coming from within Bakunin himself. The question then becomes, why did he want, need the masochistic illusion of himself as a suffering victim?

There were, I believe, two reasons, corresponding to the two sides of his essential ambivalence, the infant-hero dichotomy. With respect to the heroic side, "suffering" demonstrates power through an intriguing paradox, a reversal of opposites that was to become Bakunin's basic strategy for meeting his contradictory needs. Great suffering, which on the surface would seem to be a sign of defeat, victimization, weakness in the face of oppression, becomes in this dialectic evidence of great strength and power. Weakness is strength; impotence, omnipotence. Demonstrating a characteristic transmutation that we will see Bakunin reenact repeatedly in the future, he proves to himself, and hopes to prove to others, that he is powerful because he is able to suffer powerfully.[33] It was an ideal synthesis for Bakunin. The gentle pastels were not only preserved and allowed to prevail, but in the very act of doing so, they appeared to be their opposite, the reds and blacks of strength and power: "the worse things go for me, the stronger I will be." Recalling the paradoxical currents of 1834 (when his proclamations became most stridently aggressive at just the time that he was retreating into his "inner existence"), Bakunin constantly speaks of his "strength" during this Fichtean missionary year (1836) of deep "suffering." He is "strong" because he now feels himself in God, "stronger than ever," "strong" because he is in his own world, "strong, for I see into the future," "strong" because he is alone and thrives on this isolation, "strong" because he must be so in order to suffer, "strong" and calm because he is doing the work he loves, "strong now... because I am free, because I have entered upon the path Providence intended for me."[34] But it is and must be, to restate a central point, a strength that re-presses "animal" virility: the "great deeds" must be done with "our conscience clean." It is "strength and purity" "pure and strong," strength that "belongs to pure and lofty sentiments" in contrast to the "weakness and flabbiness" of "sensuality" that "is strong only with animal strength."[35]

With respect to the infant side of the dualism (the narcissistic roots of the masochistic suffering), it involves, primarily, the "narcissistic rage" experienced by the child against deprivation or, especially, against some persisting injury to his emerging sense of self (as discussed more fully in the concluding chapter, "Narcissus and Oedipus"). The child experiencing the rage cannot direct it against the real maternal source causing the injury, since the child is dependent on that source for survival. To protect the mother (or, rather, the intrapsychic idealized image of a fantasied "all-good" mother), the child (among other reactions) directs the rage against itself. Moreover, since the child's sense of himself in the "dual unity" is based on the mother's responses, her denial and rejection of the child become the child's rejection and punishment of himself.

There is, finally, a third source of masochistic suffering besides those associated with the oedipal and narcissistic patterns functioning separately. It concerns a particular interaction between the two patterns that, if this part of the interpretation is valid (and it is admittedly speculative), would be, I believe, the ultimate source of Bakunin's apocalyptic violence, the essential generating core that drove Bakunin on and on in his destructive fervor until the end of his life. It was argued earlier that in reaction to oedipal failure, Bakunin regressed more deeply into an aberrationally prolonged "symbiotic couple" and that it was essential that he keep the reunion free of anything sexual, animal, material, lest the "symbiotic couple" itself become the oedipally incestual union that the regression was meant to escape. That danger, I believe, was not, and probably could not be, avoided. Coming as it did after the oedipal crisis and as a means of compensating for oedipal failure, the regression necessarily carried the substance of the oedipal crisis into the "symbiotic couple," which thereby lost its pre-oedipal sexual innocence and became, in effect, the incestual union. Try as he may by his impotence, his life-long war against the animal, material, sexual world, and his various other strategies to keep the union pure and to prove himself innocent and weak, he unavoidably committed the crime by being in the sanctuary that he clung to for protection against it and, therefore, had to be punished. He was caught in a vicious circle and, with no exit from the trap, could only go on punishing himself endlessly by masochistic suffering, in fact and fantasy.

Had Bakunin kept his credo of suffering to himself, enduring the spiritual struggle in silent deprivation, he would have been his only victim. But it was impossible for him to keep his suffering a personal drama. If it was essential for him to preserve detachment and impotence, it was no less essential for him to engage in a fierce assault against society and all it represented to him, for the many reasons, oedipal and narcissistic, that are discussed throughout this study. He must, therefore, carry on in the world outside the same struggle against the flesh that he fought within himself, actively help God "triumph over matter," spread the gospel of purity and pain. That was his mission, and he continued to give himself to it unstintingly, striving relentlessly to save his sisters and the Beyer sisters from the corruption of sensuality and to lead them through the vale of suffering that he had come to cherish into the "True Life": "My friends, the earth is no longer our fatherland. Our happiness is celestial; our life, heaven."[36]

He waged his holy war on a number of fronts simultaneously, investing an awesome amount of time and energy in it. In fact, this was the *only* specific issue he wrote about that year (1836). He had first to go on protecting his sister Liubov. Although the threat to her virtue that Bakunin had helped avert three years before had faded away, a new danger loomed ahead in the person of one Vladimir Rzhevsky whose intentions, Bakunin wrote Varvara in February, would of course be welcomed by their parents, no matter how much harm this caused Liubov. To stop the courtship from going any farther, Bakunin wrote long letters denigrating Rzhevsky's character and behavior and even challenged the suitor to a duel.[37] How could he, her brother, allow "poor Liubinka to be a victim once again to our parents' false views?" In urging Varvara to help him protect Liubov from a marriage their parents were again planning for her, he wrote that Varvara, having herself experienced marriage knew "what marriage really is. You know the consequences, you know all the sacrifices which a woman must offer up to her husband. Liubinka cannot know the conditions of marriage, she cannot foresee the dreadful suffering and terrifying humiliations which a woman suffers for her husband's sake, suffering endured only for the sake of the beloved man, to whom the wife sacrifices everything—her modesty, her shyness— because the loving wife no longer lives for herself." Continuing this description of the dreadful future awaiting Liubov should she marry Rzhevsky, he used almost the same words, phrases, and images that he was to use a year and a half later, in December 1837, when he recalled the earlier dangers Liubov had faced in 1833, when their parents had first tried to arrange a marriage for her. Here, as there, he expressed his horror at the thought of this sacrifice of "an innocent and pure young girl, rich in sensitivities, whose inner life is a harmonious synthesis of the finest thoughts, delicate and pure images" and described vividly (*too* vividly) how her husband

> begins by sacrificing her to the coarseness of his beastly passion, which, blind to the gentle sensitivity necessary for the happiness of a woman in love, gradually takes from her, one after another, all her hopes, all the pleasant illusions that make up her inner life, her religion, her moral life, finally plunging her into a dreadful reality, and there, chained by duty, dead to all hope, engulfed at every moment by the personality of her husband—who must become unbearable to her—will she not be the most miserable being on earth?[38]

In Varvara's case the harm had already been done—she was already married. However, she had separated from her husband soon after the birth of their first child, and Bakunin, as we will see, was determined to keep them apart. Her husband very much wanted her back, and her parents urged her to return. Bakunin acknowledged that her husband was kind, considerate, and well-meaning, but he also denounced him as a narrow, crude, materialistic, and sensual Philistine who was completely unworthy of her and extremely harmful to her son.

Concerned as he was to keep his sisters from marrying, or, as in Varvara's case, to liberate them from the bond if already tied, it was not towards them but towards the Beyer sisters that he directed his most persistent and fervent missionary work that year. Following his own victory over Premukhino obligations and the threat of a "fussy" job, it was the freedom of the Beyer girls, especially Alexandra, from their mother's control that most consumed his talents and energies as a Fichtean teacher, guide, and priest during his first months in Moscow. Conditions at the Beyer winter apartment that year were strained unbearably, with mother Beyer going to all lengths—spying, fits of hysteria, threats of beatings (according to Bakunin)—to protect Alexandra from an unpromising alliance with Fedor Rzhevsky, the brother of the would-be duelist Vladimir, and force her into a marriage worthy of her station.

Desperate, Alexandra saw only one way out: she would get herself to a nunnery. No, Bakunin told her, that would be a meaningless self-sacrifice, a monstrous self-deception, and above all an intolerable loss of freedom. "You are too intelligent to believe that one might please God by voluntary imprisonment, by useless sacrifice, by passive prayer. The essence of God is freedom, and he wants people to be free, for only in freedom does he reveal himself to them."[39]

To save her from this "slavery,"[40] from a life no different from that in the army barracks,[41] he bombarded her with admonitions and instructions; told her how to deal with her mother—now appeasement, now defiance; denounced her brother—"a swine"—for taking the mother's side; devised schemes for getting her away from home on the pretext of visiting Varvara; urged his sisters to write Alexandra; provided them with the necessary arguments—tell her, he instructed Varvara, "that you need her friendship, that she can help you raise your son and ease your suffering";[42] and on his evening visits to the Beyers took command himself in the impassioned confrontations with this mother who was so "stupid, immoral, incapable of feeling, loving nothing."[43]

The main thing was to get Alexandra, and also her sister Natalie (who "could do nothing against my will"[44]), away from their mother's wrath. He outlined in precise detail alternative contingency tactics, sent urgent letters to his sisters instructing them in the parts they were to play, censored Alexandra's letters, tearing up at least one of them that did not fit his strategies (in it she had asked advice from Varvara), and, in general, attacked his objective with all the care, determination, and enterprise of a military operation. In the end, he succeeded in having Alexandra stay with Varvara at her husband's estate near Premukhino.

From the monastic fortress of his own inner purity, he had fought hard for the world's purity, for "God's triumph over matter." Here, in these battles in defense of Liubov's and the Beyer sisters' virtue, were Bakunin's first "great deeds" done with "conscience clean." The formula worked: by making the "pure and virginal" his cause, he could take the risk of displaying "manly" power (otherwise denied him because of its oedipal implications). Having found the right arena, he could now let his passions "rage" and "seethe" without guilt or fear, demonstrating expertly in these domestic battles for purity all the skills and traits of character that he had been expected, but failed, to demonstrate in the army and in conventional society. But besides treating these family quarrels as though they were decisive military conflicts, and already revealing the boundless energy that was later to become his trademark, he also displayed through them a later aspect of his character that is far less known—his extreme authoritarianism. The following examples of his dictatorial domination should be enough to show this trait and show as well still another essential continuity joining these early, apolitical years to his later life as a revolutionary.

You must believe me, I demand from you fulfillment of my will, for this will is the wish for your happiness. Answer me. Believe in me. I am not mistaken. Feeling guides me. Give me your word. Bend to me. I demand this of you again, Alexandra. I will be your providence.... Believe in me completely or do not believe in me at all, but for the sake of all that's holy let there be no middling way....Do not think that having given yourself in friendship to someone you are not giving him as well eternal rights to yourself....You assume that you could succeed in deceiving me and hiding from me what is going on in your soul. What madness, my dear friends! Deceive me, one who has learned to read your souls, to notice the slightest shifts within them, to foresee all your feelings, even all doubts.[45]

He must again "possess your souls, your souls entirely, as I possessed them before."[46] Natalie, as we saw, "could do nothing against my will."[47] Her mother, too, was for a time under this control, or so he claimed:

We have her firmly in hand....She cannot take a step without our permission....She must be managed, that's the crux of it. Since our last talk, she is simply afraid of me, and I will not relax my power. I am very courteous, very respectful, even very attentive with her, but she is fully aware that I understand her through and through, that I will not let her do as she pleases, and for some time now she has done everything she can to ingratiate herself with me in spite of the fact that she can't stand me.[48]

Once Tatiana asked whether they could not love each other in spite of holding different views. He assured her that was impossible, for true friendship "means agreement in convictions: it can exist only given this single condition."[49] And why should he not claim such despotic rights, since "My 'I' is divine and is conscious of its divine origin. It commands circumstances. It rules them....I will take care of everything."[50] Still, when the young ladies balked at his tyranny, and complained that he was trying to force them into directions they did not choose to follow, he could hardly even understand the accusation.

This means that I forced you? Is it possible that you do not understand how deeply those words insult me, one who lives only in freedom and loves only freedom? I force you—how little you have understood me, Alexandra! I want everyone to be free. I would begin despising myself were I even to consider forcing, tyrannizing anyone.[51]

If, at the time, the target of battle for this lieutenant manqué was the institution of marriage, the main bridge joining sex to society, then the officers leading the enemy camp were, perforce, the parents who guarded the bridge. Nothing inspired him to flights of impassioned rhetoric or provoked his rage more than the subject of parental authority. The theme came up constantly in his letters. It was the only subject he referred to when describing a salon dispute in which, as we saw, he and Chaadaev took the same side in defense of children's rights.[52] In his meetings with the young man he tutored for a month, he did his best to "tear him out of that apathetic and moribund sphere into which his father's life and practical ideas have plunged him."[53]

Whether in the persons of his own parents, who had constantly tried to "prune" his soul down to social customs, who refused to see in his divinely chosen path anything but selfish egoism, and who did everything they could to defile the purity of his saintly sisters, or in the person of the Beyer sisters' mother, who was working strenuously to ruin the lives of her daughters in the same beastly way—parents emerge from his letters as demons incarnate. As for himself, "parents do not exist. I renounce ours."[54] He would have nothing to do with the "dogmatism" according to which one must "'honor thy father and mother;' one must sacrifice oneself for one's mother; one must load this cross on oneself, carry it and thus merit paradise."[55]

His parents responded in kind, if more gently. His father said he was glad to learn that his son had decided to earn his way by giving lessons (this was in April, the month the lessons began—and ended): "God please you have enough ability and patience for this," for "teaching is an honorable profession." However, he went on, showing how little he thought of his son's character as well as how little he knew how to encourage improvement in it, teaching "demands vast knowledge and unwavering steadfastness" and "the assumption that leads you from one lesson to twelve and from one week to all the following weeks seems to me not entirely well-grounded." While never doubting "the kindness of your heart," he said, twisting the blade, he felt that "an intellectual fever has always dominated you." And then, in a prophetic remark with chilling precision: "We will see, in the end, whether good prevails over Ahriman [Lucifer]."[56] A rare note from his mother was appended to his father's letter:

> For a long time I have been unable to write you. My heart has been too heavy. I do not want to reproach you. But if you are not entirely estranged from the feelings and obligations of a son to his parents, from the love for parents who have found all their joy in love for their children, then you must yourself know how guilty you are before us, and also that your actions and your offensive letters can hardly persuade us either of your love or of your respect for us. I am unable not to love you. [Love for you] is fused to my very life, and the way to my heart is always open to you, no matter how antagonistic you are to me. I bless you and embrace you.[57]

What we are witnessing through this year of Bakunin's Fichtean mission is Bakunin at war against parents, his own and the Beyer sisters', in the name of "freedom," that is, purity and virtue. Will he, his sisters, and the Beyer sisters be sacrificed to the vile "animal" world, or could they be saved for the "pure and virginal"? It is the same battle between "body" and "soul" that, as he had said several years earlier, "fills the pages of humanity's historical fate" and decides "the bloom or ruin" of individuals and whole peoples alike.[58] Leading the camp of the "pure and virginal," he was at one and the same time the Fichtean "priest of truth," struggling for "God's triumph over matter" as Jesus had done, and the fearless artillery officer, planning, mobilizing, maneuvering, and attacking as he had been taught to do in the army he had deserted. Exhilarated by the challenge (and freed by the purity of the cause from oedipal constraints on such displays of power), he sounded every bit the mighty crusader he now set out to act.

> I am a man because I want to be one, because I am called upon to be one. I have no other aim besides becoming a man, and I will crush everything that impedes my way to it. Damn all these conditions forged through man's degradation. And damn all these relative ideas, senseless but no less effective in limiting his will. One must destroy, pitilessly and without exception, everything false so that truth may triumph. Its reign will come. And all those who were weak, all those who were frightened by the pitiful deceptions that shackled them, all those who stopped midway, all those who bargained with truth, will not be allowed to enter. They will repent their errors. They will lament their weaknesses. No, my dear friends, I will make no more concessions. They almost destroyed me....[59]

There was no room for compromise, because "there are only two ways of looking at things: either everything is sacred, everything must be sanctified, or everything is a wretched farce, absurdity, and putrefaction. Between these poles there is no middle....Man cannot and must not rest content with the golden mean."[60] If doubts arise, then one must "crush them all. Rise up against them.... So crush them all."[61] And if this uncompromising zeal meant that he must remain alone, then so be it, for then at least one can "say to oneself: 'I am alone. My soul belongs to me; its secrets are not soiled by the stares of the indifferent.'" Moreover, as with all suffering, there was happiness in this isolation, "a happiness that is most bitter—a Satanic happiness!" "But," he went on to reemphasize his main point here, "the golden mean attitude which serves to embellish the lives of ordinary people—oh, that is unbearable, horrible....I do not want it, for it exhausts one's soul, deprives it of all its strength, all its energy."[62]

We must stop here a while and take a longer look at these Promethean forays against compromise and the "golden mean." Those familiar with Bakunin's work will see at once how much these declarations anticipate the essential feature of his later revolutionary tracts; while those familiar with the gnostic-apocalyptic tradition will realize how clearly this aspect of Bakunin's personality and proposals reflects a characteristically gnostic rejection of an evil, material world as totally unredeemable and destined to utter annihilation. It is important, therefore, to keep in mind that this all-or-nothing, fundamentally gnostic, assumption underlying Bakunin's revolutionary outlook was well developed long before he became political. Enough has been said already about the roots of his personality to understand why there can be no compromise, no meeting ground, no contact with the "dark, filthy, and vile" world, why he can only flee it or destroy it. The "golden mean" "exhausts" his soul and "deprives it of all its strength, its energy" for the same reason that, earlier, any "sensual thought" had only "to penetrate my heart" for "my feelings to dull and my soul to be cast again into black gloom, anguish, suffering, self-laceration, and, when strength is exhausted, silence."[63] Strength and manhood lay only in the complete avoidance or destruction of the fallen "animal" world.

The roots of Bakunin's gnostic apocalypse, in short, were psychological—psychopathological—and not political in any way. Linking these militant pronouncements with similar declarations Bakunin had made during his army years, we can see some details of these roots. There is still, as before, a strong element of oedipal bombast and bravado serving the same purpose of concealing the contrary truth underneath: the more violent he sounds, the more virile he must be. Then, there is the factor of vengeance and the oedipal and narcissistic rage it channeled. More important than either the bravado or the vengeance, however, is the positive appeal and apparent pleasure that he comes to experience in the fantasy of violence, something he himself began to touch on when he referred to the "Satanic happiness" he found in his lonely and bitter war against the "dark, filthy and vile." This aspect of his violence is only now beginning to appear in his writing. As the appeal of violence in and of itself strengthens, we will see that, in addition to the pleasure it afforded by venting rage and staging bombast, violence becomes a source of masochistic suffering discussed above and a surrogate sexuality. We will see as well that this pseudo-sexuality is essentially passive or, as Bakunin defined sexual traits, feminine. But there still remained several other ingredients to be added to this potent brew, mainly Hegel and Weitling, before the violence would be ready to attempt "the complete annihilation of the present social and political world."[64]

The war in which this violent strain first began to manifest itself—the war against parents in defense of Liubov's, Alexandra's, and Natalia's "purity"—led that same year (1836) to another relationship between himself and the young ladies that in some ways served his need for concealment even better than did the role of crusading "priest of truth." He became a celibate father of a pseudo-family made up of his sisters and his "soul sisters," the Beyer girls. For that was the ultimate meaning to him of the "holy commune," the organization (if one can call it that) which he now formed and which he was repeatedly to reincarnate throughout the rest of his life in a dizzying succession of "intimate" brotherhoods, "families," alliances, parties, and federations. As he initially thought of the "holy commune," it was to comprise those who were prepared to forsake as he did all animal pleasures and all conventional social institutions and expectations and to devote themselves to the pure love of God, to pure friendships uncontaminated by carnal desires, and to the familiar gateways to the spirit—religion, philosophy, music, poetry, nature.

Even before he had left Premukhino at the end of 1835, he had written to Natalie Beyer about his plans to form a religious circle. In a note added to this letter, Tatiana spoke of the great impression his plan had made on her, and she urged the Beyers' brother Constantine to join.[65] By April the following year, near the end of Bakunin's stay in Moscow, the circle seems to have been well underway, with the Beyer sisters rather than Bakunin's own sisters heading the list of loyal followers, since he had found in the Beyers "what I could not find in my own family." Describing for them what he had in mind, he wrote that they would all together "—you, my sisters, and I—form a chorus of souls, fused as one,"[66] and that he would look after their welfare with "the feeling of a father wishing only the inner happiness of his children."[67] In the quarrels between the Beyer sisters and his own sisters, often over which set was most favored by "father" Bakunin, Bakunin usually supported the Beyers, who "are for me much more my sisters than they are; for you [the Beyers] are my soul sisters."[68] Paralleling his own elevation of spiritual fatherhood over "animal" fatherhood, he honored this "kinship of souls" he felt for these "true sisters, sisters of my soul" above the "involuntary, physical, unconscious kinship" he had with his own sisters.[69]

The purpose of the circle was as lofty as the souls that formed it: "to expand more and more the sphere of our love, of our bliss, to purify our souls from everything earthly, incessantly ennobling them, making of them worthy offerings of eternal love, to elevate thereby earth to heaven, endlessly to realize in the external world the idea of the fine, the lofty, the noble...."

Even that was only the beginning, for "feeling God within ourselves...having received communion through his divine love, we feel ourselves to be divine beings, free, and predestined for the liberation of enslaved mankind, the liberation of a universe that is still sacrificed to the instinctual laws of unconscious existence."[70] Again, it is "God's triumph over matter" that is at issue: mankind is to be liberated not from enslavement by some imperial state or oppressive economic class, but from "the instinctual laws of unconscious existence." He could hardly be more explicit as to the basic motivation for his revolutionary career. What he envisioned now and, however concealed, thereafter was a union of pure, virginal, celibate souls destined by God to purge the world of all that was "dark, filthy, and vile," all that was animal, matter, sexual.

Neither this first, embryonic crusading order nor the many that were to follow would have been possible, of course, if Bakunin had not possessed the overwhelming charismatic attraction he unmistakably had for so many, then and thereafter. Tatiana, for example, could hardly find words to express her gratitude to him for "this God whom you are teaching us to understand" or to say "how much we owe to you and how much right you have to our friendship." "Oh, Michael, never doubt it, be assured that without it we would not be able to live, that it is as necessary for us as is the air we breathe....My dear friend, nothing can ever separate us." Natalie Beyer, too, Tatiana told him, had come to understand "the inner life about which you preached to her so much, and she wants to strive towards this celestial harmony....These days that have drawn all of us completely together have shown me that your efforts have been crowned with success....Yes, Michael everything depends on you....You can, you must ressurrect their splendid souls."[71]

Nor was Tatiana alone among his sisters in her gratitude and devotion to her brother. A few days earlier, Liubov had written: "You have given us a new life. You have helped us to see the purpose of our existence and yet you are not here to take joy in the fruits of your labors, to share with us our happiness, to inspire us with strength and bravery, because, to tell the truth, many impediments remain for us to overcome." And from Varvara, in a note appended to Liubov's letter: "Your little flock is waiting for you. Really, Michael, I do not know just what you have done to become so indispensable. May God bless you."[72]

Such ecstatic devotion may not be so unusual for that ardently romantic era, when not to wear one's heart on one's sleeve meant risking the charge of not having a heart. But the sentiments that Bakunin expressed to his sister Tatiana during the summer of 1836 reflect much more than fashionable effusion. Tatiana seems to have taken the first step when she wrote a letter to her brother that (while no longer extant) was so impassioned that she insisted he burn it. He was euphoric:

> No, my enchanting friend, no one will see this letter, but I will not burn it. Oh, I will save it always and not for even a moment part with it. Away with all doubts! You have returned to me the sister I adore.

> Nothing will ever separate us! If you could only know, if you could only sense even half of the bliss that your letter granted me....Ah, how I want to see you again, to press you tightly, tightly to my heart, to tell you things that one cannot say in letters, to express in my eyes what words cannot express. I feel now that I love you more than anything in the world, that you have become my one idol on earth. And you ask me not to write to you! But, little silly, you ask the impossible. How could I do this? How—learn that you love me, feel my whole soul renewed through this news and then be silent? This would be beyond my strength. No, my lovely one, I have disobeyed this order; I cannot observe it.[73]

Feeling as he did, there was something he had to know: Was she in love with anyone else "perhaps with Sologub or Koslovsky....Answer me quickly, tell me the truth, I beg you, I implore you to do this!"[74] About a week later, he again asked her not to be angry with him for replying to a letter she had wanted him only to burn. He simply could not help himself, it was impossible "not to tell you how I love you and how I have always loved you, how I suffered at the very thought of your indifference to me and how impossible it would be to replace you in my heart with anyone else."[75]

And, again, from Tatiana:

> And so you are ours again. You again belong to your sisters who adore you....You no longer reject our love. You give us your trust again. Oh, thank you, a thousand times thank you! If I had wings, I would fly into your arms to press you to my heart....Oh, Michael, never doubt us again! If you only knew how many bitter tears you caused us to shed.... So you are again ours. But will it be forever? Will you not again tear yourself from our embraces? Michael, let us vow to each other everlasting friendship and trust.

As for his suspicions about her feelings toward Sologub or Kozlovsky, "Who could have inspired in you the assumption that I could love one of these gentlemen?" All she had said, she recalled (prefacing her remark with "just see how brave I am, that I'm not afraid to provoke your displeasure"), was that he, Michael, had "no grounds for despising or hating the count." But she wanted to drop the whole matter, since she did not want "to try your patience."[76]

So far, all the members of his little family seem to be young ladies. What about men, his own brothers for example? This raises another interesting aspect of Bakunin's convoluted strategy towards—and against—power. In his relationships with his brothers and with the only male who seems that year to have played some marginal part in the intimate circle, Vissarion Belinsky, Bakunin surprisingly comes forward in strong defense of his father's fundamental values. Although, for example, his brother Nicholas had asked Michael, according to Tatiana, "to guide him, to teach him what to do, to clarify for him the great aim of life,"[77] Michael made no attempt, in response, to deter him from his advance along conventional paths. On the contrary, he urged Neverov to keep an eye on him and see that Nicholas' "excessive ardor" was not "wasted on senseless swagger" nor on "attacks against things that are, under present conditions, inevitable." Nicholas must learn, Bakunin went on, that "only those courageous actions are worthy of respect that lead directly to a definite goal,... that he must preserve himself for genuine service."[78]

Bakunin sounded even more like his father, advising his brothers as their father had earlier advised him, when three of his younger brothers—Paul, Alexander, and Alexei—decided they had had enough of Tver gymnasium and planned to run away, to Moscow, much as he himself had done. They, too, along with the rest of the Bakunin offspring, admired Michael immensely, and on his trips to Tver they had bitterly complained to him about the discipline and rote formalism of the school, learning from him in return all about "the true religion, about man's great destiny." "The more we know Misha," Alexander said, "the more we feel him necessary for us. He has raised us high above our earlier position, and we enjoyed for the first time a happiness that we had not known.... We now really understand man's great destiny."[79] For a while they went on suffering gymnasium life hoping that their parents would heed their pleas and let them go to school in Moscow, to live there with Michael. The answer was an absolute no, their father "would rather die than let you go to Moscow with Michael, whose views and advice have already had such a pernicious influence on you," Tatiana wrote them. Their father's only wish, she went on, was that "Michael, with his good heart, will in time free himself from his errors, and, while awaiting that time, he does not agree to entrusting his children to him." So, Tatiana urged them, "bolster your courage, do not crumble under the iron hand that has come down on you...obey this necessity with the noble manliness that characterizes the truly great man." In short, "be real men, be Christians, do not fall from the heights on which Michael has already placed you."[80]

But how should the boys interpret this code of manly courage, determination, and fortitude? Should they heed their father and sister and prove their manliness by stoic submission to necessary circumstance or should they follow Michael's example and prove their manliness by rebelling against those circumstances? They chose the second way and decided to run away from school, go to Moscow, force thereby their expulsion, and leave their father no choice but to accept the *fait accompli*. Their midnight escape got as far as the coach that was to carry them to Moscow and freedom. But the driver reneged (either he lost his nerve or, more likely, raised the price too high). At once everyone knew everything, and there followed the expected cacaphony of accusations, warnings, angry confrontations, and harried messengers rushing hysterical notes back and forth between Tver and Premukhino. The boys stood their ground defiantly. Their grandmother, with whom they were living in Tver, intended "to scold us like children," Alexander wrote, and assumed that "we would, as we used to, just stand there listening, eyes downcast, to her sermon! No! It was not going to be at all like that!" They would simply leave if she treated them that way, they warned her. And they did so, as, screaming at them all the way, she followed them down the stairs and out into the street. They ignored her until she told them to come back and hear what she had written Michael. It was exactly what they might have expected, Alexander continued. She went on blaming him for everything, until they told her to stop and left the house again, this time followed by her injunction never to return.[81]

Their father was furious. He sent his son-in-law Diakov, Varvara's husband, to set things right and told him to use physical punishment if need be to force the boys to stay at school and apologize to their grandmother. And Michael? In September, before his brothers' bold dash to freedom, he had seemed to encourage just such audacity: "Do not limit yourself only to a consciousness of man's destiny. This consciousness must be vitalized by action. Remember, faith without deed is dead.... Without action, without an externalized expression of the inner world there is no consciousness, no life. So act, friends, do not let what I have awakened in you die."[82] If the boys expected, as well they might from such letters, that Michael would support their action, they were sorely mistaken. He was, of course, pleased by this evidence that "your life had not gone rotten, that you hunger for life, and that you want to act." But, he went on, stating again the views he had expressed to Neverov concerning Nicholas:

> Every action must have its direct, definite aim, entirely consistent with the laws of reason and with the conditions around you, and in this respect your undertaking distressed me greatly. What was your purpose? Was it liberation from gymnasium life and for life in Moscow? Considering well the way you went about achieving your goal, and acknowledging that our parents' approval would be necessary, do you really think that you would be able to get it this way?... No, my friends, true religion consists in its provision of strength for every condition, in its preserving one from baseness even in the worst circumstances.... Don't berate the gymnasium any more, it is unworthy of you and offensive to me. Make up with grandmother, ask her forgiveness; it is necessary.

Perhaps they had misunderstood him, he wrote in a second letter when he learned that, in spite of his reproof, they were still refusing to return to school.

> I spoke to you of moral freedom, of that freedom which consists in the rooting out of all bad habits, all wrong tendencies by the power of spirit; while you have been thinking of another freedom, which because of your age, your studies, the poverty of your resources, cannot yet exist for you. . . . Shame on you, gentlemen, it is distressing, most distressing. You must write letters to father and mother; do not find fault with the gymnasium any longer; and ask their foregiveness; be three times more diligent, prepare yourself for every single one of your gymnasium lessons. Do not talk to just anybody and everybody about the rights of man. . . .[83]

The young men could not have chosen which was the *real* Michael Bakunin, since both opposing attitudes were genuine, the one that had prompted bold independence and the one that scolded them and told them to be good boys and behave themselves. While acting the part of a conventional father in counselling his brothers and adopting the role of a celibate father in his "holy commune" were clearly attempts to conceal (from himself, first of all) the fact that he could never fulfill a parental role in reality, that he could never replace his father, this pose of virile power and authority had already become as indispensable to him as was the reality of impotence and no less an essential part of his life and character.

When the dust of the boys' escapade had settled, we find them back at school, and little more seems to have come of the event. The same cannot be said for the aftermath of another conflict in which Bakunin was involved that fall (1836) one that was to begin by providing him another occasion for appearing to share his father's values, but which ended by radically undermining the whole intricate network of intellectual deceptions and decoys that had been supplying him with such tactics. His antagonist in this contest was Vissarion Belinsky, Vissarion "Furioso," as his friends called him, for reasons that will soon be obvious. In spite of their shared intensities, two more different individuals than Bakunin and Belinsky could hardly be imagined. The one, Bakunin—a tall, haughty, overbearing, well-groomed, self-assured aristocrat, pundit and pastor, detached sage and ecstatic evangelist, free of all responsibilities, cozily settled in the gentle and eternally faithful realm of inner bliss and as disdainfully indifferent to social and political concerns as to everything else in the corrupt, illusory, material, animal, external world. The other, Belinsky—a short, frail, taut, erratic, petty-bourgeois journalist, forever tormenting himself by pangs of failure and inferiority, endlessly ground down by overwhelming obligations and abyssmal poverty, and trapped, inextricably, however much or often he struggled to get out, in the cruel vise of social and political reality.

Belinsky's childhood had been as dismal as Bakunin's was (on the surface) idyllic. His father, the son of a provincial priest, was a caustic and irascible ship's doctor who had retired to become a country doctor in a remote province and who escaped awareness of incompetence, steadily reenforced by his wife's taunts, through hard drinking and by humiliating his obviously more gifted son. A scholarship to Moscow University in 1829—the year Bakunin began military school— liberated Belinsky from provincial and familial oppression, but only to cast him into the tyrannies of prodigious overwork, poverty, squalor, and serious illness. After three difficult years, he was expelled, officially because of "poor health and lack of ability," unofficially, at least in part, because of a play of his, *Dmitri Kalinin*, that the censors turned down as "contrary to religion, morality, and the Russian laws."[84] Out of school, he at first barely managed to scrape along translating popular trivia. Then his luck seemed to turn with a job on *Telescope*. But the work was massive, harried, and miserably paid, offering him no way out of his freezing room where he drudged alone, bundled up in scarves and blankets, constantly coughing, plagued by the continual pounding from a blacksmith's shop below, the fumes, stench and din of a laundry business next door, and the filth and foul air of the building and neighborhood. Later that year another speck of light broke in when Stankevich said he wanted to meet this young man who had been "expelled from the university for writing a play."[85] With this, Belinsky became a regular member of that circle of "young men distinguished by intelligence, education, talent, and nobility" and, as a result, was somewhat able "to forget my misfortune."[86]

Through the early 1830s, therefore, the years Bakunin was sinking ever deeper into loneliness and despair as his military ordeal neared its end, Belinsky was beginning his increasingly illustrious career as an esteemed publicist. The two men first met, it seems, in March 1835,[87] when Bakunin, still officially on army assignment, spent a few weeks in Moscow, as we saw in an earlier chapter. Obviously catching something of himself in Bakunin ("seething life, restless spirit, active striving after truth"),[88] Belinsky was at once drawn to him. For the rest of the year after that March meeting the two had little to do with each other, and Belinsky is merely mentioned on occasion in Bakunin's correspondence with Stankevich. However, when Bakunin came to Moscow to settle after he left Premukhino in January 1836, their relationship grew much closer, partly as a result of their being members of Stankevich's circle and partly because of Bakunin's translation of the Fichte articles for *Telescope*, which Belinsky apparently asked him to do and which Belinsky liked very much—they were full of "life, strength, energy," he said.[89]

Later that year, Bakunin, three years younger than Belinsky and pleased by this friendship with the older and already prominent writer (and, for a time, even editor of *Telescope*), invited him to spend that summer (1836) at Premukhino. Belinsky seemed awestruck at the prospect of entering "that holy and mysterious atmosphere"[90] that Stankevich and Efremov had visited the previous summer and that had gained an almost legendary reputation among members of the circle as a paradise of love and beauty. Moreover, he desperately needed a rest. Besides suffering, as he periodically did, a broken heart, his overwork, wretched living conditions, and constantly increasing obligations (including now the responsibility of maintaining and educating his brother and a nephew) had so aggravated his illness (tuberculosis) that his doctor had ordered him South. Stankevich blessed the visit, for it would enable Belinsky "to come to know moral happiness, the possibility of harmony between the inner and outer worlds—a harmony that has seemed inaccessible until now, but in which he now believes. How this pure sphere of gentle, Christian family life softens the soul! . . . The Bakunin family is an ideal family, so you can imagine what effect it will have on the soul of someone who is no stranger to divine sparks!"[91]

At first, things went as well as Stankevich had predicted, to judge from Belinsky's recollections of the visit. "I felt myself in a new realm, saw myself in a new world. Everything around me breathed harmony and bliss, and this harmony and bliss partly penetrated my soul." He recalled especially the joy he had felt when they had all gathered together in chorus around the piano, when "it seemed to me that I was listening to the rapturous and blissful hymn of perfected humanity." It had been the "best time in my life," "a flowering oasis in the fruitless wasteland of my life"; "it was my christening, my rebirth." From the time of the visit, he said, he felt that he had "a guardian angel, a sacred angel—my memory of that paradise where I was not long ago. There, there will I retire with my fantasy, to live a sublime and transcendent life, to refresh myself and cleanse the dust from my life."[92] As for the source of the inspiration, Michael's sisters could claim most of the credit. Although Belinsky was particularly attracted to Alexandra, he idolized all of them for years thereafter as ideals of moral splendor, "strangers to all sins of the body, the flesh—envy, malice, hatred." Not even Stankevich could compare with them: "I know of no one more elevated than Stankevich, but what is he before them—nothing, even less, a thousand times less than nothing."[93]

Belinsky had double cause to be grateful to Bakunin and his family, for if the family provided him a "guardian angel," a living example of the ideal life of grace, love, beauty, and ease, so different from his own bleak and frenzied existence, Bakunin opened to him "a new world—the world of thought."[94] The "new world" of thought was Fichte: "the ideas of Fichte, thanks to you [Bakunin], convinced me for the first time that the so-called ideal life is precisely the authentic, real life, while what is called actual life is negation, illusion, nothingness, vacuity."[95] Notwithstanding this shared enthusiasm for Fichte, however, there was from the very beginning of the relationship, an essential difference between Belinsky's and Bakunin's Idealism, a difference that was soon to be the occasion, although not the main cause, for a long series of bitter quarrels between them. Even during his Stankevich period and its Schelling-Fichtean influences, Belinsky remained far more rooted in reality, as distinct from Reality, than were the other members of the circle. Although he had replaced "politics" with art and philosophy and no longer wrote plays with heroes rashly denouncing serfdom as *Dmitri Kalinin* had done,[96] he clearly showed in his apolitical articles a continuing concern with social issues that was completely missing from Bakunin's statements, at least those that have come down to us. Announcing in a typically Schellingesque rhapsody that "the whole infinite, beautiful, divine world is nothing but the breath of a single, eternal idea (the idea of a single, eternal God)," and continuing in that vein paragraph after paragraph, Belinsky would inadvertently, as it were, relapse into the *Kalinin* mood with repeated references to "strife" and "action" that were still years away from Bakunin's publications.[97]

Similarly, whereas he agreed with the others in the circle that Jesus was "the ideal of human perfectability," he also had the social concern to write, as Bakunin did not at the time, that if "a rich man, having asked of Christ the way to salvation, does not agree to distribute his wealth among the poor and follow his savior, he will be denied the kingdom of God, though he had from his earliest youth strictly fulfilled all the law's commandments."[98] And, finally, if "consciousness" was for Belinsky, as well as for Bakunin, man's "normal, natural, and, therefore, blissful state," it was not "consciousness" as experienced by the Fichtean Ego, Bakunin's detached, proud, independent "I," but a "consciousness that is possible only for humanity as a whole and which will be a result of united labors.... Every individual, therefore, is a member, a part of this great whole, its co-worker and helper in the attainment of its goal...."[99] "It is not for nothing that the entire world is joined by an electrified chain of love and sympathy and that all that lives and breathes form links in this endless chain."[100]

Both Belinsky and Bakunin, thus, had their chain and links, but how differently they are put together: for Belinsky the emphasis is on the chain, the whole, the "love and sympathy" that join the individual links; for Bakunin, the ultimate concern was still the individual link, the need to avoid being "a futile, meaningless link in the chain." Bakunin may well have taught Fichte and other "thought" to Belinsky, but Belinsky had already begun to teach Bakunin something about social and political reality.

It was just these social and political issues that, at least ostensibly, sparked the discord between the two men during that summer visit and that offered

Bakunin another opportunity to stand up for his father's values, as he had recently done in the gymnasium crisis. While dining with the Bakunin family one evening, Belinsky defended not only the French Revolution but the guillotine and its toll of "heads." "Yes," he later acknowledged, "that is the way I thought then, because I looked upon Fichteanism as Robespierreanism, and in the new theory caught the scent of blood."[101]

Consistent with his conservatism at the time, and again assuming his father's role, Bakunin joined his father against Belinsky. "From that time (with the famous phrase [about the "heads"]),"[102] Belinsky recalled, "there began a dissonance in our relationship. I began to note in you both love and hate towards me."[103] To judge from his account of this second part of his visit, the hate was decidedly more pronounced than the love. On every possible occasion, according to Belinsky, Bakunin "tormented" and "humiliated" him, made him feel inferior to the noble gentry around him, made fun of his inability to learn German, and left the room with studied indifference when Belinsky began reading one of his articles. His entire behavior was like "a stab in the heart, then, after the stab, a twist of the blade, as though you enjoyed my torment."[104]

These brief summary remarks about Bakunin's treatment of Belinsky are enough to indicate that something else must have been involved besides Belinsky's defense of Robespierre and the guillotine. Belinsky himself tells us what it probably was when he describes the various situations in which Bakunin was especially cruel. At one point in the visit, for example, when Belinsky had isolated himself for two days, immersed in painful thoughts about love in general and his feelings for Alexandra in particular, Bakunin had "persecuted" him "with cynical scoffing, laughter and crude jokes." Another time, when, during a celebration to consecrate the new Premukhino chapel, Belinsky had strolled over to Tatiana to chat, Bakunin had coldly accused him of "impudence." Belinsky was completely baffled as well as humiliated by these callous affronts, and the best he could do by way of explanation at the time was to blame it all on the shabby barrack habits that Bakunin had picked up during his military training.[105]

Had he been aware of what Bakunin's "holy commune" meant to him, of how important it was for him to hold undisputed sway over his sisters as their spiritual "father" and to preserve exclusive rights to an even more intimate relationship with Tatiana, he would have realized that what disturbed Bakunin was the fact that Belinsky was making a great impression on his sisters, that, in fact, they were becoming more attentive to Belinsky's more concrete and colorful rendering of the Fichtean world and mission than they were to that of their brother. In one letter to her younger brothers, for example, Tatiana told them of Belinsky's powerful impression on her and her sisters. Belinsky revealed "the true sacred religion" and provided them a picture of man as he should be, of the "man-God" to which all of them must aspire, following Jesus' example.[106] Later, after Bakunin had himself revealed something of his deeper feelings at the time, Belinsky understood what really had been going on. He realized quite correctly that there was something more essential involved even than Bakunin's control over his "holy commune," namely jealousy over Tatiana: "You suspected that T.A. loved me."[107]

By November, Belinsky had had enough of the torment and humiliation. What had been a "flowering oasis in the fruitless wasteland of my life," "my christening, my rebirth," had become "the worst time of my life."[108] Above all, Bakunin's hostility had showed him, he said, how foolish he had been to think that he could ever really fit into this alien manoral world, that even to try to do so was simply to play "a stupid role." Anything would have been better, he now realized, than "to have talked about truth, about art, about love, about every-thing, in a word, that I did not really feel."[109] What had that rarified, unreal world to do with the brute facts of his own hard life that clamoured for his attention?

> I tried to repress in my soul all worldly cares, all worries about external life, and while I apparently succeeded in doing so, my tranquility was deceptive. A fierce struggle went on in my soul. First of all, there were thoughts about my brother and nephew, about the fact that I had been doing nothing for them, that at the very time I was living such a splendid life, they were left in neglect, struggling to meet their needs. Then there were thoughts about what awaited me on my return to Moscow, where my resources were exhausted and where the only lifeline remaining to me was *Telescope,* and that line, hopeless.[110]

Hopeless it was, indeed; for the month before, in October, *Telescope* had been ordered shut down because it had published one of the most scathing cri-tiques of Russian society and character ever to appear legally in Russia, Chaad-aev's *Letters on the Philosophy of History.* Three days after the final issue ap-peared the chief of police ordered the seizure of all papers found in Belinsky's apartment. Stankevich, who was keeping Premukhino informed of events, tried to collect enough money to get Belinsky out of the country, but without success. When, on November 15, Belinsky arrived in Moscow from his Premukhino de-bacle, he found waiting for him, in addition to his former burdens and depriva-tions, a gendarme escort to take him straight to the police station,[111] the likeli-hood of further harrassment, and, with *Telescope* closed down, the loss of his only source of income. His situation was desperate. He tried to get a job with a St. Petersburg journal, but nothing came of it. He began work on a Russian grammar textbook, but the return, if any, would come only later. Meanwhile, the only way he could keep going was by borrowing heavily from his friends, and he despised himself mercilessly for it. He sought escape in the brothels, but found there only more fuel for the self-hatred that was consuming him. By the following April (1837) he could go on no longer. At the point of complete physical and emotional breakdown, he was again ordered South by his doctor and left for the Caucasus.

Considering his crushing experience during that last part of his Premukhino visit, followed as it was by the total disarray that greeted him in Moscow, Belinsky's distress is understandable. Yet, from the moment Bakunin returned to Moscow, in the same month (November) that Belinsky got back, he seemed even more distraught than the man he had so cruelly taunted. He was "overwhelmed by a dreadful despondency," he wrote Alexandra Beyer that month. "Everything appeared in such dark tones, so dismal, even so laughable." In his "external life" everything was "dreams and phrases," and in his "inner life" everything was "impoverished and superficial."[112] For him, too, as for Belinsky, those final months in Premukhino were to blame. Simply "the memory of those last months which I spent at Premukhino threw me into depression. To return to Premukhino is impossible for me. A kind of tremor, some sort of obscure terror seizes me at the very thought."[113] It had been a "nightmare" for him, and his reaction, he said, was like "an illness."[114] At first, he was at a loss to explain "how or why" he was so downcast.[115] Several months later, he understood:

> I do not know what to call the feeling I have for Tanichka, but I know that it inspires jealousy in me, and this jealousy tormented my whole soul. It almost led me to total degradation, Oh, if you knew, if you could understand all those dreadful humiliations that I was victim to! If you knew how I felt my fall, how I felt my weakness! I who perceived standing before me so lofty, so sublime a mission, lowered myself to such base feelings, so unworthy of me, and these feelings overwhelmed my entire being. I became their wretched slave. I lacked strength enough to rid myself of them, and I became an object of sympathy for my sisters and even for you [the Beyer sisters]! Ah, this was hell, hell with all its terrors. I lost that absolute love which was all life for me. I became an egotistical, pitiful being. Oh, how I craved death![116]

While the underlying maternal incestual bond remained hidden, enough of it had been displaced onto this uncommon attraction to his sister to show him that "there is much that is vile in me, much that is base," and make him "the victim of terrible, indescribable torment."[117]

4. CONVERSION TO HEGEL: SALVATION BY FAITH

Bakunin had performed his Fichtean mission too well. He had come too close to his disciples. Having rechanneled his "animal" passions into spiritual ecstasies and messianic evangelism, he could share them safely enough with "soul sisters" like the Beyers. Not with Tatiana, however. Closest to him in age, emerging from the same intensely emotional, romantic milieu, herself strongly attracted to her brother and making no secret about it, she drew to herself the forbidden love that Bakunin's mission was meant to deny. It was not simply "jealousy" over what he thought was Tatiana's feelings toward Belinsky, but what that jealousy revealed to him about his own feelings that had evoked the tremors, the nightmare, the illness, the craving for death, the "hell, hell with all its terror"— to use, again, Bakunin's own words and phrases to describe his reaction to the experience.

Confronted by emotions he could not bear, his recourse, once again, was flight. This time, however, it was not enough to leave Premukhino for Moscow. Nor was withdrawal from the "external" into a safe "inner" world appropriate, since it was precisely that "inner" world, the world of the Schiller-Schelling "beautiful soul" and Fichtean "I" that had now proven so unreliable. Having denounced and abandoned the "external" world in order to find and celebrate truth, beauty, and goodness as divine gifts of the trusted inner "friend," he now found himself betrayed by this inner world, crushed by its "obscure terror." There was, he wrote, "only one salvation left: to find somewhere that harmony outside of oneself that one cannot find within." The "I" had to go. The "I" that had been revealed to him by his first "intellectual revolution" now became the target of a second intellectual revolution. The man who had proclaimed,"I

84

do not leave my 'I': I am entirely immersed in my 'I', and only this 'I' binds me to God," had discovered so "much that is vile" within that "I" that he had no alternative but to submerge it in and subordinate it to that "harmony outside."[1] Over the next several months, after he left Premukhino, he devoted himself, consequently, to the task of "remaking myself entirely" in order "to destroy completely my personal 'I', to destroy everything that comprises its life, its hope, and its personal beliefs."[2] Once more fortune was good to him; for, as in his conversion to Schelling and then to Fichte, he found again exactly the philosopher he needed, one who would preserve and reenforce the many benefits he had received from the Schelling-Fichte Idealism, but who would at the same time help destroy that treacherous "I" and provide him that "harmony outside" —abstract, distant, and impersonal enough to guard him against the kind of dangerously intimate involvements that Fichte's mission entailed. He discovered George Frederick Hegel and his indomitable "Absolute."

> My dear friends, I have a fiery nature, my feelings seethe. And this means that only absolute life can bring me happiness and preserve my dignity. Departing from it, *I am capable of any crime.* I am passionate, egotistical, jealous and, finally, there is not within me those qualities that fit others for life in society. I can be happy only in solitude.[3]

A month later, in early February, Bakunin had succeeded, he said, in achieving what he had set out to do, "entirely dissolve my individuality in the Absolute."

> It is that egoism that I have completely killed. It will not be able to interfere with our relations in the future. It had brought me great suffering; the struggle with it was bitter; but this dreadful struggle within me has given me a second life, a life still more ardent and fruitful than the first one. I believe that my *personal I* has been forever destroyed....[4]

Once again, Stankevich was on hand to help him through the maze. Unable, as we have seen, to move on to Fichte's subjectivism after he had decided to give up on Kant, and plagued both by relentless illness and by a failing romance (with Bakunin's sister, Liubov, as we will see), Stankevich had found in Hegel the ideal balm and solace. In a letter he wrote to Bakunin on November 3, 1836, shortly before Belinsky and Bakunin left Premukhino, he joyously announced that he had just been informed that 13 volumes of Hegel were on their way to him from Geneva. "Now I will really have something to rack my brains over."[5] He eagerly awaited Bakunin's return to Moscow, he added, since apart from him "there was no one with whom I could talk about such things." So, when Bakunin arrived in

Moscow from Premukhino in a "hopeless mood," "overwhelmed by a dreadful despondency,"[6] Stankevich was waiting for him with a year of Hegel behind him and, ahead, 13 volumes for both of them to rack their brains over. "From now on," Bakunin wrote his sisters in early December, "my studies will be my life. I am not made for a personal life. From now on I must have nothing personal other than what is tightly bound with universal life."[7]

The five years extending from this winter of 1836–1837, when Bakunin began to study Hegel, to the summer and fall of 1842, when he wrote and published his first revolutionary tract (*The Reaction in Germany*) form a critically important period for him. At all times in his life, through all stages, he searched for ways to reconcile detachment with domination, impotence with fantasies of omnipotence, a life of poetry and a life of power, and was, on the whole, remarkably successful in his search. What is so crucial about the Hegelian period we are now entering is, first, that it provided Bakunin with what was by far his most effective and the most enduring magic for achieving this union of opposites, and, second, that the Hegelian formulas strongly favored power over poetry. As a Schelling Romantic, he had removed himself from the "unreal" world of appearances and devoted his life to nature, philosophy, and God. Moving on from Schelling to Fichte was rather like moving on from Hinayana to Mahayana Buddhism, from the Aharat, who leaves the illusory world, to the Bodhisattva, who dedicates his life to helping others leave the illusory world. In both cases, Schelling and Fichte, the response to the conventional "Apparent" world was to leave it. When Bakunin has completed his lessons with Hegel, the response will be not to leave the world, but to destroy it. When the transition is complete, we will hear not only about his own suffering, about the pathetic experiences of the vulnerable "I" crushed by a powerful, alien, external world: we will hear as well an incessant clamour for apocalyptic revolutionary violence. The pain and all its very real sources within Bakunin himself will remain, but the fantasy to discharge it will radically change: rather than picture himself only masochistically as the pure and innocent victim of cruel and implacable power or as the suffering savior called upon to help other victims escape that power, he will see himself as the indomitable victor leading invulnerable armies of former victims whose turn has come to make the oppressors pay for their cruelty by suffering catastrophic destruction. As with so many other messiahs, before and after, Bakunin will have then completed his voyage from personal anguish, through the fantasy of an infantile Eden, to the dream of a vengeful apocalypse.

But it was a dialectical voyage, as dialectical as the Hegelian charts that guided it. One arrived at one's destination only by traveling in the opposite direction. Although Bakunin's Hegelian voyage ends in proclamations of apocalyptic violence, it begins with a rhetoric of submissive surrender. The first phase, covering the years of Bakunin's supposedly "right" Hegelian reconciliation, lasted about a year and a half, from the end of 1836 through the summer of 1838. The early months, the winter and spring of 1837, seem to have been given, for the most part, to the anguished reappraisal involved in his struggle to "remake" himself. Serious study of Hegel does not seem to have begun until after he returned to Premukhino in June 1837, to spend the summer and fall. The following winter and spring (1838) were spent in Moscow, where he published his first original work, an article on Hegel's philosophy. His second Hegelian summer (1838) was again spent at Premukhino, only this time he decided to remain there through the following winter (1839).

Throughout these months of "right" Hegelian reconciliation, the good news he brought to his sisters and the Beyer sisters was his discovery of the Absolute, that "harmony outside" to which he had decided to sacrifice the "I" that had betrayed him. "My dear friend, one must live in the Absolute, one must free oneself from all the relative conditions that shackle us with trivia. . . . Live every hour in the Absolute, express it in your least activity, in your words, even gestures—here is the substance of the human ideal."[8] Committed now to the Absolute, "tightly bound with universal life,"[9] he could free himself—and this was a principal purpose of the conversion—from the cult of the "beautiful soul" and its intimacies that had proved so threatening for him:

> Only that which enters into the general life of the spirit, only that is real. And so, friends, for God's sake do not tell me any more about the individual requirements of my little soul, whether it is best for it to live with Tanichka and with Varinka, in which particular place, under what particular circumstances. . . . It is time to leave this poor, wretched effeminancy of petty feelings, this repulsive sphere of *qu'est-ce l'amour et qu'est-ce l'amitie,* in which there is *ni amour, ni amitie;* time to liberate ourselves from all these banal definitions, all these trivial conditions for happiness; time to stop talking about external and inner life. There is no such division. Such a division testifies to the absence of life. Life is integrally one. . . . Sensual souls do not live in this life: it is too vast for them. . . . Subjective little feelings, subjective impressions, joy and suffering—these are lies because they are not yet enlightened by truth.[10]

In his letters and in the first of two articles he wrote on Hegel, Bakukin left no doubt as to the personal motivations behind this second intellectual revolution: his "personal 'I' has been forever destroyed," to recall his remarks, because "it had brought me great suffering."[11] Just how severe that suffering had been is made dramatically clear in the Hegel article. On the surface, the article is an academic assault against the school of philosophy that "finds no basis for its own thought other than its own 'I'."[12] The reason he gives for his rejection of such philosophy, however, is hardly academic: the "result of the subjective system of Kant and Fichte was the destruction of any kind of objectivity, any reality, and the immersion of an abstract, empty 'I' in futile, egotistical introspection.... Such self-absorption is the source of hellish torment, unbearable suffering...."[13] As an example of this "hellish torment," he chose Byron, whose "poetry is a wail of despair, a rending cry of a suffering soul, lost in contemplation of its own emptiness...."[14]

Recalling Bakunin's own Fichtean mission, its crisis and collapse into just this "hellish torment, unbearable suffering", "hell, hell with all its terrors," it seems obvious enough that this is at least as much an autobiographical account, a barely disguised personal confession, as it is the scholarly analysis it purports to be. And as he went, so should others go. It was, he said, Stankevich's failure to move on from the "I" to the "Absolute" that was the cause of his continuing distress. "We talked about the malaise of your spirit and about your *schönseligkeit* in general," Bakunin wrote him. "In your letter to sister [Liubov] there is concealed a kind of anguish, a loss of any hope for escape.... Moreover, you, who are so clearly and profoundly aware of the harm of self-analysis, are endlessly probing into yourself."[15] The suffering of his sisters was also proof of the harm resulting from too much romantic introspection, "the sign of *schönseligkeit.*"[16] He is not at all convincing, therefore, when he laments the loss of "all that was connected with the hopes and desires that are so natural to a man" as the price of becoming "one with absolute life":[17] it was precisely because he needed far stronger barriers to defend himself against those "desires that are so natural to a man" that he was so ready now to surrender his "I" to the "Absolute."

The Absolute demanded one sacrifice, however, that one would have thought beyond him: the Hegelian way to peace of mind was peace with the world, reconciliation with reality. (As we saw, it was "time to stop talking about external and inner life. There is no such division")[18] But the trauma of late 1836 had been so shattering that he seemed willing even to pay that price. "None of us should think about how things might be better with us," he now said, one "should instead regard the external world as something given, in which he must find himself and thereby transform the external into the internal." While one might "help providence somewhat," it was not for man "to take upon himself the role of providence." In other words, he went on, correctly drawing the essential conclusion from Hegelian reconciliation: "I will never decide nor quicken anything by my own will."[19] As for his holy war against the "dark, filthy, and vile" and the "custom, propriety, and obligation," all of that now seemed, from the perspective of Hegelian reconciliation, a case of mistaken identity, of poor spiritual eyesight. When judged by the needs and intentions of Absolute Reason instead of by the "individual requirements of my little soul," it was evident that "everything is good; that there is no evil."[20]

> Only for finite, limited consciousness is there evil and unhappiness, but in this consciousness there lies as well the possibility and the necessity of liberation. So, there is no evil. Everything is good. Life is bliss.... Yes, Kostia, everything in life is good. Life is bliss, love. There is no evil in it.... Evil exists only for finite eyes, for eyes that do not see the unity.... Truth, goodness, and bliss are only in unity.... Division is only in the eye of finite men.[21]

The "finite" man, for whom "there exists a distinction between good and evil" could at best be a moral being, not a truly religious being, who "believes that divine will is the absolute and only good and who says 'Thy will be done.'"

> The moral point of view is a division between good and evil, the separation of man from God, and consequently, from reality as well.... It fears evil. It is uneasy, and there takes place within it a constant struggle between good and evil, between bliss and unhappiness. For the religious person there is no evil.... He sees it as an illusion, death, limitation, overcome by Christ's revelation.[22]

Urging his followers to cease complaining about the wrongs they thought they saw about them, he said that with respect to such difficulties he himself henceforth would "never try to find the cause outside myself, but rather find it now within myself, in that part of my 'I' that is still not enlightened and illuminated by the sun of authentic life...."[23] In other words, instead of remaking the world, "we must all remake ourselves in order to enter into the new world ... to purify ourselves in order to prepare the soul for the temple of God."[24] By showing the world the rules of reality that led to these insights, especially the rule that "'what is real is rational, and what is rational is real'," Hegel had gone far toward undoing the terrible damage done by the shortsighted, eighteenth century Enlightenment, Bakunin argued in his first Hegel article, published in April 1838. But much work still had to be done to cure the "dreadful anarchy of minds" caused by those critical philosophers who, instead of "forming [the individual] into a useful and active member of society," destroyed the individual, turned him into someone who—and the confessional note is again unmistakable here—

> wanders about in sick alienation from any kind of natural and spiritual reality, in one or another fantastic, arbitrary, nonexistent world or who arms himself against the real world and imagines that with his illusory

strength he can destroy its powerful existence, who imagines that the realization of the finite propositions of his finite judgement and the finite aims of his finite will comprise the entire good of mankind, and who does not realize, poor fellow, that the real world is higher than his wretched and feeble individuality, that sickness and evil are not part of reality, but part of himself, of his own alienation.[25]

The ultimate and worst consequence of these misguided Enlightenment philosophers was the "bloody and tumultuous" revolution they helped foment:

> Where there is no religion, there can be no state. The revolution was the rejection of any state, any legal order. The guillotine applied its bloody standard, punishing everyone who had even slightly risen above the mindless crowd, Napoleon stopped the revolution and restored social order, but he could not cure the main sickness of France: he could not restore religion, and religion is the substance, the essence of any state.[26]

And now the sickness had spread through Russia, with the result that Russian education

> instead of igniting in the young heart the divine spark that providence itself had placed there; instead of inspiring in it profound religious feeling, without which life has no significance and cannot have any, without which it is turned into meaningless vegetation; instead of forming in it a deep aesthetic sense, which preserves a person from all the dirty, unenlightened sides of life; instead of all this it fills him with empty, meaningless French phrases which kill the soul at its inception and drive out of it everything sacred and fine. . . . Is it any wonder that instead of a strong and active Russian devoted to Tsar and fatherland, such an education forms only someone ordinary, colorless, characterless?[27]

The conclusion was self-evident:

> To rebel against reality and to destroy in oneself every vital life source are one and the same thing. To reconcile with reality in all aspects and all spheres of life is the great task of our time, and Hegel and Goethe are the leaders of this reconciliation, this return from death to life. Let us hope that our new generation will also come out of their illusions, that they will cease their empty and senseless chatter, that they will realize that true knowledge is entirely inconsistent with anarchy and arbitrary views, that rigorous discipline reigns in knowledge, and that without this discipline there is no knowledge.[28]

The Russian poet Zhukovsky knew this, Bakunin went on in this revealing article, when he urged his countrymen to "make peace again with nature and life" and proclaimed that "both sorrow and joy, everything, serves a single aim." Pushkin knew it, too, when he showed through Onegin how futile it was to struggle against reality, "for reality always wins."[29]

It was all, therefore, a question of right understanding, of viewing reality *sub specie aeternitatis*, through the eyes of Infinite, not finite, man. To see evil anywhere, to divide God's reality into a blessed inner world and a vile external world as he had done before, was not to see at all. Having made his peace with the world thanks to this higher wisdom, Bakunin once more elevated the steps leading to it from the level of private experience to that of universal human destiny, in a series of dialectical scenarios, fascinating both as examples of the projection that typifies his writing (as in the above article on Hegel, for example) and for their contrast with his later revolutionary scenarios. The scenarios always involve a three-act drama. In the first act man, whether as individual or as mankind as a whole, begins in a state of blissful but unconscious union with "God." Then, in the second stage, man discovers his "I," his self, and is thereby separated from "God." Although this self-awareness and its concomitant sense of "freedom" are potentially good, they represent in this initial stage of liberation a "fall" into "emptiness, inadequacy, poverty, and falsity." The freedom born of this separation from "God" is only "a negative, empty freedom" and is therefore the cause of "incessant contradiction," a "fall into the most fearsome depression." The suffering ends and blissful peace is again enjoyed in the third stage, with "the return of the finite and fallen spirit to infinite contemplation and contemplation of the infinite." If the freedom of the second stage is "empty freedom, simply a form lacking any content," the "content" that will fill the emptiness is "God and nothing other than God." When the individual and humanity as a whole freely accepted God's reality and no longer distinguished between good and evil, accepting both as God's will, then and only then would there be both freedom and bliss. As to the way back home again, "the path by which finite man returns to the lost unity is art, religion, and, finally philosophy." Here were the doors of authentic perception that would allow mankind to fuse full and free self-awareness with full and blissful reunion and thereby attain "that kingdom of the holy spirit, the divine commune that is the result of Hegel's philosophy."[30]

In one of the scenarios, in which a hypothetical young man rather than humanity plays the lead, the autobiographical roots of the drama—evident enough in the above review—are especially apparent. The theme concerns Bakunin's theory of education. In stage one "love and harmony" should engulf the boy. In the next stage two things happen: first, the boy "shakes off the yoke of animal instinct," replacing it with such things as "nature, poetry, and art," and second, the earlier "harmony brought from home" is "subject to tempestuous contradictions." Again in good Hegelian form, these very contradictions will produce the synthesis: they "force man to suffer and compel him to reestablish harmony by means of thought."[31]

Especially notable in these scenarios is the way they mirror so precisely Bakunin's own development and motivations. How lovingly he idealizes those first narcissistic years, when "man" (i.e., he himself) "did not distinguish between himself and God," "when he contemplated God directly." But then came the "fall," when the "immediacy had to be destroyed," when he "had to separate himself from God in order thereby to come to know the emptiness, inadequacy, poverty, and falsity of his individual life." While the pains of the "fall" are in part explained by the experience of individuation, separation following preoedipal maternal identification, their sexual-oedipal sources are also evident, I believe, in Bakunin's association of the "suffering," the "tempestuous contradictions," the "terrible struggles" of this phase with the individual's "rising above the senses," "shaking off the yoke of animal instinct." (The phase of life that he identifies with the "fall," the adolescent years, is, after all, the period in which those "animal instincts" normally come into their own and flourish.) Finally, we can see Bakunin's response to the oedipal failure, his deeper immersion back into the preoedipal, narcissistic "dual unity," in his description of the third stage, which, he feels, he has now entered. It is a period when "man" "must return to God," "return to the lost unity," the period for "the return of the finite and fallen spirit to infinite contemplation and contemplation of the infinite," a time when one "builds a new and more splendid, more lofty, divine temple than the one destroyed by the storms" and establishes "a kingdom of the holy spirit." There is no place there, in that "divine temple" for those "animal instincts." Only solipsistic mind, thought, art, religion, and philosophy are welcome. The time for "animal instincts" will come later—when Bakunin shifts from "right" to "left" Hegel, and when, correspondingly, the resolution of the "terrible struggles" will be achieved not by "Thought," but by apocalyptic violence and destruction.[32]

But if we know enough about Bakunin's personality and motivations to gauge the roots (in his case) of this drama of alienation and reconciliation, we also know enough to realize that *genuine* "reconciliation" was out of the question. What place did it allow for a display of power, for those repressed "animal instincts," for the other side of the permanent dualism that was no less demanding than was the side that craved detachment and withdrawal? This is the most important question to ask of Bakunin's Hegelian period, for in answering it, and most of the remainder of this chapter will be devoted to that, we will see the principal contribution that Hegel made to the formation of "Bakunin," the exquisitely honed dialectical pivot on which a submissive surrender involved in "reconciliation" became the violent aggression required for apocalyptic revolution.

To begin with the surface, Bakunin did actually try at times during this first Hegelian period (1837-38) to reconcile himself to life and the world as they were, for he did, at least on occasion, come more out of himself and into the real world than he had before. He took more interest in the estate, at least to the extent of sending seeds from Moscow before he left it to spend that summer (1837) in Premukhino,[33] and spent his Premukhino evenings, or so he wrote, reading to his father,[34] later claiming that "all my efforts last summer and fall" were aimed at coming closer to him.[35] He repaid some debts[36] and tried, without success (judging from his letters), to stop analyzing himself so much.[37] By the time he returned to Moscow in December, 1837, he had gone far enough in his reconciliation to renew his visits to his comme il faut relatives in "their beautiful, so tastefully furnished apartments."[38]

He even fell in love again, with another cousin, Sophia Muraviev. The romance seems to have begun soon after his return to Moscow from Premukhino, when he became good friends with the young lady's father, Alexander Muraviev, a Decembrist in youth, turned Christian mystic. "I am delighted that your brother Misha is a man of such lofty soul," Alexander Muraviev wrote Varvara. "He has entirely captivated me and, so to say, has driven right into my soul." To Bakunin himself, Muraviev wrote. "I am most fond of you, respect you and embrace you with all my heart."[39] With several levels of obvious innuendo, Bakunin told his sisters about the fine impression he had made on his uncle: "He has told me that he is not only very fond of me but also deeply respects me, that if only he had a son like me all that would be left for him would be to thank providence for it."[40] As for his cousin, Sophia: "Don't laugh now, but something is stirring within me and seriously. What, surprised? It's nothing, nothing, keep quiet about it, and I will write more when I myself understand it better. Only take care: not a word to the Beyers or it will trouble them."[41]

Of course, he emphasized in another letter, his love was pure and spiritual. "And can you possibly think that love can retain for me any significance if, for its sake, I tear myself away from that which unites me to eternity, to truth? Oh no, I can love only to the extent that I live with truth and revelation."[42] "It seems that I am in love," he wrote his sisters a few weeks later, but went on again to assure them that he would not "forget the universal in life because of a splendid particular," or "abandon the cudgel, as Hercules did, and the striving towards the sublime...."[43] Leaving no doubt about the "cudgel's" primary and pure fidelity, he wrote the Beyers during these weeks of infatuation with Sophia that "My jealous wife sends you her regards, Alexandra. She bids me tell you that you are a little bold to forget that she is the only one who has rights to my love."[44] As it soon became evident, the jealous wife (philosophy and the inner "friend"

she reflected) left as little room for Sophia as for anyone else. For a time he continued to write glowingly of Sophia's charms and of the joy he felt being with
her, but he admitted after a while that he really was not sure if he did love her
and again warned love "not to interfere with what was most important and to
stay in her proper place: if she should try to dominate my entire being, then
away with her."[45]

While still unable to extend "reconciliation" enough to exchange his "jealous wife" philosophy for a natural mate, he, nevertheless, continued to insist
now that "the main thing is to be a healthy, vital, and active person." The Absolute must not be regarded as a refuge, he wrote Natalie Beyer reprovingly; it was
"not some sort of separate region where one can isolate oneself and hide from
life's vicissitudes."[46] His own life, he said, was "becoming more realistic . . . more
and more approximating a normal state."[47] Not that conditions were any more
pleasant than they had been earlier for him. On the contrary, as we will see below, "external circumstances" at Premukhino that summer (1837) were as disturbing as ever, and he had to "weigh every word" in his strained relations with
his sisters. But his response "this time had nothing in common with that oppressive state in which I found myself last year [the time of "hell, hell with all its
terrors"]. The tensions with his sisters now "had no effect whatsoever on my
tranquillity or on my strength. I had reconciled myself to my being for them not
what I had formerly wanted to be, but what they and circumstances allowed me
to be."[48] In any case, he had no desire any longer, he told Natalie Beyer, to indulge in "complaints, bad moods, dissatisfactions, in short all those wretched
trivialities of human life."[49]

In his attitude towards his brothers, which, as we saw, had always reflected
his father's prudence, he became the conservative's conservative: "How I dislike
the mental anarchy of those people who think that their personality can decide
everything."[50] Since he had himself been a principal source of that "anarchy,"
he did what he could to bring the young men back to reason: "You complain
about entering military service. I myself earlier dissuaded you, but I now advise
you to serve as zealously as possible and reach officer rank. That way your hands
will not be tied. You will be able to choose your occupation in accordance with
your needs." If they would only follow this advice, he assured them, they would
"not become a useless link in the general chain of life."[51] The irony of his using
this image in urging his brothers to keep to the straight and narrow could hardly
be more striking.[52]

If there were at the time only such statements and actions as these, expressing Bakunin's new philosophy of reconciliation, the problem would be to explain
how and why he changed from such reconciliation to his later revolutionary
posture. But attitudes and behavior reflecting submissive reconciliation were by
no means all there were during this period. In fact, at no time, not even during

his first year of reconciliation, did he ever really submit his personal desires to uncongenial "conditions of custom, propriety, and obligation" or restrain his struggle against the "dark, filthy, and vile." Nor was a "fussy, bureaucratic job" any more acceptable after reconciliation than it was before. He respected the service, he told his parents, but was it his fault if he simply did not like that kind of work?[53] Much as he continued to hope for his parents' blessing, he refused to consider it a "salary" in payment for doing what they wanted but what he despised.[54] His father had ruined his own life by heeding conventions, he told his sisters, and he was determined not to do the same.[55] Besides, his father had loved the service, while he did not, and such love, he wrote his father, should be the only reason for entering it.[56] He did try tutoring again, but gave it up even more quickly than he had before. Also, he had accepted a governmental commission the year before to translate a history text from the German for the Moscow school district, and while he told his parents that he had finished it and was expecting a sizeable return, he had in fact hardly begun it (if he had done anything at all) and in the end responded to vexed insistence from the school authorities by parcelling the job out to friends and relatives.[57] Other than occasional small gifts from home, therefore, he got along by living with his friends and again borrowing ever more heavily.

Moreover, notwithstanding his assault on the Idealists' "I", his rejection of the Romantics' *schönseligkeit,* and his admonition to the Beyers not to look upon the Absolute as "some sort of separate region where one can isolate oneself," he continued to preach the familiar Romantic litany as devotedly and devoutly as ever. As before, bliss would be theirs only when "the conviction had been firmly set that [life] is in us, and that everything apart from us is only appearance and illusion."[58] It was still as true as ever that "one must stand as high as possible above our base and lowly world in order to attain authentic and eternal happiness"; that "I am not of this world. Nothing on earth interests me any longer. I have liberated myself from it. My fatherland is more splendid"; that his friends should "keep at an infinite distance ... all those who have nothing in common with you and who try to sneak into the heavenly sphere of your life"; and that they should strive after "something more real than all that wretched reality that surrounds us."[59] Even the core commitment, "I must entirely dissolve my individuality in the Absolute" is preceded by the comment, "I must seek nothing for myself in what lies outside of myself."[60] "Dear friends," he wrote the Beyers, espousing as his new testament a carbon copy of the old,

You must once and for all free yourselves of the last trace of earthly existence. Our true life will be heaven, the paradise of the moral and intellectual world, where there are no storms and suffering, where everything is peaceful and harmonious, everything love. ... Dear friends, everything around us is empty and dead. We will unite more tightly still so as not to lose our way in this dreadful wasteland. ... Yes, bliss is near for us; the kingdom of God is not far. So let us make ourselves worthy members of this sacred kingdom where there is no suffering, no boundaries, no externals, the kingdom where all come to know and to love [one another] in a single and universal absolute love. ... Nature, art, religion, knowledge will be the steps along which you will arrive at this marvelous altar of eternal truth. Let us pray to her together, bow down before her and throw down at her feet all the partial, all the individual, all the filth that still holds us back and impedes our complete unity with her.[61]

If, therefore, Bakunin had become a devotee of Hegel's Absolute Spirit in search of a "harmony outside," he nevertheless remained as convinced as ever that the way to it was entirely inward and that the vehicle for reaching it was still the sensibility of the Romantic. The path by which finite man returns to the lost unity is still art, religion and philosophy;[62] "in poetry, in religion, and, finally, in philosophy a grand event takes place, the reconciliation of man with God."[63] And the goal, as well as the means, remained the same: "complete unity with her." It is no wonder that this "objective" Absolute in no way limited Bakunin's sense of unconstrained freedom, since it was simply the mirror of that freedom, and of the inner maternal reunion that made that freedom so desirable and so indispensable for him. For all its vaunted "objectivity," Bakunin's Absolute was no less subjective than his earlier Romanticism and Idealism had been. All that had happened was the transfiguration of that subjective world from a highly vulnerable inner escape and sanctuary into an omnipotent, all-encompassing universal power, a projection that was even more reflective of narcissistic omnipotence and the oedipal fantasy of indomitable masculine power.

Bakunin was "reconciled," in other words, as long as he was left alone to go on living as he chose to live, "free at last ... in the free sphere of the eternal Spirit," as he wrote at the beginning of his second Hegelian summer (1838), free in his own "element," "master" of his "inner world."[64] Everything was "quiet and peaceful" at Premukhino, because "harmony has returned: not an illusory, but a real harmony, based not on arbitrary authority, but on the rational freedom of each member of the family."[65] However appealing and necessary to him at the time as a philosophical and religious theory, "reconciliation" was in no way permitted to interfere with his actual way of life, his freedom to go on doing only what he chose to do. "If one's soul is at peace, and is in a state of goodness and sanctity, then that gentle, quiet harmony can prevail over the most unpleasant externality, *at least until that external world becomes so bad that it completely destroys the inner harmony*."[66] When, for example, the Beyers asked him in the summer of 1837—a high point in his "reconciliation"—when he plan-ned to leave Premukhino, he replied that that depended

> mainly on my own will, which I value above everything else, which I have succeeded in bending before the Absolute, but which I cannot submit and will never submit to any other considerations. My primary concern in this is to be completely free in all my relationships. This is necessary for me if I am to be of any use whatsoever, for the moment I feel myself to be even slightly bound and as soon as I am bound, then good-by divine tranquillity and hello storms and upheavals! But do not worry about anyone violating my freedom and trying to deprive me of the absolute tranquillity that I enjoy. I have arranged everything as it should be, and no one will dare or be able to encroach upon me.... As for my fate, everything is still so indefinite that in truth, I really do not know myself what will become of me. But the main thing is that I will do only what I think sound and right. You can be sure, therefore, that everything will be for the best.[67]

Reconciliation indeed! How little genuine reconciliation there was during the period of "right" Hegelianism is especially apparent when one realizes that Bakunin's mission to liberate his sisters from sex and marriage and his war with his parents because of it went on not only unabated but at times even more bit-terly than it had gone on during the Fichtean period. Even during those painful first months of 1837, following his flight from Premukhino, he busied himself earnestly with the plight of the Beyer girls. They had taken refuge in Premukhino, on his advice, to get away from their mother, and he demanded they stay there, vowed to ruin all the plans their mother and brother were making to get them back to their own estate, and sent his sisters alternative tactics to foil the enemy. "Do not let them lock you up in a cage," he wrote the Beyers. "We must be free in our actions and our relationships. Down with slavery and down with sacri-fices."[68] In spite of his humble Hegelian remarks about not trying to control things, he still insisted that the young ladies "submit" to him and only him "in blind faith and obedience," and he swore that as long as he lived they would never see their family estate again, never return to their "mad and evil mother and swinish brother." "They are rebelling a little and talk about their trip to Shashkino [their own estate]," he wrote his sisters, "but that will not be. I would not be what I am were I to let them go and bow down before their mother and brother."[69]

The incessant crisis in the Beyer household was not the only front to engage him during those months of "reconciliation." There were also a fast-failing ro-mance between his sister Liubov and Stankevich and the continuing struggle to

"liberate Varvara" from her husband. The Stankevich-Liubov romance had blos-
somed and faded in 1835, but not before Liubov and her parents had concluded
that the two were more or less engaged. Throughout the next year, the family
vainly waited, receiving flimsy excuses from Stankevich instead of the explicit
proposal they were expecting with increasing desperation. Bakunin told his parents not to worry, assuring them that Stankevich's love was "sacred, elevated,"
that it filled his being, that "something holy, something superhuman speaks in
him."[70] The prospects of this marriage did not seem to disturb Bakunin as did
the others. Some passing comments in a letter from Varvara may explain why:
urging that the marriage take place before Stankevich's planned trip to the West,
for cures and study, she argued that he and her sister were already husband and
wife "in heaven's eyes," even though his health forbade a marriage "in its earthly
aspect." Liubov would be his "friend" and "sister." Or, as Bakunin wrote Liubov:
"He needs a friend like you. He needs rest in a pure, ardent, and believing soul."[71]

As though this sad affair together with the endless Beyer turmoil were not
enough for the "reconciled" Bakunin, he gave much of himself during the fall
of 1837 to the task of keeping Varvara and her husband apart. Varvara herself
was by no means as certain or as insistent about the separation. She was painfully
torn between her desire for "purity" and her sympathy, gratitude, and even fondness for her husband, who had always treated her well. And there were also her
parents, whom she loved and wanted to please and who sided completely with
her husband. If only he would consent to live as brother and sister, she wrote
Bakunin, she would return to him. But she refused to violate her principles, the
religion of spiritual love that, she said, she owed entirely to her brother. Were
Diakov her son and not her husband, everything would be fine, she added, for
she did want to take care of him, did not blame him for the discord, and was
moved by the kindness and the gifts with which he hoped to win her back.[72]

After Bakunin left Premukhino in November, the conflict with his parents
grew even more intense. His parents insisted that Varvara return to Diakov as a
proper wife and stormed against Michael, "declared war" on him, as he wrote
the Beyers after receiving from his father a particularly searing letter. Written by
his mother (the influence, Bakunin was convinced, behind his father's assault),[73]
the letter accused him of corrupting the souls of his sisters, of destroying Varvara's love for her husband, which had begun to revive and grow stronger before
Bakunin returned to Premukhino in June, of turning her against her parents, and,
for good measure, of inspiring his brothers to run away from school the year
before. "And all this ends," as Bakunin reviews the letter for his sisters, "with
the admonition either to become once and for all a truly Christian son or to end
my philosophical visits to Premukhino."[74]

The fuel that seems to have heightened the flames was Varvara's plan to go
abroad in order to soothe her shattered nerves in the Carlsbad waters, but to go

with her son and without her husband. Her parents were aghast at the thought: tell her she must take both husband and son or neither, her parents advised Diakov. Only their son Michael, they were convinced, could have inspired Varvara with such an idea. Thus, Michael concluded, all his efforts "to find a true father had been in vain." Varvara, meanwhile, was desperate: "Michael, Michael, free me from this torment or give me the strength to bear it." They all depended totally on him now, she said, and on him alone:

> You are fused with every moment of our lives. All that is sacred, all that is fine is inextricably bound with you! ... Misha, Misha, what bliss to know that you love us, that we are yours and that nothing can tear us from you.... Oh, you do not know, cannot know how wonderful it is to think and to speak of you.... Oh, how happy is the one whose feelings are entirely penetrated, enlightened by eternal reason, for whom nothing is dark, for whom everything is bright.... Oh, give us this bliss, Misha, enlighten us by the light of reason and truth, give us immortal, conscious life.... Misha, you were sent to us by God. You have awakened us to eternal life and our faith in you is complete, as limitless as is life itself!

He must not abandon her now, for she looked to him now as "father to my son." She would believe in him as long as she had "faith in what is lofty, eternal ... for you have shown it to us, poured its love into us.... I would perish without you." [75]

With such boundless faith and adoration as proof of the sanctity of his mission and potency of his power, Bakunin took up his father's challenge and once more forgetting everything he had just learned about reconciliation undertook his most vigorous campaign ever for "freedom" (purity). First of all, he answered his father in a massive unfinished letter—over 20 printed pages—reviewing the whole of his early life. Until now, he said, he had been afraid to admit that "I have no father," because he had wanted to hold on to the reconciliation he had been striving for over the past year and because he needed "the love and advice of a father, especially a father like you.... I would gladly pour out all my soul to you, show you all its wounds and all its unenlightened sides, of which there are still many." But his father's letter had forced him "to doubt the possibility of realizing one of my strongest needs—to be understood by you, to show you that my love for you is real, and to repay you by complete love and complete trust for all that you have done for us and have borne for us." He now faced, he said, a hard choice: either to give up his father's love forever and end relations with him or to be utterly frank about everything. And since "it is beyond my strength to abandon all hope in your love," he chose the second option and entered upon his long self-defense.

For the most part, his case is a restatement of earlier arguments against "blind obedience," love based on duty, "a slave relationship," "the blind arbitrary will of his parents." If parents demanded of children ("of course I speak here about mature and fully developed children") what the children knew was not good, then the children had the right to disobey. "Parents who really love their children do not want their slavish submission, but their love, and love and slavery are obviously completely contrary to each other." However, should slavery be demanded, then Jesus' words should be remembered: "'I have come not to bring peace, but the sword. For I have come to divide son from father, and daughter from mother, and bride from bridegroom'." Now, of course, this code of love and freedom had nothing whatsoever to do with "vulgar license"; for "just as Christ represented the triumph of spirit over nature, so was man called upon to ascend above natural love to the sacred love which made all other love seem insignificant and illusory.... Apart from this love everything is illusory and insignificant. The whole destiny of a man is none other than the striving towards union with God, union with him through the power of Christian revelation, the power of grace from the Holy Spirit."

This spiritual ascent involved suffering, to be sure, but this was not only transitory but also good, for suffering "aroused a person from torpor" and "reminded him of the fact that he lived in a world of lies, that he would not find any satisfaction of his needs there, that their satisfaction is in another realm, not of this world, inaccessible to those bound to the wretched and putrid things of this world." Resting his case on a long series of gospel citations, Bakunin went on for several pages in this vein, insisting that everything not joining man to God must be rejected.

After this lengthy prologue on proper child raising and union with God, Bakunin undertook to show where his father had gone wrong, bringing the account, however, only down through 1835. His flaws of character and judgment, which had done so much harm to his children, were all the more crushing, Michael said, because they contrasted so cruelly with the image the children had had of him from their Premukhino childhood, when they had looked upon him as "someone great, apart from the ranks of ordinary people." [76]

Never had the conflict with his father been as severe as it was in this first year of reconciliation. "Alexander Mikhailovich will show his son no mercy if the war comes out into the open." [77] From an alternatingly blissful and brooding philosopher Bakunin had again become a fierce *l'homme engagé*. For once again freedom and purity were at stake. *"Das ist der Weisheit letzter Schluss: Nur der verdient die Freiheit wie das Leben, Der täglich sie erobern muss,"* he quoted from *Faust* in a letter to Varvara directing her to be steadfast now that the real battle had begun. As long as she lived the "universal life," in the "kingdom of grace," she had nothing to fear and could simply ignore the "repulsive" people, the "world of wretched and feeble, sickly philistinism" into which their father had unfortunately fallen.[78] It was to be an all-out struggle, and through it all, reminiscent of his struggle for the Beyers' independence (and anticipating his later political battles), there is an aura of besieged urgency and conspiratorial zeal. For example, in letters from late December 1837 and early January 1838.

My dear friends, here I am in Torzhok. In three hours I will be in Kazitsino. Be strong and unbending, as I am, for the all-powerful hand of God is with us. Be at peace, as I am.... You must go to Kazitsino and not to Ivanskoe—this is the outcome of my talks with Aunt Tatiana Mikhailovna who is a good angel and entirely on our side. I am going to Kazintsino to change Aunt Anna Mikhailovna's mind. From there I will write father a letter, full of supplication and love. I know in advance his reply. Then I will send him a long letter in which I will tell him the whole truth, in a suitable way. When I have succeeded in changing Anna Mikhailovna's mind, I will write you and you will ask her by letter to send horses for you. You will come to Kazintsino with Taniusha. I will wait for you there. Fear nothing: God and the law are on our side (December 31).... Varinka, Aunt [Anna Mikhailovna] wants you to say that you will be a welcome guest at Kazintsino. Be tranquil and full of faith in providence. Write me the results of my letter. I must hurry. God be with you. If things go as badly as they have until now, dear Varinka, then ask for horses and come to Kazintsino with your son and Taniusha. Be tranquil and steadfast. (January 2)[79]

Besides maneuvering Varvara—and Tatiana—to their aunt's estate at Kazintsino where he would be waiting for them and where, he told Varvara, she could escape "[Diakov's] caresses" without arguments or scenes and without "compromising" herself,[80] he made inquiries into the legality of Diakov's threat to stop Varvara from going abroad without him by forcing her to leave their son with him if she tried. To reassure her on this point, Bakunin gave her long detailed accounts of the legal proceedings that would face Diakov if he attempted to carry out his threat and that he would certainly want to avoid for fear of scandal. But even were he to go to court, he would lose his case, since "our government is too truly paternal, too humane and too enlightened not to take the side of the weak and the just."[81] Finally, money had to be found to pay for the trip abroad. Bakunin took this task on himself, partly by selling Varvara's jewelry and silver and partly through more borrowing from willing creditors and sympathetic friends, such as Stankevich. In the end, Diakov himself realized the futility of resisting Varvara's departure and agreed to borrow money for her in his name. She and their son would leave without him the following summer (1838). Bakunin had won.

Bakunin's war with his parents over his sisters' "purity" and with the Beyer sisters' mother over theirs was, thus, even more militantly fought and accompanied by still more aggressive statements during the year and a half of full reconciliation than it had been during the Fichtean year of active proselytizing. Nor was it any less a zealously religious war or Bakunin any less in his own eyes the celibate apostle of a militant Jesus, a Jesus who had been "born man as we were" so that we could "become God as he did."[82] He continued to see himself as living "directly in Christ and through him in the spiritual world,"[83] reminded his followers that what appeared to finite eyes as evil was only the "illusion, death, and limitation that were overcome by Christ's revelation,"[84] repeatedly quoted from that revelation in defense of his beliefs and actions,[85] and approvingly recalled Varvara's intense religiosity, her conviction that Christ had spoken to her in dreams.[85] Fortunately for his purpose, he could and did use Jesus' message to sanction all his shifting responses—withdrawing from the fallen world, summoning the pure to destroy it, or submitting humbly to it in the manner of Hegelian reconciliation. Expressing a characteristically paradoxical mixture of the first and last postures, he reminded his disciples that "Man's true value lies in his happiness: 'Where your treasure is, there is your heart as well,' the savior said, and your treasure, all of it, is not of this world and is apart from the conditions of this world. But do not conclude from this that it is there, beyond the grey heavens. No, it is here, it constantly surrounds us. We unconsciously live in it and with it."[87] As we have seen, "the Kingdom of the Holy Spirit" was "the result of Hegel's philosophy."[88]

More fateful than this mixture of withdrawal and submission, however, was the addition now, and with increasing emphasis, of the militant alternative, the not-peace-but-the-sword Jesus. We see this, for example, in the greater stress that Bakunin now put on his chosen instrument for achieving "the Kingdom of the Holy Spirit," his "holy commune." Just as it had been "to establish true friendship, this holy commune, that He had come among the people," so must the purpose of Bakunin and his followers be "to realize his teaching on earth," that is, to create "an authentic brotherhood, a brotherhood of people aiming at a single idea, people loving the good and ready to sacrifice everything for that good," to establish "the divine external world, the holy commune, the sacred church, in which man must live if he is to be man." Throughout these years, ever since, at least, Bakunin began his Fichtean mission, he had identified himself and his destiny with Jesus too often and too solemnly for one to doubt his complete sincerity in doing so. He continued to feel within himself "a sense of holy pride at the thought that these fine souls, so rich in love, who once had suffered, have received from me truth and happiness." He congratulated the Beyer sisters on their "being present at my christening into truth, present at the beginning of my eternal life." And, joyful at the thought that "the commune of the Holy Spirit is really being established among us," he reminded the Beyers that "we three—you and I as the third set down its first foundations."[89]

Miniscule though his "commune of the Holy Spirit" was, he felt certain that "everything must retreat before it, since it represents a presentiment of the sacred kingdom that will be established among us." Towards that end, the commune must spread and bring in new members: "You should be happy," he told the Beyers, "at having succeeded in planting seeds in a field that had been, until you [came], so gone to weeds.... So continue your work, dear friends, direct him [Feodor Rzhevsky] incessantly towards the truth."[90] As the tiny, mustard-seed beginning of the coming Kingdom of the Holy Spirit was to be established not in heaven but right here on earth—and he was emphatic about that[91]—the holy commune must realistically prepare itself for struggle. "Do you think that there is not much suffering ahead for us from the cold touch of the frigid creatures surrounding us? Do you think that they will not, all too often, try to destroy the harmony of our souls, the harmony that comprises our only worth?"[92] To protect themselves from those "frigid" enemies who were out to "destroy" them, the commune members must hold tightly together in a well-disciplined cell, "strengthen the bonds that join us," and "remember the words of the Savior, 'What is bound on earth, will be bound in heaven.'"[93] This union must be "eternal...all who have once entered into this commune will never leave it, and all that is joined within, will never part."[94] As for the enemy, "No mercy for those who do not deserve it.... Nothing can stand against us. We will remake everything according to our will.... Our union was concluded on the ruins, on the utter destruction of the laws of this world."[95]

If during the activist year with Fichte the holy commune had been something of a monastic refuge from the corrupt world, it, thus, began to change during this year of "reconciliation" into a crusader's castle preparing itself for the merciless destruction of that "frigid" world. Had the belligerent declarations come near the end of the period of "reconciliation," we might interpret them as signs of the impending shift to the left, back to activism. But that is not the case. They come and go throughout these months. It was precisely when he had settled down in Premukhino in the summer of 1837 to devote himself to Hegel that he first described himself as a "warrior for holy truth" and said that "our union was concluded on the ruins, on the utter destruction of the laws of this world." It was following this summer of absorbing Hegel's message about the Real and the Rational that he engaged in his most fierce conflict with his father because of his efforts to separate Varvara from her husband. If, on the one hand, he submissively counselled his followers "to have unlimited faith in God, faith that everything that happens does so by his will," he also told them, on the other (and continuing this same sentence), that "this does not mean man must just stop, fold his hands and wait for the sun to shine. No, man must act...."[96] If, as a wise Hegelian, he wrote that "none of us should think about how things might be better with us," that one "should rather regard the external world as something given," he also, still the Fichtean, announced defiantly: "Everything must become better, and what is better is what I want, which means that what I want must necessarily be." If he saw his goal and that of his intimates as "the return of the finite and fallen spirit to infinite contemplation and contemplation of the infinite," he was no less convinced that "nothing will stand in our way: we will remake everything according to our will," and that "All wills must give way before the one that appears before them as God's interpreter. Matter must submit to intellect." In sum: "You know that I never retreat. And I will not retreat now, but will, one way or another, attain my aim."[97]

The stark and persistent contradiction could hardly be missed. Learning from Bakunin of his Hegelian "resurrection," Belinsky, still recuperating in the South that summer and fall (1837), congratulated him but admitted that "I have doubts about it." How could this reconciliation be believed when "you proclaim it with the same kind of pride and insensitivity that the *parvenu* usually expresses when announcing his promotion to a new rank"? Bakunin declared his membership in the "Kingdom of God" and his liberation from the "chains of insignificance" like "someone who, by an act of desperate courage, leaped into the enemy battery, captured it, seized the flag, and, with an ecstatic pride of victory, shouts out, 'Hurrah! We did it'."[98] While Bakunin himself seemed most of the time to be able to shift easily from one side to the other, from submissive reconciliation to militant opposition, even he was sometimes trapped by the confusion, uncertain which way to go: "Circumstances do not depend on us," he began one line, but then went on immediately, "We can change them. We can give to them the divine character that lives within us." Then, back again: "But, frequently we cannot change them." And, finally, "The main thing is to be prepared for anything and never act contrary to our beliefs."[99] Beginning one statement with the announcement that he had gotten over his earlier "disdain" for reality and that he now "accepted the existence of circumstances," he ended it by declaring that, as a result of the change, "I can consider myself the ruler of all external circumstances. They must take that form, that direction, which I give them."[100]

No less fascinating or fateful than this persisting ambivalence, were Bakunin's attempts to escape it. He had submitted to Hegel's Absolute in order to save himself from the dangers of Schelling-Fichte subjective Idealism and had found in the Absolute a variety of protections he desperately needed. He would not give them up, ever. But neither would he give up his absolute freedom (nor, considering what "freedom" meant to him, *could* he give it up), and submission to Hegel's "external," "objective" Spirit clearly implied a surrender of, or, at least, radical constraints on, that freedom. How could he have both the protection of Hegel's Absolute and the unlimited freedom that had been so well served by Schelling and Fichte? The formula he first adopted worked splendidly, for a while: he divided Hegel's "objective" world into two parts, one part comprising the "really" Real that must be accepted and another part involving those things that merely "existed" and that one was entirely right in opposing: "I am not talking about what is usually understood by the word reality—a chair, a table, a dog, Varvara Dmitrievna, Alexandra Ivanovna—all this is dead, illusory, and lifeless, not authentic reality."[101] To consider such commonplace items as really Real merely reflected an undeveloped consciousness, which "concealed from us the one and only reality by surrounding us with an innumerable multiplicity of illusions—terrible, frigid, meaningless illusions that we think are real...."[102] While it was true that, as the Hegelian world view required, "everything that exists and acts is necessary," this necessity was not "that dead and soulless necessity to which those submit who are crushed by fate....No, the necessity before which I bow is sacred...."[103]

With Reality thus divided, he could continue to enjoy the protection of the objective, ineluctable, all-powerful Absolute (the really Real) and at the same time remain "free" from all the "terrible, frigid, meaningless illusions that we think are real." By viewing the world this way, Bakunin had, in effect, reversed the unfortunate relationship between the "external" world and the subjective "I" that he had suffered during his romantic Schelling-Fichte period: then, it was the inner "I" that was vulnerable, subjected to all the oppressions of a corrupt but powerful external world; now, it was the "I" that was all-powerful, invulnerable, allied as it was to "sacred" (in contrast to "soulless") necessity, while all the rest, all that the "I" opposed, all those "frigid creatures" were unreal, weak, and doomed.

What Bakunin had, in fact, been doing during his months with Hegel was exactly the reverse of what he said he was doing. Rather than destroy his "I" by subordinating it to the external world, submerging it into the Absolute, he had magnified it to cosmic proportions by making it identical with the Absolute, remodeling external, objective Reality in his own image. For what else is the "sacred" necessity and the really Real if not the composite of his heart's desires? Two quotations, the first from the Fichtean period and the second from the Hegelian, make this clear.

> *Two lives live within you.* One is human and at the same time divine....
> But there is within you another life, a species of artificial life. It is all
> the dogmas, all the formulas of mundane calculation; it is the anti-
> Christian tracts about obligation....[104]

And when I speak here of the external world, you must understand well what I mean by this, since there exists for man *two external worlds.* One is the product of his spirit which has not yet attained self-consciousness, which oppresses him, impedes his free action.... The spirit must shake off its yoke, it must freely create another external world, according to the laws of humanity and, along with it, divine reason, and this second external world will not act as an impediment to his development. On the contrary, it is the product of that development. Man must destroy the first and live in the second....[105]

In the Fichtean citation the focus is on the "two lives" that are "within you," and all that the divine life within can do is somehow liberate itself from the "artificial life" imposed by conventional society with its "dogmas" and "obligation." In the second attention shifts outwards to "two external worlds," and it is the task of illumined, self-conscious "spirit" to "destroy" the existing and oppressive external world that "impedes his free action" and replace it with a "second external world" that would not stand in his way.

Instead of "remaking" himself to suit the world as he said he must do, he had set out to remake the world to suit himself. At times, in fact, he was quite candid about it. Once, for example, when instructing his followers as to the criterion to use in deciding which "reality," among the competing claimants, really represented Truth, he advised:

Trust to your feelings, give yourself to them entirely, boundlessly, unconditionally and try to understand them.... Here is the true measure for determining what is authentic thought: If the thought does not oppress you, if it does not limit the horizons of your inner eye, if it, on the contrary, enlarges [the vision] and forces you to say "everything is splendid, life is bliss, life is a sacred holiday when the spirit, immersed in blissful and infinite awareness of itself, celebrates its divine freedom and finds itself everywhere, finds in the world nothing alien, nothing hostile to it, recognizes everywhere its own free movement"—then such thought is true. Revel in it, live by such thought, and it will lift you by wings into the kingdom of immortal, eternal bliss, and in this kingdom we will know one another and take joy and blessedness in one another.

Every thought that does not lead to this is a lie, and therefore a sin, for only falsehood is sin, and sin is slavery.

"So know the truth, and the truth will make you free."[106]

What was true was what felt good to him. It could not have been simpler, clearer, more gratifying, or more strikingly narcissistic. On another occasion, aware that such praise of feeling might be mistaken for the old *schönseligkeit*, he again distinguished carefully between the objectively Real (everything he liked) and the objectionably "real" (everything he abhorred):

> Do not think that this was that illusory and abstract probing into one-self that is always fruitless, since there is no vital thought process in it, since it always leads to a static and moribund contemplation of one's own illusiveness and emptiness, contemplation without exit, bringing in its wake only depression. That sort of contemplation is simply the result of a finite, limited probing into oneself, when one has lost the sense of the infinite and fails to understand that there is an all-powerful and beneficent force of love possessing a boundless reign over every struggle and every division. My present probing into myself is accompanied by an awareness of what is eternal and real, and, therefore, it is not illusory and not abstract and cannot lead to depression, but, on the contrary, brings with it splendid fruits.[107]

So much was he still within the cult of feeling, so much still the Romantic (notwithstanding his Hegelian critique of *schönseligkeit*, to ward off Schelling-Fichte "depression") that he subordinated Thought itself, the core of Hegelian Idealism, to the needs of right feeling.

> There are minutes, hours, sometimes whole days of revelation, when everything is so clear, so luminous, so comprehensible, when you feel within yourself infinite love. But there are also other moments, moments of critical judgement,... when everything is dark, everything vile, meaningless, and when the soul is burdened by a kind of dry indifference to everything. In the middle, between these two opposing elements of our life, there is *Thought*, which pulls one's mind out of the finite categories of critical judgement and brings it into understanding, for which there is nothing contradictory and for which everything is good, everything is fine.[108]

If one thought the world "dark ... vile, meaningless" one was not thinking correctly, for true thought, "understanding," "thought based on revelation," on the "rational eyes of the Soul"[109] made it clear that "everything is good, everything is fine." While Bakunin had already spent years with other German Idealists before Hegel learning how to achieve this joyful, narcissistic remodeling of reality by merging subject and object (i.e., making world mirror self), Hegel powerfully reenforced this radical solipsism. Since it was to be from this Hegelian base that he would soon launch his revolutionary career and through the Hegelian prism that he would see the world and justify his revolutionary vision and violence, it is essential that we appreciate the extent of this solipsism at the time. The empirical fact, he wrote, "always remains for me an alien and external object, and *if I want to destroy this externality, if I want to find myself in it* and understand it, then I must find it in the general; that is, in an idea which, on the one hand, is an objective idea, an idea actually there, and, on the other hand, *a subjective idea defined by my own spirit.*" The philosophical justification for this explicit defense of projection was still the same Idealistic assumption that he had earlier adopted from Schelling and Fichte:

> Every man in his own individuality is universal, and *possessing the universal within himself, he can ascend to it without leaving his own individuality....* When it relates to its inner world of laws, the reasoning consciousness relates to itself and becomes self-conscious, a self-knowing subject, *possessing in its ideas the complete infinite truth of the external, objective world,* so that its ideas, as subjective, are not opposed to the objective, known world of nature and Spirit, but on the contrary, penetrate it and comprise its essence.

Since, in short, "the external world ... is no more than a reflection of the internal world," genuine truth is "the *truth man can achieve without having to depart from himself.*"

Now, from an Hegelian perspective, the theorist who set out to find objective truth "without having to depart from himself," was simply doing with his own mind what the mind's source, the World Mind or Spirit, had always been doing, for, if the "pure 'I' in knowing itself knows the world objective to it," so did "the essence of the Spirit consist precisely in penetrating and finding itself in the real world that stands before it."[110] According to the basically gnostic, kabbalistic, and Boehmean fantasy that Hegel refined and rationalized, God necessarily alienated the world from himself in the very act of creating it out of himself. However, there remained in the alienated world, some aspects, traces, or sparks of the creative divinity. For Hegel, one essential expression or experience of that divine remnant in the alienated, material world was Reason, as revealed in human rationality, or at least in speculative Idealistic philosophy. In the philosophy of thinkers like Hegel himself, therefore, Absolute Spirit could find itself reflected. Stated another way, the gradual enhancement and deepening of human rational understanding through ever more complete philosophical knowledge meant, in effect, that the alienated, material realm (beginning with man) was in the process of being reunited with the divine creative Spirit, thus ending the tragic separation of created Being from the creative Spirit. (The lost individual soul would find its way back home again, without losing its cherished individuality. It is not surprising that Bakunin should find this narcissistic myth so appealing.)

In the notes that Bakunin took during his first Hegelian summer (1837), he emphasized especially, and understandably, those attributes of the Spirit that reflected this solipsistic relationship to the world and that associated the Spirit (and, consequently, its solipsistic talents) with human reason, particularly the philosophers' reason. The Spirit, we learn from these notes, "'making itself its own object,'" moves more and more back towards itself in the form of progressing human Thought, "'since Thought is its foundation, the pure element of its identity.'" At the end of the cosmic drama when Thought has reached a point of full understanding of Reality (as it does in Hegel's philosophy), the Spirit, which had alienated itself from itself by creating the material world, "'arrives at itself'." In the same way, Thought, as it advances, "enters into the pure element of itself... [and] finds, thereby, satisfaction within itself...." Or, the same thing stated even more solipsistically: "'*apriori* thought, reflecting itself and mediating itself, is Universality residing in itself. The point of departure is a free act of thought which occupies a point and begins from a point at which it is for itself its object.'"[111] Whether or not this accurately describes the ways of Spirit and Thought, it summarizes perfectly the ways of Bakunin himself, then, before, and thereafter.

No wonder he could feel and say that "necessity does not constrain [man's] freedom, because it is not imposed on him and does not limit him from outside, but comprises his own individual, personally all-embracing essence, determining all and determined by nothing from without."[112] Necessity and freedom were one and the same, since what was "necessary" was whatever his freedom wished. When, years before, he had proclaimed with romantic exuberance that his "soul pours itself over the entire universe, encompassing all in nature, the whole world," he was speaking metaphorically. Now, thanks to philosophical Idealism, what had been an expression of poetic imagery had become a statement of scientific fact. It was not only that he is projecting himself into the world, submerging the Absolute into the "I" while claiming to do the opposite; what is novel and crucial is his frank and proud acknowledgment of the projection, justifying it on the grounds of an assumed identity between the "inner world of laws" and "the complete infinite truth of the external, objective world."

Necessity and freedom were identical, as were thought and feeling, subject and object, inner and external, because they all joined in unison to tell him the same wondrous Truth—that "everything is splendid, life is bliss, life is a sacred holiday." It was, indeed, paradise—and childhood—regained. He had come to Hegel weak and wounded, wanting only solace from the pain he had suffered and protection from further hurt. He got that, but much, much more as well. Having provided the balm, the Absolute then went on to become his all-powerful ally in the struggle against "the dirty, filthy, and vile" and the "custom, propriety, and obligation," a struggle that, as we saw, continued as bitterly during the "reconciliation" as it had before and would thereafter. Moreover, not only did he now have all the vast powers of objective, indomitable, ineluctable Spirit, Reason, and History on his side, but he also found that they bent to his every wish and whim, since they were, in fact, his wish and whim, reflections of himself. In another of his favored three-act scenarios, he neatly summarized the stages he had gone through in arriving at this enviable state. He recalled the "first harmony" of "feeling" as "fine and infinite" but also as "limited and powerless" and, therefore, subject to suffering and struggle. Happily, however, "from this struggle, from this suffering a second harmony flows, one that is strong, clear, triumphant," one that "rings forth its awareness of victory, its awareness of infinite strength" and has "nothing to fear, because it no longer has any external foes." And it has no foes, he added, leaving no doubt about the basic narcissism, because it "has taken everything within itself."[113] Thus, to "take everything within itself," to "transform the external into the internal," as he had earlier put it, in no way meant "to regard the external world as something given," as he had urged others to do. Instead, it involved a narcissistic refashioning of that external world (through right "understanding") to fit the needs of the inner world. That, and not Hegelian "reconciliation," was the reason there was for him "no such division" between the "inner" and the "external." "Instinctual harmony and the harmony of feeling are reestablished in the harmony of thought, and then man *need fear nothing, since he lives in thought,* in absolute love, which is omnipotent and eternal,"[114] to recall an earlier expression of this consoling solipsism. Several years before he had said that he and his friend Efremov would be happy only when they could say that what they wanted, God also desired. He had now realized this grand ideal and consequently felt happier, stronger, and more self-assured than he had ever felt before.

Having begun his Hegelian conversion as a humble penitent, apparently willing to sacrifice the "I" that was "capable of any crime" and to accept all reality "as something given," as part of a single Absolute that knew no evil, he had become during his Hegelian "reconciliation" the "warrior for holy truth" struggling more confidently than ever in defense of "sacred" Reality against the "frigid creatures" who only seemed real. He was now the savior who, with his holy commune disciples, would "destroy" the alien, unreal externality in which he could not find himself and, "on the ruins, on the utter destruction of the laws of this world," build the "Kingdom of the Holy Spirit," where he would blissfully find only himself, and his "friend."

But we must keep clearly in mind, now that Bakunin is on the eve of his revolutionary life, what the struggle was all about. The enemy, then and later, under whatever disguise, was the same sensual foe that had earlier cast him "into gloom, anguish, suffering, self-laceration" and had made the world appear as though "through a stifling, bitter fog, gloomy, bent under the heavy hand of a fierce and pitiless fate." The enemy was still, as he identified it in his first Hegel article, "soulless flesh."[115] If "man is free only in God," it was still because "apart from God he is animal."[116] And if he yearned to follow in the footsteps of Jesus, it was because, as he wrote his father at the end of 1837, Jesus had triumphed over nature.[117] Almost all of that lengthy letter, written at the time of his most ardent campaign to separate Varvara from her husband, was devoted to an impassioned defense of chastity and celibacy. Besides saving Varvara from the fate of living "with an animal," Bakunin fought so hard to "liberate" her in order to save her son from a father who wanted "to make an animal of him."[118] What Bakunin offered her, his other sisters, and the Beyer sisters in place of this "animal" existence was, he said, "religious feeling" and the "aesthetic sense, which preserves a person from all the dirty, unenlightened sides of life."[119] But to enter this realm of sacred beauty and bliss one must "purify oneself...prepare one's soul for the temple of God"[120]: "sensual souls do not live in this life."[121] So, to repeat, "let us pray to [this life] together, bow down before it and throw down at its feet...all the filth that still holds us back and impedes our complete unity with it."[122]

As we have seen (and as much additional evidence will further testify), the narcissistic and oedipal sources of this obsessive commitment to total purity and to the millennial kingdom that would achieve and preserve it were also the sources of the suffering and violence that were already the constant companions of that ideal. The dream was, thus, from the outset, long before it had put on its political mask, vitiated by torrents of violence—violence as mock omnipotence to conceal the impotence and other results of oedipal failure, violence as vengeance for the deprivation imposed by that failure, violence as an outlet from primitive narcissistic rage, violence as a barrier to separate and protect him from society and its intolerable expectations, violence as self-punishment for experiencing the now incestual "symbiotic couple," and violence, as we will soon see, as a form of pseudo sexuality, a proxy passion in a life-long war both against the "dirty, filthy and vile" society and against the "frigid creatures," against what he himself had been forced to become in that war for purity.

The oedipal struggle of "body" and "soul" and, beneath that, the narcissistic split between the all-good and the all-bad had already become therefore, a struggle between two camps, Two Cities. In one camp, the city of light, to restate the essential dichotomy in this later, more extended form, were God and Jesus; the inner world and the "friend" within; the "pure and the virginal"; the Absolute, Reason, Spirit, History, and Thought; feeling, poetry, philosophy, art, and nature; the "holy commune" and the coming "Kingdom of the Holy Spirit."

The other camp, the city of darkness, housed all that was animal, sensual, material; the "dark, filthy, and vile"; all conventional society with its "customs, proprieties, and obligations"; its dogmas, rules, and laws; the "Apparent" world and the not really Real external world with its "frigid creatures", the "dog, Varvara Dmitrievna, Alexandra Ivanovna." Between the Two Cities, no compromise was possible, "no mercy," no "golden mean"—only destruction and ruins. Destruction was unavoidable: "only that ages and is destroyed which must age and be destroyed." Finally, concerning Bakunin's choice of the doomed and the saved, "everything that is only external must be destroyed, and only that which is both external and internal at the same time will be saved"[123]—only that, in other words, in which he could "find himself."

With the parts of his apocalyptic vision ready in hand, all Bakunin need do now to become "Bakunin" was to gather them together and translate the abstract fantasy into the language of politics, of which there is absolutely nothing yet. It had taken some five years for the fundamental projection and displacement to take place. It would take nearly as long to change the mask and the rhetoric from religious philosophy to revolutionary politics. The first step would be to discard the cloak of "reconciliation" that, while providing him the warmth he had so needed in his first months following the crisis of late 1836, had become increasingly threadbare and less and less able to disguise the robust passions that had gone on raging within him in a most un-Hegelian, unreconciled manner.

5.

REVIVAL:
SALVATION BY DEEDS

The "reconciliation," as scrupulously honored by Bakunin in his Hegelian theory as it was violated by him in his continuing Fichtean practice, reached full bloom in its second summer (1838). Completely free by then to live as he chose; happy alone with his "wife" philosophy and enjoying the pride of their first offspring (his article on Hegel that spring); inspired, guided, praised, and protected by his deified inner wife and mother that satisfied his every wish and mood, approved all his thoughts and deeds, however mercurially they leaped from submission to rebellion and back again; proud and strong in the knowledge that he had liberated his sister Varvara from her husband and his "soul sisters" from their mother, and that the "holy commune" he had sired and still sternly fathered was destined to establish the "Kingdom of the Holy Spirit"—he was content, "as happy," he said, "as it is given children to be happy."[1]

Nothing is more indicative of his contentment that summer, or of his effort to be "reconciled," than the affection he expressed towards his mother, the first such expression in his correspondence—and the last until he experienced an even stranger period of "reconciliation" years later, during his Siberian exile. When his mother went to Moscow that summer to help Varvara prepare for her trip abroad, Bakunin wrote her a light, genial letter, unlike anything he had written before, describing the family's peaceful life at Premukhino—Alesha at the piano, he and Paul reading to father, and other details of the happy hearth. "As for me, mother dear," he went on, introducing another "first" in his life, "I am slightly, very slightly getting into some of the secrets of agriculture."[2] He even went into some details concerning these "secrets" of field and workshop.

Bakunin could not have chosen a more appropriate analogy to describe his feelings that summer than to speak of the happiness of children, for it was, indeed, only as a reconciled, submissive child that he could risk a direct approach to his mother again (risk knowing the "secrets" of "enchanting mother nature," which, he told Tatiana that summer, filled his heart with rapturous joy).[3] Shielded by the rich and weighty rhetoric of reconciliation, which at least claimed his abandonment of the virile Fichtean campaign, he could dare—as one of the "children"—attempt tenderness towards his mother. It was precisely now, however, while he was beginning to show some affection towards his mother, that Bakunin's philosophy of reconciliation began to crumble. As will be suggested later, this conjunction may not have been mere coincidence.

Not surprisingly, the "slight" involvement in agriculture soon dropped off to no involvement: six weeks after telling his mother about the "slight" involvement, he wrote the Beyers that he could not take charge of the estate because it "in no way interested" him.[4] What did interest him was what he said should interest the Beyers—some place where, "as quietly as possible," they could study religion, philosophy, literature, and the rest of the romantic curriculum. He especially urged them to study Goethe's poetry and, as an appropriate accompaniment, sent them some Beethoven music and a picture of Schelling, whom, along with Hegel, "the eternal spirit" had chosen "as its organ for manifesting its eternal will and its eternal truth."[5] Goethe's *Egmont,* his letters to Bettina von Arnim *(Correspondence with a Child),* Bettina's own works, and Marbach were Bakunin's recommendations to his sisters. Even his brother Nicholas, who, Bakunin was pleased to learn, was now "in spirit ours," was advised to nurture "an aesthetic sense" by reading Goethe, Schiller, Hoffman, Pushkin, and Gogol. As for himself, he divided his time between writing more on Hegel and translating the diary of Bettina.[6] Reconciliation, in short, cost him nothing during the first months of his second Hegelian summer at Premukhino, since, as we saw earlier, while "everything is now quiet and peaceful" and "harmony has returned," it was "not an illusory, but a real harmony, based not on arbitrary authority but on the rational freedom of each member of the family." He was "free at last...in the free sphere of the eternal spirit."[7]

The "eternal spirit," however, now proved as fickle to him as he had been to her: the "harmony outside" began to betray him as cruelly as had the harmony inside two years earlier. He had hoped to be able to leave Russia with Varvara, but, alas, there was no money. (Moreover, not he, but his younger brother Nicholas was given the task of making arrangements for Varvara's trip.) For a while, he thought Stankevich would provide the funds he needed, since he had written Bakunin from Berlin that he could advance enough money not only for travel but for two years subsistence abroad. Later, however, he told Bakunin that he should count on only a summer's worth of support. Finally, he pulled out altogether, saying that he just could not ask his parents for the money, considering the large expense of his own stay abroad.

A still heavier cloud marred the beatific vista. During this summer of "real harmony"[8] his sister Liubov was slowly dying, and the whole family knew it. Since Stankevich's departure, she had gone on hoping, living only for the next of the few letters he sent her, yet dreading what it might say. "What does the future hold for me?" "Oh, if only he loves me, nothing more can separate him from me." "Your letter gave me new life." "My hand shakes, but I do not want to put the pen down." "When will I get a letter from you? God only knows the things I've been going over in my mind these two months of your silence." Stankevich's occasional responses were friendly and concerned. He was fearful for her health, and he urged her to take care of herself and to write him in detail about her illness. But there was not a word about the future marriage that, as far as Liubov, the Bakunin family, and "society" was concerned, was still to take place once Stankevich got back but that, as everyone had long since certainly guessed, would never be.[9]

In early August she died. Bakunin's reaction was strange. In letters to his mother and Efremov he shows that he had been very anxious about her illness and much involved in trying to get competent doctors for her.[10] Yet, his comments to Varvara about her death seem distant and restrained, as though an acquaintance rather than a sister had died. At the end of his letter, however, his remarks suggest a stronger impact: "My letter will seem to you a little dry. This is because I cannot shake off a kind of depressed feeling that has been with me for a while. Do not pay attention to it; it is a passing illness." A letter he wrote at the time to Efremov, who had been at Premukhino when Liubov died, was full of banter and jest, with no mention at all of Liubov. But here, too, the ending may suggest deeper currents of feeling that belie the light mood and tone: Why had Efremov not written him, he wondered: "Are you ill? Have you died along the way?"[11]

Indeed, Bakunin's "passing illness" did not pass so quickly, and the banter with Efremov turned out to be whistling in the dark. For a time, on the surface, life and mind remained as they had been. He continued to live quietly at home, immersed in his studies—his "only concern"—and preaching reconciliation with reality as the only way of coming to know oneself and attaining true freedom.[12] By mid-September, however, a month after Liubov's death, it was evident that the walls of his tranquillity were giving way. Once again, we read of "my doubts, my weakness, my spiritual blindness."[13] Probably reflecting as much his own mood as his concern for hers, he wrote Varvara that he had for some time been wondering how Liubov's death had affected her, whether Varvara possessed "enough faith and love to bear this loss," "this dreadful negation." He hoped it would not cut her off from that "infinite heaven in which all the profound secrets of life are resolved."[14] He fought hard, determined not to let this "dreadful negation" destroy his bliss and the "reconciliation" that had brought it. For help, he turned to an old ally he had not called upon since the Schelling-Fichte years—his cult and dialectic of suffering:

> He who has only suffered a little has not yet drunk up the full cup, at the bottom of which lie faith and love....When one has lost simple, childlike faith, it cannot be regained otherwise than through intense suffering and torment, which, having gone to their extremes, must at last return him to the bright realm of infinite love, enriched by all the infinite negations of life, to the realm where there is no dread....And if, immersed in the most terrible struggle with the tempest, with the most powerful dissonances in the soul, we say that life is fine, and if our words are not empty, mechanically spoken phrases, but the soul's living voice maintaining faith in redemption and enlightenment, notwithstanding all possible storms, then this is a great, a gigantic step in life.[15]

He assured Varvara, resting his case on a lengthy quotation from Hegel, that contradiction and its resolution represented "the most sublime superiority of living nature," that "what remains from the very beginning only positive, is and will remain, lifeless," that only through "negation and suffering" could life become positive. Had not Jesus himself suffered gravely when he thought that God had forsaken him? And think, he went on, of the great suffering a mother experiences in bringing new life into the world. "Human life in general is a life of struggle, dissension, and suffering, for the grandeur and the strength of reality can be known only by the grandeur and the intensity of the contradiction from which the spirit makes its way towards self-concentration."[16] For those aware of this, "there is no death, everything is life, endless, blissful life."[17] Every other approach to life, he wrote his brothers, all thoughts that oppressed one, were "lies" that had to be destroyed "by the force of thought; thereby would the devil's inspiration be driven off."[18]

In dozens of different contexts this tenacious faith in the redemptive power of suffering as the way to triumph over "the monstrous nakedness of pan-destructive, omnipresent, and omnipotent death" pervades Bakunin's letters far more during the months following Liubov's death than at any other time, before or after. The lesson is always the same: an all-embracing cosmic dialectic makes crucifixion the price of resurrection, or, as he said in another context, sin the path to grace. It was to the sick, the weak, and the poor that Jesus had come, he reminded his family, not to the strong and the rich. One must bless one's suffering as a "purifying flame, as a rebirth into a new life on a new earth, under a new heaven."[19]

Although his adoration of suffering was thus able to hold back for a time the torrents of doubt, restless anger, and other influences that were soon to devastate his Hegelian refuge, it is apparent already that the "dreadful negation" of Liubov's death, "the monstrous nakedness of pan-destructive, omnipresent, and omnipotent death" had now confronted him with an elemental discord that he had been struggling to deny and thereby corrupted, fatally, his "right" Hegelian harmonies. Once again, in other words, a major reorientation in his life and thought was associated with a profoundly traumatic experience involving a sister. His first "intellectual revolution," which had turned him away from the world and into an inner life to be "reborn," "fed and nurtured," occurred just a few months after his bitter conflict with his parents over plans for Liubov's marriage. Similarly, it had been the crushing experience involving his incestual attraction to Tatiana that had forced him to abandon, in theory, Fichtean heroism in favor of Hegelian submission. And now we find Liubov's death at the precise period in which we see the first major crack in the "right" Hegelian structure, the first signs of another fundamental shift, this time from "right" to "left" Hegel, from reconciliation to violent opposition.

The basic cause of his intense reaction in the first two cases, I have argued, involved a sister-mother substitution. This may also be the ultimate explanation for the powerful impact Liubov's death made on Bakunin, coming as it did in the same months that Bakunin had come closer to his mother and was "as happy as it is given children to be happy."[20] Whether or not Liubov's death, Bakunin's new happy-child approach to his mother, and the beginning of the end of his "reconciliation" are linked in this way, the fact remains that Bakunin's "right" Hegelianism does start to collapse at this time (mid-1838) and was thenceforth to be highly vulnerable to a variety of other attacks that now, from outside and from within Bakunin himself, joined to dismantle it. The first of these attacks to ally with the "dreadful negation" in assaulting Bakunin's "right" Hegelianism was a furious onslaught that Belinsky launched against Bakunin that September and October (1838). After Belinsky had returned to Moscow the previous September (1837), following his post-Premukhino recuperation in the Caucasas, he had repeatedly urged Bakunin to write him, offered to retract his earlier criticisms, and warmly invited him to stay in his apartment when Bakunin came to Moscow.[21] "Your return to Moscow will be a happy holiday for me.... Ah, Michael, how I would like to see you sooner. The presence of a person of strong faith gives faith, and faith is—everything."[22] For a week after his arrival in November 1837, Bakunin lived with a family whose son he was tutoring, but then he moved in with Belinsky. Except for a trip he made in early March (1838) to the Beyers' estate, he remained with Belinsky until mid-March, when he moved to the apartment of a new friend, Botkin, a dapper, sophisticated, and erudite tea merchant's son who had helped Belinsky down from Bakunin's Fichtean stratosphere. Aside from Belinsky's anguish over borrowing money from Bakunin and Bakunin's occasional taunts about Belinsky's attraction to his sister Alexandra, everything went well enough at first: "In a word, our friendship was never better," Belinsky recalled in a later review of their turbulent relationship.[23]

Superficially, the occasion for renewing the conflict was a disagreement over Belinsky's editorial policies on the Moscow *Observer,* for which Bakunin had written his essay on Hegel, an essay that, as Belinsky wrote Stankevich, "destroyed the *Observer* by giving it a faulty direction at the very outset, turning readers away, and utterly ruining it in public opinion."[24] According to Bakunin, however, it was not his article, but Belinsky's editorial incompetence that ruined the journal, his lack of "objective content and reality."[25] As the dispute progressed, Bakunin, or so Belinsky claimed, began "to abuse me behind my back," and then insultingly moved out of Belinsky's apartment, "not saying a word to me, left me and went to Botkin's as though sneaking away." He was sure, moreover, that Bakunin was spreading rumors about him and forming a "coalition" against him.[26]

After Bakunin left for Premukhino in the summer of 1838, Belinsky, in his own words, "became more and more ferocious in his hostility towards him." He remained attached to the Bakunin family, however, and daily visited Bakunin's mother and sisters when they came to Moscow to bid Varvara farewell. On one such visit, Bakunin's mother invited Belinsky to Premukhino again. Belinsky wrote Bakunin about it: the ferocity, apparently, had mellowed with time. Bakunin replied in a friendly way, repeating his mother's invitation; Belinsky went; they were "ecstatically reconciled";[27] and on his return to Moscow Belinsky began again writing Bakunin letters that were in Belinsky's words, "dithyrambs of love."[28] With Liubov's death, however, the polemics started again, more embittered than ever, and inspired Belinsky to compose several essay-length letters, or "dissertations," as he and Bakunin referred to them. These massive letters, written in September and October, 1838, contain the most penetrating insights into Bakunin's character and motivations that have come down from that period.

Expressing once more his doubts about Bakunin's "reconciliation" with reality, he charged Bakunin with not even knowing enough about reality to either accept or oppose it. Reconciliation as he, Bakunin, lived it meant "not to know reality, but only to chatter and make a lot of noise about it. It all sounds terribly wise, but there is nothing at all natural, immediate in it."[29] The opposite of "simple, normal" people who say little about reality but who live it constantly in their daily lives, Bakunin could "*think* wonderfully well about reality" but knew nothing about putting that thought into practice.[30] The cause of Bakunin's trouble, Belinsky acutely sensed, was his "denial of simple, instincutal feeling," his need to "determine by thought" what others "understood directly and easily." However much he might admire Goethe's romantic heroes and see in them "a revelation of life...you yourself do not feel the desire to live, if only a little bit, like them." Consequently, while Bakunin might be able to "explain reality to others," "you yourself let it pass you by and only exclaim, with up-turned eyes, what a stench!" Nor could Bakunin bear the sight of authentic emo-tional life in anyone else, Belinsky charged: "Your subjectivity and abstractness lead you to frenzy whenever you notice in one of your friends the rustle of this kind of joy of life—right away you see this as a fall." Rather than make "life a test of thought," Bakunin made thought a test of life: "ideas are dearer to you than man."[31]

Demonstrating still more insight, Belinsky saw as well the potential danger that lay hidden in Bakunin's abstract zeal.

> You burn with an inexhaustible love for God, but God as the substance of all existence, as a universal torn from its particular manifestations: you have never loved individual subjects and objects. As in Indian pan-theism where there lives only Brahma, gestating and devouring every-thing, where the particulars are Brahma's victims and toys, transient shadows, so it is with you that ideas are higher than man, his form of thought higher than his immediate being, and you sacrifice him to your all-gestating and all-devouring Brahma.[32]

Catching also the other side of Bakunin's essential dualism (and the likelihood, therefore, that the danger would not remain potential), Belinsky realized that Bakunin would hardly be satisfied with the quiet, detached life of the mind, "reconciliation" notwithstanding. For all his facade of placid acceptance, Bakun-in was a man of too much "strength, elemental power, restlessness," a man motivated by "an incessant striving to go beyond, dissatisfied with the present, even hating the present and himself in the present."[33] Bakunin "craves move-ment, and he seeks turbulence and battle," Belinsky wrote Stankevich at the time. But in his battles, Belinsky went on, Bakunin shows that "he lacks any sense of reality" and always moves "to the extreme, because the point of depar-ture for his efforts on [his sisters'] behalf were more a thirst for some kind of action, a wish to play the hero, than it was love for them and their happiness... where one should have moved quietly, he clamoured and crashed; where there should have been simplicity, there was bravado and bombast."[34]

What seemed to distress Belinsky most of all, however, since it related most directly to his own relationship with Bakunin, was what he considered Bakunin's authoritarianism. How they had all "groaned under" this domination and had forced themselves "to believe in the infallible truth of your ideas!" "I will never forget...what undisguised coldness and what undisguised disdain you began to show me when I flatly told you that I wanted to live *my own* life, according to my own mind, to develop myself independently...."[35] Thus, while ready to acknowledge in Bakunin "a powerful spirit, a deep, extraordinary spiritual life, superior gifts, infinite intensity and vast intelligence," Belinsky was clearly more struck by what he saw as Bakunin's "monstrous pride, a pettiness in relationship with friends, childishness, frivolousness, inadequate sincerity and tenderness, a lofty opinion of yourself in comparison with others, a desire to subjugate, to dominate, a willingness to tell others the truth, but a revulsion against hearing it from others."[36]

Interspersed with these blows against Bakunin's character and against his illusory "reconciliation," Belinsky offered advice, accompanied by examples from his own and others' lives, of authentic reconciliation, since he, too, had come under the sway of the Rationally Real. The contrast between the two reconciliations is striking and shows again how little genuine reconciliation there was in Bakunin's "right" Hegelian phase. To accept reality, as Belinsky interpreted Hegel, meant to live "a life of simplicity; not the life of an extraordinary being, born to astound the world, but that of a simple, ordinary person." Bakunin need only look to his own father for a splendid example of the right approach to life, Belinsky said. "He knows life and life knows him, and it has already, in many things, proved him right over you and will prove him right in many more things—as you will see, perhaps very soon."[37]

Botkin could also serve Bakunin as a model, for he too "lives completely outside of his finite 'I,'" "involves himself in all sorts of interesting activities" "takes care of his apartment," and "if he is sometimes sad, it is without soul-crushing suffering."[38] What characterized the lives of both men, Bakunin's father and Botkin, was the fact that each had agreed to be "a useful member of society." That above all was for Belinsky the hallmark of real reconciliation with reality, and that above all was what Bakunin utterly rejected.

> The drama of life is so arranged that people of all roles are needed. Certainly, my role as well is necessary. If it depended on me, I would have asked for another one, but, you see, they do not like these requests, they insist that I be not what I would like to be, but what they want. So, I will play the role that was given me....I am no longer a candidate for membership in society, but a member of it. I feel it in me and myself in it, attached to it, grafted onto its interests, poured into its life, fusing my life in its own and giving my entire life in tribute to it. I know

there is in me the strength to live and to find fascination in life. I want to work and to feel both the desire and the strength for it. A man must have something to do in life.[39]

To prove to himself that this was not mere talk, Belinsky took a job as a teacher in the State Mining Institute in Moscow and wrote Bakunin a glowing account of how wonderful it felt to be involved in just the kind of "fussy, bureaucratic job" that Bakunin continued to abhor and avoid. How fine it was to teach the aspiring clerks "how to write clear and efficient business-like letters concerning the mining department." Besides the pleasure of doing a useful job, there was also the entirely new joy of relationships with ordinary people around him: "By looking at people not through a theory prepared ahead of time, but by the evidence that they themselves provide, I am beginning to be able to stand in authentic relationship to everyone...to find common interests in talking with the kind of people with whom I had thought I could never have anything in common." There was nothing more unrealistic, he went on, "than to concentrate in one or another circle, like some secret society that is different from and antagonistic to everything outside."[40]

The difference between this reconciliation and Bakunin's could hardly be greater. For Bakunin, comfortably settled and cared for at Premukhino, reconciliation was an abstract concept to be shaped and reshaped to suit every occasion except one—actual acceptance of real obligations and constraints. For Belinsky, it was a practical justification that made such obligations and constraints bearable and eased the unavoidable surrender of desire and will to the brute facts of an harassed and impoverished life:

> Reality is a monster, armed with iron claws and iron jaws: whoever does not voluntarily surrender to it will be seized and devoured by it.... The higher a man's dreams, the more forceful will be his rebellion against the society to which he belongs, and the more terrible will be his reconciliation and his punishment....Reality revenges itself with venom and disdain. We constantly meet victims of its vengeance. Free individual actions, unreconciled with external necessity, deviating from the life of society, produce collisions....Yes, live not as you like, not as you think you should, but as the ruler decrees, and that ruler is—civic society....I recognize personal, autonomous freedom, but I also recognize a higher will. *Collision* is the result of a hostile conflict between these two wills. So—everything is and will be as it is and will be. If I stand, fine. If I fall, there is nothing to be done about it. I am God's soldier: he commands, I march....[41]

Imagine, Bakunin wrote Stankevich later about the conflict, Belinsky "has gone to the extreme of turning any ordinary, commonplace, existing being into his ideal." He had simply surrendered, he wrote Belinsky himself, *"to the opinion of the crowd,* whose stupid voice, according to your new philosophy, is the sacred voice of truth." As for that fierce portrait of reality, Bakunin countered that he could find in his "store of *transcendental* and *logical* tricks all the proof needed to amaze even your terrible reality with its iron jaws and claws."[42] And, indeed, he could and did.

Viewed without regard to the insurmountable inner barriers that compelled Bakunin to reject what Belinsky considered genuine "life" and to seek solace and protection in successive and increasingly more abstract intellectual sanctuaries, one might argue that his and Belinsky's sense of reality differed because of their contrasting views of the battlefield. As one of the common soldiers, Belinsky willy-nilly marched to Reality's orders, and, crushed by circumstance as he was, he understandably saw iron claws on the hand pointing directions and iron jaws on the mouth shouting orders. Bakunin's view from staff headquarters, which he shared with God and Absolute Reason and which looked out upon the lovely fields and gardens of Premukhino rather than on city slums, was too lofty to make out such details as jaws and claws. In fact, however, it was precisely because Bakunin was threatened by jaws and claws far more ferocious and implacable than Belinsky ever encountered that he had been driven out of life. It was because of them that rather than become a part of life, Bakunin could only escape it or destroy it.

During the "right" Hegelian phase, now coming to an end, he had followed the first strategy. For a year and one half, he had remained apart, freely pursuing his solipsistic studies and alternately using "reconciliation" to justify total detachment or simply ignoring it whenever the occasion (still mainly some threat to his sisters' or the Beyers' chastity) called for aggressive maneuvers or proclamations. Now, in this summer and fall of 1838, Liubov's "dreadful negation" and Belinsky's "stupid voice" of the crowd combined to attack this self-deceptive reconciliation. In essence, the "negation" and the "voice" made the same charge—that Bakunin was in fact denying and hiding from the reality he claimed to accept, the jaws and claws reality that included such terrible negations as the death of loved ones. As we have seen, the very devices he drew upon to repulse the attack, such "transcendental tricks" as the return of "suffering" and "conflict" into his vocabulary and concern, were themselves evidence that the attack had been successful and that the "right" Hegelian defenses were giving way.

The full transition from "right" to "left" would take time, however, and time itself, as it turned out, made a major contribution to it. Contrary to his usual yearly cycle, Bakunin decided in 1838 to remain at Premukhino through the winter rather than return to the city as he had been doing over the preceding few years. On the surface, life seemed to move along for him as tranquilly as it had through the earlier reconciled months. He seemed a model of the detached, gentleman scholar and religious sage, advising his brother on the study of Greek, planning an essay on Bettina von Arnim, writing Efremov to send the philosophical books he needed—Strauss, Bauer, Rosenkranz, Schulz, Baader, Daub, Rotscher, Erdman. His letters continue relaxed, chatty, affectionate, even to his mother: "Dear, sweet mother," he wrote her in January 1839, "everyone at home, thank God, is well. All is quiet, peaceful and moving along in the usual way. How have you managed? Was the trip to Tver all right? Have you settled things for my brothers? We await you impatiently. When you left, everything was so empty in the house.... Do not forget sweet mother, to bring the watch you bought me as a gift."[43] As the winter wore on, however, he became more and more restless. Sheer tedium, turning bliss to boredom, now became yet another force undermining reconciled tranquillity.

Even had the "dreadful negation," Belinsky's "stupid voice" of the crowd, and Bakunin's own decision to remain too long at Premukhino not made their successive assaults on his Hegelian sanctuary, it would only have been a matter of time before it collapsed. It could not have been otherwise. The other side of the dualism, the "incessant striving to go beyond," the passion that "craves movement and seeks turbulence" would inevitably have had its way. "Right" Hegelian reconciliation could no more have lasted than could Bakunin's earlier Schellingite detachment. In fact, of all the alternative postures and philosophies that he tested, these two were the least appropriate precisely because they were so true to the character he was trying to conceal; since he was in fact withdrawn, gentle, fearful, and fundamentally passive, since the pastels remained throughout his personal life the basic tones, what he needed was a set of concepts, words, and phrases that disguised these traits of character, not one that all-too-clearly testified to them and even accentuated them. Thus, in a letter from March 1839 in which he lamented to Alexandra Beyer that "I have never been as alone as I am now" and wanted, therefore, "to admit you in and to build for you a little cottage in my solitary desert," he at once went on to describe, shifting to the virile warrior posture, the "stormy future" that he saw ahead, the "new, dark clouds" that he saw for himself on the horizon and that showed him that he was "already close to the time when a decisive change in my inner and external life will come."[44]

Although Bakunin does not specify in this letter to Alexandra Beyer the source of the heavy weather, we can surmise its direction from other letters: it is coming out of the West, from Berlin, or rather from the struggle that Bakunin now sees ahead of him in his efforts to get there. If the winter doldrums, reenforcing the impact of Liubov's death and Belinsky's attack, further helped undermine "reconciliation," the urge to go West now took over as the dominant force against it. Berlin became the exclusive focus of that "incessant striving to go beyond," and Bakunin's urge to be there seemed to grow more intense by the minute during the late winter and spring of 1839. Stankevich had already been in the West a year and one half and had been sending back tantalizing descriptions of his life and studies there. Almost a year had gone by since Bakunin's own hopes of going with Varvara had been frustrated for lack of money. Efremov, too, was now planning to go to Berlin. Finally, adding still more fuel to Bakunin's determination to find some way of getting there, Botkin had been keeping him abreast of current German philosophy by sending abstracts and summaries from the *Hallische Jahrbücher,* a "left" Hegelian journal to which Botkin subscribed. (It was no doubt from these that Bakunin had gathered that list of books by prominent Hegelians—"left" as well as "right"—that he was asking Efremov to send him.)[45] From one of these summaries, for example, Bakunin had learned about the controversy then raging among German Hegelians around D.F. Strauss's *Das Leben Jesu,* a dispute which, Bakunin was confident, would be won by the conservative, "right" Hegelians who denounced Strauss. While Bakunin welcomed Strauss's extreme scepticism, it was only because Bakunin believed that "Mephistopheles must appear in the full expanse of his power in order to be completely defeated."[46]

These unfavorable remarks about Strauss are significant coming when they do, when Bakunin is already sensing "a stormy future," "a decisive change" ahead. They help reveal an important fact about this reorientation from reconciliation back to Fichtean commitment: the restless craving for action not only came before his trip to Berlin, but also before he had been won over by "left" Hegelian influences. He was still a conservative, in other words, albeit a restless conservative. Although as free and unencumbered by obligations or responsibilities as he could have wished, Bakunin's life of scholarly detachment now palled. It was time, he wrote Stankevich, "to tear myself out of the narrow sphere of individuality, to enter into a living relationship with universal life,"[47] or, as he told the Beyers, "to surrender myself to the free current of my life, surrender myself to my fate."[48] He was most likely expressing his own feelings as well as Efremov's—the identity of phrases is hardly accidental—when he wrote that Efremov was leaving Russia for Berlin because he "had to tear himself from the vile life of his family, break away from old habits, from the senseless depression, the vacuous and useless probing into himself, and give himself to the free current of life." Just as "the stay abroad will be a rebirth" for Efremov, so would it be a new "baptism" for himself, "a matter of life and death," in fact.[49] If he did not find some way to leave for Berlin, he told Stankevich, "I will imperceptibly bury myself in the philistine world of philistine reality."[50] Reenacting the crisis of late 1835, when he had chosen Moscow, freedom, and philosophy over Pre-mukhino, obligation, and agriculture, he wrote Stankevich that what he now feared most of all was that "external circumstances, familial obligations, might force him to remain in the country" and thus take him away "from the only sacred aim in my life, from that which constitutes all my life, my salvation and my humanity—away from knowledge and a life in knowledge." He knew, he said, that Stankevich and others might say "that I do not have the right to leave my family in such uncertain conditions, leave father who, perhaps, has but a little life left on earth," but he had decided "after long and painful considera-tion" that his other brothers would be able to take over his responsibilities. In any case, he could not do otherwise, for to give up his plans to study in Berlin meant to abandon knowledge, "and then I will lose all my powers." His "spirit-ual life" was his "salvation," and, he concluded, he had no right to sacrifice it.[51]

Once again, Bakunin's inner voice was adamantly pressing its claims. "No person has any other aim than his own happiness," and the only guide to it, he told Stankevich yet again, was one's own inner voice.[52] He was delighted, sim-ilarly, to learn that Alexandra Beyer had at last decided to live "for herself."[53] In reviewing the ruined life of another friend and veteran member of the old Stankevich circle, the poet I.P. Kliushnikov, Bakunin gave a particularly clear statement of his credo of unqualified yet honorable self-interest. Kliushnikov had been a happy man, Bakunin wrote, after he "left state service at the Insti-tute, gave up the empty pretense of being useful to others (not having yet done anything useful for himself), and began to listen more closely to the inner voice of his soul." His health returned, he wrote a "lot of fine poems," and he planned a trip abroad. But then he fell "into the old malaise," troubled himself about his social role, and lost all self-confidence, to such an extent that "were some peas-ant to say to him that to be happy he must plow the soil all his life, I think he would believe him and do what he said." Why had this happened? Why had he developed this "disdain for himself" and an "imbecilic respect for shoemakers and artisans"? It was because of Kliushnikov's "lack of religion," his lack of "that inner ideal world which can serve as a refuge against the blows of the alien reality that constantly surrounds us. Religion and philosophy, at least for me, constitute this ideal world, since they are the only satisfying forms of knowing truth, and I resolutely believe in the words of the Savior 'Know the truth and the truth will make you free'."[54]

And now the voice from this inner ideal world was ordering him to Berlin. He must find the money. He was willing to live "on bread and water, live in a garret, go around in old clothes,"[55] if only he could somehow get to Berlin. He had no choice, now that Stankevich had definitely said no, but to turn to his parents. The time could not have been less propitious, however, for he and his father were once again at war over Varvara's future, which Bakunin was now certain could be assured only by a final divorce. It was, in part, to see what he could do to get that divorce for Varvara that he decided in mid-July of 1839 to go to St. Petersburg.[56] He also went, however, because "nowhere else can I so well know myself and my differences from others" than in St. Petersburg. An "oppressive battle" with his parents accompanied his departure,[57] which is hardly surprising considering his intentions and his parents' feelings about Varvara's marriage. "Dishonesty, ignoble maneuvers and tricks, accusations and attacks"[58] is how he recalled this farewell confrontation that ended his longest stay in Premukhino since he had left home for the service in 1828.

Although he had planned to spend only a month in St. Petersburg, he in fact remained through the summer (again reversing his usual seasonal cycle of spending summers at Premukhino) then, in October, moved to Moscow. From the first, St. Petersburg made an "oppressive impression" on him, and his mood fell "into deep sadness," tempered, however, by the knowledge that "as a human being I carry in my bosom the whole of the infinite world."[59] Notwithstanding the "joy" he said this awareness gave him, his letters during these months in St. Petersburg reflect, on the whole, restlessness, bitterness, and despondency. Everything seemed wrong. He was burning to leave Russia but could not. He was again thoroughly alienated from Premukhino, but also lonely and depressed away from it in St. Petersburg. He was at war with his father because of his attempts to obtain a divorce for Varvara, and completely unsuccessful in those efforts. Money he had hoped to get from translations did not materialize.[60] And there was an additional crisis: while he was in St. Petersburg, his mother lay seriously ill in Moscow, where she had gone to help the younger Bakunin boys establish themselves at the university. He did not make the trip from St. Petersburg to Moscow to see her.

"Reality," in short, was once again becoming rent with contradictions, negations, struggle. The suffering that Liubov's death had first reintroduced into his world and that Belinsky's jaws and claws had so emphatically highlighted was now, as a result of Bakunin's own disappointments and distress, growing too personal and too great for the pollyannish gloss of "reconciliation." And so we learn again and again from his letters "how necessary every manner of negation is for happiness," since without it "life becomes empty, lifeless vegetation."[61] Similarly, we see once more, in a letter he sent on the eve of his departure for St. Petersburg in July 1839, Faust's proud affirmation: *"Nur der verdient die Freiheit, wie das Leben, der taglich sie eroben muss."*[62] "Yes Natalie," he wrote at the same time, "one constantly encounters negation in life, every positive value is bought at the price of negation. A person can only know and realize in himself the grandeur of man when he has borne on himself all the burdens and boundlessness of humanity. One only knows true happiness when that happiness comes after one has already drunk the whole, bitter cup of unhappiness."[63]

It was in this mood, his thoughts in a state of "strange chaos," "tormenting chaos,"[64] that he wrote his second article on Hegel. Begun shortly before leaving Premukhino for St. Petersburg,[65] the article was written in two parts, the first appearing in the prominent *Notes of the Fatherland* the following year (1840), the second never published. Taken together, the two parts reveal, the first part vaguely, the second clearly, the continuing demise of "right" Hegelian reconciliation. Throughout, Bakunin tried hard and, as we will see, not without success, to preserve as much as he could of the philosophy that had served him so well. Watching the process unfold, one has the image of Bakunin bulwarking the roof and the walls of his fortress even as he opens the windows (or, better, tears up the floorboards) to let in the threatening forces, the "strength, elemental power, and restlessness." Once admitted, however, those forces immediately take control and blow down the walls, leaving only the roof to hang there somehow, supported only by its continuing indispensability to him. But that is a later chapter in the story.

On the surface, the first part (and only part published) seems largely a repetition of the article on Hegel published in April 1838. Almost as if he is answering Belinsky's charge against him, Bakunin sets as his theme the question of philosophy's value for the philosopher: does "it tear him away from all reality," "sow doubts," and change a healthy and useful person into one sick and useless; or, on the contrary, is it "the only means for eliminating all doubt...the only means of reconciliation with reality, heaven, and earth?"[66] Vigorously contending that the latter is true, he went on at length attacking all "pedantic and lifeless" empiricists and their predecessors, the "godless, glibly liberal," "atheistic and anarchistic" philosophers of the eighteenth century.[67] Here, as in the earlier article, Hegel is celebrated as the one who revealed the "eternal, rational order" by proving through intuitive speculation the identiy of the Real and the Rational. What seems even more important to Bakunin than speculative philosophy itself, however, is the Idealist's assumption of the identity of subject and object on which such speculation is founded, the conviction that the only authentic Truth is "the truth man can achieve without having to depart from himself." I have already quoted several examples of such solipsism from this two-part article, since the theme itself is one that persisted throughout Bakunin's Hegelian years and was examined earlier.[68]

What makes this second article on Hegel different from the first is the expressions of Fichtean activism that come through so clearly. Not that the activism in itself is new: as we have seen, in practice he remained a Fichtean zealot throughout the phase of Hegelian "reconciliation" and continued to insist that "everything that is only external must be destroyed and only that which is both external and internal at the same time will be saved."[69] What is new about the second article is the emphasis. The consequences and corollaries of statements like the one just quoted are drawn out more fully and explicitly. We see this, for example, when he asks how man can resolve "the contradiction between the boundlessness of his inner ideal essence and the limitations of his external existence, a contradiction that is the source of movement, of development aimed exclusively at this resolution." The answer is even more indicative of the change underway: the resolution would come only by "the self-realization of inner rationality and *the negation of the externality that is incompatible with it,*" by "the sacred voice of the immortal spirit striving to realize its freedom and its boundlessness and *to negate the externality alien to it.*"[70] We see the same emphatic activism (so distant from the mood in which he had urged others "to regard the external world as something given")[71] in a further corollary that he draws from that "striving...to negate the externality alien" to the "immortal spirit": "living, abstractly self-aware subjects unlimited in the universality of their self-awareness, yet limiting each other in reality, encounter each other and, *motivated by the striving to realize their inner universality, their inner abstract freedom, in the world that surrounds and limits them, engage in war between themselves.... *"[72]

In effect, what distinguishes this second article from the first is Bakunin's elevation of Fichtean activism from the day-to-day world of practice to the sacred and sublime world of philosophical theory. In his actual relationships with the world around him, Bakunin had already divided Reality in two: the really Real and the merely existing world of "a chair, a table, a dog, Varvara Dmitrievna, Alexandra Ivanovna." Now, in this second article, that division enters into the realm of philosophy as part of an objective analysis of Rational Reality. "Usually, everything existing, every finite thing is called real, and in this lies the error. Only those things are real in which reason, idea, and truth are present in their entirety. All the rest are illusion and lies."[73] Reality, in other words, was not at all what it meant to those who "will always prefer a piece of beefsteak as something absolutely real to an idea which, for them, will always remain an illusion."[74]

As a "right" Hegelian he had preached that Reality was Rational, that evil was only in the eye of the unenlightened beholder, and that one should look into oneself and change oneself if one was distressed and not blame the world and seek to change it. Now, on his way to becoming a "left" Hegelian he is willing to state in a well-considered philosophical article (and not simply as a statement in a letter, reflecting the mood of the moment) that not all that exists is rational or, consequently, "real." The stage is already set, therefore, for the next advance—to *make* the world "rational" and "real." Love, goodness, truth, reason, and harmony are no longer constant and eternal Realities to be understood by illuminated Thought and blissfully contemplated; they are already well on their way to becoming goals to be achieved by destroying the alien "externality". The direction of human development, both social and individual, is no longer transcendentally upward, but historically forward, and the arena for the "stormy future" is already less Bakunin's own soul (which he has already conquered by repression) than the world.

Reflecting this descent from Absolute Reason to historical reality, Bakunin gave considerably more attention to history in this second article, mainly in its first part, than he had given it at any time before. For over two years, from the beginning of 1837 to mid-1839, Bakunin had little interest in history, even less than he had had in his pre-Hegelian days. The first article on Hegel, for example, focused almost exclusively on epistemology, logic, and religion. Why, after all, be concerned about historical change if Reality, properly understood, was already fully harmonious and rational? If complete understanding was accessible to right thinking, and if that understanding revealed a rational world without evil, then there was no alien externality to fight and no need of time and history in and through which to fight it. It was only after Bakunin had run out of "transcendental tricks" to combat the jaws and claws of reality that had begun increasingly to harass him, that he heard again the call to battle. This time, however, thanks to Hegel and in contrast to the Fichtean crusade, the battle would be carried on not as an escape *from* history, but as a struggle *in* history, and with history itself as an indomitable ally.

True, there is nothing really specific yet in Bakunin's use of history, no definite historical examples from, say, the works of Guizot that he was reading at the time. But he does refer now, and repeatedly, to history and not only to nature, cosmos, and personal fate when discussing the Spirit's manifestation and realization. He includes "the law of progressive historical development" as one of the partial laws to be encompassed in the overall unity of knowledge achieved through speculative introspection, and he puts the laws of history on the same level of importance as the laws of mathematics and natural science. Of course, in stressing again and again the necessity of understanding mankind's past, present, and future as well as understanding nature, mind, and religion, it is Hegelian, providential, "necessary" history that Bakunin has in mind, the historical flow as grasped by those who understand Rational Reality, not the history of ordinary historians who, he says, see in it only "a game of chance."[75]

By the time he wrote the second part of the article, the change had gone far enough to allow the honorable reinstatement of Fichte and his ego philosophy. Fichte was right to celebrate the first time his son said "I," Bakunin wrote, since that marked the advent of his self-awareness, the advance from feeling to thought. However, it is essential to keep in mind that this return to Fichte, which, as we will see, is even more emphatic in Bakunin's letters at the time, in no way indicated disillusionment with Hegel. What we have here is a very successful and fateful merger of the two. Fichte will once again be recruited to help provide personal inspiration to the warrior for holy truth, who is once more beginning to prepare himself to battle and suffer. This time, however, he would not be fighting alone nor in defense of a vulnerable inner world of romantic sensibilities, but in alliance with the indomitable power of Hegel's Absolute Spirit in opposition to the weak, trivial, unreal, illusory world of the chair, table, dog, Varvara Dmitrievna, Alexandra Ivanovna, and others of the "crowd" who prefer illusory beefsteak to rational and real ideas. While Bakunin now welcomes again the ardor and heroism of Fichte's militant ego, he remains as opposed as ever to what he repeatedly identifies in this second Hegel article as Fichte's "one-sided subjectivity:"[76] the new "I" is to be an objective "I," as invulnerable and omnipotent as the Absolute Spirit itself.

During the months he was writing the article, through late 1839, the thoughts and mood of his letters clearly reflected this new, "left" Hegelian orientation. A new word begins to make its appearance—the central symbol of the "left" Hegelians—Action. "Not complaints, but action and life is what is needed," he told his sister Alexandra.[77] He even admitted his error in spurning the action involved in fulfilling obligations, although still taking care to leave to himself free choice as to which responsibility he would shoulder:

> Action, *die Tat*—this is life's only fulfillment. There was a time when I rejected every kind of *obligation*, and from one point of view I was right: there is no truth in obligations that have no other basis than cold duty, for such obligations are the compulsion of slavery, the negation of the infinity of the inner spirit. Love is the essence, the beginning and end of life. But love that does not go beyond the inner spirit, that does not go beyond possibility to actuality, such love is *schönseligkeit* love and there is no truth in it either; for truth must also be actual. And so, from this point of view, I was completely wrong; I sinned against truth when I rejected responsibility.[78]

Those around Bakunin sensed the change and warmly encouraged it. T. N. Granovsky, who returned to Moscow in late August 1839 after two years of study in Berlin, where he had been Stankevich's closest friend, wrote Stankevich in December that Bakunin had become less "abstract" than Granovsky had remembered him. He was also much impressed by Bakunin's second article on Hegel, which he read in manuscript and which he found "intelligent, simple, and to the point." In fact, even though Granovsky had just spent years of study at the very center of Hegelian thought, he conceded to Stankevich that "in these things" Bakunin "had gone much farther" than he had.[79]

Granovsky's entry on the scene at this time points to still another important influence in reorienting Bakunin's views. The "Westerners" were coming back, after the long, bleak hiatus that followed the Decembrist failure and the repression of the miniscule opposition circles that had vainly tried to carry on the struggle. In addition to Granovsky, Nicholas Ogarev also returned about this time, having received a pardon in May 1839. By the end of September, Botkin told Bakunin of his friendship with Ogarev, and Bakunin himself seems to have begun at least occasional participation in a revived Ogarev circle either at the end of 1839 or at the beginning of 1840. By that time, the end of 1839, Bakunin was moving so fast that he was criticizing Granovsky for his friendly visits to the Kireevskys, a foremost Slavophile family.[80] Further encouragement in this same direction, leftward, continued to come from Berlin itself, by way of Stankevich's letters to Bakunin, in which he had good things to say about such leading Hegelians on the "left" as Feuerbach and the Polish philosopher Cieszkowski.[81] In the case of Cieszkowski, about whom more will be said in the next chapter, one sees a convergence between the two leftward influences active at the time on Bakunin—from Berlin and from the revived Russian "Westerners"—for Ogarev's lifelong comrade Alexander Herzen had been captivated by Cieszkowski the previous winter (1838-39)[82] and had shared his zeal with Ogarev. Ogarev, in turn, may well have discussed Cieszkowski's views with Bakunin at gatherings during the winter of 1839-40.

An important, albeit indirect, indication of this "left" Hegelian impact on Bakunin during these months in late 1839 is a distinct change in Bakunin's judgement of Strauss's work. No longer did he mock him as easy game for the established "right" Hegelians. Instead, he now took him quite seriously, even though he still thought him too critical (a sign that Bakunin had still some distance to go before becoming "Bakunin"): "Read Strauss," he urged his sisters, "love him, but do not believe him entirely. As far as I can judge, it seems to me that he is at the stage of *Werden* and that in him the negative process of critical reason still prevails. . . ."[83] Another comparison similarly demonstrates how important these months were in Bakunin's first steps to the left. Whereas he had been conventionally conservative enough in July of 1839 to be a welcomed and appreciative guest at the home of one of Nicholas I's most prominent police functionaries, L. B. Dubelt,[84] he was at the year's end beginning to associate with Dubelt's foremost enemies. He now realized, as he wrote his brother Paul in December, that "glory comes at a high price—as my illustrious friend Peter Grigorevich Chaadaev declared when, as with Tasso, they judged him insane."[85]

(The reference is to Chaadaev's house arrest as "insane" for having published his scathing attack on Russia's past and present, mentioned earlier.)

No doubt these new influences made the constraints that kept him from going to Berlin all the more intolerable, especially since, as in Granovsky's case, they confirmed Bakunin's high opinion of his own intellectual talent and promise. He must get away: "the inner voice speaks louder and louder within me and obedience to it constitutes all my happiness and my glory."[86] But he was still trapped with no exit in sight. He might then have turned to his parents—he was soon to do so—but the times were even more unfavorable for such an appeal than they usually were. Besides the battle that had accompanied Bakunin's departure from Premukhino in July of that year (1839), because of his plans to obtain a divorce for Varvara, and the fact that he had not made the effort to visit his seriously ill mother in Moscow while he was in St. Petersburg, there was a new family crisis that had made his parents still more furious with him. Botkin and Alexandra Bakunin were, it seems, in love. The tea merchant's son, who the elder Bakunin made quite clear could never be considered a possible suitor for a daughter of nobility, had first been attracted to Alexandra during a summer visit to Premukhino in 1838, when he went there with Belinsky, Efremov, and another friend. After he saw her again, during the Bakunin family stay in Moscow in July 1839 (while Bakunin was in St. Petersburg), the infatuation became serious. A flood of sentimental, ecstatic, mournful, self-lacerating, and blissful letters ensued—all kept secret from the elder Bakunins. Then, in October, Alexandra's aunt came upon one of the letters and promptly showed it to Alexandra's parents. They were outraged, of course, although less because of the secrecy than because of the social distance between the two principals.

It was now Alexandra's turn to experience the contrary pulls, the anxiety, and the illness that Varvara and Liubov had suffered. Bakunin was called to arms again: "only you are left to protect her, to be her defense among these aunts and uncles," Botkin wrote him. "Go to her, go to her, you will resurrect her—for God's sake, I implore you. Drop everything. I have sent 400 rubles. . . .But move, move, time is precious. She may be dangerously ill."[87] Although Bakunin did not go, and thus avoided another direct confrontation with his parents, he did, at first, support Botkin and advise Alexandra to marry him if she loved him. This was enough to bring most of the blame down on him, as we see in a letter from his mother to Alexandra: "Were Michael a good son, he would have been the first to warn us about all this and not allow a sister to enter into correspondence with a young man; but he knew, was silent, and went on borrowing money. . . ." Bakunin's father agreed completely: "The affair was begun by you," he wrote his son, "since, had you warned us in time, as it was your duty as a son to do, none of this would have happened."[88]

Bakunin's views about the Botkin-Alexandra romance are not as clear as they were with respect to his other sisters' relationships. There are indeed suggestions, and from both Belinsky and Botkin explicit and angry accusations, that he tried to ruin the relationship by turning it into a choice for Alexandra between Botkin and himself, between "husband and brother."[89] According to Botkin, he is supposed to have written Alexandra that "Botkin will try to take you from your brothers."[90] Similarly, Belinsky told Botkin that "in Petersburg, he [Bakunin] revealed to me, bluntly, not even aware that it was something to be concealed, that she would be willing to marry you on condition that she have no marital relations with you."[91]

In his own letters home, however, Bakunin does not seem to be that opposed to the marriage. Perhaps it is because Alexandra had assured him of her faithfulness to her brothers, declaring that—as Bakunin quoted her in a letter—"whoever wants to take you from me will be laying a death shroud over all the rest of my life."[92] Another reason, it seems, is that Bakunin had come to link the marriage with his own trip to Berlin: "my trip to Berlin cannot be realized before your union with Botkin."[93] Does he expect Botkin to provide the money? Or was it rather a way of easing the guilt he may have felt for leaving by providing a substitute support for the family, a man gifted with the sense of responsibility, not to mention the money, that he lacked? In any case, it seems more than coincidence that, while speaking about a restoration of the old Premukhino warmth and intimacy that he expected would follow the marriage, Bakunin should assure his sisters that there would be "atamans" to take care of them (the name for the leaders of Cossack villages).[94]

What principally comes through Bakunin's comments about the Botkin-Alexandra troubles, however, is neither his opposition to the marriage nor his support of it, but rather his wish to be done with it and with all the other endless Premukhino intrigues and crises. "I cannot be a judge in this matter and am, therefore, taking myself out of it and leaving it to fate or chance. I am now only concerned with a way of getting to Berlin. I have to get out of all the trivial life of family and friends and completely immerse myself in universal life."[95] Even his "holy commune" now seemed dull and trivial when set against the "universal life" that he was sure awaited him in Berlin. "I am no longer fit to preach to others," he told his sisters at the time; "I need to preach to myself. During the time that I was preaching to others, many evil foes lay hidden in my soul which I must drive out."[96]

It is not known what the young ladies thought of this rather perfunctory adieu, but there was at least one erstwhile recipient of Bakunin's ministry who was not at all ready to let him just pack up and leave like that. Vissarion (Furioso) Belinsky felt it time for another massive barrage. "I hate Bakunin," he told

Botkin, mainly because of the "strange, fantastic, fanatic, abstract, barbarous, and *slavish* attitude" towards himself that Bakunin had encouraged in his sisters, for his "oppressive authority," his intolerable need "always to be right and never at fault." "The main flaw of your whole life," he wrote somewhat more gently to Bakunin himself, "is the fact that you are in no way called upon to exert your personality on others, and yet you consider yourself called upon to do just that. You cannot stand it when anyone does not think or do as you do."[97] What now seemed to disturb Belinsky even more than Bakunin's authoritarianism, however, was what Belinsky considered Bakunin's extraordinary irresponsibility, his habit of "living at the expense of others," his life of "indolence and inaction, consoling himself with resounding phrases about spiritual experience, lofty ideas, high calling...."[98] As for Bakunin's Berlin plan, that too in Belinsky's opinion was just another way of avoiding "making his peace with reality." If Bakunin had been serious about Berlin, he would have "acquired the money by giving lessons or by taking the candidate's and master's examination and then leaving, as Granovsky did, on a government stipend. No, he is deceiving himself....Is he going to fly there through the air and live on air?" And where was the "will," Belinsky asked, that Bakunin was "forever lecturing" everyone else about? "There is not even a shadow of it, not even an illusion of it....He has enjoyed lording it over others, fighting with his parents and bragging about these fights.... but is this really will?"[99]

It was still, ultimately, the same quarrel over what "reconciliation" with reality really meant. Whereas Bakunin's "reality" allowed him a life of "indolence and inaction," or, as Belinsky wrote Botkin, the opportunity to make "a lot of noise about philosophy and himself, about himself and philosophy."[100] Belinsky's reality was made of much sterner stuff. "It demands that I read vile trivia of useless mediocres, write reviews of them for the use and pleasure of the esteemed public of Imperial Russia, and, moreover, that I do this reading and writing without knowing German. And then there are the hemorrhoids, headaches, cramps, nausea, trembling hands and feet."[101]

In short, still "jaws and claws." Striking hard and cruelly at what could only have been a particularly sore point with Bakunin, Belinsky contrasted Bakunin's escape from reality with his brother Nicholas' genuine reconciliation with and involvement in life. "Here is the real, full man, a complete man!...He has in him strength, power, life, action. He is *complete,* integrated. For him words and deeds are one and the same. He does not rant and rave about himself, nor pinch little sensations out of himself so that he can then analyze them, usually while lying in bed, and wallow in this rubbish." "Woe to the man," he went on, "who limits himself to being merely a man, who does not add to this abstract and bombastic rubric the title of merchant, landowner, officer, bureaucrat, official, artist, or teacher. Society will punish him for it."[102] It was "barbaric and sense-less rubbish" to believe as Bakunin did that "simple, normal, and full natures characterize cattle and philistines."[103] Belinsky also further developed insights he had earlier used in disclosing the dangers inherent in Bakunin's character and relationships: no doubt Bakunin's "motives are pure and fine. . . .But what differ-ence does it make to me whether a brigand cuts my throat for money or a reli-gious schismatic does so for the salvation of my soul, that is from love for me? The result is just the same—my throat is cut. He is an unfortunate man, born for grief to himself and to others."[104] In the end, the attack unleashed in February and March, 1840, came down to a challenge: "I hope you are able to get to Berlin. . .and that you completely achieve your aim. But only then will I believe in the reality of your aims. . . .I no longer believe in words, but only in deeds, in facts."[105] Then, a final thrust of the rapier: "Nicholas [Bakunin's brother] will be in Berlin at government expense—wonderful!"[106]

When the first part of Bakunin's second article on Hegel appeared in early 1840, Belinsky again changed his mind somewhat, or at least his feelings, about Bakunin. It was a fine article, he wrote Botkin in April 1840, "as fine as" Bakunin's first article on Hegel had been "vile." "That man can and must write," Belinsky continued, "he will do much to advance the thought of his father-land."[107] The following month, Kraevsky, the editor of the *Notes,* expressed similar delight with the article in a letter to Bakunin thanking him for "the splendid article, which is for me nothing less than a model philosophical article in the Russian language." Since Kraevsky "could not hope to read or publish in Russian anything better than it on the subject of philosophy," he urged Bakunin to send him the second part so that he could include it in the July issue.[108]

Shaming Bakunin into turning words into deeds, as Belinsky did in his Feb-ruary and March assault, and acclaiming him, as Belinsky, Kraevsky, Granovsky, and doubtless others did for his work on Hegel, had the same effect: they all heaped still more fuel on the "burning thirst" for Berlin that was already at white heat. He had to get away. "I will live on bread and water," he vowed again to his sisters in February 1840. "I simply cannot stay here another minute. I can and I must study, because in sacred, divine learning is my entire life, all my joy and my strength."[109] Everything would change if only he could find some way to be in Berlin. A "golden period will begin when I finally pull myself out of these narrow limits of our reality and immerse myself exclusively in the vital atmosphere of European life, where divine thought breathes everywhere—in sci-ence, religion, art, nature, people. Oh, I expect a baptism, a transforma-tion. . . ."[110]

By the end of February, the wings of such ardor had sent Fichte soaring even higher than Hegel in Bakunin's esteem, making Fichte once again "the real hero of modern times" and inspiring Bakunin, as he wrote Alexandra Beyer, to spend all his time reading him. He had always "deeply loved" Fichte, he went on in the letter, envying "his amazing strength, his ability to remove himself from all secondary and external circumstances and from public opinion in order to move directly and tirelessly to his determined goal. . . .There is in me something of the same sort, but I still need to develop my strength, the ability to depend, calmly, on myself and to act independently of and in opposition to everything external. Yes, I feel this, with profound joy I feel this. The former, strong, inspired state of my soul is being reborn within me. I am returning to my vital source. I am again becoming myself."[111] He now wanted nothing more to do with "abstract innerness," with an "empty *Jenseits:*" "The *Jenseits* is only complete when the *Disseits* is complete."[112]

But yearn and strain as he might, he still had absolutely no way of finding the money to leave Russia, much less to pay his way while abroad, and by this time his parents were so upset with him that they were not even answering his letters.[113] He repeatedly sank into despondency, filling the emptiness as best he could in the way that would later become habitual for him and lead to his legendary proportions: "For days I have been plunged, most of the time, in oppressive melancholy, perhaps because. . .I have been eating all this time with great appetite."[114] He seems to have been too impatient even for study, or at least this is one way of interpreting the comment of his new friend Ogarev to the effect that he was ready to drop his Hegel for a good chess game anytime, which, as one of his biographers put it, was comparable to someone else drowning his sorrows in drunken orgies.[115]

Stankevich again came to mind. Two years had passed since he had turned Bakunin down. Maybe his situation and attitude had changed. Encouraged by some favorable remarks Stankevich made about him in a letter to Granovsky,[116] Bakunin tried again. Complaining that his only strength, "a kind of abstract spiritual strength has been broken by the vile trivia of routine family matters, by the vacuous strife with family and friends and, perhaps, by my own insignificance," he assured Stankevich that Berlin would bring him "rebirth, baptism of body and spirit." Either that or nothing: if he were unable to go to Berlin, he would be "completely indifferent" as to what happened to him, "whether I finish my life as an artillery lieutenant or a state counselor."[117] Instead of an assurance of funds he had hoped from Stankevich, however, all he got, and that after a two-month wait, were echoes of his father's counsels: "You must be able to resign yourself at least for a little while. . . .You could work, in the meantime, for some periodical. I cannot give you any other advice. . . .Misha! Try to get to Berlin—if you fail at that, try to do something else. But don't just give up!"[118]

Perhaps anticipating this rejection, or simply unable to wait longer for a response from Stankevich, Bakunin decided at the end of March 1840 to turn once more to his father, in another pamphlet-length letter arguing his case. Since he had just told his sisters, in connection with the Botkin-Alexandra events, that the only feeling he now had for his parents was "disdain" and that "I have no father,"[119] it must have been an exceptionally difficult and humiliating letter to write. It is also a particularly important letter, for it gives us a good idea of Bakunin's thoughts and intentions on the eve of his career in the West, as well as some insights into several additional, and not very admirable, traits of his character. Although he knew, he began the letter, that his parents felt only "absolute disdain" for him and that they had accused him "of the most vile crimes," he believed nonetheless that he now deserved their support because he had become "more sensible, more prudent" than he had been at the time of the earlier family quarrels. He now realized, for instance, that "life itself demands external realization, reality" and that if unrealized, "any inner life, however true it might be... decays and turns into a sickly, impotent life." Moreover, he continued, sounding now even more like Belinsky, since "every citizen must be useful to his fatherland, an active member of his state," he, too, was in search of "an activity that, while providing me an honest piece of bread and a calling in society, would also enable me at the same time to be useful to my fatherland, useful as far as I am able." He was no longer the person he had once been, he said, for he had "already come out of that enthusiasm which led me to think that a man can, with impunity, tear himself away from all social conditions and which made every specific definition seem to me a constraint on the boundlessness of man's inner life."

The question, then, was to choose the appropriate activity. He knew, he said, that his parents wanted him to take over the estate, as, he added, his father had done in his youth. But he could not do that, for while his father's "inner development had already achieved its authentic completion" when he had settled down, his own had not. He could not take over the estate even though "I understand so well the sanctity of familial obligation" until he, too, had achieved that full inner development by satisfying his "limitless need for knowledge, a need that forms the core, foundation and inner essence of my entire spiritual existence." Nor could he do both, continue studying while managing the estate, because "I must give myself entirely to my activity in order to attain real results." For the same reasons, he could not take advantage of the two other occupations open to him, the military and the government. With respect to the military, moreover, "it would be absurd after four years of retirement" to become a lieutenant again, and, as for a government job, with his "low rank and without a university diploma" he would be assigned nothing more than "copying papers." In any case, he could not force himself into an occupation. He had tried that twice before, he reminded his father. The first attempt had caused him a week of drinking and thoughts of suicide; the second, a "long and painful ordeal" of self-analysis resulting in the realization that he could not "tear" himself "away from serious study, since to live and yet not know is for me a thousand times worse than death."

Still, he knew that he must do something, that otherwise, "without money, with no position in society and, in spirit, a dilettante, I will be condemned to an empty, useless and tormented life." Fortunately, there was one occupation in which he could continue full time study and still have a profession: he could, he told his father, become a professor. That settled, the next problem was, how? Attending the university seemed the obvious answer. But, no, that was out of the question,

> first, because it would be absurd were I, a man of 26, to sit on the bench alongside youngsters and be in the same grade as my brothers; second, because I would have to start with the first year and waste four years studying many courses that would be useful only for the examinations and not for my future; third, because during these four years I would have to abandon my own subjective studies in order to devote myself to other subjects that are useless to me; and, fourth and finally, because, as all of the young professors admit (and also the government itself, which, dissatisfied with our universities, sends professors abroad for their education), not one of the Russian universities can provide a classical, scientific education, for the attainment of which there remains to me only one single means—*Berlin.*

In case this did not persuade his father, Bakunin added a tactical advantage in going to Berlin. For a doctorate, it would be necessary to earn both the candidate and the masters degree. In Russian universities, however, "the candidate's examination was the most difficult and uncertain...because it demands *excellent* answers in all subjects for all of the four years of a particular faculty, answers to the most specific and trivial questions." The thing to do, he had learned from "some young professors" in Moscow, was to get a degree from Berlin, which would take three years, then return to Russia to take the master's examination, which was "much easier and more relevant" than was the candidate's examination. After that a Russian doctorate would present no difficulty, and he could go right on to a position in "either philosophy, history or law" and "maybe even enter government service" while awaiting his professorial appointment. Given the chance, nothing would hold him back. He would work day and night, count every kopek, and dress and socialize only within his means. Also, of course, "orgies and the disorderly life usually excused in young people as a necessary attribute of youth are simply repulsive to my very being....I am incapable of finding poetry or satisfaction in the filthy swamp of sensual pleasure."[120]

His father's first response, which came about a week after Bakunin sent the letter, did offer some small financial hope, but ruined whatever joy that offer may have brought him by sending along with it the usual scolding. The elder Bakunin did not, in fact, accuse his son of "the most vile crimes" ("all your actions while not criminal are completely irrational"—what "crimes" did the son have in mind?). But he did express the expected disdain: "You are like some new Don Quixote, in love with a new Dulcinea and carried away by her imagined charms, having completely forgotten all your obligations."[121] About a week later, in early April, Bakunin learned from his sisters that their parents were prepared to give him only about a third of what they had suggested in their letter to him.[122] While he accepted, "of course,"[123] he decided at the end of the month to go to Premukhino to see if he could get more. But instead of receiving firm assurances of more, he learned that any support at all was dependent on more income coming in from the estate.[124]

At this point Bakunin took an audacious step, unusual even for one as carefree as he was about borrowing. At the end of March, about the time that Bakunin wrote his lengthy appeal to his parents, Alexander Herzen arrived in Moscow to spend a couple of months there before going on to St. Petersburg, where a position in the Ministry of the Interior had been acquired for him. For the six preceding years, it will be recalled, he and Ogarev had been paying for their modest flirtation with Schillerian rebellion and loyalty to the Decembrist heritage—Ogarev by banishment to his country home in Penza and Herzen by banishment first to Viatka, at the edge of Siberia, and then, for the final two years, in Vladimir, nearer Moscow. As we have seen, Ogarev was permitted back in 1839, and by the end of that year, or early in the next, Bakunin had come to know him. When Herzen arrived in early 1840, he met Bakunin, probably through Ogarev, learned about his dire need to go abroad and his want of money to do so, and in a conversation suggested to Bakunin that perhaps he and some friends might help. As soon as Bakunin learned in Tver that his parents were either unable or unwilling to promise him enough for the trip and for maintenance abroad, he wrote Herzen, not even waiting until he got back to Moscow for a personal meeting, and asked for a large loan. "I do this because I am taking money from you not in order to satisfy one or another stupid or empty fantasy, but in order to attain the human and the only aim of my life."[125]

The gambit worked. Herzen—and Ogarev along with him—agreed to make this large contribution to Bakunin's liberation and destiny. Although the full amount was not given at once, enough was advanced, and sufficient assurance given for the balance, for Bakunin to feel himself able at last to make his leap to freedom. Considering Herzen's earlier radicalism and Bakunin's reputation as the author of impressive articles defending Hegelian "reconciliation," one might well wonder why Herzen should want to help Bakunin advance his philosophical career. Actually, changes in both men had brought them much nearer together. In the years preceding his exile and, then, during the first period of the exile, the Viatka years, Herzen had himself ascended through a Schelling phase and beyond, into the lofty reaches of mystical love and religious rebirth. He had begun to descend during the last two years of exile, while in Vladimir, and by early 1840 had arrived back at the kind of vague, diffuse, ecstatic Saint Simonian Christian socialism he had espoused before his exile.[126] It was during these same years (1838-40) that, as we saw, Bakunin was similarly coming down from his transcedent sanctuary of "right" Hegelian reconciliation, on his way back towards the explicit activism to which Herzen was also returning. In addition, what may have inclined Herzen all the more favorably towards Bakunin was Herzen's dissatisfaction with Belinsky's credo at the time. Besides writing his lengthy critiques of what he considered Bakunin's sham reconciliation, Belinsky was publishing in late 1839 and early 1840 some boldly conservative articles that for Belinsky reflected a genuine "right" Hegelian reconciliation, including, *inter ali*, a zealous defense of Tsarist autocracy. The articles had infuriated Herzen, who, because of them, broke relations with Belinsky. Since Bakunin and Belinsky were again engaged in another bitter dispute (Belinsky's February-March attack), Belinsky's enemy became Herzen's friend.

In any case, whatever the reasons for Herzen's generosity, Bakunin now had what he desperately needed, and he moved with stunning speed. Two weeks more in Moscow, about a month home for farewells, then he would be off to Europe, to return, he said, after three or four years, "renewed."[127] His letters in May and June show how far he had already moved away from his family, with the exception of his father and Tatiana. Those to his other sisters sound formal and strained. Of his brothers, he refers mainly to Nicholas, with whom "we are least of all familiar"[128] and whose friendship with Bakunin's enemy Belinsky he mentions repeatedly. (Bakunin apparently got an added bit of satisfaction from thoughts of leaving Russia because of the painful burdens he believed his departure would impose on Nicholas: "Let Nicholas experience all that you and I have experienced over these past few years,"[129] he wrote his other brothers when he learned about another quarrel between his mother and sisters.) As so often before in his letters, his most tender remarks were reserved for his father: "Friends, dear brothers and sisters, do not forsake father. We are all obliged to repay him for all the suffering he has borne. Try with all your strength to become as close to him as you can. This will give him some pleasure during the last years of his life."[130] For the Beyer sisters, he had the familiar explanations. Using his brief infatuation with Sophia Muraviev to define again his views on conventional "love," he wrote them that this period of his life had passed and that "in my heart there is no more place for love." Still, it was good to know that when "moods of depression and suffering befall me, I can pour them out into your heart without danger of being misunderstood."[131]

Stankevich's letter arrived just then. Since Herzen and Ogarev had solved, temporarily, Bakunin's money troubles, the sting of disappointment from Stankevich's refusal to provide support was eased. Telling the Beyers about the letter, Bakunin mentioned Stankevich's praise of him for helping Varvara and told them about Stankevich's plans for study in the fall. This last point especially aroused Bakunin's interest: "He then talks about his present and future studies. In general, it is obvious that he is a bright fellow. I have fallen far behind him. But just wait—I will catch up!"[132] He could easily do so now: the night before Bakunin wrote this to the Beyers, Stankevich, too weak to complete a trip to Lake Como, died in the village of Novi, on the road to Milan.

"And so, dear Stankevich, I will at last be in Berlin," Bakunin wrote in reply to the friend who was no more. He confessed again that he felt grieved to leave his family, but he could not stay any longer: "my soul had finally reached such a state of illness that not a single healthy spot remained in it."[133] He promised to write Stankevich as soon as he arrived in Berlin, and he asked Stankevich to advise him as to what he should study at the university. Also, if Stankevich intended to write his Hegel professor, Werder, with whom Bakunin, too, planned to study, he should remember to put in a good word for him. Too preoccupied with his own plans and preparations, perhaps, he somehow forgot to say a word about Stankevich's own hopes and dreams that he had shared with Bakunin in his letters or about the illness that had already killed him.

To expedite travel arrangements—boat tickets had to be purchased, money had to be deposited ahead of time in a Berlin bank—he turned to Botkin.[134] By the last week of June everything was ready, and, in the highest spirits, he arrived in St. Petersburg three days before his boat was scheduled to sail. Hoping to leave on good terms with Belinsky, he went to his apartment to say good-by personally. But the scene was set for quite a different encounter, perhaps the most deeply humiliating experience Bakunin had yet suffered. The circumstances go back a little way. In late 1839 Bakunin had unwittingly chanced upon an embarrassing scene at the Ogarevs: N. Katkov was sitting on a bench, Ogarev's wife was standing next to him, and he was resting his head against her knees. Bakunin left the room at once, but, so his accusers charged, told others what he had seen, much to the dismay of both Katkov and Ogarev. From that time on Katkov hated Bakunin bitterly. For the rest of the story we have Belinsky's account, and to get the proper perspective on it we should know that, after a brief revival of the friendship in April, Belinsky was once again furious with Bakunin—this "monstrosity," this "abstract hero born to bring ruin on himself and others, a man with a fine mind, but completely without a heart, and with the blood of a rotting salt cod." The issue was as familiar as the fury: Bakunin had been so "vile" as to write his sister Alexandra "that marital relations were loathsome and thus frighten the poor girl....Oh my God, my God, what a crude, insensitive, dirty, vile nature! And this man once accused me of being a sensual, dirty person and was offended by my expression *sleep with a woman....*"[135]

With Belinsky's attitude in mind, we can turn to his story of what happened the next month, during Bakunin's last three days before departure. On the day of his arrival in St. Petersburg Bakunin had gone to visit a friend, Panaev, where he unexpectedly saw Katkov. Both Panaev and Katkov received him coldly. The next morning, Katkov, angry and excited, went to tell Belinsky about the meeting. Belinsky had already learned that Bakunin was in town and that he planned to call on him. Rather than wait at his apartment, Belinsky and Katkov decided to go to Panaev's in the hope of finding "our abstract hero" there, but, just as they were leaving, they saw him in the courtyard on his way to Belinsky's flat. Belinsky tried, unsuccessfully, to avoid his embraces, and Katkov began at once denouncing him as a malicious gossip. Bakunin, "as though suddenly struck by lightening," moved back, sat down, and demanded "facts." "'What do you mean facts! You have degraded me to nothing. You are a scoundrel, sir.' Bakunin jumped up. 'You are the scoundrel!...Eunuch'!,'" Katkov shot back. With that last blow from Katkov, Bakunin "shuddered, as though from electric shock," rushed for a cane, stood there a while without looking at Katkov, "then, seizing the moment, struck Katkov across the back with the cane...with this outburst of strength and courage, both left him—and Katkov slapped him twice in the face." They agreed to duel, and Katkov left, then returned, and said to Bakunin: "'If there is in you a single drop of warm blood, do not forget what you said.'" Having reluctantly agreed to be Katkov's second, Belinsky went to see Bakunin to make arrangements. Instead of discussing the details of the duel, however, Bakunin gave him a note to give to Katkov. "In the style of a eunuch and ona-nist," Belinsky told Botkin, "it took him almost two pages to say what could have been said in two words; namely, since by Russian law the one who survives a duel must go into the army, it would be better to have the duel in Berlin." This maneuver by Bakunin "to get out of it" especially repelled Belinsky, who was now ready "to wipe the scoundrel from the face of the earth."[136]

Bakunin had gone to Belinsky's in friendship, hoping to smooth over past discord, but he had met instead only an alliance of enraged enemies. Herzen's friendship, which he gratefully acknowledged in his last letter home, was still too new to ease the wounds inflicted on him by those with whom he said he had once been so close. There was still, he thought, Stankevich, whom he had "always distinguished" from the other members of the circle and whom he now all the more looked forward to seeing again. Until the renewal of his ties with Stankevich, however, his only friends were those at home, the very bonds that he had been doing his best to weaken in preparation for his new life. So it was to them he turned for solace and farewell during his final night before sailing. He now realized, he wrote, "how inseparable and sacred are the ties that join me to you. Do not forget me, love me dear friends. I have no one else besides you, besides your little world. . . .In my brief stay in Petersburg, I have realized at last that the former circle of my supposed friends no longer exists for me. . . .I am yours, friends, entirely yours and will belong to no one else again other than to you and to truth. . . ." Then, after a few light and gentle words of paternal advice to each of his brothers and sisters, Bakunin ended this letter to Premukhino—his last letter home before leaving—with a final gesture towards Tatiana: "Dear, fine, wise Tatiana, good-by, dear, sacred friend, be as happy as you can and never take your love from me; it is more than necessary to me. Everything that in any way enters your life must be known to me."[137] As for the Alexandra-Botkin romance, his final words were that if his sister did not marry Botkin "I will cross myself, with all my soul."[138]

Perhaps now more appreciative of their loyalty and devotion to him, it was to the Beyers that he wrote his final letter, apologizing for not seeing them before he left and pledging his eternal friendship to them and to their brother Constantine. But even in these last remarks to the Beyers, his final words—the last he was to write in Russia until his return in shackles a decade later—were of his family: "It was sad parting with father, sisters and even with dear mother, who has recently show me that, in her own way, she loves me."[139]

The next morning, accompanied only by his new benefactor Herzen, Bakunin went to the port at Kronstadt and boarded. But fate had still another dose of gloom and disappointment for him: the boat had barely left port when a sudden gale forced it back to shore. Refusing to disembark, he remained to wait out the storm alone on deck. As Herzen left the dock, he saw him standing there, "his tall, strong figure wrapped in a black cloak and drenched by the rain."[140]

His dream of so many desperate months had come true. He was on his way to his "rebirth," a new "baptism," the "golden period" of his life. Premukhino and his family were left behind, and with them the "reconciliation" that had been disintegrating over the previous year and a half. Suffering, conflict, negation, *die Tat,* and Fichte were already back in force, not only in actual daily life, which they had never really left, but also in his theory of life and world. He had decided, as he had earlier written his sisters, that if he failed to get the money to go abroad, he would give up everything, including even his books, "put on a military uniform and leave for the Caucasus," where at least he would find "vital action and a vital, dynamic existence." To do otherwise, to remain where he was would mean "quiet and gradual debasement into philistinism."[141]

Such remarks, especially when associated with the variety of other evidence that similarly reflects the renewal of Fichtean activism that had been growing steadily stronger through 1839, inevitably raise doubts about his academic intentions. There is no reason to question his sincerity when he outlined those intentions to himself and to others, such as we saw in his long letter to his father. Philosophical study had indeed become "the core, foundation, and inner essence" of his life. Moreover, given the persistently solipsistic and narcissistic nature of these studies and the fact, or so I have argued, that in this "wife" philosophy he had found a seemingly safe way back to the maternal "friend" that had "fed and nurtured" him, we can well understand the source and intensity of this compulsion, so great that any life apart from "study" was "a thousand times worse than death." So uncompromising was this need for a purely subjective mirror in which he could always find himself (and, therefore, the "friend" as well) reflected in what he read, that he could not bear the idea of a customary university curriculum, since that would require him "to abandon my own subjective studies in order to devote myself to other studies that are useless to me" —an act of infidelity to his "wife" and an intolerable separation from his "friend." In the infantile fantasy that was directing the course and form of his life, he could not separate himself, "tear" himself away from the "warmth so sweet" and live.

We should keep in mind, moreover, that his friends regarded him at the time not as an activist, but as a speculative philosopher. "It is a good thing that Michael has stopped being active," Granovsky wrote Stankevich in February 1840. "He is capable of achieving a great deal in science (he has gone far since I left: a real talent for speculation); but in the sphere of active life, he can do nothing at all."[142] Similarly, it will be recalled, if Belinsky saw a bright future for Bakunin, it was because he felt that Bakunin would be able "to advance the thought of his fatherland." As for Bakunin himself, even without the testimony of that letter to his father, it is clear from his other letters that he envisioned his "golden age" as one of intellectual achievement based on a continuation of much the same kind of introspective speculation that had occupied him almost exclusively over the previous five or so years. In fact, looking back over those years, he now complained that "various circumstances have not permitted me to get into the interior of my spirit and to live exclusively my own life." What he longed for in Berlin, he said, was "the construction of a new temple," a period free of "illusions and trivia," and "a broad free sphere of life and truth." If he expected a "golden period," "a baptism, a transformation" from "the vital atmosphere of European life," he defined the contents of that atmosphere not as politics, but as "science, religion, art, nature, people."[143]

But which, then, was it to be, "vital action" or "limitless need for knowledge"? Everything that had been happening inside him and in his relationships with the world outside from late 1838 strongly favored "vital action," notwithstanding the unquestionable genuineness of his ardent commitment to "knowledge." But where would he find an arena for this revived Fichtean "vital action" given his uncompromising rejection of the customary social involvements and occupations? And should this need for "vital action" keep him from fulfilling the plans he had outlined to his father, that is, achieve the necessary academic degrees and then return to Russia for that professorial position, how could he go back home? To do what? Finally, and I believe most important of all, if he abandoned his "wife" philosophy along with the "reconciliation" that had become the ground, frame, and sanction of the marriage, what would take her place, the place of the "friend" within and the narcissistic intellectual routes to her he had so painstakingly constructed all these years? He was now 26 years old. Does the urge to "vital action" perhaps mean that he no longer needs to be "fed and nurtured," that he is now at last, as he leaves Russia, breaking away from this infantile dependency? Not at all, to judge from statements such as the following, all written in these neo-Fichtean months:

> Go more deeply into your bright, inner world, close it off strongly with a monastic fence and do not look beyond that fence: everything out there is vile and banal, while in you all is good and light. Only take care, leave a little hole in it, or else your brothers will come and search long for you, search, and search, and search, but not find you for a long time. Finally, Alesha will suddenly notice the hole and will crawl into it, and after him Sasha and then Pasha. But then, trouble: Pasha's head has grown so fat with philosophy that he will get stuck in the hole and you will all have to help him. So...they will all come to you, sit down, and begin to tell stories. But I, poor fellow, will remain here alone. So take care, girls, do not forget me altogether.

> My inner life is reestablishing itself within me, enriched by the long and painful wanderings of my spirit outside of itself. Now it has returned, and I have built a splendid mansion with sturdy gates and locks so that nothing alien to it can again penetrate into its forbidden temple.

> Anyone not wanting to lose himself in the endless multiplicity of external life must acknowledge a principal, inner source of his life and surround it with a strong, high wall, inaccessible to ever-changing ex-

ternality, so that he can cross behind the wall whenever things go bad
for him in the outer world.[144]

How little has changed from the time of his first "intellectual revolution" of
1834! Now, as then, we see a frightened boy disguising the fear from himself and
from the world by heroic vision and rhetoric. And now, as then—in the 1834
remarks about being "fed and nurtured" with "warmth so sweet"—the sources
of his troubles are remarkably clear. The "monastic fence," the "little hole" in
the fence, the long search for the hole until it is found, the "sturdy gates and
locks," and the "strong, high wall" protecting the "mansion," the "forbidden
temple"—even were it not for the countless echoes of such images and attitudes
in virtually everything Bakunin said, wrote, and did, those few quotations perhaps would be enough to disclose the roots of his character and world view.
With respect to the specific period in which it was written, there is one point in
the first quotation that may be particularly important. Pasha (Paul) finds it difficult to crawl into the hole, because his "head has grown so fat with philosophy."
Leaving the deeper analysis of that remark aside, Bakunin's saying it at the time
he is preparing to move away from philosophy and to begin his career of action,
die Tat, may reflect his dissatisfaction with the passive way his "wife" philosophy achieved the desired reunion with the inner friend. But the remark may also
reflect his fear that apart from philosophy he might not achieve the reunion at
all: Pasha does, after all, make it back in, whereas he, "poor fellow, will remain
here alone."

Thus, while the boy and his problems remain much the same, the ways he
sought over the years to resolve the agonizing contradictions changed repeatedly
and dramatically. In 1834 he had retreated inwards, first into Romanticism and,
then, into a Schellingite Idealism, trying to disguise the passivity of this retreat
by promethean declarations of opposition and stoic endurance. Finding the disguise inadequate, and Schelling too fragile for heroic pose and purpose, he then
tried to bring withdrawal and action together by adopting the role of Fichtean
"teacher" and "guide," becoming "active" in the task of inspiring other pure
souls to withdraw as he had from the corrupt world of animal sensualism and
social constraint. The results of that first activist crusade, however, had been disaster: the "hell" and "terror" of his incestual attraction to Tatiana. The third
attempt, his flight to the sanctuary of "right" Hegelianism, was the reverse of
the first: now it was the rhetoric that spoke of tranquil and passive reconciliation, while his actual life remained as involved in Fichtean combat as it had been
before the Hegelian conversion. The present chapter surveyed the events and
conditions that undermined this third attempt at resolution: Liubov's death and
the consequent return of suffering and negation to his "reconciled" world (as

well as, perhaps, the blow it may have struck against the strategy of returning "home" as one of the "children"); Belinsky's successive attacks against his pollyannish view of reality, his blindness to the "jaws and claws," and, in general, his sham reconciliation; the increasingly fierce conflict with his parents over his efforts to break up Varvara's marriage and, then, over the Botkin-Alexandra romance; the effect of time itself, which merely by passing brought on the reverse swing of the pendulum, the shift from the passive to the active phase of his essential dualism; and, probably most important of all, the basic inappropriateness of a philosophy of passivity and reconciliation for someone who must above all *appear* all-powerful and who had too much rage for passive reconciliation.

The sum effect of these and related factors reviewed in the chapter was to prepare the ground for Bakunin's fourth attempt to integrate his conflicting needs. In essence, the new strategy would repeat the Fichtean strategy of aggressive external proclamations and actions, disguising the continuing inner fear and withdrawal. This renewed aggressive posture, however, would differ in two ways from its Fichtean predecessor. First, as discussed earlier, it would draw its strength and enormous confidence from the Hegelian heritage, which Bakunin tenaciously retained as he moved from "right" to "left." Second, it would be directed not toward bringing others, the "holy commune," *out of the fallen world,* but toward summoning them *to destroy that world.* Once fully worked through, this fourth strategy was to last him a lifetime. Along the way, moreover, it would solve the problem of what to do after divorcing his "wife" philosophy: it would provide him a much more gratifying spouse to take her place—"our common bride—the revolution," as he was soon to call her.

6.

REVOLUTIONARY
NOVITIATE

The farewell humiliation suffered at Belinsky's was soon forgotten in the joy of freedom at open sea and the rush of new sights and sensations. The quintessential romantic was in his element:

> I stayed on deck almost the whole time, not taking my eyes off the grandiose and, for me, utterly new vista. . . . I recall the poems of Heine that so well express this stark yet profound northern beauty, and also Walter Scott's *Pirate*. Everything is somehow sad, mournful, yet also grand, boundless, powerful—the life and beauty of the North. . . . I will be entering a new world—with faith, with a fresh, warm feeling, and open to all impressions.[1]

He had only a few words now for the old world left behind, a reference to those oppressive final days and his customary assurance of the "mutual, inseparable love" that bound him to his brothers and sisters. It was only Tatiana who was spared this ritual courtesy. Instead she was granted the most explicit admission of his love for her that he had ever allowed himself: " 'The laws condemn the object of my love.' Taniusha, this concerns you. Dear, good girl, write me soon and love me as you have."[2]

From Lübeck, where he landed, Bakunin went to Hamburg, together with an army officer and an artist he had met on the boat. "Again there is faith," he wrote Varvara, whom he would soon join in Berlin, "again hope. Everything around me is so new, so original, everything breathes such joyful, vital life. I am hurrying now to Berlin where I must begin my new life." As for the old life, good riddance to it. It had "produced in me an oppressive, persistent despondency, and forced me to hide within myself": "things were not well with me. I was ill and feel now the need of baptism. I expect this rebirth in Berlin, and I believe I will find there what I seek."[3] Sensing, perhaps, Varvara's doubts about his leaving Premukhino, he went on in this first letter to her since his departure to assure her that their brother Nicholas "will replace me and be a strong support for our sisters." Also, there were other "atamans" coming along: "Moreover, our other brothers as well have already grown up." Nevertheless, he acknowledged feelings of guilt over leaving his father, who had become "so soft, meek and indulgent" and who "was so sad at parting with me that I would have been prepared to stay, were I not convinced that by staying I would have been a burden both to myself and to the entire family."[4]

For three days Bakunin remained in Hamburg with the colonel and the artist, then he and the colonel took a coach to Berlin. Once in Berlin, the fresh, exuberant overture to his new life ebbed into deep melancholy. The appalling news of Stankevich's death, which greeted his entry into Berlin, was itself enough to drag him rudely down from the heights. The tragedy is mentioned often in his letters now, and almost two months after he had learned of it, it was still overwhelmingly with him—"his death brings terror."[5]

In addition to the distress at the loss of one of his few kindred spirits, he was burdened now with the sundry prosaic chores of settlement, especially the strains and tensions of setting up house in Berlin with Varvara and her son and of taking care of both of them during their frequent illnesses. Had he been swept at once into the university student's life his high spirits might have remained longer aloft, but classes would not begin until October, and, in the meantime, notwithstanding the new and, one would have thought, vibrantly stimulating environment, he lived "a completely quiet" life, as he wrote his family and friends back home. In fact, he became much more withdrawn and resigned than he had been during his final year in Russia, when he had been constantly agitated by his successive campaigns for chastity and his frustrated yearning to get to Berlin and to the rebirth he was sure awaited him there. Now he was in Berlin. Everything should have changed. But everything remained much the same. He spent his days reading philosophy, under the occasional guidance of Stankevich's professor, Werder, at least until Werder left for his summer vacation a short time after Bakunin's arrival. Fortunately, at just about the time Werder left, Bakunin met and soon became fast friends with another young Russian student of philosophy who had come the year before to study in Berlin, Ivan Turgenev. Much more enthusiastic than Bakunin at the time, Turgenev probably helped keep Bakunin's mood from falling even lower than it did.[6]

Letters from home only made matters worse, for while they no doubt pleased him by reaffirming his sisters' and brothers'—mainly Tatiana's and Paul's—extraordinary devotion to him, they also probably exacerbated the guilt he felt for leaving. "You see, Misha," Tatiana wrote him in July, "the reason for all our happiness, all our joy—is always you. I want to believe that life will reward you for all that you have done for us. Alesha says that we are now like a flock without its shepherd. . . . It is true, without you nothing is right. . . . I do not know why, but never before had I been so deeply, so hopelessly depressed as I was this summer."[7] It was Paul, however, who was the most disconsolate after his brother's departure, and "only you can pull him out of it. Your presence revived him. Your firm belief saved him from his oppressive thoughts. . . . Misha, arouse him; call him back to life. Oh, why does he not have your strength!"[8]

Finally, in this list of depressing influences on Bakunin's first months away, there was the duel with Katkov he had postponed. Not paying one's debts was one thing among his peers, but reneging on a duel was something else again. "And now, in a letter from Efremov," Belinsky wrote Botkin in mid-August, "in which he informs me of Stankevich's death, there is a request that I persuade Katkov to put off the matter [the duel] indefinitely, because [Varvara] is in Berlin, and Michael is her only support, etc., etc." One can imagine how his enemies greeted what to them could only have seemed ignominious evasion. Ogarev, who, as Herzen's closest friend, had contributed to Bakunin's liberation fund, now bitterly regretted having helped him (the "reptile") and told Herzen not only that he would give nothing more, but also that he would keep clear of Bakunin altogether.

> Even to shake hands with this kind of person is vile. It was a wise thing you did not to become close friends with him. . . . Moreover, in spite of my disagreement with Katkov, I must be just to him: he is to Bakunin what nobility is to baseness. . . .
>
> It is a shame he is so intelligent; that is, one cannot in good conscience discount his head as one can his heart. It's quite incredible; for example, 1) Botkin's testimony: he alternatively smoothed then spoiled his [Botkin's] relationship with [Bakunin's] sister so that he might travel around and live the whole year at Botkin's expense; 2) Stankevich's evidence: when Stankevich, feeling that he did not love Bakunin's sister, declined the marriage . . . Bakunin demanded from him 3,000 and then 15,000 rubles; 3) hypocrisy towards us so as not to lose the money, and toward Katkov so as not to lose Botkin. Before Berlin he refused to fight Katkov, and from Berlin he wrote that he could not because he was— the only guardian for his sister, who had come to Berlin; 4) he opened Granovsky's letter to Efremov . . . then thanked Granovsky for remembering him—which was just plain stupidity; 5) for six years, not receiving money from home and not working, he lived in Moscow at other's expense. So, as you see, all this testifies to the greatest of scoundrels, to whom I am resolutely ready to refuse my hand.[9]

What is true and what is baseless rumor in this indictment is less important here than the fact of this reputation itself and the likelihood that Bakunin was well aware of it, which would also account for his not turning again to Ogarev or Herzen for the rest of the promised loan, choosing to depend instead on small amounts from home, heavy borrowing, and living with friends.

Writing his sisters in early August, Bakunin summarized the depressing effects of this series of disappointments, burdens, and humiliations.

> We have remained alone. Around us stretches nothing but a vast waste-land on which we come upon caricatured *shadows of our own inner life,* shadows which we mistakingly take for kindred spirits. Now we know very well what sort of souls these are, and how little they are kin to us. We feel ourselves isolated, but in this isolation we are not alone. From the infinite depths of eternal truth there flows into us the fullness of the true, spiritual and blessed life.[10]

Besides the faithful inner "friend" (the "eternal truth" flowing "into us"), there was still, as always, the credo of redemptive suffering, first to ease the anguish by proving it inevitable and beneficial, then, by enabling Bakunin to prove to himself that he was strong because he could bear the anguish, to lift him out of it, back upwards again to proud and joyful self-assurance: through suffering, rebirth. "Life is fine," he wrote his childhood governess in late October, "but it is also difficult, very difficult. Man must suffer to be a man. But suffering is the animating, the vitalizing principle of existence. It illuminates ordinary experience, elevating it to the spiritual. Without suffering, without negation, everything would be dead and motionless. That is why we do not complain but rather rejoice in our being chosen to bear truly human suffering...."[11] "Do not be sad," he advised the Beyer sisters after a lengthy review of their disappointments in life, "do not complain about your fate, but be glad that it has been given to you to experience the suffering and the joy of sacred human life."[12] But more than anyone else now, it was Varvara whom he deemed worthy of admiration and praise for having endured her sorry lot with stoic fortitude. Even her frequent illnesses became, in this dialectic of pain, reason for gratitude: "after this attack she began to feel even better than she did before, so that in some respects it was even beneficial for her."[13]

No doubt reflecting both his own unhappiness and his customary way of handling it, he again urged his sisters not to fall into excessive introspection, "a kind of egoism, a vile poison,"[14] but to overcome misery by "the infinite force of will." But will to do what? His fresh, new hopes had gone sour almost at once. Months of dreary routine had already gone by and "rebirth" seemed as far away as ever. At times he eased back into detached reconciliation: "live quietly, peacefully, enjoy what the present provides you, do whatever you can in the present, do not demand too much of yourself, do not give yourself too great a will, and do not think and worry too much about the future."[15] More often, though, he remained true to his new conviction that man "must live and act," "become finite and concrete," "bring truth and universality into current, actual existence," and "raise that existence to truth as truth's dependent manifestation." Only by living a life of active realization could he feel himself both "completely free" and "forever reconciled with God."[16]

In the meantime, however, the "finite and concrete" were still infinitely theoretical and general. Besides working on Hegel's *Logic* that summer, he copied some lecture notes, which he borrowed from another student.[17] But the focus of his thought and the character of his life during those first months are reflected not in occasional references to Hegel, but in his extensive quotations from the didactic, inspirational, religious thoughts-for-everyday *Laienbrevier* by one Leopold Schefer (a German writer, poet, teacher of mathematics, and philosopher) which he sent his sisters with his warmest recommendations.[18] Similarly, in a letter he wrote to Herzen at the end of October, the first letter Bakunin wrote his benefactor since leaving Russia, he seemed more concerned with German music (which he adored), German "philistinism" (which he despised), and the latest works of Russian literature (Pushkin, Gogol, and Lermontov) than he was with philosophy. The letter is also of interest for offering yet another indication of his surprisingly inactive life at the time: "You will of course want to know how I have spent these three months. Most of the time was given over to worries. . . . There are many newspapers at the coffee shops and I read them all, one after another."[19] Six days remained before classes at the time he wrote that letter.

Once classes were underway, however, his spirits rose quickly to their former heights. "Almost every minute I am immersed in my beloved studies, so that I do not even notice how time passes. . . . The static freeze that had begun to threaten the flow of my inner being has gradually disappeared. I feel myself alive and free."[20] All day long, from six in the morning until late at night, or so he wrote his family, he attended lectures and studied in his room, across the corridor from Turgenev's room, which he rented after he and Varvara gave up their joint apartment. In the evening—"every evening," both he and Varvara recalled—Bakunin and Turgenev went to Varvara's, where, together with a few other friends, they sang, read together, joked, and argued. Their circle was small and select, comprising—besides Bakunin, his sister, and Turgenev—only Werder and a Mlle. Froman, of whom Varvara was especially fond, even to the point of provoking in her brother jealous doubts as to whether Varvara preferred Mlle. Froman to himself, a suspicion Varvara vigorously denied.[21]

Consistent with his happier mood, Bakunin even tried now to broaden some-what this scanty social life. Recalling a year later one such venture into the world, and showing us what he may have meant when he spoke of living a concrete, finite life, Bakunin wrote of "how, realizing that our life, for all its amplitude, was still abstract, ideal, we [he and Turgenev] decided to throw ourselves into the real world in order to live and act, and how, as a result of that noble decision, we went off the next day to Mlle. Solmar's, he in a green velvet Don Juan styled coat, and I in a violet, and similarly velvet, jacket."[22] A fellow student provides another glimpse into the more "finite" side of those first months at the univer-sity, when he, Bakunin, and Turgenev met several times a week to study and chat over tea and sandwiches. As to political themes in these conversations, the mem-oirist cannot recall having heard Turgenev "express the ardent hopes or desires for the abolition of serfdom that some now claim he did express. Even Bakunin himself, who went very much farther in his wishes than Turgenev, regarded the liberation of the peasants as something for the distant future."[23]

Although the author of these intriguing remarks, written almost 40 years after the event, does not tell us in what ways Bakunin went so much farther than Turgenev, one can assume from Bakunin's other associations at the time that opposition politics were already involved. Since the end of 1839 Turgenev had been a frequent guest at one of Berlin's most influential salons, the home of Mme. Frolov, where he met such leading defenders of Prussian constitutionalism as Bettina von Arnim—an old favorite of Bakunin's—and Varnhagen von Ense, dip-lomat, writer, and prominent enthusiast for all things Russian. Through Turgenev and Werder, another participant in the Frolov salon, Bakunin soon came to know these illustrious Berliners and to pay frequent calls on them.

Until this time, Bakunin had concerned himself only with the romantic, lyrical side of Bettina, since he had come to know her mainly through *Goethe's Correspondence with a Child,* reminiscences based on letters Goethe had written to her when she was in her 20s. But now, in 1840, when Bakunin first came to know her personally, it was her outspoken liberalism that most distinguished her—her open appeals to the new monarch Frederick William IV for a Prussian constitution and freedom of the press, her successful influence on him to appoint the brothers Grimm (whose liberal sentiments had cost them their Göttingen professorships) to Berlin University, and her defense of a mayor who had sup-ported the cause of starving Silesian weavers, after they had destroyed a factory owner's machinery when he answered their plea for bread by recommending straw as cheaper. To Varnhagen, she was "the hero of the period, the only free and strong voice." For her audacity, she was even sentenced to a brief prison term, which, however, she never served, thanks to her brother-in-law Savigny, then Minister of Justice. (One evening Savigny dropped in while she was entertaining her liberal friends: "Just imagine, Savigny came to take my daughters to the ball; I wanted to introduce him to my democrats, but he was frightened and waited outside, walking around in the dark.")[24]

Much more prudent, Varnhagen was careful in what he said and where he said it, usually consigning his bolder thoughts to the secret and safe pages of his diary. But he was no less dismayed and irritated by the new monarch's assault on what little civil and political freedom remained from Frederick William III's repressive reign. As the editor of an Hegelian journal and a long-time admirer of Russian literature and culture, he heartily welcomed visits from young Russian students, such as Stankevich and Granovsky, who had earlier come to study Hegel in Berlin. Bakunin first visited him in mid-October of this first year abroad: "Herr von Bakunin visited me, while I was still in bed. He had lost a letter [of introduction] to me from Neverov. Only fragments of his translation of Bettina's letters were published, the rest of the manuscript was lost." Nevertheless, Bakunin impressed Varnhagen as "an alert young man, noble and of independent mind," and Varnhagen felt the same about him when he visited again about three months later: "Yesterday a visit by Herr von Bakunin, with some noteworthy reports about Russia. A solid young man, of noble spirit!"[25]

Together with Bakunin's remarks to Herzen about reading all the daily papers, these visits to Varnhagen, also beginning in October, and to Bettina, which Varvara says were frequent,[26] indicate at least a beginning of Bakunin's contact with political opposition movements—his first contact, for that matter, with politics in general. It was a fortuitous juncture of events, for it was just that summer of his arrival in Berlin, the summer of 1840, that the liberal opposition movement, aiming at a constitution for Prussia and a bill of civil rights, first ventured forth again after almost 20 years of timid retreat in the wake of the severe punishments suffered by those—mainly university students—involved in the opposition of the early 1820s. The immediate cause of this reawakening was the crushing disappointment that liberals experienced soon after Frederick William IV succeeded his father to power that summer. First, contrary to the liberals' expectations, he refused to carry out his father's promise to introduce a constitution, as many other German states had earlier done (partly in fearful response to the French Revolution of 1830). Then, after replacing a relatively mild and tolerant Minister of Culture with a relentless defender of Prussian order and Protestant orthodoxy, he went on to intensify restrictions on the press and universities, the home ground of the students and professors who now comprised Bakunin's daily milieu.

Unquestionably the most powerful influence on Bakunin during this period, his first semester at the University, was that of one of those liberal professors, Karl Werder. If anyone was midwife to his rebirth, Werder was. Only five years older than Bakunin, Werder had already been teaching philosophy for about seven years at Berlin University and making a great and enduring impression on young Russians like Granovsky, Stankevich, and Turgenev. Besides winning favor through his youthful enthusiasm, charm, and intellectual brilliance, Werder seems to have attracted the Russians because, as a gifted playwright as well as an eminent and original philosopher, he succeeded in doing what Bakunin and his friends had been trying to do for years, blend philosophical "science" with Romantic sensibilities.

Although Bakunin warmly praised the products of both sides of his talented teacher (the one producing a book on Hegelian logic and the other a play entitled *Christopher Columbus*), what really drew his admiration was the fact that the two sides fused so well, that Werder's philosophy was not abstract and impersonal, but alive and vibrant. "What a wonderful man," Bakunin wrote Herzen. "In him, the spirit, knowledge, takes on flesh" thereby creating a "living, free union of knowledge and life. Not the dead letter, but the fruit of a religious, inner striving. I hope to become close friends with him, and I expect from him much of value, both intellectual and moral."[27]

The principal theme of Werder's two works that year, *Logic* and *Christopher Columbus,* suggests another reason, besides the fusion of logic and life, for Bakunin's praise: the spirit that took flesh in Werder's philosophy and play was the spirit of absolute freedom, a spirit that Werder saw threatened by narrow-minded philistines in the same way that Bakunin had always seen his own lifelong struggle cruelly and unjustly misunderstood and abused.

> No sooner does someone strive to become free in spirit, to remake himself in the image of God, than he is at once pursued by the guardians of the dead letter, those who, properly speaking, are themselves dead. They overwhelm him with abuse and damn him as a heretic. Thinking that they offend him, they denounce him as a free spirit and even say that he deifies himself. Free Spirit! As if this were not to his honor.... Anyone, in effect, whose heart is filled with God can expect, without fail, to be defamed and treated as an atheist.[28]

Further echoing Bakunin's own renewed sense of himself as a Fichtean "warrior for holy truth," Werder regarded the practice of philosophy as "a divine service and nothing but that." Philosophy was "in no way the passive edification of an indolent heart...a cowardly nostalgia, a commodious cloak to cover hypocrisy. Just the opposite—we want to elevate ourselves through it towards a humanity blessed with divine force, but also blessed with the strength of heart and the courage of liberty." One must follow the lead of the great poets, prophets, and philosophers, Werder taught, for their courageous will reflected both the free will of God and the free, self-determining world mind, Absolute Reason. Rearranging Hegel's concepts of Being, non-Being, and Becoming, Werder's *Logic* transformed Hegel's pattern from an ultimately conservative set piece into a mighty, progressive, epic drama. In Werder's version, non-Being (vision, ideal, hope) appeared as the knowledge that Being had of its as yet unrealized potential, its free, active, self-creativity. It was "the frontier of Being," which, by representing what was yet to come out of existing Being, was in this sense a "negation" of that existence, albeit a negation that "denies only in order to affirm." Here, in short, was just the kind of Fichte-Hegel blend that Bakunin had been moving towards as he searched for a new philosophical rhetoric to ground and to express his own merger of Fichtean subjective voluntarism and the Hegelian objective Absolute, i.e. "vital action" and "limitless ... knowledge."

The play, *Christopher Columbus,* ("a marvelous, profound work," in Bakunin's words)[29] was an illustrative enactment of this cosmic unfolding on the humbler scale of human destiny. In effect, it showed Absolute Reason, Spirit, becoming flesh in the person of one of its great men, one of Hegel's "geniuses," who by their enormous exertion of will were able to move mankind from the realm of existing Being (the known) into unknown, unchartered non-Being. As must all great men who performed this divine service, according to Werder, Columbus found himself surrounded by lesser men who, failing to understand either him or the opportunities he offered them, blocked his advance at every step of the way. Although they defeated him, he remained their moral superior.

Inspired by Werder, and aroused both by the general excitement of university life and by his introduction to real, opposition politics, Bakunin was ready now, as he had not been that summer, for the long waited "rebirth," for another momentous "intellectual revolution." At the end of January 1841, in his first letter home in almost two months, Bakunin told his brother about it:

> I have not written anyone because a new revolution is occurring within me. I am passing through a transformation. The dust has settled, and clarity and strength once again reign in my soul. This winter I lived a remarkable life. The rebirth, to which I was so drawn, has already begun to express itself in my soul. The feeling of age that had so oppressed me has disappeared. I feel myself once again young and vital. My former faith and my strength are gathering as though for a resurrection—and all this is reenforced and enriched by the rational insight I have gained as a result of the most difficult hours of my life.[30]

The "rebirth" was only beginning, however. Even as late as the following May, three months after this letter, he still saw himself passing through the transformation. "My friends," he wrote the Beyers, "I have not written to you for a long time.... All this time I could not write. I experienced much that is new, splendid, and difficult, and I am still not able to give a clear account of any of it, either to you or to myself."[31] The vagueness, to judge from these letters, reflects less a reluctance to tell his family and friends about the change than his own uncertainty as to what it all meant and where it was heading. Another bit of information coming out of these months in early 1841 clarifies the situation somewhat. In a letter to Efremov, written a month before his letter to the Beyers (and advising Efremov to watch out for the German merchants because "these damned philistines with their stupid laws are terribly proud when it comes to petty property"), we find "Neue-Brandenburg" given as the inside address and, at the bottom of the letter, a note from a young man whose family lived there, one Herman Müller-Strübing. This was Bakunin's first recorded encounter with a real revolutionary, real enough, at any rate, to have earned Müller-Strübing five years in prison (1835–40), a charitable reduction from an original sentence of death commuted to life imprisonment. Other than the fact that Müller-Strübing, like Varnhagen, took it upon himself to introduce visiting Russian students to Prussian life and politics, this is all we know of the young man's relations with Bakunin at this time, but it is enough to suggest the direction of Bakunin's political progress. Moreover, the fact that Müller-Strübing had invited Bakunin to visit his family and the playful tone of the note he added to Bakunin's letter to Efremov suggest that the friendship between the two had begun sometime before, closer, that is, to the onset of Bakunin's new "intellectual revolution."[32]

But where did Bakunin invest this activism? Was he actually involved in some way in local Prussian opposition politics? There is no evidence at all to suggest he was. What evidence there is shows that he directed much of his revitalized faith and strength right back into their familiar channels, back home to Premukhino and into its endless intrigues and entanglements. In his January letter to Paul, the one in which he spoke of his new intellectual revolution, he deplores the fact that "We have subjected ourselves so much to philistine reality that every free, expansive decision seems wild to us," whereas, he went on, it was much more "wild, impossible and unpardonable to fold our hands, do nothing, and leave everything to the philistine and the ruinous course of everyday life." There must be "faith, more faith" in "our thoughts, feelings, and aims, which rise out of the depths of our souls" and which "struggle against the ordinary, everyday life." We must cease dismissing them as "illusions, vacuous fantasies.... No, it is not they that are the illusions; it is this ordinary life that is the most dreadful phantom, shackling us by wretched, little—yet powerful—invisible chains. By the force of faith and the force of will, the permanent companion of faith, we must throw off these chains."[33] But to what cause is this heroic outburst dedicated? What new struggle? It was nothing more political than a campaign he had undertaken to find some way—and to urge his brother Nicholas to find some way—to have Paul and Tatiana leave Premukhino, in the face of their parents' opposition, for a brief visit with him in Berlin! Nicholas must do everything he could to attain this goal: He must "act, quickly and powerfully."[34]

The Fichtean mission was indeed on again, and no less impassioned than it had been four years earlier, with Bakunin still in the role of general-from-afar instructing his sisters and brothers on the tactics and strategy for liberating, this time, Paul and Tatiana,[35] at least long enough for them to spend some time with him abroad. Disclosing again some of the subtler needs, motives, and earlier experiences interwoven in his militant engagements, he spurred Nicholas on, after giving him detailed battle instructions, by saying, "So now dear Nicholas ... aren't you pleased with this easy opportunity to distinguish yourself on the home front of our own family? ... So brother Nicholas, rise up, arm yourself and act. Here is a wide field of action for you.... Act together, in common council, so that there is a plan, so that there is unity in your action. Send them off to us as soon as possible. We await them in Berlin...."[36]

Thus, although he had been in Berlin for some nine months and although the new intellectual revolution was already well underway within him, the primary battle field was not Prussia but Premukhino, the enemies were not Frederick William IV and his reactionary minister Eichhorn but mother and father, and his allies were not Bettina, Varnhagen, and Müller-Strübing but Paul, Tatiana, Varvara, and Nicholas. Once on the offensive again, there was no shortage of Premukhino causes to champion. During his first, depressing summer abroad, he had weakened to the point of agreeing to Varvara's return to Russia, even though there had been no divorce and no assurance that her relationship with Diakov would not revert to what was for him conjugal bestiality. Now that he felt himself again, strong and self-assured, he stood adamantly against anything of the sort. This, too, was to be Nicholas' assignment: he must make father realize that any kind of reconciliation between Varvara and her husband was out of the question.[37]

As for Bakunin's own relations with his father: "He will always more or less see me as the enemy of his peace. Yes, Nicholas, this thought sometimes rends my soul, and I am very, very sad. But what is there to do?"[38] As long as his parents remained willing to sacrifice their children out of "respect for customary conventions," his duty, he said, could only be to fight them. Turning again to his second-in-command, Nicholas—whom he regarded, however, as "rather phlegmatic, lazy"—he asked:

Do we have the right to submit to their will? Must we not in fact rip this philistine, commonplace conventionality to pieces and fulfill our sacred duty, heeding the sacred voice of love? Yes, Nicholas, I experienced situations in which, in order to save our sisters, I had to oppose father's will, to offend him. It was distressing, hard for me, but I did not waver, because within me love spoke and acted. And love alone is sacred and true. Everything else, whatever it is called, is vulgar, stupid, dirty and sinful.... Believe me, Nicholas, I would pay dearly for the possibility of surrounding our poor old father with love and tranquility. Nothing is as necessary for me as his belief in my love, as his blessing. But what can I do?[40]

It would be absurd, certainly, to conclude from the themes of these letters that Bakunin ignored what was going on around him, that his interests were as absorbed by Premukhino squabbles as the letters indicate. His remarks to Herzen about reading the daily press, his visits with the liberals and Varnhagen's description of him, his fellow student's comparison of his views and Turgenev's, his friendship with Müller-Strübing, his comments about a new intellectual revolution in process within him, and, most of all, the content and character of his first publication abroad, which he was to begin writing later that year[41] (1841) all indicate another side of his life that does not come through his letters. Still, on balance, the picture remains one of a young man tentatively testing the margins of a vague new world, an innocent abroad whose interests and concerns, sentiments and thoughts are just about what they were before he left Russia. "We remain here as orphans,"[42] he wrote home in May 1841, all the more so since Turgenev, his closest Russian friend in Berlin, was preparing to return home to Russia just a few days later.

That summer, his second in Europe, Bakunin and Varvara decided to vacation at Ems, mainly for Varvara's health. After sending dozens of letters searching for them, their brother Paul also joined them there. Troubled by his prolonged depression, their parents had decided to let Paul spend some months with his brother, hoping the change of scene might help him. As for Tatiana going along, they would not even hear of it. Other than some routine socializing, we know little of Bakunin's life that summer. When we do hear from him again, however, in early September, we find him telling the family that he had "changed a great deal," although not "with respect to the inner necessity of my life."[43] Assuming that the direction of the change was still leftward, the Müller-Strübing direction, the change was soon to be dramatically accelerated. Early in the morning after writing that letter, Bakunin, with "the whole family on my hands"[44]— Paul, Varvara, and her son—left for Dresden, where, whether by chance or prearrangement, he met Arnold Ruge, one of Germany's most prominent "left" Hegelians and editor of the *Hallische Jahrbücher,* the journal that, via Botkin, had first introduced Bakunin to the early rumblings of the "left" Hegelian movement.

While this was Bakunin's first meeting with one of the leaders, it could hardly have been his first encounter with the movement itself. It is inconceivable that, even though he makes no mention of it in his letters, he could have missed the commotion this Hegelian heresy had raised in the minds of the university students he met daily in the classroom and, more often, in the cafes, especially since the direction the dissident young philosophers were following was the same one he had been taking now for about two years: from contemplative reconciliation to vehement criticism, from Hegelian thought and understanding back to Fichtean will and action. Since the publication of D. F. Strauss's *Life of Jesus* in 1835, a new generation of Hegelian professors and students had been at work, at first gently and haltingly, then, at the end of the 1830s, more and more stridently, transforming Hegel's "royal Prussian state philosophy" from a plea for reconciliation with existing institutions into a (rhetorically) merciless attack against the Establishment as well as against Hegel's "one-sided theoretical, quietistic Spirit," to quote Ruge.[45]

The impact of this political and philosophical movement on Bakunin cannot be overestimated. Although he had already been on the road back to Fichtean activism for two years before arriving in Berlin, there can be no doubt that the "left" Hegelians did more than simply quicken his progress in that direction. By effecting a synthesis between Action and the Absolute, Fichte and Hegel, the "left" Hegelians strongly reenforced the work already well begun by Werder in providing him a powerful conceptual framework and foundation that were to remain—in consort with the earlier Schelling Idealism—his basic guide and sanction for the rest of his life.

D. F. Strauss, Count August von Cieszkowski, Moses Hess, Bruno and Edgar Bauer, Ludwig Feuerbach, Max Stirner, Arnold Ruge—these were some of the leaders of the Hegelian migration leftwards. For the old guard, Hegel's prominent epigonoi, the Master had already achieved all that philosophy could achieve, leaving his students and successors no more to do with philosophy but "thoughtfully working out its material in the manner which the lately departed so clearly and precisely indicated."[46] Having learned that the Real is the Rational, that there could be no genuine distinction between "is" and "ought," the philosophers, in the words of another loyalist, "should quietly take over Hegel's doctrines, avoid all extremes, and, in the knowledge that their philosophy was world-historical and final, reconciling all contradictions, not get involved in the struggles of the moment: a position of positive quietism."[47] As we can see from a letter one student sent his father in 1830, this was indeed a blissful formula for those whose temperaments inclined them towards such "positive quietism":

Hegelian philosophy has reached apriori what Christianity and world history teach aposteriori.... Now I behold the Eternal Being just as it is, with thorough certainty, and all my longing is quenched. You will believe me mad if I say that I behold God face to face, and yet it is true. The other world has become this world: man is a luminous focus within the Eternal Light; and equal beholds equal. Since I am all being, I behold all being. And as I rest upon God's heart, I am bliss already now....[48]

"Like the blessed gods," the "left" Hegelian Bruno Bauer recalled in 1840, accurately capturing the mood of the time in spite of his obvious malice towards it, "the disciples dwelled with patriarchal peace in the Empire of the Idea which their master had bequeathed them for contemplation. All the dreams of the millenarians concerning the fullness of time seemed to have come true."[49]

If the Master's brilliance forced his immediate heirs to close their eyes to new philosophical ventures, it had, understandably, no such effect on those more distant in time from the awesome source of illumination. Moreover, however appropriate and welcome this gentle and undemanding legacy was for the elders —of all ages—it was entirely unacceptable for those who had still to make their own mark, to cut their own swath, for those, in short, who insisted on adding a future, their own, to Hegel's past and present. The student coffee shops along the Friedrich Strasse and Dorotheen Strasse were no place for mellow, nostalgic ruminations or for "thoughtfully working out" inherited doctrines. The young men who spent their days and nights at Hippel's Weinstube or the notorious Doctors Klub had no intention of turning their lives into footnotes, however glorious the text.

Furthermore, they lacked that particular past that had frightened Hegel out of his own youthful liberalism and had sent his whole generation rushing into the consoling arms of "positive quietism": They had not experienced the terrors of the French Revolution, which had persuaded their fathers that the "Reason" of the Enlightenment was, in fact, dangerously irrational. Against the background of that violence and chaos, even Prussian politics in the decades immediately following the Napoleonic occupation seemed eminently sane and even progressive, especially when compared with the reaction that swept Austria under Metternich, France in the Restoration, and even England. To the elders, therefore, Hegel was not at all far from the mark when in 1818, at the time he accepted his chair at Berlin University, he described Prussia as one of the most advanced states of the time.

But royal liberalism, such as it was, could not withstand the fears aroused by the new wave of revolutions that swept Europe in 1830. As always, the first to suffer were the thinkers of dangerous thoughts. The free thought and religious toleration, for which even Heine had commended Hegel's Prussia, were now subject to the harsh resolutions of Carlsbad that called upon all governments to impose rigorous censorship, fire liberal professors, and suppress student political organizations. To the academics under attack, especially those teaching philosophy and religion, the Real and the Rational suddenly seemed to be going their separate ways. Philosophy had no choice but to turn "critical" again.

As might be expected, the rebels, the "left" or "young" Hegelians, justified their rebellion against the elder, "right" Hegelians by claiming to be the only true Hegelians, defenders of the real Hegel. Their aim was not to reject Hegel in the interests of political action, but to use Hegel in its support. It was exactly the union, in short, between the Absolute and Action that Bakunin had himself been approaching since mid-1838, and that Werder had been exemplifying during Bakunin's first year in Berlin. The dissidents' stratagems for moving Hegel from right to left, for revealing what they claimed to be the inner "esoteric" Hegel beneath the speciously conservative, "exoteric" facade that Hegel had prudently thrown over his philosophy, were straightforward and brilliant. First of all, if, as Hegel and his conservative successors claimed, philosophy and reached its apex in Hegel's own thought, then it was obvious that the next task facing philosophers was to move from thought to action, to "realize" those philosophical insights, to advance from theory to "praxis." The moderate Hegelian C. L. Michelet put it this way in his *History of the Last System of Philosophy in Germany,* which he wrote in 1837: "As far as thought is concerned, the reconciliation is completed. It only remains for reality as well to elevate itself from all sides toward rationality.... Thought thus ceases to be the last stage of the World Spirit's development.... The world emerges from thought and is developed further by it. As philosophy teaches us, truth, in order to become ours, has to become our own activity; and by means of truth transformed into activity, we shall reach freedom."[50]

The following year, the Polish Count August von Cieszkowski, whom Stankevich had mentioned admiringly to Bakunin in one of his letters, argued this basic "left" Hegelian position more emphatically in his *Prolegomena zur Historiosophie:* "Absolute idealism has achieved all that it is possible for philosophy to achieve....Philosophy must therefore now be content *primarily* with being *applied,* and just as the poetry of art has been transformed into the prose of thought, so philosophy must descend from the heights of theory into the *battlefield of practice.* Practical philosophy or, to put it more accurately, the philosophy of practice—the most concrete action of life and social conditions, the development of truth in concrete activity—is the future lot of philosophy as such."[51]

Thus, to quote Moses Hess, "The task of the philosophy of spirit now consists in becoming a philosophy of action."[52] In place of his former, "right" Hegelian three-stage scenario of human development (innocent harmony, conflict, and a higher harmony reached by Thought) the "left" Hegelians provided

Bakunin with just the formula he needed for his Hegel-Fichte fusion: a first phase of feeling and imagination, a second of thought and philosophy, and a third, (the stage mankind was then entering) of will and action. "Reality" was no longer to be understood by Thought and accepted as "something given"; it was to be achieved by *die Tat*.

Moreover, and this is essential, the "acts" were not to be "blind instruments either of chance or of necessity,"[53] but actions guided by an infallible knowledge of Absolute Reason in its future unfolding. Rather than abandon Hegel's Absolute and dialectic, the "left" Hegelians claimed far more for them than did the Master himself: while Hegel argued the possibility of objective, certain knowledge only for what had already taken place, the "left" Hegelians did so also with respect to what was to come in the future. Thanks to Hegel's great discoveries, mankind, guided by the philosophers, was now able "to make its own determinations perfectly identical with the Divine Plan of Providence."[54] As for the obvious rejoinder from the "right," that the Real was already the Rational, that what now existed was meant to exist, and that all talk of radical change testified only to a sadly defective philosophical vision, the "left" answered that this was a grotesque and sinister misreading of what Hegel really meant: since the Real must indeed be the Rational, they argued, all that was manifestly irrational in the unjust and unfree existing society was not really Real and should, therefore, be destroyed and replaced by genuinely Rational and Real institutions. This was just the kind of distinction Bakunin had been making with respect to "a chair, a table, a dog, Varvara Dmitrievna, Alexandra Ivanovna."

It was in their views concerning the way philosophers were to play their new, active role that the "left" Hegelians most clearly showed their loyalty to Hegel and to German Idealism in general. Even though their aim was to change reality and not merely to understand it, they still believed that ideas determined existence and that a change in mind would soon bring about a change in life. The task of the philosophers, consequently, was to raise the consciousness of the age by a constant barrage of radical "criticism" (the key word for the "left") that would tear away the deceptions that kept the old society going. Once the prevailing evils and irrationalities had been unmasked, the system built on them would come tumbling down. In Bruno Bauer's words: "Once the kingdom of ideas is revolutionized, reality cannot hold out.... Without passing through the fire of criticism, nothing will emerge into the new world.... Criticism is the crisis that breaks the delirium of humanity and lets man understand himself once more.... As soon as the critique has cleared our heart and made it free and ethical, the new world will not be far away." Or as Bauer said in a letter to Marx, "the terror of pure theory must clear the field."[55] Nor was the "terror" limited to the extremism of critical rhetoric. The cataclysmic social breakdown provoked by "criticism" would be correspondingly terrifying: "the catastrophe will be frightful; it will of necessity be a great one, and I would almost go so far as to say that it will be greater and more monstrous than that which accompanied Christianity's entrance on the world scene."[56]

Arnold Ruge, the man Bakunin came from Ems to see in September 1841 and the editor of *Hallishe Jahrbücher,* the journal principally identified with this new and aggressive radicalism, had steered his journal far more to the left since the time (1839) when Botkin began sending copies of it to Bakunin. The journal had now reached the point of declaring that "All reforms in the system of government, even the best of them lead to nothing.... There must be a complete change in the system."[57] When, in March 1841, the government had ordered the journal closed down because of its "libertinism," "destructiveness," and other dangers to the public mind, Ruge had immediately moved the press from Halle to Dresden in Saxony, changing the title from *Hallische* to *Deutsche Jahrbücher.* Only further embittered by the repression, Ruge vented his rage in increasingly more violent rhetoric. This in turn caused the more moderate contributors to quit, leaving the journal even more in the hands of such extremists as Bruno Bauer. As one of the moderates wrote in 1842, "What happened to this journal, which began so excellently, is a great pity. Ruge has let himself succumb completely to radical theories.... The *Jahrbücher* has come to the point where no contribution is accepted unless it is written in a brusque, dictatorial, atheistic and republican tone."[58]

This, then, was the situation when Bakunin arrived in Dresden eager to see the man who also, like himself, wanted to "resurrect Fichtean activism out of the rotten contemplation of Hegelianism"[59] and at the same time "tear" the Germans "out of their rotten, immobile golden mean in which they have so long been resting."[60] Enthusiastically responsive though he naturally was to this call for a war on the "golden mean," Bakunin was not in complete agreement with Ruge and the other "left" Hegelians. There was one essential issue on which he differed sharply from them—religion. From the beginning, that is from Strauss' *The Life of Jesus,* religion had been a primary focus of the "left" Hegelians' analysis, since, as good Hegelians, they considered religion to be the source of the prevailing attitudes and ideas in every society and, therefore, the ultimate foundation of society. Only by undermining the Christian foundations of the present moribund social system, consequently, could it be radically transformed. Taking his cue from Hegel's treatment of ancient Hindu and Greek religions, Strauss had begun the assault by portraying Jesus as a purely mythological symbol. Feuerbach went on to do the same with God, arguing that God as well was simply a fictional anthropomorphic construct that embodied not just human attributes and ideals, but the very best of what was human. Pathetically, man had abstracted his finest traits, gathered them together, projected them into this fabricated divine image, then abjectly submitted himself to this fiction of his own making. The existing, evil society would come down and a new, rational, just, and free society would arise in its place only after man had reclaimed for himself and his world all those ideals that he had foolishly locked up and alienated in his religious fantasy. They must be returned to him and seen as his own ideals to be realized by man himself and not as divine gifts offered through grace, but only at the cost of individual and social enslavement.

This was, indeed, later to become a central theme in Bakunin's own world view. But now it was totally foreign to him. While, for example, he praised Ruge for his "unusually developed will and clarity of judgment," he felt that Ruge "errs in being one-sided in everything that concerns religion, art and philosophy."[61] On his way back to Berlin after a month and a half stay in Dresden, where his "family" remained for the winter, Bakunin once again, as so often before, chanced upon a work that he felt much closer to his own thoughts and feelings than were the atheistic broadsides of the "left" Hegelians. Unhappy, as he said in his account of this trip, at the thought of leaving "my poor orphans" (Paul, Varvara, and her son) and wishing "to put an end to this melancholy which, you know, does not suit me, I decided to read Lamennais and had only read a few pages when the most vital, the most expansive life filled my soul." He spent the entire trip to Leipzig "enraptured" by the book, *Politique à l'usage du peuple*, returned to it on the way from Leipzig to Halle (although he lost the first volume and urged Paul "without fail" to buy him another copy), and plunged into it again that night in bed during his layover in Halle.[62]

Politique à l'usage du peuple, a collection of articles Lamennais had written for the daily *Le Monde* during the four months he edited it, gave Bakunin the combination he needed at the time—a powerful denunciation of existing society generated by a passionate religious devotion. In part, the message was his own. There was the same ardor, the same vocabulary and imagery celebrating "brotherly love," "grand and sacred duty," a truly "Christian society, human society," "the universal advance of humanity" and so forth. In part it was not yet his, but would be soon—Lamennais' impassioned attack on social inequality and injustice. In part, it was not his and never would be—Lamennais' admonition against class violence and his appeal to both sides for reconciliation, understanding, forgiveness. In spite of these latter differences, the mere fact of finding political radicalism joined with religious affirmation was enough to win Bakunin's favor.[63]

Left-wing denunciation alone was not enough: "criticism" by its very nature, Bakunin argued, could only be a negative force. It could not inspire a new vision.

Only religion could do that. As he wrote in his enthusiastic appreciation of Lamennais, the only role for "thought and reflection" was "the negation of that which, having lost its living soul, no longer belongs to the present, but to the past." They could tear down but not rebuild. The new construction could only be done by "someone who gives expression to a simple, and, therefore, universal, practical and vital principle of a new religion, a new life, a new reality." "Encompassing all present reality," he went on, "and indicating, with the most devout conscientiousness and without mincing words, the incessant and omnipresent contradictions within it, Lamennais is guided by that simple love and that profound unwavering faith in the future of humanity that constitutes the only basis for any authentic apostolicism." Rather than follow other "left" Hegelians in turning politics against religion, he had found in Lamennais an authoritative justification for his belief that "politics is religion and religion politics."[64]

Both the attraction to radical "politics" that he had acquired that year and his continuing evangelic faith, his search for a new "apostolicism," were reflected in the course of study he was then planning for his second year at the university. Besides continuing work with Werder on Hegel and, significantly, Fichte, and taking a course with Ranke on modern history, he was eagerly anticipating a course called "the Philosophy of Revelation" to be given by none other than Schelling himself, whom the government had invited in the hope that his romantic Idealism would counter the frightening implications that the atheists on the left had drawn from Hegel's rationalist Idealism. "You cannot imagine with what impatience I await Schelling's lectures. For a year now I have read a lot of him and have found in him such an immeasurable depth of life, of creative thought that I am sure he will now reveal to us much that is profound."[65]

His letters home that winter term (1841–42) reflect the new direction his life had taken over the previous months. In contrast to his first year at the university, a time of "youth," the current year, he wrote, was to be a time "for manliness, reality, deeds," a time of "bloody contradictions." "Contradiction" had now become "the most profound basic law of all life and all reality," and "to reject this basic law would mean to remove from life all divine meaning and reduce it to the philistinism of ordinary, everyday life." "Contradictions constitute life, the fascination of life, and whosoever is unable to surmount them cannot master life.... Life is splendid, filled with mystical, sacred meaning, filled with the presence of the eternal, living God only because it contains these contradictions.... If life did not include those contradictions in itself, then all those who crave truth and significance in life would have to shoot each other in despair."[66]

In April 1842, with the end of the winter term, Bakunin ended as well his university career and returned to Dresden and to Ruge, ready to begin his manly deeds, his first revolutionary confrontation with the "bloody contradictions" of the time (and still embraced by "mystical, sacred meaning" and "filled with the presence of the eternal, living God"). It was one of the most momentous and fateful decisions of his life thus far, perhaps even his point of no return. Why did he make it? Why did he not go on with his studies and carry through the program he had so precisely and elaborately outlined to his parents—get his preliminary degree in Berlin, return to Russia for the higher degree, and take a position that would allow him to earn an honorable living, win the respect of his parents, serve his country, and so on? He had already made a fine beginning. He had not at all "failed." The favorable impression he had made on Werder, Varnhagen, and others, his earlier publications in philosophy and the beginning of a reputation they had brought him, even his rather conservative defense of religion and speculative philosophy, all seemed to assure him success. Yet, excellent prospects notwithstanding, Bakunin could not carry out his intended program. The reorientation that had been in process within him since mid-1838 and that had inspired his unshakeable determination to go to Berlin was hardly consistent with a life of tranquil scholarship. Even had circumstances in Berlin been other than they were, even had "right" Hegelianism still held sway and secure positions, whether in the West or in Russia, still been available to a hard-working, ambitious, and successful young philosopher like himself, it is just about inconceivable, knowing what we now know of the man and his psychological constraints, to imagine him taking his degrees, then settling into a responsible "philistine" professorship— that "fussy, bureaucratic job," that "insignificant link," the kind of prospect that led people "to shoot each other in despair," and that had earlier led him to drink and thoughts of suicide.

But if he was no longer interested in pursuing an academic career, how could he bring himself to return home? What would he do? How would he face his parents and his friends? Or were his prospects any better in the West? At a time when young philosophers of the "left" like himself were losing their jobs, even had his "limitless" passion for knowledge gone on being "the core, foundation, and inner essence" of his life, his chances of building an academic career outside Russia were minimal at best. And with his commitment to academic philosophy and scholarship now gone, what could he possibly do abroad? Nearing 30, unable to return home, untrained for anything and as adamantly opposed as ever to conventional occupations, impoverished and now entirely dependent on heavy borrowing (mainly from Ruge)—his situation certainly seemed hopeless.

Its very hopelessness, however, made it ideal for him: with no choice at all, blocked at every turn from doing anything, he was left with only what had always been his own first choice—to remain completely apart from society, free of its obligations and limitations. He could, in other words, continue to live as he chose to live and as, in fact, he had been living ever since his *de facto* desertion from military service. But, whereas living that way in Russia had evoked the disdain of his parents and others because it had been his own choice, it was now, in the West, a detachment forced upon him by oppressive conditions beyond his control. More than that: this radical separation from society was a source of double honor; first, because he could interpret it as the price paid for noble, progressive aims and sentiments and, second, because such absolute detachment was proof that he had entered into the properly "left" Hegelian relationship with society. Since the "thesis" was to be completely destroyed by the "antithesis," according to the "left" Hegelians' revised dialectics, the only correct relationship with that "thesis," with the existing society, was none at all, other than standing apart from it in a violently "critical" posture. Finally, besides further transforming withdrawal from a source of shame to one of pride (a transformation already well begun by Schelling and Fichte), "left" Hegelian ideology provided Bakunin with an invaluable illusion of promethean virility. By allying himself with the now revolutionized Absolute as it prepared the cataclysmic birthpangs of the new world, the next painful leap forward in humanity's spiritual and social ascent, and by adopting a rhetoric of boundless violence appropriate to this imminent apocalyptic transmutation, Bakunin could feel himself "virtually" omnipotent.

The "dialectic" had worked its miracle for him as it was to do for countless others thereafter. Complete withdrawal from society no longer meant a loss of honor and power; it became the only acceptable way to them, a source of power and honor incomparably greater than those available to others, like Bakunin's father, who had exchanged childhood freedom for genuine social responsibility. The "left" Hegelian dialectic had simultaneously gratified Bakunin's two contradictory needs: his need to remain apart, to be "free" of the intolerable dangers of involvement, and his no less compelling need to feel himself "strong," "a man." Freedom, detachment, honor, and power—the new formula provided them all. As a Schelling romantic he had enjoyed detachment, but at the cost of honor and virile strength. As a Fichtean missionary he had gained a sense of honor and power, but at the cost of losing detachment, of coming too close in his human relationships, and he had suffered sorely for it. As a "right" Hegelian, the least tenable of all the combinations, he had entangled himself in a double deception by a feigned "reconciliation" that implied, first of all, as Belinsky realized, full civic and occupational participation, not narcissistic detachment, and that, secondly, required a submissive acceptance of things as they were, not a continuing Fichtean rejection. Now that Bakunin had been converted from "right" to "left" Hegel, this contradiction between his theory of "reconciliation" and his actual detachment and opposition was removed. Bakunin could now remain completely free and detached (as required by the dialectic), at the same time enjoy a feeling of enormous power and honor through his violent and noble rhetoric, and do all this with the full approval of the Absolute and his "eternal, living God."

Blessed now with this best of all possible world views, he devoted himself in the months following his stay with Ruge to proclaiming it to the world in his first genuinely revolutionary publication, *The Reaction in Germany*. Published in October 1842, it was clearly one of the best articles Bakunin ever wrote, as well as being one of his most revealing. Everything he was later to write is already substantially here. The fact that it is so abstract and lacks any specific discussion of social, economic, or political events or conditions makes it easier to appreciate the deeper undercurrents that motivate it: they are less disguised by a spurious facade of "realism." Paradoxically, as his later publications become more "realistic" in their apparent concern with "real" social, economic, and political themes, they also thereby more effectively conceal their subjective source: while seeming to become more "concrete," they in fact become more "abstract," more distant from their psychological roots.

Structurally and thematically, the article presents a classic apocalyptic vision: the present society is all bad; the future "new heaven and new earth," to quote from the article, will be all good; the transition between the two must involve catastrophic violence; to be among the saved, one must follow the selfless saviors who know the truth and the way; the saviors are in no way responsible for the terrible destruction, since that is the will of God, History, or Nature, depending on the particular form of the apocalyptic drama one favors; and, finally—and the central focus of the article—the zealots' principal enemies are not the rulers of the "fallen" world, but the moderates who seek only to reform rather than destroy that world. The purpose of the article is to announce the apocalyptic struggle that has already begun and to denounce the enemy camp. Mankind was on the eve of a cataclysmically violent time and would soon witness "a storm of destruction," "ruthless negation," "the complete annihilation of the present political and social world," "the restless and ruthless annihilation of every positively existing thing."[67]

While, of course, the reactionaries would be among those doomed in the imminent annihilation, it is not against them that Bakunin aimed his attack in the article. In fact, those he calls the "consistent reactionaries" do not come off too badly at all. Bakunin rather likes them: for one thing, they agreed completely with him that there could be no compromise between the two sides in the struggle, the "Positive" and the "Negative" (i.e., "reactionaries" and "democrats"), that "they get along no more than do fire and water." The "consistent reactionaries" were, therefore, "sincere, honest; they want to be whole men.... Just like us, they hate everything that is halfhearted, for they know that only a whole man can be good and that halfheartedness is the putrid source of all evil.... They hate, just as we do, all uncertainty, for as practical, energetic beings, they can breathe only in a pure and clear air."[68] Moreover, Bakunin was grateful to these "consistent reactionaries" for provoking the opposition into determined action: by shaking the Negative out of "its peaceful self-orientation," the reactionaries were doing "a holy service.... They awakened the Negative from its philistine repose, to which it is not fitted, and led it back to its great calling, to the restless and ruthless annihilation of every positively existing thing." Revealing, perhaps, still more of the personal sources behind this indulgent treatment of the extreme "reactionaries," Bakunin went on to concede that "they *are really striving* to want the good, that, indeed, in their nature they are called to the good, to a vital life, and that they have deviated from their true destiny only owing to an incomprehensible misfortune." "They are really to be pitied, since the source of their endeavor is almost always honest."[69] (Bakunin's parallel ambivalence towards his father readily comes to mind here.)

It was not, therefore, the adamant defenders of tradition that he set out to attack here, but rather those he called the "compromisers," the moderates in the middle. The fury and disdain he felt towards them was limitless: they were nothing but "half-men" who were out to stifle "the only vital principle of our present time ... the creative and pregnant principle...." Lacking "energetic purity, a purity for which the consistent, ruthless Positivists at least strive," and "more rotted than these by the speculative disease of the time," the compromisers wanted only a process of "endless gradation" and tried to persuade each side to concede something in order to ease the contradiction. As a result "they rob it [contradiction], or rather want to rob it, of its motion, of its vitality, of its whole soul, for the vitality of contradiction is a practical power incompatible with their impotent half-souls." For them the great power struggling to achieve a new world was not a "power to which every vital man must ruthlessly surrender himself in order to remain vital, but only a theoretical toy." "Are you whole men?" he asked them. "Has modern speculation, the epidemic of our time, left a single sound part in you, and are you not permeated by this disease and paralyzed and broken by it?"[70]

Bakunin could hardly be more explicit about the psychological roots of his new-found violent politics. Impotent, asexual, in constant flight from anything "animal," yet for that very reason driven to pretend immense power and virility, he uses violent rhetoric as a substitute for the genuine "power" he lacks and conceals his malaise from himself and from others by lashing out against the "half-men," the "impotent half-souls," who were "paralyzed and broken" by the "speculative disease," lashing out, in short, against himself. (As we see repeatedly, crime and punishment—self-punishment—are one and the same in this psycho-drama.)

The attack against the "compromiser" also served another essential purpose in his strategy at the time. The "endless gradations" and the compromises advo-cated by the "half-men" necessarily involved a direct and continuing participa-tion in society, and that was doubly intolerable: first, because it jeopardized his complete freedom and, second, because it required participation in *real* power. If we recall that "freedom" meant for him first and foremost freedom from the sexuality he loathed and from the social and familial institutions largely sustained by it, and that (as I have argued earlier) this same revulsion motivated his lifelong avoidance of genuine power, its obligations and its possessions, we can under-stand why he had to preserve complete detachment. He must put on his power-ful act in society by refusing "powerfully" to play any part at all, by standing defiantly aside and subjecting everything to the "terror of pure criticism." The enormous appeal the dialectic had for him (and for so many others as well) was in part due to its capacity to justify and rationalize this contradictory posture, to show Bakunin and others how to experience simultaneously both unqualified freedom and a feeling of vast power (however self-deceptive). The gifts provided by the dialectic represented, therefore, a further enrichment of the already sump-tuous heritage that German Idealism had left him (namely, the talent for acquir-ing total knowledge of reality while maintaining total detachment from it and the honor of leading pure souls out of the fallen world).

It would honor Bakunin more, of course, to see in his defense of the "all-embracing principle of unconditional freedom" an impassioned plea for basic political freedoms, for the civil rights and representative government, for exam-ple, that the political opposition in Germany was fighting for at the time. But that would completely distort the truth both of the article, which reveals noth-ing of the sort, and of the man, who was never concerned about such trivial goals. Thanks to the fact that so much of his early correspondence has come down to us, we know what being "free" meant to him. His own need to be free (i.e. "pure") had earlier motivated his own "liberation" and, then, the "liberation" of his sis-ters and friends. Now, in Berlin, he broadened the scope of his emancipation campaign by attaching himself to the political conflict underway in Germany at the time. Yet, the very way he talks about that conflict in the article shows how little he has to do with it or it with him and his real motivations. He ascends so high above the actual, day-to-day political conditions and events that they are no longer even visible in the article. Many years earlier, he had declared a war be-tween the "pure and lofty" "soul" and the "body" with "its own tendencies, its own demands" and wrote that "the struggle between these two elements, which form man, fills the pages of humanity's historical life" and that "the victory of one or the other decides ... the bloom or ruin of a people."[71] Here, in *The Reaction in Germany,* he speaks of the "contradiction between freedom and unfreedom" as the "eternal contradiction, which is the same at all times except that it increases in intensity and develops itself ever more in the course of history." Once knowing what Bakunin's absolute "freedom" really means to him, we see how little difference there is between the earlier and the later declarations. Only the imagery and the symbols have changed: the thoughts, feelings, and fears behind them remain the same. He is still at war against what he calls here the "wretched nakedness" of reality. And this will continue to be the case when, as we will see, Bakunin moves on to adopt other symbols and still grander "liberation" movements of oppressed nations and exploited classes. There was no more genuine concern in this article for practical political freedoms, of the kind actually being fought for by "compromising" German liberals in the 1840s, than there was concern for social and economic justice of the kind one finds, for example, in the works of Lamennais at the time or, for that matter, in the articles Marx was writing in those same months, articles like "Debate on the Thefts of Timber" and "Debates on the Freedom of the Press."

Repeatedly throughout *The Reaction in Germany,* the concealed Bakunin reveals himself beneath the disguise. By far the most fascinating and significant example of this self-revelation, even more striking than the disclosures that come through the attacks on the "half-men," is the way Bakunin's essentially passive character manages to show itself even in his most vehement revolutionary declarations. The "Negative" [the Revolution], he writes "lovingly surrenders to the Positive in order to consume it, and, in this religious, faithful and vital act of denial, to reveal its [the Revolution's] inexhaustible and pregnant nature." Similarly: "a man is really intelligent and moral only if he surrenders himself wholeheartedly to this Spirit and is permeated by it"; "the great present-day contradiction is not for them [the compromisers] the practical power to which every vital man must ruthlessly surrender himself"; "they are not permeated by the practical spirit of the times"; "have you [compromiser] ever discovered under the ruins which surround us this world you long for, where you could wholly surrender yourself and be once more born anew in this great communion with all humanity?"[72]

Even allowing for idiosyncracy of style, it is at least highly unusual for an heroic, "violent" revolutionary out to destroy the existing order of things to speak repeatedly of "loving surrender" to the Spirit "in order to consume it," being "permeated by it" in order to reveal the Revolution's "pregnant nature" and be "born anew." To appreciate the significance of these phrases and the attitude they represent, we should recall the way Bakunin described his first "intellectual revolution" some eight years earlier, when he spoke of turning inward, into his studies, where he watched himself being "fed and nurtured," enjoyed "the warmth so sweet that poured" through him, and felt himself being "reborn." By the time he wrote *The Reaction in Germany* he had divorced his "wife" philosophy and in this pivotal work denounced "speculation" as "the epidemic of our time," a "disease" that "left no single sound part" in a person, that left him "paralyzed and broken."[73] Philosophy, even with the sublime talents that Hegel and the other Idealists had bestowed on it, could neither provide enough reds and blacks to disguise the broken, paralyzed, unsound part nor offer a satisfactory outlet to the "passions" that continued to "rage." So, Bakunin now, in *The Reaction in Germany,* assumed a new, violently activist posture. Or so it seemed, for the bizarrely passive way he described the revolutionary experience indicates that at the deepest level there was really no change at all, that rather than achieve a genuine identification with virile male power, he was essentially continuing his earlier identification with what he defined as feminine passivity, with, in other words, the same maternal "friend" of his Romantic and Idealist phases. The revolutionary, the "Negative," to recall his remarks, "lovingly surrenders to the Positive [established power]," "surrenders himself wholeheartedly to [the] Spirit and is permeated by it," and as a result of this surrender and permeation is "born anew."

The basic passivity of Bakunin's revolutionary experience (a theme that will remain with us throughout the "revolutionary" phase of Bakunin's life as it had been a leitmotif of his "philosophical" phase) is also clearly evident in *The Reaction in Germany* in Bakunin's unexpected and repeated criticism of his own revolutionary cause. Fierce as he is in his tirades against the "compromisers," he clearly does not like the fact that "evil passions are awakened also in us through this fight," and spends almost as much time criticizing the uncompromising "Negative" as he does advancing its claims. He does not want to "attack anyone personally," because within everyone is an "inner core" that is "inviolable." Even when he must criticize, he does not want to do what the reactionaries do, "deny all that is good, all that is human" in the opposition. He insists on being "just and impartial," since "one-sidedness must be partial and fanatical in its utterance, and hate is its necessary expression." His party must transcend "this one-sided, merely political existence" and "not only act politically, but in our politics also act religiously...." To the extent, in fact, that the "Negative," the party of "Democracy," also suffers from the one-sidedness that "transforms into hatred, by their very utterance, all the good sentiments that are innate in every man as man," it, too, must be destroyed in the coming confrontation. During the revolutionary stage, when the only aim of "the Negative" is "the annihilation of the Positive," "democracy does not yet exist independently in its affirmative abundance, but only as the denial of the Positive, and, therefore, in this evil state, it, too, must be destroyed along with the Positive, so that from its free ground it may spring forth again in a newborn state, as its own living fullness." [74]

What Bakunin had done, in effect, was to reverse the relationship between reality and disguise from what it had been during his years as a philosopher: rather than try as he had done then, unsuccessfully, to distil a virile warrior out of a passive philosopher's life, he would now try to distil a passive philosopher's life out of a warrior's code and commitment. Having tried to make the passive life of a philosopher look active, masculine, powerful, he was now beginning a lifetime career of experiencing revolution passively—not only in the more super- ficial sense of remaining totally apart while appearing to be totally engaged (the gift of the dialectic), but also in the deeper and more pathological sense of ex- periencing revolutionary violence and the pseudosexuality that, as we will see, it represented for him, not as a man, but as a woman (permeation, pregnancy, lov- ing surrender, etc.). This strategy of militant detachment, one of the main attractions that had drawn him to the "left" Hegelians' dialectics, was expressed in *The Reaction in Germany* in such phrases as "energetic purity" or "ruthless surrender." The dramatic ambivalence of that last phrase captures Bakunin's needs and intentions perfectly. The important word is "surrender"; passivity, withdrawal, fear are still the ground of his being. But the surrender must be "ruthless" and therefore, somehow, be evidence of strength and power. It is here especially that we should recall the character and role of Bakunin's cult and plea- sure of suffering, by which he had similarly tried to prove how powerful he was by showing himself and others how powerfully he could suffer and passively, masochistically, endure; how much a man he was by how stoic a suffering victim he could be.

Finally, with respect to this first revolutionary declaration, Bakunin leaves the reader little doubt as to its apocalyptic character: he explicitly upbraids the compromisers of his time in the words that "the author of the Apocalypse said to the Compromisers of his own day. 'I know thy works, that thou art neither cold, nor hot. I would thou wert cold, or hot. But because thou art lukewarm, and neither cold, nor hot, I will begin to vomit thee out of my mouth'." [75] And what, if not apocalyptic, should one call his appeal for "the complete annihila- tion of the present political and social world" as the way to "a new, vital and life-creating revelation, a new heaven and new earth, a young and magnificent world in which all present discords will resolve themselves into harmonious unity!" [76] Religious exaltation of this sort infuses the entire article. Bakunin's debut as a maximalist revolutionary did not mark a break with his religious zeal, but rather its intensification. In the service of his cause, which he himself identifies here as "a religion," he sees himself and his comrades as "precursors of the future religion," fulfilling their "holy priestlike office."[77] "Indeed," he writes, "for us alone, who are called the enemies of the Christian religion, for us alone is it reserved, and even made the highest duty even in the most ardent of fights, really to exercise love, this highest commandment of Christ and this only way of true Christianity."[78] While the "compromisers" were denounced as "immoral men" because of their reluctance to let violence continue to the final "annihilation" of the old and the glorious creation of the "new heaven and new earth," the revolutionaries who had "no other program than the destruction of whatever order prevails," were compared, a little later, to "the first Christians, weak in numbers, but strong in truth."[79]

From a war between "soul" and "body" and the repression of the "sensual thought" that had cast him down "into black doom, anguish, suffering, self-laceration";[80] through the Fichtean period of the "holy commune," its war against everything "animal" and its hopes for a new, pure world to be built on the "utter ruins" of the old; to the Christian apocalyptic vision of a "new heaven and new earth" to arise after "the annihilation of the present political and social world"—that, basically, is the story of Bakunin's formative years, from Premukhino and the barracks to Berlin and revolution. *The Reaction in Germany* is a climax and summary of that story.[81] Having now adequately politicized his inner drama and, with the help of "left" Hegelian dialectics, constructed a world view that adequately met his need to be violently passive (through "ruthless surrender"), safely isolated yet omnipotently powerful, all later additions to and alterations in that world view would be largely cosmetic changes in costume and setting.

Bakunin's letters home and to friends during the months following his move in April 1842 from Berlin and the university to Dresden, Ruge, and work on *The Reaction in Germany* echo the dominant themes of the article and amplify its subtler message. They sustain the celebration of action, of "manliness, reality, deeds,"[82] that had begun to appear in his letters months before he left Russia and, except for those early summer doldrums, had continued to accompany his "rebirth" and "baptism" abroad. "To live," he wrote Varvara in June, "means not merely to ponder wisely but to be, that is to be a really authentic, active human being. Only the deed represents real life, and an authentic deed is possible only when there is authentic contradiction, only when there are authentic impediments."[83] Divorced now from his "wife" philosophy and dedicated to the "miracle of the living deed," he would henceforth have nothing more to do, he said, with the "fumes and wastes of theory in which I had lived for so long" and would instead concern himself only with "reality in all its wretched nakedness."[84] "Man must act," he wrote his brother Alexander, "always act in order to be a real man."[85] The members of his "holy commune" must now learn that Truth. They, too, must "tear themselves free from this world of illusions, powerless feelings, and lifeless thought" and realize that "only reality can satisfy us, because only reality is strong, energetic." They must abandon "hypocritical idealism" and "do battle passionately and bravely with the bountiful—although at first alien—waves of real life." They must, therefore, submit their "theoretical pride" to the "evangelism of simple action," abandon "dry reflection" and "that theoretical pseudo-wisdom that is ruining you and which I had done so much to develop in you."[86] Everything that he had taught them, he now apologetically acknowledged, had been "merely an illusion that must now be destroyed."[87] As for himself, that destruction had already been completed. He was now, as he put it, "a good soldier" who now realized, as he urged Paul to realize, "that life is a great task, with great obligations."[88] "I do not want happiness—nor do I think of happiness. Deeds, deeds—expansive, sacred deeds—this is what I want. A broad field stands before me. Mine will not be a trivial destiny."[89]

Such Fichtean zeal is what one would have expected to find in Bakunin's letters during these months surrounding the writing and publication of *The Reaction in Germany*. But there was also at the same time a quite different tone and mood that, while the reverse of the zeal, should also come as no surprise to those attentive to Bakunin's other voice, the passive side of the dualism that had found its way even through the heroic bombast of that virile-sounding article. In telling his brother Nicholas in October 1842, the month the article came out, that he would "never return to Russia," he went on to say that he was determined "to make something of myself and not ruin the only career remaining to me."[90] Yet, he began his new "career" not in a mood of buoyant optimism that one would have expected from the author of *The Reaction in Germany*, but in one of anguish and despondency. All he could see ahead of him now was "a lonely, sad, and difficult future": "so gloomy and so futile does my future sometimes seem to me." "At times it is dreadful for me. Everything ahead seems so empty and dreary. I will be alone, without love, perhaps even without human sympathy.... Loneliness has always been there ahead of me, and sooner or later I had to enter this wasteland."[91] His mood darkened still more after his brother Paul left Dresden, a few weeks after *The Reaction in Germany* came out. With Paul gone, "only alien faces surround me. I hear only alien sounds. The native voice is silent. It is true, I did not realize that I loved him so. I did not realize that I am still bound to you. I am writing you as I weep, weeping like a child.... I had not known before what tears were. Only leaving Kazitsino [in 1828, on the way from Premukhino to military school] did I cry as I do now."[92] After seeing Paul ("my spiritual son") off at the Dresden station, Bakunin was overwhelmed by such depression that "several times I wished for death."

You see how weak I am. Give Paul back to me; see him, spend some time with him, then return him to me. Let him come back next spring. There are so many of you together, but I am—alone. I need Paul, and I know that he needs me. He cannot live without me. He loves me more than all of you do. He is used to reading what is in my heart. Alone I will grow completely hard. Do you see how weak I am? *I ask this of you as a woman, since I am at this moment as weak as a woman.* This will pass, I know, and soon. But only its expression will pass; as the innermost essence of my heart, it will never pass.[93]

Despondent loneliness was not the only depressing feeling that darkened his entry into his last remaining "career." There was also deep fear, not so much of an unknown and insecure future, but a fear of being killed. Considering the place, the time, and the substance of his activism—opposition journalism—this seems, to say the least, excessive. A censored article, suspension of a newspaper, even expulsion from this or that town, or, at the very most, prison—such were the real risks that opposition publicists like Ruge faced. But the reprisal Bakunin feared as punishment for his virile activism was, as he wrote Alexandra Beyer, the loss of "one's head."[94] That he was quite serious about this fear is apparent from his other letters that spring and summer (1842), in which he time and again talked about dying, no doubt terrifying his family in the very process of supposedly trying to allay the fears he was arousing. "What are you so frightened about, dear friends. Look, I am still not dead, and God alone knows if I am to die so soon or not. In any case, I am not yet really thinking about preparing myself for the attack nor do I think that I am ready for it, in the way that any good soldier must be prepared for his task. Why paint all of this in such dreadful and sombre colors?... It is possible that I will be killed, but I do not consider this an absolute necessity."[95]

Nevertheless, he wrote elsewhere, this did not mean that death should be shunned, for "death is present in its positive significance at the most sublime and blessed moments of life.... A man must continually die in order that he continually live.... Only for a life deprived of grace is death an evil negation, and life—an evil continuity. For the man penetrated by grace, death is the life of life, the source of its luxurious fullness and of its self-conscious immortality."[96] "If everything is ordinary," he wrote Tatiana, "then life is not worth living; and if not, then death is not so terrible, but has instead a great, sacred, splendid meaning."[97] "A man always finds himself in danger of losing his life," he went on. "This fate is the inevitable destiny of everyone, a destiny bound in the strongest way with the nature of man, with everything that is grand and fine in life.... If death is evil, if it is even in the least degree terrible, then there is no sense whatsoever in life.... Better one moment of real life than a series of years lived in moribund illusion."[98] Providing something of a logic for this death-life "mystery," as he called it, he appealed to individual "immortality," in which, he said, "I believe unconditionally." Death, according to this "mystery," was part of a profound spiritual dialectic: "self-negation is the universal and sublime law of all spiritual life. In contrast to material life, which only possesses what it takes to itself, spirit possesses only what it gives away. And death, the total destruction of individuality, is the highest realization of this mystery, and therefore as well the highest realization of personality."[99]

Notwithstanding the clarion ring of this preference for "one moment of real life" over "years of moribund illusion," for a "great, sacred, splendid" death over everything "ordinary," we have seen enough of Bakunin's style and character to recognize it as largely bravado. The thinly disguised reality lies beneath, in the fear that generates this whistling in the dark and in such poignant little fantasies as the one he wrote his brother Alexei at the time: "permeated by a great and compelling task that we share, we will live in a Gothic castle, on top of a high, steep, inaccessible mountain, a castle with an immense store of food, wine, and tobacco and surrounded by a fine garden to suit our taste."[100]

Those few lines say it all and, after what we have already seen, need no comment. As so often before in his past, the loneliness, fear, and uncertainty that strengthened his hold on religion also drew him closer to Premukhino, especially to Tatiana. "Yes, Tatiana, you are mine, and I am yours, before all the others. I have long known this, but it has been a long time, a very long time since I have felt it as keenly as I do now.... Continue to write to me, friend, help me to come out of myself and to speak with you, and you will then see how strong, how constant, and how impassioned is my love for you."[101] To remind her of himself now that he had decided not to return to Russia, he sent her his portrait and asked her to hang it in her room. Later in that letter he once more confessed his love for her: "You told me last summer that were you not my sister you would have fallen in love with me. I say to you the very same: I love you, friend, deeply love you."[102] (A qualification corresponding to Tatiana's "were I not your sister" is glaringly absent.) To his father as well he continued to express deep affection. "How my heart broke when I bid father farewell," he again recalled, "how painful it was for me to abandon our poor, old, saintly father.... I am now entirely excluded from his heart. If he only knew how much I love him. Watch over him, friends. He suffers. He was worthy of a better fate."[103]

No less constant than this expression of tenderness towards his father, are the animosity and disdain that he shows towards his mother during these first years abroad, particularly as he begins his life as a revolutionary. In his first letter home after arriving in Berlin, the time when he had lovingly described his father as "so soft, meek, and indulgent" and had recalled how sad he had felt 'o leave him, he spoke of his mother as "a child of nature, partly corrupted by a faulty upbringing." Although he had come to believe when they parted that "she loves us," he nonetheless considered her to be "a constant offense against aesthetic feeling, completely lacking in femininity."[104] Later the accusations grew more impassioned: "Oh, how much harm mother—who ruined all our lives —did to [Tatiana] ! How many crimes she has piled up behind herself! Let merciful God forgive her. As for me, I cannot forgive her."[105] The hostility reached a high point after he had written *The Reaction in Germany* (the period of intense loneliness and fear in which he had spoken so affectionately of Tatiana, Paul, and his father).

> Don't say that I am unjust to Mother. In the first place, I know her better than you [Nicholas] do: I could tell you and prove to you such things as would make your heart turn over.... Weakness, together with bad instincts, bad motivations, transformed by long habit into second nature —such weakness is the source of every sin, all evil acts. Remember that Mother has on several occasions tried even now, when her vulgar nature and her unclean tendencies are still balanced by father's noble (although, unfortunately, also somewhat spoiled) nature, remember that she has even now tried several times to subject our sisters' pure, sacred world to her unclean world....[106]

What is the cause of such hostility now? What had happened to make him so certain now that, as he says, "she does not love me, that she cannot stand me"?[107] (He had not seen his mother for over two and a half years). Two specific reasons for his anger are mentioned in this letter to Nicholas. While seemingly trivial in themselves they do (especially the first reason) point the way to an explanation for Bakunin's rage against his mother. Once, while his father was lying ill, she had told someone "as despicable as Sergei Ivanovich, and in the presence of the children, that a time might come when she would need protection."[108] Another time, "on the very day of Liubov's death," when Liubov wanted Natalie Beyer to come up to her room, their mother, who "hated Natalie...made a scene in front of our sisters." Why did the recollection of such events now lead Bakunin to accuse his mother of "bad instincts, bad motivations" that were "the source of every sin, all evil acts"? Why did he now attack her, so long after the alleged events involved, as a "child of nature" and denounce "her vulgar nature and unclean tendencies"? Turning to the "despicable" outsider when his father was dangerously ill rather than to Bakunin himself as the eldest son does indeed suggest the real cause of this rage, but it lies much deeper than that occurrence and its superficial offense.

What is involved here first of all, I believe, is another consequence of Bakunin's shift in strategy, away from refuge in his "wife" philosophy and into the struggle for "the complete annihilation of the present political and social world." During his "right" Hegelian "reconciliation," after he had changed his role from a Fichtean hero to one of the children, he had been tenderly affectionate to his mother. Now, having donned again the costume of a powerful, "good soldier," he expresses only violent hatred for her. No objective reason is given for the change, no specific event or change of attitude on his mother's part, that is anywhere near adequate to explain the force and duration of his rage, but the reason is one that corresponds in his mind to words and phrases like "sin," "evil," "corrupted," "bad instincts, bad motivations," "offense against aesthetic feeling," "vulgar nature, unclean tendencies." I have argued earlier, when this reorientation first began in 1838-39, that the hostility and the corresponding terminology were the result of his return to the posture of a virile warrior. As a submissive, asexual child he could approach her safely, innocently, but as a man seeking "manliness, reality, deeds," "action, *die Tat,*" "a vital dynamic existence," he must avoid her, drive her away, hate her (just as he must appease with tender words of devotion the father he feared and whose image, in everything representing conventional individual, familial, and social life, he spent a lifetime trying to destroy.) Since, finally, the return to battle meant another claim to virility, sexuality and, thus, the revival of incestual dread, he projected the threatening emotions from within himself onto the one he saw as the temptress, blaming her for the "evil," "sin," and "unclean tendencies" that once again loomed before him and for which he feared the ultimate punishment, the loss of his "head" and death.

Yet, at no time did he need her more than now. His loneliness and his constant concern with his own death, those touching fantasies he shared with his sisters and brothers about the castle, the high walls, the gates and locks, the expressions of timid passivity that come through the bravado of *The Reaction in Germany*—all make it abundantly clear that he was no more ready now than he had been before to end his childhood bonds. Since he could neither go on accepting the role of a submissive child (for the various reasons we saw earlier) nor cease in fact being one (the castle, gates, locks, the "immense store of food," etc.), he again had to find a rationale for having things both ways. He had to appear active, revive his claims to "manliness," yet avoid the "terror" and "hell" that had punished his earlier, Fichtean display of power as well as the "sin," "evil," "bad instincts," "bad motivations," and "unclean tendencies" that now threatened him as he returned to the virile battlefield. The dialectic provided just the right formula for the magic. In the same way that the dialectic allowed him to imagine himself powerfully and honorably committed to society precisely because he kept completely apart from it and violently denounced it, so did it allow him to strengthen his bond with the maternal "friend" by means of hatred, a bond that is at least as strong as love, yet one that guaranteed to him the indispensable protective distance. To hate is to be simultaneously attached and separate, and the more one hated, the stronger was the attachment and the more distant the separation. Thanks to the dialectic, he could enter a new fantasy world of power protected both by a rigid barrier against involvement and a strong maternal love-hate bond. One might carry this argument a step further: once the inner pendulum had begun to swing back from "reconciliation" to "manliness," at the end of 1838, it may well have been his need to preserve the bond with the "friend," while at the same driving her away (as the revived "virility" required), that made the dialectic so attractive to Bakunin in the first place. In other worlds, first may have come the psychoanalytically familiar process of experiencing love and attachment by way of their opposites, hate and negation, then the apocalyptic miracle that allowed him to see himself lovingly tied to the world as one of its saviors precisely because he called for its destruction, that (to quote the most famous passage of *The Reaction in Germany*) allowed him to transmute the "passion for destruction" into a "creative passion."

From the beginning of this analysis, the interaction between Bakunin's sexual malaise and his social theory and practice has been a continuing theme. There is now, however, a certain completion, a sense of resolution, in both the personal and the social spheres. As a Schellingite, Fichtean, and "right" Hegelian, Bakunin had also molded the world outside to fit the world within, but, as we have seen, there had been in all those postures a deep contradiction and strain between the opposing needs. Now, in the "left" Hegelian resolution, everything fit precisely *because* of the glaring contradictions. He could appear to himself and to others as a powerful man like his father (thereby denying his impotence and redeeming his flights and failures), yet at the same time remain a child safely distant from genuine social power and responsibility (and their dangerous associations). He could express violent hatred towards the maternal "friend" within, as he must do, yet bind himself to her all the more ardently through the very passion of that hatred. Distance joined and destruction created in this dialectical world of "ruthless surrender."

Through the good offices of the dialectic, embattled opposites were now symbiotically joined, each strengthening its opposing pole. He could rightfully feel, therefore, that "all contradictions, all suffering, are already, even now, divinely resolved."[109] Henceforth, since the contradictions had been largely resolved (by permitting full expression to both opposing sides), what would be important to him would not be the success or failure of a particular undertaking in the real world, but rather how well that undertaking, strategy, or program played its part in the inner pattern of those dialectical resolutions. Now, as earlier, the only relevant reality was in his own self. What had changed was the path to that inner reality. It "is no longer accessible to theoretical construction; only free action can understand it." The point is, however, that this "free action," the "manliness" and the "deeds," were as much the affair of his solipsistic, personal fantasy world as "Thought" had been in his years of philosophical Idealism. The external world does not set the problems to be solved; they are his own, and they are not even problems, but rather patterns to be ritualistically repeated. What reality provided was no more than the raw materials and the successive arenas for the performance.

This constant solipsism is also apparent, I believe, in the images of God that continue to accompany him as he moves from thought to action. Although God is now portrayed as a God of becoming and action instead of a God of being and contemplation, what is important in the present context is the character and locus of that action: "The person of God, as well as the immortality and dignity of man—and in my opinion they are all closely connected—can be understood only through practice, by means of free action that gives birth to itself out of the original depths of the personal spirit and out of its self-fertilizing, self-engendering creativity, because God is nothing other than miraculous self-creativity.... Only such action, action that burns and consumes itself within itself reflects a simple, innocent heart, a clear realization of the eternal personality of man."[110] The actions of God and immortal man—and Bakunin—are, thus, self-fertilizing, self-engendering, self-creating, self-consuming actions that give birth to oneself. Once again, the images and the composite portrait project the essential narcissism and show that the new "manliness" and "free action" concern, primarily, not the world outside, but the child's fantasy world inside and its claims of infantile omnipotence. In that magical world nothing is impossible. All wishes are granted, even those most deeply concealed: "'In the realm of the finite there exists the condition that everyone remain what he is. If he commits evil, he is an evil person....'" By contrast, in the realm of the infinite, there reigns the *"'spirit that can turn something that has happened into something that has not happened.'"* Thus, "for me as for the infinite, the past already no longer exists.... Man rises to his ... blessed homeland where he is pure, holy, and worthy, not because he has not sinned, and not because he will never sin again, but because in his awareness of his authentic infinite essence, in the realm of the eternal Spirit, he casts off his sin."[111] Or, in still more Christian terms:

> we are all sinners, great sinners, but sin need not frighten us; we need
> not perish in weakness and depravity from a dirty awareness of our dirty
> sins. Were we not sinners, grace would not be needed. For grace is given

not according to good deeds, but according to one's sins, from which come an awareness of one's individual insignificance and the need, the striving toward purification by the force of grace and love.... And it is also true that there is no fall so great that there can be no rising from it, a chance for *complete restoration* of the original, lost purity. Christianity is a religion for sinners. It is the great mystery of redemption from sin and death....[112]

The "warrior for holy truth" was now ready for his second crusade—ready but also frightened, often despondent, and very lonely. At some level he knew that he had been forced to cut himself off from the very world he was now committing himself to save, that, as he wrote the Beyer sisters, his "heart, in spite of the passion languishing within it, is surrounded by a thick husk of ice that repels even those who might wish to come close to me, and very few people are able to break through it." "I know that there is in me something repulsive and that it is very difficult to love me."[113] The love he strongly felt within himself, he told Tatiana, using again one of his favorite images to describe his plight, "has been covered by an impenetrable, cold crust that often repelled people from me, and I myself often find oppressive."[114] Rare occasions, such as Paul's return to Russia, "cracked the husk covering my heart,"[115] and he then could weep "like a child" and implore "like a woman," but as a man he suffered what he called an "impotence of expression."[116]

A month after *The Reaction in Germany* appeared, he sent Natalie Beyer a cross to remind her of his "prophecies" and told her that he too would now wear one. At the same time, he asked that his brother Alexander draw portraits of his brothers and sisters and send them to him, adding that he was also sending them a portrait of himself—"let it belong to all of you, but *especially to Tatiana.*"[117]

7. "APOSTLE OF LIBERATION"

Three months after the publication of *The Reaction in Germany,* Bakunin's fear got the better of him, and he fled Dresden "like partridges away from a hawk."[1] What he was most afraid of, he said, was his forced return to Russia, "which seemed to me death!... nothing but gloom, frigid moralizing, torpor, stagnation."[2] Once away, he realized that his flight from Dresden had been "somewhat hasty."[3] Friendship as well as fear may have played some role. In October, the poet Georg Herweg, one of the most flamboyant bards of a new "Young Germany" movement, visited Dresden and so impressed Bakunin by his romantic politics, so much like his own, that Bakunin used Herweg's departure as the occasion for his own. Had Herweg "gone to America," Bakunin later wrote, "I would have gone with him even there."[4] The fact that Herweg, whom he had only just met, was the only one he knew west of Berlin and Dresden shows just how isolated Bakunin was as he entered upon his career as a rebel. Even the depth of that friendship at the time is questionable: in November, the month Herweg left Dresden for Berlin, Bakunin asked Paul and Turgenev, who were then also in Berlin preparing their return to Russia, "Does Herweg still remember me?"[5]

By mid-January, following in Herweg's footsteps, he was settled in Zürich—very comfortably settled "in a small apartment on the very shore of Lake Zürich. Before me lay nothing but the lake and mountains, eternally snow capped.... Sometimes I lie for hours on end on the couch and look at the lake, at the mountains, especially fine at sunset, and follow the slightest changes in the panorama, and the changes are incessant...." "My windows are open, and before them, just steps away, lies the marvelous Lake Zürich—the mountains, the village, the woods

184

around it, engulfed in a light, soft, translucent, luxuriant haze—the lake, mirror-clear, reflecting the rays of the sun."[6]

But neither the surrounding beauty nor his friendship with Herweg, whom he loved, he said, "as a brother loves a sister,"[7] but who was busy with plans for his forthcoming marriage, could hide or assuage his loneliness, now deeper than it had been since those painful barracks years. The anguish seemed to grow now with the distance from home. As he had wept and pleaded "like a child," "like a woman"[8] for Paul's return to him, so did he now alternately order and implore Paul "to come back quickly and bring Tatiana to me.... Do you remember how we talked while we were still together? What times we would have were we now in Premukhino." "I am waiting for you, Paul, and, if possible, bring Taniusha to me." "Your obligation, friends, is to use all available means to see to it that Taniusha comes abroad. This is a sacred obligation." "We will see each other sometime? Is it really true that there is no way for you [Tatiana] to come abroad, so that you could teach me to live economically? You would be my housekeeper, Taniusha, and how tranquilly and well we would live. Paul, bring Taniusha." "Dear sister! Taniusha, Sasha, don't forget me, I am depressed, deeply depressed now. I walked along the lake for two hours this evening. It was already dark. Black, heavy clouds. Damp, cold gusts of wind. High waves. The sea—blue-gray. Then, together with a young boy, I set two sails and quickly flew across the entire lake, and I felt good and happy and wildly fantasied that I had decided to sail home so that I would not forget reality." Not only did Paul and Tatiana not come, but they seem to have stopped writing: "for more than two years," he wrote Paul in March and Tatiana in June 1845, "I have not received a line from you, not from any of you."[9]

As they had during his army years, fantasy and imagination could partly fill the void—he could dream of his sailboat carrying him back home, though fear of the "hawk" made actual return seem like "death" to him, or imagine Tatiana setting up house with him abroad. And he could go on "constantly," "incessantly" reading George Sand, who had become for him at the time "a prophet bearing revelation": "for me reading George Sand is like belonging to a cult, like praying."[10] Fantasy could do even more for him than generate wishful thinking and heighten the pleasures of romantic fiction. So powerful was it in his case that it enabled him virtually to conjure up those he missed, a variation of the narcissistic magic that solipsism had taught him ("The pure 'I' in knowing itself knows the world objective to it;" authentic truth is "the truth man can achieve without having to depart from himself.") "Do you know, Paul, I have noticed in myself a strange characteristic: the personality of those I love fuses so with my own, that even in their absence, in fact especially in their absence, I involuntarily see with their eyes and feel with their feelings. How would you explain that to me?" Once while walking along Lake Zürich, he went on to say, giving an example of this gift, "it almost seemed to me that I was you, that it was your joy that I felt, that I was expressing quite spontaneously, involuntarily, your thoughts, in a word that I was for a certain span of time both you and myself. I live here very much alone...." "My 'I'," he similarly wrote to Varvara, even more remarkably disclosing the hidden "dual unity," "my own, personal inner world involuntarily co-mingles you within itself, without any effort at all. When I say I, I say we. I do not exist apart from you. This has become still clearer to me since the time of my separation from Paul, and especially in my present isolation."[11] "Without in the least losing my autonomy," he told Paul in connection with this experience of merger, "I become ever richer and fuller."[12]

While fantasy could ease his loneliness, at least on occasion, it was powerless against his by now habitual poverty. A humiliating campaign to get money and to hold off clamoring creditors, even as he searched for new ones, fills the greater part of his letters that first year in Switzerland and provides further insight into his childlike dependency on others to take care of him. When money he had hoped to receive from home—from his own family and from Turgenev—failed to arrive, he got Ruge to lend him large amounts, promising that Turgenev would repay him. Turgenev refused, and Ruge was stuck with the bills: "I wish with all my soul that you get out of this difficult situation and convince your father that he should not let you and other members of your family stay abroad so long without financial support." (Bakunin was approaching 30 when he got this scolding from Ruge.) Bakunin was sorry, of course, that Ruge's "affairs were in a state of disarray" because of him, but Turgenev "had promised me...."

He seemed unable to do anything except go on writing IOUs, albeit dreading as he did so that once they became due, his creditors "will have the right and the opportunity to put me in prison": *"adieu mon honneur et ma liberte car on me mettra au prison."* On second thought, that appeared to him to be not so bad: his honor might, in fact, be restored by imprisonment. "I not only will not evade this unpleasantness, but, on the contrary, I will seek it out as the last resort to prove to them [creditors] that I had no intention of deceiving them." Other than passively suffering imprisonment or simply "dying of hunger," there seemed two other possible escapes. First: "Paul, my situation is so unbearably difficult that had I less faith I would really shoot myself." But that would leave his debts unpaid and was, therefore, too dishonorable: *"je suis esclave, je n'ai pas meme le droit de disposer de ma vie."* Which seemed to leave only one way out: "I will become a worker... earn my bread through my own labor... work in the sweat of my brow."

That, too, alas, was impossible: for "what work could I choose? I am still so inexperienced, I have still so little practical and theoretical training...." Write for a living? No: "To disseminate one's ideas and convictions must be a sacred vocation, and would one not risk demeaning it by making it only a means of subsistance?" Perhaps, he said, had he a reputation he might be able to earn an income writing without "being forced to betray" himself, but "no one knows about me yet." Write a book about Russia? Absolutely not! First of all, a book like that would take a year to write and "during all that time I would have to live at someone else's expense, and for me that's impossible.... Whether such pride is good or bad is irrelevant, for I have firmly resolved never again to be financially obligated to anyone. Yes, dear friend [Ruge], this pride in unlimited independence is for me the one essential condition, the condition *sine quo non* of my personal dignity, and the latter is the only possession that I saved at the time of my shipwreck. I must keep it pure of any stain, from the least sign of dirt." Should this reasoning (to save honor he must pay debts; to pay debts he could write a book; to write a book he must be financially dependent; such dependency would "stain" his honor) be lost on Ruge, he had another argument against writing about Russia: "I would never write a book on Russia out of need: that would contradict my love for my country."[13]

At a few points in this elaborate defense, so reminiscent of his letter to his father explaining why he had to go abroad to study, he got beneath excuses and nearer the real reasons: "I cannot bear the chilling constraints of deadlines by which time my work must be done," "I must tell you, dear Ruge, that I feel a kind of revulsion at the idea of writing as the only source of income," and, especially, those remarks already quoted about staining, dirtying his honor. As always, it is still a question of absolute "freedom," a freedom that still involved protection against stain and dirt. Impoverished, lonely, and with absolutely no prospects at all ahead, he remained as convinced as ever that his will reflected divine will, that what he felt like doing and only that was the voice of God, signposts of his providential destiny. In this generous dialectic, to do only what he wanted to do meant to forget himself, to sacrifice himself humbly to divine direction. To challenge, resist or disregard this inner voice and directive, *not* to do what he wanted to do, was to be selfish, cowardly, blasphemous, and dirty: "the source of my decision is clean; I am doing this out of the inner necessity of my being...."[14]

In the end, if money did not come from home, he would have no choice, he said again, but to become an ordinary laborer: "I'll wait another month, maybe even two. Then I will sell all my clothes, everything that belongs to me as a member of the educated class, except for books and a little furniture, of sentimental value, and become a real proletarian, an artisan." Of course, it would be hard, but "with the help of a resolute will, more than that—a passionate, religious will— one can overcome all difficulties." Should he actually be forced into this, he hoped Ruge would take over his debts—in return for another promissory note. But, if Ruge did not mind, could he please make out the note for two and a half instead of the two thousand talers that he owed, so that, after the debts were repaid, "a little something will remain with me... enough until summer, since by spring, my parents will have already found a way to send me money, because at that time there are always many people travelling abroad." Somewhere along the way, the proletarian disappeared, and needless to say, nothing more was heard about "working in the sweat of my brow."[15]

Depressing as these circumstances were (mainly because of the loss of honor: "they no longer trust me; they consider me a liar and a cheat"), he refused to let debts get him down or threaten his resolve. "Our obligation to our creditors and to ourselves," he wrote Paul, "consists in taking all honorable means available to us towards payment of our debts. But it doesn't follow from this that we must fall into despair in the event our efforts fail. Believe me, nothing will force me to lose my belief in my worth and faith in my future."[16] One reason, perhaps, for the brighter mood of this particular letter was the fact that he had just returned from a fine ten-day vacation with some new friends, the Pescantini family, who had a home on the island of St. Pierre in Lake Bienne: "I was as happy as a child—I strolled, sang, climbed mountains, enjoyed nature, translated Schelling, read some Italian, fantasied, built castles in the air and waited for you, Paul."[17]

What about active politics? Did the beautiful countryside around Zürich soften his determination now to struggle for "the complete annihilation of the present social and political order"? Did loneliness, nostalgia, constant money troubles, or delightful Swiss vacations turn his attention away from his new apocalyptic vision? On the contrary: "Thank God the time of theory is past," he wrote his sisters after a month in Zürich, and continued, soaring ever upward:

> Everyone more or less feels this. The dawn of the new world already shines on us. Let us be worthy of renewal. Let the thought that all our suffering is not in vain sustain us. Is it worth talking and fussing about our own suffering when the entire world is suffering the birth pangs of a new and spendid world? Humanity, the grand mysteries of humanity that Christianity revealed, and that, notwithstanding all its errors, Christianity preserved for us as a sacred mystical treasure, all these profound yet simple mysteries of eternal life will be from now on tangible, real, present actuality. And all who suffer must bless their suffering, because only suffering can make us worthy of that new world that we sense within us.[18]

The apocalyptic ardor was even further enflamed that winter, (1842–43) by new inspirations. It was at that time, after the appearance of *The Reaction in*

Germany but before his flight from "the hawk," that Bakunin seems to have gathered his first serious knowledge of socialist and communist theories from Lorenz von Stein's *Der Sozialismus und der Kommunismus des heutigen Frankreichs.* As he later recalled, von Stein's work "made almost as strong and all-encompassing an impression on me as Dr. Strauss's *The Life of Jesus* had earlier made. It opened up a new world to me into which I threw myself with all the passion of someone suffering great hunger and thirst. It seemed to me that I was hearing the annunciation of a new paradise, the revelation of a new religion of loftiness, honor, happiness, and liberation for the whole human race."[19] Rather than satisfy the "hunger" and "thirst," von Stein's revelations only further whet Bakunin's appetite for more, which he happily got almost immediately after settling in Zürich, from, as Bakunin introduced the new fare, "the *first* German communist work by some tailor named Weitling (*Guarantees of Freedom and Harmony,* Wilhelm Weitling, Vevey, December, 1842)." Bakunin was ecstatic over what he discovered in the book. Werder had helped restore and update Bakunin's renewed Fichtean dedication. Bettina, Varnhagen, Müller-Strübing, and Ruge had helped shift the arena of salvation from Premukhino to Europe and the goal of salvation from spiritual to temporal liberation. Bruno Bauer and other "left" Hegelians had helped give "politics" the uncompromising, maximalist, and violent vocabulary that heroism required. Lamennais, finally, had added divine blessings. Still, it was all largely theory. Where was the action, the *praxis*? Indeed, a German "liberal" movement had begun, but that involved the unspeakable compromisers, the "impotent half-souls" that Bakunin had chosen as the target for his revolutionary debut, *The Reaction in Germany.* It was hardly the force that would effect the "ruthless negation," the "storm of destruction."

Here is where Weitling came in. Building on foundations that had just been laid by von Stein, Weitling gave Bakunin a force that could do the required demolition job—the people. It was not the second part of the book in which Weitling set out his plans for a communist society that attracted Bakunin. He made that quite clear in an article he wrote on the book later that year: "This is no free society, not a true, living union of free people, but rather a form of unbearable oppression, a herd forcefully consolidated and pursuing exclusively materialistic goals...."[20] The one passage from the book Bakunin chose to quote in a letter to Ruge shows what it was about Weitling and "the people" that so excited him: Only in the people, Weitling insisted, was there "the audacity to put the arm of destruction to work...." For now was the time that "without in any way concerning ourselves with construction... we begin decisively, more and more resolutely to get rid of the old rubble as well as any new timber, any new foundations, in which even the slightest remnant of the old evil is concealed.... We must not waste any time.... The break between good and evil must be effected by catastrophic means."[21] It would be difficult to compose a more accurate statement of apocalyptic transmutation.

If God and the Absolute were still in charge of the overall strategy, still directing the drama, it was the "people" who were henceforth assigned the role of carrying through that strategy by the "catastrophic means" appropriate to an apocalyptic "break," fulfilling thereby the "sacred goal of realizing the society of brotherhood and freedom, realizing the Kingdom of God on earth."[22] Nothing of value, Bakunin was now convinced, could be achieved apart from the people, "the only ground from which alone all the great acts of history have taken place, all the liberating revolutions."

> If anyone is alienated from the people, all that he does is, from the outset, damned to defeat. It is only possible to create, to really create, where there is a truly electrifying contact with the people. Christ and Luther came out of the *simple* people, and if the heroes of the French Revolution set with a mighty hand the first foundations of the future temple of freedom and equality, they were able to do so only because they were reborn in the tempestuous sea of the people's life.[23]

The German "Democrats" would not have been defeated in their first foray against the "castrated philosophers,"[24] he himself and others would not have had to flee Dresden, and Ruge's journal would not have been shut down, he told Ruge, "had we not been leading an isolated life in the clouds of academic theory and had the people been on our side."[25]

The entry now of the "people" into Bakunin's fantasy may account for another important change that began that winter. Although the "people" came not to replace but to fulfill the apocalypse, their coming nevertheless coincided with the beginning of a subtle but unmistakable secularization of the fantasy. What, he asked in his article on Weitling's communism, is it that has preserved "the sanctity of concord and love" since Christianity had ceased to play the leading part it had once played in European life? And his answer: "The holy spirit of freedom and equality, the spirit of pure humanity revealing itself to the people in thunder and lightning at the time of the French Revolution and like seeds of new life scattered everywhere by means of the revolutionary wave." The personal God of the spirit and of immortality that had been so important to him and that had survived both "right" Hegelian abstract formalism and "left" Hegelian atheism was now giving way to a deified secular idealism, a "holy spirit" of "pure humanity," which would henceforth be worshipped with no less devotion and honored with no less suffering than had the former God. The revelation that had come through the "thunder and lightning" of Paris was as holy and compelling as was its divine ancestor. "We were born under the revolutionary star. . . . We are on the eve of a new struggle all the more dangerous because its character is not only political, but religious. Why indulge in illusions: we are speaking of nothing less than a new religion, a religion of democracy, which began its new struggle, its life and death struggle, under the old banner of 'liberty, equality and brotherhood.' "[26]

Secularization, thus, meant nothing more than a change of names, as had been the case earlier when Bakunin had chosen to call his desires "objective" instead of "inner." While continuing to preach faith in God, he now urged others to believe as well "in the star that until now has constantly guided us,"[27] in the "mysterious force": "contrary to all the rationalists and all conventional truths there lies concealed in existence an incalculable mysterious force that guides to their goals all those who really thirst for life. . . . Never lose faith in this benevolent miraculous force that creates the unexpected."[28] In time, the "mysterious force" will follow its predecessors into oblivion, but then, too, nothing will have changed. The underlying needs and motivations always remain the same, whether projected and sanctified in God, Providence, the Absolute, Fate, Destiny, the Mysterious Force, Eternal Revelation, or, later, Nature and History. Whatever guaranteed the fulfillment of his destiny and vision and thereby allowed him to demonstrate his power and manliness was fine with him. "If it really came to me to achieve something significant, then no sacrifice could be considered great enough to offer up in gratitude for this fate. But if I am destined by nature to spiritual impotence, then, speaking honestly and not just talking, it is then completely immaterial to me whether I die one way or another."[29] Or, as he expressed it to Ruge that May 1843, in words more appropriate to the messianic hubris involved:

It is given to thinkers and poets to anticipate the future and to construct among the ruins and the putrefaction that surrounds us a new world of freedom and beauty. . . . There are only a few people noble enough to surrender themselves totally and irrevocably to the creative work of truth, the truth that liberates. There are only a few who have the capacity to transmit to their contemporaries these deep and intimate feelings and thoughts. But should even one of them succeed in becoming the voice of truth and captivate the world with his silvery voice, he would be assured of victory. . . .[30]

The "people's" revolution and the apocalypse became one and the same and the only means of achieving the Kingdom of God on earth, the holy spirit of freedom and equality, the religion of democracy, the birth pangs of the new and splendid world, the sacred mystical treasure, the new world of freedom and beauty. "I speak with you in the name of God, who wants to have you among his children," he had told the Beyer sisters years before. Now, he speaks as "the voice of truth," the great liberator who "captivates the world with his silvery voice."[31] But, to stress again the essential point here, he in no way abandoned his Christian apocalypse when he moved on to his people's revolution. The two continue in tandem, explicitly (as in *The Reaction in Germany*) for many years to come and implicitly for the remainder of his life. Thus, he could go right on referring in good conscience to the Gospels in defense of his ideals of a secular communal brotherhood, continue sending religious tracts to Tatiana, see in the Christian crusades analogies for the forthcoming social revolution, describe "true communism" as "the divine essence of Christianity," and liken himself and his revolutionary comrades to Jesus' martyred disciples—"seeds of new life scattered everywhere by means of the revolutionary wave." "To find a real person in our time, where we, the true democrats, the apostles of liberation are so few, when we are scattered across the face of the earth and suffer in anguished loneliness, to find a person and to befriend him is true happiness...."[32]

In guiding Bakunin to the "people," Weitling did more for him, however, than provide a weapon of destruction that made his fantasied conversion of impotence into omnipotence appear more realistic than it had in the purely theoretical *The Reaction in Germany*. In his portrait of the people and their revolutionary violence, Weitling introduced Bakunin to a world of passion that at once became a substitute for passions long denied him. "What a feeling, what indefinable bliss such striving and such power gives a person," he exclaimed to Ruge. "Oh, how I do envy you in this work, even your anger.... Oh, were I only in a position to be able to act together with you! To give all my life and blood for the liberation of the people!" Similarly, while spurning "the theoretical cosmopolitanism of the last century" as "cold, apathetic, rationalistic, lacking ground or passion...a dead and barren, abstract, theoretical construction, without even the tiniest spark of productive, creative fire," he praised Weitling's revolutionary communism for its "passion and fire.... In it are concealed a warmth and flame ...flame that can no longer be extinguished." One need only recall, if nothing else, his repeated references to "an impenetrable, cold crust that often repelled people from me" to appreciate the strength of this new attraction to the people's "passion and fire," "warmth and flame."[33]

Taken separately, such remarks, as well as phrases like "castrated philosophers," "truly electrifying contact with the people," and "reborn in the tempestuous sea of the people's life" might be viewed as no more than stylistic flourishes.[34] But considering them together and along with the many corresponding passages we have seen already and the corroborative echoes from other corners of his life and personality, the conclusion can hardly be avoided that much more than style is involved here and that the story these statements tell has little if anything to do with German politics at the time, or with any politics, then or thereafter. Now as always in his life, reality is a quarry from which he takes only what raw material he needs, then molds that material exclusively to fit those needs. What he takes from Weitling is an invaluable opportunity to immerse himself in the "passion and fire" of the people's violence and to gratify thereby the long repressed emotions that such violence served.

The "passion and fire," however, were still confined to theory. Nothing was happening. To be sure, the fantasy was getting richer by the month, as it absorbed new revolutionary imagery. But the actual content of his life and of the life around him remained unchanged throughout that first "revolutionary"year in Switzerland. He did spend some time with Weitling, who came to Zürich in May, and also became friends with several local radical politicians and journalists— August Follen and Julius Fröbel for example[35] —but his life style that year was hardly that of a revolutionary struggling to liberate the people. In fact, he spent much of that summer and autumn enjoying a delightfully bourgeois lakeside resort vacation with the Pescantinis at Nyon. He then went to Berne, where he remained through January 1844 with another friend, Adolf Reichel, a young German pianist and composer he had known in Dresden and who was, in Bakunin's words, "a stranger to everything political."[36]

Who can say how long his life would have gone on this way—bourgeois in fact, revolutionary in fantasy—had the "hawk" he had escaped not swooped down on him in his gentle sanctuary. Soon after he had met Weitling, the messianic tailor was arrested, less for his *Guarantees of Freedom and Harmony* than for a book he had just completed in which Jesus played the part of an illegitimate child turned revolutionary communist. Bakunin's name appeared in Weitling's papers and, therefore, also in the official reports, first those of the Swiss police and later those sent by the Russian envoy in Berne to his St. Petersburg superiors. In early February 1844 the sequence (slowly unfolding while Bakunin was enjoying himself at Nyon) climaxed in an order from the Russians in Berne directing Bakunin to return to Russia at once. Bakunin quickly left Berne and, together with Reichel, moved to Brussels, where he remained, except for a short trip to Paris in March, until July of that year, when he moved permanently to Paris.

From the time the order came in February 1844 to leave Berne, until another order came four years later at the end of 1847 to leave Paris, Bakunin lived in a vague political no-man's-land. It is a difficult period to assess, difficult to see in its own perspective, apart from what was to happen in the epochal revolutionary years that followed (1848-49). On the surface, judging by the names of those he met and talked with those years—a veritable who's who of the European "left" —these would appear to be intensely active, radical years. Lamennais, Proudhon, Pierre Leroux, Karl Marx, George Sand, Louis Blanc, Cabet, and so on—he met them all. Nor should that be surprising: he was the first more or less permanent Russian political émigré, now that he had refused to obey the order to return home, and was, moreover, known as the author of a powerful revolutionary article in Ruge's journal. Even without those credentials, however, his aristocratic standing and his eloquence, intensity, and captivating self-assurance would have doubtless won him entry. But beyond an occasional visit or discussion with these luminaries, what was he doing? Actually, the years were remarkably uneventful and unproductive,—empty years, except for two short items that he published in the local papers, until Bakunin made a speech in November 1847 that signaled the end of this inactive period and the beginning of the ensuing storm.

What "action" there was in the first Paris year (1844) began with a meeting of radicals in late March, during his brief trip to Paris from Brussels. Marx, Blanc, and Leroux participated, as did Botkin, visiting Paris at the time. Nothing came of this. Then, after coming permanently to Paris, he collaborated on a German radical journal in Paris, *Vorwarts,* and lived for a time with a brother of one of its editors. But there is no evidence of just what Bakunin did, and the editor's memoirs have nothing to say about his role. The only publication in 1844 that included something by him was Ruge's first—and last—issue of the *Deutsche-Französische Jahrbücher,* which Ruge had hoped would replace the *Dresden Deutsche Jahrbücher,* but the publication by Bakunin in it was simply his letter to Ruge of May the previous year discussed above.[37]

At the end of January the following year (1845) he was in print again, in a letter to the editor of *La Réforme.* Significantly, it is a letter written in reaction to another blow against him from the "hawk": as punishment for refusing to obey the will of the Tsar and return to Russia, he was deprived of his aristocratic rank and privileges and sentenced in absentia to Siberian exile. Since, as he wrote that October, he "favored Paris over Siberia," he chose to remain there "permanently."[38]

As Weitling had helped Bakunin find in the "people" a hero in his drama that was more convincingly real and powerful than the vague "left" Hegelian "Negative," so did this Tsarist harassment now crystalize for him a villain more concrete than the "Positive." His counter attack occupied two fronts, the nobility and the people. First, he scoffed from above at the autocracy for withdrawing rights and privileges that it had never truly given and at the gentry who foolishly thought they had such rights. Rather than being proud possessors of genuine rights, the gentry were distinguished only by their "lack of all noble impulses," their demoralized submission to unlimited power. They were as much enslaved as were the slaves they owned, worthy only of disdain. "And they call themselves aristocrats!" But, there was hope that all this would soon end. For there were among this generally wretched aristocracy some, "especially among the youth," who were motivated by "higher aspirations," "who suffered from this humiliating condition," and who were taking steps already to liberate themselves from it by closely and sympathetically following the advance of civilization and freedom in Europe and with all their strength trying to come nearer to the "people." There were, in other words, others like himself "striving to preserve, to bolster and maintain in themselves, and to ignite in others, the sacred flame of great and noble instincts."

Moreover, these noble youth had good reason to expect success, since the Russian people, in spite of all they had suffered for so long, also "possessed completely democratic instincts and habits." More important for the revolution than democratic habits, however, was the people's strength and capacity for violent revolution:

> In their semibarbaric nature one feels so much energy and sweep, such an abundance of mind and passion that knowing them one cannot but be certain that there yet stands before them a great world mission to realize.... The Russian people are moving forward, sire, against the evil will of the government. Scattered but extremely significant peasant risings against the landowner, multiplying to threatening proportions, unquestionably support this contention. It may well be that the moment is not far off when they will all flow together into a great revolution, and if the government does not hurry and liberate the people, much blood will flow.[39]

These remarks (including the hesitant note at the end of the statement) represent the completion of Bakunin's revolutionary posture. Early as this was in his career, all the basic patterns, themes, and dynamics were already in hand, or in mind. The world was sharply divided into good and bad. The enemy was the Russian autocracy and, by association, every comparable organization of power. Salvation would come from an alliance between a few at the top, those noble youth with "higher aspirations," with "great and noble instincts," and the many at the bottom, the people. The upheaval would be bloody, cataclysmic, apocalyptic. Finally, with respect to the concluding hesitancy, since the violence, "the passion and fire," always was associated in his unconscious with forbidden emotions, he was to remain fundamentally ambivalent about it. This theme will become especially familiar as Bakunin's revolutionary career develops, although we have already seen something of the ambivalence in *The Reaction in Germany*. While Bakunin would design several variations on this general revolutionary scenario in the coming years, the essentials would remain unchanged to the end, since they now satisfied his own inner needs and that, not correspondence with the real world, is all that mattered to him.

He was now ready for the revolution. But there was none on the horizon, especially none that might "annihilate" the "hawk" in the East. Still, a beginning had to be made, and the obvious place to begin while in Paris was with the principal contingent of Tsarist enemies there: the Polish refugees, smarting from earlier defeats and as determined as ever to revenge themselves, to liberate their homeland, and to get back home as victors.[40] They, of course, warmly approved of Bakunin's own—a Russian's—attack on their Russian oppressor. Some contacts were made after his *La Réforme* letter appeared, but they were few and short-lived.[41] As Bakunin later explained it, he was "Russian in spite of everything, even more a democrat, vis-a-vis the Polish emigration and people in the West in general, and dubious as well of the phrases and the hollow, futile, bombastic displays, which I have always disliked. And so I ended for the time being my relations with the Poles and saw none of them at all until the spring of 1846." Recalling his earlier domination over the members of the "holy commune," his belief that his will was God's will, and his uncompromising insistence on absolute independence, one can understand how he would find authentic cooperation with others difficult, at best: "The thought that I am now alone encourages me: when someone is alone, he is prouder." "I liked my independence too much to allow myself to become the slave or blind instrument of any secret society at all, not to mention any society whose views I did not share." (And as with the Poles, so with the German radicals: "I kept apart from them and decisively made it clearly known that I would not enter into their communist union of artisans and wanted to have nothing in common with them.")[42]

With the pride of independence, however, went the loneliness. When he broke his tentative ties with the Poles in early 1845, he was left with nobody, no cause, no movement. Once again he struck bottom. "Nowhere else have I ever felt so isolated, so estranged...so disoriented as in Paris," he later recalled:

> My life in Paris was hard, very hard....I found myself all of a sudden in the middle of a foreign land, in a spiritual atmosphere without any warmth, without family or relatives, without any field of action, without anything to do and without the least hope for something better in the future. Split off from my own country, and prohibited from returning...there were days when, by evening, I felt so depressed that I would quite often stop on the bridge that I usually had to cross to get home and ask myself whether it wouldn't be better for me simply to throw myself into the Seine and thereby drown this useless and joyless existence.[43]

Once more his letters home are filled with plaintive declarations of love and yearning for his sisters and brothers, scoldings for their not having written him now for years, questions about their life and times, directed to each in turn (except for Varvara: about her "I simply won't say anything; she has again become a wife"), and nostalgic recollections of the Premukhino joys he had shared with them. He had "suffered greatly, greatly and often fallen into despair," but "these memories are my greatest treasure: they preserve and sustain me."[44] If only Tatiana might come! "How I would look after you, if only we could be together, how I would try to set your heart aflame. Dear friend, give your grief to me: it is I who have the inalienable right to it. Let me hear a living word from you. Let me into your heart, your feelings.... Dear friend, for some time I have been having a fantasy—for, really, nothing is impossible for those with will and love enough—maybe, after a few years, we will meet in Paris and live together."[45] There were tender words as well for his father, the one who, in spite of the "wrongs he had done me," had inspired in his children a "love of nature and a sense of the finer things in life." He was "our guardian-angel."

But guardian against what or whom? "Without him, mother would have ruined and corrupted us."[46] Lonely and depressed, wanting, it would seem from these letters, only to be home again, he once more drew closer to his mother in the only way he could now that he was the manly revolutionary—by the same love-hate bond that he had drawn upon for solace when he had first entered upon this "last remaining career."

> You must all be together, all be happy in spite of our enemies; or, to put it better, our enemy—mother, for whom I have no feeling in my soul but damnation and the most profound disdain. She is the source of what is unclean in our family. Her presence, even her existence, is an offence to what is sacred.[47]

In exposing his pain and need to Paul, Bakunin revealed with extraordinary clarity the link between this original, primary "enemy" and his successive later political "enemies":

> How's father? I feel sorry for him. He also had the capacity for another kind of life. Is he still alive? Soon I will write him a final farewell letter without any practical, selfish aim, but only to say good-by to him and say a few words of love and farewell. As for our Mother, I damn her. In my soul there is for her no room for any other feeling but hatred and the deepest, unmitigated disdain—not for myself, but for you, whom she ruined. Don't call me cruel hearted. It's time for us to leave the

world of fanciful and powerless sentimentality; it's time to become real
people and to be as constant and forceful in hatred as we are in love
itself. Not forgiveness, but implacable war on our enemies, because they
are the enemies of all that is human in us, enemies of our dignity, of
our freedom. . . . Yes, the capacity to hate is inseparable from the capacity to love. We must forgive our enemies only after we have thrown
them down and utterly triumphed. But as long as they remain on their
feet, no mercy and no respite![48]

The roots of Bakunin's apocalypse are once again clearly evident—in the
transition, without pause, from the principal "enemy" (mother) to "enemies
of our dignity" in general; in the ferocity of the anger towards someone he has
not seen in five years; in the explicit association that he twice makes here between the "capacity to love" and the "capacity to hate"; and, particularly, in
the reasons, never stated but unmistakably implied, that he gives for his fury:
she was "the source of what is unclean in our family," "an offence to all that is
sacred," as she had earlier been "a constant offense to aesthetic feeling, completely lacking in femininity," a woman of "vulgar nature" and "unclean tendencies" whose "bad instincts" were "the source of every sin, all evil acts." Certainly, such rage, maintained at such intensity over so long a time and distance,
could hardly have been only the result of her trying "several times to subject our
sisters' pure, sacred world to her unclean world." It was his own oedipal dread of
being drawn into her "unclean world" that inspired such otherwise inexplicable
outrage, strong enough to assault "even her existence." (The oedipal source may
also be implied in his suggestive description of how he will triumph over his enemies "only after we have thrown them down . . . . as long as they remain on their
feet, no mercy and no respite." One recalls a similar double-meaning in the way
he had earlier lamented Liubov's fate were she to marry a "man who will with
hellish lust take off of her, one after another, the covers of sacred modesty. . . .")
    No less revealing than this direct association between "mother" and "en-
emies," the hate side of the love-hate dualism, is an association Bakunin made
between his beloved and the "people," the love side of the dualism, and the fact
that he made these two associations in the same letter.

I am passionately in love. I do not know if I am able to be loved as I
would like, but I will not despair. In any case I know that they [sic] do
care for me a great deal. I want to, I must deserve the love of the one I
love, loving her religiously, that is actively. She is now enslaved by the
most terrible, the most shameful slavery, and I must liberate her by
struggling against her oppressors, by enflaming in her heart a sense of
personal worth, by inspiring in her a need for freedom and a demand

for it, the instincts of indignation and independence, by evoking in her a consciousness of her own strength and her rights. To love means to desire freedom, complete independence for the other person: the first manifestation of authentic love is—the complete liberation of the object of that love. Only that being can truly love who is *totally free, independent not only of all others but also, and even mainly, of the one who loves that person and is loved in return*.... Should love involve dependency, then it would be the most *dangerous and repulsive* thing in the world....[49]

First of all, who is the object of this ardent love, the "they" that he fears may not yet care enough for him, the enslaved "her" he must liberate, as he had sought to liberate—using precisely the same language—his sisters and the Beyer sisters? Even the Soviet editor of Bakunin's letters, who strains mightily to preserve an image of normality and rationality in his notes on Bakunin, concludes that he is talking about his love for the "people" and argues at length against those who try to make one or another woman Bakunin knew at the time the beneficiary of these vows. (Were a particular woman involved, she would surely have appeared elsewhere and often in his letters. Also, who are the "oppressors"? And why if there is one particular woman is the pronoun "they" used when referring to the beloved?)[50] The sexual-incestual roots of his love for the "people" may also be seen in his insistence (and in the same letter in which he so venomously attacks his "unclean" mother) on total separation rather than intimate union as the essential attribute of true love and in the fact that he uses such an otherwise bizarre expression as "dangerous and repulsive" to describe a love that lacks this separation, this "total freedom" of the beloved "mainly" from the one who loves her.

In spite of his depression, loneliness, and nostalgic reminiscences of home that prompted these revelations, Bakunin had no intention of returning to Russia (how, in the light of all this—and Tsarist punishment—could he?) or of moderating his stand as "an implacable enemy of existing reality."[51] "'All or nothing'—that is my motto, my war cry, and I have not retreated one single step from its demands."[52] He remained ready for the revolution, but, in the mid-1840s, there was still none in sight. Perhaps in search of some kindred spirits, after the failure of his first approach to the Polish émigrés, he decided in 1845 to join the Freemasons. Considering his own synthesis of Enlightenment and Christian ideals and his attraction to small, detached, inspirational circles, there is nothing unusual about this step at the time. His religious sentiments and pronouncements continued as strong and as prominent as they had ever been, notwithstanding the increasing secularization of his millennial vocabulary. The only political activities he was later to recall from that year (1845) were those of two new German religious sects, the *Lichtfreude* and *Deutsche-Katholichen,* which had "excited the imagination of the masses" and which had "translated the thoughts and needs of the time into the language of religion, that is, the language of the people." Moreover, he added, in their collective communion, which they had inherited from the time of the early church, the *Deutsche-Katholichen* were openly preaching communism.[53]

It was also a religious theme that he chose when he decided in January 1846 to send a letter to the press in order to "bring myself again to the attention of the Poles, who had already forgotten about me."[54] Taking the "persecution of Catholic nuns in Lithuania" as a pretext for the new foray, he provided his French readers with a brief history of Russia's oppression of its Catholic and Uniate subjects in the Baltic, White Russian, and Ukrainian provinces, emphasizing the courageous resistance put up by the religious dissidents and picturing in passing the dire fate "of the defenseless women accused of heresy and disobedience to the Emperor."[55] After the letter appeared, in *Le Constitutionnel,* he took another step toward bringing himself again "to the attention of the Poles," by going to Versailles to meet with Polish émigré leaders. His plan was to offer them his services in promoting revolution among the Russians in the parts of Poland, Lithuania, and Podolia that were under Tsarist control, a revolution to be followed by a "federated republic of all slavic states.... federated, that is, only administratively, but centralized politically."[56]

Several points are noteworthy about this, his first, specific revolutionary proposal: his focus on Russia as the principal enemy, his advocacy of political centralization ("federation" was only administrative), and, especially, his astounding audacity in offering to undertake an enterprise of such vast proportions at a time when he had absolutely no contacts, no funds, no organization, no preparation, no serious knowledge of the current realities—nothing. Although more will be said later about this remarkably quixotic disregard for even the most elementary preparations, it is important to emphasize it here, since this is his first genuinely revolutionary gesture. "Reality" was still within him. Whatever he intuited as true and real was true and real: man could still know the truth "without leaving his own individuality, can know the universal, the true, and realize it by the force of his own free will." Had Bakunin been at any time seriously concerned with affecting the real world, with succeeding in his revolutionary actions, this disregard of objective conditions might be held against him. But that was never his intention. All that was important was to demonstrate to himself and to others that he had power, manliness, virility. As we will see later, the worst thing in the world for him would be to succeed, to face the challenge and obligations of actual political power. That would not only mean a loss of freedom, but also the assumption of his father's role and all its intolerable implications. As we have already seen, and as we will see increasingly in Bakunin's later encounters with power, it was not only through impotence and total separation from the world of "custom, propriety, and obligation" that Bakunin sought to escape that oedipal danger, but also through avoidance of any position involving explicit power and responsibility. To protect himself from that "most dangerous and repulsive thing in the world," therefore, meant not only to avoid his mother, but also to avoid having his father's manly power and authority. Of course, as I have tried to show and will continue gathering evidence to show, Bakunin never ceased searching for ways to achieve and experience what he was compelled to avoid: to return to his mother, for example, through the dialectical bond of hatred; to enjoy the honors of power and potency by the similarly dialectical path of suffering, detachment, and defeat; to fantasize control of indomitable revolutionary organizations that, however, were kept harmlessly secret and "invisible."

Because of sharp disagreements "in our views and national sentiments," no more came of this second approach to the Poles that had come of the first, and Bakunin "once again remained completely inactive."[57] The doldrums this time lasted a full year and a half. By late summer of 1847 he had even come to feel that "Paris, at least right now, is not a place where one can really feel oneself alive." His interest had ebbed, he went on in this letter of August fifth, and he found himself feeling "lazy, my primordial national sin." The horizon was, at best, hazy, uncertain: "I have still not come to anything definite. I am still involved only in a search for life and truth, and anyone at my age who still finds himself in the process of developing, does not much feel like writing about himself." He was now 33, living with and off Reichel. The Paris years, indeed, had not been good to him. But he refused despondency: "you should not for an instant think that I am disheartened, that I have lost the joy of life, or in any way changed my former outlook. On the contrary, I think that I am in every way stronger." Moreover, he concluded, however bleak things looked then, "the moment is not far off when we will have to act."[58]

By the beginning of the next month, the haze began to clear. True, the Polish émigrés seemed to him to be blundering badly by directing their revolutionary plans only against Russia rather than against the other two oppressors of the Poles as well, Prussia and Austria. Moreover, he thought that they spent too much time in cafes drinking and that they should "display a little more dignity and restraint." By contrast, however, events were moving along all right in Italy ("the Pope seems to be, nonetheless, a sensible, efficient man"), in Switzerland, and especially in France, where a series of recent troubles, which Bakunin listed, clearly signaled an "approaching storm."[59]

Although he was aware of the political crisis brewing in Paris that late summer and fall, he did not involve himself in it, preferring instead to concentrate on the struggle that really concerned him, "the Polish-Russian movement" and its principal target, the "hawk" in the East. Having now no contacts with the Poles themselves, he had to limit this involvement once again to that of an outside intellectual, writing something, as he said in a letter he was doing, about the forthcoming revolutionary alliance of Russians and Poles against the Tsar.[60] It is surely significant that on the eve of the Paris revolution of 1848 he gave his attention not to a real revolution ready to explode on his doorstep, but to a nonexistent revolutionary alliance far away in the East—still the location of the real battles that were taking place within him. It was "in the service of this great cause that I decided to dedicate my feeble talents and all my convictions and my strength."[61] Perhaps it was because he concentrated on this imaginary conflict and alliance and not on the genuine struggle then beginning in France that he continued to be so despondent: "It sometimes seems to me that a famous Swedish doctor froze me for some better time, so frequently does all feeling for life and consciousness leave me.... Aren't you really weary of Russians and just plain bored with all this barren exaltation, this Platonic love of freedom, these splendid dreams...to be realized, maybe, in two or three centuries off someplace in Turkey or Asia?"[62]

A few weeks later, in November, too ill to leave his room, he was visited by two young Poles who came to invite him to give a talk at a celebration commemorating the Polish revolution of 1831. He accepted "with joy," ordered a wig (it seems his illness had required a head shaving), spent three days writing his speech, presented it at the end of that month, and, mainly because of the later reverberations of the speech, was catapulted to fame as a revolutionary leader. The focus of that speech was the same as it had been in the pieces he had sent to *La Réforme* and *Le Constitutionnel,* the Russian autocracy. The alliance that was to bring the tyrant down was also basically the same—the young Russian noblemen who were "ashamed" and "repelled" by their position and the "people" who were "only superficially corrupted" but who possessed an "inner virginal beauty," an "unknown treasure." To this core alliance, Bakunin was now adding the support of the Polish nationalists, not so much because the purely Russian alliance (nobles-people) seemed to him unrealistic, which would not have troubled him in the least, but because the Poles in Paris were the closest kin to his private cause, the only ones abroad he could work with and thereby prove that he had really descended from theory to practice, that he was at last manfully active. Also, they were the only ones around who could save him from his desolate isolation and loneliness. "I come to you as a brother, and you will not reject me (shouts from all sides: 'NO! NO!)." The essential and astounding fantasy of the entire enterprise is apparent enough from the main theme of the speech: "Gentlemen, in the name of this new society, the real Russian nation, I offer you alliance.... I lack the legal authority to speak like this to you, but, I feel, and without the slightest pretentiousness in the claim, that at this solemn moment the Russsian nation itself speaks through my mouth. (Applause.)"[63]

He had been away from Russia seven years. He had no "revolutionary" contacts there, received few letters even from his family, and knew now even less about the country than the little he had known when he was there. He was completely alone and impoverished, had just written Herweg about his loss of "all feeling for life and consciousness," and had indicated deep discouragement over "barren enthusiasms" for utopias three hundred years off. Yet, there he stood, speaking in the name of the Russian people, offering the Poles a grand alliance, promising them not only victory over their common foe, but, rising higher and higher, the "liberation of all Slavic peoples languishing under a foreign yoke," and—higher still—the "final collapse of despotism in Europe!"[64] How would he do it? For an answer, one need only recall a few of his earlier declarations: "All wills must give way before the one who appears before them as God's interpreter." "Everything must become better, and what is better is what I want, which means that what I want must necessarily be." "Here is the measure for determining what is authentic thought: if the thought...forces you to say 'everything is splendid, life is bliss.'" "The pure 'I' in knowing itself knows the world objective to it." *"Ce que je veux, Dieu le veut."*[65]

A long spiral voyage was now completed. The Premukhino drama was the first stage. It was too personal, too intimate, and led to the "terror" and the "hell" of late 1836. Two years of withdrawal and Hegelian "reconciliation" followed. Then came the gradual descent (carefully maintaining the defensive Hegelian distance and abstraction all the way down) from the coldly schematic Positive-Negative confrontation, through Weitling's "people's" violence, down to what now seemed to be a concrete national movement of Poles in alliance with a revolutionary movement of the Russian "people" and radical young nobility. What we see at the end of the voyage, however, is the same Premukhino conflict, thinly disguised, that we saw at the beginning. Bakunin's first important political statement, his address to the Poles, was basically a new version of the old drama he had been acting and reenacting for years. In place of his parents and all parents there is now the "hawk," the imperial despot, and, by association, all despots; in place of his "pure" sisters and the Beyer girls to be saved from their "fate worse than death," there are now the "people" with their "inner virginal beauty" and "unknown treasure" to be liberated in the coming "storm of salvation." It is only the "storm" that, in a sense, differentiates the present variation from the youthful Premukhino variation: the "left" Hegelian-Weitling influence had provided him, in the theory of absolute negation and the practice of the people's revolutionary "passion and fire," an outlet for those "passions that seethe within" that had not been available in Romantic *schönseligkeit* or in the successive Idealist philosophies he had earlier tried. Even the fine points are still there, for example, the barely visible weakness and passivity peeking through the bombast: the autocracy would fall, he assured the Poles, not so much because any organization he might now be initiating would bring it down, but rather because it would collapse from within—"the Russian government day by day by its very own actions weakens and disorganizes itself to a terrifying extent."[66] Both parts of this last remark are intriguing, the emphasis on self-destruction, precluding as it does the need of active opposition on his part, and that surprising word "terrifying," which may reflect the elemental fear of having to replace the overthrown authority, recalling what authority symbolizes to Bakunin. It is above all, however, the pose of omnipotence that has not changed since the "holy commune" days. Instead of God speaking through his lips, it was now the Russian people. He had done, in fact, what he vaguely hinted at in his letter to Ruge four years before: "should any one of them succeed in becoming the voice of truth and captivate the world with his silvery voice he would be assured of victory."[67] That he did in fact captivate his Polish audience is certain. Why should they not warmly applaud this dazzling prophet who so fervently echoed their own hopes and dreams, bolstered them with fantasies they would never have dared imagine, assured them with such boundless confidence "an early liberation, a speedy return to your home"?[68]

His illusions fed their dreams, as their enthusiastic praise fed his illusions. And so it would continue throughout Bakunin's life, with the illusions becoming ever grander and the applause ever louder in this strange ritual of symbiotic self-deception. His eloquence (and, as his fame grew, his prominence) confirmed other dreamers' fantasies, while their applause and admiration became the confirmation for his own. It was his very distance, his radical alienation from the very causes he so zealously championed, that allowed him to soar so high and gain thereby such commanding influence: His tones were silvery because they came from so far away. Driven by violent energies that had nothing at all to do with the adopted movements, energies generated deep within his own tangled personality and early life, and unrestrained by practical considerations necessary for genuine success, he freely fashioned his borrowed programs into compelling fantasies far beyond the daring of those less driven by illness from within and more constrained by reality from without. Without the applause and the support his fantasies might well have collapsed, and without the fantasies it is doubtful that his fragmented self would have survived. They had become and would remain the structure of his sanity.

Befitting the almost mythological aura his career now began to assume, his November hubris was followed immediately by severe punishment, with the Russian state, appropriately, in the role of the jealous god. Enraged by this attack from one of their own, in support of the state's most relentless enemy, the Polish nationalists, Russian authorities pressured French authorities to expel Bakunin from Paris. But that was far less painful or damaging for him than were the rumors the French and Russian authorities now began to spread about his character and past life, to the effect that he had been a Russian agent who had been fired because he talked too much. The consequences of these two attacks against him were to compete with each other for years to come: while the slander did serious damage to his image among other revolutionaries, the expulsion had just the opposite effect of what was intended—it brought him Europeanwide fame.

If one were to choose a single event to mark the beginning of Bakunin's illustrious career, the honor should go to this December fourteenth directive ordering him out of Paris. The leaders of the opposition to the Guizot government (the February revolution was only two months away now) used the expulsion as evidence of how low France had fallen under a government that so readily did the bidding of the Russian state. The speech itself, which might otherwise have remained only a glorious memory for the Poles who had heard it, was published by *La Réforme* on December fourteenth, the day of Bakunin's expulsion—in connection, that is, not with the Polish national struggle, but with a French political struggle in which Bakunin had not at all been involved. Four days after *La Réforme* published the speech, it printed a defense of Bakunin and a protest against French submission to Russian pressure. Similar declarations, each further spreading the heretofore barely known name of the gallant martyr, were delivered at successive opposition banquets. Finally, on February fourth, Vaven, a National Assembly deputy and its presiding officer, vigorously defended Bakunin and the Polish cause. In response, the French government, in the person of the Minister of Internal Affairs, Duchâtel, sinisterly spoke of "serious reasons" for the expulsion that could not be divulged without going "into personal details." An outrageous slander of "this man of outstanding intelligence and profoundly democratic convictions," *La Réforme* replied. With each exchange, Bakunin's image bloomed. From Brussels, where he had gone when he left Paris, he himself challenged Duchâtel ("man to man" and "speaking in the name of all my suffering and oppressed brothers") to back up his innuendo with facts or withdraw the slander. In the meantime, Bakunin said he would go right on doing his "duty," confident in having the "sympathies of all those who suffer and hope."

When Bakunin wrote this from Brussels, he was already preparing "a new triumph" to keep the accelerated momentum of his destiny going—another speech announcing "an imminent European revolution, a terrible cataclysm" and proclaiming a "great future for the Slavs." "Let us prepare," he concluded, sounding very much the artillery officer preparing his troops for battle, "and when the hour strikes let each of us do our duty." But as rapidly as his fame spread now, so did the ruinous slander concocted by French and Russian officials. "At the time," he later recalled, "the Poles were more suspicious of me than ever." Besides the earlier rumor of his being a former agent, the French added a new one, to the effect that, as Bakunin recounts it, he had refused to return to Russia not because of political beliefs, but because he had been guilty there of financial fraud.[69]

The rumors and the effect he felt they were having made his weeks in Brussels an unhappy period, in spite of his rising prominence, and caused him to doubt what he was doing and where he was heading.[70] Perhaps reflecting these tensions and uncertainties, his actions during these months in Brussels reveal several unflattering traits that were to remain with him throughout his political life. He became a secretive intriguer, drawing close to one leader or faction as he criticized another. He wrote, for example, to one émigré Pole against others ("I won't even bother to talk about Constantine Zalecki: he's kind, but really laughable") and even against an old acquaintance, Lelewel, who had befriended him years before and who had set up his Brussels speaking occasion, the "new triumph" ("As a person, I deeply respect him ... but he is a broken man and a complete nullity in politics. . . . Moreover, he has made friends with a Polish yid, someone named Lubliner"). With the Pole to whom he was confiding these sentiments he was all sweetness and light: "Candor, complete honesty has been the basis of all my relations with Vladislav and with you and will always continue to be so. . . . With others, I am sometimes diplomatic, really against my will, and, perhaps, there may still be many times that I am forced into this by people that I will have to deal with. But with you two—never."[71] It seems fitting that at precisely this time he was at work on an article about Belgian Jesuits and was himself, as he recalls, "the focus of Jesuit propaganda" aimed at converting him to Catholicism. As for Lubliner, the "yid," Bakunin had a few more words about him in a letter at the time to Herweg: "a Jew here who is trying to pass as a Pole ... and one of the most unbearable creatures one could imagine."[72] (Except for the anti-Semitism, the atmosphere of secrecy, manipulation, and intrigue is once again reminiscent of his earlier correspondence with his sisters and the Beyer sisters).

Events soon spared him sinking any deeper into this mire. The "terrible cataclysm" that he had predicted occurred in Paris on February twenty-third. One is tempted, here at least, to praise him for insightful prediction; but, then, one recalls that he had been predicting imminent catastrophe for at least five years now, and that he would go on predicting it for most of his life, as do all prophets of apocalypse. He left for Paris at once, on the twenty-third, but could not arrive until the twenty-sixth, because the Belgium train stopped at the French border and he had to walk the rest of the way. His description of the "paroxysm" that his first direct, "electrifying contact" with the people brought him could serve as a classic expression of apocalyptic rapture, even though it was written several years after the event and under circumstances (his "Confession" to the Tsar) in which he might be expected to have toned down descriptions of his revolutionary ecstasy.

> Sire, I cannot give you a clear account of the month I spent in Paris, because it was a month of spiritual inebriation. Not I alone, but everyone was intoxicated. Some from insane fear, others from insane rapture, insane hopes. I got up at five, at four, in the morning and went to sleep at two. All day I was on my feet. I took an active, resolute part in all the assemblies, meetings, clubs, marches, demonstrations—in a word, I inhaled the intoxicating revolutionary atmosphere through all my senses, through my pores. It was a feast without beginning or end. I saw everyone and no one, since everyone was lost in a single vast, aimless crowd. I spoke with everyone, but cannot remember what I said to them or they to me, for at every step came new impressions, new adventures, fresh news. . . . It seemed as though the whole world was turned upside down. The improbable became the usual; the impossible, the possible; the possible and the customary—senseless. In a word, one's mind was then in such a state that were someone to come and say 'the good God has just chased the devil from the heavens, and proclaimed there a republic' everyone would have believed him and none would have been surprised.[73]

Three times in the few pages he gives to these heady days in his "Confession," he speaks of a "miracle": first, with reference to the power "that fell into their hands by some sort of unexpected miracle;" then, in discussing the conservatives, who as a result of their unexpected defeat came "to believe in all the miracles and impossibilities even more than did the democrats;" and, finally, with respect to the "profound instinct for discipline" he discovered among the workers, so remarkable that "were these French workers to find a leader worthy of them, able to understand and to love them, he would be able to accomplish miracles with them."[74] It was, for him, the ideal revolution: all power miraculously bestowed, as the old aeon crumbled by itself and the children of the new heaven and new earth enjoyed their endless "feast." No wonder he felt that he had been "present at the birth of a new world," as he wrote in a letter to *La Réforme* on March thirteenth, a world in which "yesterday's utopia became from today on the only thing possible, rational and practical."[75] "There is a lot of mysticism" in his politics, he admitted to a friend at the end of 1847. "But," he went on, "who is not a mystic? Can there be a drop of life without mysticism.... We go on existing within a vibrant, living sphere, surrounded by miracles, by life forces, and each step we take may be the one that calls them forth, without our even knowing it, often even independent of our will."[76]

The real "miracle" of the revolution that made "the impossible, possible" for Bakunin and that so intoxicated him had nothing to do with French politics. It was the miracle he himself had discovered for resolving, through the "paroxysm" of the "people's" revolution, some of his own deepest contradictions and for gratifying, if only in fantasy, some of his most deeply repressed emotional needs. It was no longer only through a fantasy of revolutionary violence, but also through actual participation in revolution that he could enjoy at least the illusion of immense power and sacred honor, while at the same time remaining absolutely free and (recalling the meaning of "freedom" for him) chaste.

Moreover, by falling "passionately in love" with the "people" and experiencing an intoxicating "paroxysm" through the "electrifying contact with the people," their "passion and fire," their "warmth and flame," he not only found a way to release repressed "animal passions," but also a way of maternal reunion, a reunion that was both narcissistic and, by the dynamics argued earlier, incestual. There is much more than coincidence of style involved in Bakunin's repeated birth and oral imagery, in his being "reborn in the tempestuous sea of the people's life;" his earlier prophecy of being among the "first born of a new mother;"[77] his description of how, in response to von Stein's book on the people's revolutionary movements, he once again "threw" himself into his study, driven by "hunger" and "thirst," and sensed in the experience another rebirth, an "annunciation;" his recollections of the pleasures of revolution as pleasures enjoyed at a "feast without beginning or end" (both parts of the statement are revealing); and his later repeated references to his "thirst for revolution."[78] Setting these comments alongside the comparable statements of 1834, when he first used this oral imagery of "being fed and nurtured" with the "warmth so sweet" and being thereby "reborn," what we see is another lucid reflection of the merger of pre-oedipal and oedipal patterns that was the ultimate root of his character and pronouncements. Bakunin is passionately in love with the "people" as both nurturing mother (feast, birth, hunger, thirst) and electrifying, intoxicating, sensual wife, able to provide the long-denied "paroxysm," the "passion and fire." Both "warmth and flame" are needed, the narcissistic "warmth so sweet" and the sexual-incestual "passion and fire." Bakunin practically acknowledged this sublimation of blocked sexual passion into revolutionary "paroxysm" when, for example, he wrote the Herwegs in September, 1847, that "soon things will be fine, soon life will begin for us, and we will again, together, be *healed* and able to work with the free scope and zeal that all three of us crave.... I await my, or, if you will, our communal bride—the revolution. We will be truly happy, that is, begin to be our true selves only then, only when the whole globe is engulfed in flame."[79] Or, as he was to express the same substitution somewhat later: the revolutionary force will "renew both the world and us, brothers, open the way for us to pour out vigorously our inner fullness like fresh spring juices into the stiff, frozen life of the people of Europe.[80]

In spite of the compelling force of these and so many similar expressions of Bakunin's apocalyptic violence, we should not forget the other side: although the wellsprings of the violent rhetoric and the need for "passion and fire" are very real and irrepressible, no less so is the passive, detached, fearful side, however muted and (relative to the violence) infrequently publicized that side is. We saw this, for example, in the *Reaction in Germany*, in spite of its fierce proclamations and predictions.[81] It is also evident in Bakunin's repeated descriptions of the end of the old regime as a process of breakdown from within rather than from direct confrontation and defeat by opposing forces, i.e., by Bakunin himself: power "fell into their hands by some sort of unexpected miracle,"[82] the Russian government "by its very own actions weakens and disorganizes itself to a terrifying extent,"[83] and other examples we will see later.[84] In this same connection, finally, we should recall that Bakunin made his remarkably swift rise to worldwide revolutionary fame less as a result of what he himself had done than as a consequence of what had been done to him, the harassment he had undergone at the hands of the French and Russian authorities, his suffering.

This relationship between Bakunin's suffering and his fame, both growing together, each dependent on the other, was to become a pattern in his later political life, as suffering and olympian, messianic pride had gone together in his youth. If less were known about him, one might draw analogies from Greek epics and tragedies and speak of areté and até, heroic power and retribution. But he has told us too much about himself for that. Suffering is not punishment for his heroic action: his suffering *is* his heroic action, and its roots and proper context lie elsewhere than in Promethean power. His celebration of suffering, as we have seen, had been a constant theme in his earlier life, both before and after leaving Russia. Throughout the desolate 1840s, as one might have expected, the word and the corresponding mood are ever present in his letters: suffering continued to be described as necessary, richly beneficial, and pleasurable. If he favored George Sand over his former favorite Bettina, it was, he said, because she knew more about the "great suffering that exists in real life." While one might argue as to whether or not his difficulties at the time were really crushing enough to warrant the anguish, the point is not the fact of his distress, but the fact that he feeds it, cherishes it, makes the most he can of it in order to convey to himself and others the image of himself as an innocent victim of circumstance, suffering vastly and unjustly, but manfully carrying on, indeed, growing stronger and better with each blow. He is still, in short, proving his virile power by proving his capacity to suffer powerfully.

But if passivity repeatedly accompanies violence, so does the violence continually flow from passivity. Rather than diminish the violence required for the display of virile power and the supply of "passion and fire," as one might assume, the passivity and the need to suffer (or at least to appear to himself to be suffering) only fed the flames. First of all, in order to imagine himself (and actually to live his life) as a powerful sufferer, he had to portray the world to himself and to others in such a way as to provide the appropriate conditions for his own victimization and for the victimization of his beloved "people," whom he had been summoned to liberate—and to suffer still more in the process. It was probably as much the real suffering of the people (a mirror for his own subjective, psychological pain and self-punishment) that drew him to them as it was the people's capacity for vengeful violence and the opportunities that violence provided as an outlet for his own vengeance and narcissistic rage, as a vehicle for his pose of virile power, as a substitute sensuality for his repressed "animal passions," and for the other ends that violence so well served in his complex drama. Also, given his extreme solipsism, his by now habitual narcissistic remodeling of the world to reflect himself, he inevitably saw the world as engaged in the same drama of purification and redemption through suffering, rebirth through pain, that he himself had been experiencing through most of his life. If he must suffer to prove that he is pure (to punish himself, that is, for the fact that he is not), so must the world.

History has always been rich in lessons to make us fearfully suspicious of heroic sufferers preaching love, yet prophesying catastrophic destruction. To Bakunin this was the ideal combination, the very one that, to his mind, Jesus and his apocalypse exemplified. For over a decade now he had been convinced, as statements from his letters and articles cited earlier amply testify, that in his pursuit of an apocalypse of his own that would purify the world, he was being true to authentic Christianity as he understood it and to the message and the model of Jesus. No valid sense of Bakunin is possible apart from his constant sense of himself as a Suffering Servant and Savior. It is not hubris and nemesis that we are dealing with here, but the contours of Calvary—unless they are the same.

Intoxicating though the "paroxysm" and the "feast" had been in Paris that winter of 1848, they could not last. The French democrats, Bakunin himself realized, now had to "sober up, for they had to get to work and strengthen the power"[85] they had won. And that was clearly not for him. Moreover, although he had been in France some five years and was on friendly terms with various factions in the opposition, he had never gotten seriously enough involved in French politics to be in a position now to make any meaningful contribution to the new France, even had he chosen to do so, of which there is no sign. Watching, enraptured, the demise of the old world was one thing; getting down to work in and with the new world was something quite different—the "fussy, bureaucratic job" and (by the association discussed earlier) "the most dangerous and repulsive thing in the world."[86] Besides, his calling was elsewhere, in the East: "after two or three weeks of this intoxication, I sobered up a little and began to ask myself, what should I do now?" His mission, he answered, "was at the Russian frontier."[87]

But if his "thoughts naturally belong to Russia," as he wrote to *La Réforme,*[88] the Revolution belonged to France. Somehow the two had to be linked; "revolution" and "Russia" had to be brought together. Again intuition and imagination solved the problem easily: the revolution begun in Paris simply would "spread everywhere," for when France "is inflamed and aroused, the blaze rages everywhere." Soon, "maybe in less than a year," the revolutionary blaze would spread eastward engulfing Austria, Italy, Germany, Poland, and so on, not stopping until "all of Europe, *not excluding Russia* was transformed into a federated democratic republic. Impossible, they will say? Careful now! That word belongs to yesterday, not today." Far from being impossible, it was not even very difficult: the revolutionary movement would sweep ahead "without even taking the trouble to overthrow all the phantoms of oppression, falsehood and deception accumulating in Europe over the centuries, but simply chase them away without effort and just about without any turmoil at all." "No one would dare oppose it in open battle."[39] Victories, at no cost to the victors. More miracles. The enemy just melts away as the apocalyptic blaze spreads on ineluctably. Everything for nothing: the other side of all-or-nothing. It is still infantile omnipotence concealing an essential impotence. Since the "phantoms" would be "chased away" "without effort" (presumably as "the good God has just chased the devil from the heavens"), preparation and provisions were of little importance. Still, he had to begin something somewhere, and since there were rumors, unfounded, that a revolutionary government had been established in Poznan, he decided to go there to see "if a war with Russia had broken out yet."[90] Did he know anyone there? he was asked in a conversation *en route* that he himself relates. "Except for several young men whom I often met at the University of Berlin, I don't know anyone." Did he have any contacts with the Russians? "None at all, but I put all my hopes on propaganda and on the powerful spirit of the revolution, which has now conquered the whole world."[91]

"Spirit of revolution," "the holy spirit of freedom and equality, the spirit of pure humanity," "the revolutionary star," "mysterious forces," the Absolute, Providence, God—different names for the same power in his private dream language. And the fantasy grew and grew, feeding on itself. Recalling in his "Confessions" the reasons for this trip to the East, though perhaps distorting the account somewhat to curry favor and forgiveness from Tsar Nicholas, he claimed that he was motivated by fear of an alliance being formed in a newly "liberated Europe against Russia," aimed at "driving Russia back into Asia." "That," he said elsewhere, "was too much for me, a Russian. I wanted a European war, a war against the Russian state for the liberation of Poland, but not for the destruction of the Russian people, whom I cherish with all my soul." His aim was "to work simultaneously on the Russians and the Poles in such a way that this war would not be allowed to degenerate into a war of Europe against Russia." He would turn the war from one of "Germanized Poles against the Russian people" into "a war of liberated Slavs united against the Russian Emperor."[92]

The megalomania of all this must surely astound. Other than the notoriety that French and Russian harassment had given him, he had nothing. Except for some 2,000 francs that the new French officials had loaned him (which "I was not able to repay"),[93] he had no funds whatsoever. He had lost what contacts he still had with the Poles,[94] those left, that is, after the disputes, suspicions, and intrigues. And apart from a letter of introduction Herweg had given him to a German opposition leader and his own ties with Ruge, he had no serious connections with the German movement. Finally, as we have seen, he was just as ill-prepared with respect to Poznan and Russia. Yet, there he was on his way to move whole nations this way and that, to change one nonexisting alliance he disliked into another he desired, to prevent a war against the Russian people, and turn it—by himself—into a war of "liberated Slavs" (which fantasy had already accomplished) against the Tsar.

The return voyage eastward began March thirty-first, when he left Paris for Frankfurt with the introduction from Herweg to the German leader he hoped to meet there. He arrived still aglow with the excitement of Paris, "like a madman," in his words, "still feverish" with revolutionary ardor.[95] Although, or, better, because, Frankfurt was at the time seriously engaged in the real and tedious work of laying foundations for what the liberals hoped would be a constitutional government, Bakunin "remained in total isolation" and left for Berlin after a week and a half. He stopped for a week at Cologne, to wait for his luggage to catch up with him, and there calmed down a little: the passions of revolution could not survive the "philistine quiet" that reigned there.[96] Next came Berlin, where he arrived on the twentieth of April. He had planned to stay two days then continue on to Poznan. The police kept him to his schedule by arresting him on the twenty-second, because of his ties with Herweg who was supposedly then on his way to Baden with a revolutionary legion. In spite of his ties with Herweg and the general tensions of the times, Bakunin was released in return for a promise not to go to Poznan or remain in Berlin. Moreover, the police not only returned his false passport to him, but gave him another one. Perhaps this is a measure of how serious a revolutionary threat he was considered at the time.[97]

The following day he was in Leipzig, where he met Ruge, urged him to abandon his "philistine" intentions of running for the new Frankfort Parliament, and, by pressuring him into missing the meeting that was to select candidates, did actually help ruin his chances that time. "Don't worry about it," he said in response to Ruge's irritation, "after the Slavic revolution we will compensate you for the ingratitude of the Saxon philistines."[98] That done, he was on his way again, on the twenty-fourth, to Breslau, arriving the twenty-sixth. Here he set to work on his Polish-Russian alliance. Once again, however, the relationship collapsed almost as soon as it began. "I felt myself a stranger among them, and the more sugary their words, the colder my heart became and the less we were able to understand each other. . . . Finally losing patience, I began to keep away from them. . . ." Relations with the Germans were not much better. Although they warmly greeted him, he recalled, they were in his opinion just "playing at politics": "there were no conspiratorial groups or serious politics. . . . Their clubs were nothing but schools for elocution or, more precisely, schools for chitchat." So passed the month of May. With Poznan forgotten and nothing else in prospect, "I remained bored and anxious, awaiting the right moment."[99] Not surprisingly, the anxiety and feeling of "coldness"—a favored image, as we have seen, for Bakunin when describing himself—intensified as he moved homewards again, towards the "hawk." "The farther North I go," he wrote from Cologne "the more depressed and fearful I feel. The dark Russian power is there."[100] Similarly, in his "Confession": "my soul got colder and colder. At Cologne a vague, indescribable anxiety seized me."[101] He is again approaching the world of "hell, hell with all its terrors," and we should keep this "vague, indescribable anxiety" in mind as we enter the denouement of this, Bakunin's first real campaign as an "Apostle of Liberation."

All he could do now was wait, as he had waited through the mid-1840s, wait to be "permeated" again by the "holy spirit of freedom," wait for the next "electrifying contact" with the people's revolution. The wait was not so long this time: "there was talk about a Slavic Congress. I decided to go to Prague in the hope of finding there an Archimedes point for my activities."[102] The phrase "Archimedes point" was well chosen. The revolutionary "blaze" that was to "spread everywhere" and sweep Reaction away "without effort" had not yet behaved as it should. A new force was needed, but Bakunin, isolated and powerless as he was, had none. To make up for the lack, he decided, as he was often to do later, to make use of other movements and organizations, such as the Prague Congress that he now joined and tried to mold in his own apocalyptic image.

For the organizers and leaders of the Congress, the word "impossible" belonged to the world of today as well as yesterday: they saw no "miracles" on the horizon. Moderates and liberals, they had a sane regard for circumstances that limited the range and the speed of their action. Like it or not, Central and Eastern Europe was a maelstrom of conflicting national and class aims. Bohemians, Slovaks, Moravians, Poles, Ruthenians, Germans, Magyars, Serbs, Croats, Jews, Rumanians all viewed the loosening of traditional Prussian and Austrian imperial authority only from the perspective of their own particular interests. Bohemian liberals in Prague and German liberals in Frankfurt both fought for representative government at home but disagreed completely about relations between the two movements: Frankfurt liberals saw Bohemia as part of the coming united Germany, while the Bohemians made the avoidance of that fate one of their principal aims. Contrariwise, any move toward Czech independence, however much this might please the Czechs, confronted the influential German element in Bohemia with the prospect of drowning in a Slavic sea. Then there was Russia to consider. If the Czech and Hungarian independence movements resulted in the complete collapse of the Austro-Hungarian Empire, Palacky and other Czech leaders of the Congress were convinced that Russia would move in to fill the vacuum. For such reasons as these, leaders like Palacky and Thun, the chairman of the committee organizing the Congress, believed that the best that could be expected, the goal that would best respond to these constraining realities, was an autonomous Czech state within a preserved Austrian Empire.

Until his arrival in Prague at the end of May, a few days before the Congress opened, Bakunin had neither concerned himself with any Austro-Hungarian affairs, spent any time there, nor, if we are to credit his own words, known until then "a single Slav" other than Poles and Russians.[103] But, *"Ce que je veux, Dieu le veut,"* and what they both wanted was simple and clear: All the Slavs should unite against all the tyrants—Austrian, Prussian and, the ultimate target, Russian. As for the age-old conflicts that divided the Slavs, they were a result of the Slavs having "forgotten the sacred bonds of race and blood that unquestionably should have united them for the realization of their common destiny."[104]

In Paris eight months before he had spoken only for the Russian people. Now, in June, he speaks for all Slavs. "Begin your union this way," he told the delegates at the Congress, or at least says he told them: "Proclaim that you, Slavs, not Austrians, but inhabitants of Slavic land in the so-called Austrian Empire, have come together and united at Prague in order to lay the basis of a future free and great federation of all Slavic peoples and that, in the expectation of being joined by Slavic brothers in the Russian Empire, in Prussian lands, in Turkey, you Czechs, Moravians and Poles of Galicia, Ruthenes, Silesians, Slovaks, Serbians, Croations, and Dalmations have concluded among yourselves a powerful and permanent defensive and offensive union...." In addition, they should demand from the Hapsburgs the withdrawal from Italy of all Slavic troops and should send envoys to Hungary "to resolve peacefully the Slavic-Hungarian question." Besides achieving "the complete destruction of the Austrian Empire," his "other and more important goal was to find in the union of Slavs the point of departure for an extension of revolutionary propaganda to Russia." From beginning to end, Tsarist power—and what it represented to him—remained the real enemy: "Only by way of the liberation of Poland will the Russians be able to achieve political and national freedom," he told the Polish-Ruthenian section of the Congress to which he was assigned.[105] Not that the overthrow of the Tsar would mean the end of Russian power. On the contrary: "In the Slavic union I saw the fatherland writ large, for the day that Russia joined it, Poles and Czechs would of course be obliged to cede it first place."[106]

The evidence concerning Bakunin's participation at the Congress is too contradictory to allow definite conclusions. His initial participation was a result of the failure of the invited Russian participant to attend and, then, of the defeat of a proposal by Palacky and other leaders to limit participation to Austrian Slavs. As a voting participant Bakunin was assigned to the Polish-Ruthenian section and was elected its chairman. The protocals of the section, however, show him playing a marginal role in it, even urging other members on occasion to stop giving such enthusiastic attention to what he considered trivia. Such minor issues would be solved when the Slavs won their freedom, he told them, but that would come only via Warsaw and Moscow. In only one discussion is he recorded as having taken an active part, that concerning the needs of Russian religious sectarians in Bukovina.[107]

Choosing to avoid general meetings of the Congress ("vacuous and absurd") his own committee work ("where the Poles played at parliamentarianism the way the Germans played at revolution"), and the special caucuses ("I did not attend these"), he was once again alone. "I once more felt that sadness come over me, and I began to find myself as isolated in Prague as I had earlier been in Paris and in Germany." There was only one way to go now: "Being convinced that I would find nothing, not even in the Slavic Congress, I began to gather people outside the Congress and formed a secret society."[108]

His "holy commune" remodeled to suit his new role, it was the first of his long series of secret revolutionary organizations. Although we know little about the organization, we do have some hints regarding the kind of organization he had in mind from other things he wrote at the time. While he once more spoke of "federation," the mechanics of that "federation" again (as in Paris) had a decidedly centralist character, at least as he described them in his "Foundations of a New Slavic Policy," which he presented to the Congress. A "Slavic Council directs all of Slavdom as a supreme authority and high court: everyone is obligated to submit to its directives and carry out its decisions. . . . Slavic peoples who wish to become part of the federation, must completely relinquish their sovereign power and turn it directly over to the Council."[109] Regarding the internal system of each of the federated units, they were to be free to follow their customs, needs and circumstances, as long as they fulfilled the principal requirements of the federation, "universal equality, universal freedom and brotherly love."

He elaborated on this political structure (so reminiscent of his "holy commune" authoritarianism) somewhat more in describing it later to Tsar Nicholas. He wanted a republic, he said, but not a parliamentary government, since that would mean only a conflict between competing interests and a consequent paralysis of all effective government. A "dictatorial power" was far preferable, one that would be "exclusively concerned with the education and elevation of the masses." It would be "free in spirit and in the character of its actions, but without parliamentary forms." It would "print books with liberal content, but without freedom of the press." "Surrounded by those who shared his views and enlightened by their counsel," the dictator would be "limited by no one and by nothing." Such a dictatorship must not, of course, be confused with traditional monarchic rule, for this new dictatorship "in the spirit of its establishment must do all it can to make itself unnecessary as soon as possible, having as its aim nothing other than the people's freedom, independence, and gradual maturation." Monarchic rule, on the contrary, only wanted to keep its subjects in a state of "perpetual childhood." There were still, he acknowledged, several questions that had yet to be decided. For example:

> What would come after the dictatorship? I did not know, nor did I believe that any one now could even guess. And who would the dictator be? One might think that I myself was ready to assume that high position. But such an assumption would have been entirely unjustified. I must say, Sire, that except for enthusiasm, at times fanatical (but fanatical more as a result of circumstances and unnatural situations than by my nature) there were not in me either the brilliant qualities or the powerful vices that make both illustrious political leaders and great criminals against the state. . . . I do not say that I lacked pride, but it was never a dominant characteristic of mine: on the contrary, I had to overcome myself and, as it were, go against my own nature when I undertook to speak publicly or even write for the public. I lacked as

well those enormous vices à la Danton or à la Mirabeau, that vast, insatiable depravity which, to satisfy itself, is ready to turn the whole world upside down. And if there was egoism in me, it consisted entirely of a need for movement, a need for action. There has always been in my nature an essential flaw—a love for the fantastic, for the unusual, for unheard of adventures that open to me a limitless horizon and whose outcome no one can foresee.... There has always been in me much of Don Quixote, not only in my political, but also in my personal life.... With such traits of mind and feeling I could never have thought of myself as dictator.... More than once I told the Germans and Poles, when I heard them arguing about future forms of government, that "We are summoned to destroy, not construct; construction will be the task for others who will be better, more intelligent, and fresher than we are."[110]

For those familiar only with the legend of Bakunin, this defense of dictatorship may come as a surprise. In the context of Bakunin's real life, personality, and abundant statements on party organization, they are familiar, appropriate, and even predictable. Dictatorship had been the "politics" of his first "organization," the "holy commune"; the plan he brought to the Poles in Versailles in 1846 was "centralized politically";[111] and some form of rigorously authoritarian rule was to characterize the plans for all his later secret societies. Nor is there any contradiction between his penchant for dictatorial organization and his insistence on absolute freedom. They reflect, in fact, one and the same personality, only in different contexts. For what is "dictatorship" if not the preservation of absolute freedom, of arbitrary action for the dictator? What freedom is for Bakunin when he sees himself standing apart, dictatorship is for him when he sees himself taking part. It was just another way of being out and in at the same time, comparable to the "left" Hegelian dialectical posture and such contradictory phrases as "ruthless surrender." There is nothing psychologically inconsistent, in short, between Bakunin's authoritarianism and his insistence that he himself could never "become the slave or blind instrument of any secret society," that he never "lowered" himself "to the point of being the agent of any one whomsoever or the slave of another's ideas."[112] When his disdain for the "vacuous and absurd" parliamentary assemblies and all its "philistine flabbiness"[113] inspired him to think of forming a "secret society" of his own, his thoughts understandably moved toward dictatorship as the only arrangement that could preserve for him this same uncompromising independence. Dictatorship also plays an obvious role in the dialectical dualism that underlay all Bakunin's politics: it is another mask of omnipotent power disguising the reality of frightened isolation and detachment. However, since the purpose of such "dictatorship" was ultimately to preserve this absolute detachment, it paradoxically exposed the impotence it was meant to conceal, in the same way that passive violence, "ruthless surrender," as we saw, only accentuated the gentle pastels that *The Reaction in Germany* was supposed to deny.

This same paradox is even more evident in the above quotation from the "Confession," where Bakunin explains why he himself cannot be the dictator he proposes. First there is the powerful pose, the proposal of dictatorship. Then the hasty retreat—he is shy in public and must "overcome" himself and go against his true nature when he speaks; he might be fanatical, but not to the extent of turning the world upside down; he is too quixotic, too strongly drawn to the fantastic. If one assumes that Bakunin was consciously intending to distort his attitudes and motivations in the hope of winning reprieve, then one would have to say that he was being truthful in spite of himself, that intentional deception had opened the door to concealed truth, so accurately would the "deception" correspond to the reality of his character. But the case is less involved than that, for there is no reason to assume that he was engaged in deception here or, for that matter—as will be argued in the next chapter—in most other sections of the "Confession." What this extraordinary self-awareness does show is that he had come to realize (or even had sensed all along) that he had indeed been engaged in fantasy, that the violent apocalyptic appeals to turn the world upside down were radically contrary to his essentially passive, nonviolent, timid, nature, that, in brief, it was all dramatic theater with himself playing a most unsuitable, promethean role. Again and again in his "Confession" he displays this striking self-awareness:

> I was at one and the same time deceiver and deceived, deceiving myself and others with me, doing more or less violence both to my own mind and to the good sense of those who heard me. I was not born a charlatan, Sire, quite the contrary, nothing is more repugnant to me than charlatanism, and a thirst for the simple and pure truth has never been extinguished in me. But the unfortunate and unnatural situation in which I found myself, by my own fault moreover, sometimes forced me to be a charlatan in spite of myself. . . . In a word, I wanted to believe; I wanted to make others believe. This spurious faith, forced and artificial, was not gained without effort, without painful struggles. More than once, at moments of loneliness, I was overcome by searching doubts, doubts about the morality and the possibility of my activity. . . . I stifled the voice of conscience within me and dismissed my doubts as unworthy.[114]

To return to the Prague act, the secret society lasted only a few days, crumbling along with the rest of the resistance under the force of Austrian troops before it had time to do anything or even properly organize. The troops had moved in to quell a rising, mainly by students, that occurred on the last day of the Congress, June twelfth. The students' aim was to established the independent republic that the more cautious and realistic Congress delegates had rejected. Although general histories occasionally give "Bakunin's fiery speeches"[115] an important role in this rising, the historian of the Congress itself, while mentioning the influence of other Congress radicals, states that not one source of the time mentions Bakunin.[116] Bakunin himself, in fact, contends in the "Confession" that he had "tried to make the students understand the necessity of giving up this impossible enterprise" which would only "provide the Austrian army the opportunity for an easy victory." However, such prudence (and here, too, there is no reason to doubt him) did not keep him from adding his powerful voice and Russian songs to the preinsurrection festivities the night before the rising, or from bursting into the Polish caucus on the day of the rising to tell his fellow delegates that "this was not time·to meet, but to fight," or from going himself to the barricades with a rifle to fire "a few times." But this was not Paris. Even at the barricades, he recalled, he was skeptical and "never ceased being a kind of outsider, not expecting any significant results." Still, the show must go on. So, doubts and alienation notwithstanding, he advised the rebels once the rising had begun how best "to overthrow the government in City Hall . . . and replace it with a military committee provided with dictatorial powers."[117]

The conclusion was foregone. A week before the rising, the commander of the Austrian forces, Windischgraetz, had already massed his troops and artillery around the city and was well-enough prepared to let the insurrection spread, the better to crush it completely when he chose to do so. An artillery barrage on June sixteenth followed by a reign of martial law finished the job. On the eighteenth Bakunin was on his way again to Breslau, where he remained until his return to Berlin on July fifth. There things went from bad to worse. Everything had gone wrong in his political life. Now it was the turn, again, for his personal life to suffer. The day after his arrival in Berlin, the *Neue Rheinische Zeitung,* edited by Marx, carried a report claiming that George Sand had evidence to prove that Bakunin really had been, and perhaps still was, a Russian agent, and the one chiefly responsible for the arrest shortly before of several Poles. Two days later, Bakunin wrote George Sand asking her either to make the alleged evidence public or to help him dispel the slander. The following day he wrote an open letter of protest in *Allgemeine Oder-Zeitung,* which was reprinted in Marx's *Neue Rheinische Zeitung* on July sixteenth. A letter from Sand, dated the twentieth, was published in *Neue Rheinische Zeitung* on August third. It completely exonerated Bakunin.

The whole ugly affair was overwhelmingly painful for him. It was bad enough when such slander was spread by word of mouth by French, Russian, and Belgian authorities. But now it was printed for all to read, and printed in just those journals that were read by everyone who really mattered to him. He knew that once the rumor was in the air disclaimers could never fully clear him, especially among that group he was counting on as his key "Archimedes point," the Polish nationalists, the ones he had allegedly betrayed. Most of July was devoted to writing and rewriting drafts of letters to various journals in the hope of at least mitigating the harm done. But he did not feel it was doing any good: "It seemed to me at all times that everyone considered me a spy, and I was prepared to hate everyone and to keep away from all of them. Never, Sire, were things so hard for me as they were then."[118] The honor that had meant everything to him, that he had so strenuously been building and buttressing all these years, now seemed irrevocably lost. He must and would do anything he could to restore it: "I swore not to give up my plans, not to deviate from the road I had taken, but to advance along it without looking back, until the day when my death would prove to the Poles and Germans that I am no traitor."[119]

But where, now, did that road lead? Wherever he turned he saw "reaction everywhere."[120] Months of embittered and frenzied uncertainty followed. When Varnhagen von Ense visited him at the end of July, he found him doing research on the Balkans.[121] In early August he was encouraged by events in Germany: "At last we can breathe deeply.... Revolution has turned out to be stronger than intrigue.... I join with you [Ruge] and say 'we' not 'you' and call your German victory, 'our' victory."[122] But about a week later, the German revolution had become "an illusory struggle, a struggle of shadows pretending to be real, yet constantly aware of and willy-nilly revealing limitless weakness." Then, in this same letter to Herweg, he recalled Paris and Proudhon, "the only man in Paris ... who still understands something."[123]

Through all his uncertain flitting here and there, from illusion to illusion, his main hope continued to rest on the collapse of the Hapsburg Empire: "the destruction of Austria is the question of life for us—the Slav—and for the entire revolutionary party."[124] It was here, however, that he was to experience his next and, in some respects, his worst blow yet. In September 1848 the Croat patriot, soldier, and governor, Baron Josip Jelačic invaded Hungary supposedly to liberate Slavs from their Hungarian overlords, whose dedication to freedom from Austria was nicely balanced by their denial of freedom to their own minority Slavs. This, surely, was a cause that should appeal to the bard of pan-Slavist liberation, but he was hesitant: "We would very much like to know where you [Bakunin] are now, why you are not with us as you promised. We waited impatiently for you in Zagreb, and when you did not show up, we thought that something unpleasant had happened to you and were worried."[125] Judging from these remarks, by a Slovak professor and long-time foe of the Magyars, it appears that Bakunin had at first supported Jelačic, and it was probably due to that early support that members of Bakunin's Prague secret society had done the same.[126] But if he had, he soon changed his mind when he discovered that the Slavs he had praised so enthusiastically (so much so that he had become "something like a guarantor of the political reliability of the Slavic peoples")[127] were under Jelačic actually helping the Hapsburg Emperor crush Kossuth's Hungarian revolution. "What are you doing, brother," Bakunin answered the Slovak professor, "you are sacrificing the great cause of the Slavs and are only serving the Emperor and the Austrian aristocracy.... You have declared revolutionary war, [but] you are serving reaction...."[128]

Since what was uppermost in Bakunin's mind now was the restoration of his own revolutionary honor, we can well appreciate his dismay at watching his guaranteed Slavic democrats serving the cause of reaction. He planned to go to Hungary himself, he said, to see what he could do, or at least "to get a better picture of this terribly complicated Slavic question," but he could not "because my friends in Russia have until now been feeding me not with money but with promises and fine words."[129] He wanted to forget the whole thing, like a bad dream: I "no longer had any relations with the Slavs, except for one insignificant letter from Ludwig Stur [the Slovak professor] which I would have liked to answer, but could not since I did not know his address...."[130] Alternately, he searched for some justification for the early support of Jelačic. After all, he wrote, "Kossuth himself was even less a democrat," since he was willing "to be reconciled with Innsbruck [the temporary quarters for the Austrian Emperor] and to serve the court against Vienna [in rebel hands], against the Poles, and against Italy, provided that the Innsbruck court satisfy his own Hungarian demands."[131] He tried to exorcise the pain of fact by the magic of illusion: On the tenth of September an article appeared in the Berlin *Reform* reporting the conclusion of a fact-finding trip to Vienna and including the sentence, "it is sad that here, where the Germans are democrats, the Slavs came forward as enemies of democracy." Taking this sentence as his theme, Bakunin drafted, but never finished, a defense of the Slavs. The Slavs were democrats, he insisted, because they just had to be: "Simply by reason of the fact that Slavs have been until now the most oppressed race in all of Europe, they are, as it were, sentenced to achieve democracy...." They had to be democrats "notwithstanding everything that at first sight contradicts this," because "as a result of their liberation, the entire world order, based on privilege and despotism must undergo a radical alteration."[132] He had found an "Archimedes point," and he would not let the mere facts of reality take it away from him.

The times were bad indeed: "It was a most difficult time for me. Without money, without friends, openly denounced as a spy, alone in a large city, I had no idea what to do, and it came to the point of my not knowing how I would live the next day."[133] Even more than in July, he was anxious to do anything he could to help him regain his honor, now doubly challenged, by the Jelačic betrayal on top of the cruel allegations of his own treason to the revolution.

> Although political conditions had clearly changed to such an extent that I had almost completely ceased to hope or expect, I could not nor wished to return to Paris, the only asylum remaining to me, before I had demonstrated by some tangible act the sincerity of my democratic convictions. To redeem my stained honor I had to hang on right to the end. I became spiteful, misanthropic, fanatic, ready to leap into any dangerous enterprise whatever, provided it was not dishonorable. My entire being was obsessed with revolution and a passion to destroy.[134]

He tried Breslau again but was ordered to leave—not only Breslau but all of Prussia—under threat of being turned over to the Russians. He chose Dresden but was denied permission to remain even the short time he intended staying. There was one refuge left in the area—Koethen in Anhalt. A small enclave hidden away in Prussian lands, it enjoyed one of the most liberal constitutions in Europe and had opened its doors to political nomads like Bakunin. It was a chance for a well deserved rest, and since "no one took any interest in politics" there, he did nothing, he says, but "hunt rabbits and other wild game. It was for me a period of repose." "Until the month of December, I remained completely inactive and I would not be able to say anything about this period other than the fact that I lived in a state of futile hope, having firmly decided to seize the first opportunity to act."[135]

These recollections are extraordinary, for it was just during this period of rabbits and repose that he wrote his most fervently apocalyptic declaration to date—*An Appeal to the Slavs.* The cause of this apparent discrepancy between mood and action is suggested by the reasons he gives for writing the *Appeal:* "to prove to the Poles and to the Germans that I was not a Russian spy, ... to pave the way to the possibility of a new rapprochement" with them, and "to remind those in Prague about myself."[136] For all its inflamed passion, in other words, the *Appeal* seems to have been almost a cooly calculated maneuver (entirely consistent with rabbits and repose) in the interests of what had become his most pressing concern—the recovery of his lost honor. The raging passions that flood the *Appeal,* therefore, may have been largely artificial, pumped in for effect, in the same way that his impassioned speeches came to him not naturally but only, to recall his own words, after he had overcome himself and gone against his nature. No doubt as he got into the work, deeper springs of emotions were tapped by association, and these give the piece its occasional ring of authenticity.

Nevertheless, the proclamation as a whole sounds forced and strained against the background of earlier declarations that seem in comparison fresh and spontaneous. The shriller and more bloodcurdling the violent rhetoric, in fact, the less believable it is, The playacting that is virtually acknowledged in the "Confession" is apparent in the *Appeal,* both in the circumstances of its composition and in the work itself.

He had become, in short, self-consciously aware of his capacity to inspire, or, more accurately, the capacity of a role he could play to do so. When he wanted to, as he did now, he could come on stage, perform his part with consummate skill and enjoy the applause. The soaring ideals, the apocalyptic exhilaration, the complexly interwoven theories that were once unconscious projections had already congealed into a repertoire of fixed scripts, complete with appropriate gestures and emotions. But the fact that he had grown increasingly detached from the role does not mean that he needed it any less. However uncongenial, however much it required him to "overcome" himself and "go against" his own nature, the role had by then become indispensable to him, the only way he now had to release the repressed emotions and quiet somewhat, if not resolve, the warring contradictions within him. The sanctuary that he had first built in escaping from life and the world and that he had later hoped to turn into a fortress to destroy that world had become instead his own prison, and from behind its "high walls," "locks," and "gates" he was more and more to become, as the years went on, the bondsman to his own fantasy, a bystander and witness to his own emerging legend. The legend was to grow larger and brighter, until it became the heroic fiction of history books and revolutionary hagiography; while the man himself was to diminish and dim, becoming ever more childlike, helpless, and pathetic.

The inspiration for writing *An Appeal to the Slavs* seems to have come from his old friend Müller-Strübing, in a letter he wrote Bakunin in mid-October:

> How badly your Czech friends are behaving themselves! You must speak out loudly against this, my friend—It is your obligation to do it! The Slav must raise his voice in the service of democracy and must formally denounce these perfidious crusaders of nationalism with their deceptive patriotism. You must openly disavow them. You must come forward with an appeal to Slavic democrats. Now is not the time for laziness! You'll say to me, "Hell, whether I'm lazy or active won't make any difference anyhow. I'm just one of many. If I don't do something that doesn't mean it won't get done—others can do it just as well or even better." Your situation is exceptional: what you don't do, just won't be done; since you represent Slavic democracy, you are a force, or at least can become one.[137]

While Bakunin had been enjoying his "laziness," the Jelačic scandal had deepened: after leading Slavic troops against Hungarian rebels, he and his forces had allied with Windischgraetz to crush the German rebels in Vienna. The aim of the *Appeal* was to right this grotesque wrong by returning the Slavs to the democratic path they were meant to follow. The pitch and tone of the broadside are high-voltage apocalyptic.[138] It is as though each failure extended the horizon and exacerbated the frenzy of Bakunin's messianic message. From speaking for the Russian people in November 1847, through speaking for the Slavs in Prague in June 1848, he now, at the end of 1848, is speaking for all the people—Slav, German, Magyar, and so on—against all the tyrants:

> Everywhere the old order is crumbling to the ground with a fearful crash.... Revolution and chaos reign everywhere! A new spirit, emerging at first as the spirit of destruction, has penetrated down to the deepest and darkest levels of the people and shakes the nations.... It is necessary now to destroy this old world that is collapsing under the weight of its own injustices. It is necessary to wipe all of this off the face of the earth in order to have a clean place for the new world. A new world, brothers, a real and complete liberation for all individuals as well as all nations—the beginning of political and social justice—the kingdom of love, of brotherhood, the boundless kingdom of freedom.... We must destroy the material and cultural conditions of contemporary life, overthrow from top to bottom our antiquated social world, which has become impotent and sterile, unable to contain and support such a vast scope of freedom. We must first of all clear the air and totally transform the atmosphere in which we live, because it corrupts our instincts and our will, binds our hearts and minds.[139]

Once again employing, as we see here, images that unmistakably disclose the real motivations and sources of these declarations, Bakunin repeatedly summoned the "new spirit with its destructive, disintegrating power,"[140] which, since Weitling, he had identified entirely with the "people." He conceded that the character of recent popular risings in Galicia was conservative rather than revolutionary, but, in spite of that, he remained as convinced as ever that the "people," the peasantry

> conceals in its womb the embryo of a new and unprecedented force, a volcanic fire, whose explosion will bury beneath tall mounds of lava the well-ordered, artificial gardens of your diplomacy and your reign, shatter your power in a single instant, blind Tsar, exterminate it without a trace. The peasant rising in Galicia is nothing, but its flame spreads ever deep-

er beneath the earth, and already among the peasant masses of the vast
Russian kingdom gigantic craters flare up. It is in fact Russian democracy with its tongues of fire that will devour the state and by its blood-
red glow illuminate the whole of Europe. The miracle of revolution
will arise from the depths of this flaming ocean.... In Moscow, out of
a sea of blood and fire, the constellation of revolution will ascend on
high in splendor to become the guiding star for the benefit of all liberated humanity.[141]

While, presumably, the peasantry of all nations were destined for this glorious
task of extermination, it was specifically the Slavs who were to spark the "world-
shattering revolution." "To create miracles, the Slavs must become like fire.
Agitate among the Slavic masses without restraint or second thoughts. Ignite in
them a sacred flame. Advance like apostles of awakening Slavdom."[142]

The old world must be completely annihilated. A new "kingdom of love, of
brotherhood ... the boundless kingdom of freedom" would arise from the ruins.
The transmutation from one to the other must be catastrophically violent. And,
as the fourth principle of the *Appeal's* apocalyptic litany, there could be no compromise between the doomed and the saved. The rejection of any contact with
the "dark, filthy, and vile" world that had been a leitmotif in everything he had
written before, whether in private letters or public pronouncements, was dramatically reemphasized in the *Appeal.* "The world is divided into two camps. There
is no middle road running between them.... The world is divided into two camps.
Here, *revolution;* there, *counterrevolution....* Each one of us, you and I both,
brothers, must decide on one of them. There is no middle road. Those pointing to
such a road and glorifying it are either deceiving themselves or deceiving others."[143]

As for himself, the choice had been made long ago. He rejoiced in it and tri-
umphantly urged others to follow his lead. At one point in the *Appeal* his evangelism becomes a virtual love song to his "bride—the revolution."

... throw yourself bravely and completely into the embrace of the revolution. In her there is everything—your awakening, your resurrection,
your hope, your salvation, your future. In her and only in her! Trust
her! ... Only in her is there life. Apart from her—death. Only the one
who follows her and does her work will see his efforts crowned with
success, for she alone distributes all the glorious rewards of battle. Whoever is against her must sooner or later perish and not see the day of salvation. She tolerates no ambivalence, no duplicity, no playing around a
little with her and a little with her enemy, no wavering, doubting, hypocritical hedging. She demands that you surrender yourself totally, unre-
servedly, believing in her and belonging to her completely.... She alone

can create a full life, provide unshakable confidence, give strength, create miracles. ... Believe in the revolution. Give yourself to her completely, and unconditionally![144]

Tyrannically possessive, the queen of the "deepest and darkest" realms, concealing in her womb the embryonic volcanic fire, his "bride—the revolution" was, nevertheless, the divinely good mother and wife, giving birth to new life and a new and splendid world, healing him by intoxicating paroxysms. Twice before he had enjoyed her, first in Paris and then in the Prague street rising, when, as he recalled in the *Appeal,* "the noble youth whose triumphant songs still ring in our ears and who were inspired by the grandest and loftiest sentiments" took to the barricades, and when, "under the fire of Austrian artillery, we proclaimed the overthrow of all tyrannies and the onset of the era of Slavic democracy."[145]

In contrast to the beloved "bride—the revolution" there was also, however, another feminine presence in the *Appeal to the Slavs,* an evil force (the all-bad image). Identifying her with the old world destined for destruction, Bakunin denounces Jelačic for being so foolish as to think that he could cooperate with her. Jelačic was blind not to see that "instead of using her for yourself, you yourself will be used, that once she has beaten her present enemy with your help and finished him off, she will once again enslave you." "Just take a close, hard look at the face, twisted by evil ... and you will be seized by disgust and horror at the enticements of this procuress and be shaken back from her in dread and revulsion."[146] No, one must not look to her as an ally: "How could she possibly be an ally of that demonic force that will renew both the world and us, brothers, open the way for us to pour out vigorously our inner fullness like fresh spring juices into the stiff, frozen life of the people of Europe."[147]

Given what these symbols and images represent, it is not surprising to find him reacting in "horror and distrust," "dread and revulsion" to this evil "procuress" and her "enticements," denouncing her for being "hypocritical and treacherous" and for so long having "led the people on lead strings" like infants, and identifying her with "her mother, that same old despotism." Nor is it remarkable that he calls even his cherished "bride—the revolution" a demonic force: even in this complexly camouflaged and sublimated guise of revolutionary politics, the "animal passions" they permit him to release remain evil, still denizens of the "deepest and darkest levels," like that volcanic flame secretly spreading deep "beneath the earth." The violence of the people's revolution was always to express for him the "devil in the flesh," not because its "sea of blood and fire" implied political violence, killing, and the like, but because the "blood and fire," meant sex and sex meant incest.[150]

As for the "traitor" Jelačic and his Slavic alliance with the Austrian army against Hungarian, German, and Italian rebels, they seem to fade away into insignificance in the glare and passion of these messianic visions. Although much space and many arguments are spent on proving to the Slavs that they must shift sides at once and join the rebels against the empire, this all becomes almost incidental in comparison to the vision of the "new crimson dawn," the end of the "thousand year sleep" that carries Bakunin higher and higher in apocalyptic ecstasy. Even on the mundane level of actual politics, Jelačic is upstaged by Russia and its "blind Tsar." So central was the theme of Russia in this declaration to the non-Russian Slavs that a portion of the *Appeal* reprinted in a radical Leipzig journal was given the title *Revolution in Russia.* It was this part that also most impressed the *Appeal's* Polish translator: "Marvelous! I wept reading what you wrote about your people."[151] We have already seen above, in descriptions of those mounds of lava, gigantic craters, tongues of fire, blood-red glow, flaming ocean, and sea of blood and fire one such moving passage. Vienna had become as Poznan and Prague had been before, another "Archimedes point" to "overthrow Tsarist Russia and wipe it from the face of the earth"—the "goal of my life." And so: "I turn to you in the name of a Slavic people of 60 million [Russia], in the name of 60 million of your brothers" against a "calculating and heartless despot." "His hour has struck....I say to you that the despot's intrigues are more and more shattering against the granite breast of the revolutionary spirit" as it "moves forward invisibly, and like an Asiatic plague sweeps away all barriers and defenses."[152]

The composite of images and the interplay of characters again disclose the inner drama. The enemy is the "blind Tsar" and his "well-ordered, artificial gardens." (We will see later, in connection with Bakunin's "Confession," other associations between the "blind Tsar" and Bakunin's blind father). The force that will destroy the tyrant, "wipe him from the face of the earth," is the "people," his Slavic "brothers" (brothers against the father) and that "volcanic fire" lying at the "deepest and darkest" level. This "demonic" force, heretofore stifled by the "heartless despot," is "no longer in a deep sleep, but only slumbering and already beginning to awaken."[153] Even without this force, however, victory is assured because the enemy is so weak: "impotent and sterile," "old, decrepit," "blind," "crumbling under the weight of its own injustice." It is helpless above all precisely because the forces that will destroy it are hidden, elusive, insidious, spreading "beneath the earth," "moving forward invisibly." Again we have victory without direct confrontation, omnipotence via impotence and victory achieved, moreover, by a beloved revolutionary force that is at the same time demonic, evil ("an Asiatic plague").

Although he waited uncertainly before publishing the *Appeal,* Bakunin was anxious to have it read once it did come out, and in a most businesslike way he mailed packages of the brochure to friends for distribution.[154] In a letter accompanying a copy to Herweg, he succinctly summarized the core of the enterprise, both in its public and in its personal perspective: Only an "anarchic peasant war" could now save Germany, not the "so-called democratic leaders" with their "constitutional and republican phrases" and their fear of the "so-called evil passions of the masses." As for himself: "I am not afraid of anarchy. I wish it with all my soul. It alone can tear us from that damned middle way in which we have had to go on vegetating for so long."[155] Indeed, his months of Anhalt vegetating were now over. Renewed by his Anhalt rest and now buoyed by the *Appeal,* he returned to battle, more ardent than ever. "My political fever, further intensified and inflamed by my earlier failures, by my bizarre and intolerable situation and, finally, by the victory of reaction in Europe, reached at this time its highest paroxysm. I was entirely transformed into a thirst for revolution."[156]

Aglow again, he left Anhalt for Leipzig in December of 1848. Soon after arriving, he chanced upon two Czech students from the University of Leipzig, Gustav and Adolf Straka, who, before meeting him, "had no thought of politics. . . . I changed their way of thinking. I uprooted them from their peaceful pursuits and persuaded them to become instruments of my activities in Bohemia."[157] Their first assignment was to go to Prague and invite some Czechs to a Czech-Polish-German meeting he was planning. He would himself contact the Poles. The results: one radical came to the meeting from Prague, none from Poland (even worse, "no one even answered").[158] Never mind. He would himself arouse the Bohemian masses, the peasants—"nothing seemed easier"[159]—and provoke thereby "a radical, absolute revolution; in a word, a revolution such that even if defeated afterwards, would have thrown everything topsy-turvy. The Austrian government, after winning, would have found nothing in place." The nobles and the "hostile clergy" would be exiled. Part of the land would go to the peasants, "in order to win them to the side of the revolution," and the rest would be used to help finance the revolution. All property titles and other legal documents would be destroyed. Debts under a certain amount would be annulled. The revolution would be, in short, "terrible and unprecedented," even though—a most important point—"it would be directed against things rather than against people." This accomplished, Bohemia would then become a "revolutionary camp" powerful enough not only to safeguard the revolution in the country itself, but also to take the offensive, starting out from Bohemia and inciting the Slavic peoples along the way.[160] Since the new government to be established in Prague would have to be capable of these awesome undertakings, it would, of course, have to possess "unlimited dictatorial powers":

> All organizations, all journals and all signs of chatterbox anarchy will also have to be abolished. Everyone must submit to a single dictatorial power. The youth and all able-bodied persons will be divided into categories according to character, capacities and individual tendencies and

sent throughout the country in order to provide a provisional organization, revolutionary and military.[161]

Nothing could be clearer. All he had now to do was to make it work. While he was still in Anhalt he had met two alleged members of a German revolutionary "Central Committee," d'Ester and Hexamer, who had come with him to Leipzig and who, supposedly, were collaborating with him on the grand design of a Slavic–German revolutionary alliance. Himself impoverished, he turned to them for funds to get the Bohemian rising under way, "but their income could not even cover their own political expenses."[162] In fact, they were probably as isolated as he was, "Central Committee" notwithstanding. As for the dedicated Czech who actually came to his Czech-Polish-German meeting, Emmanuel Arnold, a journalist, he could only stay one day and, as Bakunin put it, wasted most of it "in useless discussions" with d'Ester and Hexamer over calling a Slavic-German Congress, which Bakunin "energetically opposed." But Bakunin succeeded, he says, in winning Arnold over, and he sent him back to Bohemia with instructions to form a secret society.[163] Bakunin had already prepared an outline of its organization: three separate groups to work with the petty bourgeoisie, the youth, and the peasantry; each group to be ignorant of the others' existence; all groups to submit "to a strict hierarchy and absolute discipline"; and, at the top, the inevitable "Central Committee." "These three societies would be linked by a Central Committee composed of three or, at most, five members: myself and Arnold, with the rest to be elected.... The revolution once achieved, my secret society would not disperse, but, on the contrary, reenforce itself and expand, gathering together those who were really strong and vital, until, little by little, all Slavic lands would be encompassed."

With regard to the other major partner in the grand alliance, the Germans, he appointed a Viennese student

to organize, on the same plan, among the Germans of Bohemia, a society of which I would have been the secret head, without at first appearing to be part of its Central Committee. If my plans were successful, consequently, all the important threads of the movement would be concentrated in my hands, and I would have been sure that the revolution planned for Bohemia would never depart from the path that I had charted for it.

Finally, the postrevolutionary government:

First of all, I wanted to know intimately the people involved [in the government], know about them and their situations. I did not know whether or not I would openly take part in it, but it would seem to me that I would surely have to do so, directly and intensively. It was not egoism or ambition that led me to deviate from my former shyness, but rather the conviction, resulting from a year-long experience, that no one among the democrats I knew would be capable of taking into consideration all the conditions of the revolution or of taking all the decisive and forceful measures that I regarded necessary for victory.[164]

Is this Bakunin or Lenin? Where is the bard of freedom? If one looks closely, he is still very much there, hiding—in the coy uncertainty about assuming power, even about "appearing" to belong to the leadership, in the almost-hoped-for defeat that will let him and his revolution play their part then run away, and in the pathetically small-scale operation that he is actually involved in, so ludicrously disproportionate to his grandiose fantasy. No doubt fully aware that he had nothing at all to work with, he tried again to use an already established organization, a new "Archimedes point," in this case the so-called Slavic Linden Society, "the center of all societies and Slavic organizations in the Austrian Empire." As unconcerned as ever with reality, he was certain that it would be "easy enough to take over the Slavic Linden Society, which would then become...a powerful and effective instrument for reaching my goals."[165] Arnold was given the job. For some reason, however, he never let Bakunin know how things were going.[166] Bakunin's only recourse was to go to Bohemia himself, which he did in March of 1849. On the way, he stopped at Dresden where he met two émigré Galicians, Kryzanowski, whom he had known in Brussels in 1847, and Heltman. The prerequisite for friendship between Bakunin and the two was the same as it had been for his friendship with d'Ester and Hexamer—their disbelief in the various rumors about him.[167] Once that was out of the way, the two men agreed to have their "Central Committee" send representatives and money to Dresden to help prepare for Bakunin's Bohemian revolution. As it turned out, however, the representatives sent by the "Central Committee" were none other than Kryzanowski and Heltman themselves, and they came, it goes without saying, empty-handed.[168]

But that blow was to come a little later. First the Bohemian failure had to run its course. In spite of the detailed instructions he had given Arnold, Bakunin found on his trip to Prague "that nothing was ready, literally nothing." Arnold claimed poor health as the reason, but Bakunin "always thought, to the very end, that he [Arnold] had simply done nothing whatsoever, even when he gave the appearance of being active." Bakunin was even more discouraged after one evening spent discussing politics with some Czech radicals, who turned out to be just another group of "incorrigible chatterboxes," a defect, he believed, they had acquired from the Germans. Still, their philistine formalism did hold one advantage for him: "ceding to them all the external signs of power, it would not be much trouble for me to take over power itself, once the revolution had broken out."[169]

Contrasting the grandeur of his purpose with the sparseness of his means, he might have been expected to feel disheartened by the visit. Not at all: "My short stay in Prague was enough to convince me that I was not wrong in hoping to find in Bohemia all the necessary factors for a revolution crowned with success." Upon his return to Dresden, accordingly, he gave the Straka brothers their battle orders, "detailed and complete instructions concerning all the necessary preparations for the revolution in Prague and in Bohemia in general." To begin with, they were "to organize at once secret societies in Prague" and to select from the workers a reliable force of "500, 400 or 300 men, depending on possibilities." Money? He turned to his fellow conspirators, Kryzanowski and Heltman, but all they had brought back from their "Central Committee" were best wishes. "No one gave me a kopek, except for Röckel...who was able to contribute a little by selling his furniture."[170]

Enriching the tragic comedy with still more absurdity, the "leaders" had ceased cooperating with one another or even telling each other the true state of affairs in their respective corners of the conspiracy ("when I received unfavorable news I did not mention it, and when the news was good, I exaggerated it"). Hexamer, moreover, turned out to be "a doctrinaire democrat and utopian," who was mainly interested in starting a newspaper; while d'Ester was "superficial," "lacked both sufficient intelligence and enough character to be a leader of a party," and "was more interested in his election to the second Prussian legislative assembly" than in preparing for revolution. Bakunin had come to realize, moreover, that their Central Committee "had done absolutely nothing" for the success of the planned revolution. The Germans, finally, were dismissed as hopelessly undisciplined, each group going its own way, ignoring completely the directions of their own Central Committee: "anarchy prevailed—a consequence of Protestantism and of German political history as a whole. Anarchy is the fundamental nature of the German spirit, character and life."[171]

So, nothing was ready there either. "Leaders should have been designated; a revolutionary hierarchy set up; the peasants should have been propagandized and drawn into the revolutionary movement."[172] The Straka brothers remained "my only hope for the revolution in Prague."[173] Still, he remained firmly confident "that I would soon be summoned to Prague."[174] Taking advantage of his friend Röckel's departure from Dresden to Prague, for reasons we will turn to below, he urged him while there "to speed up as much as possible the preparations for the insurrection of Prague."[175] The results, as recalled by Röckel, were predictable:

In Prague, however, I found things completely different from the way they had been described to me. Czechs and Germans were more hostile to each other than ever. . . . And the great battle in Hungary found no sympathy among the Bohemians. . . . The different nationalities glared at each other jealously and instead of joining forces against the common enemy, they were convinced that each would gain from the repression of the others. . . . Rather than the powerful, widespread organization that Bakunin imagined himself to be leading and through which he assumed he could set the most powerful forces in motion, I found scarcely a dozen very young people.[176]

Penniless, powerless, at odds with even his few allies—Arnold, d'Ester, Hexamer, Kryzanowski, Heltman—with no one except the young, inexperienced Straka brothers ("whose mind I had, so to speak, to reshape and fill with my own spirit in the course of more than two months of daily, even hourly meetings"),[177] Bakunin still went on waiting in Dresden for his summons to the great revolution that would usher in the new world and his own "invisible" reign. Looking back over these months some years later, Röckel caught the essence of the madness: "Whatever he begins to hope for and strive for becomes through his impatience an illusion of something already attained."[178] Bakunin himself, referring specifically to these frenzied months after the *Appeal,* put it even more incisively, echoing dozens of earlier expressions of the same solipsism: "I reasoned as follows: the revolution is necessary, consequently it is possible." He realized, he admitted in this account of the period, that all his plans were "ridiculous." But he could not help himself.

I no longer belonged to myself. The demon of destruction had taken control of me. My will or rather my stubbornness grew with the difficulties, and instead of these countless obstacles frightening me, they excited my revolutionary thirst, driving me into tireless and feverish activity. I was doomed to my demise. I foresaw it, and I rushed towards it joyfully. By then I was already sick of life.[179]

There was another reason now for frenzy and despair besides the unmitigated failure of everything he had tried. At the very time when his political impotence was becoming ever more apparent, his arch rival, the "blind Tsar," was putting on an impressive display of his own enormous strength. In the *Appeal* and, during the months immediately thereafter, in a quasi-sociological series of articles on Russian conditions[180] Bakunin had assured rebellious Europe that Russia was in no condition to come to the aid of reaction, that Tsarist troops were too filled with shame at their role of oppressor and with hatred toward the Tsar to be used for such repression. Reality again argued otherwise: several weeks after Bakunin's articles appeared, Austria announced that Russian troops were on the way. In the weeks that followed, three Russian armies marched in and crushed the Hungarian rebellion. Bakunin struck back with another *Appeal:* "Arise, Slavs! Russian troops are here. They have invaded Austria...."[181] All internicine Slavic strife and all nationalistic discord that had divided the multinational revolutionaries against each other must now end. Magyars, Slavs, Germans must all join now to drive the Russians back.

Such was the situation—Russians advancing, Slavs fighting Germans and Magyars, Bakunin helpless, the imminent Prague revolution nowhere in sight— when fate, with masterful irony, threw a revolution right at Bakunin's feet, in Dresden, where he had planned nothing and expected nothing. The "final act,"[182] as Bakunin aptly put it, now began.

In his "Confession" Bakunin disclaimed any part in preparing the Dresden revolution.[183] While there is no reason to doubt him—he admitted far worse throughout the "Confession"—it is certain that he did meet with German radicals there and that he influenced the editors of a leading opposition journal, the *Dresden Gazette.*[184] There is no contradiction here, however, since most of the actual leaders of the Dresden insurrection were worlds apart from the revolutionaries Bakunin was meeting. The Dresden rising was a bourgeois, liberal, constitutional movement, as were most of the revolutions in the German lands during 1848-49. An all-German constitution, freedoms of speech, press, and religion, equal representation, a withdrawal or reduction of privileges from the nobility— these were the general concerns of all of them.

At the center of the struggle in Saxony[185] at this time (spring of 1849) was the demand by the elected, liberal Chamber of Deputies that the King of Saxony accept the Frankfurt Constitution. It was by then a late and futile demand. The Frankfurt Assembly had been powerless since that March, when Frederick William IV, King of Prussia, had declined the offer to lead the proposed united constitutional Germany: he would have no "crown from the gutter," no "dog collar." That April he showed that he had the power to practice his disdain. When an impatient Prussian parliament demanded a further liberalization of their own constitution as well as Prussian acceptance of the Frankfurt Assembly's all-German constitution, he simply dissolved it and wrote a new election law assuring a conservative Prussian parliament. At the same time, on April twenty-eighth, he promised military aid to any other royal authority in Germany who needed help in resisting their own local constitutionalists.

For the King of Saxony the offer came just in time. On the twenty-second of April, the *Vaterlandsvereine,* representing some 75,000 citizens, had met in Dresden and had voted against imposing any taxes until the Saxon King accepted their constitutional demands. On April thirtieth, having by then learned of the Prussian action and promise of aid, the Saxon King dissolved the Chamber of

Deputies. (It was then that Röckel, fearing the loss of protection he had enjoyed as an elected Deputy, decided to leave Dresden for a while and when Bakunin used him for his phantom revolution in Prague.) Faced with a great public outcry at his actions, together with a temporary shortage of Saxon troops, on duty in Schleswig-Holstein, the Saxon King urged Frederick William IV to rush the promised Prussian forces. That same day, an angry but unarmed, crowd attacked the Dresden arsenal, claiming the need of arms to defend Dresden against the "foreign troops" on their way from Prussia. The guards fired, killing five. A second assault was made, this time armed. One officer was killed and several soldiers wounded. That same night, May third-fourth, the King fled, and, on the fourth a Provisional Government was formed.

Although the insurrection had begun, the main Saxon forces had not yet become involved and the Prussian troops had not yet arrived. The rebels seemed to have won, but it was unclear just what. Nor was it at all clear, under these circumstances, what the Provisional Government should do. It was, on the whole, a moderate government, chosen by a meeting of former Chamber Deputies and made up of three men—Bürgermeister Todt, a constitutional monarchist and close friend of the Crown's ministers; Heubner, chairman of a district council; and Tschirmer, a lawyer. Only the last of these, Tschirmer, seemed to relish the excitement of the insurrection and the opportunities for personal glory it offered. At first the moderates prevailed. A truce was arranged and negotiations begun. From a realistic perspective, the rebels' prospects were not very promising: the Saxon troops had remained loyal and were on their way, as were the Prussian forces; the town militia stayed neutral, against all pleading from the rebels; the arsenal was still in government hands; and throngs of townspeople, guessing what lay ahead, were already streaming out into the countryside. True, the barricades were going up, manned by exhilarated youth, intellectuals, and, it is said, some workers. Reasonably sure of the outcome of any clash between the barricades and a combined Saxon-Prussian force, the Crown's negotiators were firm in their demands: the leaders must give themselves up, especially those in the Provisional Government; all weapons must be surrendered in 24 hours; the barricades must come down and the streets cleaned up; and the town must be reimbursed for its expenses. These were the costs the insurgents would have paid had they quit then. The costs that were eventually paid for not retreating from this hopeless situation was, five days later, over a hundred soldiers killed and about another hundred wounded on the King's side; and, for the insurgents, 250 killed and some 400 wounded.

According to an account published later in the *Dresden Gazette,* the journal of Bakunin's friend Wittig, Bakunin was delighted by the insurrection when it broke out on May third, but he was convinced that it would fail and was, in any case so intent on leaving Dresden for Prague that "his friends had a hard time convincing him to stay."[186] As Bakunin recalled the events, down to the fourth he had taken no interest in the rising at all, since its bourgeois leaders were only planning "legal" demonstrations. It would be "peaceful, without bloodshed, inoffensive, and in no way a revolution." Only on the fourth, after the King had fled the night before and the Provisional Government had been set up, did he decide that "the movement had become a revolution" and that he had a role to play. All during the fourth he played his part: he strenuously urged the Provisional Government to end the truce and the "useless negotiations," to take the offensive, and to conquer the city. He himself, he said, would lead a detachment and capture the arsenal.[187] By the next day, the fifth, he had won Tschirmer to his point of view,[188] and by noon, according to Todt's later testimony, Bakunin was in the Town Hall leading a revolution, together with Heltman and Kryzanowski: "separated behind a fire screen from the rest of the group, they were feverishly active."[189] Faced with what seemed a choice between ignominious surrender and disastrous defeat, the moderates, Todt and Heubner, were hesitant and confused, uncertain as to what to do next and so "made way for the democrats," as Bakunin expressed it.[190] Perhaps this remarkable Russian nobleman and artillery officer, bursting with confidence, rich in revolutionary experience, and ready to bring in others no less experienced (Heltman and Kryzanowski) was right. Why not give him a chance?

Had Bakunin not been on the scene, had he not persuaded a trapped, desperate, and inexperienced group of moderates that he could save them and their revolution, would they have chosen to fight that futile and costly battle? And why did Bakunin get involved? Nothing could be farther from his own political aims and ideals than those bourgeois, constitutional goals. "I have very little interest in parliamentary debates," he had written Herweg two months after the Prague fiasco. "The epoch of parliamentary life, of national, constituent assemblies, has already passed.... I do not believe in constitutions and in laws. Even the very best of constitutions would not satisfy me. We need something else— passion and life, and a new, lawless and, therefore, free world."[191] Once the Dresden insurrection had failed and the rebels were fast retreating, Heubner asked Bakunin straight out what his own politics were. As forthright as ever, Bakunin answered that he opposed all government, that he had only contempt for the Dresden rising, and that it was his admiration for Heubner himself that had brought him into it.[192] Since that last remark is probably untrue ("Heubner was completely unknown to me,"[193] he later stated) and since the aims of the revolution were the opposite of his own, we are still without a motive.

One of his reasons for getting involved, once he saw that it was, in his terms, a real revolution, may have been his hope of using Dresden as he had hoped to use Poznan, Prague, and Vienna, as an "Archimedes point" for his grander aims, mainly his war against the Tsar, all the more urgent now that Russian troops were heading his way. It was, in fact, with this prospect of making the Dresden insurrection a spark for the larger conflagration that, he said, he had persuaded Heltman and Kryzanowski to join him. Also, part of the deal he had made with Tschirmer, behind the backs of Todt and Heubner, was a promise of money and arms from a victorious Dresden Provisional Government to support Bakunin's Bohemian revolution. (In their memoirs, Röckel and Richard Wagner also give as Bakunin's main concern the prospect of using Dresden in his Slavic-German-Magyar revolutionary war against the Tsar).[194]

This is certainly a plausible and perhaps even sufficient reason for his involvement. But in his "Confession" he suggests, in passing, another and, I believe, more decisive reason, one which corresponds even closer to his experiences, mood, and intentions during the preceding months. He was tempted to leave Dresden at first, he says, because the likely defeat of the rising would expose him to arrest, if only because he was there illegally. "But," he continued, "it would have been disgraceful, absolutely impossible to run away.... I had sent the Straka brothers to Prague, sent them and many other people into obvious danger, so I did not have the right myself to avoid peril." To stay, however, meant to fight, and to fight to the end: "Once I had decided to remain, neither my character nor my situation could allow me to remain an inactive, indifferent spectator of the Dresden events."[195] Basically, in other words, the same concern for his tarnished honor that had flooded the *Appeal* with such rage now sent him into the Town Hall on May fourth, gave to his arguments that day their compelling force, and thereby helped carry the insurrection to its disastrous end. We should recall his own description of his mood a few months earlier: "To redeem my honor I had to hang on right to the end. I became spiteful, misanthropic, fanatic, ready to leap into any dangerous enterprise whatever, provided it was not dishonorable. My entire being was obsessed with revolution and a passion to destroy." His bravery throughout the events is above question. He stayed with Heubner after the other leaders, including Heltman and Kryzanowski, had fled. Why? Partly because he "could not bring [himself] to abandon poor Huebner," but also "and more important" (in Bakunin's judgment), because he was "more open than were the others to vile suspicions and had already been slandered more than once."[196] It was "for honor's sake" that he had to see it through, he told Heubner when it was all over.

The insurrection followed its predictably doomed course. Bakunin had won the trust of the Provisional Government by optimistically assuring them that victory would be theirs, since they could win before the Prussian troops arrived and since there were enough armed citizens to take care of the Saxon force. When he saw that "the citizens have left together with their arms and the people have lost their enthusiasm," he did not blame his own poor judgment, but the Provisional Government's waste of a day, the fourth, in negotiations.[197] Similarly, when he learned that instead of the 500 or, at least, 300 men that he said he would need to attack the arsenal he could get only 50 men, he did not blame the people's lack of enthusiasm for the rising, but the commander of the rebel troops, who, he was convinced, simply refused to send the available men: "I was then and am now even more convinced that Heinze acted like a traitor.... He contributed to the victory of the [Prussian] troops to a much greater degree than did the troops themselves...."[198] From the fifth to the ninth the Prussian soldiers advanced steadily, methodically, and, by all accounts, with extraordinary cruelty—not only against those at the barricades, but also against noncombatants seen along the way. In spite of a brave defense, encouraged by Bakunin's and Todt's exhortations at the barricades, the Prussians rolled forward, crushing one barricade after another. As early as the sixth, Heltman, Kryzanowski, Todt, and Tschirmer had all run off, although Tschirmer later came back for a short time.

Unwilling to accept the fact that the adventure had been hopeless from the start, Bakunin went on blaming others. Tschirmer was nothing more than "a scoundrel and a coward," and "Tschirmer and Heinze had so ruined things that only a miracle could have saved the democrats." "I gathered the barricade chiefs several times to try to bring about some order; to concentrate forces in preparation for an offensive, but Heinze smothered all my efforts in the bud, so that all my intense and feverish activity remained useless."[199] On the evening of the seventh Heinze was captured. His successor, Stephen Born, could do no better. After another day and a half, in the early hours of the ninth, the Provisional Government ordered a general retreat to the town of Freiberg.

In many ways, in spite of the defeat, this "final act" was Bakunin's finest performance. Throughout those four difficult days he seems to have remained a cool, efficient, hard-working member of the central command. He was no longer the Bakunin of Parisian revolutionary "intoxication." He was doing, as best he could, what he felt he must do in a cause that was not his own, without any of the exhilaration, the "paroxysm," of his Paris or even Prague days. It is instructive to compare his mood with that of his friend and revolutionary comrade, choirmaster Richard Wagner: "I experienced a sensation of vast, indeed extravagant, delight.... The view from the Kreuz Church steeple was splendid and the combination of bells and cannon, intoxicating."[200] Nothing of the kind has come down about Bakunin, either in his own description of his feelings at the time or in accounts of him given by others. For once, he just did his job.

And he did it, significantly, with minimal violence. Notwithstanding the desperate situation, the provocation of Prussian ruthlessness, and the illusion of

treason all around, there was nothing approaching a reign of terror or even excessive violence from his side. Some 70 suspects were arrested and imprisoned—
mainly former officials and aristocrats—"but they were very well treated," according to a recent scholar who has studied the events closely,[201] and were hardly being prepared for the guillotine that rumor had Bakunin building for them
"in the yard of a little house."[202] With respect to the only major act on the part
of the rebels that has been ascribed to terrorism or barbarism, the burning of the
Dresden Opera House, it has been justified by others on purely military grounds:
since it held a commanding position overlooking the area under the insurgents
control, it would have been unreasonable to expect them simply to surrender it
intact when they were forced to abandon it. Bakunin was also accused of burning civilian houses, and while he denies this, he says, reasonably enough, that he
would certainly have done so if he thought it might save the revolution. "I have
never understood how one could grieve more over houses and [other] inanimate
things than over people." Other evidence has him rather more extreme on the
issue: "Oh, houses—the only thing they are good for now is for burning." "What
are houses to us? Let them all be blown sky high!" Another witness, however,
claims that it was Bakunin who stopped them from blowing up the Royal Palace
in spite of its strategic position. There is similarly conflicting evidence as to
whether or not Bakunin wanted to bring all available gunpowder into the Town
Hall, their command post, and then blow up the building and all the insurgent
leaders inside in case of defeat. Finally, there are references to some harsh threats
he allegedly made against a city official who opposed the gunpowder idea.[203]

Assuming that even the worst accusations about the houses, the Opera House,
and the threats are true, is this all that one would have expected from a "blood
and fire" fanatic under enormous pressures and on his way to world "annihilation"? Demonstrating in practice a distinction he had already often made and
would later stress repeatedly, he might be prepared to destroy "things" but not
people.[204] Even assuming he really suggested blowing up the rebels' headquarters
with the rebels inside, it was a characteristically suicidal fantasy, destructive of
himself, not of the "enemy." Recalling later the arrest and imprisonment of the
Straka brothers, he lamented that "their ruined lives, for which I alone was the
cause, weighs like a great sin on my soul. . . . It is for this alone that I must answer
to God."[205] The sincerity of this regret is entirely believable. Although the fiercely revolutionary rhetoric and vision by now dominate the mask and the fantasy,
they have barely, if at all, touched the man himself. As in *The Reaction in Germany* and in numerous other publications and actions, it is the nonviolent, passive side that, however hidden and seemingly incidental, still reflects what is most
authentic in the man.

Nothing demonstrates the force of the fantasy more than Bakunin's actions
after the retreat from Dresden. "Reaching Freiburg and wishing to continue the

war on the Bohemian border, I hoped for a Bohemian rising."[206] A line, in these circumstances, surely worthy of the brave knight of La Mancha to his good squire Sancho Panza! But the helmet was, after all, really a basin: "everyone was exhausted and had completely ceased believing in success."[207] Since honor precluded either surrender or escape, Bakunin heard rumors that fresh recruits were on hand in Chemnitz. Arriving there thoroughly done in, he and Heubner collapsed in sleep. The curtain came down: "instead of the expected help, we found treason: the reactionary citizens arrested us in our beds during the night...."[208] So ended the Dresden insurrection, the Bohemian rebellion, the Slavic-German-Magyar revolutionary alliance, the fall of the Austrian, Prussian, and Russian Empires, and the birth of "the kingdom of love, of brotherhood... the boundless kingdom of freedom."

8.

DARK NIGHT
AND APOSTASY

He could now rest. The "final act" was over, at least for that season. His performance had been brilliant, and he had good reason to take satisfaction in it. He had held firm under fire and had stayed to the end, carrying out his duties with more than enough courage to redeem his honor and to prove, as he had set out to prove, that he was a "good soldier" and not a Tsarist agent. Moreover, lurid accounts of him in the conservative press, echoing his own apocalyptic rhetoric (especially in the *Appeal*) were now depicting him as a titanic demon, as ruthless as he was powerful, the leader not only of the Dresden rising but of a widespread, secret, and fierce revolutionary movement.[1] Rumors mated and multiplied, compounding themselves into fictions that were just the opposite of the man and his "organization." He was, thus, no longer alone in fabricating this reverse image of himself. The promethean fantasy, until now propagated mainly through his own violent declarations, was becoming a "reality," first in the press, then to the world, and, finally, for history.

Understandably, his enemies responded to the fiction rather than to the facts no less than did his admirers, doing even more than they to build it up. Although he had put up no resistance whatsoever to his arrest and throughout his years of confinement lived the life of a model prisoner, compliant and cooperative at all times, he was guarded as though he were indeed Lucifer incarnate and really did command a forceful revolutionary organization ready to rush to his rescue at the first opportunity. The elaborate, panic-ridden precautions taken to forestall the expected imminent rescue attempts, especially during transit trips between prisons, would be ludicrous were it not for the additional hardships they imposed on the prisoner.[2]

Yet, strangely, he does not complain during these first prison years. Although the time was surely ripe for another deluge of heroic suffering, there is little of the sort in his prison letters. It would be describing his mood as more depressed than it was even to speak of "resignation." To say that he was "happy" would be going too far, but, if we listen to what he himself says, this is the right direction to follow in summing up his state of mind at the time. His letters from the prison fortress at Koenigstein, where he was moved at the end of August 1849, having spent the first two prison months in Dresden, reflect more contentment than his letters had shown for years.

> As for myself, I am well and tranquil. I study mathematics a lot, am reading Shakespeare now and studying English .... I feel quite well, of course as far as that is possible in prison. I am treated here extremely humanely, and I, from my side, try to avoid anything that might be used as an excuse to change this treatment; and while I am not joyful, I am also not unhappy .... Thanks to several friends, I have here almost everything that one could desire, within reasonable limits—a comfortable room, books, cigars ....[3]

No doubt, as he went on to say, he would gladly have agreed to live in a forest and eat black bread in exchange for freedom, but he seems to have accepted that loss, too, with remarkable ease. He quickly organized his time, turning his confinement into a period for study—mainly mathematics,[4] which he talks about a great deal in these letters from the fall of 1849. While he calls it "positive" knowledge and contrasts it to the "abstract" philosophical study that he says he can no longer bear, it is obvious that his absorption in mathematics serves at least in part the purpose that his philosophical interests had served in earlier periods of isolation. Once again, as in his army years, he could depend on mind and spirit to free him from oppressive reality, for, unlike the body, "thoughts are duty-free, unconstrained by any fortress walls, and so they can roam the world over."[5]

Viewed from the perspective of his real life and motivations rather than from that of rumor and later mythology, his calm and even contentment is not so surprising. A decade earlier, having already exchanged philosophy for action, he had come to Germany in search of rebirth, a golden age, and a grand destiny as leader and savior. The overwhelming loneliness and depression he had suffered in Paris in the mid-1840s when he was deprived of action and the glorious sense of power and honor he experienced when he had been involved in revolutionary action at the end of the 1840s are proof enough of the strength of that need. But, compelling though it was, it was always balanced by a still more essential need to remain apart, always free to withdraw to his "Gothic castle, on top of a high, steep, inaccessible mountain," his "splendid mansion with sturdy gates and locks so that nothing alien to it can again penetrate into its forbidden temple," his "bright, inner world" closed off "with a monastic fence" and "a strong, high wall inaccessible to ever-changing externality," so that he could "cross behind the wall whenever things [went] badly for him in the outer world."

And things had gone very badly for him in that outer world. As he wrote a friend during those first months in prison, "To be frank, I had little to be happy about in Germany during the past two years. I have often been in the most difficult situations. Alone, very often without money, I was, in addition, vilified as a Russian spy and at the same time, from the other side, considered to be an insane, violent Jacobin. The fact that I was regarded as a Russian spy, moreover, drove me to some intentionally careless steps, confused everything, and landed me in trouble." So badly had things gone for him, in fact, that "for many years now I have not had any great desire to live. I live out of a sense of duty . . . ."[6]

What is involved here is not simply exhaustion and rest after long battle, but rather reprieve from the obligation of playing a rigorously demanding role that was the opposite of his true self. Well, the role had now been played, admirably and honorably. He had dared *to seem* powerful, not enough, of course, to win power and possession, but enough at least to feign virility and experience "electrifying" "paroxysm" with his beloved people's revolution. (The ferocity of his declarations and the extremism of his aims, while seeming to demonstrate power, in fact virtually guaranteed by that very extremism that he would never really have to possess it.) Then, having dared to appear virile, to challenge authority for possession of the "people," he was duly and severely punished by defeat and imprisonment. So, the slate was clean. He had paid a high price for his audacity, and could feel free again, reprieved into prison, safe for a time behind his "monastic fence" and "strong, high wall."

In the meantime, as he spent his days in study and relative comfort (all things considered), official investigations into his role in Dresden proceeded. Especially illustrative of his calm, detached mood that first prison year is his failure to help his counsel prepare a defense. After first refusing to give the lawyer a statement reviewing his own side of the events, he decided to write one after all but turned it in weeks after the attorney had already argued the case. In mid-January 1850 he, Heubner, and Röckel were sentenced to death, but he had been assured beforehand[7] that this was only a dramatic gesture to make the forthcoming monarchic clemency, commuting the sentence to life imprisonment, all the more merciful. Clemency, however, first required an appeals trial. Another defense had to be prepared. The attorney begged Bakunin to write something, anything, for him. Again nothing came, until three weeks after the second defense had been presented.[8]

What Bakunin sent then was an abbreviated version of the statement he had begun working on, belatedly, for the first trial. The precis is a bold reaffirmation of the principles that had guided him through the revolutionary years. As a loyal Russian, he said, he had given his life to the liberation of the enslaved masses both in Russia and abroad. But, he added, one could not really separate the struggle geographically this way. A free Russia meant a free Europe; an enslaved and despotic Russia, a dominated Europe. The same was true for Germany: there must be a free Germany, not an imperial Germany controlling Slavic subjects. Everyone should be free, and all should join in defense of civilization and human rights. After this preamble, Bakunin gave a brief survey of his travels and policies, beginning appropriately with the November 1847 speech in Paris and pausing along the way to deny emphatically the charge that he had plotted the assasination of Tsar Nicholas I: "Could anyone find in the course of my life even the slightest capacity in me for murder?" Concerning his remaining in Germany after the Prague failure, he said he wanted to stay close to the "only theater where I could act." As for the Dresden rising itself, he had not taken part in its preparation in any way, was surprised by it and prepared at first to leave, could not have been a leader in it since he did not know Dresden that well, and had remained only because he "considered flight disgraceful."[9] Once the appeals court confirmed, as expected, the death sentence of the lower court, the way was clear for the king's grace. It came on June twelfth. That same night Bakunin was turned over to the Austrians.

Although the longer self-defense, from which the summary statement was drawn, never played any part in Bakunin's actual defense, it is a fascinating document in itself. It is much the longest work he had written so far, covering over 60 printed pages.[10] To say that it attempts a political history of the modern Western world is only a slight exaggeration. It includes a survey history of Russia, a lengthy review of sectarian religious movements in Russia considered as a form of political opposition, a close look at the role of the people in the defeat of Napoleon, a discourse on German history and current German conditions, along with advice for a sound German foreign policy, an analysis of the complex interdependency between foreign policy and domestic politics in Russia and Germany, some passing swipes at liberals and Jews, a summary of the past, present, and future of Austria, Italy, Poland, and Galicia, and a bird's-eye view of eighteenth and nineteenth century European ideologies and political trends. It was, he said, his "political testament." His main resource in preparing it was, he said, "the nature of things."[11] In part, it is indeed a trial defense, in the sense that it explains the broad historical and contemporary forces that supposedly guided and justified his politics during the revolutionary years (1848-49). But that purpose was adequately served by the short precis, and, in any case, this encyclopedic survey was hardly what his attorney needed or wished from him. Other motives lay behind this "testament." What Bakunin seems to be attempting here, and would soon try again in his "Confession" to the Tsar, was to bring to the world, or at least to the eminent personages who would read the document, evidence of his own outstanding talents as a global strategist and policy maker. It represents, in effect, the beginning of another shift in his intellectual career, one that would take him back again not only towards reconciliation with authority but, for a time, to a radically new synthesis between power and rebellion—fascism.

There is some evidence even during that first prison year to suggest that he was having second thoughts about his revolutionary views, for example, the remarks quoted above about how unhappy he had been "during the past two years" (i.e., the revolutionary years) and how he had even felt life itself a burden at the time. Later in that same letter, written in February 1850, he critically reevaluated his grand revolutionary design of 1848-49: "I was alone, with nothing but my sincere good will, and perhaps one could reproach me for being quixotic even to think of such a gigantic undertaking." Second thoughts about his own revolutionary plans in no way implied doubts about violent change, however. He was still convinced that "the slightest human progress, each new vital growth has been the result of a flood of human blood" (and in expressing this conviction he still revealed as clearly as ever the personal motivations behind it):

> Storms in the world of morality are as necessary as they are in nature. They cleanse and rejuvenate the spiritual atmosphere. They stir slumbering powers. They destroy what is due for destruction and bestow new and everlasting lustre to that which is eternally alive. It is easier to breathe in a storm. Only in struggle can you know what a man can and must do. And such a storm was surely necessary for the contemporary world, for it had come very close to suffocating in its own polluted air.[12]

Both the "final death struggle" and, its rationale and goal, the "more youthful, splendid world"[13] were still imminently at hand, but, having come to realize how "quixotic"[14] his earlier fantasy had been, he was now open to new formulas for achieving the apocalyptic miracle, especially, as we will see, if they might hold as well possibilities for his own release from prison.

The Saxony prisons in Dresden and Koenigstein, were havens of comfort and indulgence compared to those that followed: first one in Prague from mid-June 1850 to mid-March 1851, then the most severely repressive of all of them, the prison fortress of Olmütz, Moravia, where Bakunin was at times chained to the wall. He went on with his mathematics, however, and, judging from his bearing before his Austrian interrogators, maintained his spirits and his hard-won honor. Once more he was ritually sentenced to death, then given life imprisonment instead, and immediately, with even more than the usual excessive precautions, shipped out of the country, this time into the hands of those he had most feared, those who had meant "death" to him—the Russians, the "hawk," the "bear," the "blind Tsar."

A week later, at the end of May 1851, he was back in St. Petersburg, in the Peter-Paul fortress. After the dreadful Olmütz experience, his return home was by contrast an improvement, particularly since he was met by such "noble, humane and indulgent treatment,"[15] instead of by the merciless punishment he had been expecting. Two months after his arrival, an opportunity came for him to express his gratitude for this unexpected leniency. Through an aide, the Tsar, for reasons known only to himself, sent Bakunin a gentle, paternal letter, assuring him that his life was not in danger and urging him to confess his sins to the Tsar as he would to a father confessor.[16] Bakunin's response was his famous "Confession." For his admirers, as well as for revolutionaries in general, it has been a source of deep shame and embarrassment ever since its revelation. While generally agreeing that it was a hoax, a deceptive ruse—the possibility of it being quite sincere is usually too scandalous for consideration—they divide over whether or not such obeisance was justifiable, even as a means of deception. However, set in its own prison context, considered against the background of Bakunin's life until that time, rather than his life as a revolutionary that still lay ahead, and judged in the light of the real man and not the promethean fiction, the document stands as a fundamentally honest and forthright statement of Bakunin's thoughts and feelings at the time.

Rarely, on record, did Bakunin talk about the "Confession." He referred to it once in a letter he wrote from Siberia to Herzen, in December 1860, and again in remarks he made to a close friend, Zemfiri Ralli, who mentions it in his memoirs. In neither case does Bakunin say what his staunch defenders were to say and what he might easily have said to clear himself; namely, that he was lying in order to deceive the Tsar and thereby win freedom for continuing the revolutionary struggle. "I thought a while, then decided," he wrote Herzen, "that had there been a jury, an open trial, I would have been obliged to sustain the role to the end, but that behind four walls, in the power of the bear, I could without shame soften the forms, and so asked for a month's time and agreed to write something like a real confession, rather in the nature of *Dichtung and Wahrheit.*"[17] What was Dichtung and what Wahrheit? Bakunin himself may have pointed the way to an answer in the two sentences that come after: "My actions were in any event so well-known that it would have been useless to try to conceal them"—Wahrheit, and "Thanking the Tsar in the proper terms for his indulgent attention"—Dichtung. If Dichtung had meant much more than that, if it had referred, that is, to all the self-effacing, self-lacerating, and contrite statements that fill the "Confession" and cause his apologists so much anguish, then surely he would have made that quite clear. Similarly, in the remarks recounted by Ralli, Bakunin does admit that the "Confession" had been a "great mistake"; however, the reason he gives is not that he had feigned repentance as a way of getting out, but that he had been such a "Slavophile" in his statements and had given so great a role to Russia in the coming struggle for Slavic liberation. It was this, he said, that he feared would be misunderstood by the Tsar. There is not a word about putting on an act to free himself. In fact, the only talk of an "act" comes in his comment to Herzen about sustaining a firm *revolutionary* "role," were there a jury to see it, which squares well with his "charlatan" comments in the "Confession."[18]

To come to grips with this important issue, it would be best to divide the contents of the "Confession" into credibility categories. By far the greater bulk of the work is a review of his revolutionary life in the 1840s. Since this is basically the same account that we find in his letters as well as in the statements to his attorney and to his Saxon and Austrian interrogators,[19] there is no reason to doubt its essential authenticity. Then, there are a whole series of fascinating self-analyses, probes into his own personality and the motivations for his actions. Some of these have been quoted earlier, in connection with his life in the 1840s, so well do they summarize the character of what he was doing and saying at the time—his being at once deceiver and deceived, his acknowledged love of the fantastic, his basic shyness, his tendency toward the "quixotic," and so on.

In deciding whether or not to accept these and comparable remarks at face value, one should keep in mind only what had come before in Bakunin's life, since that is all that was in his mind: five or so years of suicidal loneliness and frustration in the 1840s, a brief year and one half surge of revolutionary "paroxysm" generated mainly by personal causes that had only recently and tenuously been connected to larger social and political issues, then, crushing failure and unhappiness deep enough to lead him to question life itself, and, finally, two prison years to think it all over. Given his short-lived, ultimately disastrous and psychologically guilt-ridden association with the revolution, there is nothing improbable about a decision to turn back, reconsider his relationship to it and begin to work out a new formula for satisfying his contradictory needs. Viewed from this perspective, *his* perspective at the time, there is ample reason to accept the sincerity of this retrospective reappraisal that he shared with his "father confessor," especially since it also held out the chance of earning forgiveness and release.

Apart from the vastness of the crime, You must find it very amusing, Sire, that, unknown and powerless, I set out alone on a war against

You, the great Tsar of a great kingdom. I clearly see now my insanity and would laugh at myself, it I were up to laughing .... But at the time, I saw nothing, thought about nothing, and advanced to my certain ruin as one possessed .... Recalling now with what paltry means I imagined I could carry through a revolution in Bohemia, it strikes me as comic. I myself do not understand how I could have hoped for success. But nothing could have stopped me then. I reasoned as follows: revolution is necessary, consequently it is possible.[20]

Accepting as authentic his account of the events, his self-analysis of his motivations, and his belated awareness of just how fantastic his plans and actions had been, we are left with a final category of statements, his groveling, obsequious submission to the Tsar's grace.

Yes, Sire, I will confess to You as to a spiritual father from whom one hopes for forgiveness, not here but for another world, and I ask God to inspire me with simple, sincere, words from the heart, devoid of cunning and flattery, words that are worthy, in short, of finding access to the heart of Your imperial majesty .... Sire! In this confession I have concealed nothing from You, nothing, not a single sin, not a single crime; I have bared my entire soul before You. You have seen my delusions, how I fell from one madness into another, from error into sin, from sin into crime.... I will speak before You as I would speak before God, whom neither flattery nor lies can deceive.... And now, I turn again to my Tsar and, falling to the feet of Your imperial majesty, I implore you ... do not let me rot in eternal prison confinement![21]

Given the revolutionary code of prison defiance, one can understand why other revolutionaries might not forgive Bakunin such obeisance, even were it nothing more than deception. But was it deception? Merely "Dichtung"? If he were so calculating and cunning in his attempt to win the Tsar's favor, why would he have emphasized as much as he did throughout the "Confession" the violence of his revolutionary war against Tsarist Russia? And, surely, he could have covered the main points in his revolutionary plan without going on as long and as vehemently as he did about the evils in Tsarist Russia. Given his situation at the time, his preceding prison years, and the main currents of his life and mind until then, even this abasement may well have been entirely sincere. Difficult as it is to bear in mind (considering what was to come), we must realize just how brief and tenuous Bakunin's revolutionary ties had been in the 1840s. Failure and disillusionment, continuing religious devotion and a profoundly religious temperament, a not unreasonable hope that his initial good treatment together with the Tsar's paternalistic invitation to confess might point the way to freedom—these all could well have joined to bring him to this stage of devout contrition.

One other factor may also have played its part here. Indeed, if the speculation supporting it is correct, it may have been decisive. Several times in the
course of confessing to the Tsar, Bakunin spoke in terms of a son doing penance
before his father. "Gifted with a fervent imagination and, as the French say,
d'une grande dose d'exaltation. . . . I caused my aging father much grief, for
which I now repent with all my soul, even though it comes late." "But it is less
difficult than it is painful for me, Sire, to speak with You about what I have
dared to think concerning the direction and spirit of Your rule, painful in all
ways: painful because of the position I am in, standing before You, Sire, as a
condemned criminal; painful to my pride, since I can hear You, Sire, saying 'the
boy is chattering away about things he doesn't understand!' And most of all,
painful to my heart, since I stand before You as a prodigal, estranged, corrupted
son before his offended and angry father!"[22] Is he, in fact, through the mirror of
the deeper drama and conflict that had guided so much of his life, standing
before his father, repenting before him? The similarities between his attitude
toward his father and his relations now with the Tsar are impressive. A radical
ambivalence defines them both—warm, glowing praise, well suited to disarming
hostility and avoiding punishment, and furious denunciation accompanying an
assault on everything the two potentates stand for. Also, with regard to both his
blind father and the "blind Tsar," the son sharply separates the "abstact" role of
the enemy from his "living, sublime person."[23] Not only, for example, does he
assure the Tsar that "there has never been in my heart even the slightest shadow
of hatred against You," but he goes on to recall that, while he was in military
school, he had "passionately loved him" and had been ecstatic when the Tsar
once visited their camp. Even later, after he had become a revolutionary and was
"obligated to hate Emperor Nicholas," the hatred was only "in imagination, in
thought, not in my heart." "The impressions from youth are not easily effaced,
Sire."[24]

Throughout the earlier chapters of this study we have seen that precisely the
same recollections of early love towards his father, or at least professions of it,
remained intact in spite of a constant verbal barrage against him as the personification of familial and social control. "Blind obedience," "a slave relationship,"
"blind arbitrary will"—the phrases and the sentiments behind them appear in his
relations with his father years before they appear in his "Confession" to the
Tsar. In fact, his adolescent confessions to his father and his later voluminous
letters to him (his 1840 defense of his need to go abroad, for example, or his
1837 remembrances of paternal things past, benevolent and tyrannical) read like
veritable rehearsals for the later "Confession." Nor was the "Confession" the
first occasion of this merger between father and Tsar. Why had he turned against
the Tsar in the first place? It was not because of a *socially-conscious political*

outrage over the Tsar's oppression of the Russian masses or Polish people, but a *personally-conscious filial* outrage at being told to go home and threatened with disinheritance.

We must keep in mind how late the concern for the oppressed masses or national minorities entered Bakunin's rebellion. Its essential form and dynamics were already well established long before he took any interest whatsoever in politics, much less in the fate of the "people." It is only the cast of characters that change: tyrannical father, tyrannized sisters, and liberator son become tyrannical Tsar, tyrannized "people," and revolutionary. The drama was the same, and so was the fear. No wonder that as he moved eastward on his way back to the "hawk," he repeatedly suffered an inner "coldness" for reasons he cannot explain and that once in the hands of the "bear" he rejoiced at the good treatment, certain, as he stated again and again in the "Confession," that he really deserved to die for his "crime" and "sin." (How strikingly like, incidentally, the time Bakunin had mistakenly assumed his father had accused him of the worst crimes or the day he came home late for supper, paralyzed with dread of what he thought would be his father's wrath, then overcome with relief and love for him when he was spared punishment.) Transferred back into this personal setting where they belong, the contrition, penance, abasement, and confession are as "true" as was the narrative of his "objective" political actions. He can confess now, unburden himself at least somewhat, because he had undergone the catharsis of punishment. Having now suffered real pain, especially in Olmütz, and not just the fantasy pain of his familiar credo, he could forgive and, for a time, accept himself, and having found that the father-Tsar was not the monster he had dreaded, he could forgive and accept him as well, confess before him, and be home again. A new period of reconciliation had begun.

Expressing his second reconciliation in terms strongly reminiscent of his first, he once again bowed before the indomitable force of history, lowering the "impotent arm" he had dared raise in rebellion:

> I understand that history goes its own mysterious ways; that it has its own logic, which often contradicts the logic of the ordinary world; that it is redemptive, although it does not always correspond to our private desires; and that—other than a few exceptions, extremely rare in history, that are, so to speak, permitted by Providence and sanctified by the approval of posterity—no single person, however sincere, honest, or saintly his convictions might seem to be, has either the mission or the right to raise his rebellious thought and impotent arm against this inscrutable higher destiny. I understood, in a word, that my own ideas and actions were to the highest degree comic, senseless, impudent and criminal.[25]

But the reconciliation this time was not simply a replica of the reconciliation of the late 1830s. He did not merely withdraw from the battlefield as he had done (or at least claimed to have done) in the earlier reconciliation. His strategy this time was more involved: if he could not win in his revolution against power, he would try to bring power over to the side of the revolution. Bizarre as this might seem, it was this enterprise—the attempt to persuade the arch-despot, the "blind Tsar" (or one of his viceroys) to lead the war against despotism—that Bakunin undertook in his "Confession" and, as we will see, in most of his letters and relationships during the subsequent years of his imprisonment and exile. Actually, from the "right" Hegelian perspective, so evident again in that preceding quotation, this was not really so strange. The state, according to Hegel, was the highest embodiment of Absolute Reason as it advanced dialectically in its "mysterious way"; the power and victory of the Tsar were, therefore, proof of his Rational Reality; there was no reason why authoritarianism could not be used for good as well as for evil; and, as we have seen, Bakunin had himself usually chosen dictatorship as his midwife for the birth of the kingdom. Therefore: "I asked [myself] why does the present government, the autocracy, armed with limitless power, unconstrained by law or, in fact, by any rule outside of itself, by a single competing force, why does it not use its omnipotence for liberation, for the elevation and enlightenment of the Russian people."[26]

It would be incorrect, however, to say that this thought came to him only after his imprisonment. According to the "Confession," he had written the Tsar an even wider-ranging proposal after the Prague failure, "imploring" him "in the name of all the oppressed Slavs to go to their aid, take them under your powerful protection, be their savior, their father, and, proclaiming yourself Tsar of all the Slavs, raise at last the Slavic flag in Eastern Europe, to the dread of the Germans and all other oppressors and enemies of the Slavic peoples."[27] That appeal, he went on to say in the "Confession," echoed the hopes of all other Slavs, including even the Poles who, "deceived by the French revolutionary government, deceived by the Germans, insulted by the German yid,.... rush to the protection of the Russian Emperor and ask him to be gracious enough to unite all the Poles of the Austrian and Prussian provinces to Russia."[28] (Even in his own plans for a revolutionary Slavic union, as we saw and as he recounts in the "Confession," the Poles and Czechs were expected "to cede first place" to Russia.)[29]

What he was offering the Tsar was something still grander than hegemony over Eastern Europe, however, for "I thought, I hoped, that the Magyar nation, forced by circumstance, by its isolated position among Slavic peoples, and also by its own more Eastern than Western character, that all the Moldavians and Wallachians, finally that even Greece as well would enter the Slavic union, and that there would thus be created a single, free Eastern state, something in the way of a reborn world of the East in opposition, but not in enmity, to the West, and that its capital would be Constantinople."[30] To show how seriously he took this whole line of thought, he devoted to it a substantial portion of the "Confession," humbly explaining to the Tsar why it would be so much better for him, for the Russian people, and for the Russian state if he were to stop pursuing his misguided reactionary policies and instead lead the way in this universal liberation.

In terms of the inner drama, this was the full realization of what his successive plans for dictatorship had always implied. By playing the role of counselor to the Tsar, he could identify himself with power and share its virility not by possessing it himself, but by attaching himself to it as a subordinate (and powerless) helpmate. And through the fantasy of the Tsar as enlightened savior as well as all-powerful dictator (the dream-like combination of opposites that had always been implicit in his fantasies about himself) he could enjoy this new alliance with real power at no loss to his revolutionary honor. Revolutionary Tsar. Absolute power and universal revolution combined. Omnipotent father and rebellious son. Here, indeed, seemed the ideal wish-fulfillment, the perfect dream synthesis.

Nicholas read the confession attentively, making marginal notes along the way, but was not persuaded to improve the lot of the "repentent sinner," as Bakunin signed himself. He did, however, grant one request, that Bakunin's parents and his "one beloved sister" be permitted to visit him.[31] Since his father, 84 years old and now completely blind, was not up to the trip, brother Nicholas went in his place, taking the "beloved sister," Tatiana, with him. The meeting took place that October, two months after Bakunin completed the "Confession."

For the next half year after the "Confession," there is a break in Bakunin's correspondence, or at least in the letters that have come down to us. Once they are again available, beginning in January and February 1852, they provide additional evidence of the authenticity of the "Confession," for its being, in general, an honest and sincere statement rather than a cunning deception. Regret, contrition, and repentence fill these letters to his family as much as they do the "Confession," in some ways even more so. Blaming his fall mainly on the influence of German philosophy, he urged his brother Alexander to learn from his mistakes and to realize that the only result of such abstract philosophizing is a "mass of false ideas." "A person is never so stupid," he wrote, "as when he thinks only about himself" and, still worse, "constantly criticizes and insults other people, turning them into our enemies. That is the story of my life. You recall, surely, what a crank I was in Premukhino for all outsiders." Rather than end up a "dreamer and chase after illusions," Alexander should devote himself earnestly to a "life of work," and not fret about "his lost freedom, about his abstract studies, about his useless and aimless fantasies." His own life was now over, he went on, having "no aims, no future." Except for thoughts about Premukhino, all the more intense now, he said, after the family visit and his parents' forgiveness of their "profligate son," he would now "try not to think at all, for thoughts torment and oppress me too much with vain regrets and repentence that comes too late."

All he could do now was "smoke cigarettes, read novels and tell [himself] stories. To a certain extent, it is the life of an opium smoker, an eternal dream, sometimes a bad dream of a ruined Don Quixote, sometimes a fantastic dream in the spirit of Hoffman...." The only good he could do now was to sit there, "like a post with the warning 'do not take this road'." But that road now lay in the past; his punishment and suffering had "purified" him; and "I swear that were I now offered my freedom on the condition that I resume my former aimless and frantic life...I would not agree to it." All that he wanted to do now, he said, was to share the lives of his family at Premukhino through their letters, which he urged them to send more often, and "let the world completely forget my existence." He now had nothing but the best to say about everyone at home, even Varvara's husband, who he hoped would write him. His father, "friend and benefactor of hundreds of immortal souls, yet at the same time caring for the needs and education of his own family," is the model he now advised his brothers to follow. How fortunate they were to have with them "our kind, wise, father who knows so much, whose advice and experience will not be lost on you as they were lost on me...."[32]

This change of attitude is especially evident in his advice to Alexander and his new wife, Lisa. In page after page, he gently advised them to adopt precisely that life of "custom, propriety, and obligation" that he had always abhorred. Besides keeping away from philosophy and attending to the business of the estate, Alexander is to dress properly, listen to the wise counsel of his father and elder brother, Nicholas, avoid introspection, and learn to laugh at himself. He should be innovative in managing the economy of the manor and, as others in their class, conscious of the responsibilities of the landed gentry, since his privileged position was "a public function, a form of service, political and moral at the same time, almost religious, that is temporarily entrusted to the gentry by the government more as a duty than a right." While such privilege and power could be abused, it also gave one "the possibility of doing much good: it all depends on one's ability to get down to work and not chase after impossible reforms, disdaining those that are easy to realize."

Having thus warned Alexander again against being "quixotic," he went on to provide him detailed instructions on how one should deal with the peasants, given their "natural suspiciousness, obstinacy, ignorance, fanaticism, prejudices" They must be treated as "children, children by nature of their ignorance." But they must not be forced to act against their will: they should be treated with love and respect and won over only gradually, patiently. "The method of applying forceful measures is quicker, but I prefer my own because it is less abrupt, more civil, and, besides, will lead to better and more durable results, for it is based on the convictions and the voluntary agreement of those to whom and for whose welfare it is applied." However: "I am not preaching weakness. On the contrary, I am convinced that along with much good will and, especially, constant justice, a great deal of severity is also absolutely necessary. The Russian peasant considers it a failing not to deceive where deception is possible and despises those they deceive.... Although I am not at all very fond of corporal punishment, I think that, unfortunately, it is still completely necessary. If you have to order a whipping, dear friend, then do so. But never do the whipping yourself. That would be vile."[33] (Once again, nonviolent violence).

It is difficult to know how long this mood lasted. The letters for the rest of that year (1852) and through 1853 are few, brief, and rather curt. Jesus and God are still with him, and he can still "praise God every day for having returned me to Russia." He continues declaring his devotion to Premukhino, still loves Tatiana "more than everything in the world" and laments the fact that she has ceased writing him, shares the family's deep grief over the deaths of Alexander's young wife, Lisa, and Varvara's husband, and concerns himself with the proper education of Varvara's son to make sure that he becomes "not only an intelligent, but a worldly man, a complete gentleman."[34] Nevertheless, except for remarks to Lisa in a letter from May 1852, the letters are terse, rather heavy, and not at all like the January and February letters.

The reasons for this shift in sentiment may be found in letters he wrote in February 1854. Taking advantage of a visit from Paul and Tatiana that month, he secretly gave her some letters, at considerable risk to her as well as to himself. Two years had passed since the reconciliation of January-February 1852 (and two and a half years since the "Confession"), two years of unrelieved tedium and loneliness, largely in solitary confinement, made worse toward the end by serious and painful illness. It was more than reconciliation could bear. As bliss had turned to boredom in the first Hegelian reconciliation some 14 years before, in 1839, so did resignation turn, for a time, to renewed rebellion during this second reconciliation.

He had no strength to go on any longer, he said in the clandestine letters. Scurvy, pounding headaches, hemorrhoids, and feverish hours struggling to catch his breath had utterly exhausted him. They had also left their mark on his appearance. He was "terribly disfigured." His teeth had fallen out and his face had become heavily bloated. His brother Paul was shocked, and he himself could not bear to look in a mirror. But worse still was the by-now unbearable isolation and immobility. He felt as though he had been "buried alive." Nothing could be worse. Death would be a deliverance, he said repeatedly with only slightly veiled hints of suicide. "Even Napoleon would sink into stupefaction and Jesus Christ himself grow embittered" after years of such conditions. He craved action now as never before, he said. "A flaming thirst for movement and activity" consumed him, and he felt himself "capable of any sacrifice and even heroism." He told Tatiana that he would "begin again what led me here, only with more wisdom and more caution" and that his ordeal "had in no way changed my former convictions, but, instead, made them more fervent, more determined, more unconditional." (In another secret letter, however, he qualified the envisioned heroism somewhat with a significant vow: "I promise you that if they free me, I will remain tranquil and undertake nothing unorthodox while father is alive."

Remaining on this elemental level a while longer, his thoughts then moved, in the next line, to Tatiana. "I love you, I deeply, deeply love and respect you. I even envy your son a little [Lisa's child, who, with his encouragement, Tatiana was raising]. Let me also be your son, while I am here, and so come back more quickly.")[35]

In mid-March 1854, about a month after Tatiana's and Paul's visit, Bakunin was moved to another prison, Schlüsselberg, on Lake Ladoga, and while he remained isolated and under strict supervision his material conditions improved considerably. His daily ration was increased, and even included a jigger of vodka for dinner, and he was permitted to receive more packages from home, citrus fruit for the scurvy, a variety of reading materials, and, except for occasional lapses, an adequate flow of his indispensable tea and tobacco ("Turkish, please, the same kind that you once sent me, Baerutski Strong, from the Fortun Factory, at Zhako's house in Bolshoi Morskoi").[36] Best of all, he had won the affection and sympathetic attention of a general's daughter, who acted openly as intermediary between Bakunin and Premukhino for letters and supplies. Besides arrangements for these supplies, expressions of family affection, and criticism of Tatiana for not writing, the remaining letters that year (1854) mainly concern the heroic role his brothers were playing in the Crimean War and the family's fears for their safety. His joy and pride in their heroism seemed quite genuine, and may well have been an important stimulus behind his rekindled "flaming thirst for movement and activity... sacrifice and even heroism," the revived Fichtean passion in the secret letters. "It is hard to imagine more flattering or more honorable praise" than that received for defending Sevastapol. "And the promise of a Cross of St. George on top of it!" "They are all fine young men, and each one of them, given the chance would fulfill his duty with intelligence, dedication and strength. I am sure of that, and I know also that, through the special blessing that we have *inherited from father, all that they have, they have in common; and whereas such things as a medal or a wife cannot be shared,* the honor and happiness, acquired by one, is enthusiastically shared by all. You, dear little mother ... and you Tatiana ...."[37]

Although their father had the honor of seeing his son Alexander enter the service, he did not live to share the glory of his success.[38] He died December 4, 1854, at the age of 88. "I am entirely guilty, dear Elizaveta Ivanovna [the general's daughter]. I should have answered you long since and returned your journals, but the sad news struck me so hard that for a while I lacked the strength even to move a finger .... Is mother well? Tatiana? ... I am returning number 32 of *Revue des deux Mondes*...." Except for one other reference to his "deceased father" in another letter to his benefactress, this is all we have of his response to his father's death.[39]

Almost immediately after her husband's death, Bakunin's mother began a strenuous campaign first to be permitted to visit her son, then to win his release. The visit was arranged for early March 1855, delayed that long because of the death of Tsar Nicholas on February eighteenth and the succession of Alexander II. Together with Michael's brother Alexei, she spent some three weeks in St. Petersburg and five days at Schlüsselberg, during which time she met with Michael in the office of the prison commandant.[40] She now took the main part in the family's efforts to free him: "my principal hope is now in you, my dear mother."

Bakunin had again felt himself able to approach his mother affectionately even before his father's death, perhaps because he once again, as during the Hegelian reconcilation of 1837-38, had dropped the pose of powerful, virile warrior. There had been, indeed, those desperate remarks in the letters he had given to Tatiana in February 1854, but in the context of everything else he wrote during these years in successive prisons and, then (as we will see) in exile, those sentiments are markedly the exception. (However those secret letters are interpreted, moreover, they can be readily explained by the severe degeneration of his conditions and mood in the months immediately preceding Tatiana's 1854 visit, conditions that, as we have seen, had been significantly improved.) In his first letters following the "Confession," the January-February, 1852 letters (those in which he so thoroughly defended "custom, propriety and obligation"), he gave his first indication of this revived good relationship with his mother: "As for you, dear mother, thank you, thank you for wanting to come. I have deeply wronged you and keenly sense how much generosity and love there is in your forgiveness."[41] With his father's death, his mother's visits with him in Schlüsselberg, and her energetic efforts toward winning his release, he became still more expansive and daring in expressing his tender feelings towards her. "After you left," he wrote her following a visit in August 1856, "I walked and walked, lay down, again walked a long time, thinking only of you, then sat down and wrote you these lines, as though I were chasing after you with my thoughts and my heart to say good-bye to you one more time, and having written, became calm.... You are so kind, understanding. One feels oneself so free with you, that some outsider might think, looking at our manner with you, that you are to us—an older sister, not a mother. *But that is not dangerous,* because along with all the love, the confiding of everything, and the freedom in our behaviour with you, not one of us even for a moment forgets that deep, religious respect that children have towards their mother...."[42]

Neither her efforts, nor those of his brothers and of the many influential friends the family turned to for help did any good. The state was adamant, refusing any moderation of the prisoner's punishment, much less his release. Desperate, Bakunin decided to beg again. First, he implored Prince V. A. Dolgorukov, head of the gendarmes, to give him permission to write Alexander II in the hope the Tsar would "lighten" his punishment and give him a chance to be something useful after a life "that has brought nothing but harm to others and to myself." Although, he said, he had nothing but his word to prove to Dolgorukov the honor of his motives, he assured him that his word bound him as much as did the fortress walls. Besides, "it is already too late for me to return to an active life, even if I so desired. My strength is broken. Illness has crushed me. It is only that I do not want to die in a dungeon."[43] Permission was granted, and Bakunin wrote his second confession.

In comparison to it, the first "Confession" seems strong and dignified, perhaps because of the heroic revolutionary career it surveyed, the audacity of advising the Tsar on foreign policy, and a certain firmness, even in the more submissive sections. The plea to Alexander II is a forlorn dirge of a spent and broken man. He simply begs for clemency. The years of isolation in "the silence of the tomb," the "profound, inexpressibly painful regret over my having destroyed, irreparably and senselessly, any chance of ever being a support for my family, as my five brothers are, and an active servant of my government," a full awareness of just how "empty, useless, harmful" his past had been, the humiliating comparison between his own shameful inaction in the current war and the courageous service of his five brothers—it was all, he lamented, more than he could bear. If he could efface this sorry past through some "purifying service," he would do so, willingly paying with his own blood for his crimes. But "illness has made me incapable of anything," and, with nothing to offer in return, he can only implore the Tsar to spare him the fate of dying in prison, to grant him a chance "to breathe one last time in freedom, gaze at the clear sky and the fresh meadows, see the house of my father, bow down before his grave, and, devoting my last days to my mother, broken with grief because of me, prepare myself for a dignified death."[44]

The plea was sent February 14, 1857. On the nineteenth, Tsar Alexander decreed that Bakunin be allowed to exchange prison for exile to Siberia. Three days later, he sent another letter to Prince Dolgorukov with a "new and last request." Could he not stop over for a day or so at Premukhino on his way to Siberia? That request was also granted, and on March eighth Bakunin left St. Petersburg for Premukhino, where, according to one account, he spent a gloomy, almost wordless day, mainly playing games with one of the nannies, or, according to another, "talked a lot, laughed joyfully, reminisced about the past, sang various songs along with the others, joked and laughed some more."[45]

What was to happen during the ensuing three years of Siberian exile would show that the eight years of prison life he was now ending had all but wiped out the eight preceding years of faith in mass revolution, that, in other words, the lament to Alexander II was as sincere as the "Confession" to Tsar Nicholas had been. Two prospects were open to a well-born political exile like Bakunin. He could join his fellow revolutionary exiles, such as the Decembrists and members of the Petrashevsky circle,[46] or, taking advantage of his class and connections, he could join the guards. Continuing the conversion already well begun in the "Confession," Bakunin joined the guards, while trying, of course—he was still Bakunin—to make them appear a higher order of revolutionaries. The argument that all this, too, was sham and deception, sand in the eyes of gullible officials, to help conceal a carefully thought-through plan of escape that he steadily realized step by step over three years not only lacks evidence and adequate plausibility, but denies the complexity of the man. For a person to feel and live at different times, or even simultaneously, sharply contrasting convictions, and to live and feel each of the opposites as intensely and authentically as the other is hardly unusual even among ordinary mortals. For extraordinary personalities like Bakunin (and many others among the Russian intelligentsia) it is practically the defining character trait. In other words, Bakunin's "Confession" of 1851, his philistine sermon to brother Alexander, his desperate letters of February 1854, and his doleful plea to Alexander II of 1857 all mean just what they say at the time they appear, however different the moods they express. Since, for many people, ambivalence of one sort or another is virtually the pulse of life itself, these comments are truisms and would be entirely unnecessary here were it not for the simplistic, one-sided revolutionary mold into which both critics and friends have long tried to squeeze Bakunin.

It is, admittedly, difficult to believe that Bakunin spoke and acted as he did during his years of exile, that, at the very outset, for example, while in Omsk *en route* to Tomsk, he could write to the head of the Third Section (the secret police) to say how "touched I was by the kindness and attentive care" shown him by his guard. "In his appointment as my companion to Siberia, I could not but see a continuation of that expansive, noble, and truly Russian kindness which has called me back from death to a new, proper life and which, Your Excellency, I dare to hope, will not leave me in that distant prison."[47] Another letter he wrote on that trip is, on the contrary, all too familiar. "Only one thing somewhat troubles me," he told his mother, "it seems that the money you gave me for the trip was not enough, not even for the first year. I will have to make household arrangements for myself; buy a little house, perhaps; learn how to run it, to buy and sell; in other words, to stand on my own two feet. And you know what an impractical person I am when it comes to such things."[48] (He was now 43 years old.)

He actually did this time go through the motions of finding employment. He had to do something, he wrote a gendarme general who was passing through Tomsk, not only to free his family from the burden of supporting him, but also because his "entire life, devoted to abstractions and finally entangling itself in illegal activities, has gone by without my having done anything useful for [his family]."[49] Siberia was just the place to "renew" "prodigal sons" like himself, he went on, seemingly exhilarated by the prospect. But, he said, without capital there was only one respectable enterprise he could undertake, gold transactions, and for that he needed permission to travel long distances from Tomsk. Would the general help him get that permission? "The rest of my life I will try to prove the purity of my motives and the depth of my gratitude...."[50] The general did what he could, assuring his superiors that Bakunin had "sincerely and profoundly repented his former crime, is fully cognisant of the mercy the Emperor has shown him, and by his behavior has earned general praise in the town."[51] This time, however, Dolgorukov said no. Bakunin would have to stay in Tomsk.

Denied gold, he turned again to tutoring. His students were the children of a Polish nobleman who had known better times. One of them, a girl of 17, so attracted Bakunin that he decided he would marry her. The 26 year difference in their ages apparently troubled neither of them. The gap between his own parents' age had been similarly wide (he 40, she 18), and, in any case, his intentions were only "to care for her as the flower of my old age,"[52] since he did have, as one biographer, Steklov, gently puts it, that "certain physical characteristic" that made him "incapable, apparently, of conjugal life."[53] (The girl, Antonia, was later to have children, three of them, but all by Carlo Gambuzzi, Bakunin's close friend, fellow revolutionary, and financial benefactor during the second phase of his revolutionary career in the 1860s and 1870s.)

Why did Bakunin get married? To his mother he explained it as "new proof of my turning towards the right principles of a proper life, and a sure guarantee of my firm resolve to abandon everything that in my past life caused you such great anxiety and resentment."[54] Also, the argument is often made that the marriage, too, was part of his constant, overriding, secret plan to escape: In order to marry and then support a family, he must have an income, and the only source for that open to him, or so he claimed in his letters to the authorities, was the gold industry, far to the East, the direction, that is, of his Pacific escape. He does, in fact, use precisely this argument in his letters requesting permission to be free to travel on business.[55] Even were this the case, however, there can be little doubt about the reality or intensity of the love he came to feel for Antonia. His later letters and actions show that he was constantly and tenderly concerned about her welfare and longed for her when they were apart. Perhaps the best way to understand the marriage is to recall Bakunin's love for Tatiana through the years and especially his fantasy of their living together abroad.[56] In the underlying psychodrama of his life, Antonia may have played the role originally designed for Tatiana, a role that was also easier for him to share now that his father was dead and his mother once more approachable, for reasons discussed earlier. Moreover, since there were no family, consanguineous ties between them, Antonia was a much less threatening substitute for the mother than Tatiana had been. (Bakunin's comment about his mother being like a sister to him may also be relevant here). And if the difference in age, making Antonia more like a daughter than a wife to him, helped disguise the substitution, the fact that his mother had been comparably distant in age from his father helped achieve it. Finally, the absence of sexuality neutralized the danger of the substitution, even as it helped to prove that one was taking place.

Besides being able to use the marriage to support his appeal for travel permission, Bakunin could also use it as evidence of his having turned over a new leaf. Repeating the assurances he had recently given his mother, he told his captors that "my intention to marry should itself be enough to prove my resolute decision to devote the rest of my life to peaceful and legal activities."[57] Still stronger evidence of that change, however, was his general behavior. In a report sent in mid-April 1858 by the governor general of western Siberia to the Ministry of Internal Affairs, Bakunin's behavior is described as irreproachable, reflecting "a most humble attitude" and "a sincere repentance for his errors."[58] Reenforcing the continuing appeals by his family and their influential relatives and friends, such humility and contrition on his part persuaded the government to make things easier for him. While not yet allowing him free movement, he was offered a rank in government service that would facilitate his finding at least clerical employment. Predictably, he rejected the opportunity: a "fussy, bureaucratic job" was no less fussy in Siberia than it had been in European Russia.[59] And at a deeper level: "it seemed to me that once I put on the cockade, I would lose my purity and innocence."[60] So, instead of taking a government job, he went on making appeals to officials like chief of police, Dolgorukov: "Your eminence!

My entire fate and the chance of any happiness in my future life now depends on you. Do not refuse me. Be now my succor and savior as you were already once before .... Only your word can now resurrect me .... "[61] This, too, failed, and he had to remain, for a while yet, in Tomsk, still "behaving quietly and properly."[62] In October he married Antonia, although he had told Dolgorukov in the above letter that he could not marry without the requested permission for free movement eastward.

At the beginning of the next year (1859) he took another step back towards a quiet and proper life. It was a time of political ferment in Russia, the years of intense discussion and preparation for the "great reforms" of Alexander II. Wishing to be a part of it, Bakunin reentered the world of political journalism, but now as a cautious liberal, rather like his father had become after he had sown his own radical oats. His opening statement came in a letter to his old friend-enemy Katkov, who was at the time editing a successful and influential liberal journal. Expressing joy over the impending thaw in Russian life and agreement with Katkov's fondness for English liberal institutions, he cautioned Katkov against being so pro-English as to discredit Russia by comparison. The freedom and property that the English cherished were indeed splendid, he said, and the Russian government was quite right in its plans to free the serfs and provide them with private, not communal, land. But Katkov should not forget Russia's own Slavic mission to liberate the oppressed Slavic peoples, who shared "a general, instinctual expectation that Russia would save them."[63]

Reflecting his habitual ambivalence towards power, he argued in another letter to Katkov that power, both at home and abroad, should limit itself to unofficial guidance. The privileged landed elite, for example, should continue their prevailing influence, but this influence should not be institutionalized into explicit, legal dominance. The same held true for relations between Russia and the other Slavic peoples, and Russia must therefore end its oppression of Poland, Russia's Ireland. However, he was pleased to tell Katkov that he had met a number of remarkable Poles who, for all their desire to see Poland free, "are *completely* convinced now that conspiratorial methods are fruitless and that if there is to be a Polish revival it must be along a normal, broad path, one founded on rational development, both morally and materially .... "[64] As for himself, he was married, "completely happy," and preparing to move to Eastern Siberia, where his cousin Muraviev-Amursky, governor general of eastern Siberia, had found him a position.[65]

Under the pressure of insistent family appeals (Muraviev's mother and Bakunin's were first cousins) and probably impressed both by the very favorable reports on Bakunin's behavior and by Bakunin's heroic reputation and olympian bearing, Muraviev was to be Bakunin's Siberian guardian angel, a guardianship for which Bakunin was to repay him handsomely, as we will see. The position Muraviev had obtained for him was in Irkutsk, with a Siberian business magnate named Benardaki, who, mindful of the ways Muraviev could favor or hinder his many ventures, was delighted to take Bakunin on. Although it is unclear just what Bakunin did, if anything, he stayed with Benardaki's Amur company until November, then quit. He said he did not like the management policies.[66] When he gave up the job, however, he did not give up the salary, and for the next two years continued to receive regular payments from Benardaki as well as loans from him,[67] even though he did no service at all in return.

In the meantime, he lived on in Irkutsk with Antonia and her parents, sister, and brother, the whole family having accompanied them from Tomsk, and continued to enjoy Muraviev's protection. But Muraviev was not his only friend and benefactor among the authorities. Through him he met other prominent and useful people, for example, the young general Ignatiev, chief of staff Kukel, provincial governor Izvolsky, and Muraviev's second in command, Korsakov, whose sister was later to be Bakunin's sister-in-law (Paul's wife). Their doors were always open to him, and he spent much time with them, to the chagrin of other exiles who had expected something quite different of the great revolutionary. "I exposed the activities of the pseudo-democrat Bakunin," the Decembrist exile Zavalishin later wrote, "showing how the pseudo-liberal hobnobbed with despots, and I broke off all relations with him. This pseudo-liberal and pseudo-democrat Bakunin, who, having told me that one could not deny the abuses and coercion in Muraviev's relations with the people, said that one could still excuse him everything because he was a revolutionary, this Bakunin was welcomed at the home of Muraviev and Korsakov and published articles in defense of Muraviev in the *Bell.*"[68]

The last reference is to one of the most scandalous episodes in Bakunin's life, from the revolutionaries' perspective. In April 1859 a duel took place in Irkutsk between a top official and a lower clerk. The clerk was killed. Critics of the government, including one of the most prominent of all the exiles, Petrashevsky, called the event outright murder and pressed for an investigation. Muraviev was away at the time of the duel, but when he returned, he tried to force the opposition to keep quite. Hoping to win support for their case, the local intelligentsia sent an account of the affair to friends in Paris who used the information for an article denouncing Muraviev in the leading émigré Russian periodical, the *Bell,* edited by Bakunin's erstwhile benefactors, Herzen and Ogarev.[69]

Even before arriving in Irkutsk, and months before the duel, Bakunin had come to idolize Muraviev, a "noble, effective, energetic, and in all respects remarkable man, the sun of Siberia, whose disappearance would plunge everything into stagnation and gloom...." As for his critics, those "scoundrels Zavalishin and Petrashevsky," they were out to vilify a man who would prove to be "one of the best and most indispensable people in Russia."[70]

In three letters that Bakunin wrote to Herzen at the end of 1860,[71] the first of which was another of Bakunin's characteristic pamphlet-length discourses, he expanded this praise into a reverential panegyric that would have made Nero blush. Governor General Muraviev was as "noble as a knight, pure as few people are in Russia" with a

> daring, broad, fiery, decisive mind and a native-born gift for captivating, ardent rhetoric... the most courteous conversationalist, always lively, incisive, kind to such an extent that not only women but men also fall in love with him. In fact, one cannot help loving him: he himself loves and hates so passionately and has so much heart; he is all heart.... And add to that, self-sacrifice and exceptional disregard for his own interests—a man of princely generosity.... There is not a drop of egoism or vainglory in this remarkable man, he seeks the essence, not the form of power—another similarity with Peter the Great, of whom, in his elemental genius, he so often reminds me.... His doors are open to everyone at any time, and to each he gives his memory and his heart.... He can see right through your soul, even when you choose not to open yourself to him.... He seems born to command, gifted with all the capacities of a first-class general: quickness and clarity of mind, spirit, resourcefulness at the critical moment, military knowledge, a steadfastness, and most important of all, a daring, dashing, instinctually heroic decisiveness—all the guarantees of victory are combined in him to the highest degree.[72]

"Here and ready is the savior of Russia, and you are his enemies!"[73] To prove how wrong Herzen had been in printing articles against Muraviev, Bakunin reviewed at length all his hero's many accomplishments, as a military leader and as the man who virtually single-handed had turned the Amur River into a thriving trade artery and dramatically developed the great mineral and other riches of eastern Siberia, in part through favoring "private industry" against state economic direction.[74] Sleeping little, always working hard and efficiently, Muraviev forced others as well to work effectively, both the common people, "helpless as children, lacking all initiative,[75] and the bureaucrats, "trivial philistines with puffed up positions, fools trying to look profound; half-educated, crude, vain, and petty egotists with patriotic phrases, who rose to the top and kept themselves there through baseness and intrigue; mechanical, routine formalists, lacking even the thought of vital, authentic action."[76] In short, Muraviev "had accomplished miracles, especially miraculous considering this is slumbering Russia, accustomed to replacing deeds by words and dreams."[77]

But it was not simply because of these great achievements and attributes (so reminiscent of Bakunin's own fantasies about himself, or at least his potentialities) that Herzen should honor and support Muraviev instead of denouncing him and aiding his enemies. What was truly remarkable was the fact that Muraviev was also a "convinced democrat." "Both by his deeds and his convictions, he is entirely ours," "a red general," "the only one with strength and authority in Russia who, in the full sense of the word—and I am not in the least exaggerating—we can and must, without qualification, call *ours*," "unconditionally ours." "He is our strength and the best and strongest of us: in him is the future of Russia."[78] To prove his point, Bakunin gave Herzen a summary of what he thought was Muraviev's progressive program, lauding it enthusiastically as he went along: liberation of the serfs with land, a jury system, elimination of classes, freedom of the press, broad public education, local self-government, and, with respect to the form of central government, "the destruction of the ministries" to be replaced "during the first period not by a constitution and not by a blabbering gentry parliament, but by a temporary iron dictatorship, under one name or another...."[79] Muraviev, notwithstanding his position, had nothing but disdain for the privileged classes, believed in and loved only the people, and hoped "that the peasant's axe will bring Petersburg to its senses and open the way there for the rational dictatorship that he is convinced is the only way to save Russia, rotting in filth, theft, mutual oppression, sterile chatter, and philistine triviality."[80]

The aims of the "red general," the future "iron," "rational dictatorship," were not limited to Russian domestic life. "He regards dictatorship as necessary also for reestablishing Russian power in Europe, and he would first of all want to direct this power against Austria and Turkey in order to liberate the Slavs and establish, not one pan-Slavist monarchy, but a freely, yet strongly, united Slavic federation. A friend of the Hungarians and a friend of the Poles, he is convinced that the first step in a rational Russian foreign policy must be the reestablishment and liberation of Poland."[81]

Who were his enemies? Who had turned Herzen and others against him? First of all, the liberals whom Muraviev disdains: "He is a simple democrat, and has nothing in common with them."[82] The accusations of these "lying correspondents" who have misled Herzen were as empty as they were themselves. They accuesed Muraviev, for example, of paying high human costs for his enterprises. To begin with, the charges were false: the peasants supposedly abused by him through forced labor were actually, as a result of his policies, living in a "kingdom of heaven" compared to their life before, when they were exploited and controlled the way Russian peasants were controlled by the "White Russian yid."[83] Moreover, even were the accusations correct, "what does a temporary sacrifice like that matter when compared to the immense results obtained."[84]

"Muraviev, by nature a revolutionary, can, as dictator, sometimes sacrifice private good and even personal will for the general good and general freedom."[85]

As for Muraviev's more illustrious critics, exiles like Zavalishin and Petrash-evsky, Raevsky, Lvov, and "the yid Rozenthal," they were even worse "scoun-drels" than the liberals.[86] Petrashevsky, for instance, was simply an "adventurer," a "pig with a man's head," who felt at home, like "a pig in filth," only in a tavern. Posing as a revolutionary activist, he was really a coward, who fought with ink rather than blood, enjoyed getting people into quarrels with each other, had a passion himself for litigation, carried the art of intrigue to the point of genius, loved to cause a scandal or do something vile simply for its own sake, and did not pay his debts. Bakunin knew that it was hard for Herzen to believe that "a political prisoner might be a scoundrel," since he assumed that to be "a poli-tical prisoner meant to be one of the best men in the realm. . . . But the time for such a fiction was surely over now."[87]

Muraviev could not have wished for a more devoted or articulate advocate. Why did Bakunin take on the task? There is no question here, as in the "Confes-sion," about sincerity. These were closed letters sent to Herzen by courier, with the intention of publishing a defense of Muraviev in response to his *Bell* critics. Bakunin was, of course, grateful to Muraviev, who had gone to Tomsk to see him, publically supported him there (according to Bakunin), arranged a place for him in Irkutsk and (through Benardaki) two years of comfortable support for which he did nothing, and persistently tried to win him a complete reprieve. In part, it was a repetition of the gratitude he had felt when, instead of the dire punishment he had feared after his transfer from Austrian to Russian hands, he had experienced a marked improvement in his conditions. A still more dramatic improvement followed his transition from Schüsselburg to Tomsk, and he was accordingly grateful to those he felt responsible for it.

But this would hardly have been enough to inspire such adoration. Bakunin said what he did about Muraviev because Muraviev had become both the ideal he had always had for and of himself (as his idealized portrait of Muraviev clearly shows) and a personified resolution of his own basic ambivalence. What he had earlier hoped to find in Nicholas I he now was sure he had found in Muraviev, a fusion of authority and revolution, and all that those two symbols meant to him at various levels. In effect, this merger, essentially a continuation of attitudes clearly apparent in the "Confession," represented yet another attempt to solve his fundamental conflict. Having tried unsuccessfully to be "healed," first by turning romantically and philosophically inwards and becoming a Fichtean savior, then by submerging himself in active, "ruthless surrender" to the people's revolution, he was now attempting to transmute impotence into omnipotence by attaching himself to those with genuine power. Once more, however, as in the first two strategies, the very means—in this case the role of sychophant and, as suggested earlier, "helpmate"—reveals the passivity, the impotence, that the strategy was designed to conceal. (The ambivalence even comes through the portrait of the hero, who, as we saw, sought only the "essence, not the form of power.")

The results of this latest strategy, however, are even more disturbing than were the puerile, solipsistic messianism of the romantic escape or the cataclysmic violence of the revolutionary role, for the ultimate implication of his praise for the "red general" was nothing less than nascent fascism. Most, or even all, of the ingredients are already there—plans for a "rational," efficient, "iron dictatorship," achieving "miracles" of economic growth, social welfare, and national glory, and exercising a dominant influence over a "strongly united" federation of all related peoples (Slavs); scorn for the "babbling" parliaments and hatred of liberals and Jews; devotion to the "people," "helpless as children" whom the "savior" loves and believes in and who, in turn, trust him alone, but who, alas, may have to be sacrificed by him at times for the larger good. He even found a place for a dislocated and disenchanted middle class in his forthcoming revolution from above: "I believe in the middle class—not the merchants, who are more rotten even than the gentry—but in the real, officially unrecognized middle class, constantly taking shape from the displaced people who have lost their jobs, from shop clerks, petty traders, the children of the clergy...."[88] As for the rest of Russia's privileged class: "The Russian Revolution will be terrible, yet whether you like it or not you [Herzen] must call it forth, for it alone can awaken us from this ruinous lethargy and bring us to real passions and real interests. Perhaps it will bring forth and create vital people, since the majority of today's prominent people are good only for the axe."[89] Alexander II's reforms only scratched the surface of that evil and decay: "They say that Russia is beginning to thaw, but beneath the ice there is always a lot of muck and dung, and it stinks."[90]

When, in November and December 1860, he sent these letters to Herzen, Bakunin was hopefully looking forward to a full pardon and permission to return home to European Russia. Muraviev had assured him, he said, that he would be free the following spring. Once free, he would go back to Russia "in order to search out people, renew old friendships, and begin new ones," in preparation for the revolution that he was sure would soon follow the changes underway both in Russia and in Western Europe. He now knew just the kind of people to look for to lead the revolution: the Muraviev type, men like the young general Nicholas Pavlovich Ignatiev, a man of about 30, "daring, decisive, energetic and competent to the highest degree,"[91] or like the retired lieutenant G. N. Potanin, "wild, naive, sometimes bizarre and, though still very young, gifted with an independent—albeit not yet fully developed—mind, a love of truth, that at times leads him into quixotic indiscretions... an unbending persistence, love for work and a capacity for relentless effort, and, finally, an utter indifference to everything that people call the comforts and pleasures of material life."[92] Now (1860), in his last months as a prisoner, military officers like Muraviev, Ignatiev, and Potanin are the type of "good soldier" he idolizes (heirs of the "warrior for holy truth") and would so much like to be himself. A decade later their place will be taken by revolutionaries like the young, energetic, steadfast, hard-working, fearless Nechaev. The characteristics will be much the same, for in the basic plot of Bakunin's inner drama, the change from Ignatiev or Potanin to Nechaev is, once again, no change at all.

In January 1861 Muraviev was relieved of his post and recalled to St. Petersburg. With him went Bakunin's hopes for release that coming spring, as well as the guarantor of his relatively easy life in Siberia. Moreover, the previous October he had quarreled with another of his protectors, Kukel, who had broken off relations completely with him, and Korsakov, Muraviev's replacement, had sided with Kukel. "In his behavior toward Kukel," Korsakov later wrote, "as well as on many other occasions, Bakunin revealed a thoroughly bad side of himself."[93] Since hopes for release now seemed futile, he tried to get permission for at least a short visit home, for half a year of even four months, he told his relatives, urging all of them to use their influence to help him. A series of other letters sent that winter suggests that he had already put his hopes elsewhere than on the indulgence of the state, that with the departure of Muraviev, he began planning some way of escape.

The main evidence for this revolves around his zealous efforts at the time to obtain a large amount of money. His most likely source was still his "employer," or patron, Benardaki. Before getting more from him, however, Bakunin felt he must first repay what he owed—the two year pension as well as the additional loans he had taken from Benardaki. Taking full blame for what was obviously a favor to Muraviev (the two-year unearned salary to a cousin) and showering only praise on Benardaki, Bakunin assured him that his own brothers would make good all the debts; since, "cherishing my honor, I could not accept a single kopek for doing nothing."[94] It was necessary to repay Benardaki, Bakunin wrote his brothers, in order to reestablish his own financial credit with him. That, in turn, was essential, for if he were freed and allowed to return to European Russia, Benardaki could loan him what he needed for the trip, or, if he were not freed, "then I would hope that he would give me a business commission along the Amur as far as Nikolaevsk"—precisely his later escape route. He was convinced, he said, that he could return Benardaki 100 percent profit on his investment.[95]

Covering himself in the event this plan failed and Benardaki proved unreceptive to the Amur proposal, Bakunin simultaneously wrote Katkov again, telling him of the debt and of his brothers paying it off for him but adding as well a new scheme: since his brothers would be unable to provide him money for some other debts once they had repaid Benardaki, could Katkov and his friends collect among themselves a fund on his behalf, a kind of political relief fund? "If it is impossible for you to carry this out," he concluded, "then I will have to stay here in Siberia."[96] Finally, in this vigorous campaign for money, he applied to the government for an allowance he had hitherto declined (a small sum regularly given to political exiles), asking payment for the period 1856-59 even though it was not due him for 1856 and the first two months of 1857, the period preceding his exile. In the end, nothing came of any of these efforts except for the last: Korsakov agreed to pay him the exile pension, although only for 1859. But more important, Korsakov also gave him a letter permitting him to sail down the Amur to Nikolaevsk.

One way or another, he was now determined "not to rot away in Siberia." Since he had not been allowed to return to life in European Russia, he would escape to renew the life he had led in the West, or, in his words, having "given up regular planetary motion, I must again become a comet."[97] (Perhaps a scholar who studied Bakunin's life in Siberia is right when he says that, considering how much Bakunin had changed over the years, he "would surely not have been a very dangerous member of society had he been returned to Russia.")[98] Taking advantage of Korsakov's trusting permission to go to Nikolaevsk and justifying the trip by procuring a trading commission from a merchant, Sabashnikov, Bakunin left Irkutsk on June 5, 1861.

Six months of perpetual motion followed, highlighted by breathtaking audacity and incredible good luck: a month down the Amur to Nikolaevsk—seven weeks from there, first on a Russian then on an American ship, to Yokohama, where he remained for two weeks—five weeks for the Pacific crossing to San Francisco—about a month by way of the Isthmus of Panama to New York—and, finally, after a month or so visiting New York and Boston, another month across the Atlantic, arriving in London in late December, six months after the flight of the comet had begun. Fortune had smiled on him all the way. Heeding Korsakov's written permission, a lieutenant Afanasev, aide to the governor general of the maritime provinces, allowed Bakunin to go to a port where he was able to transfer to an ocean going vessel. The aide soon learned, however (from a merchant Bakunin had turned to for money), what Bakunin's real intentions were and sent a messenger out to advise all local authorities to be on the lookout for this "political criminal" who had been allowed to travel "on his word of honor" not to escape, but who now was trying to do just that.[99] Unfortunately for Afanasev, who later paid for his part with two months imprisonment, the officer he charged with the message gave it to another officer, who fell ill and, not being told the message was urgent, waited to deliver it until he recovered—until, that is, Bakunin was well on his way.

Had the officer not fallen ill and had the message arrived in time, Bakunin, in all likelihood, would have spent the rest of his days carefully watched in Siberian exile or even returned to prison. As it was, he was now a free man, in London, ready to begin the second phase of his revolutionary career under the auspices and with the blessings of Alexander Herzen, the man who had seen him off over 20 years before to begin his "golden age." Having failed in his fascist fantasy of merging authority and revolution by the "iron dictatorship" of the "red general" he had no choice now but to try and go back, after a year or so of fluctuating ambivalence, to the same old drama he had already played out in the 1840s.

9. RETREAT TO ARMAGEDDON

On the surface, the rhythm of Bakunin's second revolutionary campaign seemed to recapitulate that of the first. Like the 1840s and early 1850s, the 1860s and early 1870s opened with several transition years (1861-63), blending themes that had come before with those that were to prevail later, moved into a relatively quite three year preparatory period (1864-67), peaked in two years of intense activity (1868-70), and climaxed in a long period of retreat (1871-76). Although apparently the same, there were, however, several important differences in the two patterns. One, the more obvious difference, was in the denouement. While Bakunin suffered defeat in both periods—Prague and Dresden in the 1840s and the Lyon fiasco, the Nechaev scandal, and the Baronata and Bologne humiliations in the 1860s and 1870s—in the final years of the second campaign he experienced a triumphant success in his battle with the principal authority he challenged during that period, Karl Marx. But, as one might have predicted, this success against authority only deepened the depression that weighed so heavily on the last years of his life and hastened his final retreat from politics.

Besides this difference in ending, the second revolutionary period was also different from the first in a more fundamental way, one associated with the retreat from politics: the withdrawal did not, in fact, wait until the climactic years, but was subtly and intermittently underway throughout this second period, notwithstanding Bakunin's continuing revolutionary performances. Nor should there by anything surprising about this gradual retreat: Bakunin was nearing 50 years of age when he escaped and in broken health as a result of his prison and exile hardships, his voracious appetite, and his passion for tobacco and tea.

One need only compare an 1862 portrait of Bakunin, on the eve of his second revolutionary phase, with one from 1842, the time he began his first campaign, to appreciate the effects of those punishments and abuses. What is amazing, on the contrary, is the fact that he did not at once retire completely, that he had the capacity to go right on with this promethean performance, that his need, in short, for more "paroxysm" and "electrifying" contact with the people's "warmth and flame" remained as compelling as it did for so long. The withdrawal, therefore, was not a steady and persistent process: each retreat was followed by a return to action, which, however, led in turn to another retreat, usually deeper and longer than the one before. The retreats, moreover, as would necessarily be the case with Bakunin, were disguised to look like just different forms of attack. What makes the play as a whole especially dramatic is the fact that the fame and power that his intermittent activism brought him only hastened his flight from them. By the time the fame and the power reached their peak— the time of his victory over Marx—he had no more use for them at all, not even as camouflage.

If the acts of the drama in its second performance were in general arranged as they had been in the first performance some 20 years earlier, the stage and the audience this time were much grander. Instead of the 26 year old aspiring student of philosophy who arrived in Berlin in 1840, the man who landed in London that December 1861 was a world-renowned martyr and hero. As soon as Herzen learned, from San Francisco, of Bakunin's escape, he proclaimed the news in bold type on the front page of his journal, the *Bell*. His arrival in London was blazoned in its headlines. Most of the first two pages of the following issue were devoted to a biographical sketch of his life and long martyrdom. A notice in the next issue announced the sale of portraits of the great man, and a full supplement, longer than the rest of the paper, was attached to a subsequent issue to provide space for Bakunin's first publication since his escape, a proclamation *To Russian, Polish, and All Slavic Friends.*[1] What he had done to achieve this extraordinary surge in fame was what he had done to initiate his international prominence in the first place in late 1847—he had suffered. And since the suffering was so much greater, so was the fame.

In addition to unrolling the red carpet for his arrival, Herzen did what he could to help him get settled, among other things taking up a collection on his behalf both to pay the debts that Bakunin had incurred along his escape route and to maintain him now that he was free. Botkin and Turgenev were among the contributors, the latter even agreeing to provide Bakunin with a yearly subsidy. Herzen had hoped that Bakunin himself would at least help with his own support, perhaps by accepting some of the many offers that came to him now for memoirs and accounts of his thrilling escape. Bakunin did, in fact, inform his family that "however unpleasant it is for me to talk about myself, I will write them" and that by such publications, together with earnings from brochures, he would be able "to stand on my own feet." However, as Herzen wrote Turgenev, "the money is gone, and he does little work." Once more, all he could do to help himself was to turn to his family, assuring them that "with this all financial dealings between us will end."[2]

Bakunin was now even more desperately in need of money than he usually was, for he was eager to arrange for Antonia's trip from Irkutsk. If there were any doubts about his love for her earlier, his stream of letters those first months in London telling her how he missed her and urging, imploring, demanding that various people help her come to him would remove them.[3] In spite of the considerable attention and time that he gave to his efforts to bring Antonia to London—arranging her departure from Irkutsk, her stay at Premukhino (where he doubted she would be treated well), and her permission to leave Russia (which he also doubted)—this was only a side issue in comparison with his renewed revolutionary activities. "Deprived of political life for 13 years," he wrote George Sand at the time, "I crave action...."[4] He took up exactly where he had left off in 1849. In the years since then "the world has rested," he said (as solipsistic as ever) in his letter to Herzen from San Francisco announcing his escape, and it was now time to renew the old war, the battle of Slavic liberation, "my *idée fixe* since 1846."[5] His interests, henceforth, Herzen wrote in his *Bell* biographical sketch, would be "exclusively Slavic-Russian."[6] Similarly, in a letter that May (1862) Bakunin declared himself to be a "pan-Slavist," albeit in the "positive" sense of the word.[7] He surrounded himself with revolutionaries from all countries—Poland, Serbia, Czechoslovakia, Bulgaria, Hungary, Italy, France, England, Russia—corresponded with leaders who were not in London (like Garibaldi), and sent couriers back to Russia with highly incriminating letters (that helped the police in their efforts to locate the revolutionaries).

Any news that reached London of a possible revolution anywhere at once became for Bakunin the bell for the next round in the struggle—rumours from a priest of the Old Believer sect about sectarian resistant movements against the state, assurance from a former Russian army officer that Russian soldiers occupying Poland were ready to rise, plans for a coming *Zemsky Sobor*[8] as told by a former serf, a variety of accounts of imminent Polish revolutions narrated by competing Polish national committees, descriptions of nonexistent Russian underground organizations with hundreds or even thousands of members scattered throughout the land and ready to go, even anonymous letters from police agents feigning support for "the cause" in the hope of enticing from Bakunin information about the opposition movements. It was all so exhilarating that Bakunin found it hard just to sit in London and watch. Irritated when told by one Russian émigré that things were quiet all over—in Italy, Austria, Turkey—he asked in disbelief if he would have to go to Persia or India to get some action. "It is enough to drive you mad. I cannot sit still doing nothing."[9]

Fortunately for him, there were, indeed, serious rumblings in Poland. That was enough: the Austrian and Turkish Empires, he told his *Russian, Polish, and All Slavic Friends,* were crumbling, and "from the ruins," the "new leaders" of "a new civilization" were offering a new life of freedom to all Slavic peoples as well as to the Italians, Greeks, and Magyars. " 'The time is near,' as the religious sectarians say." The Russian troops stationed in Poland were restive and just waiting for the word to rise against the Tsar, he assured his readers. All of Russia, in fact, was now ready for revolution. The social, economic, judicial, and administrative reforms of Alexander II had done little to change the oppressive system. Their only real importance was to make clear the division between "the party of reform and the party of radical revolution." Nor could the Russian state defend itself any longer, no more than could the Austrian or Turkish Empires defend themselves against their rebellious national minorities. The spirit of Russia's religious dissidents and their implacable defiance of the alien Germanic state imported into Russia by Peter the Great had spread to the entire Russian people, who no longer even feared the despised regime and its Germanic bureaucracy. ("Germanic Petersburg is as ruinous for the Slavs as are Berlin and Vienna," he wrote in a short *Bell* editorial at the time.)[10] As for the gentry, they were, with some few notable exceptions, as vacuous and inconsequential as ever, and to look to them for the defence of the state meant to see "the powerless defending the powerless." The state and its supporters did not understand this yet, but they would "when the axes flashed." So let them go on "playing the parliamentary game," for "the awakening was near, and it would be terrible."[11]

Once the "axes" had cleared the way and the "new civilization" had emerged from the ruins, the people would at long last attain complete freedom—full freedom of movement, the free use of the land (to which both individuals and communes would have access without payment) freedom of religion, freedom of assembly, and the freedom of self-government, by way of institutions rising "organically, from the bottom upwards, through the free consent of independent communities, beginning with the commune, the social and political unit that was the cornerstone of the entire Russian world, and continuing up to the regional, state and even federal all-Slavic government."[12] Once the "great and free all-Slavic federation" had been achieved, all Slavs would join, not only to help each other against foreign enemies, "especially against the Germans," but also to help those like the Italians, Magyars, and Greeks who similarly suffered the tyranny of Austria and Turkey.[13] As for the unity of Russia, the Tsar need not worry, for "all our neighbors will be incomparably more closely and strongly united with us than they are bound to us now."[14]

The enemies were, thus, much the same as they had been in the 1840s—the Empires of Austria, Prussia, Russia, and Turkey. The allies, too, were the same— Russian peasants, oppressed Slavs, and non-Slavic minorities in southeastern Europe. Finally, the goal was also largely the same—complete freedom of all peoples, voluntarily joining in a great free federation, with Russia, as the first among equals. In one basic way only did the program now differ from what it had been in the 1840s: the means for achieving the goal. Between 1849 and 1861 lay the "Confession," Bakunin's Siberian identification with Muraviev, and his hope for revolution from above, if not from an illuminated Tsar, then from the "red general." As further evidence that those ideals genuinely reflected his sentiments at the time, we find them continuing as a main current of his thought for several years afterwards. If only the Tsar would take the lead in the people's struggle for freedom, he wrote in another article that year (1862), *The People's Cause: Romanov, Pugachev, or Pestel?,* if only he would lead them "against the gentry, against the bureaucrats, and against everything German," he would see Tsarism elevated to "unprecedented heights of power and glory" and the Tsar become "the people's hero," "the idol of the people." Were the Tsar to rule not with force but with "a broad, expansive, noble and truly strong Russian heart," he would see that "all Russians and, yes, even all Slavs, would reach out to him, ready to serve as a pedestal for his historic greatness." Even now, in spite of everything, the great majority of the people "still have great faith in the Tsar" and consider him a "symbol of the unity, grandeur and glory of the Russian land." Other peoples, he said, may look to heaven for salvation; for the Russians, their salvation must be earthly, and "the earthly god is the Tsar." "The Tsar is the ideal of the Russian people, a kind of Russian Christ, father and provider of the Russian people" who was kept from doing the good he would do only because "he himself, poor man, is unfree, bound by malevolent boyars and evil officials." Let him free himself and the people by turning "against the gentry, against the bureaucrats, against everything that wears a German outfit."

The way to this liberation, he went on, had already been prepared by Russian history, through such institutions as the *Zemsky Sobor,* the popular assembly of the late sixteenth and early seventeenth centuries that had for brief periods participated in Tsarist governments. "There can be no doubt that were the Tsar to summon *now* a *Zemsky Sobor,* he would at once find himself surrounded by people truly dedicated to him." "If, at this fateful moment, when the question of life and death, of peace or blood, is to be decided for all of Russia, a people's Tsar, a just Tsar, a Tsar who loved Russia more than himself, was worthy of the people's deep love, and was prepared to build the nation according to the will of the nation, what could that Tsar not do with such a people! Who would dare rise against him?.... Guided by such a Tsar, the *Zemsky Sobor* would build a new Russia." Beyond that, "in alliance with Poland and the Ukraine, having broken all the hateful German ties, and having audiciously raised the all-Slavic banner, he would become the redeemer of the Slavic world!"[15]

A remarkable feature of Bakunin's continuing revolution from above was its relative nonviolence: the Tsar could lead "a revolution without shedding a drop of blood." "We are also prepared to follow him [the Tsar], because he *alone* can fulfill and bring to an end the great, peaceful revolution, not spilling a single drop of Russian or Slavic blood. Bloody revolution is sometimes necessary because of human stupidity, but it is nonetheless an evil, a great evil and a great misfortune, not only for the victims themselves, but also with respect to the purity and perfection of the goal for which it was carried out."[16] That year and the next (1862–63) Bakunin frequently expressed this opposition to bloodshed, reminiscent of the many similarly nonviolent statements he had made earlier.[17] He even opposed the actions and proclamations of extremist revolutionary organizations then beginning to form in Russia, those charged, for example, with starting a series of fires in St. Petersburg. Besides doubting that the fires really were started by revolutionaries, as the government claimed,[18] he denounced all such actions for, as he put it, responding to stupidity at the top with barbarism from below. Similarly, he argued that violent revolutionary proclamations, such as "Young Russia,"[19] reflected a tendency on the part of young radicals to lose themselves in "a world of abstractions" and indicated as well both a lack of discipline and the radicals' distance from the people. What he found particularly galling, however, was the fact that people were attributing the fires and the proclamations to his own influence. Finally, he vigorously opposed any assassination attempts, calling them a "terrible blunder," the work of "undisciplined youth."[20]

But what if the Tsar refused to come to his senses and went right on with the customary Germanic domination instead of serving the Russian people and other Slavs? Then the "axes" would flash, and even though Bakunin "cannot even think of the thousand of victims without shuddering," he could see ahead only a bloody revolution under the leadership of "a self-appointed Tsar like Pugachev or a new dictator like Pestel"—although there was still a chance that, perhaps, "the *Zemsky Sobor* would save Russia." Whatever the ultimate leadership, however, the opposition must prepare itself in case the Tsar did in fact continue to "betray" Russia. Above all, they must end their separation from the people and their disdain for them. At present, because of this detachment from the people, the influence of the revolutionaries on the people was, he said, practically nil. But he was sure this defect would soon be remedied, that the revolutionaries would find their way to the people, for they "passionately strained to be with the people" and understood that "to live apart from the people was impossible."

Our life is empty and aimless. We have nothing to do, no field for action, and if there exists any future for us, then it is only in the people.... We must love the people more than ourselves.... Passionately love, surrender all our soul.... To be at one with the people, to fuse with them in one soul and one body is a difficult task, but for us it is unavoidable and inevitable.... It is only by joining them that we can free ourselves from impotence.[21]

In addition to reflecting once more the concealed meaning of Bakunin's "passionate love" for the "people," such passages suggest that of the two ways to "free ourselves from impotence" and be "healed"–joining the "red general" at the top or "surrendering" to the people's "warmth and flame" at the bottom–it was the latter that brought with it the apocalyptic violence. While the "axes" were bloodless when he identified himself with the "red general," his vocabulary explodes with cataclysmic violence when he describes the "paroxysm" of the peoples' revolution. There are several reasons for this. First of all, revolution from above under the aegis of the "iron dictator" shifted the emphasis away from the people and thus deprived Bakunin of the "bride" that had been (and would soon be again) the source of the "paroxysm." Moreover, identifying himself explicitly with the "red general" Muraviev and other military leaders like him was a brazenly virile display of genuine power and therefore required a severe constraint on the very power that he was demonstrating. So, the "red general" must achieve a revolution "without shedding a drop of blood." However, precisely because it provided no "paroxysm," no violent apocalyptic annihilation, the merger of authority and revolution that Bakunin had worked out in Siberia and, as we see here, retained for a short time thereafter, was inadequate and inappropriate for him in the same way that Schelling and "right" Hegel had been.

Nor was the role of powerful and successful leader, in the manner of Muraviev, consistent with the masochistic dimension of Bakunin's character–the cult of suffering, the martyrdom proclivities, the "ruthless surrender" to the Spirit that "permeates" him, and the many other modes of thought and behavior through which Bakunin sought to prove his power by suffering powerfully, by being the innocent, powerless, victim. Bakunin's pseudo-sexual "paroxysm", I have argued, was not primarily derived from the pleasure of imagined aggression that one would associate with victorious leadership, but rather from the masochistic pleasure of passive suffering that Bakunin could experience, or imagine himself experiencing, by identifying himself with the people as victim, by making and being prepared to make enormous sacrifices on its/her behalf, and by imagining the vastly greater pains still to come in the anticipated apocalyptic catastrophe. Moreover, since, beneath all the layers of disguise, the violence remained for him essentially sexual, and since all sexual experience remained forever incestual, evil, filthy, demonic, Bakunin had to punish himself for it by imagining still more masochistically violent scenarios, which only meant more "paroxysm", requiring more punishment, and so on.

In depriving him of the opportunity for masochistic suffering, the Muraviev-heroic posture also limited the scope of his feminine identification, since, as we saw, in experiencing the "paroxysm," the people's "warmth and flame" masochistically rather than aggressively, Bakunin was identifying himself not only with the victim in general but with what to him was a feminine role. One should recall in this connection, Bakunin's frequent identification with women (whom he saw almost exlusively as suffering, innocent victims); the character of his adolescent correspondence with his sisters; his placing that important message in the postscript where, he felt it necessary to say, a woman would put it; his weeping "like a woman" for Paul to return to him; his passive "surrender" to the spirit of revolution to be "permeated" by it; and his persistent flight from roles identified at the time with male authority and responsibility, preferring to remain a dependent. These and other signs of what Bakunin and his period characterized as feminine traits and themes are too glaringly present in Bakunin's personality, ideas, and actions to be ignored.[22] He, of course, was compelled to spend a lifetime trying to repress and disguise them under mountains of aggressively heroic declarations, programs, organizational plans, and absurdly quixotic forays. In every case, however, the basic "pastels" and the masochistic passivity managed to announce themselves clearly and distinctly, usually through the very declarations that were supposed to conceal them.

(In this revolutionary masochism and the related identification with the woman's role—in Bakunin's view—as passive, suffering victim, pleasure and pain were fused into a single experience, as they were in Bakunin's earlier cult of suffering. Masochism punished him for the oedipal crime even as it provided the "passion and fire" that fueled its gratification. Passive suffering helped preserve the desired feminine-maternal identification inherent in the narcissistic "symbiotic couple" while punishing him for the incestual character that, as discussed earlier, that "couple" had acquired. The rejection of male roles and the assumption of a feminine identity as a means of avoiding the oedipal crime only led to the perpetration of the crime in the narcissistic refuge. It was through the functioning of such vicious circles as these that Bakunin was driven all his life back and forth between radical detachment and radical destruction, that he was forever locked in dialectical dualisms of permanently contradictory opposites. By repeatedly calling his cherished revolutionary passions "evil" and "demonic," Bakunin, in effect, acknowledged this melding of sexuality, violence, pleasure, and punishment. While he could not live without the two fantasies that structured and guided his thoughts and actions—the fantasy of infantile maternal reunion (the millennial end) and the fantasy of omnipotent violent power (the apocalyptic means)—he knew at some level that both were, as he experienced them, incestual and therefore damned. In short, he was never to be "healed," neither through the therapeutic guise of revolutionary hero, red general, Tsar liberator, and party militant, nor that of innocent, infantile, passive, suffering victim.)[23]

As we saw before that analytic detour, Bakunin showed in *The People's Cause: Romanov Pugachev, or Pestel?* that he still leaned towards the nonviolent, chaste, revolution from above: "we would most of all be willing to follow the Romanovs"; if a Pugachev mass rising from below were to occur, "then God please there is in him [Pugachev] the political genius of Pestel, for without it, he will drown Russia and, in addition, Russia's whole future, in blood."[24] To judge from his descriptions of Bakunin at the time, however, Herzen never noticed this relatively moderate side and saw only the same frenzied millenarian who had impressed the world by his quixotic audacity and heroic suffering over a decade earlier.[25] As Herzen recalled, Bakunin did his best to make him see the radical light, to transform the *Bell* from a journal of criticism to one of active revolutionary leadership. "Propaganda was not enough, there ought to be immediate action; centers and committees ought to be organized; to have people closely and remotely associated with us was not enough, we ought to have 'dedicated and half-dedicated brethren,' organizations on the spot—a Slavonic organization, a Polish organization. Bakunin thought us too moderate, unable to take advantage of the situation of the moment, insufficiently fond of resolute measures."[26] They argued constantly over the *Bell's* party line, Herzen advising patience and prudence, Bakunin demanding clear and extreme action, and Ogarev leaning now to one side, now to another, although in general seeming to favor Bakunin's militancy.

The conflict climaxed in their response to the Polish rising that began in late January 1863. For months before, Herzen, Ogarev, and Bakunin had been holding discussions with representatives of a Polish Central Committee in London regarding the Russian response to the forthcoming rising. In July 1862 a Russian officer, Andrei Potebnia, had brought to London assurances that many Russian officers stationed in Poland were sympathetic to the Polish demands. The month before, in June, three Russian officers had, in fact, been shot for their support of the Polish movement. Similarly, several young Russians appeared on the scene at the time claiming to represent a secret revolutionary organization in Russia, Land and Freedom, which might also be expected to help the Polish cause, as well as use it as the occasion for advancing their own struggle against the Tsar. "Are there many of you," Herzen asked one such Land and Freedom representative. "That is hard to say . . . . Some hundreds in Petersburg and three thousand in the provinces." "Do you believe it?" Herzen then asked Bakunin. " 'Of course. But', he added, 'well, if there are not as many now, there soon will be!' And he burst into a roar of laughter."[27]

Since Herzen had little confidence in any of this and even less, therefore, in the success of a Polish rising at that time, he urged the Polish leaders at least to postpone it.[28] Such evidence of support for the rising was more than enough for Bakunin, however. In August, a month after Potebnia's visit, he went to Paris to offer his and Russia's services to the Polish general, Mieroslawski. As the general described the strange encounter, Bakunin presented himself as the "plenipotentiary delegate of a powerful Russian secret conspiratorial organization who was in a position to strengthen our uprising on the Vistula by some 70,000 Russian troops, to surrender Modlin into our hands, etc. It seems that he [Bakunin] had just been wondering himself at the time how he might use those 70,000 Tsarist soldiers. So, he promised to form them into a Russian legion in order to start a revolution in [the Ukraine] and then in Russia."[29]

Mieroslawski's decision to have nothing to do with this "dangerous madman" apparently meant little to Bakunin. He returned to London, published a manifesto ordering Russian troops to retreat from Poland and not oppose the rising, and waited for his chance to get more actively engaged, to "fulfill my destiny," convinced, as he wrote his brother Alexander that November, that "I will soon play out the last act of my drama." "Preparations are under way everywhere," he told Alexander, "war and revolution, and in Russia, God willing, there will soon be a *Zemsky Sobor.* We'll try not to get ourselves killed right at the beginning, so that, maybe, we can manage to do something of value. A lot of electricity is gathering in Europe, western and especially, eastern."[30] Notwithstanding his awareness that "the prospects for success were slight," he was more than ever eager to immerse himself once more in the "electricity," even if it would mean his death. "And do you know what I pray?," he went on in this same letter, "that in case of failure as many Russians as possible die in the Polish struggle, so that our brotherhood will be sanctified by deeds and blood, and it would be a joy to die with them." Such, indeed, was just the advice he gave to the Russian officers themselves in his efforts to spur them on to courageous defense of the Polish cause: "If it is your fate to die, then your death will serve the common cause. And, God knows, maybe your heroic deed and your rejection of all the calculations of cold reason will unexpectedly be crowned with success."[31] In

October, undeterred by his disappointing meeting with Mieroslawski, Bakunin wrote to another Polish leader assuring him that when the rising began he would be there along with "the party of my Russians,"[32] referring, perhaps, to the Land and Freedom revolutionaries that fantasy had furnished along with the rebellious Russian troops.

For Herzen, Bakunin's response to the rising was simply more of the quixotic romanticism he had already come to expect from this man who, to quote Herzen, always "took the second month of pregnancy for the ninth....He longed to believe, and he believed." "I saw that he was in the middle of his revolutionary debauch, and that there would be no bringing him to reason now....Beyond the insurrection in Warsaw, he already saw his 'Glorious and Slavic [*slavnuiu i slavianskuiu*] Federation,' of which the Poles spoke with something between horror and revulsion. He already saw the red flag of 'Land and Freedom' waving on the Urals and the Volga, in the Ukraine and the Caucasus, and even, if you please, on the Winter Palace and the Peter-Paul fortress." It seemed as though Bakunin were rehearsing for a theatrical performance, not a real-life insurrection and revolution, Herzen said elsewhere, echoing Bakunin's own reference to his involvement in the Polish rising of 1863 as an "act of my drama."[33] Ogarev was more direct: "You want to do something harmful, because it gives you something to do, even though it hurts the cause."[34]

Bakunin predicted that the rising would begin in the spring of 1863.[35] For once, reality outran his fantasy: it broke out in late January, with a Polish attack on garrisons of the Russian troops that he had assured Mieroslawski were ready to side with the rebels against Tsarist occupation. Bakunin at once wrote to Polish national leaders explaining to them how wrong they had been to have launched this attack, how ready the Russians would have been at the first sign of the Polish rising to rebel themselves in the name of land and liberty, how much more difficult it would now be to bring over the Russian troops. Nevertheless, he was still prepared to do his part. First of all, he would agitate among Russians in the border regions, Russia's western provinces, in order to convert Russians from enemies to friends of the Polish revolution. However, he admitted, this would be difficult, since the rising "had caught them unprepared." Also, he would form a Russian legion in Poland itself under the banner of the Land and Freedom Party, whose existence and influence he now seemed to take for granted.[36] Bakunin wrote the Polish leaders repeatedly to offer his help. They refused even to answer him. "For the past three months," he informed them in early February, "I have sent you letter after letter asking you to tell me whether or not I should go to Poland. I did not receive a word in reply," other than indirectly from friends in London whose advice was "to stay in London, since there was nothing for me to do among you."[37]

Notwithstanding this indifference and still believing that the rising had little chance of success, he decided to go anyhow.[38] With the financial backing of a Polish count, a Canadian passport, and a fine departure dinner of soup, fish, and "veal cotlett with tomate [sic]," he left London for Copenhagen on February twenty-first, hoping he might meet some "really active Pole" there and planning to wait for instructions, from Herzen perhaps, or from the Polish leaders.[39] If "after three days, well, let's say four or five days," no instructions came, he would move on to Stockholm and there "await favorable news."[40] In other words, he left London for the Baltic as he had left Paris for Poznan, to start a revolution completely empty-handed. When the first week of waiting was up, he went to Stockholm, to wait some more, spending the time on yet another diversionary plan to help the Poles—inspiring Swedes to spark a national rising in Finland.[41]

At last his orders came. On the twenty-second he was told of a 150–200 man expeditionary force of Polish revolutionary émigrés and foreign sympathizers that had sailed from London the day before.[42] The plan was for the ship, the Ward Jackson, to head for the Finnish coast and then go on to Lithuania, distributing arms to the rebels as it went. Bakunin was to meet the ship at Helsingborg (on the southeast Swedish coast, north of Malmo) and help the expedition by provoking revolution along the rest of the route. The ship arrived in Helsingborg on the twenty-fifth, expecting to pick up Bakunin then leave. But Bakunin was not able to get there until the next day. The plan, after he finally arrived, was to leave at once for Gothland Island and then use small fishing craft to sail across to Lithuania. In the meantime, however, the weather had turned bad, and the ship was forced to remain in Helsingborg two more days. In boarding again, as one participant recounts the event, a "separate boat" was used to carry Bakunin's luggage. "Was this a joke or did he really mean it? There were cartons, bags and boxes of all sizes, eight pieces in all, and with all this he was off to war!"[43]

The amazed Pole need not have worried: there was to be no war. The British captain of the Ward Jackson had had enough. The vile weather, the arguments among and the threats from the rebels, the grumbling among his own sailors about the polluted water they had to drink, the approaching danger not only of Russian vessels (now fully aware of the expedition) but of any official stop-and-search, since the ship had left London without proper papers—all of this together convinced Captain Weatherley that it was time to go home. Instead of Gothland, he sailed to Copenhagen and refused to go any farther. The best the expedition could do then was to find a Danish crew to sail them all to Malmo, where Bakunin ended his role with a fine speech to a cheering crowd and a banquet that evening honoring freedom-loving Poles and Swedes.

A few days later Bakunin left for Stockholm where he would meet Antonia. She had at last arrived in London from Russia, and, learning this, he had wired her at once to come to him in Stockholm. She arrived there in May. As for the other rebels: the ship and its arms were sequestered by the Swedish government and went up in flames while in harbor; a contingent of 32 of the volunteers decided in June to continue the mission and set out on a faulty boat, which sank, taking 24 lives with it. "And now," one survivor and the author of his account goes on, "we are in England, literally dying of hunger.... Help me, Zhiro and Bompar: I want to die a worthy death for Poland, not die here of poverty. Here is a list of those who perished...." The 24 names followed.[44]

Sweden welcomed Bakunin as a fearless hero. Since they had been Russia's Baltic rival for over a century and were eagerly hopeful of regaining Finland after its liberation from Russia, the Swedes were strong supporters of the Polish cause and even more enthusiastic about someone like Bakunin who had suffered so much in his lifelong war against Tsarist tyranny. The newspapers competed with each other in their praise of him, at least during the first months of his stay. He was granted a private meeting with the King's brother and, perhaps—reports vary—with King Charles XV himself. A banquet was held in his honor. The themes of his address there were mainly those of his publications the year before, especially *The People's Cause: Romanov, Pugachev, or Pestel?*. Old Russia was tottering, rotted from within by its own corruptions, and a new, young Russia was rising. If the impending revolution did in fact break out in Russia, the Tsar himself would be to blame. He, the Tsar, was the real revolutionary. "Could Robespierre or Marat have done more?" As for people like himself, "We are the true conservatives. We are terrified of blood. But since it is necessary that it flow, it is better that it flow not for the destruction, but for the happiness of Russia and Poland." "We, the ones they call revolutionaries, we are not necessarily even republicans," he went on. "If Emperor Alexander II were to choose to stand openly at the head of the political and social revolution in Russia, if he were to choose to give freedom and independence to Poland as well as to all the provinces that do not want to be a part of the Empire,... then, gentlemen, far from struggling against him, we would be his loyal, his most ardently dedicated servants." Since the Tsar refused to understand this, however, the Russian people would have to speak for themselves.

And it now had the organization to do so, the Land and Freedom Party ("which I have the honor to belong to...and to represent before you"), a general, national party that included members from all provinces and all classes, "generals and officers, high and low government officials, landowners, merchants, priests, sons of priests, peasants and the millions of sectarians." This society "of all Russians of good will whatever their wealth or position" was now "properly and powerfully organized, striving to constitute itself, so to speak, a state within a state. It is organizing its own finances, its own administration, its own police and soon, I hope, it will have its own army." As for the program of this phantom power, it was simply his own: all land to the peasants, with the state repaying the owners; a federation of free, autonomous provinces, with the village commune at their base; an end to military recruitment, to be replaced by an armed citizenry; and, to put all this into effect, the summoning of a *Zemsky Sobor,* with delegates elected from all Russia without respect to class, wealth, or position.[45]

The contrast between the glorious reception he received in Stockholm and the denigrating indifference with which he felt he had been treated by Herzen and the Polish leaders made that treatment all the more humiliating to him. Failing in his efforts to radicalize the *Bell* or to become, as he had expected, "the third in their union" (the union of Herzen and Ogarev) and believing himself to have been deliberately kept in the dark about plans he was sure Herzen had been making with the Poles, Bakunin was hurt and indignant. "There is, all the same, strength within me, noble and useful, which I know to be there, but which you choose not to see." Even before the Ward Jackson episode, he had bitterly resented the "haughty, systematic, offhanded disdain" that he felt Herzen showed toward his recommendations. Then came the Ward Jackson. Why had Herzen not told him about that venture before he, Bakunin, left London? "You treated me as though I were a child, alerting me only at the last minute ... sending me here and there.... Keep in mind that I am not a child, that soon I will be 50 years old and that it is improper, rather, impossible to be your [errand] boy...."[46]

As was his wont, given his ambivalence toward power and conflict, each time he broke with Herzen during this period, he apologized. In mid-1862: "I am wrong, Herzen. I beg you, don't be angry. Because of an inherent awkwardness, a harsh word slipped from my tongue when there was no such harsh feeling in my heart." And now again, a week after the Ward Jackson scolding he had given Herzen: "Well, friends, I am wrong. You are right, and in relationship to you I am still a complete fool. The insulting expressions in my last letter were really not right. Having sent the letter off, I remembered them like a stab in the heart, and I wanted to take them back, but too late.... I see now that you were in no way to blame.[47] It was Cwierczakiewicz's fault." The other leaders of the expedition were also incompetent, at best, no better, that is, than the Dresden leaders had been. Lapinski, brave as he was, was unscrupulous. Demontowicz was so ill and beaten down that he could hardly move or talk.[48] Mazurkewicz was a "scandal-mongering intriguer." Bobchinski was a "gossipy old lady." The "little yid Tugendbold" was Lapinski's flunky and spy. As for the rest, they were just youngsters "happily going off to die."[49]

Reconciled with Herzen, Bakunin spent the rest of his time in Sweden doing what he could to improve the distribution of the *Bell* and other propaganda materials through Sweden to Russia. As for Poland, the Ward Jackson fiasco was enough for him for awhile. Although he wished the Poles well, he now concluded that "we Russians, it seems, must keep out of any direct involvement in their affairs."[50] The Russian foreign office tried to pressure Sweden into expelling him, as other governments had done before, and may even have been preparing a publication to discredit him, with excerpts from his "Confession."[51] The publication never appeared, however, nor did the Swedish government give way to the pressure. Bakunin went on freely carrying on his propaganda work until October 8, 1863, when he and Antonia returned to London. He had no intention of remaining there, however. His failure to win enough respect and confidence from Herzen and Ogarev to make him an equal member in the Herzen-Ogarev partnership, much less give him principal control of the *Bell's* policy, as he apparently wanted, eliminated whatever attraction London may have held for him.[52]

There is reason to believe, in fact, that he had never really planned to stay there. As early as June 1862, nine months before the Ward Jackson disaster, he had written Antonia that as soon as she arrived in London they would go to Italy where they could live "more cheaply, pleasantly and with a lot to do." She could also count on having a maid. He wrote her again about Italy two weeks later, this time mentioning his plan to form an alliance between the Slavs and Italians (both "natural enemies of the Germans") in order to satisfy "my special passion—the destruction of Austria." Towards this end, he told her, he was already engaged in a friendly correspondence with Garibaldi.[53] In his February 1862 proclamation to his "Slavic Friends," moreover, it was Italy that he mentioned first when he announced the awakening of the world from its long rest following the 1848-49 debacles.[54] In fact, "the avidness with which he followed Garibaldi's [activities] while in Irkutsk," as Herzen wrote of Bakunin,[55] and his keen interest in and frequent meetings with Mazzini in London, suggest that his intention all along may have been to settle not in England but in Italy.

Leaving London at the end of November, with letters of recommendation from Mazzini and other Italian leaders, the Bakunins made their way leisurely through Belgium, France, and Switzerland, arrived in Italy in early January 1864, then, after brief stays in Turin, Genoa, Livorno, and the island of Caprera (for a three-day visit with Garibaldi), settled comfortably in Florence. From the outside, the life Bakunin lived in Florence seemed that of a retired gentleman radical. His days and evenings were relaxed and expansive, enriched by a flow of congenial visitors: the Hungarian revolutionary émigré Count Pulsky, the Mazziniite Count Mario, the Russians who either lived there or were passing through, such as the scientist L. I. Menchikov (who later recalled the "completely bourgeois" style of the Bakunin residence), the artist Ge, the sculptor Zabello, and so forth. Besides the Menchikov description, there are several entries in the diary of the Pulsky governess to give us a glimpse into the cosmopolitan company that enlivened Bakunin's semiretirement.

> 13 February: Today's company was even more polyglot than usual in its composition. Hungarians—the Tarnóczys; Germans—Frau Urich and her daughter, and Fraülein Assing; the Russians Herzen, Bakunin, and Fricken (a Garibaldian of 1860); a Polish antiquarian, Rizski; a Swiss or French family, Quatremolle; a young Frenchman whose name I don't know; Garcia (a Spaniard...a Garibaldian of 1860); an American; and finally a crowd of Englishmen and Englishwomen, and, as always, Italians...glory to God, ten nations.
>
> 20 February: Again a large company in the evening, few English this time but more Italians, Russians, Poles, and Germans. The famous singer Boccardi performed. The Tarnóczys also came.
>
> 23 February: Bakunin and Schiff. An evening at the Schwarzenbergs—Hegelians. Matter is only an abstraction—we know what the will is.[56]

As for politics, these were clearly transitional months, a period of moving away from aims and patterns that had occupied Bakunin during 1862–63, the first two years after his escape, and towards those that would direct his life thereafter. During his brief stay with Garibaldi on Caprera, Bakunin had no doubt continued to press for the anti-Austrian alliance of Slavs and Italians that he had earlier mentioned to Antonia and in his correspondence with Garibaldi and that, in fact, had already been tried when a Garibaldian detachment fought with the Poles the year before. Occasionally, in the first part of the Florentine year, Bakunin also wrote about a Slavic-Magyar-Italian united front. But his real views on the future of the Polish national movement were probably expressed in a letter that April (1864) in which he said that "the first and unquestionably the most painful act of the Polish revolutionary tragedy" was over.

The same fluctuation and uncertainty were evident in his attitude towards the other source of hope in the 1862–63 period, the Land and Freedom Party and its Russian revolutionary potential. While he went on for a time helping Herzen find a southern route for smuggling the *Bell* and other revolutionary literature into Russia, he now wondered whether the Land and Freedom Party had not been an "illusion" all along and asked Ogarev in March if he still believed in its existence. Finally, regarding these recent themes in his political outlook, his close friendships at the time with the Hungarian émigré, General Gyorgy Klapka, who was a supporter of the "red prince" Jerome Napoleon, and with Karl Vogt, a defender of Napoleon III, suggest that he still had not yet given up his "red general" scenario (notwithstanding a cool and awkward meeting he had had with Muraviev himself in Paris on his way to Italy). But there was no one around to play that role. To judge from his warm appreciation of Garibaldi, Bakunin might have cherished some hopes along these lines for the Italian hero, but Garibaldi's recent failures and his deep skepticism disqualified him: "in every gesture or expression he clearly revealed profound melancholy." And when Bakunin had asked him why, "he answered, with a Christlike sorrow, 'The harvest is ripe, but the reapers are few.' "[57]

If the past left little hope, no signs to indicate a promising political direction to take after the failure of 1863, the present in Florence, genial as it was, offered still less. Bakunin had indeed been warmly welcomed into the Mazzini and Garibaldi circles, led by one Giuseppe Dolfi, the town baker to whom Garibaldi himself had recommended Bakunin. But their aims encompassed nothing more lofty or powerful than a parliamentary, constitutional republic, the aims of the "compromisers" Bakunin had always despised, and notwithstanding the less violent tendencies that had continued after Siberia (the *Zemsky Sobor* theme, etc.) he basically had no more in common with them than he had had with the "compromisers" of Prussia or Saxony in the 1840s. No wonder, therefore, that he sounded so despondent in a letter he wrote in mid-March 1864 to a friend, Countess Elizabeth Vasilevna Salias de Turnemir:

> Civilization is rotting, barbarism has not yet grown strong enough, and we are sitting *entre deux chaises*. It is difficult just to go on living until the great day of Nemesis, until the terrible judgment, which this vile European society will not escape. Let my friends build: I thirst only for destruction, because I am convinced that to build in the midst of carrion with rotten materials is wasted labor and that only from vast destruction can there arise new materials and with them new organisms. . . . For the forseeable future there can be no poetry other than the harsh poetry of destruction, and we may yet be happy, if it is given to us to witness that destruction. It would be worse if instead of destruction there were peaceful putrifaction. Our era is in all respects a transitional, unfortunate era, and we, disconnected from the old and not joined to the new, are unfortunate people. But we will bear our misfortune with dignity, for complaints will not help, and we will destroy as much as possible.[58]

Those remarks are important for several reasons. First of all, they testify to his depressed mood at the time: They are, especially those final lines, the thoughts and feelings of an embittered old man. But the statements are significant for another reason as well, one that is indicative of another basic shift in

Bakunin's political posture. They show that the apocalyptic vision is back again in full force. Not only had it been noticeably absent during his prison and exile years, but it had been displaced, or at least markedly subdued, during the London and Stockholm years (1862-1863) when Bakunin was actively involved in the day-to-day politics of specific national liberation movements. The return of apocalyptic expectations is also indicated in Bakunin's April 1864 letter in which he said that the first act of the Polish "revolutionary tragedy" was over. Another act was just then beginning, he went on to say, but this time it would involve nothing less than "a red, social, geological revolution."[59] Considering this comment along with the apocalyptic, "terrible-judgment" vision reasserted in Bakunin's letter to Countess de Turnemir the month before and setting both in the context of the national liberation failures, what we see is another basic reorientation in Bakunin's life and thought—away from the concrete national struggle of 1862-63 and back to the general, abstract, universal upheaval with its apocalyptic devastation that he had envisioned in the early 1840s, the time of *The Reaction in Germany*.

Moreover, and more to the point of the interpretation underlying this and the following chapter, this return to an abstract "Nemesis" reflects not only a move away from specific national liberation politics, but away from politics altogether. However unrealistic Bakunin had been during his year in London, (1862) and his involvement in the Polish rising the following year, his concerns were at least focused on identifiable movements, conditions, events, and leaders. Now such tangible politics disappeared due to the failure of the Polish rising and the predominance in Italy of a bourgeois republicanism and constitutionalism that meant nothing to him. Nor did he seem interested, yet, in finding any new political enterprise, revolutionary or otherwise. Had active revolutionary work been his concern, then, as one contemporary noted, Milan or Naples, not Florence, should have been his destination. Also, according to another source, he had begun writing his memoirs while in Switzerland *en route* to Italy,[60] hardly something he would do were he seriously planning to devote himself to revolutionary activism, but very much in keeping with retirement. Apocalyptic devastation, "Nemesis," in other words, precisely because it appeared to be such violent politics was really no politics at all, but rather Bakunin's attempt to disguise the fact—and, again, first of all from himself—that he was going to Italy with Antonia to begin a slow withdrawal that would occupy the rest of his life, albeit a withdrawal interspersed with intervals of zealous revolutionary outbursts.

Apocalyptic maximalism, however, was only one part of Bakunin's camouflage. The other was the organizational form, the "secret society" that he now began to fashion for the purpose, so he claimed, of setting the people aflame and sparking thereby the final conflagration. Ultimately rooted in the same motivations that had made him the father of his Fichtean "holy commune" some 30 years before, the "secret society" had already become his favorite political organization, in Paris in 1846 and in Prague, Anhalt, and Dresden in 1848–49. No doubt the elite organization had become even more attractive to him after the failures of the "people's" revolutions of 1848–49 and the inspiring encounters with powerful personalities like the "red general" and other military leaders Bakunin had befriended in Siberia. Almost immediately after his escape, he turned to it again. In May 1862, for example, he said that "we must cover [our] Slavic brothers with a network of secret societies, and these secret societies must encompass within themselves everything vital, advanced, energetic, everything that feels and thinks.... Afterwards, all these secret societies must be united into one and put in motion at the same time in Italy, Poland and Russia."[61] The Polish rising the following year set those plans to the side, but now that the national movement had failed, he could return to his plan for a network of secret societies. Moreover, his new residence, Italy, provided an additional stream of influences in support of this organizational form. Conspiratorial secrecy had been dramatized by leaders like Buonarroti and Pisacane, by political movements on the left (Carbonari) and on the right (Calderai and Sanfedisti), and by apolitical "bandit" associations that were soon to win Bakunin's admiration.[62]

Besides providing him this rich Italian conspiratorial tradition to go along with his renewed apocalypse, Florence offered him two models of such an organization ready at hand—the Falangia Sacra of the Mazzini republicans, who had established a branch in Florence in 1863, the year before Bakunin arrived, and the Freemasons. As we saw, Bakunin had already become involved with the Freemasons in Paris during the mid-1840s, and they may even then have helped turn his thoughts toward the secret revolutionary organization that he had recommended to the Polish émigrés at that time. He had also encountered a number of Masons in London and Stockholm, among them the Polish revolutionary leader Josef Cwierczakiewicz, the Czech Josef Demontowicz, and a Swede and Frenchman who were later to play parts in his career, August Sohlman and Alfred Talandier.[63] Since he had little if any interest in the modest political aims of the local Florentine republicans, it may have been the Freemasonry of some of those leaders (such as the baker Dolfi, Grand Master of the Florentine Freemasons as well as a Mazzini leader) that drew Bakunin to them. Attracted by the secrecy, the ritual, the intimacy, and the social commitment of the Florentine Masons (who the previous year, 1863, had moved to the left of the dominant Concordia Brotherhood and had formed their own lodge, *Il Progresso Sociale),*[64] Bakunin found in them a reincarnation of his "holy commune" of the 1830s blended with his revolutionary ideals of the 1840s.

As evidence of the seriousness of his Florentine masonic involvement, he rose steadily up the ladder of degrees—from the twenty-third degree of the Scottish ritual to the thirty-second, near the top. Notwithstanding this dedication or the probable influence the organization had both on Bakunin's thought and on his later secret societies, the Florentine Freemasonic movement had for him two basic flaws—its aims fell far short of the apocalypse and, even more important, it was not under Bakunin's personal control, and all his efforts to remodel it in his own image were unsuccessful.[65] For a secret society to meet the needs of his semiretirement, it must not only provide an atmosphere of familial intimacy, which the Freemasons did, but also help him display the mask of apocalyptic violence (needed especially now to disguise the de facto retreat) and allow him to play the part of father of the family, submitting to his will and whim as his sisters and "soul sisters" had done some 30 years earlier.

His consequent dissatisfaction that first year in semiretirement was already apparent in his March letter to the Countess de Turnemir. Although the apocalyptic vision had returned here in full glory, it was not accompanied, as it had been earlier, with the exultant optimism and the summons to self-confident battle that had characterized Bakunin's earlier apocalyptic declarations. Instead, the letter is a dirge of defeat and despair. Even the destructiveness comes through more as the spiteful vengeance of someone left out or behind than as the just and sacred punishment by God's or history's vanguard. The Florentine mix was not yet quite right.

In September 1864 he returned for a visit to Stockholm. The reasons for the trip remain unclear, although they seem to have involved a search to fill the gaps still left in Florence. First, with respect to more action, having felt again "electricity constantly building up" in Europe,[66] he may have gone to Stockholm to get closer to it, since Stockholm had been the location of his last "electrifying" contact with revolution, or at least with its marginal charges. Second, regarding a more appropriate "secret society," he was able to recruit along the way a number of followers who were to become part of a "secret society" better suited to his revived apocalyptic and authoritarian fantasies than were the Florentine Masons. A third possible reason for the trip may have been related to publication contracts he made with the Swedish press so that, as he wrote Premukhino, he would at last (yet again) be able "to stand on my own feet."[67]

Except for writing, in his words, "two short pages" a week[68] for the Swedish press, he does not seem to have done very much with these business arrangements. One reason, perhaps, for sending so little to them when he returned to Florence was that he had arrived home with something far more important to do—establish a secret revolutionary international. Although he may have begun working on it before the trip (it may have been, as we saw, one reason for the trip), he devoted himself to it much more zealously after his return. The reason for the intensification was his experience in London on his way back to Italy from Stockholm; more specifically, his meeting on November 3, 1864 with Karl Marx. Bakunin arrived in London from Stockholm on October seventeenth. Three weeks before, on September twenty-eighth, a packed meeting was held in St. Martin's Hall to establish the International Workers' Association. Sensing as a result of several earlier meetings "a revival of the working class," Marx had decided to set aside his research for a time and, in contrast to his usual attitude toward such activities, to take part in the gathering. He was elected to the central coordinating committee and to a subcommittee charged with preparing a program and a constitution for the new organization. His famous *Inaugural Address* was the main result of this early involvement in the International. In it he reviewed the workers' plight and struggle, urged "a fraternal bond of union between the working classes of different countries" as a necessary base for success, and, especially important for what was to come, called for a struggle against capitalism by political means, including the conquest of political power through representation in bourgeois parliaments. Bakunin's arrival came right in the middle of this historic ground breaking.

Learning of Bakunin's presence in London from Bakunin's tailor, Marx wrote him and suggested a meeting. Bakunin replied warmly, welcoming the invitation. His later comments about their meeting indicate a strong remnant of distrust beneath the superficial reconciliation: Bakunin did not really believe Marx's disclaimer of involvement in the repeated revivals of the old Tsarist-agent slander against him. Marx, for his part, seemed more sincerely enthusiastic. "I like him very much," he wrote Engels. He was especially impressed by what he called Bakunin's complete break with nationalism in favor of socialism, so impressed, in fact, that Marx urged Bakunin to come out actively in favor of the International and against Mazzini's nationalism when he returned to Italy.[69]

Judging by its aftermath, the meeting had a tremendous effect on Bakunin. He would indeed go back and challenge Mazzini, but he would do so not only on behalf of the fledgling International, but also as a leader in his own right, a leader of his own entirely different "International." Who could be better suited than he himself for the role of leader of an international? He was the internationalist *par excellence,* a man without a country, at home in all of them, widely travelled, and intimate friend of militants throughout Europe. On this last trip alone, he had added handsomely to his following—men like August Sohlman in Sweden, Alfred Talandier in London, the Reclus brothers in Paris, and more.[70]

The example of the London International, reenforced by the discussion with Marx, came at just the right moment for Bakunin. To return to Florence as a defender of the local Mazzini and Garibaldi republicans would have meant committing himself to the "compromisers'" struggle for a parliamentary republic. Never an acceptable program, it was least of all so now that he had returned to his apocalypse. Freemasonry had been more promising, but, as noted above, suffered from similar shortcomings.[71] As for simply representing the London-based International as Marx was expecting him to do, Bakunin was surely no more willing to be Marx's "boy" than he had been willing to be Herzen's the year before. Again combining diverse influences into a program and direction uniquely his own, Bakunin adapted, then merged into a distinctly Bakuninist secret international, his earlier ideas about secret organizations, the London workers' International, the Florentine Freemasonic organization, and the various other secret societies in Italy noted above. What he needed, what had been lacking in his Florentine semiretirement, and what he earnestly devoted himself to preparing after the Stockholm-London trip, was an international organization that would appear forthrightly revolutionary and violently powerful (commensurate with the revived apocalypse, the "Nemesis," the "thirst for destruction," the "red, social, geological revolution"), that could thereby disguise his retreat and, consequently, permit him to continue enjoying it, that would disguise the disguise (that is, conceal the deceptive—but still dangerous—fantasy of virile power under a cloak of secrecy), and that would be totally under his mock-paternal control, on the model of the "holy commune." Through the secrecy he kept the power powerless (i.e., chaste), while through the solipsistic control he would know that he could narcissistically always "find himself" in his new pseudo-family, find, that is, the "friend" within.

So secret, so powerless, and so narcissistic were these successive international revolutionary societies, in fact, that they seldom got farther than his private notebooks! However, fantasies though they were (for the most part) the enormous amount of time and the intense concern that he was to give to them (and, in fact, had already given to them in the 1840s) testify to their great, indeed, indispensable, importance for him. "You reproach me for inactivity at a time when I was more active than ever," he wrote Herzen in July 1866. And the "exclusive object" of that activity, he went on, was "the foundation and formation of an international revolutionary-socialist secret society."[72]

To judge from the writings that have come down from those years, the work that so exclusively preoccupied him was a series of drafts and redrafts of organizational charts, membership regulations, party aims, sacred "vows," and so on for his new "secret" International, the International Secret Society for the Liberation of Mankind, the International Brotherhood, the Sacred Union for Freedom. This series of texts—*The International Secret Society for the Liberation of Mankind, The Organization of the International Revolutionary Brotherhood, Essential Points of the National Catechisms, Revolutionary Catechism,* and a variety of other fragmentary drafts of similar statements of goals and rules—provide some important missing links in his apocalyptic message. During the 1840s he gave us his vision of the cataclysmic upheaval that would annihilate all existing institutions, but he said little about what would come next, the look of his new heaven and new earth. Also, while he was certain that the destructive force would come from the enraged masses and their "warmth and flame," he had only begun experimenting with the "Archimedes point" that would allow him, weak and isolated as he was, to spark the mass rising—the "secret society." The texts of the mid-1860s filled these gaps almost completely, so much so, in fact, that everything he was to write or do along these lines for the rest of his life was essentially repetitions, elucidations, or realizations of what they say.

To begin with paradise, we can consider these documents[73] as the first of Bakunin's later-day beatific visions of the ideal anarchist kingdom to emerge from the apocalyptic ruins. Absolute "freedom," the constant theme throughout his life, beginning with his youthful flight from society's "dark, filthy, and vile" "custom, propriety, and obligation" and ending with his final anarchist declarations, remains the base and the crown. In the new society, no man or woman "will in any way have to search for any sanction for their actions other than what they find in their own conscience and reason, determine them by anything other than their own will, and be responsible for them only to themselves, first of all, and, then, to society to which they belong, but only to the extent that they freely consent to being a part of it." Not only would there be full freedom for the individual, but also "absolute liberty for associations not excluding those that, by their aims, are, or seem, immoral or even that aim at the corruption or destruction of individual or public freedom."

Consequently, all powers, authorities or institutions that limit this absolute freedom must be destroyed—"such as official churches, permanent armies, centralized powers, bureaucracies, governments, parliaments, universities, state banks, as well as aristocratic or bourgeois monopolies ... all the political, military, administrative, judicial and financial institutions that today make up the life and power of these states ... the criminal and civil codes now in use in Europe, since they are all equally inspired by the cult of God, state, and family." Moreover, "having itself ceased to exist and being, therefore, unable to repay its debts, the state could no longer force anyone to repay theirs—the [repayment] would then naturally revert to a matter for one's own individual conscience."

Repayment would be difficult in any case, since besides "confiscating the possessions of all the reactionaries," the revolution "would deliver to the flames all
legal documents, whether relating to court cases or property or debts." Sex,
marriage, and family, finally, would be freed of legal forms and formalities, becoming "natural" relationships.[74]

While society would protect children against delinquent parents, among
other things assuring them complete equality of education, Bakunin conceded
that nothing could or should be done about the inequality of talent and that
there would also be individual differences in wealth, as long as one's wealth came
only from one's own energy and prudence. Equal education and—an essential
concern throughout—the complete elimination of inheritance would gradually
narrow these differences, and they could be expected to diminish still more once
the age-old division between the privileged educated classes and the uneducated
laboring masses came to an end, once "the man of science labors and the worker
thinks."[75]

There would, of course, be a governing social apparatus to take the place of
the old oppressive system, but it would be organized not "as today, from the top
downwards and from the center to the circumference, but on the principle of
free federation, beginning with the free individuals who formed the associations
(the autonomous communes) and followed by the autonomous communes that
formed the autonomous provinces, the provinces that formed the regions, and
the regions that, in freely federating among themselves, formed the countries,
which in their turn formed, sooner or later, the worldwide, universal federation."[76] The essential content and structure of these layers of freely associating
federations would be economic, or syndicalist, rather than political. Society
would be divided "no longer as nations, but as groups organized on the basis of
production...." As was the case with many other reformers and revolutionaries
of the day, including Marx in his *Inaugural Address,* Bakunin was at the time
greatly impressed by and placed much hope on producers' and consumers'
cooperatives, the model and basic building blocks, he believed, of the coming
people's socialism.[77] Three other principles—besides cooperation and bottom-
upwards federation—complete the essentials of Bakunin's anarchist socialism in
this period: (1) all land belonged to society and could be used only by those
who worked it; (2) all products belonged to those who produced them; and (3)
wealth belonged only to those who earned it. The emphasis on economics as a
basis for organization and federation, however, in no way "impeded individuals
from freely associating for any purpose whatsoever: religious, political, scientific,
industrial, artistic—or even for the corruption or exploitation of innocents and
fools, provided that they are not minors."[78]

Bakunin's readiness to accept inequalities that resulted from differences in ability, energy, efficiency, or prudence, to employ inheritance laws rather than forced levelling as a means of narrowing the gap, and to distinguish between the "duty" of respecting others' liberty and the "virtue" of helping them all show that "freedom"—and what it particularly represented to him—was too inviolable even to be qualified by communal ideals. As for the possibility that this insistence on absolute freedom might in practice contradict his no less absolute commitment to equality, such problems could be easily handled by the same intuitive deductions that had always reconciled his opposites and resolved his contradictions. As much the philosophical Idealist as ever, thought is still fact; to say is to solve. Consequently: "there can in no way be liberty without equality"; "the liberty of each is realizable only given the equality of all"; "man is truly free only so far as his liberty, freely acknowledged and reflected, as though in a mirror, in the free conscience of all others, finds confirmation for its infinite extension in their liberty." Nor does he worry about the effect of absolute liberty on the social order, since "the order and unity that were destroyed by violence and despotism will be reborn from the womb of liberty" and "taking liberty as a base, one arrives necessarily at union.... One for all and all for one." Similarly, the patriot need not fear a loss of his own nation's well-being as a result of exchanging sovereignty for universal federation; for "the prosperity and happiness of his country far from being in contradiction with those of other countries require for their realization that there prevail among the destinies of all these nations an all-powerful, ultimate solidarity."[79]

Automatically by now, as predictably as night follows day, paradise implied catastrophe, the Word meant the sword. It is the elemental logic of apocalypse, and Bakunin is hardly alone, therefore, when he abruptly moves from his millennial kingdom to "demonic" violence. Inspired by his trip to Stockholm, London, and Paris, by the impressive example of the nascent International and Marx's role in it, and by his own determination to form an international of his own Bakunin had purged his apocalypse of those despondent, embittered, and vengeful strains that came through so clearly in mid-March 1864 in his letter to Countess de Turnemir. No longer was it the task of revolutionaries to "bear our misfortune with dignity" and realize, without complaining about it, that they were simply born at the wrong time. Instead, their task was once again "to electrify the passions of all the masses" when the "hour of the great revolution will have rung out anew," to "ignite a war of extermination without mercy or respite ... not letting down the sword until they have destroyed all states and all the old religious, political and economic institutions in Europe and in the whole civilized world."[80] Needless to say, the revolutionaries were again sternly warned against all such "impotent" tactics as "conciliation" and "negotiation." Nor should we be surprised to see that, while summoning the people to the appropriately apocalyptic "war of extermination without mercy or respite," Bakunin also gently assured the world that "there will be no cold, systematic terror—it will be a war against functions and things far more than against people ... and once the enemies of the revolution were deprived of the means to do harm, it would not be necessary to take bloody measures against them. ..."[81]

No less important now for Bakunin than his refurbished apocalypse, was his detailed work on the organization that would guide humanity through the cataclysmic ordeal, his "secret society," the International Secret Society for the Liberation of Mankind. Its universal, apocalyptic mission is clearly spelled out at the outset: "The aim of this society is the unification of revolutionary elements of all lands for the creation of a genuine sacred union of freedom in opposition to the sacred union of all the tyrannies of Europe—religious, political, bureaucratic and financial."[82] The postulate of vigilant secrecy implied several corollaries, no less essential for a successful revolution—the revolutionaries must have "the same philosophic, religious, political, and social convictions," "the same grand principle, broad and elevated enough in order to become for those who acknowledge it a kind of religion";[83] there must be a severe code of discipline; the whole apparatus must be kept in order by an efficient system of centralized direction.

To assure that centralized direction, a "provisional central junta" would control the organization at its early stage, until there were some 70 members, at which time it would call a constituent assembly, which would in turn create an International Directory and Supreme Council. These highest organs would then choose the regional and provincial "juntas," and each lower body would be entirely subordinate to the one above. "The national families are to have the position of apprentice in relationship to the international families, with respect both to ideas and to revolutionary practice." "The members of the regional committees owe absolute obedience to the national junta, which appoints, suspends and removes them."[84] At several points in his organizational scheme the clash between freedom and authority is particularly dramatic, or psychodramatic if we recall the sources of the ambivalence. In describing, for example, the relative power of the lower bodies vis-a-vis those of the bodies immediately above, he begins by stating that the higher will in no way interfere with the lower. Yet, he then goes on to say that the higher will establish a code to which the lower must adhere.[85]

There is no such ambivalence, however, when it comes to assuring unity through a common program and set of regulations: every organ and all the members are obligated to swear allegiance to Bakunin's organizational system, his

Revolutionary Catechism, and all his substantive and organizational aims and theories involving the means and ends of the coming revolution. "No European people will rebel anymore except to realize the ideas of political and social emancipation, and they must adopt our program as their correct expression."[86] As their basic laws and principles, the International Councils in each country must adopt "our *Revolutionary Catechism* [and our] provisional organization, including the provisional rules of the international society," and they must do so without making "the slightest change" in any of those rules.[87] Besides being strongly centralized because of the "secret organization" and the "common program in all countries,"[88] the organization would necessarily be centralized as a result of a number of other indispensable requirements. While, for example, the communes, at the lowest level of the hierarchy, were theoretically free to federate or not, they would in fact have to join "for the common defense" and in order to carry out simultaneous uprisings. The same would be the case all the way up the scale to the single international,[89] the federation of nations. Moreover, since isolated revolutions that occurred apart from the direction of the International "secret organization" were doomed to fail, any such rising was to be judged "treason, a crime."[90]

Finally, there were the vows to be taken by the "brothers" in the secret "families," national and international. Two categories of "brothers" were defined—the active and the nominal brothers. The active brothers, from whom alone the leadership could be drawn, took the more stringent oaths:

> I swear on my honor and my conscience to accept with complete and unqualified conviction all the principles, philosophical, economic and social, theoretical and practical, of your *Revolutionary Catechism.* I accept as well all the organizational forms, all the precepts, and all the laws that form parts of your Rules and Regulations. I submit to them in a provisionally absolute manner reserving the right and the duty to oppose at the next Constitutional Assembly all the secondary points on which I have a different opinion, but accept in advance the decisions of that Assembly as definite and supreme.
>
> I consecrate from this time forward all my strength, my efforts and my life to the service of the federalist and socialist world revolution, which can have no other foundation than these principles, and since I am convinced that I can serve them in no better way than through my participation in the open and secret activity of an international revolutionary organization, I ask to be included among you.
>
> I swear loyalty and absolute obedience to the international organization and promise to it zealous activity, care and discretion, silence regarding all secrets, the sacrifice of my own egoism, self-love, ambition and my personal interests, and the complete and unlimited surrender to

its disposition of all my strength and power, my social position, my influence, my fortune, and my life.

I submit in advance to all the sacrifices and assignments that it will impose on me, certain that it will demand nothing of me that is contrary to my convictions and my honor or beyond my personal capacities. Throughout the time that I am charged with a function or mission I will unconditionally obey the orders of the immediate leader who has entrusted me with it and swear to carry out the mission with all possible speed, precision, energy and foresight, stopping only at what seems to me to be truly insurmountable obstacles.

I subordinate from now on all my activities, public and private, literary, political, official, professional, and social to the supreme directives that I receive from the committees of this organization.

Such were the first set of vows. The following set mainly concerned relations between the "brothers." In the final vow, the candidate agreed to accept against himself "the vengeance of the Society" if he betrayed his oath or even forgot it.[91]

Yet this was the same Bakunin who wrote in these same texts, "To be free is the right, duty, value, happiness, and mission of man. It is the fulfillment of his faith. Not to have freedom is not to be human. To deprive a man of his freedom and of the means of achieving and using it is not only to murder him, but to murder humanity."[92] Back and forth the contest went, with the advantage going now to freedom, now to domination. He proclaimed, again and again, unlimited freedom and complete democracy, including universal, equal suffrage, the right of every individual or group to free, voluntary entry into the association and withdrawal from it, and the gradual emergence of higher levels of association only if and only as long as that was the wish of the participants at the level below. Then, he prepared in painstaking detail his secret, tightly disciplined, completely centralized militant organization in which the higher organs, from the central "junta" down, gave the orders and in which the members swore total submission. Not that this was something new in his life. The dualism and ambivalence that now defined his organizational schemes had in the same (if less explicit) way characterized the earlier Fichtean "holy commune." Everywhere in these organizational texts one hears echoes both of his domination of his sisters and "soul sisters" and of his unquestionably sincere assurances that such domination was the farthest thing from his mind, that all he wanted was their "freedom." The declarations of freedom against all authority and the proposals for authoritarian controls, the "families" and the "brothers," the apocalyptic war of extermination and the timid flight from violence, the "two camps" and the implacable refusal to compromise—all these, and not merely the attack on inheritance (even as he vigorously insisted on his share of his own) or the quaintly millennial demand for the liquidation of debt, reflect entirely personal needs and feelings as much as if they had been poems or paintings. As always, the story those projections and displacements tell is the opposite of what they appear to tell—not strength and assault, but weakness and retreat. The utopian goal is still the idealized Premukhino childhood (and the narcissistic roots of that fantasy) that had sustained him 30 years earlier during his oppressive army years. And the means, the abstract, universal, cataclysmic "two camp" Armageddon that would clear the way for that regained childhood paradise, is still the heroic virile mask he had worn in the barracks, in *The Reaction in Germany*, in the *Appeal to the Slavs*, and in all his other promethean soliloquies.

Besides so clearly echoing the "holy commune" of the thirties, the "secret societies" that were henceforth to play an ever greater role in Bakunin's apocalyptic vision served the same purpose that the dialectic had been serving since the early 1840s, a vehicle for similarly transmuting impotence into omnipotence. As a "left" Hegelian dialectician, he had proved his powerful social role by remaining completely apart from society. Now, imagining himself the planner, organizer, and director of a vast international network of secret societies, he could lead his "brothers" and "intimates" through the apocalyptic death and rebirth of society, while situated comfortably, first in Florence, then, after October 1865, in Naples. The secret society was even more suitable for him now, at his age, than were the dialectics. Whereas the dialectics focused only on the "bloody contradiction" and imminent Gog-Magog upheavals and, therefore, gave priority to immediate action, the emphasis of the "secret society" was on gathering "brothers" and "intimates," the formation of a new "family." However inspiring, exhilarating, and potent were the fantasies that Bakunin brought back with him after meeting Marx in London, the real function of the "secret society" (the function those fantasies were meant to conceal) was to provide Bakunin a new pseudo-family, or series of families, which—as his sisters and the Beyer sisters had done in his youth—would echo and mirror his thoughts, love, honor, and obey him, and, by sanctioning his generalship-at-a-distance, help spare him the harassments and obligations incumbent on those seriously concerned with social change. "Loving Michael Alexandrovich to the point of adoration," as the wife of one of Bakunin's new "intimates" recalled, "Cafiero was boundlessly devoted to him, acting as his nurse and governess, looking after him as after a child."[93]

As for the participants of his new "brotherhood," they were, in general, the same demi-intellectuals, the "intelligentsia," that have usually—then, before, and after—gravitated towards and become the cadre in such maximalist revolutionary fantasies. "Quite naturally," one member in the Florentine circle recalled, "there gathered around [Bakunin] a complete staff, formed from retired Garibaldi volunteers, lawyers with few court cases, and an assortment of the most ill-matched people with nothing to say, nothing to do, and even without convictions, people always changing everything—their social situation, activities, beliefs—keeping only the extreme radicalism of their desires and aims, which they themselves did not really understand."[94] Or, as Bakunin himself described his potential followers some years later, they were "passionate, energetic youth, completely displaced, with no sign of a career, with no way out."[95]

Since the purpose of recruiting the new "brothers" was to provide himself a new family, it was hardly necessary for the new recruits actually to meet the stringent, paper requirements, which served, in fact, exactly the opposite purpose, that of feigning virile power, not of providing intimate solace and approval. Thus, he could laugh off one follower's resistance to the vow taken on a dagger ("we did that for the Italians"),[96] ignore the fact that Fanelli, one of his closest "intimates," kept his place as an elected parliamentary delegate, and forgive three "active brothers," including Fanelli again, who joined Garibaldi in just the kind of patriotic foray that Bakunin now made a prime target in his campaign against Mazzini's and Garibaldi's nationalistic revolution.

At the same time, of course (for appearances had to be maintained), he kept insisting on uncompromising, disciplined dedication and revolutionary maximalism. Throughout this period, for example, he continued to urge Herzen to stop growing old so fast, to become bolder in the *Bell,* to drop his foolish faith in Russian reform from the top and in the constitutional, parliamentary programs of the liberals, and to support instead the young radicals in Russia who were beginning to organize seriously, not for superficial political reforms, but for total social transformation. Herzen had made a terrible mistake, he said, in criticizing Karakazov for attempting, in 1866, to assassinate Tsar Alexander II. While he himself did not expect much good would come of it and was even willing to agree with Herzen that only harm would result, Bakunin would not criticize the attempt itself, understanding, he said, the intensity of police oppression that provoked it. Karazazov was still one of us, he insisted, as were all the radical youth, in spite of "their unpleasant, disorderly, even dirty sides," since they felt "a real passion for equality, work, justice, freedom and reason." Whatever their shortcomings, they remained "heroes," "pioneers of a new truth and a new life."[97] As to Bakunin's accomplishments in Europe during these Neapolitan years of work on his secret international, he boasted great "positive results." "We have friends in Switzerland, in Norway, in Denmark, in England, in Belgium, in France, in Spain and in Italy; there are Poles and even several Russians. In southern Italy the majority of Mazzini's organization, the Falangia Sacra, has come over to our side."[98]

Once again, as in the days of his own "holy commune," a pseudo-family of "intimates" that he could paternalistically inspire and guide (this time by correspondence from his hilltop rooms overlooking Naples rather than from Moscow or St. Petersburg) took on the appearance of a militant front-line regiment rather than the monastic sanctuary it was. Unfortunately for his real intentions, however, this time the "network" of "intimates" was to achieve remarkable success on its own and as a result offer him the opportunity for genuine leadership that was finally to drive him completely out of politics. In short, little had changed since the days of the first "holy commune": the "secret society" was necessary, he wrote, for "otherwise we ourselves would reveal to our enemies our projects, which are to a certain extent illegal, our plan of action, the condition of our strength, and also our weak sides."[99] The "weak sides" that he was afraid to reveal and the reason he knew his "projects" were "illegal" had no more to do with objective political or social problems than his theory and practice had ever had or would ever have. Because of its real source and purpose, even this highly sublimated fantasy of power had to be severely constrained, kept strictly "secret." As usual, Bakunin's mask exposes and highlights what it is supposed to hide.

It was mainly due to these entirely personal benefits that he derived from the "secret society," "brotherhood," "family," and "alliance" that Bakunin was attracted to them in the first place. In spite of all the sound and fury associated with his work on his secret international, therefore, what appears to be Bakunin's first, preparatory steps into his most famous revolutionary crusade, the one that involved him in conflict with Marx over control of the International, was primarily a further step *out* of politics.

Shielded by his revived apocalypse and by his work on the organization that would lead it, he could continue his Italian retirement in good conscience. "We live here quietly," he wrote Countess de Turnemir soon after he returned from his Stockholm-London trip. "We work little. Each week I send up to two short pages to Stockholm and earn thereby 100 francs and sometimes more for the week. Antonia has started to study seriously. Sometimes we go to the theater and, rarely, we visit friends.... In a word, we read, study, write, sometimes chat and pass the time quietly, innocently, but quite pleasantly."[100] The following year (1865) we have a similarly idyllic scene, this time from Antonia, as she describes their summer at Sorrento:

> Life here flows peacefully and regularly as before. We rise early, Michael bathes, then has coffee and grapes.... The entire morning Michael writes, while I read.... At three Michael takes a nap. I wake him at four, and we go swimming at five. At six we eat, then at seven take a walk.... We return at nine for tea on the terrace, after which Michael takes up his work again, and I, mine; I, until 12; he until one or even two."[101]

In October 1865 Bakunin and Antonia moved to Naples, where they lived near the sea, at the edge of town, on a hill overlooking all of Naples and beyond.[102] Thus comfortably established, and having acquired a generous benefactress in the person of one Princess Zoe Obolensky, Bakunin's life flowed on as smoothly and tranquilly as his revolutionary programs were rocky and stormy. It is not surprising, therefore, that one finds a most uncharacteristic new word in Bakunin's political lexicon—patience. "One needs a great deal of patience and restraint here. If we but see a millionth part of our goals fulfilled we will, at least, be as content to die as Samson [!] died." And if not? Well, "then let it be that we should not have lived entirely in vain but have left after us at least some living trace.... Thanks to constant effort, I can say that there have been enough consoling successes, especially recently."[103] He realized, he wrote in an earlier letter, that "in order to achieve only the basic points [of the program] at least 50 years or perhaps over 100 years would be needed. But, like the Jesuits, who having created secret societies with the best organizations in the world, then worked relentlessly, fiercely for over two centuries...so have we founded a society for a long period that will surely outlive us and that will disband only when the entire program has been carried out."[104]

Years before, as a Fichtean father of his "holy commune" he had balanced the needs of childhood and manhood by remaining freely, irresponsibly, and comfortably detached, while self-deceptively enjoying a sense of power and honor as God's instrument, chosen to show others how to leave society as he had. Later, as a "left" Hegelian revolutionary he had exchanged thought for action, withdrawal from society for the revolutionary annihilation of society. Now, as he begins his final revolutionary phase, we find him combining both of these earlier postures: withdrawing into his revived holy communal secret societies, while continuing a fiercely apocalyptic pose with its appropriate vision of universal destruction—sometime in the future.

From this perspective, therefore, there is a clear continuity joining Bakunin's prison and exile years with the decade that followed. But the direction of that continuity, contrary to the conventional interpretation of Bakunin in this period, was towards further retreat. This was most obviously apparent in the hope, which Bakunin continued to cherish even after his escape, for a bloodless revolution from above, led by a radicalized Romanov. It was no less the case, however, as this chapter has shown, with respect to the opposite scenario that replaced that bizarre hope, the apocalyptic, axe-flashing revolution from below and the secret brotherhood that would lead it. The abstract extremism was so far removed from any concrete political involvement, that Bakunin was left freely detached in his Florence-Naples retirement, which he shared with the secret brotherhood that helped make the retirement look like militant engagement.

Following the progress of Bakunin's career until this point, we see a great circular voyage. He began as a shy and lonely young man who compensated for and attempted to conceal his inadequacies by becoming, in the 1830s, God's warrior for holy truth. Then, in the early 1840s, having replaced his "wife" philosophy by his "bride" revolution, he became one of history's apocalyptic saviors *(The Reaction in Germany)* and, somewhat later, the defender of the "people's" cataclysmic destructiveness (Weitling). Finally, in his most forceful and heroic performance, 1848–49, he was the fearless revolutionary leader of all repressed national minorities in rebellion against all the repressive tyrants. Then, with his arrest, imprisonment, and exile, the direction shifted into reverse. His first step backwards came when he replaced the national masses, as the principal revolutionary force, with the enlightened good Tsar and "red general." As we have seen, this scenario continued for a short time after his escape. The next regression came when, following the failure of the Polish rising of 1863, both the national movements and the good Tsar gave way to the renewed apocalypse, the "Nemesis," the "red, social, geological revolution." With that, he had returned to the early and mid-1840s. Then, beginning in late 1864 and continuing in one form or another almost until the end of his life, came the "secret societies" and with them his return to the "holy commune" of the Fichtean days.

Having reached that stage in his regression (and there were still several more steps back to take), Bakunin once again had reversed the relationship present in his "right" Hegelian posture. At that time, the late 1830s, the facade had displayed reconciliation, while the inner reality, his actual day-to-day life, had continued the romantic rebellion of the Fichtean crusade. Now, in the mid-1860s, it was the rebellion that was, for the most part, the deceptive mask (as it had been in the beginning of the "left" Hegelian 1840s), while the reality of his life, the life he lived in Florence and Naples, was one of withdrawal and at least relative serenity. Thus, rather than leave "our common bride—the revolution" as he had earlier left his "jealous wife" philosophy, he now, in effect, arranged a *ménage à trois* with both of them. For appearance's sake, and for the basic needs that made such appearance necessary, he would go on living with the revolution—secretly. But, at first haltingly then steadily, he also would return home again, to the family (his "intimates" in the "secret societies") and, as we will see, to "Thought," the eternal mirror of himself and his "friend."

One wishes, after all Bakunin had been through, that he could have gone on enjoying his militant inaction (a later-day variation of his "ruthless surrender"). And perhaps he might have, had the real world let him. But it did not. For one thing, his benefactress, Princess Obolensky, was forced to leave Italy in the summer of 1867 and move to a town near Geneva: her estranged husband had decided he had supported her radical politics and her irregular romances long enough. Also, as a reason for leaving Italy, Bakunin was once again facing a scandalous charge that would force him, as he wrote Herzen, to sue, duel, or leave. The charge was counterfeiting.[105] Yet, even apart from these inducements from the real world outside there was probably enough strength remaining in the fantasy world inside to drive him back into the fray. For the same reasons that he had been compelled so often before to exchange a too telltale passivity (Schelling, "right" Hegel) for the act of action, that he had left the sanctuary of his Florentine semiretirement some three years earlier, in 1864, and that he had responded so zealously at that time to the stimulus of Marx and the International, the pendulum would no doubt have swung back in time and sent him back on stage once more.

In any case, he left in August 1867 together with his restored apocalypse and several of the devoted apostles from his Italian secret society to begin a new ministry in Geneva. It was an ideal location. Liberal Swiss policies had made it a haven for radicals in flight from more repressive regimes and a preferred site for political conferences and intrigues. Herzen, for example, had moved there from London, together with the *Bell,* in March 1865, and Bakunin had on several occasions written him to say that he, too, planned to move there. Finally, in June 1867 a group of European liberals and radicals, concerned about a Franco-Prussian war looming ahead, had arranged for a peace congress to be held in Geneva that September. It would be a fine opportunity for Bakunin to repeat his stunning and fateful success of 20 years before, when, in November 1847, he had addressed the Polish émigré community in Paris and had thereby begun his meteoric ascent. The curtain, in short, was about to rise on Bakunin's next and most illustrious act—his duel with Marx.

10. THE INTERNATIONAL: ZEALOTS AND PHARISEES

Conventional interest in Bakunin usually begins at this point and focuses on the next five years, the period in which he fought Marx in the International, collaborated with Nechaev—the Russian "savage" and "fanatic" (Bakunin's terms),[1] participated in and perhaps even triggered the hapless Lyon putsch, and wrote his principal anarchist works. His fame now soars and spreads, gaining for him in a remarkably short time the enormous and enduring influence that won him his large, permanent, and constantly expanding place in history.

Yet, these are not really creative years for him. As we will see, everything that he was to do now he had done before, although usually on a less grandiose scale. His ideas are either repetitions or variations of earlier themes, old wine in familiar, if sometimes larger and more colorful, bottles. Even the occasional flash and brilliance are afterglow. Once again, moreover, the success and fame came as often as not from his being used and abused by others to advance local causes rather than as a result of his own accomplishments. He is still more the passive recipient of his prominence than its maker. Conditions and "the times" are now more congenial for the role he had been playing for years, and, consequently, he now becomes even more the revolutionary celebrity. But, to round out this synopsis of what is to come (and further develop the theme of the preceding chapter), no sooner does his performance begin to have its great impact than the man behind the mask grows weary of the role, one that had long been essentially alien to him, however much he had been condemned to play it. Thenceforth, as the role became the cherished property of others, friends and enemies, he withdrew more and more into himself and into his secret family of "intimates."

The *deja vu,* the sense one has during this period of having seen it all before, begins with Bakunin's participation in the work of the League of Peace and Freedom, whose opening Congress in September 1867 may have been one of the reasons for his leaving Italy when he did. If, as suggested earlier, the occasion recalled November 1847, the character and constituents of the Congress were Prague 1848 all over again. A largely moderate, bourgeois, pacifist group of European intellectuals had gathered to search for ways of averting the Franco-Prussian war that they saw ahead and, in general, to plan and build a road to lasting peace. Bakunin's prominence earned him immediate and enthusiastic recognition at the Congress and election to the committee charged with working out a program.

As at Prague, however, the solutions he urged at the opening Congress, in his committee, and at the second Congress the following September, were as irrelevant to the immediate aims of the Congress as his maximalist declarations had been to the similarly restricted aims of the Prague deliberations. Building on themes he had developed in Italy, mainly in response to Mazzini's nationalism, republicanism, and theism, he argued at the 1867 Congress that there could be no peace until nationalism, patriotism, and the state were eliminated. This must be the main work and goal of the League. "In essence, all centralization, whether religious, bureaucratic or military were identical"; "every centralized state no matter how liberal it might be, even if it were a republic, is of necessity an oppressor, exploiting the people and the laboring masses in the interest of the privileged class." Finally, and the essential point with respect to the aims of the League, "it [the state] needs armies to repress the masses, and the existence of this armed force drives it into war." Peace would only come, therefore, when the people abandoned their narrow, nationalistic, patriotic sentiments, began to think in terms of "universal justice," the "absolute kingdom of freedom," and destroyed the existing states so that "from the ruins of these entities, organized from above by despotism and conquest, there can arise free systems, organized from below upwards, a free federation of communes into provinces, provinces into nations, and nations into a United States of Europe."[2]

Having introduced his views at the first Congress, then restated them at a banquet afterwards, he further developed them during the following months into one of his principal theoretical works, *Federalism, Socialism and Anti-Theologism,* which he proposed that the League's program committee, of which he was a member, adopt as a statement of the League's basic aims. The work is the 20-year belated drop of the other "left" Hegelian shoe, the vigorous assault against religion that had long been missing in Bakunin's "left" Hegelianism. It is to this attack that he devoted most of the pamphlet, with his denunciation of the state taking second place and his statements on socialism only a distant third. As was everything he wrote from first to last, it was essentially an impassioned defense of absolute "freedom" against even the slightest limitation, since "this little part that you cut off is the very essence of my freedom, it is everything."[3] Although heavily repetitive, the arguments are often perceptive and forceful, and would still provide fine grist for those choosing to work this mill. For the League members hearing them for the first time, these arguments to the Congress seem to have been powerfully effective, so much so that, as we can see from a statement of aims published by the committee in June 1868, part of Bakunin's program did in fact win the committee's approval.[4]

Supported by the program committee and hoping for similar success with the full League Congress when it would meet again in September 1868, Bakunin expanded his political horizons. He had come to Switzerland with a program to realize and the beginnings of an organization to achieve it, the secret brotherhood that he had formed in Italy and that, in the persons of several of its members, he had brought with him to Switzerland and into the League. But the bourgeois, pacifist League was hardly the instrument through which he and his "brothers" could do their apocalyptic work. A series of strikes in Geneva in March 1868 and the organization the strikers turned to for support pointed to a much more promising agency—the International. Although there had been little contact between Marx and Bakunin since their meeting in late 1864, Marx had sent him a copy of volume one of *Capital,* with a personal dedication, shortly after the League's first Congress.

In July Bakunin joined the International, urged close affiliation between the League and the International, and persuaded the League's president to invite members of the International who were planning to attend the International's third Congress in Brussels to attend as well the second League Congress, since both would be meeting in September (1868). Bakunin was quite candid about his intentions. He was not planning to "drown our League" in the International, but to have them work together as complementary organizations, with the International "concerning itself if not exclusively, then at least principally, with economic questions," while the League would handle "political, religious and philosophical questions," as well as "prepare the issues and, thereby, clarify the political direction." As a result, and this surely was the intent of it all, "we would have the power, the entire revolution in our hands."[5]

The plan could not be simpler or more explicit. He and his "brothers," especially those who were in the League with him, would control the League (had he not already won over the program committee?) and the League would, in turn, become the policy director for the International. Here was as grand a network of "Archimedes points" as he could want, and one that left all the threads in his hands, secretly of course, much as he had planned in 1848-49.

Once more, however, reality refused to play the game. Quite aware of what was going on and of the dangers for itself, the General Council of the International, i.e., Marx and his aides, had the "impertinence," as Bakunin put it, to spurn the league's offer of collaboration. Then, another blow: the League, apparently less enthusiastic about *Federalism, Socialism and Anti-Theologism* than its program committee, refused to adopt Bakunin's views as its own. Defeated, he and his supporters, 18 members, abruptly and noisily quit the Congress and the League.[6]

Failing to win the League over to his point of view, Bakunin reacted as he had when he had failed to win over the equally alien Prague Congress: he went underground. On September 25, 1868, the same day that he left the League, he and his "intimates" gathered to form a new "international," or rather to further organize and adapt their earlier Florence-Naples "brotherhood" and "family." Its essential ideas, as well as its principal founders (Fanelli, Gambuzzi, Tucci, for instance) were much the same as they had been during the Italian period. Compromising between Bakunin's wish for an entirely secret organization and the other members' preference for a public association, the founders decided to have both forms.[7] As finally worked out, the "Alliance," as the organization as a whole came to be called, reflected several levels of secrecy and intimacy, that is, degrees of "family" ties with Bakunin. It is important that we appreciate the place of this Alliance in Bakunin's later years, since it was the main issue around which his controversy with Marx revolved and a central focus for our evaluation of Bakunin's use of power.

The principal aim of the organization was still "the destruction of all existing states, together with all their political, juridical, bureaucratic and financial institutions," the end of the "the existing order of things based on property, exploitation, domination and the principle of authority," including, with reference now to the "impertinent" Marxists, the authority of Jacobin statist revolutionaries. Yet, one could not imagine a more rigidly centralized, authoritarian revolutionary organization than the one Bakunin proposed as the weapon for carrying out this destruction of all authoritarianism: the voluntary, freely-federated society formed from the "bottom upwards" was reserved for the new world, after the old world had been destroyed by a rigorously disciplined, martial organization formed strictly from the top downwards. The organization had two overlapping forms, one secret, involving only the "intimates," and one public, the Alliance of Social Democracy. Even in its open, public mode, the Alliance was to be a highly centralized organization, with all decisions on the national level approved by the central committee. Since it was the real controlling body, the secret organization was even more tightly centralized than the public organization, with, first, a Central Committee, then a "central Geneva section" acting as "the permanent delegation of the permanent Central Committee," and, finally, within the central Geneva section, a "central Bureau," which was to be both the "executive power...composed of three or five or even seven members" of the secret organization and the "executive directory" of the public organization. As for the initial formation of this key Bureau, it was "provisionally elected by all the founding members of the Alliance, most of whom, former members of the Congress of Berne [the League], have returned to their countries after having delegated their powers to citizen B."[8]

Over 30 years had passed since Bakunin had formed and dominated his "holy commune," his first vehicle for universal liberation, yet he is still acting the part of a pseudo-father over his "brothers," "intimates," trying hard all the while, however, to conceal this demonstration of power carefully from struggle against all power. As with power, so also with violence; here as well he must continue to have it both ways. He insisted, on the one hand, that the Alliance members be filled with "revolutionary passion and have the devil in their flesh," since the imminent revolution would mean "death to the rulers, exploiters and guardians of all kinds," a destruction so vast as to leave "no stone on stone." Far from being fearful of "releasing what people today call evil passions," he depended on those passions as the force which the revolutionaries must "electrify." On the other hand, again as in the Italian version of these plans, he continued to play down violence against people. The revolutionaries must be "merciless with respect to positions and things," but not to human beings. Not the people themselves, he argued, but their functions and possessions were responsible for mass oppression and deprivation, and even if members of the dominant class must be judged guilty, their guilt was as much the responsibility of the society that had formed them as was the guilt of any other criminal, and it would be both immoral and harmful to the cause to take vengeance on them. In fact, those like the Jacobins and Blanquists who struck out more against people than against possessions and functions were in his view simply showing that they were interested in taking over those same state functions and class possessions.

The "evil passions," the "devil in the flesh," the call for "death to the rulers" and for a cataclysm leaving "no stone on stone" must somehow carefully spare people in the apocalyptic assault on the old world. One can only assume that the miracle would be achieved, the axe would be kept bloodless, by the same magic that would keep the revolutionaries from becoming dictators even though the purpose of their "invisible network" was to "prepare, organize and accelerate the revolution." Besides being vital sparks to "electrify" the masses into revolution, the revolutionaries would have to remain in action during the "transitional" period that, Bakunin candidly acknowledged, would necessarily follow the revolution in order to protect it against reaction, to spread the revolution to other countries (since revolution could succeed only if universal), and simply to keep things together, given the predictable social breakdown: "It is necessary that, given the popular anarchy that will constitute the very life and the entire energy of the revolution, there be some organ to achieve unity in revolutionary thought and action. That organ must be the secret and universal association of international brothers." As to the number of "brothers" he would need for the universal revolution that would leave no stone on stone, 100 well-organized revolutionaries could take charge of the overall revolution, with an additional 200 or 300 working in each of the major countries.[9]

Bakunin set to work on several fronts simultaneously. First, he coopted other members into the central Bureau, since only one of the founding members remained in Geneva with him. With his *état-major revolutionnaire,* as he called the Bureau, now in hand, he began recruiting the troops. On October twenty-eighth (1868) a meeting was held formally establishing the public Alliance and enrolling about 85 members into it. At weekly, Saturday, public meetings thereafter, attended by 20-25 members on the average, Bakunin propagated his views on the state, read from his works, reported on his trips, commented on current affairs in the Swiss and international labor movement, and, above all, urged his audience to abstain from all political participation in the existing system and to concern themselves instead with bringing it to a revolutionary end.[10]

Work on and in the Alliance was only part of Bakunin's task in the months following its formation. The Alliance, in fact, was meant at that time to be more than an end in itself. It was also to be a means for gaining control of Marx's International, which Bakunin had earlier tried and failed to control through the League. The League having failed, Bakunin and his "intimates" reverted back to their own Florence-Naples "brotherhood" as the means of winning power over the increasingly prestigious and genuinely influential and powerful International. Referring later to this shift from the League to the International, Bakunin wrote: "The tool was tried, proved to be a bad one, and had to be rejected. The only thing to do then was to find another. The International Association of Workers naturally presented itself as that better tool."[11] Having joined the International in July, 1868, while still in the League, he then coopted important Swiss members of the International into the Bureau of his Alliance, among them Johann Philipp Becker, a veteran of the workers' movement and Marx's friend; Charles Perron, co-editor of the Geneva organ of the International, *L'Internationale;* and François Brosset, president of the Geneva branch of the International.[12]

The effect of his revolutionary fame, of his charisma, and of his eloquence on leaders of the local Swiss labor movement seems to have been overwhelming, at least at first. "One of our friends recalls very well with what pride Henri Perret [general secretary of the International's Geneva branch] showed me his name at the bottom of this famous Address, adding, confidentially, that he was not the one with the talent to write such fine things, and that the Address came from the pen of Bakunin, whom Henri Perret enthusiastically admired at the time."[13] The "Address" referred to here was a fiery declaration Bakunin had sent on October twenty-first to the "brothers in Spain," summoning them to the banner of the International. However, while he wrote in the name of the International, he and other Alliance "intimates" who were simultaneously in the International worked primarily to promote the aims and interests of their Alliance. It was more as representatives of the Alliance than of the International, for example, that the veteran "intimates," Fanelli, Aristide Rey, and Elie Reclus were in Spain that winter organizing sections of the International in Madrid and Barcelona. Similarly, it was as President of the Bureau of the Alliance and in the name of the central Bureau that Bakunin himself corresponded that December, 1868, with Albert Richard, an "intimate" from Lyon who had joined Bakunin during the earlier League disputes.[14]

From this foundation—a secret Bureau directing his international Alliance and exerting simultaneously a strong influence in the Geneva branch of the International through overlapping directorates—Bakunin made his boldest move yet. Acting through Marx's friend Becker, he officially applied that November (1868) for admission of the Alliance as a whole into the International, on terms that would allow the Alliance to retain its organizational integrity, hold its own Congresses, and so on. The International would gain considerably by the merger, Becker said in a letter accompanying the application, since the Alliance could make up for the International's lack of "idealism."[15] The two organizations would complement each other, Bakunin later wrote, since the International could continue its fine work with the masses, representing necessarily only the "germs" of the full program, while the Alliance, at a higher level of development, would preserve the ideals of the program and thereby be in a position to give the International a "really revolutionary direction." As he later was to describe the relationship between his Alliance and the International, the Alliance was to be "a secret society formed within the International in order to provide the International a revolutionary organization, in order to transform it, together with the popular masses that were outside of it, into a force sufficiently well-organized to annihilate reaction."[16]

After a month had gone by with no response to the proposed merger, Bakunin wrote Marx one of his by now characteristically ingratiating letters, praising Marx for his insight in following the road of "economic revolution" and assuring him that "my fatherland is now the International" and that "as you can see, dear friend, I am your disciple and am proud of it."[17] It would be wrong to dismiss this as entirely a cynical maneuver, a ruse to help spare the Alliance the same rejection that the International had earlier dealt the League. That may have been part of it, but if so, it was the lesser part. For a proper understanding of Bakunin's ambivalent judgment of Marx, one must set it alongside Bakunin's similarly ambivalent relationship to most of the other powerful authorities in his life, such as his father and Tsar Nicholas I. Bakunin is as sincere in his high praise of all three of them as he is in his strenuous efforts to obliterate the foundations of their power. A related aspect of this relationship between Bakunin and Marx's International, which will emerge more clearly as the story unfolds, is evident even now in a striking image Bakunin used in a letter he wrote to his "intimate" Richard on December 22, 1868, the same day that he wrote the above letter to Marx. The International, he told Richard, is a "mother to us, while we are only a branch, a child."[18]

While it is unlikely that Bakunin's deference to Marx would have in any case improved the chances of his Alliance-International proposal being accepted, the letter reached Marx too late. The very day that Bakunin wrote these letters to Marx and Richard, the International's General Council arrived at its decision to refuse to let the Alliance into the International unless the Alliance ceased being a parallel International. Bakunin's Geneva Alliance group could join and even keep the name Alliance, but only as one of a number of Geneva sections of the International already in existence, not as the center of an independent international organization.

Why had Bakunin wished to join the International yet remain apart?, the Council of the Belgian branch asked in a letter to the Geneva Alliance sent in mid-January. If the International did not reflect his views, then Bakunin should leave, they said. If it did, then he should be totally committed to it. As it was, his actions, however high-minded the motivations for them might be, were divisive and in other ways seriously harmful to the cause of the working class. Moreover, the Belgian Council asked, what right did he and his Alliance have to assume the role of "moral guides" for the rest of the International? "Do you not understand that the workers established the International precisely because they wanted no kind of patronage, whether from Social-Democrats or from anyone else; that they want to go forward on their own without advisers; and that if they accept into the Association [the International] socialists who, because of their birth and privileged situation in the present society, do not belong to the disinherited class, it is only on condition that these friends of the people do not form a group apart, a kind of intellectual protectorate or an aristocracy of intellect, in a word, *leaders,* but instead remain part of the ranks of the vast proletariat masses?"[19]

It is difficult to judge how much of a blow this rejection was for Bakunin, since, as we will see, it had little effect on either the structure or the activities of his Alliance. In fact, it helped him mold the Alliance into the completely secret organization he had wanted it to be in the first place. Moreover, his views and his supporters were enjoying enough success in Switzerland at the time to compensate for this setback, which, in any case, could be considered temporary. The first weekend in January 1869 some 30 sections of the International in Switzerland (from Geneva and from the Jura mountain towns) met to form a federation, *la Fédération romande*. Among those elected to the Central Committee were three from Bakunin's secret Bureau (Brosset, Duval, and Guetat) and two other Alliance members (H. Perret and Guilmeaux), while the editorial board of the Federation's new journal, *Égalité*, included Bakunin himself and four other Alliance members (H. Perret, C. Perron, Guilmeaux, and J-P. Becker).[20]

One reason for the success of the Alliance in Switzerland, that is for Bakunin's success in winning a strong following there, was the gradual radicalization of the Swiss labor movement that had occurred in the 1860s. Throughout its first years, the Swiss labor movement was gradualist and distinctly nonviolent, as one can see from the statements of early leaders like Pierre Coullery.[21] This moderation, however, mainly reflected the attitudes of only one section of the working class, the relatively well-paid workers in the Geneva watch and jewelry factories. Conditions were much bleaker for two other segments of the working class—the urban construction workers, mainly migratory workers from other countries, and the still independent Jura craftsmen, scattered about the Jura mountain towns like Le Locle, Chaux-de-Fonds, and Saint-Imier and facing stiff competition from the more productive factories in Switzerland and abroad.[22]

One expression of the radicalization was a spreading disenchantment with the power of the vote, the power of "bourgeois" elections, as a means of improving working-class conditions. For leaders like Coullery, electoral "politics" were not only the best means for labor progress, but the means favored by the International's London leadership. Aware of the power of "political privileges for the defense and perpetuation of economic monopolies," Marx in his *Inaugural Address* had urged "the political organization of the working men's party" in order to gain "political power," and ever since then Marx had made participation in political elections, wherever they were available to the workers, an essential means, along with the trade union struggle, for the liberation of the working class. Unfortunately for Coullery and for other labor leaders who thought as he did—but most propitious for Bakunin—the vote did not yet seem influential enough to achieve significant economic gains. Whether Swiss labor continued its traditional alliance with the progressive "radical" wing of the bourgeoisie or, as it more recently had done, decided to run its own independent labor candidates, the workers fared badly at the polls and were therefore deciding in increasing numbers "from now on to abstain from any participation in political elections" and to turn instead "to the revolutionary path."[23]

As for the construction workers, since they were, as mentioned above, mainly transient migrants and, therefore, not voting residents, they could not in any case rest their hopes for improvement on the vote. Poorly paid as they were, in comparison with their fellow workers in the watch and jewelry workshops, and dependent only on strikes as the means of pressing their claims, these construction workers provided a particularly receptive audience for Bakunin's revolutionary strategy, his propaganda of absolute "abstention" from any and all "bourgeois" politics and concentration exclusively on the coming social upheaval that would end all such central politics.

Besides offering this rich soil for his efforts, the Swiss labor movement provided Bakunin with several devoted and tireless lieutenants who must be credited with much of his success in Switzerland at the time. Of these, by far the most important was his devoted disciple, ally, and later chronicler, James Guillaume. A young man of 25 at the time, son of a state councilor who was in charge of public education in Neuchâtel, and himself a hard-working ascetic, Guillaume had first been impressed by Bakunin when he heard him speak before the League in September 1867. When Guillaume came to Geneva for the *Fédération romande* meeting, he accepted Bakunin's offer to stay with him at Bakunin's apartment. The match was perfect for both of them: Bakunin found another admiring "intimate," while Guillaume acquired an international luminary to support his own militant "abstentionist" position in Jura politics. Guillaume immediately turned the new friendship to his advantage by inviting Bakunin to visit him in Le Locle. Bakunin promised that he would come, but not until February, since he was preoccupied with other concerns at the time.[24]

The difficulties that forced him to postpone the trip were serious indeed, and his response to them presaged another important shift in his mood and actions soon to come. Something of a rebellion against his leadership had taken place involving a number of his closest followers. Although the malcontents included some recent Geneva recruits, the core comprised the Russian-Italian colony settled in and around Vevey, members of the old Florence-Naples "brotherhood" who still hovered about Princess Obolensky and were financed by her and by another of Bakunin's benefactresses, one Olga Levashov. During his year's work on the League (1867-68) Bakunin, too, had lived in the area, at Clarens, continuing, as in Italy, to enjoy the generosity of the Princess. In a letter he sent to the rebels on January 26, 1869, he told them that he knew they were planning to meet apart from him, no doubt to exclude him, he said, from some new organization they were probably forming. He was at a loss to understand, he went on, why they were doing this, but he linked their action to some "vast conspiracy" against him that he felt had begun soon after the League's Congress in September 1868. What Bakunin may have had in mind here was the success of a recent rival of his, Nicholas Utin, whom he had excluded from his Alliance, but who had been able to win control of a Russian periodical (the *People's Cause)* that was financed by the Vevey colony and, thus, in effect, to supplant Bakunin. Touching indirectly on what may have been a key motive for the split, his own tendency to dominate whatever organization or group he was involved in, he went on to comment on what the opposition alleged to be his "dictatorial rule." "It is my most profound conviction that the one who is dictator in fact, although not, of course, by law, is always the one who acts—and only as long as he acts—in the spirit and interests of society." And while the other members, he charged, had been "sleeping and theorizing in their dreams," he himself "had been working like a black over the past four years and almost always utterly alone, not because I wanted to keep you from participating, but because you were more or less lost in apathetic theorizing."

Whatever the reason for the split, Bakunin was sorely hurt by this rejection of him by some of his oldest friends. This is apparent throughout the letter, but especially in his threatened response to this rejection: he would participate actively in their next Congress, he said, but until then "I have decided to leave the Central Directory of the International Brotherhood as well as retire from the central Bureau and public activities of the Alliance and, until the next Congress, not take part, either directly or indirectly, in the activities of its various societies." Not only did he need "some rest" after having worked all alone for so long, but he must now "seriously work in order to have some means of subsistence and be in a position to feed my wife." Because his family in Russia had either been unwilling or unable "to send my share of the inheritance, I have lived over the past three or four years by borrowing large sums from the kind and noble Princess," but "now I no longer have the possibility of turning to the same source of help."[25]

For anyone else, this plan to retire just four months after the beginning of the campaign (the founding of the Alliance) and at a time when everything was going so well would seem strange indeed. In Bakunin's case, it was further evidence of his characteristic response to genuine authority and responsibility, the kind he was rapidly acquiring as a result of his success in the Swiss labor movement. In late January 1869 it was still only a threat, however. He settled matters with the Vevey rebels by dissolving the "Brotherhood" for what he called its bourgeois and republican tendencies, continued to preside over the Geneva Alliance section, and went to Le Locle, as he had promised Guillaume. While in Le Locle, he delivered a series of lectures on philosophy, nationalism, and the history of the bourgeoisie, and enjoyed a most enthusiastic welcome from the local socialists ("in the shops, the union halls, and private homes people were talking only of him"). Everything about him overwhelmed the Le Locle socialists—his immense size, his harrowing stories of prison and escape, his reputed audacity and courage, his incessant smoking (what would you do if because of the revolution you had nothing to smoke, he was asked: "I would smoke the revolution!"), his violent eloquence ("I drink to the destruction of the public order and to the unleashing of evil passions"). The admiration was mutual: "I must tell you that you have conquered me completely," he wrote young Guillaume. As a result of the great impression he had made in Le Locle, new sections of the Alliance were formed in Le Locle, Chaux-de-Fonds, and Saint-Imier, and Guillaume's journal *Progrès* became the Alliance's official journal.[26]

Never before had Bakunin been in such a strong position. His supporters controlled two radical journals, *Égalité* and *Progrès*. He held sway over the Alliance section in Geneva. He enjoyed the significant backing of the Jura craftsmen and the Geneva construction workers and directed, when he chose to do so, a network of "intimates" in Switzerland, Italy, Spain, and France who comprised his secret international Alliance. Moreover, since these scattered "intimates," together with the members of his Geneva section, all belonged as well to the International, he was also, in effect, gradually building a base for himself and his policies inside the International, thereby moving closer to what certainly *seemed* to be his goal, to what he often enough said was his goal: the control (secret, of course) of the International ("the mother to us") in order to give it a "real revolutionary direction."

The "mother," however, was firmly under the control of the authority who had already come to be regarded as the father of the International, Karl Marx, and Marx had rejected Bakunin's proposal to unite the two bodies, the "mother" International and his Alliance. Bakunin's Bureau was split over a response to the rejection. Several wanted to break from the International completely. Bakunin, on the contrary, saw no reason for giving up this splendid "Archimedes point," and his view prevailed. At a meeting in late February 1869, the Bureau decided to accept the conditions laid down by London, to "dissolve" the Alliance as an international network and to turn its local sections into sections of the International.

The Alliance would, thus, enter the International "without any organization, bureaus, committees and congresses other than those of the International Workers' Association,"[28] or so the Bureau said in a public announcement of the dissolution. In fact, no such dissolution occurred at all. Clandestine correspondence in code, such as it was, continued to flow from Bakunin's pen to his "intimates" in other countries, discussing, among other things, tactics for strengthening the Alliance's influence within the International; and the secret Geneva Bureau continued to exist alongside what now became the Geneva Alliance section of the International. (Confusion was inevitable. For example, we read from the minutes of an Alliance meeting on March 5, 1869: "The minutes of the last meeting were read and approved with the condition that mention of the founding of the Alliance in Spain must be made more precise in the next meeting, since it is unclear whether the aforementioned Fanelli was speaking about the Alliance or about the International Workers' Association.")[29] March brought another strong boost for Bakunin's cause. A wave of strikes involving the construction workers and printers swept Geneva and led to several violent confrontations. The International sections and the radical journals, like *Égalité* and *Progrès,* were concerned with little else that month.[30] Given his strategic position in the movement at the time, it was a golden opportunity for Bakunin to consolidate his gains and push further ahead toward genuine power.

Then, that same month, just when the opportunity for real authority was rapidly taking shape for him in the Swiss and, through it, the West European labor and socialist movements, Bakunin suddenly immersed himself in an entirely new enterprise, one that turned most of his attentions eastward again. The inspiration behind this dramatic and, from the perspective of conventional politics, badly ill-timed reorientation, was a 22 year old revolutionary desperado named Nechaev, who arrived that March from Russia aflame with fabricated stories of his own revolutionary deeds, arrest, and escape and no less spurious evidence of an imminent Russian revolution. If the 55 year old Bakunin had been "conquered completely" by the 25 year old Guillaume in January, he was virtually hypnotized into prococious senility in March by this "Boy," as Bakunin affectionately called Nechaev throughout their engagement. In mid-April he tried to explain the infatuation to Guillaume:

Right now I am preoccupied with what is happening in Russia. Our youth, perhaps the most revolutionary in the world, with respect both to theory and practice, is aroused to the point that the government has been forced to close the universities, academies and several schools in St. Petersburg, Moscow and Kazan. I have here now a specimen of these young fanatics who know neither fear nor doubt, who take it as a matter of principle that many, many of them will have to perish at the hand of the government, but who will not rest for an instant until the people have arisen. They are admirable, these young fanatics—these believers without a God and heroes without speeches!... Here in

[Switzerland] we must proceed differently. There are no such conscious youth here: they are completely reactionary. And the workers are still firmly bourgeois. They will become savage, I have no doubt, but it is necessary that something happen to transform them.[31]

Although the motivations drawing Bakunin into his bizarre relationship with Nechaev are complex and will be more fully discussed as this chapter proceeds, one important reason for the appeal is apparent in this early description of Nechaev and in the accompanying comparison between the Russian "fanatics" and the "bourgeois" Swiss youth and working class. Bakunin may indeed have been strikingly successful in his work during the half year or so after leaving the League, in September 1868. But where was the "electricity" and "paroxysm" in presiding over Geneva Alliance meetings or in lecturing to small Swiss audiences? They were no more to be found in such gatherings than they had been present among Berlin academics in 1841–42 or Florentine Freemasons in 1864. Bakunin could drink a toast to unleashing "evil passions" and look forward to the Swiss youth and workers someday becoming "savage," but as for the people and the events that filled his daily life, they were tediously placid and banal, and that went for the self-styled Swiss socialists as well as for the bourgeoisie. If he had looked for his "bride—the revolution" in Switzerland, he had looked in vain. No wonder this young "fanatic" swept him off his feet!

One should also recall again Bakunin's age, older than his years after the prison ordeal and his subsequent illnesses. As his letters to Ogarev at the time reveal, he was very sensitive about growing old, watching age mock the pose of power that had meant so much to him. Two years before, in a heated dispute with Herzen over Herzen's attacks on just such young extremists as Nechaev, he had urged Herzen to think young and avoid the conservatism of the old, and twice in a long letter he sent to Nechaev he referred to his own age as a reason for his not being able to keep up with the "Boy's" revolutionary zeal. In effect, Nechaev was a new version of the "red general" and his martial comrades, another genuine warrior blessed with all the virile virtues that had drawn Bakunin to the Siberian strongmen, Garibaldi, and Andrei Potebnia.[32] Even after Bakunin had learned the truth about the "Boy," how Nechaev had used, deceived, blackmailed, disdained, and generally humiliated him, Bakunin continued to cherish him as "a man of rare energy," "one of the most active and energetic men I have ever encountered," "a force because he has immense energy," so much superior in his rough ways to the intellectuals in their "white gloves" who "dabble in a dilettante fashion." Implying that, age notwithstanding, he had no more need for those "white gloves" than Nechaev had, he told Nechaev that "He who wishes to retain his ideal and virginal purity should remain in the study, dream, think, write discourses or poetry. He who wants to be a real revolutionary in Russia must take off his gloves; no gloves will save him from the deep and all-embracing Russian mud.... Whoever is frightened of horrors or dirt should turn away from this world and this revolution." Consequently, he shared completely Nechaev's dedication to violent mass revolution since "the people's depravity is natural, forceful and vital.... That is why I am on the side of popular brigandage and see in it one of the most essential tools for the future people's revolution in Russia."[33]

The phrasing and the choice of words make the message as clear as it is pathetic. As is so often the case in Bakunin's declarations, the reds and blacks highlight rather than conceal the pastels as they are supposed to do. To pretend to lose "virginal purity" Bakunin must pretend to "take off" his "white gloves" and sink into the "horrors," "dirt," and "depravity" of the "all-embracing Russian mud." While able, thanks to Nechaev, to enjoy once again the passions of apocalyptic fantasy—albeit vicariously—that had been denied him in Switzerland, the fantasy itself is still, as it always was and would continue to be, too obviously a surrogate for "animal" passions to be anything but dirty, horrible, and depraved, even at the safe distance that fantasy and abstract theory assured. While he praised the brigand as "one of the essential tools," he also admitted that "I recognize the necessity, but, at the same time, am fully conscious of my incapacity for this task.... For myself, I cannot tolerate either brigandage or thieving, or any other anti-human violence."[34] (Fantasy aside, his own "white gloves" must never come off.)

Irresistibly drawn, Bakunin surrendered totally to Nechaev's personality, and during the four months they lived together, he came to love this "Boy" of "virginally pure integrity." He continued to love him, moreover, even after Nechaev had rejected him and treated him like "an invalid," to be used when needed, then discarded, to use Bakunin's description of the relationship. "How deeply, how passionately, how tenderly I loved you and believed in you!" "I loved you deeply and still love you, Nechaev." While "feeling instinctively the presence of *deceit*" in Nechaev's account of what he had already done as a revolutionary and what he planned to do, Bakunin had "consciously and systematically refused to believe it." Reexperiencing what he had gone through much earlier in his relations with the Land and Freedom Party, he had doubted, he said, the very existence of the organization in Russia that Nechaev claimed to represent, but, he continued proudly, "you will do me the justice of admitting that I never asked you indiscreet questions.... I believed and believe in you." "I unconditionally submitted to the authority of the Committee [Nechaev's] as the sole representative and director of the Revolution in Russia," he told his readers in one of the revolutionary tracts he wrote during this Nechaev phase, even though he later asked Nechaev straight out, "Did your organization really exist, or were you only going to create it somehow or other?" Bakunin had not asked any questions and had gone along on faith, because it really made little difference to him and to his needs whether such an organization existed or not. What mattered was the opportunity once more to act as though a Russian revolution were imminent and to pretend to play a part—if only through Nechaev—in it, such as he did when he gave Nechaev a membership card declaring Nechaev "delegated with plenipotentiary powers by the Russian section of the general Revolutionary Alliance—Number 2771," all of which, of course, was pure fantasy.[35]

Of the half-dozen publications written for their Russian readers during the first period of the Bakunin-Nechaev association, March through July 1869, only two are firmly attributed to Bakunin. The first is, fittingly, an appeal to *The Young Brothers in Russia,* published in May 1869, in which Bakunin urged Russian students to leave their universities, "go to the people," and become "the midwife of their [the people's] spontaneous emancipation." Electrified by the "Boy" and his exciting revolutionary stories, the Bakunin of the *Appeal to the Slavs* now returned to celebrate "this pitiless commitment to destruction and this coldly impassioned resolve before which the souls of our enemies tremble and the blood runs cold in their veins." "The end of this infamous Empire of all the Russias is near." "One can sense the approach of a new bloody confrontation, of a final battle to the death between the Russian people and the state." Stenka Razin, the leader of the great peasant rising of the late seventeenth century, had shown the way, he repeated again and again, and the youth of Russia must follow his example, turn away from the university studies through which the state tried to "castrate" them, and take the lead of the new peasant upheavals.[36]

The second of Bakunin's Russian publications that spring and summer (1869) was a brochure he called *Science and the Vital Question of Revolution.* Written, apparently, in July, it is largely a summary of his by-now familiar views—his defense of true revolutionary socialism against the reformers and state socialists (i.e., Marx), his distinction between those acquiring socialism from books and those learning it from life, his attacks on the division between the uneducated masses and the educated exploiters and a demand that the masses be fully educated so that they could end the exploitative class society, and his two fundamental postulates that the unjust society would end only with the end of government itself, the state, and that the masses, after centuries of submissiveness, were now ready to rise.[37]

Of the works born of their collaboration that year (1869) one centrally important publication, the *Catechism of the Revolutionary,* has been considered by some to be Bakunin's, by others, Nechaev's. Recent scholarship has tended to favor Nechaev's authorship.[38] From the approach followed in this study, many statements throughout the *Catechism* do seem quite inconsistent with Bakunin's character. For example, among the tasks assigned to the local revolutionary organization is the use of "prostitutes" as sources of information; the revolutionary is required "to destroy with his own hands everything that stands in the way" of the revolution; such emotions as "friendship, love, gratitude and even honour must be stifled in him"; "He is not a revolutionary if he fells pity for anything in this world"; the worst of the revolutionaries' enemies must be "condemned immediately to death," while the less dangerous enemies "must be exploited in every possible way.... We must make them our slaves"; the organization "will employ all its power and all its resources in order to promote an intensification and an increase in those calamities and evils which must finally exhaust the people and drive it to a popular rising."[39]

The gap between such lines and even Bakunin's most extreme statements is very real and very wide. What one does not find in Nechaev, at least in his revolutionary tracts, is precisely the "other side," the passive and pacific side, that almost always comes through Bakunin's works as a counterpoint to the violence. However, the essential parts of the *Catechism* are entirely consistent with Bakunin's views. The centralized organizational structure of the ultra-secret movement, the necessity of total dedication on the part of the revolutionary, his "cold and single-minded passion for the revolutionary cause," the walls of secrecy raised even within the movement separating its various levels, the goal of a revolution "that eradicates the entire state system and exterminates all state traditions of the regime and classes in Russia"[40]—all this is pure Bakuninism. Looking back on their collaboration after their split, Bakunin wrote Nechaev that "your programme, at least during the last year [1869–the *Catechism* year], not only resembled, but was identical with my programme.... Our programmes were truly identical. I was convinced of this not only by our daily conversations, but by the fact that all my writings, conceived and printed while you were here, evoked in you a sympathetic response precisely on the points which most clearly expressed our common programme, and because your writings, printed last year, bore the same character."[41] In the second phase of the collaboration, during the winter and spring of 1870 (to be discussed later), this similarity of views became even more apparent as Bakunin vainly tried to keep up with his "young savage!" So close did their views come, in fact, that had the *Catechism* been written in 1870 rather than 1869, the argument for Bakunin's authorship would be stronger.[42]

As though recharged by Nechaev's energy, Bakunin returned later that spring (1869) to his western fronts (including the "firmly bourgeois" Swiss movement) with renewed vigor. He continued directing the Geneva branch of the Alliance, published articles in Guillaume's *Progrès* and in *Égalité,* the journal of the *Fédération romande,* and intensified his secret contacts with his international "intimates" (the Alliance International that was supposedly suspended) in preparation for the Basle Congress of the International, to be held that September (1869). His management of the Geneva Alliance meetings gives us a good example of the kind of "dictatorship" he had justified in his attack on the Vevey "Brotherhood" and that the "Brotherhood" members apparently had found as intolerable as had Belinsky and, at least at times, the Beyer sisters. The role he played at these meetings, as reflected in their minutes, verges on the comic, so much were they his own one-man show. He presided, proposed the questions to be discussed (e.g., the expulsion of members who miss three meetings, the right of the Committee to coopt new members to fill vacancies), and carried the votes, either unanimously or with only token opposition.[43]

Besides dominating these branch meetings, Bakunin was able during these months to determine the policy of a radical journal, as he had wanted to do with Herzen's *Bell.* The opportunity came in June (1869) when the regular editor of *Égalité,* Perron, gave up his position for a time due to personal reasons, and Bakunin replaced him. Bakunin used the occasion to publish a series of articles through which he apparently hoped to attract the "firmly bourgeois" Swiss radicals to his cause. With this particular audience, however, Bakunin had to tone down his declarations and demands; these were moderates in Switzerland, not "young fanatics" in Russia. Still, taken together, the articles proclaim his familiar message. The target remains the "impotent" bourgeoisie, and Bakunin now sees "only one role left to it to play, namely, to die as quickly and gracefully as possible,"[44] to commit "voluntary suicide."[45] Since the time of Bakunin's attack against the bourgeois "compromisers" of 1842, however, the despised bourgeoisie had gained an "illigitimate child," an "heir" for Bakunin's lance: the "bourgeois socialists," those, he said, who tried to defuse the hatred of the exploited masses by settling for trivial concessions that in no way weakened established power and privilege.[46] Among the main culprits were local Swiss labor leaders like Coullery[47] who deceived the pepole into believing that their lot could be improved through participation in bourgeois elections, who placed their hopes in more education within the bourgeois framework, and who favored reformist activities such as the cooperative movement, which actually benefited only a few by coopting some workers into the bourgeois style and status and, thus, represented a form of treason to the working class as a whole.[48]

In radical contrast to this bourgeois socialism, the new compromisers, stood "revolutionary socialism": here was the "legitimate child of [bourgeois] radicalism," but a child that "disdains the temerity of its father, accuses him of inconsistency and cowardice."[49] To demonstrate this disdain and to prove his own courage and constancy, the true revolutionary must vow, among other things, "to subordinate personal interests, even those of family, as well as beliefs and political and religious activities to the supreme interest of our association" and "to remain faithful always to labor solidarity, for the slightest treason to this solidarity is considered by the International as the greatest crime and the greatest infamy that a worker can commit."[50] Fulfillment of these vows would lead to the self-liberation of the working class and with it "the overthrow of everything that now exists."[51] Towards this end the workers must avoid participation in bourgeois political institutions in their separate countries, join in the International to overthrow bourgeois societies everywhere, and create on their ruins the *"universal economic republic."* Reflecting the Nechaev influence and the revolutionary prospects in the East that Nechaev had revived for him, Bakunin now included Russia, too, in this workers' alliance.[52] There, in Russia, the forces for revolution were already gathered in the "mass of young students," who filled "the prisons, police stations, the dungeons of the secret sections [the secret police], and the fortresses," in the activities of what was now "a legion," a "falange of several tens of thousands" of revolutionary youth, and in the pent-up fury of the oppressed masses. "A little while now, two years, a year, maybe even a few months, and these two movements [the masses and the revolutionary students] will unite, and then, then you will see a revolution that will surpass, without doubt, everything that we have known of revolutions until now."[53]

Of course, the other side was there, too: while surpassing all other revolutions, his would also be, somehow, the least violent. "It would not require the death of the individuals who comprised [the bourgeoisie], but its death as a political and social body.... Less blood-thirsty than were the bourgeoisie, we want to massacre ranks and objects, not people."[54] (The other side of this coin is Bakunin's hope that, as we saw, the bourgeoisie would commit "voluntary suicide," "die as quickly and gracefully as possible," and thus spare him even the thought of destroying them.) In an article he wrote for *Progrès* at the time he supported his by-now characteristic attack on the state and church with detailed ethnographic and zoological evidence to prove that they and their inherent violence represented an early, "animal" stage of human development.[55]

Not much is said in these articles about the good society that would emerge after the bloodless massacre of ranks and objects. But we are assured that state, church and class would end, that inheritance—the subject of a separate article[56]— would no longer be permitted to divide people at birth into rich and poor, and that a just education for all would preclude the division between those who worked and those who thought, since everyone would do both. Bakunin was particularly antagonistic here towards the intellectual elite—now that he was again trying to take off his "white gloves" and was no longer, to recall an earlier rendition, "paralyzed" by the "speculative disease." "In our view, of all the aristocracies that have oppressed—each in turn and at times all together—this so-called aristocracy of intellect is the most odious, the most despicable, the most impertinent, and the most oppressive."[57]

Relatively mild though these articles were, compared to what Bakunin was writing at the same time for Nechaev's fictitious Russian revolution, the Swiss moderates who subscribed to *Égalité* were vehemently critical of them and lodged successive protests against Bakunin's editorship of the journal. What they wanted at the time was another alliance with bourgeois radicals in preparation for upcoming fall (1869) elections, and this extremism could only scare off the prospective electoral partners.[58] Discord between Bakunin's Alliance and the Geneva moderates reached a critical point at the end of July when Bakunin came across a statement on strikes issued by the Committee of the *Fédération romande* that he considered intolerable. Without denying that strikes were necessary, justified, and often effective, the statement called attention as well to their dangers. "These constant wars" could not only use up all the funds and energies of the workers' movement, but they could provoke as well bitter hatred towards the workers and even lead to a "more or less brutal intervention" by the government, with the result that labor would "lose in a moment of legitimate anger the fruits of four years of struggle and hard work...." "A strike is a calamity, that is, a war, and must therefore be called only in specific and clearly defined cases," and even then only "after having exhausted all other means of achieving an amicable accord...."[59]

Nothing could be more distant from Bakunin's strategy and tactics, especially during this Nechaev period. At a general meeting of his Alliance section, Bakunin and his supporters decided to announce through *Égalité* that the Alliance "not only neither regrets nor fears provoking the bourgeoisie as a result of strikes, but, on the contrary, desires just that, in order to awaken in both the working class and in the bourgeoisie a consciousness of their mutual antagonism, with the inevitable result of eliminating the bourgeoisie."[60] "The social revolution is knocking at our doors," Bakunin had written a wavering "brother," Fritz Robert, the month before. "We must gather and tighten our fraternal ranks so that it will find in us a falange able to prepare it, speed it up as much as possible, and, when it breaks out, serve it."[61]

Unlike the Geneva moderates, Guillaume and his Jura friends were solidly behind Bakunin. Among the four resolutions voted by the Jurassiens in a Le Locle meeting at the end of May, one called for the formation of "an organization more effective and substantial than the International so that the proletariat can oppose the coalition of the state and the bourgeoisie with a power capable of victory," another declared "that the International must completely abstain from participating in bourgeois politics," and a third supported two other favorites of Bakunin, "collective property" and "the abolition of the right of inheritance," both of which had especially provoked the ire of the moderates.[62]

Gratifying as was the Jura support, however, it was hardly the "falange" needed to prepare, speed up, and "serve" the revolution that he heard at the door. For that Bakunin needed his latest and best "Archimedes point," the International. In late June, when his collaboration with Nechaev was in full progress and he had just begun the articles in *Égalité* that so disturbed its more moderate readers, the Alliance submitted its official acceptance of the General Council's terms, agreeing to dissolve the International Alliance of Social Democracy. The day before, however, we find Bakunin writing Guillaume that "Richard from Lyon has arrived here today. I am extremely satisfied. He is completely ours."[63] The "ours" refers, of course, to the "dissolved" International Alliance of Social Democracy. The next step, having feigned acceptance of the General Council's terms, was to prepare his now entirely secret international Alliance for the fourth Congress of the International, to be held in Basle on September 6-12, 1869. To organize his caucus, he wrote "all our friends" in July urging them to arrive early for a meeting on the sixth. They should come in full strength, he told Richard, because "the Germans" would bring with them "a lot of doctrinarism and bourgeois socialism."[64] He himself planned to arrive on the third, so that he could make arrangements with "some Belgian friends" before the Congress.[65]

As the Basle Congress approached, Bakunin suffered several local reverses. Probably the most unpleasant for him was a revival in the first week of August of the accusation (spread this time, he said, by Liebknecht and Bebel) that he was a Russian agent whose escape from Siberia had been aided by the Russian government and that he had formed the Alliance in order to harm the International. A "jury of honor" must be formed, he insisted, to clear his name yet again.[66] In addition to this unpleasantness, he had to face growing discontent among some members of his own Geneva Alliance section, particularly, so it seems from the record, against his insistence at the July meetings that the section's committee draw up its own list of Basle delegates for the workers' subsequent approval rather than have the list openly voted by the workers themselves (from the bottom upwards).[67] If resentment was growing against him from within the Geneva Alliance section itself, it was spreading even faster among members and leaders in other Geneva sections of the International, so much so that the Central Committee of all Geneva sections, at a meeting held August sixteenth, refused to admit his Alliance section into its Federation of the Geneva Canton, in spite of the fact that some three weeks earlier the General Council in London had accepted the Alliance's June twenty-second submission to its terms.[68]

Far from being able to impose his own list of candidates for Basle, when the elections were held August twenty-first to twenty-third Bakunin himself was not chosen as one of the three delegates to be sent by the Geneva sections. He did go, however, as a delegate from both Lyon, arranged by Richard, and Naples, arranged by Gambuzzi. (When his own Geneva Alliance section decided to send its delegate they selected, instead of Bakunin, another "intimate" of the secret Alliance international, the Spanish doctor Sentiñon who was visiting Geneva at the time and was already a delegate for Barcelona.)[69] Thus, Bakunin was to attend this, his first and only, Congress of the International, not as a representative of the legal Geneva Alliance section recognized by the International, but as a result of his secret international Alliance network that had officially been dissolved as the price of entry into the International.

Then, the climax to this series of disappointments and losses: Nechaev left western Europe in early August and returned to Russia.[70] A few weeks later, at the end of August and just a few weeks *before* the Basle Congress towards which so much of Bakunin's efforts that spring and summer seemed to have been aimed, we find Bakunin again writing (as he had the previous winter) of his plans "to retire in solitude with Antonia," to leave Geneva after the Congress and settle in some warm, quiet retreat across the mountains in Ticino. And it was not simply to recuperate from anticipated confrontations at the Congress: the plan was to withdraw for "at least a year of silent, studious, and profitable retreat."[71] More will be said later about this second strangely ill-timed plan to withdraw, a plan which Bakunin this time carried out. But between late August, when he spoke of this year-long retirement, and October, when he was able to begin it, stood the Basle Congress.

More radical than the previous Congress, three-quarters of the delegates voted for collective ownership of land as well as capital. The Congress then split into those, following Marx, who wanted state control over income and products and those, like Bakunin, the Jura representatives and other Alliance member delegates who wanted income and products to go "to the communes, to the free associations of free workers." (In the course of arguing his case, Bakunin unexpectedly advocated "construction of an international state of millions of workers on the ruins of all national states." When Guillaume asked him how he, the enemy of any kind of state, could call for an international state, he said, as Guillaume recalled, that "the phrase international state, expressing as it does a self-contradictory idea and impossible to realize, is equivalent to the negation of the state. Even while seeming to make a linguistic concession to the partisans of the state, he believed that he was thereby undermining the very foundations of their theoretical conception. His formula was equivalent to a demonstration by way of absurdity.")[72]

Although a vote was not taken on this question, it already pointed the way to the coming conflict between Bakunin's faction, which supported local, communal control, and Marx's "state socialists," as Bakunin was already calling them. At Basle, however, it was another issue that sharply divided the two camps—the question of inheritance. The elimination of the right of inheritance had been a principal focus of Bakunin's articles and lectures for years now, and it was due to his pressure and influence that it had been put on the Basle agenda. In recognition of his role in pressing the issue, he was made a member of the commission to consider it and was the "spiritual father" of the commission's proposal to make elimination of inheritance a central plank in the International's platform.[73] The delegates from the London Council supported the position Marx had argued ever since the *Manifesto:* after the workers' victory and the collectivization of property, the whole question would simply disappear, since there would be no great wealth to bequeath. In response to this argument of law reflecting economic changes, Bakunin contended that in this case a prior change of law should alter economics. Moreover, he argued, while there would be serious resistance from the peasants if one tried to take the land from them outright, the resistance would be much less if the right of inheritance were first abolished and private property allowed to die a slow death. Continuing in this unusual role of a cautious and patient gradualist, he went on to compare the Marxists' focus on the future, when all property would be collective, with the commission's proposal to "start from where we are." "They have said a lot to us about being practical. Well, now it is in the name of practicality that I ask you to vote for the abolition of the law of inheritance."[74] Although neither the commission's proposal nor that of the General Council won a clear majority, it was apparent to all at the Congress that Bakunin and his supporters had directly and successfully challenged Marx's leadership. (The commission received 32 votes, with 23 against and 13 abstentions; the General Council got 19 votes, with 37 against and 6 abstentions.)[75]

Why was it on this seemingly trivial, marginal issue that Marx and Bakunin first came into direct, public conflict within the International?[76] Without Bakunin's virtual obsession with this question it might never have been raised at all, but rather, as one delegate argued at the Congress, be set aside, like the law of contract, for the revolutionary future to handle. Why was it so important to Bakunin that he was even willing to reveal himself as a moderate if that might help? The answer, once again, is found in personality, not politics. Given his own constant dependency and its psychological sources, what better way to conceal them (and mainly from himself) than this war on inheritance? Moreover, with Marx now assuming the part of the hated and feared authority in Bakunin's perennial reenactment of the basic dramas, an attack on inheritance, the symbol and substance of filial dependency, became an ideally suitable ground for his battle with Marx. Or rather, pseudo-battle. For just as he had never ceased praising his father, while attacking everything he stood for, and just as he had gone right on demanding that Premukhino send him his share of the inheritance, even while he fought vigorously against all inheritance, so did Bakunin now not only continue to praise Marx warmly, but he also accepted precisely then (coincidentally?) a commission to translate Marx's *Capital* as a principal source of income, a commission, it should go without saying, he never carried out.[77]

The position Bakunin took in a third controversy at the Congress has also been judged highly unusual for him. Eccarius, a delegate of the London General Council, had proposed that the General Council have the right to expel any section that acted contrary to the spirit of the International. While protecting local sections of the International against their exclusion by national committees (in order to guard militant sections like his own against the kind of regional conservatism that prevailed in Geneva), Bakunin accepted the right of the London General Council to suspend existing sections. As the official report explained his action, "Bakunin wants to emphasize the international character of the Association and for that it is necessary that the General Council not be without authority."[78] From the perspective of Bakunin's real, and not mythological, views on revolutionary organization, his position on this issue is entirely appropriate: strict centralism and obedience, *top downwards,* was the very essence of a sound revolutionary party, as he time and again described it, and if one takes seriously his stated intentions, he hoped to see the International become just that kind of genuinely revolutionary body, mainly through the growing influence of his Alliance network. Even during the Basle Congress, Bakunin and his "intimates," Guillaume and Aristide Rey, searched out recruits for his secret international Alliance. They were especially anxious, as Guillaume recalled, to see if "there were among the French delegates elements suitable for entering into a revolutionary organization," since "it seemed to us very desirable that this organization [the "secret international organization"] should be more extensive, particularly in Paris and in the principal French towns."[79] Bakunin turned fiercely against such centralization in the International only when it became clear that Marx would continue to control it and to use his control against Bakunin and his supporters, (much as Bakunin was soon to turn against Nechaev's "Jesuit" approach to intraparty relations mainly because Bakunin himself became one of its victims.)[80]

From his mood and actions after Basle, one would hardly have guessed that the Congress had been something of a triumph, that he had successfully challenged the power of Marx and his followers in the International. Surely, were Bakunin seriously trying to win control of the International from Marx, he would now change his mind about leaving Switzerland "to retire in solitude with Antonia" or at least greatly shorten the period (a year) he planned to be away. In fact, he did just the reverse: he was not only still determined to leave, but during the month and a half that remained before his departure, he kept away from the movement completely: "I just about never, or very rarely, attended meetings of the International, and I only spoke once, on the eve of my departure. As for the Alliance Section, I only took part in one discussion after my return to Geneva from Basle, and that was in order to ask the Committee of the *fedéral romande* for admission [of the Alliance section of the International] into the *Fédération romande*."[81] The fate of that request was only more reason for him to stay and fight, if he were really committed to the battle with Marx. Even though members of the *Fédération romande* central committee belonged as well to the Alliance, the committee decided to postpone action on the request because of the hostility towards the Alliance that had been building up in Geneva.[82]

To add still another blow to further depress these last days before his retreat to Ticino, Bakunin was confronted with another assault on his character. Hardly had a "jury of honor" been arranged at the Basle Congress to clear his name, when Moses Hess published a new set of accusations in an article appearing in the Paris press on October second. Not only was Bakunin, so Hess claimed, the leader of a strongly pan-Slavist faction in the International, but between Bakunin's party and the rest of the International there lay "all the difference that exists between civilization and barbarism, between liberty and despotism, between citizens who denounce every manner of violence and slaves accustomed to intrigues involving brute force."[83] Moreover, it was Bakunin's intention, the accusation went on, to achieve a dominant influence for his Russian party in the International in order to alter its policies and principles in this barbaric and despotic direction. Towards this end, Hess charged, Bakunin had deceived the International by pretending to comply with its conditions for admitting the Alliance. Rather than openly oppose the organization he disagreed with, Bakunin preferred to enter it and secretly work to turn it into an instrument for his own demogogic extremism.[84]

The very day that article appeared, Bakunin was writing Ogarev from Locarno, where he had gone to find an apartment for the year-long retirement that he planned to begin October seventeenth. With its "friendly warmth, beauty and ingenuous, charmingly childlike simplicity" Locarno was a veritable "kingdom of heaven," especially compared to "the dry, thick, drab atmosphere of Geneva.... The carefree, unconstrained freedom, the simplicity and the warmth (like Nice), the air and the beauty—In other words, precisely the kingdom of heaven." He was in such an "enraptured state of mind," in fact, that he feared "the gentle life and air might lessen, soften my savage socialist vindictiveness. Really, it is hard to be angry even with the bourgeoisie here, since they are so simple, live so closely with the people and share their interests...."[85]

Thus, three times during that year of fervent activism we see Bakunin thinking about and planning retirement: in January before Nechaev arrived, in August when Nechaev left (and before the Basle Congress), and, finally, in October following the Basle Congress, when after completely detaching himself from the movement while waiting for his chance to leave Geneva, he retired to his "kingdom of heaven" and its "childlike simplicity." These facts require a closer look at the character of Bakunin's revolutionary zeal that year. It was more than coincidence that Bakunin was carried away by Nechaev's extremist fantasies so soon after he had first mentioned retirement. What we see here is a repetition of the pattern Bakunin followed in 1864-66, when he had made withdrawal from politics look like militant revolutionary dedication by reviving his apocalyptic rhetoric (the "red, social, geological revolution," etc.) and by devoting so much of his time to planning his secret society. It was argued earlier that Nechaev's energy and fantasy provided Bakunin a source of fresh revolutionary exhilaration that had been missing in Switzerland, where "the workers are still firmly bourgeois" and where there were no "conscious youth" even among the Swiss radicals. However, against the background of these repeated references to retirement (and recalling the earlier Italian pattern), we can see as well another aspect of Nechaev's appeal: Nechaev's revolutionary extremism not only allowed Bakunin to experience again an "electrifying" "paroxysm" unavailable in Switzerland, but also, and no less important for him now, it allowed him to escape the increasingly burdensome (and psychologically threatening) consequences of his success in Switzerland. He rushed so eagerly and gullibly into Nechaev's deceptions not so much because of his impatience with the "firmly bourgeois" Swiss, in other words, but rather because of his distress over the remarkable success he had had in the Swiss labor movement, because of the psychosexual meaning that success, visible power, had for him. As in the earlier Italian years, therefore, what seemed on the surface to be a vital burst of power and political commitment during these months of Bakunin's infatuation with Nechaev and his revolutionary fantasies was actually a further step in Bakunin's continuing, if intermittent, retreat from genuine power and commitment.

As for his ongoing participation in the Swiss movement during the Nechaev months (his editorship and articles in *Égalité,* his publication for *Progrès,* and his preparations for the Basle Congress), they find their explanation in the fact that *they lasted only as long as Bakunin was with Nechaev,* that Bakunin was ready to give them all up after Nechaev left (even though that was before the Basle Congress), and that he did actually withdraw, leaving behind the many unused possibilities for real authority offered him by his achievements, both at the Congress and in the Swiss labor movement that preceded the Congress. In short, his heightened activism, energized enough to keep him working enthusiastically even among the "firmly bourgeois" Swiss, was the effect of Nechaev's influence on him, a spillover, as it were, of the renewed apocalyptic pose that lasted only as long as the source, Nechaev, was present.

More specifically regarding the Basle triumph, success there only fortified his determination to withdraw. The revitalized zeal of the Nechaev months had indeed inspired him into active preparations for the Congress. But that zeal was mainly part of the act Bakunin was then performing together with his costar Nechaev, in an effort to disguise a withdrawal from the power and responsibility he was rapidly acquiring. Unfortunately for him, however, both his followers and his rivals thought the performance real, and by their actions for and against him they succeeded in offering him still more of that very power he was trying, once again, to escape. The last thing he could tolerate was genuine control. It was only from a safe, "free," chaste distance that he—the "child"—could "compete" with Marx for the "mother" International, that he could attack all that Marx stood for, as he had attacked from afar all that his father and the equally "blind" Tsar had stood for. The "child" could no more *replace* Marx in power over the "mother" International than he could replace his father or the Tsar. The pattern of his relationship with all three was essentially and significantly the same: underlying fear, assault from a distance, appeasement and ingratiation. Public, explicit authority was still "the most dangerous and repulsive thing in the world." He could not even fantasy it openly: only in "secret" could he reign over his paper "families" and in secret prepare to fight Marx. It was probably, in fact, the trauma of having dared so much at Basle that made him withdraw so quickly from everything after the Congress, without even waiting for his retirement to begin, and that kept him from ever attending any other Congress of the International.

What Bakunin now needed, in the fall of 1869, following the Basle Congress and the threatening accomplishments leading him into it, was another Premukhinolike sanctuary, in a place of warmth, beauty, and leisure; a secret family of "intimates" who would visit him, correspond with him, and help, through their praise and collaboration, make his fantasies look real; and the freedom again to prove his powers through safely detached and irresponsible apocalyptic declarations, without running the risk of assuming the heavy and psychologically dangerous leadership that his achievements in Geneva, the Jura, and Basle had offered him. He had given two years to serious politics, from the fall of 1867 when he arrived in Geneva and joined the League of Peace and Freedom to the fall of 1869 when he went south again, to Ticino. That was more than enough for him.

Anxious as he was, however, to leave Geneva and retire to his new-found "kingdom of heaven," he had to stay on a while longer. He must refute the charges of Hess and the rest of the "German Jews" who, he said, were all— except for Marx—out to get him. While he was "in no way either the enemy or the detractor of Jews," he told the editors of *Le Reveil,* to which he sent his response to Hess's criticism, he was convinced by "ethnographic history" that Jews were "*par excellence* exploiters of other people's labor" and, therefore, "completely opposed to the interests as well as to the instincts of the prole- tariat." "I know very well," he went on, "that in frankly expressing my personal thoughts about the Jews I expose myself to enormous dangers. Many people share [these views], but very few dare to express them publicly, because the Jewish sect, far more formidable than Catholic Jesuits and the Protestants, con- stitute a real force in Europe today. They reign despotically in commerce and in the banks and have overrun three-quarters of the German press and a very sig- nificant part of the press of other countries. Too bad for anyone careless enough to displease them!"[86]

Of course, he did not mean, he said, that only Jews were exploiters or that all Jews were. After all, Jesus, Saint Paul, Spinoza, Marx, and Lassalle were all Jews. He was only criticizing "Jewish pigmies" like Hess or Borkheim ("some sort of maniac" who, in 1868, had attacked Bakunin in a German radical paper "edited in Berlin exclusively by Jews"), those "lacking all moral sense and all personal dignity," those "German Jews skilled in the art of slander," who had been spreading such rumors about him since the early 1850s, when "a meeting took place in London in which emigrant German Jews" organized this campaign against him.[87] As for the charges themselves, he dismissed them as patently groundless. How could he be accused of being a pan-Slavist, he asked, when he had written so vehemently against Tsarist Russia? How could he be accused of trying to undermine the International when he had just written a long series of articles in *Égalité* defending the International's principles? Concerning the Alli- ance, all that existed of it, he assured the public, was the Geneva Alliance sec- tion of the International. He was, to be sure, opposed to the International's emphasis on politics rather than social revolution, for one had only to see the sad fate of Garibaldi's and Mazzini's hopes to realize how little improvement came from exclusively political change. And why, finally, did Hess come down so hard only on the Russians? Why concentrate on them and prophesy a "barbaric" invasion from Russia, a destruction of Western civilization by Russians when it was the German states that were the real expansionist powers?

Why had he spared Marx in his assault? Herzen asked. Bakunin replied that, first of all, it would be neither just, since Marx had contributed such "great services to the cause of socialism, which he had served energetically, intelligently and sincerely for almost twenty-five years," nor sensible, since Marx was still "an unquestionably useful man in the International." Moreover, it would be poor "tactics" to attack him now: although the time was near when he would have to confront Marx on the issue of "state communism," were he to do so now, he would lose, for Marx would have three-quarters of the International on his side. "In this war," Bakunin concluded, he must first split off the lesser foes, *"Divide et impera,"* then "I would have the majority with me."[88]

The day before he explained these tactics to Herzen, Bakunin's fury against the Jews was further stoked by a dispute with his old rival among the émigré Russian community in Switzerland, "the little Russian Jew Utin," "the Maccabee and the Rothschild of the International in Geneva."[89] The argument took place at a meeting on October 27, 1869 at which Utin eulogized the English trade union movement. Bakunin, in rebuttal, minimized its value and contrasted its reformist aims with what he considered the International's goal of complete social transformation to be achieved through social revolution. The argument was all the more painful for Bakunin, because it was clear that two of his followers, Perron and Robin, sided with Utin and were reorienting *Égalité* policy, which Perron and Robin now determined, in Utin's more moderate direction. With Bakunin's departure for his "kingdom of heaven" two days after the trade union debate, this trend away from his extremism grew more pronounced, and he soon lost his influence on *Égalité*. If he had remained in Geneva, he later wrote, this shift of his followers away from the interests of the more radical construction workers towards those of the moderates would not have occurred. But he had not remained.[90]

After finally leaving Geneva on October 29, 1869, he stayed for a time in Lugano, but finding Mazzini and his entourage there, he decided to go right on to his "kingdom," Locarno. For money, he depended partly on Marx's *Capital,* which he had undertaken to translate for a substantial advance (an ironic and revealing arrangement, as we saw, considering the role Marx played in Bakunin's psychodrama and the importance and meaning of the "inheritance" issue in their conflict)[91] and, later, on loans from a special revolutionary fund controlled by Herzen and Ogarev. He could not then turn to Gambuzzi, (his follower, benefactor, and father of Antonia's children) he told Ogarev in December, because Antonia was leaving Naples (and Gambuzzi) at the time in order to be with Bakunin in Locarno.[92] After a slow start, the *Capital* translation advanced smoothly, and he seemed to be attending to it responsibly.[93] It was again, as it had been in Florence and Naples two years before, a quiet and relaxed time. But there were also bouts of depression, to judge from his letters. Drawing out the implications of his retirement and disclosing a little more of the motivations behind it, he seemed to feel that his revolutionary days were over. He wrote Ogarev that even if the old guard like Ogarev and himself lived to see the revolution there would be "little personal consolation" for them, since "other people, new, strong, young...will cut us off the face of the earth, having made us useless."[94] (It is as though he already sensed what was to come in his relationship with Nechaev.) A subdued, nostalgic air hovers over these Locarno letters to Ogarev. Ghosts from the past reappear—Stankevich, Granovsky, Belinsky, Neverov, Werder.[95] In his recollections of Granovsky, one finds a poignantly transparent attack on the self he himself once had been and at heart always remained: "Granovsky was also an idealist.... But there was not in him a single drop of real Diderot or Danton blood, real love of the people. He lived and died by doctrine and by a sentimental humanistic fiction. He loved humanism, but not living people.... I read several of his letters to his sisters and cousins—what lofty soulfulness, what repulsive worrying about oneself, about the impression he was making while carrying out his mission...."[96]

Still, he stoically insisted, they must go on with the struggle to the last breath: "think of the revolution," he told Ogarev, "think of this universal mass vengeance," and hope that "fate would grant us both the chance to end with a death like Samson's."[97] Practicing what he preached, he continued to maintain active contacts with his secret Alliance "intimates" in various countries. He was especially concerned about the fate of the Geneva Alliance section after his departure, for even if, he conceded, one considered it "an *imaginary* center of propaganda and action for Italy, Spain, southern France as well as for the Swiss romande," still, "some imaginary existences are very useful...."[98] As time went on, moreover, the pendulum again was gathering strength for its swing back. He seemed envious of the activities others in the network were undertaking—at the end of November, 1869, for example, Guillaume was giving Sentiñon a guided tour of the Jura towns, and the following month the two of them went to visit Richard, Bastelica, and Palix (all "intimates") in Lyon.[99]

Bakunin was, of course, fully aware of all this. Two days before Guillaume and Sentiñon left Geneva for Lyon, he wrote Richard of their coming.[100] Using a "coded" language, which as before, revealed much more of the deeper truths and motivations of his life than did the political play he was acting and trying to conceal by the code, he went on in this letter to Richard to express both his eagerness to get moving again into something really, electrifyingly, revolutionary and the force behind it. "Try to come to an understanding with them [Guillaume and Sentiñon] on all points, so that we can cease being a pleasant fiction and finally become, if not yet a reality, at least the beginning of a serious reality. This angelic existence between heaven and earth is beginning to bore me greatly, and I know you to be enough of a realist to assume that it bores you equally. So, let us give ourselves a body, but do so in such a way that this body also conforms to our soul, so that the latter does not find itself forced, in the manner of Egyptian metempsychosis, to live in stupid and impure animal bodies...." Altering the imagery but disclosing the basic disorders no less graphically, he went on to advise Richard: "let us live with others as do parasites. Let us nourish ourselves on their life and their blood without allowing ourselves to be absorbed by an alien existence."[101]

We see again in such passages the double bind in which Bakunin had long since trapped himself. Through a sequence of substitutions, the revolution, the people's violence, and, now, the International (as representative of the people's revolutionary violence) all came to symbolize for him the "body," virile power, his mask of omnipotence. However, they also meant to him "our communal bride—the Revolution," the beloved people whom he must "passionately love," merge with in "one soul and one body," and a "mother" on whom the "child" must depend, on whose "life and blood" the "child" must "nourish" himself. This combination of meanings necessarily involved an irreconcilable contradiction. Since the main purpose of his participation in the International was to use it as an "Archimedes point" and mask of power, he had to approach it as a virile man, a warrior claiming leadership, not as a "child" after "nourishment." Virile leadership, however, was just what was forbidden him: to try to acquire a powerful "body" through joining with and controlling the "mother" International meant to recreate the very danger that he had been running from all his life. At best, therefore, he could conceive of the alliance, of linking "soul" and "body" and merging "heaven and earth," as he put it, only after he assured himself that these would not be "impure animal bodies."

His method of meeting this dilemma, so familiar in his life, was, as always, to try to have things both ways: to attempt as long as he could, as we will see, to remain influentially inside the International, opposing those of his "intimates" who wanted to break with it, while at the same time keeping a safe distance from real control of it. The needs of the "child" for "nourishment" once again prevailed over the youth's need for a virile "body": it was only as a child, never as a man that he could approach the "mother." He must and would continue to spurn the opportunities for power that his success was making ever more available to him, hiding instead in a succession of new secret, intimate, safe, little revolutionary "brotherhoods," distracting himself from the challenge of authentic authority through renewed fantasies of world-shattering revolutions that were abstract, distant, intangible, and unreal enough never to pose the multiple threats that serious enterprises such as the International and the genuine labor movement posed to him.

In mid-December, 1869, two weeks after sending this letter to Richard, Bakunin began hearing rumors that sent him soaring again to the heights he had enjoyed during the Nechaev months earlier that year. "Where is our dear, bright, noble adventurer, my Boy [in English] and what is he doing?" Bakunin asked Ogarev. "You write that he is on his way to Geneva, but just today I received a letter from N. N. in which I was shocked by the line—'Is it true that Nec. is dead...?'" Another two weeks, and another rumor: "they have arrested our Boy." Reassured by Ogarev a few days later that this was not the case, Bakunin prepared for the reunion: "I have bed and board always ready for him." Then the great day came—Nechaev had returned! "When I received your note I jumped for joy so high that I almost broke the ceiling with my old head." He "absolutely must see the Boy," but he could not travel to him for lack of funds and also because Antonia was expected to give birth at any moment. "And so I will wait here for our Boy, or, rather *boevoi* [warrior] . I have waiting for him blankets, bed, table and room, and also the deepest secret....Good-bye, I await the Boy."[102]

In the five months that had passed since their last collaboration, Nechaev had put the essential principle of the *Catechism* to its ultimate test. He had formed the basic cell of a secret, centralized, and rigidly disciplined organization that was to expand into a conspiratorial network capable of sparking and directing a mass peasant rising that he expected to occur on February 18, 1870, the ninth anniversary of the Emancipation. One party member, Ivanov, resisted his domination, threatening to break away and form another organization. With the collusion of four other members, Nechaev killed him. Discovery of the body led to widespread arrests, but Nechaev managed to escape and in January, 1870 was again in the West, ready to begin phase two of the Bakunin-Nechaev affair. Repeating the experience of the year before, when Nechaev gave Bakunin the revolutionary charge he had been denied by the tepid Swiss labor movement, Nechaev now again pulled him out of his Locarno semiretirement, which had already begun to pall.

For the next half year, Bakunin once more surrendered himself totally to the direction of the ruthless young fanatic, eagerly accepting everything Nechaev said about the strength of his "organization" and the imminence of the mass Russian revolution. Bakunin's principal contribution to their collaboration this time was an appeal *To the Officers of the Russian Army*. If in writing to Ogarev a few months earlier, he had doubted that they would even live to see the great rising, he was now again on the very eve of the apocalyptic climax: "the hour of the final battle approaches. . . ."[103] Whether the battle would be relatively blood-less or not depended on whether or not the army joined the revolution. If the army came to its senses, understood its ties with the masses and joined the mass revolution, then the battle would take few lives, since the people, "magnanimous in its victory," would forgive most of the former exploiters and parasites and, for the most part, only expel them. If not, if the army opposed the masses, there would inevitably be "all the horrors of merciless destruction and annihila-tion."[104]

Still favoring, therefore, a bloodless liberation, Bakunin did what he could, redreaming his Siberian and 1863 fantasies, to recruit the army into the revolu-tion. First, he devoted a number of pages to the shining example of Andrei Potebnia whose conscience had turned him against the Russian state in support of the Polish revolution and who, unlike the Decembrists, had realized that no victory against tyranny was possible without the participation of the masses. Then he gathered a variety of arguments to persuade other young army officers to follow Potebnia's example. Among the arguments used to prove that the duty to disobey was often morally more compelling than the soldiers' duty to obey was the following: "Well, what if the commander orders [an officer] to kill his father, rape his mother or surrender his sister to the pleasures of some general, grand prince or, if you will, even the Tsar. Must the officer obey even then?"[105] To prove to the officers that mass revolution was indeed possible, Bakunin went on to describe at length the powerful organization—Nechaev's!—that was already on hand and prepared to organize and direct the mass rising. It was "a secret organization," "a kind of general staff of the revolutionary army," "strong in the discipline, the passionate dedication, and the self-sacrifice of its members and unconditionally obedient to all the orders and directives of a *single Committee* that knew everyone, but was known by no one. . . . The members of that Committee had vowed total self-sacrifice. . . . Renouncing, once and for all, all personal property, all official and public authority and power, and, in general, any form of social prominence, they destined themselves to eternal anonymity, granting to others the glory, the external brilliance and the clamour of public action, while leaving for themselves, although again collectively not individually, its essence, as do the Jesuits, only not with the aim of enslaving but of liberating the people. . . ."[106] (Thus, once again, "invisible" power and "bloodless" annihil-ation: the persistence of the basic pattern never falters.)

To assure solidarity and discipline, the members were ready to accept "the renunciation of their lives, their views, and their wills," agree to the rule that once having joined the organization "leaving it is impossible," that "entering it, each must know that he surrenders himself to it, with everything, with all the strength, resources, capacity, and life that he has, and *irretrievably.*" Consequent-

ly, "the organization must look upon those leaving as traitors...." To tighten
security still more, each member must vow to carry out "all orders and instructions received from above," while "speaking about the activities *only with the
one* with whom he is directed to speak." Of course, there must be no "parliamentary chatter," for that could only "form opposing parties within the organization," demoralize it, waste precious time, and, by its debilitating effect, keep
the organization from taking the decisive actions it had to take. So strong and
determined was this secret organization with its "iron discipline" that Bakunin
was "completely convinced that there was no power that could now destroy
it,...that it is so firm and elusive that neither force nor cunning could undermine
it." Finally, as to the period after victory, he emphasized again that power and
leadership must be hidden, invisible, that "not one single member of the Committee will come forward or occupy a visible post. The Committee will remain
secret, putting in people from outside the organization, perhaps even those who
are strangers to the organization as a whole, satisfied with the fact that they are
carrying out its predetermined plans."[107]

Central as these passages are for understanding Bakunin's "politics," they
were not the focus of his appeal to the Russian officers. As he does so often in
his writings, Bakunin seemed to get stuck on a side issue about a quarter of the
way through the article, in this case a discussion of what went wrong in the
Polish rising of 1863. In the end, most of the article was devoted to that theme,
even though Bakunin said, when he finally did get back on track, "But what is
now approaching is not a Polish, but a Russian revolution. Therefore, the task
before us is a thousand times easier than it was for the Russian officers stationed
in Tsarist Poland in 1862. Today it is the Russian people who are rising."[108]

So exhilarated was Bakunin now, that his praise for Nechaev and Nechaev's
alleged "organization" surpassed even the heights reached the year before:

> How those boys are working over there [in Russia]; what a disciplined
> and serious organization and what strength for collective action—where
> all individuals are effaced, having renounced even their names, their
> reputations, their vanity, their glory, accepting only risks, dangers, the
> hardest privations, but also thereby the consciousness of being a force
> that can really act. Do you still remember my young savage?.... They
> are all like him. The individual has disappeared and in place of the indi-
> vidual, there is the legion—invisible, unknown and omnipresent, every-
> where active, dying and being reborn each day anew.... The individuals
> perish, but the legion is immortal.....[109]

Here was yet another chance to prove that he was not "weak and incompetent," as he called those who failed to move forward with this new opportun-

ity. "We really have acted like idealists until now," he went on to say in this letter to Ogarev, written on February 21, 1870. "He who wishes to do something great, must be greatly daring. We must become practical and efficient—and not let ourselves be condemned to weakness by our own helplessness and poverty.... Otherwise it would be just as well for us to retire and become monks."[110] The first and most important task of the new campaign, however, was to protect Nechaev from the police. Virtually following Nechaev's orders now ("Today, at his insistence,... I wrote...."),[111] Bakunin sent a protest to *Progrès*, denouncing the Swiss police for helping the Russian government in its search for Nechaev and for calling him and others "assassins," whereas in reality they were only people "unfortunate enough to displease the Russian government." Nechaev's "crime, if there was one, was that of a political activist.... But they say he killed. Who says so? The Russian government. But is it not being extraordinarily naive to believe what the Russian government says?..."[112] Besides writing this article, Bakunin urged his friends and "intimates"—Perron, Becker, Reichel, Vogt, Talandier—to activate similar public campaigns on their own against the continuing harassment of Russian émigrés by the Swiss government.[113]

This defense of Russian émigrés soon broadened into an effort to form what Bakunin and Nechaev saw as an entirely new organization, one that would be centered in Zürich and would be concerned above all with countering "the vile things written about Russians and Russia in the best European press."[114] But how could Bakunin give himself fully to this grand cause as long as he was burdened by his obligation, reenforced by a sizeable advance payment, to translate Marx's *Capital?* Nechaev took care of that with ease: in mid-February he wrote a letter to the man, Liubavin, who had obtained the commission and advance for Bakunin, ordering him in the name of "the Committee" to release Bakunin from the contract at once or else the Committee would have recourse to "less civilized methods."[115] While it may be true that, as is generally argued, Nechaev did this without Bakunin's knowledge, Bakunin seems to have accepted his sudden liberation without protest. In any case, once free, he threw himself passionately into the new enterprise. In March (1870) he published another brochure directed to "the Russian youth," entitled *The Universal Revolutionary Alliance of Social Democracy.*[116] As was the case with much of his work now, it was a restatement of his basic arguments against the "state socialists" as well as against those moderate socialists who thought that a liberal, parliamentary, constitutional system could solve real social problems or that the future just society could emerge out of the expanding cooperative movement.

Publishing pamphlets or articles in other people's journals, such as *Der Volksstaat, La Marseillaise,* and *Progrès,*[117] was useful but not enough. Nechaev and Bakunin wanted an outlet of their own. Although born of a sad loss, the opportunity for acquiring one seemed at hand. On January 21, 1870, Herzen had died, opening the way not only to a renewed publication of the *Bell*, this time under Nechaev, Bakunin, and Ogarev, but to the funds to finance it. A special revolutionary fund had been placed under Herzen's and Ogarev's control by a Russian landowner, named Bakhmetev, who was sympathetic to radical causes. During Nechaev's first stay in Europe, Bakunin had persuaded Ogarev, and both had prevailed over Herzen's better sense, to give half the money to Nechaev's "organization." The other half was still there. In his efforts to help Nechaev get both the *Bell* and the balance of the money, Bakunin involved himself in one of the most unflattering episodes in his life.

Since prospects for a new *Bell* would be helped immensely if Herzen's name could be used, Bakunin and Nechaev worked strenuously from the end of February through March trying to persuade Herzen's daughter Natalie to announce her support for the venture, allow her name on the title page, and even, as Nechaev suggested, become the editor.[118] While knowing, Bakunin wrote Natalie, that condolences were futile after such a loss, he asked her to allow him, "as an old man," to suggest a way to ease somewhat her pain—help them "continue Herzen's work" by resurrecting the *Bell*. Those like himself, he went on, "the practical workers, who are humbler, less gifted, and of lesser repute" wanted to do this because it was "the finest monument we can erect to his memory." Her participation, moreover, would save her from "leading a life of idle dilettantism." Whereas she now had "no aim in life," she would then be working "for the Russian cause," "for the liberation of the Russian people." Finally, there was old Ogarev to consider. She must help him in this new venture: "It will be unforgivable, criminal of you, to abandon Ogarev to his melancholy solitude."[119]

On February twenty-first he was urging Natalie to join them in order to help Ogarev. On the twenty-second he was writing Ogarev to instruct him on how to bring in Natalie in order to save her. If she went on with her aimless life, "she may really lose her mind," so "first and foremost you must save her." There followed detailed instructions on what Ogarev was to write, when he was to write it, how he was to express himself—all reminiscent of Bakunin's letters to the Beyer sisters in the days of the "holy commune." He should "first of all, without raising any other points about the *Bell* or the Russian cause, have her come and settle at your place." Should she resist or question Ogarev's judgment, he must write her a letter, "not passionately patriotic, but as reasoned and skeptically as you can." Ogarev must also see to it that Natalie receive copies of a letter Nechaev published in *Progrès*. He should "get that number and dispatch it—oh so cunningly and carefully—to the Natalies in Paris, by two methods: one, in a sealed envelope, and the other, inside Russian newspapers wrapped as printed matter."[120]

The day he wrote that letter to Ogarev, Natalie had just arrived in Geneva from Paris in order, as she had written Nechaev on February twentieth, to "acquaint myself much more closely with the Cause, and see much more clearly by what means you wish to achieve your aims, before I can have *absolute* trust."[121] So important was it for the success of the new venture to have Natalie with them, that Bakunin decided to go to Geneva himself, borrowing money for the trip and the stay there. "Keep her with you at all costs; that is the only way you can save her," Bakunin wrote Ogarev on the twenty-ninth.[122] As Natalie recalled one of her meetings with Nechaev and Bakunin Nechaev "was continually trying to prove that these [Nechaev's] methods were essential. Soon B[akunin] arrived and assisted him so well in this that they almost succeeded in driving me completely out of my mind. 'What,' he [Nechaev] said to me. 'Our enemies are ten thousand times stronger than we are, and shrink from no means, and are we to think we can fight them without resorting to the same means?' "[123] "Bakunin tried every day to show me that I must be with them, if only to continue my father's work. I always made the same reply: 'I need to have a clear idea of the ends and the means!'.... I was constantly seeking an answer to the question of what I could do. Bakunin hinted at things that filled me with revulsion. For example: 'A beautiful, young lady can always be useful.' I was speechless with amazement. 'It's very simple. There are so many rich men, young and old, and it's easy to turn their heads and make them give money to the cause.' "[124] Besides, she too had money, Bakunin said, and if he allowed himself to say what he really wanted to say, "I would say in words of one syllable—leave yourself the *'stricte nécessaire'* to live on and give the rest to the common cause."[125]

It is obvious from almost everything Natalie wrote, however, that while blaming both of them for "Jesuitism,"[126] she did not consider Bakunin and Nechaev equally at fault. It was not Bakunin who "dragged—or wanted to drag—me into your 'Carbonarism'....*you* are the principal culprit," she wrote Nechaev. "Enough of accusing poor B[akunin]."[127] When Nechaev scoffed angrily at her reluctance to break with friends for the good of the cause, Bakunin took her side "and said that I should not listen to V. [Volkov: Nechaev's code name in these notes], that he did not recognize any kind of affection....Everything that was not the 'Cause' was in his opinion triviality, sentimentalism, etc."[128] And it is indeed the case that throughout these negotiations, Bakunin comes across as the moderate intermediary, tempering Nechaev's impatient and often offensive extremism, even while supporting his general position. When discussing rumors that the Herzen heirs planned a trip back to Russia and, thereby,—or so it seemed to Nechaev—a reconciliation with the Russian government, Nechaev warned: " 'It goes without saying that if you *do* go to Russia our people will be obliged to get rid of you somehow!'....B[akunin] glanced at him reproachfully and said:

'Now, what's all this? Threatening, are you? What sort of an idea is that? Well, he really is in a rage—just look at him.'" Or, as he put it on another occasion, "Now, now, calm down, you little tiger."[129]

All the maneuvers failed, however: Natalie adamantly refused to submit to an organization and program about which she was allowed to know next to nothing and which was prepared to employ means she deplored. She would not be the blindly obedient organizational instrument that the *Catechism* (as well as Bakunin's revolutionary programs) required. In the end, Nechaev, Bakunin, and Ogarev had to reissue the *Bell* without her. Getting the remainder of the Bakhmetev fund was easier, since, as Bakunin repeatedly reminded him,[130] Ogarev was codirector of the fund, and Herzen's son Alexander did not oppose Ogarev's allocating the money as he saw fit, that is, giving it to Bakunin who in turn turned it over to Nechaev.

Though indulgently critical of the young "tiger's" claws, Bakunin strenuously supported and defended him throughout these months, writing a separate pamphlet, for example—*The Bears of Berne and the Bear of St. Petersburg*—to denounce Swiss authorities for helping the Russian police track down and harass radical Russian émigrés like Nechaev.[131] (This alliance between the Bears, East and West, he argued, proved that there was no real democracy in the much vaunted representative system, that "all political organization necessarily led to a negation of liberty.")[132] In the first weeks of April (1870), however, a serious dispute took place between Bakunin and Nechaev involving the question of political extremism. However, in this case it was Bakunin who was the more militant. The issue concerned the future "color" of the *Bell*. Bakunin and Ogarev wanted it unmistakeably "red," openly socialist and revolutionary. Nechaev, on the contrary, was eager to attract as many different groups and individuals as possible into a concerted attack on the Russian government and, therefore, insisted that nothing at all be said about socialism, that the new *Bell* be either multicolored or colorless.[133] While Bakunin for a time seemed more willing to go along with him than was Ogarev, who almost came to blows with Nechaev over this, he was totally dissatisfied when the first issue came out on April 2, 1870 and said so in an open letter published in the next issue, April ninth—Bakunin's only contribution to the new *Bell* during its brief, five week revival. "What do you really want? What colors do you fly?... Who are you? Socialists or supporters of the exploitation of the people's labor? Friends or enemies of the state? Federalists or centralists?"[134]

Perhaps to emphasize his own loyalty to true "red" and his opposition to Nechaev's blurring of party lines, even if only for tactical reasons, Bakunin sent a letter to *Volksstaat* on April eighth, the same week he criticized the new *Bell*, praising again the quality and promise of the revolutionary Russian youth. Once more he based his argument on a contrast between Germany and Russia, a prominent theme in Bakunin's publications since his escape from Siberia and one that would soon virtually dominate his thought. He began by dividing Germany into four parts: the splendid scientific and humanistic ideals, the brute official reality, the feeble bourgeoisie who dreamed the right ideals but who were powerless victims of the state, and the great hope, the working class who would actually achieve the ideals of which the bourgeoisie could only dream. There was not yet a working class in Russia, he conceded, but in its place there existed a promising youth that combined a passionate idealism, which was a religion for them, with a dedication to materialism and realism, grounded on Comte, Buckle, Marx, Lassalle, Feuerbach, Darwin, Vogt, Büchner, and Moleschott. Moreover, unlike their counterparts in the West, this Russian youth ("practical idealists notwithstanding their materialism") could not look forward to careers within the establishment and so were "revolutionaries by circumstance" as well as by ideals. Whereas the purpose of the *Bell*, he said, should be to propagandize uncompromising revolutionary ideals, the kind he himself had argued in his appeals to Russian youth and to Russian army officers, the *Bell* was pursuing instead the compromising, coalition aims that had always been for Bakunin the most repugnant of all political corruptions.[135]

But disappointment with Nechaev's *Bell* was not Bakunin's only cause for dismay that April (1870), for it was at this time that he began to pay the full political price in Switzerland for his retirement the previous fall and for his almost exclusive concentration on this second Nechaev collaboration during the following winter. Since he had left Geneva, his enemies, with Utin at their head, had gained ground steadily. "*Égalité* has become a reactionary journal," he wrote Richard on April first. "Here is its program: cooperatives and the local politics of the bourgeois radicals."[136] Having won control of *Égalité*, Utin had then gone on to gain a strong influence in Bakunin's own fortress, the Geneva Alliance section, where on March thirteenth, for example, Bakunin's old ally Becker brought the majority to Utin's side on a vote to change several key points in Bakunin's program. Utin struck another painful blow two weeks later when *Égalité* announced the formation, by Utin and his supporters, of a "Russian section of the International," with the *People's Cause* (the Vevey journal Utin had earlier won from Bakunin) as its organ. To cap his successive triumphs over Bakunin, Utin planned, according to a report in *Égalité* on April second, to keep Bakunin's Alliance section out of the *Fédération romande* (the Alliance's application for admission was still pending) as well as to bring in his new Russian section as the real representative of Russian socialism in the International.[137]

Throughout this campaign against Bakunin, Utin considered himself to be Marx's devoted follower and explicitly informed Marx that his goal in this affair was to expose Bakunin, who, he claimed, "dreamed only of a personal dictatorship" and whose programs were fundamentally inconsistent with and injurious to the International.[138] With Utin's criticism of Bakunin to reenforce his own, Marx prepared a "confidential communication" concerning Bakunin and on March twenty-eighth sent it to the German Social-Democratic Party. Briefly reviewing their relationship, back to their collaboration in 1843, and Bakunin's involvement in the League and the Alliance, Marx accused him of an organized, persistent, and determined effort to take over the International, of using his international Alliance for this purpose, and of only pretending to have dissolved it.

While Marx may have made a number of errors of fact in this general attack, he surely had good reason to accuse Bakunin of wanting to dominate the International through delegates belonging to his secret international Alliance and thereby to reorient the policies of the International in what Bakunin considered a genuinely revolutionary direction. This, after all, is precisely what Bakunin himself had often said was his purpose in attaching the Alliance to the International, and this at least appeared to be the intention of Bakunin's network of "intimates" inside the International and his continuous correspondence with them. The very day, March twelfth, that Utin wrote Marx accusing Bakunin of dreaming only of a "personal dictatorship" and of programs "injurious to the International," Bakunin was once more corroborating at least part of the accusation in a letter to Richard. Denouncing what had by now become a focus in his conflict with the Marxists, the workers' participation in bourgeois elections and parliaments, he insisted that the proletariat organize their revolution apart from all such bourgeois institutions, that "in order to save the revolution, in order to bring it to a positive end," there must be formed in the midst of the inevitable "anarchy" of revolution "an invisible, collective dictatorship, *not clothed in any kind of power, but therefore all the more effective and powerful....*"[139] Or, as he expressed this by now familiar theme of invisible domination in another letter to Richard two weeks later: "we must foment, arouse, unleash the passions—we must produce anarchy—and, acting as invisible pilots in the midst of the people's storm, *we must direct it,* not by any kind of ostensible power, but by the collective dictatorship of all the allies—a dictatorship without the sash [of office], *without title, without official legality, yet all the more powerful in having none of the appearances of power*—Such is the only dictatorship that I acknowledge."[140]

In fact, Marx was quite wrong about Bakunin's real intentions, those that are so pathetically apparent in the constantly repeated formulas for secret, invisible, powerless power (all of them variations of "ruthless surrender" and the bloodless axes that annihilate without hurting anyone). Marx misread Bakunin's

aims because he judged him by himself and by other men of real power and responsible authority and because he took Bakunin's words and deeds at face value,
not realizing that they were largely fantasy revealing the reverse of what they
seemed to say, that nothing could be farther from Bakunin's real aims than taking control of the International.

During the first week of April, the same week that Bakunin was angered by
Nechaev's *Bell*, Utin's attack against what was left of Bakunin's position in
Geneva climaxed at the Chaux-de-Fonds Congress of the *Fédération romande*. It
was virtually a Geneva-Jura division, with the exception of the more moderate
Chaux-de-Fonds delegation itself, which, though Jura, sided with Geneva against
Bakunin. On the issue of accepting or rejecting Bakunin's Alliance into the
Federation, acceptance won 21 to 18. At this point, those who opposed Bakunin
and his Alliance left the hall and formed a separate organization, which, they
said, was the real *Fédération romande* because it represented far more members
(over twice the number) than did the pro-Bakunin faction that had won the
vote. There were, thus, two groups claiming to be the *Fédération romande*,
one in Geneva that included the Utin faction and one in Chaux-de-Fonds that
comprised the pro-Bakunin Jura towns and that was soon to become the *Fédération jurassienne*, Bakunin's principal base in Switzerland.[141]

The split at the Congress was not only the result of a personality clash between Utin and Bakunin. Behind it was the fundamental argument over revolutionary theory and strategy that had from the outset divided Bakunin and his
followers, especially in the Jura towns, from the more moderate International
sections in Geneva—the argument over "the abstention or participation of the
workers in local politics," as Bakunin phrased it.[142] Should his side lose in this
"great battle," he said, then he would "separate from Geneva in order to form
another Federation." Much more was involved here than a local Swiss controversy: the Chaux-de-Fonds battle was only a prelude, Bakunin wrote Richard, to
the far more important conflict to come at the next Congress of the International, where the issue would be clear and fundamental:

> Do we want the grand politics of universal socialism or the petty poli-
> tics of bourgeois radicalism, as revised from the perspective of bourgeois
> workers? Do we want the abolition of bourgeois nations and political
> states and the advent of a single, socialist universal state? Do we want
> the complete emancipation of the workers or only an amelioration of
> their lot? Do we want to create a new world or patch up the old?[143]

In the weeks following the Chaux-de-Fonds Congress, the journals of the
two factions vigorously defended their respective positions on this key issue of

participation in bourgeois politics. Insisting "that all participation of the working class in bourgeois governmental politics can have no other result than the consolidation of the existing order of things, thus paralyzing the socialist revolutionary action of the proletariat," the new organ of the Jura, *Solidarity,* called upon all sections of the International to "renounce all activities that aim at the transformation of society by means of national political reforms and direct all their activity to the federated organization of labor, the only means of assuring the success of the social revolution." Five days later, on April sixteenth, *Égalité,* now firmly in the hands of Bakunin's enemies in Geneva, argued in response that putting up "workers' candidates" in order to achieve "representation of labor" had such obvious value that they would "combat abstention from politics as having consequences fatal for our common cause."[144]

Since the time Utin had first defeated Bakunin by winning control of the *People's Cause* and the Russian colony in Clarens-Vevey, he had advanced from one victory to another. He had taken over *Égalité,* won to his side some of Bakunin's closest supporters, formed an anti-Bakunin Russian section that Marx, 'n his "confidential communication," had officially recognized, and, in effect, kept Bakunin out of the *Fédération romande,* since it was the Geneva faction rather than the *Fédération jurassienne* that won the recognition of the International. On April sixteenth Utin initiated his next attack: he proposed the expulsion of Bakunin and three of his followers from the International's central Geneva section.[145] Two days later Bakunin left Geneva (where he had gone to discuss the future of the *Bell),* and returned to Locarno.

It had not been a happy trip. The collaboration with Nechaev that had meant so much to Bakunin had ended in serious discord over the "color" of the *Bell,* while his contest with Utin and, indirectly, with Marx in London, had cost him his influence in the most important center of the Swiss labor movement. Nor was he to get much of a respite from misfortune after his return to his "kingdom of heaven." At the beginning of May 1870 a young Russian revolutionary named German Lopatin, who had been among those arrested in the aftermath of Nechaev's Ivanov murder and who had fled Russia the next year, arrived in Geneva from Paris. His purpose was to find out what had happened to the Bakhmetev fund and to regain some letters and notes in Bakunin's and Nechaev's possession that might be used against their authors.

From the information Lopatin[146] brought with him, it became at once evident that Nechaev had indeed killed Ivanov as the Russian government had charged, that his story of being arrested then escaping was a lie, and that the great "organization" he claimed to represent was pure fiction. On May seventh a meeting was held involving the principal Russian émigrés in Geneva, including Nechaev himself. About the same time, Ogarev wired Bakunin: "Serious business.

Meeting. Concerns the Boy."[147] Perhaps suspecting the worst, or maybe because he had had enough of Geneva intrigues in March and April, Bakunin was very reluctant to go. Referring in a letter on the ninth to an earlier wire urging him to come (probably to the meeting on the seventh),[148] he listed reason after reason for not going—there was no money, there were Antonia and her children to consider, why come when no one told him what was really going on and when he doubted anything serious was involved? On the tenth he assumed the burning issue involved the Bakhmetev fund and that Utin was making a row about it. He now said that he would come, but he insisted on having an apartment for his family in the country for Antonia's sake. Later that day, he added other requirements: Antonia must have a maid to help her, and the apartment had to have three beds, for Antonia, for himself, and for the children. If there was no one available with the time to search out a good apartment, then someone should be hired by the day to do so. Also, he added the next day, don't forget the linens. Hesitant as he was to go, he was also intensely anxious about the whole affair. "Where is the Boy?" he asked repeatedly, in each note. "What has been decided? How has it been decided? Where is the Boy? In Geneva or not?" Every other day he wrote Nechaev—the second, fourth, sixth, ninth, and eleventh, or wired him— the fifth and the seventh—to an agreed-upon address, but there was no response. Finally, in mid-May, he went, alone.[149]

The day he arrived, a meeting was arranged with Lopatin and Nechaev, at which Lopatin told Bakunin the truth about the Russian "organization" and the details about the Liubavin affair. However, as Lopatin later told Natalie Herzen, Bakunin wrote to him after the confrontation to say that he doubted the accusations. As Lopatin put it, Bakunin continued to believe Nechaev's "inventions" even though "their absurdity was glaringly obvious."[150] To judge from Bakunin's later account of the meeting in a letter to Nechaev, he may not at all have been so gullible: "The last trip confirmed all doubts and completely shook my faith in the honesty and truthfulness of your word. Your conversations with Lopatin in my presence on the evening of my arrival, his direct and sharp accusations, which he made to your face with a conviction which did not permit any doubts as to the veracity of his words—words which showed your statements to be lies. . . . He triumphed; you retreated before him. I cannot express to you, my dear friend, how hurt I was both for your sake and for mine. I could not doubt the truth of Lopatin's words any longer. It followed that you systematically lied to us, that your whole enterprise was riddled with rotten lies and was founded on sand."[151] If this account is accurate, then Bakunin was evidently concealing his true feelings and did, in fact, believe Lopatin when he wrote him that he did not. Moreover, he seems to have gone right on resisting a public acknowledgment of this truth for some days afterwards. On May twenty-sixth, at least a week after the meeting, he stopped at Berne on his way back to Locarno to arrange for wider distribution of the *Bears* pamphlet defending Nechaev and to urge others to come out with comparable protests.[152]

Back in Locarno, he seemed relaxed, just glad to be away from Geneva: "Ah brother! It's good here! Quiet, tranquil—one can think as much as one wants and do as one pleases," he began a letter to Ogarev on May thirtieth. He then went on to name those he was glad to be away from (especially the Russian colony that had been gathering to oppose Nechaev) and to list a variety of chores for Ogarev, mainly concerning distribution of the *Bears*.[153] There was no mention of Nechaev, other than the indirect support expressed in reference to the *Bears* publication. Yet, several days before, on May twenty-sixth, Lopatin had written him a long letter detailing once more the accusations and the proofs. Was Bakunin still avoiding the painful truth? If so, by June second he had surrendered to it, and for the next week devoted himself to writing Nechaev one of his enormous letters in which he acknowledged finally his complete acceptance of Lopatin's accusations and expressed his profound and bitter disappointment with Nechaev's policies and actions.

Long and impassioned as the letter is, however, one must look closely to see just what policies Bakunin opposed, wherein lay the differences between the "Boy" and "Matrena," a name that Bakunin sometimes used when writing the "Boy."[154] Had Nechaev gone too far when he murdered Ivanov? If Bakunin thought so, he said nothing about it. Besides, he himself had justified revolutionary terrorism in the case of Karakazov and, still more to the point, had himself called it an act of treason for anyone to leave the secret organization once they had joined and had ruled that such traitors surrender themselves to the "vengeance" of the organization.[155] Was Nechaev's revolution too violent? Was his call to "poison, dagger, and rope" (in his *The Question of Revolution)* too barbarous? Again, if so, Bakunin did not say so. The closest he came to opposing such brutality was his rejection of what he called in the letter Nechaev's *Abreki,* a term referring to ruthless desperadoes of the Caucasus. But, again, he himself seemed to be supporting much the same kind of criminal violence when he praised in the same letter the "whole wide and numerous underground world," the "world of tramps, thieves, and brigands," who were among "the best and truest conductors of a people's revolution, promoters of general popular unrest, the precursor of popular revolt."[156] (And who could be more gifted with "evil passions" and the "devil in the flesh"?)

Nor, surely, after all Bakunin had said about secret conspiratorial organizations could he complain against Nechaev on this score. Much of the letter, in fact, was devoted to describing precisely the same kind of organizational model, another centralized and disciplined "brotherhood." Beginning with a central body of about 10, the organization would slowly grow until it reached "40, or at most 70 members." Subordinate to this central organization, there would be "several hundred" "Regional Brothers," organized as "Regional Brotherhoods," who would remain ignorant of the members of the central body and "only know that there exists a Central Committee which hands down to them their orders for execution...." Together, these two organizational levels would form the "General Staff." Beneath it would be the lower "District Brotherhoods." Rigorous discipline would prevail throughout the entire organization. There would be "no parliamentary chatter" (by now a ritual insistence). Instead, all the members would be strictly obedient to their local committees as would the local committees to the Central Committee. Within the organization, "Everyone's personal intelligence vanishes, like a river into the sea, into the collective intelligence, and all members obey unconditionally the decisions of the latter." (Each of the many times one reads these statements one cannot but wonder at Bakunin's fame as the supreme bard of freedom!) As for the individual "brothers" themselves, they must be "the most intelligent," totally dedicated and obedient, cold, calculating, realistic and practical, motivated only by a passion to liberate the masses, ready to give their lives for them, free of all self-interest, vanity, and ambition, having nothing any longer to do with "material comforts and delights" nor with "ambition, status, and fame."[157]

Rather than attack Nechaev on the issue of centralized, disciplined, "top-downwards" organization, it would seem that Bakunin was trying to compete with him to see who could be the most uncompromisingly centralist. It was in this letter, in fact, that Bakunin made more explicit than he had ever done before just how permanent his party dictatorship would be, although at the same time revealing again his ambivalence towards power and the psychological roots of that ambivalence:

> Imagine yourself in the midst of a triumphant spontaneous revolution in Russia. The state and with it all sociopolitical systems have been demolished.... The turbulent filth that has accumulated in immense quantities within the people rises to the surface. In various places there appear numerous individuals, brave, clever, unscrupulous and ambitious, who, of course, try to win the people's trust and to direct it to their own advantage. These people come into conflict, fight and destroy each other. It seems to be a terrible and hopeless anarchy.
>
> But imagine that in the midst of this universal anarchy, there is a secret organization which has dispersed its members in small groups over the whole expanse of the Empire, but is, nevertheless tightly, solidly joined, inspired by a single idea, a single aim that is adopted

everywhere (according to local conditions, of course) and acting everywhere according to one and the same plan. These small groups, unknown by anybody, have no officially recognized power. But strong in
their ideas, which express the very essence of the people's instincts,
desires and demands; [strong] in their clearly understood aim, among a
mass of people struggling without any aim or plan; strong . . . in that tight
solidarity which connects all the hidden groups into one organic whole;
strong in the intelligence and energy of the members that comprise
them, and successful in having formed around themselves a circle of
people more or less devoted to these same ideas and subject, naturally,
to their influence—these groups, while seeking nothing for themselves,
neither privileges, nor honors nor power, will be in a position to direct
the popular movement in opposition to the ambitious persons who are
divided and fighting among themselves and to lead it to the fullest possible realization of the socioeconomic ideal and to the organization of
total popular freedom. This is what I call *the collective dictatorship* of
the secret organization.[158]

Besides rejecting Nechaev's *Abreki,* Bakunin also denounced his unscrupulous tactics, "your Jesuitical system."[159] A militant, disciplined, centralized
organization of individuals willing to renounce everything for the revolution was
one thing, but systematic deception was something else again. That, he said,
would ruin everything, corrupt the youth who were to form the base and heart
of the coming revolution, "our General Staff" ("if one considers the people as a
revolutionary army, here is our General Staff").[160] To fulfill their mission, he
said, these young people must be of the highest moral caliber. Nechaev's system,
however, could only "educate them in lying, suspicion, spying, and denunciation."
Never could this Jesuitical system teach them "the new and only religion which
has the power to move souls and create a collective force for salvation."[161]

This brings us nearer to the center of the quarrel but not yet all the way
there. For, as in the case of Nechaev's *Abreki,* Bakunin's attack against "your
Jesuitical system" contradicts some of Bakunin's own actions and statements
not only before the break, but right here in this letter that makes the break. He
argued in the letter, for example, that since the revolutionaries were at war,
"there inescapably arises the necessity for violence, cunning and deceit." Similarly, he said that other organizations whose aims were close to theirs "must be
forced to merge" with their own organization, while organizations opposed to
theirs "must be destroyed," and that in all such activities "cunning, diplomacy,
and deceit are necessary." "Jesuit methods or even entanglement can be used for
this—entanglement is a necessary and marvelous means for demoralising and
destroying the enemy. . . ."[162]

One might argue that Bakunin approved of such "Jesuit methods" only against the "enemy," while strictly forbidding their use within the revolutionary organization itself: they were, he said, *"certainly not* a useful means of obtaining and attracting a new friend."[163] "You, therefore, treat your friends as you treat your enemies, with cunning and lies...."[164] Was that, then, Nechaev's principal sin, the main feature in Nechaev's strategy and tactics that distinguished him from Bakunin? One wonders what Natalie Herzen would have said to this after her dealings with the two of them, especially had she read Bakunin's instructions to Ogarev about how to use her, or what Ogarev would have said had he known that Bakunin had told Natalie she should "not say everything in O[garev's] presence."[165] Also, what about those organization members whom the leaders no longer fully trusted, those who turned out to be "weak-nerved, cowardly, ambitious and self-seeking"? Bakunin: "They can be used as weapons by the society without their knowledge...."[166] When one of Bakunin's allies, Malon, proved to be unworthy in his eyes, Bakunin wrote Richard, in April 1869, a month after Bakunin met Nechaev, that "one can make use of him, without doubt, but only on condition that we keep him on the outside."[167] "Let us live among others," to recall Bakunin's remarks to Richard about the International, "and use them. But we will live with them as do parasites: nourish ourselves on their life and their blood...."[168] Similarly, with reference to Malon and Aristide Rey (another erstwhile "intimate"), he wrote: "If kept firmly outside, they can be useful and be used when needed."[169]

Ever since that letter many years before to one Polish revolutionary expressing distrust against a former close Polish ally,[170] intrigue and shifting alliances of this sort had been a constant part of Bakunin's "intimate" revolutionary life, as it had been a part of his intimate Premukhino "holy commune." In fact, until Nechaev applied his "Jesuit methods" *against Bakunin himself,* Bakunin had only high praise for the cunning Fathers: "You who love to ponder," he wrote Richard, "have you ever wondered about the principal reason for the power and vitality of the Jesuit order? Would you like me to tell you? Well, my dear, it is the absolute effacement of individuals into the will, the organization, and the action of the collective.... I do not want to be 'I'; I want to be 'We'.... Long live the collective. Long live the Jesuits."[171]

Ultimately, therefore, what turned Bakunin against Nechaev was neither his organizational structure nor his revolutionary methods, but the fact that Nechaev used some of those methods against Bakunin himself. In the course of this June 1870 letter and subsequent letters, Bakunin listed a number of Nechaev's crimes against him and others—stealing letters to be used as blackmail, trying to seduce daughters and wives to entangle them in the movement, systematically lying and spying, and being willing to "denounce a member, a devoted or semidevoted follower, to the secret police."[172] Now, as was the case with regard to similar tactics in the *Catechism,* it is highly doubtful that Bakunin would ever have recommended or even supported such things. However, would Bakunin have denounced and broken with Nechaev over them (any more than he did over the Ivanov murder) had he himself not been one of their victims?

Actually, the real blow was not what Nechaev did to Bakunin, but what those acts implied as to Nechaev's attitude towards him. By treating Bakunin as he did, Nechaev showed that "you considered me as an invalid whose counsels and knowledge might sometimes be useful, but no more, whose participation in your fervent efforts would have been superfluous and even harmful." Yet, even when he realized that Nechaev felt this way about him, he went on, more and more poignantly: "it did not offend me.... It was not my business to prove to you that I was not such a hopelessly unfit case for an ardent, a real movement as you thought." Besides, even if he were unfit, that was not his fault: it was because people like Utin had "paralyzed my activities," and because "I am getting old. Eight years of imprisonment have led to a chronic illness.... I also have a wife and children...." Not appreciating all these impediments, Nechaev had treated him as though he were "three-quarters blind," and did not even bother to get his approval before acting, as Bakunin said Nechaev had promised to do. "You should have talked to me as an equal, person to person...." All in all, as Bakunin repeatedly concluded: "I turned out to be a complete fool."[173]

Having joined with Nechaev and drawn on this "energy," Bakunin had been dismissed by the "Boy" as the "invalid" he knew he was. He pathetically tried to respond the only way he could: he struggled to hold on to Nechaev as long as possible, offering him in the June letter *"new relations on a different basis."* In spite of everything, Nechaev would be restored to his good graces if only he would "clear me entirely in the Liubavin affair," acknowledge that "I have never directly or indirectly interfered in the disposal of the Bakhmetev fund," abandon all "attempts for a rapprochement with Utin," "eradicate from your organization any use of police and Jesuit systems, confining their application to the government and inimical parties," agree to publish the *Bell* "with a clear revolutionary program," "adopt as a basis of the organization...the plan of organization and revolutionary propaganda expounded by me," and promise that "this plan of organization, propaganda and action, will be the absolute law and the indispensable basis of the whole Society in Russia."[174] The main thing now, he told his Russian friends, "is to save our erring and confused friend.... Therefore, let us save him together." He must be saved because "I repeat for the hundredth time—he is an invaluable person, the most energetic and committed of all the Russians of our acquaintance." There was good reason, moreover, to hope for

Nechaev's salvation, since "we have given him so much proof both of our devotion to the cause and our friendship with him that he cannot doubt the sincerity of our actions and our words."[175]

Natalie Herzen, for one, was aghast at this continuing faith in a man who had done so much harm to everyone: "How can you still envisage the possibility of working with him after all that has passed between you, after all that you say yourself in your letter to him?" Bakunin would not be dissuaded. On June twentieth, nearly three weeks after he had begun his long letter to Nechaev, he sent a collective letter to Ogarev, Natalie, and the others involved in their Russian circle. It shows more than any other document the extraordinary hold Nechaev still had on him, or, rather, how indispensable Nechaev was to him. Their letters had shown him, Bakunin began, that they were too hard on Nechaev, whereas he himself continued to regard him as "the most *saintly* person" because of his dedication, self-denial, energy, tireless industry, and constancy of will. If he acted like a dictator, that was as it should be, for "in my view, the man who best understands the job, who does more and [who] is utterly dedicated, is—so long as he understands, dedicates himself, and acts—a dictator by right."[176]

Bakunin now found extenuating circumstances even for the intraparty Jesuitical practices: given the conditions of struggle in Russia, Nechaev "had either to abandon the cause entirely or adopt the Jesuit system." He was sure, moreover, that Nechaev had adopted it "with a heavy heart" and that he had remained throughout a man with "a tender heart," and "virginally pure integrity." Defending the "cause" inside Russia, it was quite understandable that Nechaev should have taken the road he took, Bakunin now conceded. On the one hand, the power of the state was immense; on the other, the young people who were called upon to mobilize the revolution were in fact apathetic, sluggish, and weak. To shape them into the "Archimedes fulcrum" needed to bring down the system, they had to be "compromised to the utmost and their return to society made impossible." All their ties to family and society had to be destroyed. Only in this way could there be created "a phalanx of unsparing outlaws...with a single passion in common: *the passion to destroy the state and society.* You must admit that this fantasy is not the product of a petty mind or a paltry soul, and that it has, alas!, a great deal of validity and truth." Where Nechaev erred, he went on in this "collective letter," was not in his desire to destroy the ties these young men and women had with family and society, but in his failure to realize the need for new fraternal ties to take their place and to see that using his Jesuitical methods within the movement could only impede the emergence of these indispensable ties. Nevertheless, this flaw notwithstanding, Nechaev remained "finer and purer, more devoted, more active and more useful than all of us together," and he should not only be brought back into our ranks, but should "be at the head of our ranks."[177] As late as June twenty-eighth, Nechaev was still, in a letter Bakunin sent to Natalie, "the finest and...most honorable of us all."[178]

In defending Nechaev, Bakunin was protecting himself in several ways. He was defending, first of all, his judgment in having trusted and so enthusiastically supported Nechaev. Also, he was defending his own revolutionary views on violent revolution and tightly structured and disciplined secret organizations. But most of all, he was defending a last source of virile energy in these late years of his life, a living symbol through whom he could at least vicariously go on playing the promethean role that had been the form and meaning of his entire life. Now that Bakunin was haltingly making his way out of politics, that role, that mask of violent power to conceal the withdrawal was more vital to him than ever. Nechaev himself perceptively caught the difference between Bakunin the "invalid" and Bakunin the actor when he scolded Bakunin and Ogarev for their "warning to Guillaume about the danger of participating in a cause of which you have always been the theoretical instigators...."[179]

Bakunin gave Nechaev ample evidence for that accusation. When Bakunin praised "brigandage as a weapon of the people's revolution, as a catalyst of separate popular revolts," he went on to say, as we saw, that "I am fully conscious of my incapacity for the task." "For myself, I cannot tolerate either brigandage or thieving, nor any other anti-human violence."[180] He could insist, similarly, that his revolutionaries display "reason—cold, calculating, real and practical,"[181] and he could accept the need of breaking all ties with society—"first, career; and second, family bonds, romantic attachment, and vain social relations."[182] But he could not even in this fantasy see himself among those for whom "all tender and effeminate emotions of kinship, friendship, love, gratitude and even honor must be stifled"[183] and therefore criticized Nechaev for not recognizing "any kind of affection," for dismissing everything that did not serve the revolution as "triviality, sentimentalism."[184] Backtracking on what he himself had said must be sacrificed to the revolution, he faulted Nechaev, after their break, for scorning "human interests such as love, friendship, the family, social relationships." The essential purpose of all his "intimate" cricles, we should recall, from the "holy commune" to this latest "People's Brotherhood" that he proposed to Nechaev in his offer of a new relationship, was to provide him with just these pseudo-familial emotions and relationships.[185]

Difficult as it was to end the relationship he could not go on forever with an outstretched hand, needy and forgiving, in the hope of reconciliation. With no appropriate gesture whatsoever from the other side, Bakunin, after another brief trip to Geneva,[186] finally gave up trying. While still referring wistfully to

Nechaev as "one of the most active and energetic men I have ever encountered," "a man of rare energy," and recalling that "I wanted terribly not to break with him, for he is a man gifted with amazing energy,"[187] his letters of July and August no longer justify Nechaev or urge friends to save him, but only emphasize his flaws and crimes.[188]

Bakunin had now lost badly on all fronts. By withdrawing from the Swiss involvement, then devoting himself to the Nechaev crusade, he had weakened his position in Geneva and made it relatively easy for Utin to displace him. And now Nechaev had betrayed and humiliated him. Because of Nechaev, he had "compromised friends and was compromised in front of them" and had "spoiled my situation with regard to the Russian and the International causes."[189] It was like that summer and fall of 1848, when the Bohemian failure, the *Neue Rheinische Zeitung* allegation of his being a Russian agent, and the reactionary policies of Jelačic had so humiliated him that he was "obsessed with revolution and a passion to destroy," "ready to leap into any dangerous enterprise whatever provided it was not dishonorable," and determined to struggle "until the day when my death would prove to the Poles and Germans that I had never been a traitor."[190] Now again his image and honor had been badly stained, doubly challenged by failure and scandal—from the one side by the charges again being made against him by Marx, Hess, and Utin, from the other side by the disgrace he now suffered through the Nechaev debacle, a disgrace for which he could surely be held more responsible than he was in the Jelačic affair. And he no longer had the benefit of youth to help him regain his honor: "old age is approaching, and we have few years left in which to profit by the lesson," he wrote Ogarev on August second.[191] The pathetic tenacity with which he clung to Nechaev and to the illusions of his own energy and strength that he drew from Nechaev was as much an attempt to deny what age and illness revealed as it was to camouflage the retirement that secretly acknowledged those facts of life.

Age and illness notwithstanding, however, he could not let those successive defeats and humiliations go unchallenged. Further retirement would have to wait. While he could—indeed must—run away from power and success, he was no less forced to resist the evidence of weakness that those failures, accusations, and humiliations disclosed. More perhaps than at any other time in his life, he now needed some audacious, stirring, and inspiring deed to disprove through bold revolutionary action and sacrifice the intolerable charges hurled against him by the Marxists; to counter those successive defeats that Utin had dealt him and the weakness they revealed; to make amends for the deplorable revolutionary judgment shown by his alliance with Nechaev: to provide a substitute to play the role that the Nechaev fantasy had played in concealing his *de facto* withdrawal from politics; to dispute the testimony of age and broken health and make it absolutely clear to the world and to himself that he was not a "three-quarters blind" "invalid," not an "unfit case," that it was Utin and others like him who had "paralyzed my activities" rather than any essential weakness in himself.

He began planning his counterattack against Utin by forming, as he told Ogarev, a new Russian section of "our secret alliance," which he would use for "the final destruction of Utin."[192] Also, he looked forward to the next Congress of the International to avenge himself against Marx and the other Jews who he felt were persecuting him. By now, Marxists and Jews were synonymous for him, and both meant "enemy." "Notice that all our enemies, all these carping critics against us are Jews: Marx, Hess, Borkheim, Liebknecht, Jacobi, Weiss, Kohn, Utin, and many others are Jews—all belong to this nation, restless, intriguing, exploitative and bourgeois by tradition, by instinct."[193] The conflict at the next Congress, as he envisioned it, would involve a confrontation between his camp of Spanish, Italians, Belgians, "the majority of the French, I hope," and the Swiss Jurassiens against the enemy camp commanded by "German leaders, for the most part Jews, that is exploiters and bourgeoisie by instinct, including the school of Marx." He expected as well, he added, seemingly as an afterthought, that the English and American delegates would also be against him.[194]

Considering the months (July and August, 1870) during which Bakunin outlined his battle plans to Ogarev and recalling his needs at the time, there is a strange omission in these letters: there is no discussion at all of the battlefield that was now to provide him exactly what he needed to replace the Nechaev fantasy and once again sweep him into "a veritable delirium," one comparable to the "electrifying" "paroxysm" of 1848–49. The missing arena is the Franco-Prussian War, that, following two weeks of rising tensions between the two countries, had been declared by France on July 14, 1870. Bakunin makes only one passing reference to the war—or what seems to be a reference to the war—in a letter he wrote Ogarev on August first, in which he discussed "the complete liquidation of all our dealings with Nechaev,"[195] "Antonia is with the children from morning to night.... And I work a lot and read the papers, wondering each day, who will win?"[196] From the chatty tone and content of the paragraph that follows, ending this letter, it would appear that he was quite unaware of the revolutionary implications of the conflict.

Awareness was not long in coming, however. Perhaps inspired by the swift and dramatic defeats of the badly outnumbered and outmaneuvered French troops, he soon grasped the war's political possibilities. Whereas on August first he had been calculating the strength of his secret international Alliance for his conflict with Marx, on August tenth (after Prussian victories at Worth and Weissenburg) he was making similar calculations, in a letter to Richard in Lyon, as part of a plan for a general European revolution. It indeed seemed like 1848–49 all over again. "I have spent three days writing precisely 23 long letters," he told Ogarev.[197] "I wish the Prussians another great victory, at the walls of Metz," he wrote his friends the Reichels in one of those 23 letters, then went on to say why: "one way or another, the revolution is imminent—first in France and Italy, then, after a little while, everywhere. Long live the revolution!"[198]

In another of the 23, he virtually gave the signal for the universal conflagration to start. Using the "coded" language he enjoyed using when writing his "intimates," he told Richard in Lyon that "here is a fine occasion for realizing the business that James and François proposed in my name to you in Lyon at the end of last year, the one concerning a big business deal involving Switzerland, Italy, and Spain. My friend, *if you want to save us all from ruin*, you must get at it today. I am writing the same thing to Augustin in a very long letter. . . ." (James and François were Guillaume and Sentiñon, and the Lyon trip was the one mentioned earlier.[199] Augustin was Gaspard Blanc, another intimate in Lyon.) The letter went on to mention, also in coded names, Gambuzzi, Bastelica, and Fanelli, all Alliance members, and to say that "unhappily a great agitation reigns in Italy—people talk about the eve of a revolution. . . ."[200]

The most significant of these letters was the long one he mentioned he was writing to Augustin-Blanc. Later published by Guillaume, after editing, under the title *Letters to a Frenchman on the Present Crisis,*[201] it represents one of Bakunin's most explicit statements of his revolutionary strategy and tactics. Briefly, the argument went as follows: Under Napoleon III France would surely lose to Germany. The leader of the opposition, Leon Gambetta, must, therefore, end his truce with the government and his policy of class and political conciliation and drive Napoleon out. However, if and when he tried to do this, Gambetta would discover that the administrative apparatus was too far gone, the bureaucracy too corrupt and too reactionary to be an instrument for the necessary mobilization of the people against the Prussians. Even were he to try to rouse the people by sending out his own representatives, he would fail as had Lamartine and Ledru-Rollin in 1848, since, as at that time, the commissaries he would select would themselves be too moderate for the task. Therefore, Gambetta should limit his administration to Paris, abolish the state and all its central judicial, financial, administrative, and police institutions, call upon the French workers and peasants to rise against the local political and economic powers, and allow them to form their own revolutionary communes, to organize by themselves the defense of France, and to send delegates to a convention that would establish a new, free federation. Should Gambetta in Paris be unwilling to heed this advice, then some other prominent French city, like Lyon, should take the lead.

By taking the stage once more as the harbinger and leader of revolution, first by fiery rhetoric and then, in Lyon, by audacious action, Bakunin would restore his badly shaken self-image as well as once again experience the paroxysm of illusory power that he had enjoyed through his collaboration with the "savage" Nechaev. He would prove that he was no "invalid," just as his reckless fervor of late 1848 and early 1849 had sought to prove that he was no traitor to the revolution. Although, to recall his self-defense in his dispute with Nechaev, he might be old, ill, burdened with debts and a family, and hindered at every turn by scoundrels like Utin and Marx, he would show that he was still as powerful and, therefore, if need be, as violent as Nechaev. He, too, could call for "a savage war to the knife" (as he does in these *Letters to a Frenchman),* praise repeatedly throughout the letters the people's "savage passions," honor over and over the "devil in the flesh," urge the "unleashing" of the people's "violent passion" ("the liberty of proletarian barbarism"), and scathingly denounce those who trembled at the prospect. There must be a "spontaneous, powerful, passionate, energetic, anarchic, destructive and savage rising of the popular masses," "a furious avalanche, devouring, destroying everything"—this alone could save France, for "she has nothing left except the energy, desperate and savage, of her children."[202] While the message had a shade of novelty in this particular political context, its deeper meaning and the real drama it played out in the context of his own life were almost as old as he was.

Nor, it seems, was the "knife" to limit itself this time to the destruction of "ranks" and "things." The state would be destroyed "by destroying the influence, the official organization, and, to the extent possible, *the actual persons* of the Imperial functionaries: mayor, justice of the peace, priest, gendarme, rural constable...." He could easily understand, similarly, the joy that French workers might feel when "the German workers...came and destroyed the bourgeois institutions, monuments, power *and the individual bourgeoisie themselves."*[203] Moderate, antisocialist republicans like Gambetta were wrong to fear and impede such violence, for "battle is life and life is force." The revolutionaries must learn from the reactionary governments in Italy, Austria, and Russia, who knew how to make use of the peasants' natural, instinctual hatred of the rich landowners and bourgeoisie. The revolutionaries must now use these passions in the same way, only "direct them against their proper target," i.e. "against the invasion of the Prussians from without, and against the treason of the 'Prussians' within."[204] Nothing less than this "immense convulsive movement" of the masses would end the defeat that had "humiliated," "insulted," and "dishonored" France. Something more important even than the defense and survival of free France was at stake, however, for if only the people could "stand tall, energetic and full of confidence amidst the ruins," they would be "creators of a new world"; they would "hurl the torch of revolutionary socialism into Germany, Europe, the whole world"; they would sweep away "the government of the state, the criminal and civil law codes, the legal family, the law of inheritance," all "private debts. taxes, and mortgages," "bring an end to bourgeois civilization," and establish a society in which "there will no longer be either law or state," a society that would "progress freely, develop and perfect itself any way it chose, but always vitally and freely, never by law or decree."[205] So glorious were the prospects, in fact, that the French should rejoice at the Prussian invasion for having made them possible.[206]

"Social revolution, anarchy: today, national; tomorrow, universal." As had their predecessors of 1793, he wrote, the French could again become a people "achieving miracles." Of course, they must not "hope to renew the miracles of 1792 and 1793" as they were achieved then, by direction from above, from the Jacobins in Paris. No, "France could only be saved by a miracle of the people's energy," by spontaneous social revolution from below.[207] A new Armageddon— a "gigantic battle between the great states"—had brought the apocalypse again in sight, and the people were ready with their "savage passions," their "devil in the flesh." But who held that torch to start the blaze? Opposition republicans were too fearful to unleash the "evil passions." "They did not dare," "they did not dare anything," he charged repeatedly, "they did not dare, these bastards of Danton." People of other nations, "disgusted by their stupidity, cowardice, and weakness, only feel pity, mixed with disdain, for the French nation." "Power lay on the ground, it was only necessary to gather it up," but there was no one to do it the right way. There were, to be sure, an assortment of revolutionaries who were ready to lead a revolution from above, the later-day Jacobins. But it would be fearfully dangerous to allow them their way, for their policy of central control would either discourage the indispensable popular involvement, or, even were such involvement forthcoming, lead to the establishment of just another form of state domination after the revolution.

However, if to keep the torch in hand as the Jacobins did meant an unacceptable possession of real power, then "to hurl the torch away" and wait patiently for a "spontaneous" revolutionary combustion meant an even more unacceptable admission of powerlessness, impotence. There was only one acceptable way for Bakunin to start the conflagration, his inevitable way—to do it unseen. It was the same solution that he had been arguing over and over again ever since the 1840s, the same "invisible" power that he had just a few months before outlined to Nechaev, a "General Staff" that would not "command"[209] (the counterpart of the annihilation that would not hurt). This patent absurdity pervades the *Letters to a Frenchman.* The good revolutionaries would not lead or direct: that would be Jacobin. Instead, they would "organize the force of the proletariat," "foment...the furor of the masses," "provoke the revolutionary movement of the peasantry themselves, inciting them to destroy with their own hands the public order, all civil and political institutions. . . ."[210] In order to "extend and organize the revolution," the good revolutionaries "must not make it themselves by decrees, not impose it upon the masses, but must provoke it within the masses. They must not impose any kind of organization whatsoever, but rather, while supporting the autonomous organization from below upwards, *work behind the scenes,* using their own personal intelligence to influence the most intelligent and influential individuals in each locality, in *order that this organization conform to our principles* as far as possible. The entire secret of our success lies here."[211] Sometimes he saw the contradiction: "Organize—(I should myself have said: let it freely and spontaneously organize itself.)"[212] Usually he did not: "*organize anarchy* in the countryside."[213] At times he forgot himself and toyed explicitly with Jacobin leadership, as he did whenever he talked about the role of the secret "party" after the revolution. He was, for example, as delighted at the prospect of a fierce civil war and "revolutionary anarchy," as he had been in the June 1870 letter to Nechaev, since it would provide the revolutionaries a fine opportunity "to form a powerful party" (albeit a "small party"): "You will be, I repeat again, what you have never before been in the countryside, a party, and *you will be able to organize* extensively there a real socialism, an inspired collectivity, *animated by the most complete liberty. You will organize it from below upwards, through actions that are spontaneous, but at the same time required by the force of things.* "[214]

As for the proper balance between actions that were "spontaneous" and those that were "organized" to "conform to our principles" or "required by the force of things," there was the model of 1793. Again forgetting for a moment his bedrock opposition to a centrally directed revolution, he praised the local delegates of the 1793 Convention for the way they went about their work.:

> They did not arrive in a region in order to impose dictatorially the will of the national convention. They did this only on rare occasions, only when they arrived at a district that was decidedly and uniformly hostile and reactionary. And then they did not come alone, but *accompanied with troops who added the argument of the bayonet* to their own civilian eloquence. . . . They quickly recognized the real revolutionaries among the masses and joined with them to fan the revolution, anarchy, in order to put the devil in the flesh of the masses and *organize this popular anarchy in a revolutionary way.* This revolutionary organization was the only administration and the only executive force that the special emissaries used in order to revolutionize, to terrorize a region.[215]

The drama outlined in the *Letters of a Frenchman* is essentially the same as it was in *The Reaction in Germany,* still the classically apocalyptic scenario. The real enemies are still the compromisers, the craven Gambetta and his republican pseudo-opposition, those "Bohemian" intellectuals, with their "café politics," pseudo-revolutionaries "without deep, impassioned convictions," without "enough revolutionary passion and resolution to attempt a perilous leap."[216] The "complete reactionaries," Napoleon III or even the Prussian invaders, come off much better, even with honor, although they are no match, of course, for the real power in the land, the "savage passions" of the masses. If only the "small party" of true revolutionaries could unite with the "savage passions" of the masses, the revolution would triumph over any authority, no matter how powerful it seemed. To win the people to their side, the revolutionaries must promise them the land to be seized from the state and from the rich land-owners as well as an end to conscription and taxes; they must turn them against the priests not by attacking religion and thus offending popular religious feelings, but by calling the priests Prussian agents; they must persuade the workers in the towns to stop disdaining the peasantry.[217]

In sum, by merging—invisibly, behind the scenes—with the people's "savage passions," the "small party" would become "revolutionary giants" capable of defeating in one "immense convulsive movement" any power, no matter how well "supplied with extraordinary arms."[218] The new factor in his familiar oedipal fantasy, the one that distinguished this 1870 version from *The Reaction in Germany* nearly 30 years earlier, was Bakunin's attack on the Jacobins, revolutionaries who did not fear power. Under no circumstances must the "revolutionary giants" really rule. The protective impotence had to be maintained, and, as always, appropriate arguments could be found: To attempt "to impose communism or collectivism" would only provoke popular resistance, and "to repress" that resistance, recourse would be necessary to armed force. In the end, along with "the machinery of the reenforced state, there would soon be the state mechanic—the dictator, the Emperor. All this would inevitably follow, for it is in the logic of the case...."[219]

The argument is sound. The "logic of the case" is surely the way he describes it. But is it not at least as obvious that the "logic" of his own revolutionary strategy and tactics, with its invisible, disciplined, professional party emerging out of anarchy and civil war to organize the peasantry in conformity with the party's ideas, was the best recipe—indeed, the Leninist recipe—for achieving just such a "Jacobin" dictatorship after the revolution? It was more than naiveté on Bakunin's part to argue these contradictory aims, to denounce so eloquently and constantly the very domination that he himself had so often worked into his own party regulations and that his revolutionary strategies virtually assured. What was involved here was the radical self-deception that his basic ambivalence required. The Jacobins dared to draw the logical conclusions of revolution; they dared to assume the power and prerogatives of the overthrown authority. That was impossible for Bakunin. He could have nothing to do with explicit power, not even participation in bourgeois politics that his Marxist rivals advocated, much less the complete domination that the Jacobins had exercised. When he dominated, or tried to dominate, as he did in virtually every group in which he participated (indeed, that was a condition of his participation), he was adamant in insisting that he was doing nothing of the sort. When envisioning a party that would organize and direct the masses both before and after the revolution in a completely Jacobin manner, all rhetorical distinctions notwithstanding, he had to deny to himself ritualistically that this was what he and his "intimates" were doing. Acting "behind the scenes," being "invisible," remaining a "secret" organization, declining official titles (that is, public exposure of authority) was equivalent in his mind to avoiding power, even though he himself said explicitly and repeatedly that his "General Staff" would wield even more effective power precisely because it worked secretly.

As suggested above, with reference to Bakunin's anti-Jacobin arguments, the emphasis on "invisible" (powerless) power did represent, in one respect, a change in Bakunin's rhetoric from what it had been when he wrote *The Reaction in Germany.* During the 1840s, a rhetoric of omnipotence was necessary for a variety of reasons discussed earlier. Partly as a result of that deceptive rhetoric, however, Bakunin had acquired real strength over the 30 intervening years in the form of a broad following and, with it, the opportunity to acquire authentic power and authority. Considering his revulsion towards power (and the fact that he had for some years now been retreating from the dangerous opportunities for power that his rhetoric and tactics had brought him) what he needed now was a *rhetoric of impotence,* a theory—anarchism—that on principle rejected all power, including revolutionary power, and that thereby spared Bakunin himself from the intolerable danger of manhood that was threatening to impose itself on him. This is the major reason why his lifelong affirmation of absolute freedom fully crystallized into a "philosophy" of anarchism only in this last phase of his career. Performing in a different way the same alchemy that first the dialectic and then the secret societies performed, "anarchism" for Bakunin transmuted weakness, fear, and dishonor into strength, courage, and high virtue.

Convinced that the continuing French defeat made revolution imminent, Bakunin spurred his lieutenants on. Gambuzzi and Fanelli had written him, he told Richard on August 16, 1870, that "their capitals were ready," that "they and all their clients were unanimously convinced that never before had the time or conditions been so propitious for getting the business underway, [that] they have decided to begin." It would help them immensely if they had behind them "an international company," so that the "capitalists of southern France, Spain and a particular section of Switzerland" could contribute "their capital to this business." So, with Italy ready, even prepared to move alone if need be, southern France should get its "wine" business properly organized for this immediate "large-scale speculation."[220] (Again, one wonders in reading this Aesopian language, what is real and what is pretense: In the psychodrama he is playing, is the role of powerful international business tycoon any more a fiction for him than that of world revolutionary leader?)

"Don't lose a single moment," he urged Richard on the twenty-third. "Don't wait any longer for a signal from Paris.... If in ten days there is no popular rising in France, France is lost. Ah! If only I were young, I would be among you and not here writing letters." The Prussians were on their way to Paris and would take it unless the people armed themselves and began a "war of destruction, a war to the knife" against the invaders and the "traitors," the "Prussians inside." Only that could save France "from 50 years of slavery, from misery, ruin, degradation and annihilation." Not only France, but "universal liberty" was at stake.[221]

On September second, the main French army, with some 82,000 troops, was trapped near Sedan and forced to surrender. The way to Paris was open. Outraged by the capitulation, crowds charged the Palais Bourbon on September fourth and forced the Assembly to declare the Empire of Napoleon III at an end. With the Prussians on their way to Paris and France without an army or real government, as Bakunin explained to Richard that same day (September fourth), "France will descend to the rank of a third-rate power and be subject to the Prussian yoke." No one in Paris, neither Orleanists like Thiers and Trochu nor republicans like Gambetta could save the day, he said, and Gambetta and his friends had already wasted a month, at a time when each day was important for arming and arousing the people to the revolution that would alone save France. "They did not have the balls [*couilles*]" for the job. So it was now the turn of the French people themselves. "If they have the brains, the heart and the balls for it," they will first rise against "the Prussians outside and the traitors inside," and then "send their delegates to some place outside of Paris to form a *provisional government,* the real government for the Salvation of France." With Paris hopeless, some large center like Lyon or Marseilles must take the lead. But not under the guidance of the "bourgeois radicals," for they "lacked the brains and the balls." It must be done by the workers, and "it remained to be seen if the workers had the balls." They must now "dare in the name of humanity and of France. Their responsibility is immense, for on them depend the destiny of France and of European socialism. . . . . Hesitation would be criminal."[222]

Young or not, Bakunin could no longer go on just sitting there while this exhilarating opportunity slipped by. Two days after that last letter to Richard, he wrote his old friend Vogt, "I have decided to drag my old bones there [to Lyon]

and probably play there my last part,"[223] again revealing truth through incidental metaphor. Passing through Neuchâtel and Geneva, where he was joined by
two comrades, Ozerov and a young Pole, Lankiewicz, he arrived in Lyon on September fifteenth. On the day of his arrival, a newly elected municipal council
was in the process of replacing the Committee of Public Salvation that had ad-
ministered Lyon since September fourth, when a Republic was proclaimed in
Lyon, some nine hours before one was announced in Paris.[224] Under the chairmanship of the new mayor, a moderate republican named Henon, the council
comprised, in the main, other bourgeois republicans. For Bakunin, of course, the
end of the Empire and the free election of a local council for the new republic
meant not the end, but only the beginning of the revolution. "A real revolution
has not yet taken place here, but there will be one, and everything is being done
and readied for the real revolution," he wrote Ogarev on the nineteenth.[225]
The first steps toward that "real revolution" had been taken two days before,
when he and his Alliance "intimates" in Lyon announced at a mass rally that a
new revolutionary organization had been formed, the Committee for the Salvation of France. Bakunin now seemed to be working feverishly to carry out the
plan he had been endlessly restating for years—his "small party" of spartan
militants would unleash the "evil passions" of the people and at last bring
about the great upheaval. "I am playing for all or nothing," he wrote Ogarev in
his letter of the nineteenth.

His followers, men like Richard, Palix, and Combe, who really knew what
was happening in Lyon, were far more cautious. Richard kept urging him to
wait: Nothing was ready yet, he said, especially since the Alliance and the International networks in Lyon had been badly mauled by police harassment in the
last months of the Empire. Moreover, Richard added, Bakunin's repeated
demand that his supporters oppose any and all participation in ordinary local,
bourgeois politics and political alliances had only further isolated them from the
workers. Time would be needed to reestablish contacts with the masses and gain
their support, which was all the more indispensable after it had become clear
that the national guard, with a few individual exceptions, would support the
elected Republican Council, not the "real" revolutionaries.[226]

Bakunin would hear none of this. The people were ready, he insisted, and
had always been ready with their passionate hatred. Only a spark was needed.
Palix vigorously opposed Bakunin's violence: to depend on the violent, instinctual passions of the masses was not only "completely contrary to the French
temperament,"[227] but would entail, as Richard later recalled Palix's argument,
"all sorts of crimes and abominations that would lend the revolution a sinister
appeal, violate the grandeur of the idea by ugly instincts, and arouse against [the
revolution] all those who deeply love everything that is fine and whose con-

science is filled with a sense of justice and the good."[228] Not everyone was against Bakunin, however. Ozerov and Lankiewicz, again according to Richard's account, called for a revolution by any and all means—"fire, poison, and the knife, without explanations and without debates." Bakunin "scolded" them for this, but did not change his own demand for immediately "unleashing" the people's "evil passions." In the end he won, or, in Richard's words, "illusion triumphed."[229]

The first direct call for revolution came on the night of the 24th, when, at another mass rally, various revolutionary resolutions were decided, along with a manifesto "calling on the people to overthrow all remaining and meddling authorities," as Bakunin summarized it to Ogarev the next day. "Tonight," he went on in that letter of the 25th, "we will arrest all the principal enemies, then, tomorrow, the final battle and, we hope, victory."[230] For some reason, the arrests and the battle did not take place on the 26th as planned. Instead, another rally was held to hear a reading of the manifesto. While the handwriting of the manifesto is Richard's, the ideas, sentiments and language are Bakunin's: "If the people, organized for revolution, do not hasten to act, its future is lost. Inspired by the immensity of the danger and realizing that desperate action by the people must not be delayed even a single instant, the delegates of the federated committees for the salvation of France united into a Central Committee propose the adoption of the following resolutions." Predictably, the resolutions can be neatly divided into two parts: one destroying all power; another establishing total power, appropriately disguised. To be abolished: the administrative machinery of the state, all municipal organizations, all criminal and civil courts, all payments of taxes and mortgages. In their place: "Committees for the Salvation of France which will exercise all power under the immediate control of the people"; a "revolutionary Convention for the Salvation of France," which will undertake "the defense of the country"; the "justice of the people" (the new courts); and "contributions...proportionate to the needs of the salvation of France" (the new taxes).[231]

Other documents from these days show even more clearly the shape that the "free" society would take once the state was destroyed. One document lists the revolutionary committees to be established—"Finance and labor, banking"; "Railroad and Navigation"; "Post and Telegraph"; "Prisons and Military Forces"; "Political Justice"; "Civil and Commercial Justice." Another list separates the "good revolutionaries" from the "reactionaries," the latter including, among others, the leading Lyon republicans, with Henon at the head, and Bakunin's Swiss opponents in the International, including Utin.[232]

One manifesto, attributed directly to Bakunin, brings out the Jacobin in him and his plans even more boldly. The "revolutionary communes," it began, "will consider their task accomplished only when they have assured the triumph of the revolution" and have, consequently, "joined federally, establishing themselves as the provisional authorities. . . ." Once established, these "provisional authorities" would decree an end to all taxes, debts, mortgages, contractual obligations, inheritance, "all the codes, decrees and regulations," all government offices, and all religious organizations and associations. Unlike Bakunin's earlier programs of this sort, however, this one had teeth:

> *Article 12.* The punishment of death is pronounced in advance for all those who try, by any kind of maneuvers, to hinder the actions of the revolutionary communes or to reestablish any of the institutions that have been abolished.
>
> *Article 13.* The revolutionary communes will send delegates everywhere necessary to form new communes or to execute the promulgated decrees.
>
> *Article 14.* The revolutionary communes and their delegates will accept all claims and proposals that bear the signatures of at least one hundred citizens. However, these claims and proposals will only be put into effect if they do not hinder the development and application of the principles of revolutionary equality.
>
> *Article 15.* To expedite the execution of these decrees, a permanent revolutionary militia is to be formed by recruiting as volunteers for a period of six months or more all legitimate citizens of all ages. Soldiers and noncommissioned officers of the regular army who wish to join will be permitted to do so, but officers so desiring, must first offer unimpeachable proof of their devotion to the revolutionary cause.[233]

Five months earlier, in April, Bakunin had strenuously opposed what he considered Richard's plan, once the old regime had been overthrown, to send delegates to form "a kind of National Convention or Committee of Public Salvation for the whole of France." According to Richard's plan, as Bakunin described it, the Committee of Public Salvation "organizes a revolutionary state with sufficient force to repress reaction from within and without. . . . Our idea, our plan is completely different. . . . In a word, the revolution must be and must remain everywhere independent of the center, which must only be the expression, the product and not the source, the direction and not the cause."[234] Since April, however, he had come to feel how thoroughly he had been humiliated by both Nechaev—discarded as a "three-quarters blind" "invalid"—and Utin. Now more than ever he had to prove that he at least had the *couilles.*

Postponed from September twenty-sixth, the revolution was now fixed for the twenty-eighth, perhaps in order to take advantage of a demonstration the national workshop laborers were planning that noon, to protest a reduction of wages recently voted by the elected council.[235] Strategy was worked out at a meeting on the evening of the twenty-seventh. Debate seemed to center on the question of arms. Should the workers demonstrate with or without arms? While some argued for an unarmed demonstration, Bakunin vigorously called for arms. A vote was taken, and the majority voted for an unarmed demonstration—which did not, however, stop the later passage of a resolution making the distribution of arms optional. Another question concerned ways of taking control of a key fortress. Bakunin had a plan: use drugs to put the guards to sleep at their posts.[236]

The "revolution" began promptly at noon, in what must surely be the gentlest prelude of any insurrection on record. A small delegation of some 16 workers went to City Hall to ask the council to retract the wage reduction, but no one answered the door: The council was not to meet until later that day, at 6:30. So, "about a hundred determined men, with Saignes at their head, forced open the City Hall door and went inside the municipal building; several members of the Central Committee for the Salvation of France—Bakunin, Parraton, Bastelica and others—went in with them."[237] While the rest of the leaders gathered inside to decide their next move, Saignes went out on a balcony to proclaim to the crowd in the courtyard below that the elected council would either have to accept the articles in the manifesto (of the twenty-fourth) or resign. While there on the balcony, he also appointed the "General in Chief of the revolutionary federated army of the south of France," one Cluseret, who immediately set out to mobilize support for the revolution and urge the townspeople to come *en mass* to City Hall.

In the meantime, the other leaders argued strategy. According to Guillaume's account, Bakunin pressed for quick action, for the immediate arrest of the Prefect, the Mayor and the general of the National Guard before the National Guard had a chance to organize and attack City Hall.[238] Arrests were indeed made, but by the other side. Mayor Henon arrived and seeing Bakunin in the courtyard "put his hand on his [Bakunin's] collar to arrest him." Bakunin "thought a little, then was able to get a hold on Henon," but one of Henon's supporters, "a small man, almost stunted, puny" grabbed on to Bakunin's coattails, separated the two men, and shoved Bakunin, who "fell back into the pond."[239] Several National Guardsmen then led Bakunin down to a basement room and locked him in. The "General in Chief of the revolutionary federated army of the south of France" was more fortunate. Returning from his recruiting mission, Cluseret, too, was arrested, but another of the leaders summoned the crowd to his rescue. About an hour after Bakunin's arrest, his friend Ozerov noticed that he was missing and, gathering a detachment from the crowd, found and freed him. Then, for a while, the tide turned. The National Guard officers were forced to leave City Hall (by way of a court facing "la Place de la Comedie"); Mayor Henon was arrested, along with the Prefect and several other officials; and Richard and Bastelica, who had been taken earlier, were released. Upon arriving at City Hall, Richard found the courtyard filled with both rebels and National Guardsmen, including those who had arrested Bakunin. Bakunin, who had just been released, was walking back and forth among the guardsmen denouncing them for the way they had treated him: "They stole my wallet when they arrested me," he said. "Why argue? Arrest these bourgeois who arrested me and stole 160 francs from me," and arrest as well, he went on, all officials of the former Empire and the clerics, too. "No one moved."[240]

While this phase of the real revolution was underway, other National Guardsmen came streaming into the courtyard from all sides and told the demonstrators to go home. "There was no resistance at all." Saignes and Bastelica made a final effort to rouse the crowd, haranguing them from the balcony, but "their public was no longer there and the officers whistled." Bakunin was no more successful in his continuing efforts to get the other leaders "to launch a bloody collision." Unlike Dresden they were ready for compromise. Fortunately, so were the members of the elected council when they arrived at 6:30 to begin their regular meeting as scheduled. Some conciliatory words were exchanged, and the rebels joined the councilmen in a rousing "Long live the Republic," then left, leaving the revolution behind them and the councilmen free to get on with its business "as though nothing at all had happened." The council did, however, make one concession: it voted to give the workers back the three francs it had earlier legislated out of their wages. But the price for this victory had been high. Lyon was spared the bloodbath of Dresden, no thanks to Bakunin who had tried as hard as he could to provoke more violent conflict, but Bakunin's personal need to "play for all or nothing," "to fight or die" at Lyon, as he put it, did result in a wave of arrests that crippled the working class movement in Lyon for years to come. Also, according to Richard, it completely decimated Bakunin's own Alliance.[241]

The day after the fiasco, Bakunin remained hiding in Lyon, still believing, amazingly, that the miracle might happen. But it would have to be in the next 24 hours, he wrote Palix, otherwise France would be lost, enslaved to the power of Germany and its ally, "the knout of the Saint Petersburg Tsar." If that occurred then "Adieu liberty, socialism, justice for the people and the triumph of humanity." Still, even should that happen, he added immediately, "my conscience tells me that I fulfilled my duty to the very end." What was probably the main reason for this letter to Palix, written that last day in Lyon, came at the end: after telling Palix how he had been "brutalized," "pushed," "shoved," "pinched," "twisted," and robbed of his revolver, notebook, and wallet (65 francs this time) by the guards arresting him, he "authorized" Palix to retrieve the stolen goods for him.[242]

That same night (September twenty-ninth) he left Lyon for Marseilles, where he spent a month fluctuating between despair and renewed apocalyptic expectation, distributing blame to explain away his own costly misjudgment, and beginning a lengthy study of the "pathology" of current politics, which was to occupy most of his attention that fall and through the following spring. He tried for a while to go on hoping: there were still "three, four days," he wrote Palix, "to make a revolution that wil save everything," albeit "a revolution of vengeance and despair."[243] He must have considered this a serious possibility, for he went on in this letter to give very detailed and precise instructions on how he was to be informed of the outbreak of the revolution and summoned back to Lyon. Bakunin gave the letter and instructions to Lankiewicz, who was quickly arrested. Worse still, Bakunin had also given him a detailed code book listing the names of his conspiratorial "intimates." That, too, went to the police. "It is very bad," Bakunin wrote Ogarev: "it exposes them to great danger. . . . Using the list, [the police] have ordered everyone's arrest."[244] (The "code" once more expresses the deeper reality that the "real" words disguised: Thus, while centers of power hostile to Bakunin like Paris and Geneva become "monsieur" so-and-so, the rebellious towns like Lyon, Marseilles, and Neuchâtel are "madame." The word "friend" was coded as "useful," pillage as "borrow," kill as "heal," organize as "paralyze," arms as his oral obsession "tobacco," munitions as "coffee," and artillery as the "married woman."[245]

Hopes for his "revolution of vengeance and despair" continued through the first weeks of October. After all, he recalled in a letter of the eighth, with reference to the Lyon failure, "the beginning had been magnificent," and the defeat had been "the fault of the revolutionary inexperience of several of our friends" or, alternately, "the fault of General Cluseret," whom Bakunin charged with "cowardice and treason." In other words, Lyon had not been a real test; "it was merely a little adventure...and we will soon have our revenge." All that was needed was organization and, for that, money, which could be obtained by "forced contributions." So, "it is likely that I will soon be returning to Lyon."[246]

In a letter he began on October 20, 1870 to the recently appointed Prefect of Marseilles, he was both depressed and optimistic. Should the Prussians win, he wrote, "for those like us who are old, there would be nothing left to do but die." Whereas he had once hoped for a renewal of Europe, revitalized by a proletariat and peasantry not "used-up" or "depraved," "things in France today almost plunge me into despair, and I begin to fear with Herzen that the peasants and proletariat in France and Europe are dead also." "But no!," he went on, his stay in Lyon and Marseilles had only reenforced his faith in the people's "instincts" and "powerful energies," if only they are properly organized.[247] Three days later, however, he wrote: "I no longer have any faith in a revolution in France. . . . The people here have themselves become as doctrinaire, circumspect, and bourgeois as the bourgeoisie. . . .The situation is unbearable, and I tell you that as far as I am concerned, I have had enough."[248] He was planning that same day to leave Marseilles for Barcelona, he wrote in this letter, but then changed his mind and left instead for Geneva. From there, on the twenty-seventh or twenty-eighth he went home to Locarno, successfully defeated again, still "free."

11.   CALVARY

The next half year or so, well into the following spring (1871), was one of the darkest periods in Bakunin's life. He was utterly impoverished, driven to an incessant search for loans and, according to Antonia, deeply depressed by it all.[1] Crushed by the failures and losses of September and October, coming so soon after the humiliations suffered from Nechaev and Utin, he isolated himself completely and worked on the book, the "pathology," he had begun to write in Marseilles. "It is my first and my last book," he wrote Ogarev when he was almost done with the first part of it, "my spiritual testament."[2] In successive letters to Ogarev and Ozerov, he gave detailed instructions for its editing and urged, implored, ordered Ogarev to take scrupulous care to see that everything was done with meticulous precision.

The book, *The Knouto-Germanic Empire and the Social Revolution*, as he called it,[3] was now the only thing that seemed to matter to him. He paid little attention to what was happening in the continuing battle between his Jura friends and their Geneva, Marxist-Utin rivals. A rising in Marseilles and another in Lyon made little impact on him. Nor, in fact, were his spirits raised by the Paris Commune, when the insurrection broke out on March 18, 1871. He acknowledged the bravery of the Communards and praised their organization, wishing that the Lyon rebels had been as well-organized, but he was convinced, and said so repeatedly, that they were doomed to defeat: they could only succeed if supported by a general social revolution in the provinces, and that was unlikely. Moreover, what good could come of an insurrection in which the majority of the leaders were Blanquists, supporters of a centralized political revolution? He could hope for only one positive outcome of the insurrection, "that the Parisians,

369

in perishing, would take at least half of Paris with them." This was not the revolution for which he had been waiting. The French would have to suffer "stronger shocks," "and then perhaps the devil will awaken." As for himself and his friends, they must still go on preparing themselves "in order to be ready for the day the devil awakens." Until that time, "to spend our scanty means and those of the few others, our only treasury, would be criminal and stupid." Consequently, to turn to the first part of the letter to Ogarev from which that last quotation is taken, Ozerov should be spending less time in "feverish excitement" over events in Paris and more in preparing the first installment of Bakunin's "spiritual testament" for publication.[4]

Except for an intriguing account of European cultural and political history from the eleventh century, *The Knouto-Germanic Empire and the Social Revolution* is yet another reenactment of the fantasy that had obsessed him throughout his adult life: the apocalyptic Armageddon between "Positive" and "Negative," reaction and democracy, empires and peoples, delayed and betrayed by the "golden mean" compromisers, the German and Russian liberals, the French bourgeois republicans, and all the others who were "neither hot nor cold." A grand, stark choice confronted Europe and the world—either a "truly universal social revolution, a really great one, greater and more universal than the German Social-Democrats have ever dreamed of, will awaken the devil that slumbers in them [the people]," or slavery to the German state and its ally, the Russian Tsar, "that Germanized Genghis Khan."[5] Either "holy revolt" or universal tyranny. In parts similar in its fervor to *An Appeal to the Slavs, The Knouto-Germanic Empire* summons all true revolutionaries to arouse "in themselves this deep and powerful passion that stirs the soul and provokes and achieves that which in ordinary life, in monotonous daily existence, one calls miracles, miracles of devotion, sacrifice, energy and triumphant action. The men of 1792 and 1793, Danton especially, had this passion, and with and through it, they had the strength for these miracles. They had the devil in the flesh, and they were able to put the devil into the flesh of the entire nation...."[6]

Reflecting, perhaps, his anger over the recent disappointments, the apocalyptic miracle he now envisioned had become even more ruthlessly destructive. "The workers of France want to save France at all costs; *one must even make of France a desert in order to save her, blow up all the houses, destroy and burn all the towns,* ruin everything that is so dear to the hearts of the bourgeoisie— property, capital, industry, commerce—in a word, *turn the country into an immense tomb* in which to bury the Prussians. They [the workers] want a war to the death, *a barbaric war to the knife,* if that would do it."[7] More specifically, in response to his appropriately phrased question, "What is to be done?,"[8] he foresaw revolutionary squadrons dispersed across the land to execute the people's will. With the "devil in the flesh" and following the right "line," they will "remove at once everything that might impede the success of the propaganda. Then they must begin to *crush without striking a blow*, the whole communal local administration, inevitably infected with Bonapartism, if not with legitimatism or Orleanism—to attack, expel and, if necessary, arrest the local officials as well as all the reactionary large property owners and the priests along with them, *for no other cause than their secret connivance with the Prussians*."[9] (Thus, the revolutionaries must burn, blow up, crush and level France into a desert, but do so "without striking a blow." They must even "advise the people not to maltreat anyone." "Devil in the flesh" and "evil passions" notwithstanding, the revolution will be achieved "without much violence and without any bloodshed," for the people are "really generous" and are "incapable of cruelty."[10])

Just as his pandestruction would hurt no one, so would his revolutionary "government of national defense and its delegates" rule without limiting anyone's freedom. "Completely opposed as I am to what in France one calls discipline, I recognize nonetheless that *a particular kind of discipline, not automatic, but voluntary and conscious and perfectly in accord with individual liberty* is and will always be necessary.... At the time of action, in the middle of battle, the roles divide naturally, according to different aptitudes, as evaluated and judged by the entire collective: *some direct and command, others execute these commands*."[11] There was nothing at all in common, needless to say, between his "command" and that of the Jacobins, and their "cult of state control," which he attacked as vehemently as ever throughout the book.

Again and again, here and everywhere else, he insisted that it was not this or that form of state—monarchic, republican, or revolutionary—but the state itself, in principle, which was public enemy number one. That he did not see how his own revolutionary strategy and party organization must inevitably lead to a central domination of the most tyrannous kind, notwithstanding all the "bottom-upwards" slogans, almost defies belief. Yet, it must be so, for it is even less believable to assume that he was engaged, over all these years, in conscious duplicity, saying one thing while consciously scheming its opposite. He could not let himself see the outrageous contradiction; he had to hold on to both poles, denouncing any and all forms of power, while determined to *appear* all-powerful through his apocalyptic rhetoric and authoritarian revolutionary organizations (albeit careful to keep his "power" invisible, i.e., powerless, and to assure himself and others that he and his apocalypse would not harm anyone, almost). He had found long ago in the revolutionary dialectic a magical formula for having it both ways, being totally committed through total detachment, powerfully opposing all power, merging with the pure, good, generous masses in their violent, vengeful, savage yet bloodless revolution.

Frustrated and angered by the successive disappointments that past year—Utin, Nechaev, Lyon—his vengeance found new symbols in the heritage of past revolutionary insurrections (significantly, past religious heresies that were crushed): the fourteenth century Fraticelli, "who dared to oppose the celestial despot and take the side of Satan, the spiritual head of all revolutionaries, past, present, and future, the true author of human liberation according to the Bible, the negator of the celestial empire as we are of all earthly empires, the creator of liberty"; Wycliff, Huss, and Ziska, "the avenger of the people, whose memory still lives as a promise for the future . . . who, at the head of his Taborites, covered the whole of Bohemia, burning the churches, massacring the priests and sweeping away all the German and imperial vermin"; and the Anabaptists of Münster with their "attempts at a mystical-communist organization."[12] Bakunin had discovered his true lineage.

Neither the evil state—reactionary, republican, or Jacobin—nor the good satanic rebellions against it was the focus of this "spiritual testament," however. It was, rather, as it had been in *The Reaction in Germany*, what Bakunin saw as the essential "pathology"—the bourgeoisie and its "golden mean" compromising. This, before all else, was the sickness that kept the "devil in the flesh" asleep and the apocalypse so long delayed. The principal enemy of this apocalyptic Zealot remained, as always, not the conservative Sadducee, but the moderate Pharisee. In this instance, it was mainly bourgeois republicans in France who bore the brunt of the assault. More fearful of a people's social revolution than they were of Prussian domination, they had been unwilling, he charged, to do the only thing possible to save France—call for a popular uprising. As for their constitutional and parliamentary charade, deceptive and self-serving at best, the bourgeoisie was quite prepared to exchange it for open military dictatorship the moment the people threatened to use the parliamentary forms against the privileged class and their property. Since he devoted most of the book to an attack on the French bourgeoisie, he balanced it at the end with a lengthy assault on German cultural, social, and political history from the eleventh century on, arguing that the German bourgeoisie was even worse than the French, that "the sentiment of revolt—that satanic pride that repels the domination of any master, divine or human, and that alone creates in man the love of independence and liberty—is not only unknown to it, but repulsive to it, scandalous and frightening," that they "cannot live without a master" and are able "to live in servitude, as tranquilly and happily as a rat in cheese, as long as it is a big piece of cheese."[13]

It is from the second part of the *Knouto-Germanic Empire*, the segments written in February and March 1871, that one of Bakunin's most famous compositions has come down to us, *God and State*. Restating and amplifying themes already argued often before, especially in *Federalism, Socialism and Anti-*

Theologism (written for the League), it is one of his most eloquent and glowing defenses of Reason and, correspondingly, most passionate critiques of religion and every other form of what he calls "idealism." "God being everything, the real world and man are nothing. God being truth, justice, goodness, beauty, power, and life, man is falsehood, iniquity, evil, ugliness, impotence, and death. God being master, man is the slave....If God is, man is a slave; now, man can and must be free; therefore, God, does not exist....I reverse the phrase of Voltaire and say that, *if God really existed, it would be necessary to abolish him.*"[14]

Adopting again Feuerbach's thesis, he saw in the concept "God" nothing but a projection of the people's own ideals: "It is the generic name of all that seems grand, good, beautiful, noble, human to them. But why, then, do they not say 'Man'."[15] Man against God meant human freedom and dignity against human slavery and humiliation. In its earliest imagery, he said, this struggle was symbolized as Satan ("the eternal rebel, the first freethinker and the emancipator of worlds") against Jehovah ("who of all the good gods adored by man was certainly the most jealous, the most vain, the most ferocious, the most unjust, the most bloodthirsty, and the most despotic").[16] From the first rebellion of Adam and Eve (inspired by the heroic Satan) against the despot Jehovah, history has seen a continuing confrontation between these principles of freedom and despotism, or, as the confrontation expressed itself in the world of ideas, between "materialists" and "idealists." Whether in the form of religion versus rationalism, Germany's "idealistic" slavery contrasted with Italy's "materialistic" freedom, the idealism of abstract science (and the authoritarian rule of scientific experts) as opposed to the claims of concrete, everyday life, it was this perennial contest, and especially what Bakunin saw as the intellectual absurdities and social crimes of the "idealists," that concerned him throughout much of the book.

In setting out on this survey, Bakunin called attention to a remarkable paradox, which guided him through the rest of the work: those who considered themselves and were called "idealists" turned out to be exceptionally "materialistic" in their greed for personal wealth and power; while those who proudly claimed to be "materialists" seemed to be the most selfless servants of humanity and warriors for human welfare. At the base of this paradox Bakunin saw a dramatic dialectic: materialism represented, at the outset and in essence, man's animality; but, beginning from it, man dialectically ascended to its opposite, practical idealism. The same dialectic was true of the "idealists" only in the opposite direction: starting from what they called idealism, they dialectically descended to what was, in fact, an animalistic materialism. The rebellion of Adam, Eve, and Satan against the "idealism" of Jehovah was, thus, simultaneously a rebellion of materialism against idealism and a step upwards beyond materialism toward a new and authentic idealism. (Once more the "animal" is at one and the same time boldly proclaimed and fearfully transcended.)

Both by rebellion and by the acquisition of knowledge that accompanied it, the human being "separated himself from animality and constituted himself a man." From then on human history consisted "precisely in the progressive negation of the primitive animality of man": "... behind us is our animality and before us our humanity.... Let us, then, never look back, let us look ever forward, since forward is our sunlight, forward our salvation."[17] With such comments about "animality" we are down again to the personal roots that still provided the real meaning of the rebellion and the main purpose of the convoluted dialectics by which Bakunin tried again to honor the animal materialism he abhorred while denouncing the chaste "idealism" he lived by. The disguise of praise and honor, however, does not change the fact that the "rebel" is called Satan, the "passions," demonic. The "devil in the flesh" still means the devil *is* the flesh. As he had always done before, here, too, Bakunin tells us what he really feels about that "flesh," "materialism," "animality," and "rebellion"; they were as evil and demonic as they had always been for him and had to be denied and transcended, even in the act of being vigorously affirmed. Projecting, as he often did, his own plight onto his enemies (as he had done, for example, in his first attack against the "impotent" "half-men"), he traced the source of the idealists' troubles to their division of reality into two radically opposed parts, calling "one *divine* and the other *bestial*, representing divinity and animality as two poles, between which they place humanity. They either will not or cannot understand that these three terms are really but one, and that to separate them is to destroy all of them" (a most fitting description of his own malaise and a sound prescription for its cure).

For some time in April 1871, while completing these first parts of the book, Bakunin had been planning a trip to Switzerland but had lacked the funds for it. Near the end of the month he received a substantial new loan from Gambuzzi, left for Switzerland on the twenty-fifth, and remained there until the middle of May. Since he could now expect little sympathy in Geneva, he decided to stay in the Jura, at Sonvillier in the Val de Saint-Imier. While there, he delivered a series of lectures, repeating themes he had been working on over the past months for his book—attacking the French bourgeoisie and the Jacobin tradition, debunking bourgeois parliamentary democracy, outlining the great mission and future of the proletariat, wrestling with the contradictions between absolute liberty and social solidarity, and explaining the failure at Lyon. More than ever before, he now stressed the difficulty (as he was also doing at the time in his book) of winning the conservative, uneducated, and religious peasant to the side of the revolution ("you must teach him, you must save him in spite of himself").

Moreover, it was not only the peasants who were at fault, for, as he told Guillaume, who visited him in Sonvillier, there were also too few workers who really had the character of real revolutionaries.[19] Still, he continued to assure his followers that the revolution would surely arrive "sooner or later" and that "we" must in the meantime "prepare ourselves," "purify ourselves."[20]

Then, at the end of May, after he had left Sonvillier for Le Locle, an event occurred that lifted Bakunin's spirits higher than they had been since the eve of the Lyon rising: on the twenty-second news came that the Versailles army had broken the Communards' defense at the Porte de St. Cloud. Day after day, Bakunin and his friends followed the steady defeat of the Communards as they fought street by street until the end. Guillaume recalled the events (as told to him) this way: "As for Bakunin, he remained strong. He expected the defeat. He feared only one thing, that in the final catastrophe the Communards might lack audacity and energy. But when he learned that they had defended themselves like lions and that Paris was in flames, he let go a shout of triumph, 'It's about time! What men!'... as he burst into the cooperative workshop, striking his cane on the table."[21] On the twenty-ninth, the day after the last Communards had fallen, he left for Locarno, arriving there June 1, 1871.

Inspired by the martydom of the Communards, he was now, for a short time, his old, militant self again. "We must not lessen the prestige of this immense event, the Commune. We must, at the present moment, defend it to the utmost, even the Jacobins who died for it," he wrote Guillaume on the tenth.[22] He had himself by then set out to do just that, composing as part of a preamble to the second part of his book a glowing eulogy for the heroes of Paris, who "as a result of being massacred, smothered in blood by executioners from the royal and clerical reaction, have only become still more alive, more powerful, in the imagination and in the heart of the proletariat of Europe"; who have given "liberty and life to France, to Europe, to the entire world"; who have "inaugurated a new era, that of the final and complete emancipation of the popular masses"; and who have "confirmed their energetic faith in the destiny of humanity by their glorious fall." Henceforth, they must be looked upon as "humanity crucified," notwithstanding the fact that the "majority of the members of the Commune were not really socialists," that the socialists were only "a minute minority" while "the rest were composed of Jacobins," albeit good, "magnanimous Jacobins" who "proved their sincerity by being killed for the Commune. Who would dare ask more of them?" While honoring the Jacobin Communards for dying so bravely, however, he stressed again at length the radical distinction between his own free, spontaneous, federated, bottom-upwards socialism and "the authoritarian communists, partisans of the absolute initiative of the state."[23] During the first, triumphant phase of the Communards' uprising, their Jacobinism (as well, perhaps, as their initial success) had severely constrained Bakunin's praise. As martyrs, defeated victims, and powerful sufferers their heroism became so attractive to him that even the sin of Jacobin statism could not tarnish it: "massacred, smothered in blood by executioners" they had become "more alive, more powerful."

His spirits aroused by seeing "Paris drowned in the blood of its most generous children,"[24] he was now ready again to take on his most hated rivals, Utin and, behind him, Marx. The conquest of *Égalité*, the split in the *Fédération romande* (and the acceptance by London of the anti-Bakunin Geneva faction in June 1870), Utin's formation of a new Russian section—also recognized by Marx—and the expulsion of Bakunin and his comrades from the central Geneva section of the International the following August on the grounds that they were simultaneously members of the Geneva Alliance Section of the International did not end Utin's campaign against Bakunin. Utin now moved to drive the Geneva Alliance section itself out of the International by claiming that it had never really been accepted into it and that the letters used to prove that acceptance were fraudulent (a charge that the London General Council itself refuted at a meeting in late July 1871).[25] When Bakunin heard from Guillaume of this latest affront, he was understandably "aflame," as Guillaume puts it.[26] He at once set aside the preface he was working on for the second part of his *Knouto-Germanic Empire* and began work on a detailed history and defense of the Alliance, in preparation for what he expected would be a great battle on the issue at the next Congress of the International, presumably that September (1871). Over the following three weeks, he worked steadily on this *Protestation de l'Alliance*,[27] as it was first called, careful throughout to balance his defense of the Alliance with assurances of his dedication to the International and his admiration for Marx.

Hardly had he finished his *Protestation* when a new challenge was thrown at him, forcing him to do battle not only on another front, but on one requiring a fervent defense of the International. The new gauntlet came from Italy, where, in the context of a dispute between Mazzini's and Garibaldi's followers over the Commune, Mazzini published, on July thirteenth, a stinging attack on the International. Having already become involved in the argument over the Commune,[28] Bakunin felt himself called upon to answer Mazzini, which he started to do the very day he sent Guillaume the final pages of the *Protestation de l'Alliance*. Written in four days, this *Response* to Mazzini was the first of a series of articles against him that Bakunin was to write during the next year.

Although it is a strong defense both of the Communards ("massacred by the tens of thousands, including women and children, in defense of a cause that is the most human, the most just, the grandest ever produced in history, *the cause of the emancipation of the workers of the whole world*")[29] and of the International, the *Response* builds up to that defense in a curious way. In keeping with the original religious focus of Bakunin's earlier attack on Mazzini, which had also been the main theme of the *God and State* section of the *Knouto-Germanic Empire*, the *Response* is primarily a critique of Mazzini's religious "idealism" and of "idealism" in general and rests on the paradox discussed above; namely, that idealism in practice leads to materialism, to the greed and power of the privileged class, while materialism leads to the kind of selfless idealism that ennobled revolutionaries like the Communards. Throughout his vigorous attack on Mazzini, Bakunin showed him great respect and admiration, however, the same kind of respect and admiration that he had just showered on Marx in his *Protestation* against Marx's London Council.[30]

The *Response* completed and mailed out, it was back to the Marxists and especially to Utin's campaign to drive the Geneva Alliance section out of the International. Then, another blow: on July twenty-seventh or twenty-eighth, while Bakunin was writing the *Response* to Mazzini, Guillaume had been deciding on a surprising maneuver against those trying to expel the Alliance section from the International. Why not voluntarily dissolve the section? After all, he wrote Bakunin explaining his position, "for a long time it had served no purpose." In fact, Guillaume argued, the Alliance section was standing in the way of fuller cooperation between its members and recent émigrés from the defeated Commune. Reconciliation and compromise were rearing their ugly heads right on Bakunin's home ground. The very thought of crumbling this way before Utin enraged him: "I will never agree to put myself in a position of being pardoned by them when it is I who should be doing the pardoning. ... It is not by a policy of cowardly concessions and Christian humility, but only by firmly and forthrightly maintaining our right that we will triumph over our enemies, for the good as well of the International."

Instead of surrendering, he began work on another defense of his organization, a *Report on the Alliance*. There was, he said, only one thing that might bring him to dissolve the Alliance section—a public acknowledgment at the next Congress of the International that past attacks on him and on the Alliance had been unjust and an expression of gratitude to the Alliance for its voluntary dissolution. Even were the Alliance section to be dissolved, however, that dissolution, he told Guillaume, must not affect the Jura Federation (the Bakuninist faction from the Chaux-de-Fonds split). Do not be afraid of conflict within the International, he urged Guillaume. Conflict can only strengthen it, especially since "some day it will no longer be a conflict of personalities, but a great battle over two principles—that of authoritarian communism and that of revolutionary socialism." The very day that Bakunin wrote this, August sixth, the remaining few members of the Geneva Alliance section were meeting to dissolve it: they did not even write him about it. It was not until the twelfth that he learned of the dissolution through a letter from Ozerov. Bakunin could do no more than rush off another series of letters denouncing the whole affair. A few weeks after the dissolution, those last members of the Alliance formed a new "Section for Revolutionary Socialist Propaganda and Action," this time together with some Communard refugees.[31]

Back and forth Bakunin moved from one front to another, writing further supplements to his *Report on the Alliance*, interrupting this to work on a second response to Mazzini, then dropping that to attack Utin. Much of these labors went in vain, however, for neither the *Protestation* nor the *Report on the Alliance* were used by his Geneva followers. Nor could they serve as a defense in what Bakunin had thought would be the next International Congress in September; for instead of a Congress, the General Council, because of the severe repression throughout Europe in the aftermath of the Commune, decided to limit the meeting to a Conference.

The Conference met from September seventeenth to the twenty-third, and all but a few attending were supporters of Marx and the London Council. Most of the substantive resolutions either directly or indirectly concerned Bakunin and the threat he and his followers, mainly in Switzerland, were seen to pose to the International. Beginning with a reassertion of the basic commitment to political participation and the formation of working class parties, the resolutions included a disavowal of all connections with the Nechaev affair, instructions to Utin to prepare a special report on Nechaev to be published in *Égalité*, acknowledgment of the self-dissolution of the Geneva Alliance section, confirmation of the earlier recognition of the anti-Bakunin Geneva wing of the *Fédération romande* as the official voice of the International, and advice to the Jura wing either to submit to that or, if it chose to remain apart, to rename their separate faction the "Jura Federation."[32]

Perhaps the battles that now followed might have been avoided or at least delayed had the International not rejected an application for admission submitted that October 1871 by the successor of the Geneva Alliance section, the new Section for Revolutionary Socialist Propaganda and Action. With that last door closed, Bakunin's Jura followers had little choice but to counterattack with their own "declaration of war."[33] On November twelfth the Jura dissidents held a Congress of their own at Sonvillier to defend what they claimed to be the original principles of the International, as it was first founded in 1864, and to accuse Marx's London Council of betraying those principles. The policies of the General Council were destroying the International, the "protestants" charged, changing it from an association of independent working-class movements into an authoritarian, centrally dominated, hierarchically structured organization completely controlled by a General Council dictatorship. Instead of dictating party orthodoxy as it had taken upon itself to do, the proper function of the Council, they said, was to act as a bureau of correspondence and a center for the collection of information concerning working-class movements in different countries. Besides demonstrating yet again that power corrupts no matter who held it, Guillaume declared in a *Circular* to all International sections, the errors of the General Council proved how wrong it was to make the conquest of political power by the working class the principal aim of the International.[34] Marx and the General Council had pushed too hard. The wedge that Marx had hoped, apparently, would chip Bakunin and his followers off the International and rid the London Council of a marginal nuisance was now set instead right at the center of the International itself, and over the next year, down to and after the Hague Congress of 1872, it was to cut deeper and deeper until it became a major factor in splitting the International in two.

However much he was affected by these controversies in the fall of 1871, Bakunin himself had little to do with them. Throughout these months, he devoted himself to his campaign against Mazzini and to the Italian involvements into which it had drawn him, that is whenever he could pull himself out from under several particularly burdensome domestic troubles that oppressed him at the time. Besides his crushing financial woes, Antonia had suffered a breakdown due to the death of her last remaining brother and her worries over the fate of her family in Siberia. Bakunin did not even learn about the London Conference resolutions until a month after they had been decided, nor did he take any part in preparing the Sonvillier Congress.[35] A letter to Ogarev in mid-November is especially important in this regard, reviewing despondently as it does the various domestic difficulties that Bakunin faced and discussing his continuing conflict with the Mazzini party but saying nothing at all about the London Conference or Sonvillier.[36]

It was, at the time, in Mazzini more than in Marx that Bakunin saw the embodiment of everything he detested—religious faith, national glory, the state, parliamentary government, and class reconciliation. His successive articles and letters against Mazzini written that fall and winter (1871–72) seem, however, relatively mild, even academic. To be sure, he expressed deep feeling when he described repeatedly the plight of the oppressed workers and the self-sacrifice of the International in its unremitting struggle for their liberation. But, for the most part, there is something rather detached and didactic about the way he developed, for pages on end, the commonplace positivism and naturalism of the period, proving that mind is matter and that man is a part of nature with nothing divine about him, tracing the course of man's anthropological progress, reviewing the advance of society from primitive hunters to the modern state, outlining basic human motivations, or, especially, his *bête noire* now, debunking all religion

beast black

and enumerating its many crimes. As he does in so much of his work during these last years, he seems to have become in his Mazzini articles the academic professor he once told his father he intended to be.

Except for some interesting new thoughts about a downtrodden Asia waiting to pounce on a depraved and divided bourgeois Europe, the social and political ideas he argued are neither novel in general nor new for him. For the most part, they are well developed in other, earlier works. It was his obsession to repeat over and over again the same truths so that all should know and be free: to prove and prove once more that all power corrupts, that all states oppress, that the state and church are forever allied, that both must everywhere and always defend the interests of the privileged class and help them exploit and stifle the people, that Satan is the divine rebel and Jehovah the demonic tyrant (a theme particularly emphasized in these tracts against Mazzini), that idealism, religion, and nationalism are the favored weapons of all class oppressors, and that the people will be free only when they liberate themselves from such false notions, join together in the International, and, on the model of the glorious Commune (which gave "the signal for future deliverance") arise in universal social revolution to overthrow all oppressive systems and create on their ruins—freely, spontaneously, cooperatively, from the bottom upwards—the new world of absolute freedom and harmonious, federated solidarity.[37]

It was not until the end of the year (1871) that Bakunin turned his attention again to his conflict with the London Council. He had received, at the end of November, a copy of Guillaume's Sonvillier *Circular* and wrote Guillaume enthusiastically that he would set to work at once distributing it throughout Italy as broadly as possible, inundating Italy with it, as he said to his "intimate" Zhukovsky soon afterwards.[38] A little later, he read another circular with an entirely different message, one that Engels had sent to Italy on December sixth openly hostile to him and his program.[39] His situation had now become quite "complicated," he wrote the editors of a socialist journal: until now he had had "to fight only one enemy" of the International, Mazzini. Now, he must defend the International against "two Popes," Mazzini and Marx.[40]

From a letter Bakunin sent to an Italian supporter, Celso Ceretti, we can see how well the Sonvillier *Circular* met his own needs in his conflict with London. Referring explicitly to the demands of the *Circular*, he wrote Ceretti that the Council must at once return to its original role as a "simple *bureau of statistics and correspondence*." There is no place for any "orthodoxy" in the International, he went on, since it was meant to be and must remain a free federation of autonomous national members whose opinions are absolutely their own. Otherwise, the International would be no different than the "Church of Mazzini." Moreover, if not even a regular Congress of the International had the prerogative to pass resolutions limiting the rights of the autonomous members, certainly the irregular, secret, and totally unrepresentative September London Conference had no such prerogative. Therefore, he concluded, all sections of the International should join in this rejection of the London Conference, *"publicly announce their adherence to the protest of the Sonvillier Congress, and insist on an immediate convocation of a general Congress."* Not only was justice on their side, he concluded, but the votes as well, for "you will undoubtedly be pleased to learn that all of socialist and revolutionary France is with us, that the Spanish have unanimously sided with us, that the Belgians lean in our direction, that the sections in Turin, Milan, and Naples have already announced their support. The Latin world is in the process of federating, organizing, and rising up in the name of liberty, against the dictatorship of the London pan-Germanists."[41]

Later that month he composed two long attacks on Marx, the first of a series of such compositions, some published, some not, that were to follow throughout the coming year (1872), the year of the decisive Hague Congress. A brief review of these two works, *A Letter to the Bologne Members of the International* and *My Personal Relationship with Marx*, will give us some idea of the substance and character of Bakunin's arguments in this momentous confrontation. The basic charge in his case against Marx was the one already argued in the Sonvillier *Circular*, that the General Council in London, under Marx's direction, had gradually expanded its functions from those of a correspondence and information bureau into those of a dominant ruling body, a virtual dictatorship. Making frequent comparisons between Marx and Mazzini, Bakunin claimed that in both cases the root of the evil was a desire for personal power, "the need to govern, educate, and organize the masses according to their [Mazzini's and Marx's] particular ideas," "religious in one case, scientific and doctrinaire in the other,"[42] in one case with faith in Italy, in the other with faith in Germany, but in neither with any faith at all in the people.

Marx's authoritarian ascent, he argued, had been gradual, advancing slowly after the first Congress of 1866, more swiftly after his setback on the inheritance issue at the Basle Congress of 1868, then reaching its high point at the illegal London Conference of 1871. The implications of this rise to power extended far beyond Marx's own career, for his domination meant the domination by the German members of the International over the Latin and Slavic members, with the English and Americans wavering in between. However, he went on, this was not really the fault of the Germans, but rather that of a particular segment of the German intelligentsia—the Jews, since Marx was represented among German and Austrian workers "by his disciple, a Jew like himself, Liebknecht, and by many other fanatical partisans, for the most part also Jews."[43]

> The Jews constitute a real power in Germany today. A Jew himself, Marx has around him—as much in London as in France and in many

other countries, particularly Germany—a throng of little Jews, more or less intelligent and educated, living mainly off their intelligence and acting as middlemen for his ideas. Retaining a monopoly on high policy (I was going to say high intrigue) for himself, he gladly leaves to them the petty, dirty, squalid work, and one must admit that in this respect, always obedient to his prompting and direction, they do a lot for him: restless, nervous, inquisitive, indiscrete, garrulous, turbulent, intriguing, exploitative, as Jews are everywhere, business agents, writers, politicians, journalists, in a word, literary courtiers, and at the same time financial courtiers, they have taken over entirely the German press, from the most extreme monarchic journals to the most extreme radical and socialist journals, and for a long time have reigned supreme in the world of money, of high financial and commercial speculations. Having already a foot in the bank, they have been gaining in recent years a foothold in socialism.... And so, the whole Jewish world, forming a single sect of exploiters, a kind of human leach, a collective, devouring parasite, organized not only across state frontiers, but even across all political divisions, this world is in fact, for the most part at least, at the disposal of Marx, on one side, and Rothschild, on the other.... What can there be in common between socialism and high finance? Well, it is the fact that authoritarian socialism, Marx's communism, wants central power for the state, and wherever there is state centralization, there must necessarily be a state central bank, and where there exists such a bank, the Jews are always sure not to die of cold or hunger.[44]

Citing Austria as an example of the Jewish threat, he recalled that in 1868 there had existed among the Austrian proletariat a "magnificent spontaneous movement," but that soon afterwards, "propagandists and agitators, mainly Jews, of the Social-Democratic Party (recently formed in the north of Germany under Marx's inspiration) began to win to their side the Austrian Jews, and together they undertook to attract, sermonize, and lead astray the German workers of Austria." To illustrate further the tactics of these "Jewish 'writers', especially skilled in the art of cowardly, odious, treacherous insinuation," Bakunin recounted his own experiences with Marx's "calumny and intrigue. No one could make better use of them than Marx, since, to begin with, he is a genius at it and, besides, he has at his disposal an army of Jews who are veritable heroes in this kind of war," such as "the German Jew Hess," "Liebknecht, another friend and disciple of Marx and a Jew like himself," "a third Jew, Borkheim, another servitor of Marx," and of course, Utin, "a little Russian Jew, a fool but tricky, shameless, brazen, and a liar and intriguer to the marrow of his bones."[45]

Such was the army supporting the "dictator-messiah Marx." But, Bakunin argued at length, it was hardly against the Bakuninists alone that Marx was mobilizing this army: Marx's aims had to be seen in conjunction with the victories of Prussian absolutism in Europe and Bismarck's plans to subordinate all Europe "to the domination of the German race." "It is this plan to destroy liberty, a plan that has posed a mortal danger to the Latin race and the Slavic race, that is now trying to win absolute control of the International. Against this monstrous claim of pan-Germanism, we must oppose with an alliance of the Latin and Slavic races...."[46]

By the turn of the year (1871-1872), Marx and Mazzini had become almost interchangeable for Bakunin as embodiments of the dual evil, church and state domination. Mazzini's theologism, he said, was obvious enough, as was his exultant nationalism. But Marx, too, by trying to impose "perfect theoretical solidarity in all sections of the international," turning the General Council into his own "collective papacy," and issuing decrees *ex cathedra* as he had done in the London Conference, was acting like the head of a church no less than was Mazzini.[47] Since one reason for Mazzini's attack on the International, the main one according to Bakunin,[48] was the fact that the International cut across national lines and undermined national identity and rights, Bakunin was in a rather awkward position in opposing Mazzini, since Bakunin, too, was now demanding the autonomous rights of the workers' national organizations against the centralist claims of the London Council. This difficulty aside, Bakunin seemed boldly optimistic about the outcome of his conflict with Marx. Since Sonvillier, the confrontation had been steadily moving in favor of "us, the anarchists." The Spanish and Belgians had already spoken in support of the Jura declarations, and in letters to his friends in Italy Bakunin urged them to begin a broad letter campaign to the Italian sections to get them to do likewise in preparation for the coming International Congress.[49]

The first weeks of February 1872 Bakunin was ill and unable to work. What he thought about those weeks we cannot say, but whatever it was it seems to have caused a shift in the emphasis of his writing away from Italy and Mazzini and further back towards the Slavic-Germanic confrontation that had occupied so much of his attention, first in the late 1840s and, then, in the years immediately after his escape from Siberia. We see this, for example, in a long work written for his Jura followers. Beginning the work with another outburst against the "little Russian Jew" Utin and the "dirty conspiracy of German and Russian Jews against me,"[50] he went on with page after page of this strident anti-Semitism, even more virulent than what we saw in his publications the previous December, which already had shown considerable flair in this genre. Since they adored a "murdering God, the most barbarous and at the same time most personally vain of all Gods known on earth," and followed a leader, Moses, "who ordered whole peoples massacred in order to establish his own power," it was "fortunate indeed for other nations that the power of the Jewish people did not equal their cruelty." Their power was still immense, however, since the Jews formed a commercial network throughout the world and, through their control of trade and usury, dominated the simple folk, those on whom "Jewish exploitation exerted its most pitiless depredations," those who were "literally devoured by the Jews." "As a result, in all these countries the people detest the Jews. They detest them to such a degree that all revolutions are accompanied by a massacre of Jews: a natural consequence, but one hardly likely to make of Jews partisans of popular and social revolution." The Jews were, instead, "unrestrained partisans of civilization" and of the state and felt "horror at the thought of the unleashing of the popular masses...." "The Jew is, therefore, authoritarian by position, by tradition, and by nature. This is a general law and knows only few exceptions, and even these exceptions, when closely examined, confirm the rule. Revolt, the source of every liberty, is alien to the character of this people. They have once and for all stigmatized and damned it in the figure of Satan."

True, "the Jewish people have never lacked high intelligence." They were "one of the most intelligent races on earth" and could boast of such great minds as Jesus, Paul, Spinoza, Mendelssohn, Lessing, Heine, the Rothschilds, and, among others, "the eminent socialist writer, the principal force behind the International Workers' Association, Karl Marx." But, along side these "great minds, there are always the small fry [*le menu fretin*], an innumerable crowd of little Jews, bankers, usurers, industrialists, businessmen, professional writers, journalists, politicians, socialists and speculators." These were the ones who had "turned German journalism into a pit of slime" with their "cowardly and treacherous insinuations, foul lies, and stupid, dirty slander." "People say of them that they eat only excrement, like certain insects that run through the streets...."[51]

From the Jews, Bakunin then moved on to the Germans. In a long and detailed survey of German weakness, greed, materialism, and slavish submissiveness, etc. he both damns the Germans and honors their rivals, the Slavs and, almost incidentally now, the Latins. Recalling repeatedly and angrily how German-Jewish social democrats, like Borkheim and Marx, had warned Europe of barbarism and brutality coming out of the East, Bakunin threw the charge right back at them. It was the Germans who were the real brutes, obsequiously submissive to their own bureaucracies, while ruthlessly oppressive in their rule over other peoples, particularly the Slavs. It was the entirely warranted hatred felt by East European Slavs against the Germans that had led the Slavs to place their hopes on Russia, thereby providing a rich soil for pan-Slavism. "And do you consider it illegitimate or bad, after all, that the Slavs look to Russian dominion for their liberation from the yoke of the Germans they abhor? But the Russian Tsar is a terrible despot! Without doubt. I would only like to know, however, if the Emperor William is any better? But the Germans are uniting for the good of universal civilization! Well, the Slavs are uniting in order to repel this civilization which they find detestable." Take the state, for instance: unlike the Germans, "the Slavs have never been a conquering race," and "no Slavic state in history was actually founded by Slavic peoples." "The Slavic peoples are peaceful, agrarian and socialist by nature and have never established States." As for Russian despotism and brutality, "from the point of view of brutality, insolence, and cruelty, I frankly think that the laurels go to the Germans who exceeded, I say, everything that the Russians have done in Poland...." Moreover, Russia could hardly be the threat to Europe that Marx and his followers claimed, since it lacked the wealth, organization, and science necessary for that.[52]

Throughout, Bakunin again made Marx and Bismarck partners in a shared adoration of the state. As always, it is the state as such that is the ultimate culprit. It was not in Russian Tsardom that the real evil and the danger lay, but in the state itself. Russia under a constitution would be no better, and if the Germans outdid the Russians in brutality, the French republicans of Versailles surpassed them both. Herein lay the essential difference between Marx and himself, he said, between the "Hebraic-Germanic" wing of the International and the federalists or anarchists, the Slavic-Latin (and Jura Swiss) wing. The Marxists wanted only to change the state, turn it into a people's state, while the anarchists wanted "the abolition of the State, of all States," "the universal ruin of the political world." "Are we right, yes or no, to repel the political world with disgust and disdain?"[53]

While a variety of other familiar themes were touched on in the article, it was the conflict between German and Slav, or, in its extended form, between the "Hebraic-Germanic" force and the Slavic-Latin force that we mainly see unfolded before us. This great Gog-Magog struggle now occupied the central place in Bakunin's world view, supplanting in importance to him even the universal liberation of the "people," and he was to return to it repeatedly in these last years of his political life. Most immediately, we see it again in another manuscript written at the time (March, 1872) on *Germany and State Communism*, in which he again challenged the claim that "henceforth only the Germanic race, including in it the Anglo-Saxons of England and America as well as those of Holland and Scandinavia, had the capacity to exist, the energy to expand and develop, and, consequently, would henceforth remain as the only legitimate representative of humanity."[54] It was by such arguments, he said, that the Germans had justified their domination, and it was as a result of such claims that "the entire history of Germany is really a struggle against the Slavic race.... But it is not only the Slavic race, for the Latin race is equally condemned in the minds of the Germans." They are condemned for different reasons, however: while the German hates and fears the Slavs because he sees in them "absolute barbarism, anarchy" and therefore opposes them with "the hatred of the old for those younger, with an instinctual fear that the Slavs may be summoned later to eliminate and replace them," the German has respect for Latins as "more civilized, more refined, and older than themselves." From this perspective, in other words, "in the progressive advance of history, the Latin race represents the aristocracy, the Slavic race, the masses, the rabble, and the German race, the bourgeoisie."[55]

Two great forces thus stood poised "for a terrible, mortal struggle."[56] On the one side, under the banner of the tyrannous and murderous God of the Jews, was all that was evil—state, church, property, domination, exploitation, "civilization," compromise, and the bourgeoisie. On the other side, inspired by the archtypical rebel and freedom fighter Satan, was all that was good—anarchism, absolute freedom, the "evil passions," the "devil in the flesh," the masses and their pure but violent instincts, and classless, communal, federated solidarity. Germany, England, Holland, Scandinavia, American and, especially, the Jewish members of these bourgeois nations versus the Slavic and Latin "races," allied with the "masses, the rabble" of the civilized nations (once the "devil in the flesh" within them had been "unleashed") and reenforced by the distant threat of the still fiercer world of Asia.

In the months that followed, Bakunin fused into a single epic struggle the approaching conflict with Marx in the International and this apocalyptic war of the "races." Whereas in his February-March 1872 letter to the Jura sections he felt the need to apologize for his long discussion of the racial conflict (explaining it by the fact that he had been "attacked by Jewish and German slanderers who had insulted him as a Russian and as a Slav"),[57] in a letter to a Spanish follower, Anselmo Lorenzo, sent in May 1872, he argued that the two struggles were inextricably joined, that "the debate that divides us today within the International is only a reproduction of the great historical question posed by current events."

> To whom does the future belong? To the principle of domination and the great states, represented essentially, historically by the conquering race, the violent and, therefore, authoritarian civilizers, the Germans... or to the principle, represented by Latins and Slavs, of revolutionary socialism and the spontaneous organization of popular liberty through the abolition of all the political and juridical institutions of the state and the federation of autonomous communes and associations?[58]

This return to Slavic concerns, becoming more and more marked as the next round with Marx drew nearer, was not limited only to abstract racial and global apocalyptic visions. In mid-March 1872, one Vladimir Holstein, a Russian medical student studying in Zürich, visited Bakunin in Locarno and several days after his arrival invited two other young activists to join them, Alexander Elsnitz and Zemfiri C. Arbore, usually known by his pseudonym, Ralli. All three had paid heavily in Russia for their political activism, the first two with expulsion from the University of Moscow and the third, Ralli, with two years in prison. The three remained in Locarno until April fourth and while there established with Bakunin yet another secret organization, a Russian Brotherhood. Upon their return to Zürich, a fifth member was added—Michael Sazhin, known as Armand Ross. Now 27, Ross has been an "intimate" since 1870, when he returned to Europe from a stay in America, his refuge after escaping a sentence of Siberian exile two years before. Ross was not at all pleased with the prospect of sharing Bakunin's friendship with three other young men like himself, especially since, he said, "all three had told me many times, and their conduct confirms this, that they are only interested in medicine."[59] The ground was thus laid at the outset for the first of a series of long, bitter, and essentially trivial quarrels that were to exhaust and demean Bakunin's final years.

Discord among his young Zürich followers was apparent from the start. When, for example, Bakunin urged that the new brotherhood support a recently formed Polish organization, the three newcomers were for it, while Ross opposed.[60] A letter Bakunin sent Ralli in May 1872 concerning this affiliation shows how quickly and deeply Bakunin had found his way into the maelstrom of competing Slavic factions that had made life in Zürich so exhilarating for its large Slavic student colony. Writing in a new number code he devised for these communications with Zürich, Bakunin approved of Ralli's decision to join the Polish Society (since it would help "our National Committee of the Alliance of Social Democracy and our International Brotherhood"), urged him to use his participation to work against Marxist influence within the organization, argued against Ralli's dislike of his Jura friends, and much more.[61]

Not content with having his followers join the Polish Society, Bakunin undertook the next month to draft a charter of aims for the group, in the form of an article written in the name of "we, the poor Polish workers." In it, he praised the past glories of the independent and courageous Polish nobility, called for a free democratic Poland, to be achieved exclusively by means of social revolution, summoned everyone to rise everywhere against the state and to form, spontaneously, a new, voluntary, bottom-upwards universal federation that would know no national boundaries.[62]

At the end of June 1872 Antonia and her children left Locarno for Siberia, to visit her parents and perhaps bring them back with her. Bakunin accompanied her as far as Basle. "Separation. For how long? For a year? Forever?" he noted in his diary.[63] Instead of returning to Locarno, he went on to Zürich and its

Russian community and remained there until mid-October, throughout, that is, the decisive Hague Congress that September. Three days after his arrival in Zürich, still another organization, a "Slavic Section" of the International, was established, with 15 or 20 members, mainly Russians, a few Serbs, a Croat, and a Czech, but no Poles, notwithstanding the fact that Bakunin had just the month before written the "Polish Program."[64] (Near the end of his stay in Zürich, he provided the Serbs as well with their "program" at a secret meeting of the Serbs that he attended. Some weeks after the meeting, one of the delegates wrote, "I know I was wrong in not resolutely opposing Bakunin and not telling him that he should keep out of Serbian affairs since he doesn't understand a thing about them.")[65]

The revival of the eastern connection did not mean that Bakunin was entirely abandoning his association with the International. The part he was taking among the various Slavic organizations in Zürich at least appeared to be that of a leading member of the International, as one can readily see, for example, from the references to it (and to the Alliance as well) in discussing the "Polish program." While much of his correspondence with his "intimates" in Europe during these months has been lost or destroyed,[66] enough remains to suggest an outline of his activities with respect to the International at the time, the period leading up to the Hague Congress. In a letter to F. Mora, sent in early April 1872, we see Bakunin stating again the principal points of the Sonvillier resolutions and Guillaume's *Circular*, opposing "dictatorship, government, authority" (since "human nature is such that any domination becomes exploitation") and, therefore, opposing the London Council.[67] That letter also shows that his "dissolved" Alliance was still very much alive: "You know, of course, that in Italy recently the International and our cherished Alliance have gained very much ground."[68] In the letter he sent to Lorenzo (in which he had forthrightly set forth his vision of a universal "racial" confrontation), there is a similar reference to the Alliance: "I ask only that you do not mention a word about the Alliance in your reply, because the Alliance is a secret that none of us can divulge without committing treason."[69]

With prospects of a "great battle, a decisive battle" with the Marxists just ahead, he thus seemed to be activating his secret weapon, his network of "intimates" in Spain, Italy, the Jura (where he made three trips in July and August),[70] and, now, among the various Slavic émigrés in Zürich. For four weeks, beginning on May twentieth, two of his principal Italian "intimates," Cafiero and Fanelli, had been with him in Locarno, probably working out details of their strategy for the fall International Congress. It was their assumption at the time that the Congress would be held in Geneva, but while they were meeting among themselves in Locarno, the General Council was also meeting and, on June eleventh, chose instead the Hague, Holland as the Congress site.[71] The reason for the choice was clear to Bakunin: "it is to block the delegates from Italy, Spain, the South of France, and the Jura," because of the high costs of travel, and thereby assure a Marxist majority.[72] Their own strategy would be as follows, he went on in this letter of July sixteenth to Gambuzzi: the Jura Committee "will invite the friendly federations of Italy and Spain to join it in its protest and its request [to hold the Congress somewhere in Switzerland]. If after that London refuses, it will invite the Italians and the Spaniards to do what the Jura would then do, namely, send no delegates to this Congress, but rather send them to a Conference in Switzerland of dissident and free sections in order to declare and preserve their independence and to organize their intimate Federation, the Federation of autonomous sections and federations *within the International*." The Spanish, he added, had already indicated their support and their willingness to "demand, as we have also done today, the abolition of the General Council."[73]

What is most interesting about Bakunin's approach to the coming conflict is not his radicalism, but rather his moderation, his reluctance to break with the International, to go any farther than demand "autonomy" "within the International." In his May letter to Lorenzo, he was already predicting that the Congress would result in a "horrible scandal," but that he would have an impressive minority of Spaniards, Italians, French, and Belgians behind him and that "this minority will save the liberty and even the existence of the International."[74] Later that month, on the twentieth, he similarly asked Ralli whether Guillaume had told a Jura Congress meeting earlier that month about "my proposals concerning the character and the limits of the International."[75]

Given this apparent unwillingness to break with the International and establish a competing organization, one can well appreciate his displeasure when the Italians, meeting at Rimini August fourth under the chairmanship of Cafiero, voted to abstain from any participation in the coming Hague Congress. While the other resolutions passed at Rimini no doubt greatly pleased him, vigorously opposing as they did the General Council, the London Conference, and the control over both by "the German Communist Party" with its "authoritarian communist doctrine,"[76] he was dismayed by the forthright conclusion of those resolutions: "we deplore" he said, the Rimini appeal to the antiauthoritarian sections of the International (i.e., those against Marx's London Council) to send their delegates on September 2, 1872, not to the Hague, but to Neuchâtel in Switzerland, in order to open there the general antiauthoritarian Congress.[77]

The tactics decided on by a Jura Congress meeting at Chaux-de-Fonds in mid-August were much more acceptable to him. Calling for the abolition of the General Council and for "the suppression of all authority in the International," the Jura declaration instructed its delegates to walk out of the Congress if their proposals for reorganizing the International were not accepted and expressed solidarity with other "antiauthoritarian" delegates from Spain, Italy, France, and elsewhere who protested "loudly and clearly" against the authoritarian tendencies in the International.[78] (The "loudly and clearly," according to Guillaume, belonged to Bakunin.)[79] Although Bakunin attended this Jura Congress, it is unclear just whom he represented. As Guillaume writes, there were several Russian and Serbian students, and "Bakunin, who was a delegate from some section I no longer recall, accompanied them."[80]

Bakunin, in short, wanted the rhetoric of the Rimini extremists but the practical prudence of the Jura. His final position on the eve of the Hague Congress is evident in a letter he wrote Gambuzzi on August thirty-first. Rejecting the Rimini decision and favoring the Jura tactic of withdrawal by the antiauthoritarian delegates "in the name of the autonomy and liberty of their respective federations," Bakunin went on to say that they should withdraw "while at the same time proclaiming, solemnly affirming, both their own individual solidarity and that of the federations *with the International*, with the proletariat of the whole world."[81] Even were withdrawal to become necessary, Bakunin continued, emphasizing the point, the antiauthoritarian delegates would gather at another Congress "in order to form there a closer alliance of the federations, *not outside of but within the International.*"

Why was Bakunin so reluctant to break with Marx's International and establish an "antiauthoritarian" International, as his Spanish and Italian disciples wanted to do? Why did he try to "save" the International, restrict himself to redefining its "character" and "limits," seek for no more than "autonomy," and insist repeatedly that whatever happens the solution must be found "not outside but within the International"? The answer, again, can be found in Bakunin's attitude toward public leadership, towards power visibly and responsibly managed. To campaign vigorously against Marx's authority was one thing; to practice power, to organize and direct an International, as Marx—the "father of the International"—did, was something else again, and something unthinkable for Bakunin. An "autonomous" status within the International was enough, for it provided him the dual benefits he had to have from any enterprise or situation— freedom to remain apart, without either responsibility or visible power, and the possibility, precisely because of this irresponsible and powerless detachment, to attack powerfully. All of that would be lost if Bakunin actually carried through the implications of his Alliance network and either won control of the International from Marx or established a new International of his own. (Moreover, and more essential, were he to supplant Marx, he would no longer be a "child" within the "mother" International, he would be a man in possession of that mother, always "the most dangerous and repulsive thing in the world."[83] The drama, ritualistically repeated in all situations, never changes.)

A further, if relatively incidental, indication of Bakunin's ambiguous conflict with Marx during these months preceding the decisive Hague Congress is Bakunin's remarkably mild reaction to the main blow the Marxists dealt him during these pre-Hague months, their publication of *The Alleged Schism in the International*. In it, the Marxists blamed him and his Alliance for virtually all the opposition and "intrigue" against the General Council, reviewed what the authors considered to be the machinations of Bakunin and his followers from 1868 (when Bakunin joined the International) to the Sonvillier *Circular* of 1871, and responded to his charges against the Council for alleged centralization. Throughout, the authors continued to do Bakunin the honor of making him the prime mover of specific events and more general political currents with which he had little or nothing to do. Unwilling to realize that the sources of opposition to the London Council were much deeper and more widespread than the deeds of one or another "intriguer," Marx and his aides thus helped Bakunin's fantasies achieve for him the very power that the Marxists erroneously thought he already possessed (but that he had, in fact, always been careful to avoid and was still avoiding by his Slavic preoccupations during these critically important pre-Hague months).

Although a serious and offensive challenge, especially threatening coming as it did just a few months before the Congress, and one that gave Bakunin a fine chance to reply, point for point, to all the charges that the Marxists had been levelling against him over the past four years, Bakunin responded only with a brief letter to the Jura *Bulletin*, calling the charges a "pile of excrement," noting the earlier occasions on which he had been "condemned by the furious synagogue" of "German Jews" and "the little Russian Jew," and vowing to appeal to a jury of honor at the coming Congress. He would not respond in detail now he said, because the charges did not deserve reply, and because he did not want to harm the International by making the quarrel public.[84]

Bakunin did not attend the Hague Congress, but Marx did, and he came well supplied with evidence against Bakunin that he had been collecting from various sources, including a letter he had just received from Liubavin concerning the broken translation contract[85] and information Engels had gathered on the activities of the Alliance in Spain. Also, Marx and his supporters had been hard at work getting delegates sympathetic to their side. Nothing less than the "life or death of the International" was at stake, Marx wrote to his followers, urging them to do all they could to assure the attendance of loyal delegates.[86] Marx's strenuous preparations showed in the voting. His motion to grant the General Council power to suspend not only sections but also entire federations, under certain conditions and pending review at the next Congress, carried 36 to 6 with 15 abstentions.[87] This was a clear defeat of the "antiauthoritarians" attempt to stop and reverse the steady concentration of power in the General Council.

Bakunin and his faction fared no better on the next question, one that was of equal importance to them: electoral politics on the part of the working class and the formation of workers' parties. The resolution supporting participation in elections as well as in bourgeois representative bodies won over Guillaume's counter proposal by a similar margin, 35 to 6, with 8 abstentions.[88]

Major setbacks though these were for the Bakuninists, they did not go far enough for Marx. Assured from the outset of enough votes, the General Council had felt confident enough at the opening of the Congress "to recommend to the Congress at the Hague the exclusion from the International of members of the Alliance and to grant the Council the necessary powers to impede all conspiracies of this sort in the future."[89] In the closing hours of the Congress, a committee that had been formed to look into the accusations against the Alliance decided, four to one, that the evidence proved the earlier existence of a secret international Alliance that had functioned according to statutes and pursued a social and political program contrary to those of the International. However, the report went on, the evidence did not prove that such an organization was still functioning.[90] Finally, with reference to the Nechaev period, Bakunin was judged guilty of deception in obtaining control of the Bakhmetev fund and of intimidation in gaining his release from the *Capital* translation contract.[91]

On these grounds, a motion was formally made to expel Bakunin, Guillaume, and several others of like sympathies from the International. At this point, the Jura plan, or at least a part of it, was put into action: a statement signed by 13 delegates was read by one of the signatories, a Dutch delegate. Declaring themselves "partisans of autonomy" who sought "*to avoid any manner of schism* within the International Workers' Association," the faction announced that, henceforth, it would resist all efforts of the General Council to interfere in the affairs of the national federations, and it called upon all federations and sections to prepare to establish the principle of autonomy at the next Congress.[92] The Congress then proceeded to vote on the expulsion motions: to expel Bakunin, 27 to 7, with 8 abstentions; Guillaume, 25 to 9, with 9 abstentions. All other expulsion motions were voted down.[93]

As mentioned earlier, Bakunin did not attend the Congress. The reason, he claimed, was insufficient funds for the trip. Yet, the expenses of the Jura delegates, chosen at the Chaux-de-Fonds meeting of August eighteenth, which Bakunin attended, were paid by donations from the Jura Federation's sections, and it is reasonable to assume that he could have drawn from the same source had he chosen to go.[94] In any case, he did not and instead remained in Zürich, deeply involved in his now customary world of secret organizations. In fact, the very days, September second--fifth,[95] that the "antiauthoritarian" delegations were defending freedom and autonomy within the International, he was refining the details of what was perhaps his most rigidly authoritarian organization plan to date.

The charter for this latest, ultra-secret "International Brotherhood" opened with his usual apocalyptic call for "universal revolution," "the destruction of all religious, political, juridical, economic and social institutions that make up the present bourgeois order," and "the creation of a free humane world founded on the labor, equality, and solidarity of all human beings." To establish this "new order," "we invoke anarchy." Similarly: "since we have complete confidence in the instincts of the popular masses, our revolutionary means are the *organized unleashing* of what are called the *evil passions*, and *the destruction* of what is called, in this same bourgeois language, *the public order*," the "complete liquidation of the state" and with it all debts, taxes, and inheritance, all state agencies like the bureaucracy, army, judiciary, police, clergy, and universities, all monopolies, privileges, and properties legitimized by the state, all titles and documents concerning rents, properties, loans, births, and marriage.[96]

Although all this could be achieved only by a people's social revolution, there still had to be (as in all of Bakunin's "anarchist" plans) a revolutionary organization to carry out the "organized unleashing" of the people's "evil passions." In addition, there had to be some central directing body over these organizations "to activate, stimulate and direct them, and to make sure that they never degenerated or transformed themselves into governments, even if only provisionally." There was only one way to block the establishment of a "revolutionary dictatorship or provisional government," and that was to organize beforehand "a force, a collective, invisible organization" that, while keeping others from dominating, would itself, of course, "abstain from any governmental or official action or interference and would thereby exercise an all the more effective and powerful influence on the spontaneous movement of the popular masses, as well as on the actions and on all the revolutionary measures of their delegates and their committees." Such supervision and guardianship was to be the purpose of the new secret International Brotherhood, code name "Y." Below it, the organization would be arranged hierarchically, with international, national, and regional levels.

All levels (as always in these schemes) would have "absolutely the same program, the same policy, the same revolutionary tactics, and the same mode of recruitment."[97] Besides the customary leadership qualifications, "such as a real revolutionary passion, steadfastness, persistence, discretion, prudence, energy, intelligence, courage," the Brothers would have to be above personal ambition, vanity, narrow family or national interests and be able "to drown their own personal initiative in the collective action." Each Brother must consider the program, policies, and tactics of the Brotherhood as "his life, his dominant passion, his conscience and instinct." The Brothers must also be both "thoughtful and fervent, as cold as possible on the outside, but so ardent inside that no alien seduction can ever prevail over them...." "Whoever enters the International Brotherhood vows himself irrevocably, body and soul, thought, will, passion and action, with all his capacities, his energy, and his fortune to the service of the social revolution." "The supreme law of our Brotherhood, the whole secret of our power, is the dissolution of all our individual initiative into the collective thought, will and action.... Each Brother is on a permanent mission. Each day, from morning to night, his thought and his dominant passion, his supreme duty must be to propagate the principles of the Alliance, its extension and the growth of its power."[98]

Supreme power in this martial Alliance would reside in an Assembly, a "Constituante," and "since there would not be different parties in the Brotherhood and since the play of ambitions and personal vanities would be impossible in it, one could hope that most of the resolutions of the Constituante would be accepted unanimously." The Constituante would in turn establish a Central Bureau, which would supervise the activities of the lower level organizations. All resolutions passed by the Constituante "would be *absolutely* obligatory for all the national Councils, which would have to carry them out at all costs in their respective countries under the constant supervision of the central Bureau, which would not only have the right but the duty to call them [the national Councils] back when necessary to the strict and active observance of this plan." Each national Council would establish its own national Bureau, which "must direct the entire national organization of the country." Each national Bureau would be made up, as far as possible, of the International Brothers living in that country, those who, in all likelihood, had also been the founders of the national organizations. Finally, to leave no doubt as to the chain of command—from top downwards—the central Bureau communicates with the national Councils by means of the International Brothers belonging to them," and they in turn, as we have seen, "direct the entire national organization of the country": "The national, regional, district and local brotherhoods form, all together, the national organization of the country, at the head of which is the national Bureau."[99]

As unqualified freedom and self-determination remain the essence, indeed the entire substance, of all Bakunin's *public* goals, those his followers were at the time vigorously defending at the Hague, so do rigid discipline and absolute domination remain the basic characteristics of all his secret programs and organizational designs. He insisted repeatedly here as he had so often before that the revolutionary must "drown" himself in the collective, "renounce the harmful or sterile pleasures of isolated individual action,"[100] carry out all orders without even asking the reasons for them, and in all ways submit himself totally to the "secret," "occult," "invisible" organization, even accepting his own death sentence at the hands of the organization, if condemned as a traitor, as someone, that is, who dared "to give his hand to another revolution." That would be unforgivable. Any dealings, in fact, with other parties were strictly forbidden. The Brotherhood "will never permit any person belonging to different parties to penetrate into its *sanctum sanctorum*, nor exercise the least influence on the popular masses: any other aim, any other direction than its own could only mislead, deceive and corrupt the masses."[101] It was quite all right to make use of these outsiders: "exploit them whenever we can do so without danger... but never allow them into our intimacy" [*intimité*, changed in the manuscript from *sanctuaire*].[102]

How long would the secret, invisible, collective dictatorship go on protecting the revolution from dictatorship? "As long as there existed anywhere on earth a single inequality, oppression, exploiter, guardian, *master*." Having won a foothold in one country, the victorious organization, he predicted and decreed, would be duty-bound to help the revolutionary cause in neighboring lands, and so it would continue until the revolution was truly universal.[103]

It was ironic indeed that just at the time Bakunin was working out this latest, and last, version of his perennial secret, authoritarian network, a committee at the Hague was reaching the conclusion that evidence for the present existence of such an organization was lacking. Yet, was the committee really wrong in doubting the present "existence" of the Alliance? Did it actually exist outside of Bakunin's head and notebooks at the time? Probably not. It would be going too far, however, to say that it had never existed as an effective association. It had been real enough in Lyon, when Bakunin's correspondence with Richard and other "intimates" from afar and his later direction of their strategy on the scene certainly was effective, however misguided and disastrous. The Alliance was also distinctly influential in the Jura, Italy, and Spain, where the "intimates" actively and very successfully helped recruit members into the International who were sympathetic to Bakunin's position. And, finally, as a result of that recruitment and representation, the Alliance certainly showed its life and strength in the International's deliberations and voting.

On the other hand, it is equally clear that none of this ever approached a genuine "organization," much less the tightly-disciplined party planned in these obsessively successive authoritarian programs. At most the Alliance represented a secret committee of correspondents, with Bakunin determining the themes and direction of the irregular communications among the participants. No doubt the younger activists boundlessly admired Bakunin and adopted his ideas. For the most part, however, they went their own ways as local or national revolutionaries, and if they took Bakunin's side in the quarrel with Marx, it was mainly because the local background and the conditions of their own revolutionary struggle—in the Jura, Spain, Italy, and southern France—predisposed them to similar sentiments and aims. They used him, in fact, as he used them: They were materials for his fantasy; he, for theirs. Each echoed, reenforced and justified the other. The young militants in Spain, Italy, and the Jura were with good reason delighted by this support from the celebrated revolutionary hero and eagerly welcomed his theories and slogans for the confirmation, strength, and hope they gave; Bakunin, in turn, needed and appreciated their applause for his performance and the spurious "reality" that it lent his act.

This is what Marx and his followers failed to grasp when they blamed Bakunin's Alliance for events, trends, and Congress votes that mainly reflected the local situations and traditions of the opposition delegations. Bakunin was hardly more to blame for the shift to the left against Marx among some delegations (especially following the Paris Commune) that he was for the shift to the right among others, those, for example, from England and Germany. The International died at the Hague, notwithstanding Marx's formal, ballot "victory" over Bakunin, not, primarily, because of the decision to move its center to the United States, but because the different national federations had derived all they could from it and now saw more to be gained from concentrating independently on their own national struggles.[104] As for Bakunin's intentions as he worked out the fine points of his new militant "brotherhood" during the Hague Congress, they were still what they had been since he first began seriously constructing these model dictatorships in Florence and Naples nearly ten years before (building on authoritarian ideas he had proposed as early as the 1840s and on authoritarian practice that goes back to the "holy commune"). The new secret society had nothing to do with the International other than provide Bakunin with both a disguise for concealing his withdrawal from the struggle against Marx and a new sanctuary for that withdrawal. It was still the organizational counterpart of the other side of his disguised retreat from practical politics, his renewed apocalyptic vision, now expressed in the imminent, universal, "racial" Slavic-Germanic confrontation that had especially engaged his fancy that year. In short, challenged to decisive public combat and threatened by the opportunity for genuine power, his strategy was still to withdraw, to conceal the withdrawal under a mask of martial, apocalyptic rhetoric and organizational discipline, and, finally, to hide the mask, to keep his "act" of power "invisible," "secret." (Keeping the power gesture "invisible" was especially important to him, as we will see by his response when he thought that several "intimates" had publicized the secret brotherhood.)

The many revealing images used throughout the program—the death sentence for the "traitor" who dared "give his hand" to another revolutionary movement, the prohibition against those of differing views entering "into our intimacy"— only make more evident what this *sanctum sanctorum* really was for him. It is understandable that he should use alternately the words 'intimacy" and "sanctuary" in referring to the Brotherhood, for these words very appropriately describe just what it meant to him—another "holy commune" serving the same purpose that the original and all its other successors had served, that of a monastic, familial refuge far away from the battle disguised to look like a powerful frontier fortress militantly engaged in the battle. His fascination with abstract, universal, non-existent, "racial" confrontations and with the organizational details for equally non-existent revolutionary parties (both of which only distracted him from preparation for the *real* controversies ahead), his reluctance to carry the conflict with Marx to a complete break and himself to triumphant leadership of a new, free, "antiauthoritarian" International, his decision to settle in Zürich in the months immediately preceding the Congress and to allow himself to get entangled in a web of futile intrigues among the sundry Slavic groups, his modest response to the insulting challenge thrown at him by the Marxists in their *Alleged Schism* publication—all were further steps along a trail of retreat, rather than the preparations for conflict that, on the surface, they might seem to be. In appearance it is all strength, power, courage, and boundless dedication—conspiratorial brotherhoods with codes and vows, death sentences for "traitors," martial discipline and self-sacrifice, and all in the service of a violently catastrophic Gog-Magog Armegeddon between his own Slavic-Latin union and the Marx-Bismarck, Hebraic-German menace. In reality, however, it was another phase in the withdrawal that had been underway, haltingly, since at least the Polish debacle of 1863 and the first settlement in Italy. During the months following the Hague Congress, that retreat became clearer than ever.

On September 8, 1872, a day before the Congress ended, Guillaume and several other delegates representing Spain and Italy (Farga-Pellicer, Alerini, and Cafiero) met to discuss ways of both preserving the unity of the International and strengthening ties among the Bakuninist minority, which now included the Belgians. As Guillaume recounts the sequence of events, the ideas set forth at this meeting were then worked out in Zürich, where "Bakunin, faithful to his formalistic tendencies, wanted to make the conditions precise by means of written statutes."[105] When on the eleventh the "intimates" (Cafiero, Schwitzguebel, Farga-Pellicer, Alerini, Marselau, and Morago) arrived from the Hague, they found the Italian contingent (Fanelli, Nabruzzi, and Malatesta) already in Zürich (except for Costa, who arrived on the twelfth). The resolutions decided on the thirteenth (with a "fraternal kiss and solemn handshake")[106] were the basis of further resolutions voted upon two days later at what could easily have been, had Bakunin so desired, the first Congress of a genuinely Bakuninist International—the International Congress of Saint-Imier.

On that day, September 15, 1872, two meetings were held with only an hour between them. The first, in the morning and afternoon, was a special Congress of the Jura. Bakunin was there as one of two representatives from Sonvillier, and Ralli (using the name Rulev) and Holstein participated as two of the three representatives of the Zürich Slavic section. In the evening, the more important International Congress met. Bakunin now joined the Italian delegation. There was no separate Slavic section. No single event testifies more to Bakunin's influence than does this first de facto Congress of the "antiauthoritarians." Beginning with a scornful swipe at the General Council by refusing to recognize the three Swiss representatives that the Council had chosen to represent it, "the antiauthoritarian Congress" proceeded to pass successive resolutions against the Council and its policies. The attack was directed squarely against "the authoritarian party of German communism," its attempt to "substitute the domination and the power of the leaders for the free development and the spontaneous and free organization of the proletariat," its willingness "to trample under foot all decency and all justice," its campaign of "intrigues, lies and the most infamous slander in an effort to besmirch all those who dare combat it," and its "artificially organized" majority, which had "cynically sacrificed, for the ambitions of this party and its leaders, all the principles of the International." It was not, of course, only this particular Council and majority that was accused of domination: *no* council had legislative powers and *no* majority had the right to impose its decisions on the minority, and since this tendency to dominate was an "inherent vice" in any such organization, the central Council itself had to be eliminated. Nor would this endanger the unity of the International, for its genuine unity was based not on central control or on a compliant majority, but "on the real identity of interests and aspirations of the proletariat of all countries, on the one hand, and, on the other, the spontaneous and absolutely free association of the federations and free sections of all countries."

If, to the Saint-Imier delegates, the desire for political power was the root of all evil within the International under Marx's aegis, it was no less the source for what they considered Marx's fundamentally misguided strategy against the class enemy outside the International. Although the resolution on "political action" began by defending the right of every "autonomous" federation and section to decide this issue themselves (in contrast, they stressed, to the Council's decision in favor of forming labor parties and participating in bourgeois politics), it went on to declare that, "Rejecting any compromise in achieving the social revolution, the proletariat of all lands must establish, apart from any kind of bourgeois politics, the solidarity of revolutionary action." Free, spontaneous, social revolution from below, by the efforts of the proletariat itself, was the only correct strategy. That did not mean, however—pointing to another error they attributed to the Marxists—that trade union actions were enough. Strikes were fine, of course, since they could help raise workers' consciousness and confidence. But they could never achieve the revolutionary goal. Only a thorough revolution could do that.

It would seem from all this that a radical break with the International and an exultant establishment of a new Bakuninist International was at last occurring. That is what the Italian delegates wanted. Instead of forming a new International, however, the majority settled for a "pact of friendship, solidarity, and mutual defense" among the "antiauthoritarians" that would assure continuing communications between them and provide support for any federation or section again attacked by a Congress majority or by the Council. The aim of the pact, the resolutions "proudly proclaimed," was neither to split the International nor even to control it, but to achieve the "great unity of the International."[107] In sum, the St. Imier resolutions represent together a clear expression of Bakunin's ambivalence and consequent strategy. Circumstances, including the impact of his own message and example, had handed him at St. Imier a splendid opportunity for genuine leadership of a movement that was made to order for him, that embodied in its programs and practices most of his views. But how could leadership be assumed by someone who could never psychologically tolerate genuine leadership, who abhorred the "inherent vice" in power? Even to acknowledge the London Council's "*fait accompli* without trying to tie us again to the Council," as one Saint-Imier delegate had advised, was apparently too audacious.

Having made all the right, powerfully militant proclamations, careful all the while to preserve his undefiled freedom, his chaste powerlessness, Bakunin could leave Saint-Imier with "conscience clean" and return to his retreat, where, as his devoted follower Armand Ross said about a later retreat, "he could occupy himself with revolutionary activities in complete tranquility."[108] By now, as we have seen, his well-disguised retreat had taken him back to apocalyptic Slavism and to his new "sanctuaries"—the *sanctum sanctorum* (the new secret International Brotherhood) and the secret Russian Brotherhood that he had earlier organized with Ralli and his friends.[109]

Through the following year (1873) the prominence and influence of the Saint-Imier "antiauthoritarians" grew continuously, fed by new support from various sections of the international labor movement. In effect, the split that Bakunin was unwilling to lead took place by itself, without him. "The antiauthoritarian movement is progressing well," according to an article in the

Brussels *L'Internationale*. "The news from various countries where the Association has the most members is excellent, and soon, no doubt, one will completely forget that there is in New York a General Council,[110] the heir to the one in London and to the political views of the men that composed it. In a while, when one has better evaluated the consequences of the Hague Congress, one will recognize that it accomplished at least one thing useful and salutary: a clear and precise division between, on one side, the politicians and authoritarians, and, on the other, the workers who want the social Revolution and want only that."[111]

One after another, national congresses met to support the Saint-Imier resolutions—Spain in December 1872 and again in January 1873, Belgium in December 1872, Italy in March 1873, the Jura (again) in April 1873.[112] To such an extent had the New York Council General lost support in Europe, that it was the Jura Federation, following its April 1873 Congress, that proposed "to all the federations of the International a general Congress of the International to meet on the first of September 1873 in a Swiss town."[113] Almost immediately thereafter, the New York Council also announced a Congress of the International for that same month to meet in Geneva, warning that "if those people from the Alliance try to take part, we'll just show them the door."[114] Neither of the Congresses were, in fact, very impressive. But whereas the "antiauthoritarian" Congress was attended by some two dozen delegates from England, Belgium, Holland, Spain, France, Italy, and the Jura, only a few Swiss and Germans showed up at the Congress called from New York. The General Council itself did not even bother to send delegates.

All in all, therefore, those identifying themselves with the "antiauthoritarians" did much better that year (1873) than did their Marxist opponents. But, little of this involved Bakunin himself. His only connection now with what was going on was to write two more articles against Marx, one as a chapter in his never-ending *Knouto-Germanic Empire*. Other than that, his interests after returning from Zürich to Locarno on October 11, 1872 were monopolized by futile Slavic intrigues and disputes,[115] which included along the way the final episode in the Nechaev epic. Nechaev had been captured in Zürich and, two weeks after Bakunin had himself left Zürich for Locarno, was extradited to Russia. "He will perish heroically, and this time will betray nothing and no one," Bakunin wrote Ogarev in early November, recalling once more that "here was a man of rare energy," but also urging Ogarev to help him fight the Hague accusations by stating publicly that he, Bakunin, was entirely innocent of any wrongdoing in the Bakhmetev affair. To make sure Ogarev got it right, Bakunin sent him a draft of the statement he wanted him to make.[116]

Besides continuing to suffer these remnants of the Nechaev fiasco, Bakunin was burdened as well that fall and winter (1872-73) by depressing developments in the other Slavic enterprise that was occupying so much of his time. Intermittently through 1872, Armand Ross, the young man who entered Bakunin's life after Nechaev dropped from favor, had been negotiating with Peter Lavrov, another prominent revolutionary émigré, the possibility of publishing a new journal. Bakunin considered Lavrov too sympathetic to the state but was willing to have his own supporters work with Lavrov if a coeditorship could be arranged. Although this at first seemed acceptable to Lavrov, he later insisted on exclusive editorship. With this, the "Bakuninists" and the "Lavrists" parted. The dispute between them was further exacerbated in early 1873 by a quarrel over managing a Russian library in Zürich that Ross had initiated. The conflict took shape as one between the founders of the library, who were Bakuninists, and the borrowers, who were mainly Lavrists and who demanded that they have an equal part in running the library. When their demand was rejected, the Lavrists left the library, kept the books they had borrowed, and with them started a library of their own! To do what he could to help settle the argument, which at one point led to blows, Bakunin went to Zürich, in April 1873, and he and Lavrov, whom he met there for the first and only time, tried unsuccessfully to calm their respective followers.[117]

At the same time, to continue this highly condensed account of Bakunin's Slavic woes that year, a particularly bitter controversy broke out among his own followers over the way Ross was directing a publishing enterprise that he had started at the end of 1872. The main purpose of the press was to publish information about and material by the International for readers back home in Russia. Publications were to begin with selections from Bakunin's earlier work, for which Bakunin was to prepare a special introduction and two new articles, one on the International in Belgium and another on his own Alliance. Just when they were ready to begin publishing, however, Ralli and his friends, Holstein and Elsnitz, turned on Ross and accused him of authoritarianism in his direction of the press. Ross, in turn, again accused Holstein and Elsnitz of inadequate dedication, because of their continuing refusal to abandon their medical studies and give themselves totally to the cause. Letters flew back and forth between Zürich and Locarno, with Bakunin favoring Ross, whom he had originally suggested as director of the press. In August, Ross simply closed the door and kept the key. With that, Ralli wrote Bakunin in mid-August telling him that he must once and for all choose between Ross and the others. "I neither can nor wish to separate from Ross," Bakunin replied. "I am too closely tied to him for that to be possible. During the three years and more that we have been united in friendship and action, he has given me too many proofs of his warm personal attachment and of his still more ardent and indefatigable attachment to the common cause for me even to consider a rupture with him. . . . You three, so it seems, are very seriously united in service to this cause. Ross and I will remain, as before, united in the same aim." Further letters were exchanged, with Bakunin hoping that personal relations between him and the three of them might continue. As we will see, however, other quarrels soon erupted that made that impossible and that led instead to a break that ended Bakunin's Russian Brotherhood.[118]

Thus, Bakunin's political activities that year (1872-1873) among his Slavic "intimates" had been as unsuccessful as the "antiauthoritarian" movement had been successful without him. His writing efforts were somewhat more productive, at least to the extent of striking two strong blows—from afar—against the Marxists; one, a letter to *La Liberté* on October 5, 1872, and the other, a section in the *Knouto-Germanic Empire* given the title "Écrit contre Marx." The letter to *La Liberté* begins and ends, significantly, with references to Marx's "triumph"[119] at the Hague Congress, even though Bakunin said elsewhere in the letter that most countries now favored the "antiauthoritarians" (not, he added, because of his own influence, but because the English and the French had turned against Marx).[120] Notwithstanding this predominance of the opposition, however, the "triumphant" Marx and his followers still represented an enormous danger, because this "new Moses" was out to establish a dictatorship, to realize "the dream of [Popes] Gregory VII, Boniface VIII, [and Emperors] Charles V and Napoleon."[121]

Besides denouncing Marx in the letter as a would-be dictator of the International, Bakunin also attacked him for his moderate policies, especially his emphasis on winning political power through bourgeois elections and parliamentary politics. This, Bakunin again insisted, was nothing but bourgeois socialism fundamentally misguided for a variety of reasons. First of all, the state would remain oppressive even if socialists ran it, and if controlled by the proletariat would probably exploit the peasantry as well. Second, a political change would not necessarily lead to the economic and social changes that the masses wanted, wanted so much, in fact, that they were ready to accept them from the hands of a despot. Finally, and to this Bakunin gave most of his attention in the letter, the political aims and means that Marx advocated were simply not available to most peoples. The temperament and the history of, say, England and the United States had, perhaps, made electoral politics a realistic path for them. But that was certainly not the case for the French and the Germans, for example. "Each race and each people" had its own temperament, character, background, and conditions. The Germans, for instance, lacked "the love of liberty, the instinct of revolt. They are the most resigned and the most obedient people in the world. On the other hand, Spain, Italy, and southern France, the South of Europe in general, could be counted on for just that instinct for social revolution. Marx was thus quite wrong [this is the new theme and insight in Bakunin's works at the time] in thinking that revolution would come first in the countries that were economically most advanced, the "civilized countries." It was rather "the millions of noncivilized, disinherited, wretched, and illiterate masses... who, almost completely virgin to all bourgeois civilization, bear within themselves, in their passions, in thier instincts, in their aspirations, in the deprivations and miseries of their collective situation all the germs of future socialism."[122]

Moreover, even were it possible "to raise the political consciousness" of those who are not now receptive to Marx's political program, it would not be desirable to do so. Not only because such political consciousness would only foster hateful illusions regarding the state and politics in general, but also because it would displace "sacred revolt":

> Revolt is an instinct of life. Even the worm rebels against the foot that would crush it, and one can say, in general, that the vital energy and the relative dignity of each animal is measured by the intensity of the instinct for revolt that it bears within itself. In the world of beasts as in the human world, there is no capacity or habit more degrading, stupid or cowardly than that of obedience and resignation. And so I claim that no people on earth have ever been so degraded that they have not rebelled, at least at the beginning of their history, against the yoke of their conquerors, their subjugators, their exploiters, against the yoke of the state.
>
> It must be admitted, however, that since the bloody battles of the middle ages, the yoke of the state has prevailed over all popular rebellions, and that, with the exception of Holland and Switzerland, it has been triumphant in all countries of Europe.... And the masses? Alas, one must admit that they have let themselves be profoundly demoralized, subjugated, if not to say castrated by the harmful effects of the civilization of the state.[123]

It was not by elections, working class parties, and the rest of Marx's "bourgeois socialism" that the masses could heal their "castration," but only by apocalyptic, "sacred revolt," the way that Bakunin had long ago discovered was the only way that he, too, might "be healed."

Important as it was, however, the two-camp division within the labor movement—between Marx's "bourgeois socialism" and Bakunin's "antiauthoritarians"—was now only a small part of the much larger confrontation Bakunin saw ahead. His main contention now, as he argued in the letter to *La Liberté*, was that Marx's dictatorial, statist tendencies represented within the International a wider and much more threatening danger to the world—pan-Germanism. Reviewing once more Germany's growing power in Europe, Bakunin again drew his grim portrait of German submissiveness, authoritarianism, materialism, and narrow-minded lack of all passions, other than a fondness for dead abstractions. Marx and Bismarck, whom Bakunin again repeatedly compared with each other in these two works, were two fronts of the same enemy attack. Giving more and more emphasis to a theme that had been intermittently present in his thought ever since he had first arrived in Prussia[124] (and that had become a leitmotif in his writings after the Lyon failure), Bakunin increasingly subordinated his quarrel with Marx to it.[125]

It was this same theme that dominated his last substantial work, *State and Anarchy*, which he wrote the following year (1873). To judge from the subtitle of the book, *The Conflict of the Two Parties in the International Workers' Association*, the focus was apparently to have been the dispute in the International between the Marxists and the "antiauthoritarians" or, as he called his party, the "anarchists." Notwithstanding the title, however, it was not that subject, but the German threat that principally concerned him throughout the work. With its victory in the Franco-Prussian War, Germany, he said, had become the undisputed master of European politics. No country could come near competing. France had been reduced to a third-rate power. Russia was deceiving itself if it thought it could compete, especially if it expected the support of the oppressed Slavs. German economic wealth, the character of the German people, the organization and dedication of the German army—particularly its superbly trained officers—made German power invincible.

Nor need Bismarck worry about a threat from within. German liberalism, the only serious opposition at the time to German monarchic domination, had played itself out in successive failures (to which Bakunin gave close attention in what is the longest section of the book, as he had given most attention to comparable "compromisers" in his first revolutionary tract 30 years earlier). As for the workers' movement, it had been crippled by bourgeois socialism, first under Lassalle, then under Marx, both of whom replaced authentic revolution with foolish hopes in elections and parliaments. There were only two alternative strategies, revolution and "legal propaganda towards a peaceful reform of the state. Lassalle, as a German, a scholar, and as a man of Jewish wealth and origin, recommends the second."[126] Although Bakunin did not discuss Marx and the "two parties" of the International until the end of the book, and only then to help demonstrate the weakness of internal opposition to the German state, he made here some of his most insightful and memorable charges against state socialism, arguing that even the "reddest republic," no matter how democratic, must necessarily dominate if it governs, and that a government of workers is really a government of "former" workers turned domineering bureaucrats.[127]

If no other great power dared to challenge Germany's imperial designs, and if there were no signs of revolution within Germany itself, then what could save freedom and humanity? The answer, the cure, was the same as it had always been: social revolution, a universal rising of the masses—"violent, chaotic, and pitiless....brutal, savage"[128]—against all forms of power. Italy and Spain were ready now. As for the Russian masses, they were always ready, because they long since had possessed two of the essential ingredients for social revolution—deprivation and despair. They only needed an ideal, an aim that would spark the upheaval, and even this they already had in germ form in their demand for the land and in their communal tradition. What the Russian revolutionaries must now do was to eliminate the barriers that kept the peasants from full awareness of these ideals and from acting upon them, such barriers as their patriarchal local peasant customs and their trust in the Tsar. Once the revolutionaries had shown the people the truth about those repressive forces—and that could be done immediately without the long period of preparation that the "Lavrists" were advocating—the people would arise.

That was the direction all peoples must follow if they truly sought freedom. No other way would do, neither the traditional nationalist movements, such as the Serbians and Bohemians were then attempting to build, nor, especially, the Marxists' bourgeois, state socialism. Fortunately, he noted, the Marxists were no longer the only leaders of the working class: ever since the days of the League of Peace and Freedom there had been an organization truly responsive to the needs of the people, the Alliance, and it had gained ground steadily in successive Congresses. Although Bakunin gave a few pages, in an appendix, to the tactics of revolution, he nowhere in *State and Anarchy* approached the detail or the enthusiasm with which he discussed the coming revolution in earlier works. Only a relatively small portion of the work was devoted to it, since most of the space was given to his review of the birth and progress of pan-Germanism and the weakness of its opponents. Moreover, even that limited analysis seems less the work of a revolutionary theorist than that of a detached global strategist, a professor of international relations, an elder statesman. On every possible occasion, however remote the subject was from what should have been his concern as a revolutionary, he wandered leisurely through the diplomatic and historical details. When, for example, he discussed Russia as a potential rival against pan-Germanism, he went on at great length to survey Russia's expansion eastward, then moved on to a survey of China, and so forth.

He had spent May to July 1873 on *State and Anarchy*. Afterwards, he seemed at a loss to know what to do next. No longer involved with the Swiss Saint-Imier "antiauthoritarians" nor with the Russian Brotherhood of Zürich, which, as we have seen, was crumbling under the Ralli-Ross conflict, he thought he might go to Spain. A revolution was underway there, and while he knew his health was bad and that he was, therefore, "unfit for adventurous expeditions," as he put it, he also "always felt and thought that the best end for me would be to fall in the midst of a great revolutionary upheaval."[129] However, his "intimate" Carlo Cafiero, who he had hoped would cover his expenses to Spain (and also "become the protector of my wife and children in case I should succumb in Spain") turned him down. The would-be benefactor, an Italian militant of 27, urged him not to go, since he considered him, in Bakunin's words, "a precious being, absolutely necessary to our circle of intimates."[130] Besides, Cafiero had another idea for his mentor's immediate future. With an inheritance he had recently received, Cafiero planned to purchase a house that would serve as a secret revolutionary meeting place. Both the intensification of the reaction in Italy at the time and the increasingly conspiratorial and violent policies of the Italian militants made it advisable to conceal themselves and their meetings behind "a peaceful and very materialistic bourgeois mask."[131] Bakunin, Cafiero suggested, could be that mask!

As Bakunin recalled the plan, "I would assume even more the character of a revolutionary who had grown sick and tired of revolution, who, because of this disgust, and having lost all illusions, had thrown himself passionately into the material concerns of family and property."[132] They found an estate just outside of Locarno that met their needs ideally. Partly hidden in the trees, up a steep slope that ran down to the road along the lake, Baronata, as the villa was called, had the appearance of "a little fort," as one visiting revolutionary described it.[133] Originally (and adding further to the multiple ironies of all this) it had been a monastery. As planned, Bakunin assumed title of the villa, explaining his sudden possession of enough money to buy Baronata by announcing that he had at last received his share of the Premukhino inheritance. He even kept the truth from Antonia, who was still away in Siberia, and let her go on for over a year believing that he was the real owner.

For a while after he moved in (August, 1873), Bakunin plunged enthusiastically into the secret revolutionary work for which Baronata had been purchased and was "completely absorbed in the creation of an arm cache and a hiding place, with secret tunnels through which one could escape if necessary."[134] Then, in early September, he went to Berne where he stayed the month with his friend Dr. Vogt. Besides a chance for pleasant reunions with his former friends and for consultations with Dr. Vogt about his health, he had gone to Berne, according to Guillaume, to find out "if the Swiss government would be willing to let him finish his days peacefully in Locarno, in return for a public assurance that he would henceforth take no part in any revolutionary agitation."[135]

Was this the bourgeois "mask" Bakunin had agreed to wear as part of Cafiero's plan? It would seem so, since official status as a Swiss citizen was considered by the conspirators as a prerequisite for the disguise. Also, as a

Swiss citizen Bakunin could not easily be expelled from the country. His response to another event that month may also provide support for this view, if only indirectly. After their break with Ross, the other three members of the Russian Brotherhood, Ralli, Holstein, and Elsnitz, had set up a press of their own in Geneva. As its first publication, they printed a revolutionary work that contained, in Bakunin's opinion, the essentials of the militant program he had prepared for the secret brotherhood. He was outraged by this act of "treason," as he called it, spurned all their attempts to explain and defend themselves, and broke all relations with them.[136] Was Bakunin so angry because the revelations came just when he was trying to act the peaceful bourgeois? Or was the anger fueled by a deeper source, his need to keep all such displays of power and leadership carefully hidden?

Other evidence for the "mask" interpretation is found in a letter Bakunin wrote to the *Journal de Genève* sometime between September 20 and 25, 1873. Using as a pretext for the letter a new Marxist attack on him as well as some remarks about himself he had read in two articles the *Journal* had printed earlier that month, he wrote the *Journal* precisely the kind of public statement of retirement required by Cafiero's Baronata scheme. After reviewing the recent attacks on him by Marx, who, he said, hated him, "no doubt because of [Marx's] triple character as communist, German and Jew," he went on to say, in effect, that he had taken all that he wanted to take of that sort of abuse.

> All of that has caused in me a profound disgust with public life. I have had enough, and, after having spent my entire life in the struggle, I am leaving it. I am 60 years old, and a weak heart, which worsens with age, makes existence very difficult. Let others who are younger take up the work. As for me, I no longer feel within me either the force or, perhaps, the confidence needed to go on much longer rolling the stone of Sisyphus against the reaction that has triumphed everywhere. So I am retiring from the lists, and I ask only one thing of my dear contemporaries, to be forgotten. Henceforth, I will no longer trouble anyone's peace, and let them leave me, in turn, at peace.[137]

This, indeed, seems to be the "public assurance that he would henceforth take no part in any revolutionary agitation" demanded by the Swiss as the price for Swiss citizenship which, in turn, was part of Cafiero's plan. But was it really just a mask, a pretense at retirement? The question becomes even more intriguing and the doubts more pressing when one reads a second letter of "retirement" that Bakunin wrote shortly before returning to Locarno at the end of September. Although only a week or so separates the two letters and although both are explicit "retirement" letters, they are in tone and substance quite different.

In the first letter, Bakunin justified his withdrawal from the "lists" by the intolerable abuse he had suffered from the Marxists, the success of reaction, and his own "profound disgust" with public life. In other words, the "disgust" that had been chosen as the motivation for the new bourgeois mask.

There is nothing of the sort in the second letter, written to his Jura followers. The principal justification for retirement offered here is not defeat but victory, in particular the victory of the Jura Federation, "powerfully supported by your friends in Italy, Spain, France, Belgium, Holland, England and America," against the "ambitious intrigue of the Marxists." "The two Congresses that have just taken place in Geneva were a triumphant, a decisive demonstration of the justice as well as of the power of your cause. Your Congress, the Congress of liberty, has united within itself delegates from all the principal federations of Europe, except Germany, and has proudly proclaimed and boldly established, or rather confirmed, the autonomy and fraternal solidarity of the workers of all countries."[138] Until now, as long as this victory was in doubt, "it was impermissible for anyone to abandon your ranks." But now that this victory has become an established fact, "the liberty to act in accordance with one's personal needs is returned to everyone. And I am taking advantage of this, dear friends, to ask you to be good enough to accept my resignation as a member of the Jura Federation and as a member of the International." Of course, he went on, if he thought he could still be of service to the cause he would continue in the struggle. However, "by my birth and my personal situation.... I am only a bourgeois, [and] as such would only be able to carry on propaganda for you, ... this is no longer the time for ideas, but for facts and deeds.... Were I young, I would move into a working class milieu and, sharing the life of labor with my brothers, I would also participate with them in the great work of this vital organization." But age and poor health made that impossible, he said, so he must retire, leaving them "one last bit of brotherly advice": they must be on guard against the reactionary forces "that are represented as much by the socialism of Marx as by the diplomacy of Bismarck, a reaction that has as its final aim the pan-Germanism of Europe [and] that now threatens to engulf and pervert [Europe] completely."[139]

Whereas one might consider the first "retirement" letter as part of the Cafiero plan, it is difficult to see how the second can be interpreted that way. This was no act, no mask, as Guillaume himself later realized, even though at first he thought it was. What had caused the change from deception to sincerity? Had Bakunin learned something about his physical condition from Dr. Vogt to turn a feigned retirement into a real one? Or had Bakunin simply taken advantage, consciously or otherwise, of the mask required by Cafiero's scheme in order to complete and at last acknowledge the retirement that he had gradually and sporadically been attempting for a decade now? Had the conscious, intentional "mask" of withdrawal and nonviolence, in other words, given him the chance to take off the unconscious mask of commitment and violence that he had been forced to wear all his revolutionary life and to be—honorably—the timid and detached boy he had really been all along? What makes explicit retirement now especially ironic, yet entirely in keeping with the character of his life and motivations, is that it came at the very time, almost the very week, when his own "antiauthoritarians" had demonstrated their superiority over the Marxist International at the two Geneva Congresses, that he should use the image of Sisyphus just at the moment when the stone seemed to be holding at the top.

During the following year (1874), the first year of his Baronata retirement, Bakunin tried his best to become a good lord of the manor. His slow, intermittent regression had brought him all the way back to a mock Premukhino. He did what he could to manage Baronata as his father had hoped he might at least try to manage Premukhino. He even advised Guillaume to follow him in his reconciliation: "make peace with the bourgeoisie," he wrote him in June 1874, "and try again to get a job teaching in public education." Again one wishes that, for a change, a happy episode might be told. But it was more of the same, or worse. Failure followed failure. Here, too, his fantasy soared with its usual cavalier disregard for reality. Unconcerned about conventional constraints like costs, he spent more and more—to build an additional house higher on the hill where visitors could stay and several other new buildings, to provide for the large household and the "mass of people" that kept streaming in, to purchase animals (two cows, two horses), to try (unsuccessfully) to restore the soil and orchards, to build a new road, and so on. In no time, Cafiero's money was gone. Not even enough was left to meet earlier political commitments that Cafiero had made, for example, to Guillaume and his Jura friends for support in expanding a cooperative printers' workshop. (The Swiss blamed this unexpected refusal on Bakunin's desire to spend precious revolutionary money in order to prepare what he had called a "paradise for Antonia.")[140]

In mid-July 1874, the day of reckoning with Cafiero came. Bakunin told him how much would be needed to keep Baronata going for two years, by which time, he said, the estate should be able to pay its own way. At first, Cafiero seemed willing to go along with him, then, as Bakunin tells the story, he changed his mind and coldly told Bakunin that he would not spend another cent on Baronata. At just this time, Antonia, along with her children and parents, arrived from Russia, still believing that Baronata belonged to Bakunin. "With faith in my letters she arrived happy and at ease," Bakunin later recalled, "and I was dismayed at the thought of the despair that would seize her and her father at the first news of the catastrophe that awaited them." Had he been alone, he went on, he would have left Baronata there and then, "but the thought of the despair and the abyss into which I would have plunged Antonia and her father made a coward of me. Rather than think of my own honor, unjustly insulted by someone from whom I had least expected it, I thought of how I might save not myself, certainly, but those who were mine. As for me, my resolution was made. I decided to die." The arrangement he made to save Antonia and her family was to give Cafiero title to Baronata and all its possessions in return for Cafiero's promise to care for them, "after my death."[141]

Fortune now seemed to favor him at least with an opportunity for a hero's death. Even as he and Cafiero negotiated the Baronata arrangements, the young Cafiero was gathering arms, munitions, dynamite, and tactics for an insurrection at Bologne. Bakunin decided to join, then he changed his mind. The man he asked to tell Cafiero about this change of mind failed to deliver the message, however, so Bakunin felt, as Guillaume writes "obliged, against his will" to go after all. On the way to his hoped-for hero's death he wrote Guillaume, among others, telling him that he was going to Italy "to take part in a battle which he would not leave alive." Among other things he wrote along the way was a *Memoire justificatif*, explaining his side of the Baronata failure and blaming himself for believing in Cafiero. In it he also expressed his disillusionment with the "masses, who did not want to become impassioned about their liberation," and without "this passion of the people . . . we ourselves are powerless." As for Antonia and her family, he now decided that "I do not want to accept anything from Cafiero, not even for the sake of my family after my death": Antonia's own "dignity, her pride, will tell her what she must do. The blow she will receive will be terrible, but I count on the energy and the heroic force of her character to sustain her. . . ."[142]

Bakunin arrived in Bologne on July 30, 1874. The next nine days, until August eighth, he remained in hiding. The "insurrection" was to begin on the night of the seventh-eighth. The Bologne rebels gathered as planned outside the walls, but the expected contingents from neighboring towns either failed to arrive or came in too few numbers. It was by far the most dismal fiasco of all Bakunin's revolutionary escapades. Those who could get away fled, the rest were arrested. Bakunin, in the meantime, waited in his hiding place expecting to be called to join the insurgents once they had entered Bologne, unaware that fate had already made a farce of his heroic tragedy. When, at about four in the morning, he realized what had happened, he tried to shoot himself in the head but was stopped by a comrade who assured him that there was still a chance for success, that the rebels would try again. On the eighth a wave of arrests crushed what was left of the insurrection, and that night Bakunin was led away to a new hiding place. The next day he wrote a friend in Locarno: "My friend, my brother, it is with dread that I ask you about Antonia and her father. Tell her that in the midst of all the torments that assail me, the one I suffer because I abandoned her in such a difficult situation is the most cruel. But I had no choice. After you read my long letter, you will agree with me that I did what I had to do." He then left Bologne to begin a five day journey back to Switzerland. In the meantime, while he was still hiding in Bologne, his *Memoire justificatif* arrived. Cafiero was furious and refused to give it to Antonia. But someone had to tell her that Baronata was not hers and that, in fact, she would have to leave it. Ross accepted the assignment, and, undeterred by her rage, insisted that Baronata belonged to the revolution and not to her. She left on the ninth, first to Arona and from there to Lugano.[143]

Bakunin was now completely broken, lost, and alone. Baronata was gone. Antonia refused to have him come and stay with her. For a while he thought he might emigrate to America, letting Cafiero pay the costs. He wrote Cafiero to come to see him in Splügen, where he had stopped after crossing into Switzerland from Italy. Two weeks passed before he heard from Cafiero in a letter telling him that they should meet not in Splügen, but in Sierre, on the other side of Switzerland. Bakunin had no choice but to go. Deepening the humiliation still more, Cafiero was not there when he arrived. To pass the time, he tried gambling and lost. When Cafiero finally did arrive, the meeting, on September second, was cold and formal, strictly business. Bakunin asked Cafiero for a loan of 5,000 francs for two years at 6 percent. Cafiero agreed and also gave him 300 francs for current expenses. By then, Bakunin had changed his mind about going to America and had decided instead, as he wrote in a letter the day after the meeting, to remain in Switzerland, "having resolved irrevocably to retire completely from political life and action, public as well as secret, and to confine myself from now on exclusively to family life and private activities." With respect to the loan, he was sure he would be able to repay it in less than the two years agreed upon, first because he would earn money from the memoirs he now planned to write, second because his share of the inheritance would surely come soon, and, finally, because Antonia's sister, Sophia Losowska, whom Cafiero had wanted to countersign the 5,000 franc loan to Bakunin, "seemed to be well on her way to becoming really rich." As it turned out, his sister-in-law refused to sign the loan, and at another meeting with Cafiero later that month the loan had to be renegotiated, for three instead of five thousand francs and with another member of their circle as cosignator.[144]

That second meeting was held at Neuchâtel, on Bakunin's way "home" again: Antonia had softened and permitted him to join her in Lugano. He arrived on October seventh, a month after his failure to die in Bologne and Antonia's humiliating departure from Baronata. On the return trip, he had also stopped in Bern to consult with Dr. Vogt again and to try once more to get the official Swiss status. Since he had "renounced all revolutionary agitation," he thought that he could now obtain the necessary documents and so return home with a "full guarantee of my tranquillity." He was no more successful this time, however, than he had been the last, and so remained to the end a man without a country. Still, the months at Lugano seemed to provide him a gentle respite. Antonia was forgiving and indulgent: "Michael is the same as ever," she wrote in a letter on November tenth, "pretending to be a serious-minded, responsible man, while remaining as always an incorrigible child," or, as she put it in another letter, "Bakunin is so ingenuous that it is sometimes necessary to treat him like a child." As he apparently did wherever he settled, he quickly formed a new circle of local friends, to supplement his constant flow of visitors.[145] As for politics, however, those days were over: he had completely "withdrawn, and this time withdrawn resolutely and finally from all practical activities, from any connection with practical undertakings," he wrote Ogarev on November eleventh. Both the worsening state of his health and the no less deplorable state of European affairs, he said, made it impossible for him to participate any longer: "Bismarckism, i.e., the military, police, and financial monopolies, merged into a single system calling itself the modern state, is everywhere triumphant," and "new methods" requiring "fresh young forces" are required to fight it. Nevertheless, he was keeping busy, he told Ogarev, writing his memoirs and preparing to write "the final and full statement of my most personal beliefs." He was also reading a great deal—"Kolb's *Culturgeschichte [sic] der Menschheit*, Stuart Mill's *Autobiography*, and Schopenhauer." In general, his days were spent in meeting old and new friends, writing letters, napping, and reading.[146]

Everything seemed to be going reasonably well, except for his perennial plague—money. That remained as much a problem as ever, as well as a cause of disagreement between Bakunin, who wanted to turn to Cafiero again, and Antonia, who could not even understand how he could think of that after the way Cafiero had treated him. Bakunin argued that precisely because of the way Cafiero had treated him, Cafiero owed it to him to help. So, by way of a friend, he asked Cafiero for more money but was turned down. There was some promise of better times, however. Antonia's sister, Sophia, had left Lugano for Russia at the end of November, and one of her aims was to help Bakunin get his share of the inheritance from his brothers. On January 10, 1875 there was good news, for a change: Bakunin's brothers had agreed to allow Sophia to sell a forest as Michael's part of the inheritance. That, it seemed, would take care of the future. But what of the present? "I need, really, *absolutely need* 200 francs," he wrote that same month, "not for myself alone, but to maintain the family: it is a question of paying for rent, food, and heating.... As you can see, it is really a question of life or starvation, sickness or even death." This time his plea was successful. Cafiero gave him the 200 francs, and he was "now quite content," all the more so, he went on in this letter of thanks on the fourteenth, because of the good news from Russia. With prospects of that income ahead, in fact, he "would soon be able to exclaim: Everything is for the best in this best of all possible worlds," were it not—he added, seemingly as an afterthought—for the continuing triumph of European reaction.[147]

In a letter to Élisée Reclus, one of his rare "political" letters to come down from these final years, he reviewed at length the substance and cause of that reaction and again expressed his disappointment with the people as a force against the "fortress" of reaction. "The masses are disorganized. But how organize them when they themselves are not sufficiently impassioned about their own salvation, when they do not know what they should want, and when they do not want the only thing that can save them! There remains propaganda, of the sort that the Jurassiens and the Belgians are engaged in. That is, surely, something, but much too little, a few drops in the ocean; and if there is no other means of salvation, there will be enough time for humanity to decay ten times over before its salvation. There remains one hope: world war. These immense militarized states must surely sooner or later destroy each other, devour each other. But what a prospect!..."[148]

If the future was apocalyptically grim for humanity, however, it seemed a little brighter for the Bakunins. The money that would soon arrive from Premukhino, once the forest had been sold, inspired him to undertake a bold new venture that, he hoped, would this time really provide the "paradise for Antonia" that he had so painfully failed to provide through Baronata. With credit based on the expected boon from Russia, and with help from Antonia's lover Gambuzzi, he purchased in February 1875 a villa near Lugano, the Villa Besso. There was now no pretext for the purchase; he was no longer acting the good bourgeois for the sake of the revolution. He had simply bought a fine estate and worked very hard to make a success of it, to do at Besso what his father had done at Premukhino. His plan was to grow vegetables, fruit, and flowers. The vegetables and the fruit would be sold at the Lugano market. The flowers would be made into bouquets and young girls would be hired to sell them along the railway track near the stations in Lugano, and then, if business were good, in neighboring Gothard as well. He studied books on agriculture and chemistry, ordered great quantities of seeds, spent the winter cutting down the mulberry trees already growing on the land ("he was delighted by this first operation"), dug, walled, and richly fertilized deep pits for the fruit trees, planted them and the vegetable seeds, then irrigated and fertilized it all.[149] He was more pleased by the prospects of a flourishing estate then he had been with anything for a long time. No sooner had he begun work at it, then he enthusiastically invited his family in Russia, especially his brothers, to come and visit his "little kingdom of Heaven" where he hoped to "revive the memory of our father's house."[150]

The results were even worse than they had been at Baronata. This time he had worked too hard: he had planted too many trees too close together; he had sown too much seed ("we must not lose an inch of soil"), and, most damaging of all, he had fed and nurtured the soil with much too much fertilizer. Everything burned. Soil that had been so fertile before that it had yielded in abundance practically without labor, now gave nothing.[151] "Before entering paradise, one must go through purgatory," he said in a letter asking another loan. "It is the same with us. On the eve of becoming rich, since Sophia [Antonia's sister] has just about sold the forest, if not already sold it, we remain here without a cent." Again, five days later: "I have payments to meet and do not have a cent. It will not be long, I assure you, for the doors of paradise are already open, and we can even now see them quite near." Once more it was Gambuzzi who came to the rescue with a loan of 3,400 francs, which Bakunin promised to repay together with the repayment of an earlier loan of 2,200 francs, as soon as the money arrived from Russia. The next month, September, he worked up enough courage to visit Cafiero in Baronata, in order to follow up an agreement they had earlier made for Bakunin to buy the Baronata furniture for the new villa, on credit.[152] In December, it was Gambuzzi's turn again to help, this time by cosigning a large mortgage loan of 22,000 francs. Bakunin doggedly went on, determined to have everything ready "in our unfortunate villa" by the eleventh of that month, for Antonia had her heart set on moving in then. All he could do now was resign himself "like a fatalistic Turk, knowing absolutely nothing of what will come."[153]

A fascinating memoir by a young Russian admirer who was with him at Besso provides some invaluable insights into his activities and feelings during this last period—the last six months of his life.[154] A believer in "peaceful socialist propaganda" when she left Russia, the young woman had come to the West first to rest and restore her health and later to meet with activists in the International, including Bakunin, who she thought was still in Locarno. The place decided on by her doctor and friends as the ideal location for "complete tranquillity and isolation," as a town where she was least likely to run into any radicals, was Lugano! She soon learned that Bakunin was there, however, and after an introduction through one of his followers, she became a regular guest at the villa.

The picture she gives is a moving testament to Bakunin's fortitude in meeting the relentless pain of these final months. Suffering kidney, bladder, and prostate disorders, he almost never slept and at times could not manage the stairway or even dress and undress himself. The only way he was able to get some relief when the attacks came was by bending stretched over a table, feet on the ground. To add to his bodily misery, the ever deepening financial crisis left the family barely enough to buy necessities. "His only luxuries were tobacco and tea. He smoked all day without stop, and all night as well, except for short periods of sleep, when the pain let him sleep. He smoked while drinking tea. He bought tobacco pounds at a time, or so it seemed, and stacked it in piles on all the tables! ... 'If you are there when I die,' he often said when lighting a cigarette, 'take care now and do not forget to stick a cigarette in my mouth, so that I can take a last puff before I die.' "[155] Although there was a large, comfortable bed in the guest room, he himself slept on a "narrow iron bed" that hardly fit his "immense body." When she once asked "Why don't they give Bakunin, who sleeps so little and so poorly, that big fine bed in the guest room?" she was told that that was the "room of G[ambuzzi], *del'amico della Bacunina*." ("The psychology of his marriage, his intimate relations with his wife always remained puzzling. There undoubtedly was something pathological here." But he was, she went on, "an indulgent father to his wife and a gentle grandfather to her children.")[156]

Still, in spite of it all, he was jovial and continued to read and write. He even planned dictating his memoirs to his new admirer and recommended that she read Pascal's *Pensées*, to learn the French style, he said. Although there were at times heated quarrels with Antonia (he thought her much too severe with her children, for example), he missed her very much whenever she left on trips and waited letters from her "with childish impatience." He also got on well with her children, at least with the two girls, Marussia, the youngest and far and away his favorite, and Sophia. As for the third child, a boy named Carlo (Gambuzzi's first name), "it was obvious that he did not like" him.[157] (Years later, in 1905, Carlo committed suicide in Nice.)[158] At times, admittedly, the games Bakunin played with them were risky. He liked to start bonfires for them and get them to keep the flames going while they danced around like "savages." "Then he would go away to his room and forget the children and the bonfires." The children were all under ten at the time. Besides the companionship of his wife and the children, Bakunin was also favored with the help and boundless devotion of several followers, mainly Italian workers, who adored him and were prepared to do anything for him. This warm and genuine ease he had with the workers made a strong impression on the new visitor, but coming from Russia herself, she put this ease in a special context: "I came to the conclusion that it was precisely the fact that he was a real Russian aristocrat that helped him in these relationships. In our serf customs, there was in practice much that was patriarchal-democratic...."[159]

It seems to have been, in fact, just this aristocratic pride and unbending individualism in Bakunin that won her to his politics, away from the camp of "peaceful socialist propaganda." Once, when he had asked her rhetorically what would come after the revolution, after all the enthusiasm had been spent, he replied—"a dreary, gray barracks" in which people would be forced to do what they did not choose to do. "The power of the few over the many is terrible, criminal; but is not the power of the many over the single individual even more terrible?" But how could he then be a socialist? she asked herself. "In his speeches one feels an ardent and deep belief in the truth of socialism. His entire past confirms this belief. But can one really imagine M. A. denying himself his rights to his own self-determination? Who has ever met a more forcefully expressed individualism?" As a result of such discussions and the impassioned individualism they revealed, "there suddenly took place within me a real shift to Bakuninism and, along with this, my final reconciliation with socialism."[160] (How she solved the individualism-socialism quandary is left unexplained.)

Converted though she was by Bakunin's enthusiasm and youthful, individualistic spirit, she was no less aware that he was then "an old man weary of life...so alone, so distant from all around him." Bakunin agreed: "I am really all by myself, profoundly alone," he told her. He often spoke of death and welcomed it. "Death? She smiles at me, a big broad smile...." Of all the subjects they talked about, he liked best to tell her about his youth at Premukhino, about the time the family read *Robinson Crusoe* together, and he "often recalled his father, always with love." From her, he wanted most of all to hear descriptions of the Russian countryside, "not the characteristics of the people or the changes in customs since his time, but, for the most part, portraits of Russian nature.... If my little pictoral sketches of Russian nature were successful, M. A. would insist the next day that I repeat them: 'Please, do tell me once more about the water meadow.'"[161]

Full circle. Back to Premukhino, to nature, to the self that "tearing itself free of the mortal barriers that constrain it, pours itself over the entire universe, encompassing all in nature, the whole world," back to the "friend" within who had always been there through all the disguises. His first, "jealous wife" philosophy, his "bride—the Revolution," the "people" he was to merge with "in one body and one soul," and the "mother" International were no longer needed. "'You imagine that revolution is beautiful?' M. A. said. 'I have seen revolution up close. Oh, how repulsive it is up close.'"[162]

Besides chatting with his young visitor, listening to her descriptions of mother nature, and being lulled into fitful slumber while she read to him, as he asked her to do, "in a droning mumble as they do in church," Bakunin at times depended on her help when he strolled into town. "With his immense hand, M. A. leaned on my shoulder as though it were a cane. 'So, Oedipus and Antigone,' he said the first time he walked about Lugano with my help.... Bakunin walked with difficulty, repeating all the while with a strained laugh, 'So, Oedipus and Antigone.'"[163]

In early May 1876, the "inheritance" finally arrived, two months before his death. It was far less than he had expected, nowhere near enough to cover the debts, and a three month grace period he had received from his creditors in February was now up. His only recourse was to surrender his "little kingdom" to the creditors and move elsewhere. They would go to Italy, to Naples, where Gambuzzi lived. Antonia left first to make arrangements and to obtain, with Gambuzzi's help, permission for Bakunin to live in Italy. Bakunin would then follow, after a brief stay in Berne to consult Dr. Vogt again about his illnesses. Naples would mean his ultimate return, going back even before the Baronata-Besso-Premukhino manoral life, into complete dependency on Antonia, who now thought him a child, and Gambuzzi, the father of her children and his own provider. He would be another child in the household of Antonia and Gambuzzi.[164]

At least he was spared that final humiliation. Arriving in Berne on June 14, 1876, after getting the approval of his creditors for the trip, he was taken at once to the hospital. "I have come here to die," he told his old friends, the Reichels, who came as soon as they learned he was there. For the next two weeks, as his condition worsened and his kidneys, bladder, and heart gave out, he seemed quite reconciled to his death, to judge from the account of these last days left by Adolf Reichel. With Mr. Reichel, he discussed music (Beethoven and Wagner) and philosophy, especially Schopenhauer. With Mrs. Reichel he chatted in Russian and enjoyed the Russian *kasha* she prepared for him. The two days before the end, he would eat nothing else. On June thirtieth the Reichels wired Lugano. That same day, a few minutes before midnight, he died quietly, "tired of life," it seemed to Reichel.[165]

He was buried in a small cemetery near the center of Berne. Later, the cemetery was made into a park, and his coffin moved to a larger cemetery on the outskirts of the city, Friedhof Bremgarten. One can still visit the grave, located on a narrow path of individual graves, a little beyond the stately family plots. The tombstone stands out boldly, a tall dark stone, part smooth, part left rough and raw. The inscription is to "Michel Bakunin, who sacrificed everything for the liberty of his country." Next to the grave is that of a former director of the Bank of Berne.[166]

12. REQUIEM

What are we to conclude about this extraordinary man and his influence? Which of his radically different images should guide our judgment? Is it right that we continue to extol him as the superbly eloquent defender of absolute freedom, social harmony, peace, and brotherhood? Should we instead be persuaded by his obsessive dedication to militantly authoritarian organizations and cataclysmic universal violence? Or, finally, is it the deeper personality behind both the mask of heroic freedom and the mask of violent power that should direct our sentiments: the personality of a fearful, timid, gentle, withdrawn boy who could never grow up, for whom "freedom" always meant purity, fear, weakness, and escape, and in whose dialectical world the rhetoric of destruction and domination was always a pathetically transparent attempt at camouflage and compensation?

Of all the voices that sound through Bakunin's words and deeds, it is that of the frightened youth that is the most genuine. Nothing rings more true than his confession of how difficult it was for him to overcome his timidity and make those brilliant speeches that won him such acclaim or his talk of turning inwards, closing himself off in his "sturdy mansion with gates and locks," his "forbidden temple" with its "monastic fence" and "immense store of food, wine, and tobacco," his "Gothic castle, on top of a high, steep, inaccessible mountain." For all its bulk and ferocity, his violent rhetoric lacks the authenticity that is so apparent in his periodic appeals—virtual pleas—for nonviolence: his faulting of his own "Negative" party for the violence that circumstance imposed on it, his descriptions of his favored destructive passions as "evil" and "demonic," his

418

bizarrely passive way at times of phrasing his most violent declarations, his intermittent fantasy of authority considerably crumbling under the weight of its own sins (sparing him its overthrow), his view of himself as heroic sufferer and the pleasure that vision gave him, and his identification with what he considered to be feminine traits and modes of behavior. It is in his scrupulous avoidance of public power, not his "powerful" assaults on it or (as in the conflict with Marx) his feigned competition for it, that he reveals himself. The most obvious and compelling fact about his life is his persistent escape, from the time he ran away from the army and Premukhino obligations to the time he hypostatized escape from society into a full-blown social philosophy—anarchism.

Bakunin's "anarchism" and "freedom," therefore, for all the resounding and inspiring eloquence with which he proclaims them, do not reflect heroic strength and self-affirmation, but rather an elemental and permanent dread of society and of the psychologically intolerable demands it made upon him. To be free meant, first and last, to be safely distant from those demands and dangers, alone in the consoling embrace of the maternal "friend" within or snugly sheltered in some tiny pseudo-family of "intimates." The ease with which he denied "freedom" to party members in his successive plans for secret organizations and with which he repeatedly spoke of submerging and losing oneself in such martially disciplined organizations tells more about his real attitude toward "freedom" than do all his celebrated theories and pronouncements in defense of it.[1]

The same pathological traits that drove him out of society, however, made him return to it again and again in order to deny those traits (and compensate for the deprivations they caused him) by pretending that they were not at all his characteristics, that his personality was their exact opposite, that he was powerfully and virilely aggressive, not fearfully, impotently passive. In the psychosexual dynamics that helped generate this dialectical drama, Bakunin first completely rejected anything sexual, "animal." He then transferred this total rejection to society, because it so inextricably involved—directly (sex, marriage) and indirectly (power, responsibility)—that oedipally repulsive "animal" world. Finally, he disguised (and compensated for) the fear, weakness, and impotence by transmuting them into their opposite. His lifelong task was to discover, refine, and repeatedly replay formulas that might achieve the alchemy, fantasies of power and violence that would (1) conceal the fear and the impotence, while providing him something of a surrogate for the gratifications they denied him; (2) allow him to continue a life of total narcissistic separation from society (permanently and pathologically ensconced in the "dual unity" with his inner maternal "friend"), while permitting him to persuade himself and others that he was devoting his life selflessly as well as powerfully to serving and saving it; and (3) provide him the approval and self-esteem needed to restore the self, heal a badly weakened, fragmented ego.

The progress from Schelling's romantic Idealism to "left" Hegelian revolutionary dialectics comprised stages on the way towards discovering those formulas. He moved from Schelling's solipsistic Idealism to Fichte's heroic egoism because Schelling did not offer, as Fichte did, a facade of promethean struggle to disguise romantic withdrawal. Then he replaced Fichte by Hegel because Fichte's heroic crusade, while disguising the narcissistic retreat and the impotence, had required too intimate involvements with those to be saved and thus provoked (in the Tatiana episode) the very incestual threat that the retreat and the impotence were meant to avoid. Hegel, in his "left" mode, solved the problem splendidly, not just by letting Bakunin remain apart (Schelling) while appearing to be all-powerful (Fichte), but by allowing him to seem all-powerful precisely by remaining apart.

Viewing this development from a somewhat different perspective, we see a fascinating process of projection. For Bakunin as a romantic Schellingite, existence was divided irreconcilably into a pure, blissful interior realm (the only gateway to Truth) and a fallen, corrupt, evil outer world. Blissful though it may have been, however, the inner refuge was painfully vulnerable, exposing Bakunin after a while to his "hell, hell with all its terrors." To save himself from further assaults, he set about destroying his inner "I," as he put it, and surrendering himself to the objective Absolute, identifying himself with its indomitable power. But as we saw, what he was really doing during his two or so years of "reconciliation" with the Absolute was projecting his own subjective self into it, merging the two so that in the end the Absolute was simply Bakunin writ large. The final step in the process came with the "left" Hegelian division of that objective world into, in Bakunin's terms, the "Positive" and the "Negative." With that, the preoedipal narcissistic split between "good" and "bad"[2] and the oedipal split between "body" and "soul" merged to become the apocalyptic split between the Two Cities, the millennial "new heaven and new earth" and the fallen, irredeemable world destined for annihilation.

Philosophy as a whole, however, even in its militant "left" Hegelian form— the "terror of pure criticism"—did not go far enough in furnishing the needed mask and surrogate. So Bakunin moved on to *die Tat,* Action. But in all his action, his "act," he was always scrupulously careful to avoid political realism ("bourgeoise" or labor politics, for example), since that required mature, responsible involvement and lacked the scope and stage for promethean bravado. Instead, he clung obsessively to an apocalyptic maximalism that allowed full expression for violence, while at the same time saving him (precisely because of the futile extremism) from success and responsible authority as well as from too close involvement with the "people" he felt summoned to save.

From the time he discovered his "left" Hegelian apocalyptic violence virtually everything he said and did can best be explained by paradox, with appearances representing their exact opposite: total freedom testified to total dependency; social commitment defended social detachment; the acts of omnipotence revealed the essential impotence; materialists became the true idealists, and idealists, the true materialists; the "cold" exterior that he acknowledged for himself and required for members of his secret societies reflected ardent interiors; the hatred he unleashed against his mother reenforced, safely, his bonds with her, while the tenderness he showered on his father and other authorities disguised a lifelong war to destroy all that they represented. Often the opposites merged in stunningly contradictory phrases and concepts—the "ruthless surrender," the bloodless annihilation, the "invisible," powerless power, the non-leading revolutionary leaders, the cherished and celebrated "evil" and "demonic" passions and so on. And at the core of it all was the basic dialectic and the repression it achieved: "as every development necessarily implies the negation of its base or point of departure, humanity is...the cumulative negation of the animal principle in man."[3]

Viewing the entire expanse of Bakunin's career, from the philosophical through the revolutionary years, one sees a great cycle completed: from Premukhino dependency through romantic, philosophical Idealism to the abstract, universal, "left" Hegelian revolutionary vision of 1842 and the concrete national movements of 1848-49—then, after an intervening period of "red generals" and iron dictatorships, the sequence in reverse: from the concrete nationalistic movements of 1862-63 through the revived abstract, universal, apocalyptic visions (the "red, social, geologic revolutions," the German versus Slavic-Latin Armegeddon) and the new circles of "intimates," (the old "holy commune" refurbished) back to the would-be manorial sanctuaries of Baronata and Besso. Only death spared him the final step, the return to complete infantile dependency as the fourth child of the Antonia-Gambuzzi family.

Throughout it all, however, whether in the earlier philosophical or the later political phase, it is the "act" that must be emphasized. The violent rhetoric and the frenzied, foredoomed revolutionary escapades were always, from beginning to end, performances, with Bakunin as his own front-row audience. It is not surprising that he so often described his forays in terms of theatrical acts[4] or that he should feel it entirely proper to reclaim his wallet and revolver after the Lyon fiasco—it was only make-believe. "Always remember," he wrote a friend from Locarno in January 1873, "that revolution is made up of three-fourths fanstasy and only one-fourth reality."[5] For Bakunin's special purposes, however, "fantasy" was the most realistic strategy he could adopt, since it assured him the constant failure he needed to avoid real authority and its multiple dangers.

Ultimately, as I have argued throughout this study, this permanent "act" and its incessant contradictions reflect the interaction of Bakunin's oedipal and narcissistic disorders.[6] Since these were the roots of Bakunin's world-view, it is understandable that the millennial-apocalyptic vision should be its crown. For what is that vision if not the all-good, all-pleasurable, narcissistic infantile fantasy achieved by precisely the kind of cataclysmic destruction that Bakunin needed to pretend virility, revenge defeat and deprivation, release rage, experience "paroxysm," and through vast masochistic suffering atone for all these sinful fantasies and deeds? It has been a central concern of this study to depict and draw together the features of Bakunin's apocalyptic relationship to the world: total detachment from and uncompromising denunciation of society, incessant prophecies of its imminent and complete annihilation, denunciation of all compromising Pharisees, self-justification for the cruelty by visions of a fine new and pure world to rise from the ruins, formation of successive circles of disciples who provided him a monastic pseudo-family that he could "father," assurance that his own purity and that of his "intimates," his apostles, his cadre were in no way stained by the brutal violence that must inevitably pave the way to the kingdom of love and brotherhood. It was, in short, a classically apocalyptic vision, whether to be realized in the footsteps of Jesus (Bakunin's model down to *and through* his first revolutionary proclamation, *The Reaction in Germany*)[7] or, later, under the fascist leadership of liberating Tsars and "red generals" or the secret direction of "invisible," professional Leninist party organizations.

Given the extent—total, I believe—to which Bakunin's apocalypse as well as the rest of his theories, analyses, programs, and strategies are designed to meet his own psychological needs, what can one say about their "validity"? In one sense, *everything* Bakunin said was "true," since it all corresponds to the objective reality that was Bakunin himself. His theories accurately describe him: his programs and strategies correctly reflect his very real malaise and his attempt to alleviate it one way or another. As for the kind of reality he claimed to be treating, if the criterion of success or failure is used to judge truth or error, then the outcome of his policies in Prague, Dresden, Lyon, the Slavic-Germanic Armegeddon and so forth could hardly be considered proof of validity. Yet, all that is really quite beside the point, for even were his political descriptions and judgments "true," they would be so only coincidentally and (as far as he was concerned) incidentally, much as any other work of subjective expression in literature or the arts may happen to be "true." And the analogy here is meant to be exact; Bakunin's theories, analyses, historical surveys, and predictions are as much projections, pure creations as are the works of any other creative artist. Bakunin's only relationship with the world outside was that of a sculptor with his stone or a painter with his palette: reality was no more than raw material for fantasy.

A comparison with his Dresden friend and fellow revolutionary Richard Wagner is instructive in this regard. Wagner's impassioned declarations at the time of the rising were even more violently apocalyptic than were Bakunin's. However, Dresden ended Wagner's play with real revolutionary fire. Thereafter, he turned to the stage and orchestra pit as arenas for his fantasies. Bakunin's channel, unfortunately, was "politics," and for his plots and scenarios he had to quarry bits and pieces of reality rather than stories from ancient mythology. As a result, while Wagner did contribute significantly to the formation of Nazi fantasies,[8] it was at least obvious that his creations were make-believe; whereas in Bakunin's case, the political make-believe had (and, sadly, still has for many) the appearance of reality, since he seems after all to be talking about real events and to be proposing concrete political action with reference to them. His words and deeds may be no more than costume, mask, and gesture designed for his own inner needs alone, but they have all-too-often been taken as descriptions of reality and rational responses to it and have, thereby, motivated and justified horrendous violence done in their name and after their example.

None of these arguments about the pure subjectivity of Bakunin's theories (and one should recall here the influence of philosophical Idealism on him in this respect) is meant in any way to deny or minimize that enormous influence on his own time and continually thereafter. Although he staged his dreams and nightmares mainly for his own therapy and even sanity (and no doubt experienced, as in all good theater, the desired catharsis), countless others in search of similar self-deceptions for whatever reason, eagerly mistook those dreams and nightmares for objective portraits of reality or serious designs for social change and acted accordingly. Bakunin is hardly alone, after all, in experiencing radically ambivalent feelings about power, in being torn between a desire to retain the carefree, detached freedom of youth and a compelling need to win the honor and power of maturity, or in searching for ways to disguise an unflattering fear and weakness by violent bombast. While it is uncertain how many workers or peasants ever knew very much about him, it is undeniably true that he was, and remains, a theorist *par excellence* for that critically influential class that shared so many of his concerns and dilemmas, the class of intellectuals, or, better, demi-intellectuals—the "intelligentsia." This is not to say that this group either individually or as a class necessarily arrived at those concerns and dilemmas from the same or even similar psychological roots that brought Bakunin to them (although the possibility is not excluded). In fact, it may well have been the

energy from that particular inner turmoil in Bakunin that enabled him, compelled him, to become so skilled, insistent, and persuasive in the art of expressing
those ambivalences and formulating more or less effective fantasies to resolve
them.

To pursue this theme a while longer, there have always been two ways for
the alienated intelligentsia (perhaps a redundant phrase) to safeguard total
freedom and avoid self-estrangement. The easier way (and for society's sake
by far the most desirable way) is forthright withdrawal, the Essenic separation,
the romantic, philosophical, religious, mystical or simply self-indulgent avoidance of the world and its obligations. But that way offers too little self-esteem,
too little to satisfy the claim to honor and power, or at least to their appearance.
The second way, the way Bakunin took and that countless others before and
after him have taken, is to declare total war against the existing society in the
name of some finer society to come. As long as the rebellion is total and uncompromising—the main assumption of the "left" Hegelians' dialectics—the radical
critic who takes this second path is entirely free of those dreary day-to-day
chores and duties that constrain not only those who accept the system (the
Sadducees), but also those "impotent," debased "half men," the compromising
bourgeois liberals who are content with finding ways to reform it (the Pharisees).
Thus, while remaining "free" and unburdened, the dialectical maximalist can
enjoy at least the illusion of vast power (cataclysmic revolution with God and
history on his side) and great honor (savior of humanity, liberator of the oppressed
masses). Impresario of the Word, the apocalyptic zealot with his "terror of pure
criticism," can indulge his imagination without restraint, conjure up fantasies
of titanic and brutal conflicts to prove his strength, glow with pride and honor
in the heroic and noble roles he assigns himself, ridicule the cautious and uncertain, demonstrate his boundless compassion by drafting the floor plans of
paradise, lament the high costs of its construction, then go off for drinks and
dinner, proud and confident in his selfless devotion to the one true good cause.

To understand why Bakunin's example and words have for so long had so
great an influence on the world's intelligentsia and to realize as well just how
close he is to us, one need only recall those elite young rebels of the late 1960s
who retreated into peaceful realms of inner space and time to enrich awareness,
contemplate beauty, and nurture love, while at the same time idolizing the
world's most violent revolutionary activists—Ho, Che, Mao—and posting huge
icons of them on their walls. Demanding power and participation (in their
rhetoric), they, too, carefully avoided "fussy" burdens of routine responsibility
once it was available, preferring the spontaneity of the coffeeshop to the tedium
of responsible involvement. Saintly idealists, whose every thought was with the
wretched of the earth, they seldom, if ever, did any more than Bakunin did

actually to alleviate that wretchedness. Uncompromising individualists, they demanded complete freedom for themselves, yet lovingly extolled totalitarian societies which made such individualism and such freedom their first victims. The parallel is especially close, finally, in that the great majority of these young rebels were no more violent than Bakunin was. Rather than a velvet glove of beatific ideals disguising an iron fist of cruelty—the Nechaev-Lenin model—we have in both cases an iron fist of fierce rhetoric disguising the gentle hand of very young and very fearful children—fearful, most of all, of growing up.[9]

But if it was all rhetoric and theatrical act performed mainly for his own catharsis, should Bakunin be blamed for what others did under the influence of his soliloquies, however ferocious they may have been? Was the poet Yeats unnecessarily guilt ridden when he wrote in a poem, "I lie awake night after night / And never get the answers right. / Did that play of mine send out / Certain men the English shot?"[10] In considering this question, we should first distinguish between what Bakunin said and what he himself actually did. As I argued in an earlier chapter, I believe that Bakunin was partly, and perhaps decisively, responsible for the fact that there were so many casualties in the Dresden rising, that the leaders of the insurrection did not realize earlier the hopelessness of their cause and accept surrender terms. Moreover, if Bakunin had had his way, the same thing might well have happened in Lyon, since there, too, he urged the rebels to go on fighting, notwithstanding the absurdity of such an action under the circumstances. Fortunately, the Lyon rebels had more sense than had their Dresden counterparts.

In Prague and, later, in Switzerland (with respect both to the League Congresses and the labor movement) the consequences of his actions were less tragic in the short run but ultimately more politically harmful. In these cases, he persistently made the best the enemy of the better, discrediting the programs of the more moderate participants who were actually involved in day-to-day politics and undermining the chances for real change by proclaiming his maximalist, millennial fantasies. While there is, surely, no substance at all to the accusations of his being a Tsarist agent, one can understand the ease with which those rumors spread, since one of the most notorious and notoriously successful techniques of the agent provocateur has always been to pose as a *ne plus ultra* extremist. And is he not at least in part morally responsible for the many lives wasted in pursuit of his private fantasies and for the lives actually lost because of his no less solipsistic celebration of "evil passions," "devil in the flesh," "sea of blood and fire," "complete annihilation," "storm of destruction," "war to the death, barbaric war to the knife," "furious avalanche, devouring, destroying everything," and so on? For one as brilliant, charismatic, and eloquent as Bakunin, the pen—the Word—is indeed mightier than the sword when it summons would-be saviors to apocalyptic holocaust, mightier and, hence, more culpable. Finally, he must surely bear a heavy charge for his extreme anti-Semitism, which he helped to make almost as endemic in the populist "left" as it is in the fascist "right." Even had he not inspired barbaric violence and repeatedly designed authoritarian organizations, his anti-Semitism and its vile influence on socialist and anarchist movements would be enough to corrupt his message irredeemably.

What then of his reputation as the great, prophetic enemy of authoritarian state socialism? Indeed, there have rarely been more perceptive insights and criticisms, and certainly not in Bakunin's time, of the dangers of socialist dictatorship than those Bakunin directed against Marx in their fateful confrontation:

> We, of course, are all sincere socialists and revolutionaries; and still, were we given power, even for the short duration of a few months, we would not remain what we are now.... Human nature, the nature of every man, is such that, given power over others, he will invariably oppress them; placed in an exceptional position, and withdrawn from human equality, he becomes a scoundrel.... Take the most radical revolutionary and place him upon the all-Russian throne or give him the dictatorial power of which so many of our green revolutionaries daydream, and within a year he will have become worse than the Emperor himself.... No dictatorship can have any other aim but that of self-perpetuation, and it can beget only slavery in the people tolerating it.[11]

His keen sensitivity to the dangers of power, sharpened by the special meaning power had for him, foresaw a time when the revolutionaries would "concentrate all the powers of government in strong hands, because the very fact that the people are ignorant necessitates strong, solicitous care by the government. They will create a single state bank, concentrating in its hands all the commercial, industrial, agricultural, and even scientific production; and they will divide the mass of people into two armies—industrial and agricultural armies under the direct command of the state engineers who will constitute the new privileged scientific-political class." More prophetic still, he sensed that after all the other classes had taken their turn in power—clerics, nobility, and bourgeoisie—"the bureaucratic class" enters and then "the State falls, or rises, depending on your point of view, to the condition of a machine."[12]

Marvelous insights, all of them—*regardless of their ultimate roots and motivations* in Bakunin's personality, and they certainly deserve the celebration they have earned their author. But who is their valid target, Marx or Bakunin himself? Whose aims and means, theories and practices, would most likely result in the socialist tyranny that Bakunin so eloquently denounced in those penetrating and prophetic statements? Should the triumvirate be Marx-Lenin-Stalin or Bakunin-Lenin-Stalin? Considering again Bakunin's adoration of catastrophically violent revolution and, even more important here, his successive plans for a secret, fully-committed, professional, tightly and hierarchically organized revolutionary party, only one answer seems reasonable. The authoritarian, Leninist, state socialism that Bakunin so brilliantly assailed has, in fact, historically been the result—repeatedly—of just those maximalist theories of violent revolution and party organization that he defended all his life and urged on his followers, in opposition to the "bourgeois socialism" of his Marxist rivals.

Since Bakunin and Lenin belong to the same apocalyptic tradition, one should not be surprised to find, as well, many other similarities in their revolutionary strategies. There is, for example, besides their shared designs for party organization and violent, maximalist revolution, far more similarity than usually noted between their attitude toward the "masses" and the masses' relationship to the revolutionary vanguard, the party and its "General Staff." If Lenin appreciated as did Bakunin the revolutionary potential of the peasant masses and was as ready as he was to spark such a rising whenever the masses seemed aroused enough and the state weak enough (never mind Marxist economic, social, and political preconditions), Bakunin stressed no less than Lenin did the need for a full-time, professional, disciplined party leadership. To lead, or at least to *pretend* to do so, meant to avoid being "paralyzed," "an invalid," "blind," "castrated," "beheaded," "impotent," to use the terms Bakunin repeatedly used to describe the loss of leadership. He differed from Lenin (and the difference is basic) mainly in his ambivalence towards power, his persistent fear of power and responsibility that accompanied his authoritarian scenarios: feigning leadership and domination kept his weakness secret, but to lead openly, publicly, involved a danger that was far more threatening than the revelation of impotence, considering the true identity in his psychodrama of his "bride—the revolution," the "people" with whom he must merge "body and soul," the people whose "spontaneity," "savagery," "devil in the flesh," and "convulsive movement" were the source of his "electricity" and "paroxysm" and his only means of being "healed." He resolved the dilemma, as he did all the other contradictions and dilemmas that harassed him, by having things both ways (as one resolves contradictions in dreams). He simply went right on compulsively constructing one dictatorial party scheme after another, while at the same time taking infinite pains to keep these fantasies secret and endlessly denouncing all those who dared publicly to defend Jacobin, state socialist, or any other manner of overt leadership.

The persistence of this stark dualism is probably the most extraordinary, yet entirely characteristic, feature of his later publications. Notwithstanding all he wrote about Jacobin elitism and in defense of the "spontaneous" uprising of an instinctively socialist and revolutionary mass, for example, he also emphasized that these same masses, as a result of their long exploitation and deprivation, were "servile," "weighed down by slavish habits and a general spirit of resignation," characterized by "ignorance, wild fanaticism, and stupidity" and by "fear and obedience," "utterly unorganized," and "gifted by nature with an amazing patience that can really drive one to despair" as well as with "obtuseness [and] a lack of any awareness of their rights." In sum: "The compact mass is a human herd barely fit for development or for the propaganda of ideas."[13] Consequently, it was the task of the secret organization, from its central bureau through its national bureaus and down to the local organizations, to enlighten, arouse, and guide the "herd": "The aroused masses of people are like molten metal, which fuses into one continuous mass, and which lends itself to shaping much more easily than nonmolten metal—that is, *if there are good craftsmen who know how to mold it* in accordance with the properties and intrinsic laws of a given metal, in accordance with the people's needs and instincts... an elemental force lacking organization is not a real power...."[14]

Voluntary, free, spontaneous, bottom-upwards anarchism was all well and good for public speeches, but it was still "necessary to organize, direct, and intensify the revolutionary passions and forces of the people," to see to it that "when revolution, brought about by the force of circumstances, breaks out, there will be a real force knowing what it must do and, consequently, capable of seizing hold of the revolution and giving it a direction beneficial to the people." Lacking such organization, the workers would be "condemned to impotence," helpless against those who would "behead the working class." And "what would a disorganized and beheaded working class do then?"[15]

It was the aim of the secret organization, the "collective dictatorship," therefore, not merely "to lead the popular movement," but to remain in existence "without breaking apart or altering its direction on the morrow of the people's liberation."[16] There were many reasons why the people's "ignorance, wild fanaticism, and stupidity" required the "General Staff" to stay in office after the revolution. For one thing, Bakunin was no Tolstoyan. He honored mankind's cultural, scientific, and technological achievements and was critical only of the fact that the masses were deprived of these benefits and that the educated elite ruled. Indeed, for him the people's lack of knowledge was one of the main reasons for their enslavement by the dominant classes. Backwardness may have been indispensable for the "rude, savage force" that would carry through the "sweeping and passionate destruction" and provide the "electricity" and the "paroxysm," but it was too raw a material to use in the construction of the new society. Thus, we find even in Bakunin's revolutionary theory the telltale sign of all self-deceptive revolutionary liberators—the "transition period," "a more or less prolonged transitional period, which is bound to follow the social revolution" and which would be required for the "rational upbringing, education, and the organization of society upon a basis of freedom and justice." Once when he squarely faced the sad fact that "during the transitional period ...society will be confronted with the problem of individuals (and unfortunately there will be many of them) who grew up under the prevailing system of organized injustice and special privileges and who were not brought up with...the habit of work," he could only say that the new society "will either have to force them to work, which would be despotism, or let itself be exploited by idlers, and that would be a new slavery and the source of a new corruption of society." Fortunately, after the new world was well under way, he was sure that there would remain only a few such parasites, and they could then be either "expelled" or considered victims of "special maladies to be subjected to clinical treatment."[17] ("I am perplexed,". Dostoevsky's "possessed" Shigalev mused. "Starting from unlimited freedom, I arrive at unlimited despotism.")[18]

Finally, even the people's violence made the General Staff a necessary institution after the revolution. Once aroused, once the "evil passions" and the "devil in the flesh" had enjoyed their "chaotic and ruthless" destruction, their "terrible and bloody struggle," their "convulsive movement," would the masses be satisfied and stop? We have seen the various psychological meanings that this rage and fury had for Bakunin, and the reason, therefore, that these emotions had to be called evil and demonic even as he praised them and tried to provoke them (the reason also that a strong and persistent obligato of otherwise misplaced nonviolence accompanied his credo of annihilation). Associated as they were both with repressed sexuality and narcissistic rage, they required even in this political fantasy a powerful repressive force, a "General Staff." After the "paroxysm," the "rude, savage force" must be calmed and controlled: "once the hurricane has passed, [the socialists] will oppose with all their might hypocritical butchery (political and juridical) organized in cold blood." "We say to the worker:...begin by overthrowing and throwing to the ground all those who oppress you. Then, after you are really sure of victory and have destroyed the power of your enemies, give way to humane sentiments and lift up these poor devils, beaten and henceforth harmless and disarmed: recognize them as your brothers and invite them to live and work with you upon the unshakable ground of equality."[19]

Besides Bakunin's and Lenin's shared insistence on militantly disciplined and structured party organizations, on an inevitable and total, apocalyptic revolution, and on the role the peasantry were to play in that revolution, there were a number of other similarities that place them in the same camp. Both were consummate "opportunists," especially prepared to take revolutionary advantage of wartime dislocations: the Franco-Prussian War for Bakunin, World War I for Lenin. Also, while they come late and are few, Bakunin's remarks about the revolutionary potential of Asia and about the likelihood of revolution first occurring not, as Marx said, in the advanced nations but in the backward, antici- pate at least the revolutionary implications of Lenin's thoughts on imperialism. Finally, the enemy who provoked in both the most vehement attacks was not the reactionary on the far right, but the bourgeois liberal or bourgeois socialist in the middle, the meliorist who saw value in the electoral vote and the trade union movement. Lenin's relentless war against Western social-democrats, the heirs of Marx (by way of Bernstein and Kautsky) replaced Bakunin's no less furious campaign against their progenitors a generation earlier.[20]

Bakunin and Lenin, in short, were both apocalpytic Zealots, while their Marxist rivals, in both periods, were—in comparison—Pharisees. Marx himself nowhere made this more evident than when, in 1873, he mocked Bakunin and his followers for spurning bourgeois elections and trade unionism:

> If, in the political struggle against the bourgeois state, the workers only succeed in forcing concessions, they are compromising, acting contrary to eternal principles. One must oppose any peaceful movements, such as the Americans and the English have the bad habit of undertaking. The workers should not struggle to get a general reduction in the length of the work day, since that would be tantamount to compro- mising with the owners, who would then be able to exploit them only ten or twelve hours a day instead of fourteen or sixteen. Nor should they try any more to gain legal prohibition against children under ten in factories, since such methods would not end the exploitation of children over ten and would only commit another compromise prejudi- cial to the purity of the eternal principles. ... In a word, the workers must cross their arms and not waste time with economic and political movements. Such movements can bring them only immediate results. As truly religious men, the workers, disdaining ordinary needs, must declare as an act of faith: "Let our class be crucified, let our race perish, but let the eternal principles remain immaculate." Like pious Christians, they must believe in the words of the priest, despise the goods of this world and think only of attaining paradise.[21]

While there is, of course, an apocalyptic side of Marx's general crisis theory, other arguments in his "scientific socialism" and, more significantly, Marx's actual practice, effectively neutralize it (at least in that part of the world, the "bourgeois" West, where his theories had their birth and relevance). By requiring, as a prerequisite for an authentic socialist revolution, that society have already lived through the "bourgeois" stage, he, in effect, set down conditions that sharply reduced the chances of workers' socialist movements progressing through violent revolution to party dictatorship. High productivity, widespread education, and long familiarity with "bourgeois democracy" and civil rights have proven to be deeply uncongenial to Bolshevik means and ends. As to Marx's practice, his defense of labor participation in parliamentary elections and step-by-step improvements through trade union pressure provided workers with the experience of self-determination, which, along with the tangible gains such elections brought them, further protected them and their societies from the terrors of apocalyptic revolution and party domination. Marx in his own time was, and, for the most part, West European Marxists since have been, as Bakunin charged, "bourgeois socialists." But as such, they should not be identified as a source of (or linked to the rulers of) authoritarian Leninist-Stalinist—Maoist state socialism.

That honor belongs to Bakunin. And one wonders, in the light of all the authoritarian strains in Bakunin's theories, programs, revolutionary strategies, party organizations, and actual practice—only a small part of which has been recalled in this summary chapter—how it has come down otherwise, how Bakunin won the title of heroic champion of absolute freedom, the shield and banner of liberty against Marx's allegedly state socialist tyranny? One can, perhaps, understand how those living in Bakunin's own time might have arrived at this extraordinary misreading; for, then, much of Bakunin's authoritarian organization schemes were still concealed and, more important, the historical dynamics that were to carry such apocalyptic revolutions as he preached from the promise of absolute freedom to the practice of absolute despotism had occurred less frequently and less impressively than they have since. But the abundant authoritarian documents have been available for some time now[22] and the explanation for the tragic revolutionary dialectic that puzzled Shigalev (from absolute freedom to absolute despotism) is now a commonplace. Why, then, does this bizarre misrepresentation of Bakunin's politics still go on? One can only assume that it does so because those perpetuating the myth of the man choose to set aside or argue away, for personal reasons of their own, either the fact or the implications of that apocalyptic and authoritarian side.

One of the aims of this study has been to make that side unmistakably clear. And it is for that side, for Bakunin's unwavering attachment to revolutionary pandestruction and to secret authoritarian party organizations as the inevitable and indispensable costs of social renewal and individual liberation that he is to be most harshly judged. It is true, and I have tried at length to do justice to this truth, that Bakunin's apocalyptic violence was largely an act, camouflage, and that his long series of strikingly Leninist organizational plans and programs were, in the main, notebook fantasies. However, with respect to performing his violent role and making his violent speeches, it made little difference to those who heard him, believed him, *and acted* on that belief that he was merely performing a part to convince himself that he was other than he was. Act or not, his words spawned a heritage of cruel deeds and useless sacrifice, and the cruelty and sacrifice continued—and continues—for generations thereafter among the countless would-be saviors he inspired. As for the Leninist secret organizations and their oppressively authoritarian character, the question is somewhat more complicated. For here we are not only dealing with an act, but with an act that Bakunin usually kept to himself and to his few "intimates." Unlike the violent rhetoric, therefore, the "secret society" fantasy did less harm as far as the outside world was concerned. However, this in no way alters the fact that it was just such organizational plans as these that were later to be adopted by Lenin and that helped establish the foundations for Soviet party dictatorship. Nor does it change the fact that Bakunin was devoted to these authoritarian schemes constantly, obsessively. He worked on them in the 1840s before he went to prison and exile and, far more intensively, in the 1860s and 1870s during his second revolutionary campaign. And even during the decade in between, the 1850s prison and Siberian years, the essential authoritarianism of these plans was dramatically present in his appeals to the Tsar and to the "red general" to take the lead of the revolution and establish an "iron dictatorship." Dedicated as one might be to defending Bakunin's image and honor, these facts cannot, or at least should not, be ignored. They are glaringly there.

But what of the marvelous and inspiring rhetoric of limitless freedom and the glowing vision of the "kingdom of love, of brotherhood"? Surely he should be praised for helping to keep those liberating lights high and bright. Perhaps so, had he not bound this messianic promise to the violence and the suffering that he insisted must clear the way for its realization. By merging social renewal and social annihilation, he committed his most grievous crime: he helped—for he is hardly alone in this—to secularize the apocalypse, to transform a devastatingly brutal vision inherited from an earlier religious era into a model for our times as well, an agenda for many who otherwise claim allegiance to reason and to the temporal realization of the good society.

Why does this happen? Why do so many visionaries insist on this apocalyptic nexus of bliss and horror, beauty and bestiality? Why have there been so many who have treated this fearful merger not as myth, poetry or theater for one or another level of catharsis, but as the plot and rhythm of history and as a guide for political action? Since it has long been obvious that maximalist violence has only and always betrayed and decimated the vision it allegedly served, arguments about "necessity" are childish and worthless. Nor is this a question of turning disillusioned utopians into vengeful prophets of doom, the way, for instance, the Russian philosopher Vladimir Soloviev turned from visions of the "Divine Feminine" to visions of an imminent Anti-Christ. What is involved here is the union of the two, the alliance of the divine and the demonic—paradise as the mask of hell, Christ as the mask of Lucifer, or, still closer to the roots, the Divine Feminine as the mask of Lilith. The merger is familiar in many religions and countless mythologies, and not only in distant, exotic gods and goddesses, such as the Hindu Kali.[23] In, for example, the gnostic despair that is the source and soul of fundamentalist Christian millennialism, in whatever age it appears, suffering and violence are more than tragic means to the sacred end: they are themselves elemental constituents of that end, the polar or dialectical twin of paradise. The dream of a new heaven and new earth does not displace the pain of life and world; it justifies and intensifies that pain by sanctifying massive, fire-and-brimstone repression of oneself and centuries of brutal torment of others and by propagating for nearly two millennia the apocalyptic vision of cataclysmic annihilation as the inevitable cost of paradise.[24] For all his daring insights, the Russian essayist Rozanov missed the point when he urged Christianity to celebrate the joy of Bethlehem rather than the suffering of Golgotha. Parousia and the unleashing of Satan are inextricably joined in this cruel epic. It is the source of this strange adoration of pain and destruction by those who dream of paradise that we question. Why do the dreamers of the miracle not fantasy beatific means as well as ends, since these visionaries depend in any case on the omnipotent magic of their divine, demiurgic, or chthonic God, Spirit, History, or Nature?

Bakunin's life suggests one answer, of, no doubt, very many. Utopian fantasy, at least of the kind that Bakunin envisioned, is clearly regressive, a flight from the real world of constraint, uncertainty, and inevitable mixtures of good and evil into a fantasied childhood or infancy where (in later imagination) all is lovingly given and nothing asked, where absolute freedom and harmonious love live happily together, where subject is object, where pleasure and reality join to feed and nurture. That dream and the solace it grants (the afterglow, perhaps, in everyone of the primary "dual unity") are not only benevolent and even necessary for stability and contentment, but may also be the source of hope and effort to reshape flawed reality into their ideal image. For Bakunin, however, that dream of maternal reunion, of infantile paradise regained, was doubly corrupted by narcissistic and oedipal disorders. As a result, the dream of paradise became the nightmare of apocalypse. In the pathologically narcissistic pattern, it is the "symbiotic couple" and the "all-good," maternal image that provides the "new heaven and new earth"; the explosive fury of archaic, narcissistic rage against the "all-bad" image that provides the apocalyptic catastrophe; and the fantasy of narcissistic omnipotence that fuels the maximalism of both the blissful, all-perfect end and the cataclysmic, all-destructive means. In the oedipal pattern, paradise is the sanctuary that encompasses, sanctions, and protects the symptoms of the oedipal failure (the impotence, the romanticism, the effemin-acy, the philosophical Idealism, and the life-long flight from power and responsi-bility); while the maximalist, apocalyptic violence serves to conceal the failure, channel vengeance, and provide a surrogate passion.

More decisive, however, in forming and driving the apocalyptic vision than either the narcissism or the oedipal dynamics acting alone was their interaction, specifically, the transformation of the preoedipal "symbiotic couple" into an oedipally incestual couple. While speculative, as acknowledged when it was first discussed, that theory best fits, I believe, the facts of Bakunin's later character, statements, and actions. As such, I would regard the dynamics described, if the theory is correct, as the decisive determinant of Bakunin's personality and behavior. To review the argument once more, before noting its central role in explaining Bakunin's apocalyptic vision, I suggested at several points that in responding to the oedipal failure, the child regressed more deeply into the pre-oedipal "symbiotic couple." Besides further intensifying the child's fixation in the preoedipal, narcissistic pattern, this regression, I believe, had a still more crucial outcome: regression more deeply into the "symbiotic couple" *after* the oedipal crisis and as an escape from and compensation for oedipal failure brought with it the character and consequences of the oedipal conflict and thereby, in effect, corrupted the child-mother "symbiotic couple" into an oedipally incestual couple. The "symbiotic couple" itself became the fulfillment of the incestual fantasy that the regressive flight inwards was meant to avoid. Withdrawing from the "fallen" world to be "fed and nurtured" by the maternal "friend" within and her "warmth so sweet" meant withdrawal into the very sin the boy was struggling to escape. The refuge from evil became its scene and instrument, and all the many and prolonged purification rites to exorcise the "animal," "sensual" "filth" were in vain. The victim was forever trapped in a vicious circle that re-volved incessantly throughout his life. Since the sanctuary itself perpetrated the crime he was trying to escape, he was driven out of it and into masochistic self-punishment through violent, self-destructive fantasies and actions. However, since displays of virile aggression were no less objectionable, for the variety of oedipal and narcissistic reasons discussed throughout the study, he fled right back into the sanctuary again, back to the maternal inner "friend," back, that is, into the now oedipally incestual "symbiotic couple," which began another turn of the circle, and on and on indefinitely.

Stating this another way, and drawing the implications for the apocalyptic vision, the price of endless bliss, of the regressive "new heaven and new earth," was endless self-punishment. Since purification was itself contamination, purity and pain were forever inextricably joined. The result for Bakunin was a life of suffering (real and imagined), a true "hell with all its terrors," both for himself and, because the dynamics involved required constant displacement and projection, for the world as he saw it. In the same way that severe deprivation and martyrdom were his punishment and atonement for living his infantile, incestual reunion, so must a comparable suffering in the form of apocalyptic violence and destruction be the world's price for attaining a similarly infantile, millennial paradise.

There are no doubt many roads that lead from deprivation and anguish, whatever their causes, to the nightmare of apocalypse, and it would be unreasonable to conjecture, without an individual-by-individual inquiry, just how heavily Bakunin's narcissistic and oedipal road to it has been travelled. Whatever the more general relationship between Oedipus, Narcissus, and Apocalypse, however, the dreams and visions involved are surely *not* themselves to blame for the violence: there have been countless utopias—including anarchist— that adamently rejected violence or domination as means for their realization. The apocalypse is decidedly not the only home for vision. There has always been in our culture another, older, and opposing heritage, that of the Pharisees and their humanist and liberal heirs, those Bakunin so furiously despised. It is a tradition that cherishes the vision and strives towards its fulfillment, while shunning in principle and practice the violence and authoritarianism that betray it. For this tradition the answer is not the maximalists' "all or nothing," that so often disguises inaction, but rather the realist's "something," that accompanies serious commitment and involvement. "It is not for us to finish the task, but neither can we desist from it."[25]

APPENDIX

NARCISSUS AND OEDIPUS

The psychological model I have followed in interpreting Bakunin's personality is, for the most part, a composite of traditional Freudian drive theory (oral, anal, genital) and more recent theories of narcissism, developed by Freudians and others, concerning the emergence and consolidation of the self and its relationship with the object world. In analyzing this development of the self and its "object relations," clinicians pay particular attention to the dyadic relations of mother and child in the preoedipal years, in contrast to the earlier tendency to focus on the triadal conflict involving child, mother, and father during the oedipal phase.

According to object relations and self theory, the self takes shape as a result of the fluctuating interaction between child and mother. At first, the mother's deepest feelings as well as her actions in that relationship are experienced by the child as his own in what is called a "dual unity" or "symbiotic couple." During this preoedipal, narcissistic phase, the child knows no other object but this "self object," this fusion of self and other into a single subjective experience. There is as yet neither a "true self" nor "true objects." Gradually, and partly as a result of the inevitable frustrations of childhood, the psychologically healthy child emerges from this "dual unity," self and object separate, and the child becomes an autonomous individual. However, and this is the central point of the theory, if the emerging self is to become psychologically healthy, as defined above, it must experience an appropriate ("optimum") balance between gratification and frustration, satisfaction and disappointment. If the childhood frustrations become so serious as to be felt as persistent rejection, reflecting a basic

436

emotional inability of the parent for whatever reason to provide love, acceptance, and encouragement, the child will not develop a healthy sense of self and self-esteem and will spend the rest of his life expressing the consequences of that basic injury and attempting to repair it, usually in vain. The child's most immediate defensive response to such deprivation is to turn to its own body and its erogenous zones for compensation and subsitution. He will also express the pain of the injury by feelings and outbursts of destructive fury, narcissistic rage, not merely because of a particular need frustration, but because, to restate the main point, the child's very self is under assault: since the child and the mother are experienced as one, the mother's rejection of the child means the child's rejection of that very self that is forming within him. (Narcissistic rage, it should be added, can also result from the opposite extreme, too much "care" that threatens to "smother" the emerging self.)

With respect to this narcissistic rage, some theorists emphasize the process of "splitting," a process that, they argue, takes place naturally in all children during the earliest years, or even months, but which takes aberrational forms in cases of pathological narcissism. "Splitting" is a way of escaping a basic dilemma. All children feel frustration because of inevitable delays and other denials, but to direct the anger against the mother is to direct it against the person the child is dependent on both for his physical survival and his own emerging self. To solve the problem, the child splits the real mother into two subjectively experienced forces or images, one all good, the other all bad. Under conditions of normal maturation and satisfactory psychological environment, the split is repaired as the child gradually achieves a self strong and cohesive enough to tolerate the frustrations, at which point the opposing images come together again in a "true" object, the good *and* bad mother. (The same merger is simultaneously taking place within the child, resulting in a comparable sense of himself as both good and bad.) In pathological narcissism, the "split" is radically intensified. The anger persists as narcissistic rage since the frustration involves an essential injury to the emerging self of the child. As a result, the outer world remains permanently "bad," alien, hostile and the target of the narcissistic rage that is from then on hurled against it; while the internalized, idealized all-good maternal image remains forever a source of fantasy approval, love, solace, encouragement and other gratifications denied the child in real life, a source far too important, too desperately indispensable, ever to be given up. The "split," in effect, never mends: the fragmented and enfeebled self remains withdrawn inward away from the painful world, dependent solipsistically on an inner fantasy life and on his identification with the all-good maternal image idealized in the continuing "symbiotic couple," unable to experience the outer reality as existing apart from himself, convinced that reality hates him and hating reality in return, forever striving vainly to fill the selfless void, usually by grandiose, omnipotent fantasies.

> In cases of narcissistic personality disorder, it is not difficult to discern the defensive nature—a pseudovitality—of the overt excitement. Behind it lie low self-esteem and depression—a deep sense of uncared-for worthlessness and rejection, an incessant hunger for response, a yearning for reassurance. All in all, the excited hypervitality of the patient must be understood as an attempt to counteract through self-stimulation a feeling of inner deadness and depression. As children, these patients had felt emotionally unresponded to and had tried to overcome their loneliness and depression through erotic and grandiose fantasies. The grown-up behavior and grown-up fantasy life of these patients is usually not the exact replica of the original childhood defense because, during an excited, overly enthusiastic, hyperidealistic adolescence devoid of meaningful interpersonal attachments, the childhood fantasies often become transformed by an intense devotion to romanticized cultural—esthetic, religious, political, etc.—aims. The romantic ideals, however, do not recede into the background when the individual reaches adulthood as would be the normal, expectable course; no comfortable integration with the goals of the adult personality takes place: the dramatic, intensely exhibitionist aspects of the personality do not become securely alloyed with mature productivity; and the erotized, excitedly pursued activities of adult life continue to be but one step removed from the underlying depression.[1]

So closely appropriate is the narcissistic pattern to Bakunin's life and thought that one might prefer (and some surely will) to define him as pathologically narcissistic (or even "borderline" psychotic) and drop entirely the oedipal category. Bakunin's zealous and obsessive introversion; his eager adoption of successive philosophies that expressed and sanctioned radical solipsism and through that solipsism an unbroken merger with the "friend" within who "fed and nurtured" him all his life (the idealized all-good mother image); his multiple locks, gates, and high monastic walls with which he guarded that inner refuge; his gargantuan oral needs and penchant for oral imagery; his "cold," "frozen" heart and his explicit feeling that there was something about himself that was unlovable; his inability to have anything to do with anything or anyone in which or whom he could not find himself and his maternal "friend"; his related need to see the outer, objective world only and always in terms of his subjective self, permitting, in effect, nothing but "self objects" throughout his life; his repeated wish to submerge himself in all-encompassing wholes, which he then transformed into mirrors of himself; his rejection of "middle way" compromises in favor of stark black-white, either-or, good-bad opposites; his constant sense of himself as being an innocent victim of a permanently inimical external world; his grandiose megalomania and his fantasies of omnipotent annihilation of the hypostatized bad world, so characteristic of narcissistic rage and omnipotence, the fury and fantasy of the elementally injured child; his telltale frenzy and mock enthusiasm that so obviously disguised and so easily crumbled into profound, even suicidal, despondency; his fluctuations between ecstatic optimism based on absolute trust in the victory of the fantasied "good" (a narcissistic ego identification with the omnipotent parent) and melancholic fatalism and depression when reality crushed the illusions and he felt his trust betrayed and himself abandoned, rejected again—all this together with many other related attitudes, statements and deeds noted along the way reflect this basic narcissism.

Indeed, recent studies on narcissism could just as well have been written with Bakunin in mind, so precisely do they describe his manner of thought and action. The gentle, romantic, pastoral, undemanding Premukhino of his childhood was not, therefore, so idyllic after all. In fact, if it appeared so to him throughout his life, it was mainly because it corresponded so well (as did his "holy commune") to the inner fantasy world into which he had earlier retreated in escape from essential injuries and losses that no mere physical environment, however splendid, could repair or redeem.

If, however, the evidence associating Bakunin with theories of narcissim is abundant, it is no less so with respect to oedipal theory. The basic formation of the narcissistic disorder occurs in the years preceding the oedipal encounter. The child who has been fortunate in his "self-object," child-mother relationships and has emerged from the "dual unity" with a firm and cohesive self is well prepared to meet successfully the new intrapsychic oedipal conflict, particularly if he has a father that is supportive and takes pride in the son's assertiveness. Such success still further strengthens the self, reenforces the self-esteem already achieved in the preoedipal period. Contrariwise, the child who leaves the preoedipal years with a weakened and fragmented self, who is still locked into the idealized, inner all-good mother image and, in fact, clings more tenaciously than ever to it as compensation for the basic deprivation, is severely handicapped when he confronts the oedipal crisis.

To appreciate the extent to which Bakunin failed to surmount the oedipal crisis, one need only keep in mind that for a boy to have resolved the oedipal conflicts successfully means, basically, that he follow his father's model by assuming or preparing to assume powers and responsibilities comparable to those of his father (having accepted the guilt that this replication—symbolic parricide—

involves and, later, resolved the guilt in mature reconciliation) and by engaging in his own sexual and familial life (having freed both from the incestual associations attached to them during these early years). Nothing in Bakunin's life is clearer than the fact that he could do neither.

The consequences of the oedipal failure are doubly injurious; for not only does the boy suffer the specific maladies associated with that failure (such as impotence, fear of masculine roles, etc.), but he experiences as well another assault on his self-esteem, his already badly weakened self. The harm is further compounded if the father's personality is as unempathic as the mother's had been in the preoedipal years, thereby burdening the child with additional rejection and discouragement rather than the love and praise that the self, especially the weakened self, needs. As one of many effects of this series of failures, rejections, and other blows to the child's self-esteem, he will compensate in later years by fantasizing ever more glorious, praiseworthy, heroic achievements that are generally doomed to failure by their very extravagance and that, consequently, only further diminish self-esteem, which, in turn, generates still more omnipotent, promethean ambitions and so forth. What results, in fact, are precisely those attributes that we have seen develop in Bakunin: his impotence and effeminacy; his passive-masochistic cult of suffering; his grandiose, heroic plans and visions; his persistent aberrational attitudes towards sex and marriage; his passionate love-hate attachment to his mother; his general avoidance of responsible power and conventional male roles and his life-long dedication to destroying all such power and roles (even while strongly admiring powerful leaders and trying to emulate them in secret plans); and his successive theories, including anarchism, that expressed and sanctioned this radical withdrawal and avoidance (the oedipal counterpart to the narcissistic theories of Romantic and Idealistic return, reunion, and merger). When one recalls especially the enormous amount of time and space Bakunin gives to his attacks on everything "animal," sensual, sexual, the sexually loaded words and phrases he uses in his condemnation of his mother, the constant appearance and reappearance of sexual imagery in his writings and the character and context of that imagery, when one recalls this and remembers as well Bakunin's radically ambivalent attitude towards his father and other authority figures, it is difficult to see how narcissistic theory (without unacceptably prolix meanderings and chains of inference) could by itself, without oedipal theory, explain Bakunin.

We are not, therefore, dealing here with two alternative or contradictory theories, but rather with two complementary theories: *both* the narcissistic and the oedipal dynamics play essential roles in determining what Bakunin said and did. While it may be necessary in treatment for the analyst to establish genetic priority and decide whether a disorder lay ultimately in the triadal-oedipal or in the dyadic-preoedipal relationship, it is enough for biographical description and explanation to know that *both* were present, that Bakunin's behavior represents a composite of both sets of characteristics. In fact, while specific traits may be assigned to one or another of the two patterns, as was done in those foregoing lists, the actual dynamics should be understood as involving the mutual interaction of both. There was, first of all, the basic interaction. Pathological narcissism helped cause the oedipal failure, first, by not providing the child with the capacities needed to resolve the oedipal conflict, a self that was integrated and strong enough to experience the new ambivalent feelings and remain a cohesive self; and, second, by preserving the preoedipal child-mother "dual unity" and the internalized, idealized all-good maternal image, thereby making the demand for exclusive possession of the mother all the more intense, tightening the incestual bond, and fueling still more hostility against the rival. The basic mutuality functioned in the reverse direction as well: the oedipal failure added still another blow to the already weakened ego, strengthening the need to remain safely embedded in the world within and, most important of all, transformed the preoedipal "symbiotic couple" into an oedipally incestual couple, as discussed at the end of the preceding chapter.

These examples of the basic mutual influence linking the narcissistic and the oedipal dynamics are, however, only the beginning of their interaction. The narcissism and its projections not only gave Bakunin a sanctuary from the abhorred reality of sex, power, and alien objectivity; it also provided him, through its rage, archaic magic, and omnipotence, the fury and the primitive fantasy needed to conceal the failure under a torrent of apocalyptic rhetoric. Similarly, Bakunin's love-hate relations with his parents derive their energy and direction from both sources. Bakunin's father is resented as the outsider threatening the preoedipal and the oedipal exclusivity and also feared as the all-powerful oedipal rival. His mother (or, more accurately, the intrapsychic experience of being mothered, "fed and nurtured") is loved narcissistically as the indispensable source of life and self and, later, oedipally as a primary sexual object; but she is also feared and hated, narcissistically as the "bad" mother who frustrated the child's needs and crippled his emerging self (by deprivation, "smothering," or both alternately) and oedipally for seeming to seduce the youth into the oedipal trap. (Still narcissistically dependent on the mother, the child attempts to possess her oedipally, but withdraws in "terror" from the incestual wish and projects the forbidden wish onto the mother, blaming her as the temptress—and adding, thereby, another source of hostility to further intensify the narcissistic rage carried over from the preoedipal phase). The narcissistic-oedipal mutuality is apparent also in Bakunin's contradictory response to the oedipal failure— impotence and violence. Impotence defends the youth from punishment for incestual intent and at the same time expresses the desired preoedipal mode of union, the safe, presexual maternal union by passivity and identification. Related to that impotence is the continuing, subdued theme of non-violence, which can be understood both as a check against the narcissistic rage (ultimately self-destructive, since it seeks the annihilation of the "self-object" on which the emerging self depends) and as another oedipal defense against a dangerously masculine aggressiveness. As for the ferocious-sounding violence, it is simultaneously the voice of narcissistic rage, the camouflage in Bakunin's mock oedipal battle, a vehicle for masochistic self-punishment for both incestual desire and narcissistic rage, and a surrogate "paroxysm" for the lost sexuality.

Finally, as we have seen throughout the study, both patterns joined to shape and energize Bakunin's millennial vision and his credo of total destruction as the only means of its attainment, to form, in short, the roots of his apocalypse.[2] It is, therefore, the combined impact of both disorders, each reenforcing the other, that accounts for the extremes in Bakunin's character and the extraordinary intensity with which he lived those extremes. If his rhetoric of hatred was so violent and endured so constantly and so long it was because it was fed by so many different elemental fires. And if his fear was so deep, his withdrawal so complete, and his appetite for fantasies of omnipotent power and infantile paradise so insatiable, it was because real life threatened him so severely and because he came to trust only what he could make a part of the inner self that he had pieced together, by means of successive illusions and fantasies, from the damaged fragments his childhood had left him. In the end, what was perhaps most extraordinary about the man was his tenacious capacity to hang on and keep going, drawing strength and purpose from little else but those fantasies that his fine mind could cull from the fragments.[3]

NOTES

CHAPTER 1. ESTRANGEMENT

1. Y. M. Steklov, ed., M. A. Bakunin. *Sobranie sochinenii i pisem, 1828–1876* (Moscow, USSR Society of Former Political Prisoners and Exiles, 1934–36), vol. I, p. 52. Letter to his parents. September 20, 1831. Since a principal aim of this study is to try to form a view of Bakunin from within the man himself, it will depend heavily on Bakunin's own works, especially his personal letters, and only sparingly on secondary sources. The letters are particularly important for understanding the critical formative years, before he began revealing his attitudes and motivations in more public statements and actions.

2. Ibid., vol. I, p. 38. Letter to his aunts. November 27, 1828.

3. Ibid., vol. I, p. 154. Letter to his parents. December 19, 1834.

4. Ibid., vol. I, p. 42. Letter to his sisters. March 2, [1830].

5. Ibid., vol. I, p. 52. Letter to his parents. September 20, 1831.

6. Ibid., vol. I, p. 164. Letter to Sergei Nicholaevich Muraviev. January [1835].

7. Alexander A. Kornilov, *Molodye gody Mikhaila Bakunina* (Moscow: M. and S. Sabashnikov, 1915), p. 88, note 1.

8. Steklov, *Sobranie*, vol. IV, p. 128 (Bakunin's "Confession" to Tsar Nicholas I).

9. Unless otherwise indicated, my description of Alexander Bakunin and of the life he formed for himself and his family at Premukhino is based on Kornilov's account and on excerpts that Kornilov reproduced from Alexander Bakunin's writings.

10. A report written in April 1820 by the French ambassador at St. Petersburg, Count de la Ferronays, insightfully describes the East-West ambivalence that circumstance had imposed not only on the Tsar but on most of Russia's educated society as well. "He talks of the rights of man, of those of peoples, of

the duties of a monarch, as the disciple of a philosopher [of the French Enlightenment] can and should talk, but at the same time he enforces his most arbitrary wishes with greater despotism and ruthlessness than Peter I would have." Similarly, as the Count de Noailles put it three years earlier, "in a state of society so remote from perfection and resembling in many ways oriental governments, a young Russian officer, armed with his knout, subject to an absolute sovereign, surrounded by his own slaves, talks to you of the rights of peoples, of liberty, like a citizen of the United States!" Both quotations are from Michael T. Florinsky, *Russia: A History and an Interpretation* (New York: Macmillan, 1953), vol. II, pp. 629, 736.

11. Steklov, *Sobranie*, vol. I, p. 45. Letter to his sisters. March 17, 1830.

12. Ibid., vol. II, p. 107. Letter to his father. December 15, 1837.

13. Ibid., vol. I, p. 112. Letter to his parents. May 1833.

14. Ibid., vol. I, pp. 41, 46–47, 51, 56, 74, 114, 134, 138, 141. Letters, as dated in the text, to his sisters, sisters, parents, parents, parents and sisters, sisters, parents, the Beyer sisters, and parents.

15. Ibid., vol. I, p. 57. Letter to his parents. April [1832].

16. Ibid., vol. I, p. 155. Letter to his parents. December 19, 1834.

17. One could dip almost at random into Bakunin's letters of the time for descriptions of other episodes like the following, written some two months before his twentieth birthday, with four years of military hardening behind him. "Maria Vosilova was ill. She had the grippe. Maria Lvova was with her until eight in the evening. At eight she had to leave for home, since they were having a gathering that evening. I had brought some books for my cousins. Maria Lvova invited me, beseeched me, ordered me to go along with her. I refused and remained there, to keep my cousin, who was all alone with her mother, company and to read aloud to her. How she rewarded me for that with her eyes, her gaze, her words! She thought that I was making a sacrifice, but I considered it the greatest happiness to stay with her. The next day, when I came to ask about her health, there was no one home except Mrs. Borozdnina, who was busy laying out a vast game of patience. My cousin and I were alone in the reception room. She poured tea and we talked. She told me that Maria Lvova was angry with me for not having gone to their gathering. I asked her to get Maria Lvova to forgive me and to tell her that I could do no such thing as leave my cousin alone. 'Dear Michel' (she always calls me this), Maria said to me, 'You are an angel of kindness (this is her own expression) and I am deeply touched by the friendship you show me.' If you, dear Varvara, could only have seen me at that moment! I was happier than one could be in paradise. I was silent, but my silence spoke more eloquently than any words. And she understood me and blushed so."

Such passages from Bakunin's letters, so different in tone and character from the familiar promethean image of the man, should not be dismissed as passing juvenalia. Distant though they are from the heroic fiction, they reflect the very essence of Michael Bakunin not only during this formative period, but throughout his life. (The quotation is from a letter to his sister Varvara, written March 5, 1833. Steklov, *Sobranie,* vol. I, pp. 80–81.)

18. Again, a single illustration will have to do, a paragraph from a letter to his sisters describing three young cousins he had just met: "They are gentle daughters and adore their father, whose slightest thought is law to them. They

are very kind, very sweet, and at the same time very intelligent. They overflow with talent and are quite well educated. They adore nature, cannot bear social affairs, although they attend them of necessity, and they comport themselves there delightfully. I cannot say more of them now. As soon as I discover something new about them, I will write you. We are already great friends. I am very sincere with them. They show themselves extremely well disposed towards me. We speak much about you. They asked me for pictures of you, and I sketched them. They are burning with a desire to meet you, to get to know you. They already love you." Steklov, *Sobranie*, vol. I, p. 126. Letter to his sisters. January 25, 1834.

19. Ibid., vol. I, p. 151. Letter to his sisters. October 5, 1834.

20. See note 23 below.

21. Ibid., vol. I, pp. 102-4. Letter to his sisters. May 20, [1833].

22. Ibid., vol. I, p. 106. Letter to his sisters. June 10, 1833.

23. Ibid., vol. I, pp. 98-99. Letter to his sister Varvara. April 7, 1833.

24. Ibid., vol. I, p. 101. Letter to his sister Varvara. April 21, 1833.

25. Ibid., vol. I, p. 100. Letter to his parents and sisters. April 9, 1833.

26. For the English romantic influence, see Ernst J. Simmons, *English Literature and Culture in Russia* (Cambridge, Mass.: Harvard University Press, 1935).

27. Steklov, *Sobranie*, vol. I, p. 79. Letter to his sister Varvara. March 5, 1833. This lengthy letter (pp. 78-85) is a particularly fine example of Bakunin's romantic sensibilities as a young man, 19 at the time.

28. Ibid., vol. I, pp. 132-33. Letter to his parents. June 23, 1834.

29. Kornilov, *Molodye gody*, pp. 36-38.

30. Steklov, *Sobranie*, vol. II, pp. 105-6. Letter to his father. December 15, 1837.

31. Ibid.

32. Ibid., vol. I, pp. 110-11. Letter to his parents. May [?] 12, 1833; vol. I, p. 79. Letter to his sister Varvara. March 5, 1833.

33. Ibid., vol. I, pp. 86-88. Letter to his sister Varvara. February 8, 1833.

34. Ibid., vol. II, pp. 108-9. Letter to his father. December 15, 1837. (Another reason that Bakunin lists to explain his side of the quarrel with his aunt was her accusing him of stealing a book from her in order to get back at her for scolding him. Ibid., vol. II, p. 109.)

35. Ibid., vol. II, pp. 110 *ff.*

36. Ibid., vol. II, pp. 114-15, 120. For another and significantly similar description of the virgin's abomitable fate, see p. 66.

37. Ibid., vol. I, pp. 120-21. Letter to his sisters. January 4, 1834.

38. Kornilov, *Molodye gody*, p. 82.

39. Vyacheslav Polonskii, ed., *Materialy dlia biographii M. Bakunina* (Moscow: Gosudarstvennoe Izdatelstvo, 1923), vol. I, p. 406.

40. Steklov, *Sobranie*, vol. II, p. 107. Letter to his father. December 15, 1837.

41. Kornilov, *Molodye gody*, p. 83.

42. See above, p. 11.

43. Steklov, *Sobranie*, vol. I, p. 140. Letter to his parents. October 4, 1834.

44. See above, p. 12.

45. Kornilov, *Molodye gody*, pp. 154-55.

46. "...I chose a freezing cold winter night, drank down a lot of hot tea, perspired heavily, then, in full sweat, stripped off my clothes, went outside nude, and lay down on my side in the snow. I lay there like that for a good half hour, bitterly cold, and only when I could stand no more, got up and dressed. And what do you think happened? Nothing, neither the next day nor the day after did I catch even a little cold! Nothing at all! And so I had to go right on drudging away as before." As quoted in Z. Ralli, "Mikhail Bakunin iz moikh vospominanii," *Minuvshie gody*, 1980. no. 10, pp. 148–49.

47. Steklov, *Sobranie*, vol. I, pp. 156–58. Letter to his sisters. December 19, [1834].

48. See above, pp. 18–19.

49. Ibid., vol. I, pp. 43–44. Letter to his parents. March 16, 1830.

50. Ibid., vol. I, p. 49. Letter to his parents. August 30, 1831.

51. Ibid., vol. I, p. 57. Letter to his parents. [April 1832].

52. Ibid., vol. I, pp. 109–12. Letter to his parents. May [?] 12, 1833. (It is especially interesting to compare this "confession" with the tone and character of Bakunin's later "Confession" to the Tsar.)

53. Ibid., vol. I, p. 147. Letter to his sisters. October 5, 1834.

54. Ibid., vol. I, p. 137. Letter to the Beyer sisters. July 11, [1834].

55. Ibid., vol. I, p. 134. Letter to his parents. June 28, [1834]; vol. I, p. 146. Letter to his sisters. October 5, 1834; vol. I, p. 156. Letter to his sisters. December 19, [1834].

56. The exact wording is "I threw myself passionately into *her*." The pronoun that I translated as "it," as is conventionally done, is actually in the feminine, "her." There are neuter Russian words for "study" that are more common than the feminine word, *uchyoba*, that Bakunin uses here. We will later see other examples of what I believe was Bakunin's unconscious revelation through his choice of words and phrases of the needs, fears, and strategies that he was striving to conceal. We will also see, in the following chapter, that the "study" into which he "threw" himself at the time and for several years to come, German Idealism, was ideally suited to his need to be solipsistically "fed and nurtured" by an inner source that he would soon call the "friend" within. Also, having "locked" himself within himself, he could freely engage in his "profound probing of nature's secrets," that same nature that spoke to him "in the language of love" and of which he said, "my soul, tearing itself free of the mortal barriers that constrain it, pours itself over the entire universe, encompassing all of nature...." The latent significance of this and an abundance of similar imagery will become apparent as we see more of Bakunin's remarks and the circumstances that inspired them.

57. Ibid., vol. I, pp. 122–24. Letter to his sisters. January 25, 1834. I am translating the verb *vyroshchat/vyrostit* as "fed and nurtured" in order to convey its special nuances and implications. See Vladimir Dal's definition: "to take care of by means of attention, food so that a young plant, animal or person grows and becomes strong....To become larger by means of feeding and the consumption of food." (*Tolkovyi slovar*, 1955, vol. I, p. 310).

58. Ibid., vol. I, p. 134. Letter to his parents. June 28, [1834].

59. Ibid., vol. II, p. 109. Letter to his father. December 15, 1837. (The reference to Venevitinov is made in the long *recherche du temps perdu* which

Bakunin wrote to explain his side of the conflict with his father.)

60. Ibid., vol. I, p. 162. Letter to Sergei Nicholaevich Muraviev. [January 1835].

61. Ibid., vol. I, p. 142. Letter to his parents. October 4, 1834; vol. I, p. 154. Letter to his parents. December 19, 1834.

62. Ibid., vol. I, p. 84. Letter to his sister Varvara. March 5, 1833.

63. Ibid., vol. I, p. 154. Letter to his parents. December 19, 1834.

64. Ibid., vol. I, p. 142. Letter to his parents. October 4, 1834.

65. Ibid., vol. I, p. 135. Letter to his family. June 28, [1834].

66. Ibid., vol. I, pp. 138–39. Letter to the Beyer sisters. July 11, 1834.

67. Ibid., vol. I, p. 135. Letter to his family. June 28, [1834].

68. Ibid., vol. I, p. 144. Letter to his parents. October 4, 1834.

69. The quotations are from Bakunin's first revolutionary publication, *The Reaction in Germany,* which appeared in October, 1842. See below, p. 169.

70. "My dear wife Varvara and children Michael, Liubov, Varvara, Tatiana, Alexandra, Nicholas, Ilya, Paul, Alexander, Alexei"—thus had Alexander Michailovich, Michael's father, begun his last will and testament the year before Michael left for military school, taking Michael out of his chronological place—after Varvara—and setting him at the head of the list. Nicholas, the next eldest son, was only nine at the time. Kornilov, *Molodye gody,* p. 688.

71. In later life, Bakunin recalled one small incident (part of which we have already cited) which dramatically reveals the value contradiction he felt he had to reconcile, the contradiction between carefree, pastoral ease and stern discipline. "You rarely scolded us and, I believe, never once punished us, but the thought that you would find out something wrong we had done, the thought that you would be angry at us struck terror in us.... I remember how once while chasing butterflies without mother, we had forgotten that it was time for dinner and that you were waiting for us. How frightened we were when we remembered and found you in the dining room, sitting at the table and already dining. You did not say a word, only got up ahead of us, and we were so scared that we did not know what to do. After dinner, having rested, you called us to walk with you and talked with us just as though nothing at all had happened. We were so stunned by your kindness, so happy and joyful." Steklov, *Sobranie,* vol. II, p. 150. Letter to his father. December 15, 1837. Since, as he indicates here, his father never punished him and rarely even scolded him, why, one wonders, was young Michael "so scared" as to speak of "terror"? Did the source of the fear—as well as that "something wrong"—lay within Michael himself?

72. Steklov, *Sobranie,* vol. I, p. 155. Letter to his parents. December 19, 1834.

73. See below, p. 50.

74. Natalia Pirumova, "Bakunin and Herzen: An Analysis of their Ideological Disagreements at the End of the 1860's," *Canadian-American Slavic Studies,* trans., Marshall S. Shatz. 10 (winter, 1976); 552.

75. With respect to Bakunin's impotence, Bakunin's principal Soviet biographer and archivist, Steklov, referred to "a certain physical characteristic" because of which Bakunin was "incapable, apparently, of conjugal life"; another early Soviet biographer, Polonsky, stated categorically that "Bakunin had no children and could not have them"; Ross, one of Bakunin's closest friends and most devoted admirers, similarly acknowledged that the children born during

his marriage with Antonia were not his; Guillaume, friend, lieutenant, and later chronicler of Bakunin's faction in the International, described Bakunin as Antonia's "husband only in a legal sense"; Vyrubova, a young admirer in Bakunin's last year, considered the marriage "pathological," a "pseudo-marriage"; both Katkov and Belinsky, as we will see, called him a "eunuch"; Herzen described him, a man near 35 at the time, as an "old Joan of Arc," a "maiden" as she had been; and even his recent biographer "Jeanne-Marie," who seems to revere the man and would do nothing to blemish his image, questions the consummation of the marriage, adding that it was "a union without sexual relations, perhaps, but an admirable union." Apparently countering this testimony, there has been a suggestion that Bakunin may have had an illegitimate son while in Siberia. In fact, Bakunin's latest Soviet biographer, Pirumova, believes that she knows the grandson. Since, according to Pirumova, the claims are not documented, all one can say is... perhaps, although what we know about Bakunin's life and personality makes it all seem quite unlikely. (Because of—in Pirumova's description—the man's poor health and consequent inability to reply to inquiries, she judged it best not to disclose the "grandson's" address.) Actually, were the claims valid, they would *strengthen* the evidence for Bakunin's impotence, since they would tend to prove that Antonia's children were fathered by another man not because Bakunin was sterile (while sexually active), but because he was indeed unwilling or unable to engage in sexual relations. Finally, general impotence is, of course, entirely consistent with occasional "success," and the special circumstances and probable mood accompanying Bakunin's release from prison into the relative freedom of exile, when the event is said to have occurred, might have provided the appropriate conditions for such an exception (*if* there had been one). In short, besides being largely speculative, the claims of Bakunin fathering an illegitimate child even if valid would not displace the traditional and prevailing view of his impotence or of his profound and persistent aversion to sexuality that is so apparent in his letters. (See also Carr, pp. 239, 266.)

76. While most biographers of Bakunin make some reference to the psychological factor (with such striking aberrations how could it be otherwise?), only one author has made it his principal focus—I. Malinin, in his 80 page monograph, *Kompleks edipa i sud'ba Mikhaila Bakunina*, published in Belgrade, 1934. An indication of the conventional response to psychological biographies of this sort is the obscurity to which this insightful and scholarly pioneer work has been relegated. Although it was not Malinin's intention to follow the impact of the psychological factor on Bakunin's thoughts and actions, he was, nevertheless, the first to see and outline the underlying oedipal problem and to emphasize the decisive role it played in Bakunin's life. As he interpreted it, the oedipal influence was most apparent in Bakunin's ambivalent attitude towards authority and power: on the one hand, his vigorous opposition to his father and all other authority; on the other, his desire and efforts to replace his father and achieve power. After discussing the oedipal character of Bakunin's conflict with his father for control of the other Bakunin children, his conflict with Nicholas I in the revolutionary 1840s, and his militant war against God during his later anarchist-atheist years, Malinin turned to the roots of the problem, first by skillfully reviewing Bakunin's incestual attraction to his sister and, finally, by

discussing, more tersely, his attachment to his mother. A final section further supports the interpretation by describing Bakunin's characteristically childlike behavior. Having put off reading Malinin's study until my own was completed, to avoid being overly influenced by a work whose title indicated an approach similar to my own, I was gratified to find considerable correspondence between our general interpretations, at least with respect to the oedipal factor. There are, however, a number of differences, as will be apparent to those familiar with the work. Besides the fact that Malinin did his work long before psychoanalysis moved on from Freud's theories to later approaches by Freudians and others to "ego psychology," "object relations," and the formation and disorders of the self (see note 83 and the concluding chapter, "Narcissus and Oedipus"), he does not enter into an analysis of the ways Bakunin's shifting theories and political practice throughout his life reflected his malaise (a central theme of the present study). Also, he interprets Bakunin's attitude toward power differently than I do: whereas Malinin sees an ambivalence between Bakunin's attack on authority and his attempt to attain power, my emphasis is on Bakunin's persistent fear and avoidance of power. Finally, there is a strange—considering the general approach—omission in Malinin's account of any discussion of Bakunin's aversion to sexuality, an aversion that, as we will see, was critically involved in Bakunin's life and thought.

77. See the Introduction for remarks on the psychological dimensions of the study, pp. 2-3.

78. Steklov, *Sobranie*, vol. I, p. 133. Letter to his family. June 23, [1834].

79. Ibid., vol. II, pp. 96-128. Letter to his father. December 15, 1837.

80. Ibid., vol. I, pp. 141-42. Letter to his parents. October 4, 1834.

81. See the concluding chapter, "Narcissus and Oedipus," for further discussion of this subject.

82. During the intervening ("latency") years between the initial formation of the disorders and their later emergence in adolescence, the special mood and mode of life at Premukhino—gentle, indulgent, pastoral, romantic, evangelic—probably corresponded to his personality enough to conceal the trouble. To recall Bakunin's own description, that life was "pure and virginal," in contrast to the "dark, filthy, and vile" experience that awaited him in adolescence, in that lions' den of virility, the military barracks.

83. On the "dual unity" (or "symbiotic couple") and its relationship to the oedipus complex, see, for example, Hans W. Loewald, "The Waning of the Oedipus Complex," *Papers on Psychoanalysis* (New Haven, Conn.: Yale University Press, 1980), pp. 384-404 and David E. Schecter, M.D., "The Oedipus Complex: Consideration of Ego Development and Parental Interaction," *Contemporary Psychoanalysis* 4 (spring, 1968): 111-37. For a discussion of the "object relations" and "ego psychology" approaches by Freudians and others see the collection of articles, *Integrating Ego Psychology and Object Relations Theory*, ed. L. Saretsky, G.D. Goldman, and D.S. Milman (Dubuque, Ia.: Kendall/Hunt, 1979). This collection mainly concerns the U.S. branch of these schools, for example, H. Kohut and O. Kernberg and their followers. A fascinating account and evaluation of the British exponents—H. Guntrip, D.W. Winnicott, W.R.D. Fairbairn, L.H. Farber and others—is presented in David

Holbrook, *Human Hope and the Death Instinct* (Oxford, New York: Pergamon Press, 1971). The chapter on Melanie Klein, a seminal influence in these later revisions and refinements of Freud's early theories, is especially useful. Finally, for "Self" theory, two works by Heinz Kohut provide a good introduction: *The Restoration of the Self* (New York: International Universities Press, 1977) and "Thoughts on Narcissism and Narcissistic Rage," *The Psychoanalytic Study of the Child*. Vol. 27 (New York: Quadrangle Press, 1972).

CHAPTER 2. SANCTUARY

1. Kornilov, *Molodye gody,* Chapter VII.
2. Ibid., Chapter X.
3. Ibid., pp. 153–155.
4. Quoted in Edward J. Brown, *Stankevich and his Moscow Circle. 1830–1840.* (Stanford, Calif.: Stanford University Press, 1966), p. 5.
5. Ibid., p. 28.
6. Ibid., p. 5.
7. Quoted in Philip Shashko, *Unity and Dissent Among the Russian Westerners,* Ph.D. dissertation, University of Michigan, 1969, p. 47.
8. Quoted in Brown, *Stankevich,* pp. 19–20.
9. Ibid., p. 48.
10. Steklov, *Sobranie,* vol. II, p. 50. Letter to the Beyer sisters. July 31, 1837.
11. Quoted in Zenkovsky, *A History of Russian Philosophy,* translated by George L. Kline (London: Routledge and Kegan Paul, 1953), vol. I, p. 118.
12. Quoted in Alexander Koyre, *Philosophie et la Probleme Nationale en Russie au Debut du XIX Siecle* (Paris: Librairie Ancienne Honoré Champion, 1929), p. 122.
13. Ibid., p. 147.
14. See above, p. 23.
15. Quoted in Koyre, *Philosophie,* p. 143.
16. Ibid., p. 36.
17. Quoted in Shashko, *Unity and Dissent,* p. 51.
18. Quoted in Koyre, *Philosophie,* p. 138.
19. Quoted in Zenkovsky, *Russian Philosophy,* p. 139.
20. Ibid., p. 140.
21. Ibid., p. 120.
22. Quoted in Zenkovsky, *Russian Philosophy,* p. 142.
23. Quoted in Koyre, *Philosophie,* pp. 134–35.
24. Ibid., pp. 142–43.
25. Nikolai V. Stankevich, *Perepiska. 1830-1840* (Moscow: Alexei Stankevich, 1914), p. 571.
26. Steklov, *Sobranie,* vol. I, p. 177. Letter to A.P. Efremov. September 20, 1835.
27. Stankevich, *Perepiska,* p. 444.
28. Ibid., p. 334.
29. Ibid., p. 444.
30. Ibid., p. 578.
31. Ibid., p. 575.

32. Ibid., p. 576.
33. Ibid., p. 595.
34. Ibid., pp. 583–84.
35. Ibid., p. 587.
36. Ibid., p. 580.
37. Ibid.
38. Ibid., p. 596.
39. Ibid., p. 579.
40. Ibid., p. 576.
41. Ibid., pp. 587, 594.
42. Quoted in Brown, *Stankevich,* p. 50.
43. See above, p. 39.
44. Stankevich, *Perepiska,* p. 582.
45. Quoted in Koyre, *Philosophie,* p. 148.
46. Stankevich, *Perepiska,* p. 594.
47. Ibid., p. 585.
48. Steklov, *Sobranie,* vol. I, pp. 166–67. Letter to the Beyer sisters. April 22, 1835.
49. Ibid., p. 168.
50. Ibid., vol. I, p. 179. Letter to A.P. Efremov. November 14, 1835; vol. I, p. 181. Reply to his sisters. [November 1835]; vol. I, p. 184. Letter to A.P. Efremov. December 10, 1835; vol. I, p. 186. Letter to A.P. Efremov. December 19, 1835.
51. Ibid., vol. I, p. 169. Letter to the Beyer sisters. May 7, 1835.
52. Ibid., vol. I, pp. 179–80. Letter to A.P. Efremov. November 14, 1835.
53. Ibid., vol. I, p. 174. Letter to A.P. Efremov. July 29, 1835.
54. Ibid., vol. I, p. 184. Letter to A.P. Efremov. December 10, 1835.
55. Ibid.
56. Ibid., vol. I, p. 182. Letter to A.P. Efremov. November 27, 1835.
57. Ibid., vol. I, p. 187. Letter to A.P. Efremov. December 28, 1835.
58. Ibid., vol. I, p. 175. Letter to A.P. Efremov. July 29, 1835.
59. Ibid., p. 174.
60. Ibid. (Emphasis added.)
61. Ibid., vol. I, p. 178. Letter to IA. M. Neverov. October 26, 1835.
62. Ibid., vol. I, p. 185. Letter to A.P. Efremov. December 10, 1835.
63. Ibid., vol. I, p. 170. Letter to the Beyer sisters. May 7, 1835.
64. See above, pp. 29–30.
65. Steklov, *Sobranie,* vol. I, pp. 169–70. Letter to the Beyer sisters. May 7, 1835.
66. Ibid., vol. I, p. 175. Letter to A.P. Efremov. July 29, 1835.
67. See above, p. 45.
68. For more on this point, arguing that the danger could not be avoided, see below, pp. 64–65, 434–435.
69. Ibid., vol. I, p. 170. Letter to the Beyer sisters. May 7, 1835.
70. Ibid., vol. I, p. 175. Letter to A.P. Efremov. July 29, 1835.
71. Ibid., vol. I, p. 180. Letter to A.P. Efremov. November 14, 1835.
72. Ibid.
73. Ibid., vol. I, pp. 170–71. Letter to the Beyer sisters. May 7, 1835.

74. Ibid, vol. I, p. 172.

75. Ibid., vol. I, p. 176. Letter to the Beyer sisters. [August 1835].

76. Ibid., vol. I, p. 180. Letter to A.P. Efremov. November 15, 1835; vol. I, p. 182. Letter to Efremov. November 27, 1835; vol. I, p. 184. Letter to Efremov. December 10, 1835; vol. I, pp. 186-87. Letter to Efremov. December 28, 1835.

77. Stankevich, *Perepiska,* p. 586.

78. Kornilov, *Molodye gody,* pp. 154-55.

79. Ibid., p. 141, note 2.

80. Stankevich, *Perepiska,* p. 574.

81. Steklov, *Sobranie,* vol. I, p. 196. Letter to IA. M. Neverov. February 15, 1836.

82. Ibid., vol. II, p. 398. Letter to his parents. [March 24, 1840].

83. Kornilov, *Molodye gody,* p. 160.

84. Steklov, *Sobranie,* vol. I, p. 180. Letter to A.P. Efremov. November 15, 1835.

85. Ibid., vol. I, p. 187. Letter to A.P. Efremov. December 28, 1835.

86. Ibid., vol. I, p. 199. Letter to his sister Varvara. February 17, 1836.

87. Ibid., vol. I, p. 218. Letter to his sister Tatiana. March 8, 1836.

88. Ibid., vol. I, p. 211. Letter to his sisters Tatiana and Varvara. February 28, 1836; vol. I, p. 198. Letter to Tatiana. February 17, 1836.

89. Ibid., vol. I, pp. 189-90. Letter to his father. [January 1836].

90. See above, pp. 49-50.

91. Steklov, *Sobranie*, vol. I, p. 210. Letter to his sisters Tatiana and Varvara. February 28, 1836.

CHAPTER 3. THE FICHTEAN MISSIONARY: FIRST CRUSADE

1. Steklov, *Sobranie,* vol. I, p. 196. Letter to IA. M. Neverov. February 15, 1836.

2. Kornilov, *Molodye gody,* pp. 176-77.

3. Steklov, *Sobranie,* vol. I, p. 249. Letter to Alexandra Beyer. April 2, 1836. For Chaadaev, see below,

4. Ibid., vol. I, p. 219. Letter to his sister Tatiana. March 8, 1836.

5. Ibid., vol. I, p. 235. Letter to his sister Varvara. March 11, 1836.

6. Ibid., vol. I, p. 259. Letter to Alexandra Beyer. April 6, 1836.

7. Johann Gottlieb Fichte, "The Way towards the Blessed Life," *The Popular Works of Johann Gottlieb Fichte,* vol. II, trans. William Smith (London: Trübner, 1889); Johann Gottlieb Fichte, "Einige Vorlesungen uber die Bestimmung des Gelehrten," *Johann Gottlieb Fichte's Samtliche Werke* (Berlin: Veit, 1845), vol. VI. (See below, p. 58.)

8. Kornilov, *Molodye gody*, p. 142.

9. Stankevich, *Perepiska,* pp. 605-6.

10. Fichte, "The Way," p. 295.

11. Ibid., pp. 296-97.

12. For these and similar examples of Fichte's intellectual solipsism see "The Way," pp. 305-6, 308-9, 316, 341, 344-45, 357.

13. Ibid., pp. 369–70, 374, 464; and Fichte, "Einige Vorlesungen," pp. 330, 332–33.

14. *Telescope* (1836), no. XXIX.

15. Steklov, *Sobranie,* vol. I, p. 261. Letter to Alexandra Beyer. [April 1836].

16. Ibid., vol. I, pp. 254–55. Letter to Alexandra Beyer. April 6, 1836.

17. Ibid., vol. I, p. 221. Letter to his sister Varvara. March 9, 1836.

18. Ibid., vol. I, p. 336. Letter to the Beyer sisters. [August 1836].

19. Ibid., vol. I, p. 252. Letter to Alexandra Beyer. April 4, 1836; vol. I, pp. 323–24. Letter to Alexandra Beyer. [August 1836].

20. Ibid., vol. I, pp. 242–43. Letter to his sister Varvara. March 17, 1836.

21. Ibid., vol. I, p. 235. Letter to his sister Varvara. March 11, 1836.

22. Ibid., vol. I, pp. 341–44. Letter to the Beyer sisters. [August 1836]; vol. I, p. 346. Letter to the Beyer sisters. September 1836.

23. Ibid., vol. I, pp. 246–47. Letter to his sister Tatiana. March 17, 1836; vol. I, p. 275. Letter to his sister Tatiana. April 20, 1836.

24. Ibid., vol. I, pp. 322–23. Letter to Alexandra Beyer. August 1836.

25. Ibid., vol. I, p. 261. Letter to Alexandra Beyer. [April 1836].

26. Ibid., vol. I, p. 242. Letter to his sister Varvara. March 17, 1836.

27. Ibid., vol. I, pp. 246–47. Letter to his sister Tatiana. March 17, 1836; vol. I, p. 262. Letter to Alexandra Beyer. April 1836; vol. I, p. 224. Letter to his sister Varvara. March, 1836.

28. Ibid., vol. I, p. 262. Letter to Alexandra Beyer. April 1, 1836; vol. I, p. 300. Letter to the Beyer sisters. May 7, 1836; vol. I, p. 252. Letter to Alexandra Beyer. April 4, 1836; vol. I, pp. 259–60. Letter to Alexandra Beyer. [April 1836].

29. See above, p. 58.

30. Ibid., vol. I, p. 227. Letter to Alexandra Beyer. [March 1836]; vol. I, pp. 353–54. Letter to the Beyer sisters. September [1836].

31. Ibid., vol. I, p. 303. Letter to the Beyer sisters. May 9, 1836; vol. I, p. 320. Letter to the Beyer sisters. August 3, 1836; vol. I, p. 312. Letter to the Beyer sisters. [July 1836]; vol. I, p. 238. Letter to the Beyer sisters. March 16, 1836; vol. I, p. 235. Letter to the Beyer sisters. March 11, 1836; vol. I, pp. 328–29. Letter to his sisters Tatiana and Varvara. August 10, 1836. (See also vol. I, p. 260. Letter to Alexandra Beyer. April 1836. For other similar indications of this sense of himself as a—if not *the*—Jesus of his time, see the index under "Jesus."

32. Ibid., vol. I, pp. 208, 211. Letter to his sisters Tatiana and Varvara. February 28, 1836; vol. I, p. 214. Letter to the Beyer sisters. [February 1836]; vol. I, p. 220. Letter to his sister Varvara. March 9, 1836; vol. I, p. 286. Letter to Alexandra Beyer. April 26, 1836; vol. I, p. 295. Letter to the Beyer sisters. [August 1836]; vol. I, p. 300. Letter to the Beyer sisters. May 7, 1836; vol. I, pp. 328–29. Letter to his sisters Tatiana and Varvara. August 10, 1836.

33. See the index under psychologyimasochism.

34. Steklov, *Sobranie,* vol. I, p. 329. Letter to his sisters Tatiana and Varvara. August 10, 1836; vol. I, pp. 322–23. Letter to Alexandra Beyer. [August 1836]; vol. I, p. 358. Letter to Alexandra Beyer. November 11, 1836; vol. I, pp. 242–43. Letter to his sister Varvara. March 17, 1836; vol. I, p. 267. Letter to his sister Varvara. April 12, 1836; vol. I, p. 245. Letter to his sister Tatiana. March 17, 1836.

35. Ibid., vol. I, pp. 322–24. Letter to Alexandra Beyer. [August 1836]; vol. I, p. 273. Letter to Alexandra Beyer. [April 1836].

36. Ibid., vol. I, p. 326. Letter to Tatiana and Varvara. August 10, 1836. This letter is in general an excellent example of Bakunin's intensely religious sentiments at the time.

37. "Once again, through Efremov, I set the place and time, the weapons— pistols, the distance—five paces. He tried every means to avoid the duel.... [But] seeing that he would have to fight and fight to the death, without seconds who might be able to end the duel, he agreed to my conditions and promised in writing to say nothing to the Beyers, to end every and all relationship with my family, and no longer to regard himself as an acquaintance of mine." Ibid., vol. I, p. 207. Letter to his sister Varvara. February 24, 1836.

38. Ibid., vol. I, p. 202. Letter to his sister Varvara. February 17, 1836. For excerpts from the 1837 letter, see above, p. 17.

39. Ibid., vol. I, p. 231. Letter to Alexandra Beyer. March 1836.

40. Ibid.

41. Ibid., vol. I, pp. 233–34. Letter to his sister Varvara. March 11, 1836.

42. Ibid., p. 234.

43. Ibid., vol. I, pp. 240–241. Letter to his sister Varvara. March 16, 1836. It would be useful to illustrate this with at least one example of Bakunin's encounters with the Beyer sisters' mother. "While we were talking, we heard dreadful, piercing shrieks from the parlour.... We found the mistress of the house rolling on the floor, her whole body shaking, and uttering terrifying wails.... Alexandra wanted to run away, not knowing where. I held her back. I took both of them upstairs so that their mother would not be able to use force against them.... Madam, seeing that all her tricks led nowhere, that her daughters (because of my insistence and that of Vladimir Konstantinovich [Rzhevsky] with whom I am again friends) did not throw themselves at her feet, got up as though nothing at all had happened, for a time pretended that she had lost consciousness, asked her daughters to come downstairs, began to abuse herself in the crudest terms—'I am vile, base, loathsome, stupid'—and at the peak of this outburst suddenly asked if I were there and if I had seen her hysteria." Ibid.

44. Ibid., vol. I, p. 276. Letter to Alexandra Beyer. April 1836.

45. For these and other comparably authoritarian displays during that spring and summer (1836), see Ibid., vol. I, pp. 226, 247, 276, 277, 293, 295, 304–6, 333–36, 339, 341–42, 345–48. The letters are either to the Beyer sisters or to his own sisters, Varvara and Tatiana.

46. Ibid., vol. I, p. 339. Letter to the Beyer sisters. [August 1836].

47. See above, p. 67.

48. Ibid., vol. I, p. 241. Letter to the Beyer sisters. March 16, 1836; vol. I, p. 244. Letter to his sister Varvara. March 17, 1836.

49. Ibid., vol. I, p. 263. Letter to his sister Varvara. April 12, 1836.

50. Ibid., vol. I, p. 303. Letter to the Beyer sisters. May 9, 1836.

51. Ibid., vol. I, p. 310. Letter to Alexandra Beyer. July 15, 1836.

52. Ibid., vol. I, p. 249. Letter to Alexandra Beyer. April 2, 1836.

53. Ibid., vol. I, p. 301. Letter to the Beyer sisters. May 7, 1836.

54. Ibid., vol. I, pp. 223–24. Letter to his sister Varvara. [March 1836].

55. Ibid., vol. I, p. 237. Letter to Alexandra Beyer. [March 1836].

56. Kornilov, *Molodye gody,* pp. 215–17, note 1.

57. Ibid.

58. See above, pp. 29–30.

59. Steklov, *Sobranie,* vol. I, p. 224. Letter to his sister Varvara. March, 1836.

60. Ibid., vol. I, p. 338. Letter to the Beyer sisters. [August 1836]; vol. I, p. 333. Letter to the Beyer sisters. [August 1836].

61. Ibid., vol. I, pp. 305–6. Letter to the Beyer sisters. May 24, 1836.

62. Ibid., vol. I, pp. 242–43. Letter to his sister Varvara. March 17, 1836.

63. See above, pp. 28–9.

64. See below, p. 169.

65. Kornilov, *Molodye gody,* pp. 196–97.

66. Steklov, *Sobranie,* vol. I, p. 350. Letter to the Beyer sisters. September 3, 1836.

67. Ibid., vol. I, pp. 338–39. Letter to the Beyer sisters. [August 1836].

68. Ibid., vol. I, p. 261. Letter to Alexandra Beyer. [April 1836].

69. Ibid., vol. I, p. 302. Letter to the Beyer sisters. May 9, 1836; vol. I, p. 298. Letter to the Beyer sisters. [May 1836].

70. Ibid., vol. I, p. 329. Letter to his sisters Tatiana and Varvara. August 10, 1836.

71. Kornilov, *Molodye gody,* pp. 222–23.

72. Ibid., pp. 224–25.

73. Steklov, *Sobranie,* vol. I, pp. 271–72. Letter to his sister Tatiana. April 15, 1836.

74. Ibid., vol. I, p. 272.

75. Ibid., vol. I, p. 279. Letter to his sisters Tatiana and Varvara. [April 23, 1836].

76. Kornilov, *Molodye gody,* pp. 214–15. (It is interesting to note that while Tatiana speaks of *all the sisters'* love for him, he speaks only of his love for *her*).

77. Ibid., p. 261.

78. Steklov, *Sobranie,* vol. I, pp. 356–57. Letter to Y. M. Neverov. November 4, 1836.

79. Kornilov, *Molodye gody,* p. 252.

80. Ibid., pp. 256, 259.

81. Ibid., pp. 262–65.

82. Steklov, *Sobranie,* vol. I, pp. 351–52. Letter to his brothers. September 11, 1836.

83. Ibid., vol. I, pp. 354–56. Letter to his brothers. November 1836.

84. Brown, *Stankevich,* p. 85. Judging from Belinsky's description of the play to his father, the censor's rejection is hardly surprising: "In this work, with all the ardor of my heart, a flaming love for truth, in a burst of indignation and detestation for injustice, I have presented a vivid and true picture of the tyranny by which some, seizing hold of an unjust and destructive privilege, torture others. The hero of my play is a passionate man, with wild and unrestrained zeal. His thoughts are free, his deeds daring, and as a result, he dies." Belinsky even had the audacity in this land of serfdom and in the reign of Nicholas I to have his hero declare: "Who gave destructive power to some people to enslave by force the will of other human beings like themselves and take away from them their most sacred treasure—freedom? Who permitted them to abuse the rights of nature

and humanity? A gentleman can either for fun or dissipation strip the skin off a slave, sell him as cattle, exchange him for a dog, a horse, a cow, or separate him for the rest of his life from his father, mother, sisters, brothers and from everything that is dear and precious to him." (The contrast between such declarations and Bakunin's entirely apolitical, romantic, and evangelic thoughts and statements at the time—and for years to come—could not be greater.) The quotations are as translated in Shashko, *Unity and Dissent,* pp. 40–41.

85. Brown, *Stankevich,* p. 87.

86. Ibid.

87. V.G. Berezina, "Belinskii i Bakunin v 1830-e gody," *Uchenye zapiski Leningradskogo Gosudarstvennogo ordena Lenina Universiteta* (Leningrad; 1952), no. 158, seriia filologicheskii fakultet, p. 37.

88. V.G. Belinskii, *Polnoe sobranie sochinenii* (Moscow: Academy of Sciences, 1952), vol. XI, p. 328.

89. Ibid., p. 329. See also, Kornilov, *Molodye gody,* p. 235.

90. Belinskii, *Sobranie,* vol. XI, p. 329.

91. Quoted in Brown, *Stankevich,* p. 85.

92. Belinskii, *Sobranie,* vol. XI, pp. 173–75, 213, 220–21, 255.

93. Ibid., pp. 161, 175, 180, 197.

94. Ibid., p. 221.

95. Ibid., p. 175.

96. See note 84 above.

97. For example: "There is no merit without strife, no reward without merit, and no life without action! Mankind represents what individuals represent; it struggles every minute, and every minute improves itself. The torrent of barbarians that flooded Europe from Asia resurrected life instead of suppressing it and renovated the decrepit world; powerful nations sprang up from the decayed corpse of the Roman empire and became the vessels of benefaction. What are the campaigns of Alexander, the restless activity of Caesars and Charlses but the movement of the eternal *ideal* whose life consists in incessant activity." V.G. Belinsky, *Selected Philosophical Works* (Moscow: Foreign Language Publishing House, 1956), pp. 16–17.

98. Belinskii, *Sobranie,* vol. II, p. 248.

99. Ibid., p. 250.

100. Ibid., p. 251.

101. Ibid., vol. XI, pp. 320–321.

102. Ibid., p. 321.

103. Ibid., p. 333.

104. Ibid., p. 206.

105. Ibid., pp. 207–8, 334.

106. Kornilov, *Molodye gody,* p. 245–47.

107. Belinskii, *Sobranie,* vol. XI, p. 209.

108. Ibid., p. 243.

109. Ibid., p. 213.

110. Ibid., p. 174.

111. Y.G. Oksman, *Letopis zhizni i tvorchestva V.G. Belinskogo* (Moscow: Gosudarstvennogo Izdatelstvo, 1958), pp. 131–32.

112. Steklov, *Sobranie*, vol. I, p. 358. Letter to Alexandra Beyer. November 11, 1836.

113. Ibid., vol. I, p. 386. Letter to his sister Varvara. January 10, 1837.

114. Ibid., vol. I, p. 422. Letter to the Beyer sisters. [spring 1837].

115. Ibid., vol. I, p. 358. Letter to Alexandra Beyer, November 11, 1836.

116. Ibid., vol. I, pp. 295–96. Letter to the Beyer sisters. Authorities dispute the date of this letter, which Bakunin left undated. Kornilov believes it was written in 1837, Steklov, in 1836 (Kornilov, *Molodye gody,* pp. 209–10, 373–74). I strongly support Kornilov's dating, mainly because the substance of the letter, especially the sections quoted here, are consistent with and, indeed, echo passages in Bakunin's 1837 correspondence with Belinsky, the Beyer sisters, and Bakunin's own sisters. Compare, for example, his letter to his sisters, April 24, 1837 (Steklov, *Sobranie,* vol. I, p. 424). Also, Steklov's argument for rejecting Kornilov's dating seems very weak to me. It is clear from the opening lines of the letter, Steklov argues, that it could not have been written in 1837 "because it says there that a year had passed since they had become good friends, and they had first become good friends in March 1835." In fact, what Bakunin wrote is that "a year had already passed since our relationship, our friendship got its real beginning." Enough has been seen above to know what Bakunin meant by "real beginning." He would hardly have used the phrase to refer to his evenings with the Beyers during that short visit to Moscow in 1835, when he was still in service. The phrase is far more appropriate for the time he began his Fichtean teacher-priest relationship with the young ladies, that is, in 1836, a year before Kornilov dates the letter (thus, "a year had already passed....").

117. Ibid., vol. I, p. 424. Letter to his sisters. [April 24, 1837].

CHAPTER 4. CONVERSION TO HEGEL: SALVATION BY FAITH

1. Steklov, *Sobranie*, vol. I, p. 424. Letter to his sisters. April 24, 1837.

2. Ibid., vol. I, p. 376. Letter to his sister Varvara. December 22, 1836.

3. Ibid., vol. I, pp. 386–387. Letter to his sister Varvara. January 10, 1837. (Emphasis added.)

4. Ibid., vol. I, p. 398. Letter to his sisters and brothers. February 4, 1837.

5. Stankevich, *Perepiska*, p. 620.

6. Steklov, *Sobranie*, vol. I, p. 371. Letter to Alexandra Beyer. December 16, 1836.

7. Ibid., vol. I, p. 360. Letter to his sisters. December 8, 1836. (See also, vol. I, pp. 372–73. Letter to Alexandra Beyer. December 16, 1836.)

8. Ibid., vol. I, p. 366. Letter to his sister Varvara. December 15, 1836.

9. Ibid., vol. I, p. 360. Letter to his sisters. December 8, 1836.

10. Ibid., vol. II, pp. 51–52. Letter to the Beyer sisters. July 31, 1837.

11. See above, p. 85.

12. Bakunin's first original publication, this essay on Hegel, was published in the *Moscow Observer* the following March (1838). It served as an introduction to several lectures by Hegel that Bakunin had translated, also for publication in the *Observer*. Steklov, *Sobranie*, vol. II, pp. 166–78.

13. Ibid., vol. II, pp. 170–71.

14. Ibid., p. 175.

15. Ibid., vol. II, p. 151. Letter to N. V. Stankevich. March 8, 1838.

16. Ibid., vol. II, p. 142. Letter to his sisters. [February 1838].

17. Ibid., vol. I, pp. 398-99. Letter to his sisters and brothers. February 4, 1837.

18. See above.

19. Steklov, *Sobranie*, vol. II, p. 24. Letter to the Beyer sisters. June 24, 1837; vol. II, p. 75. Letter to his sisters. [December 1837].

20. Ibid., vol. II, p. 62. Letter to Beyer sisters. September 4, 1837.

21. Ibid., vol. II, p. 70. "My Notes." Written September 4-November 9, 1837; vol. II, p. 41. Letter to Constantine Beyer. July 19, 1837.

22. Ibid., vol. II, p. 72. "My Notes."

23. Ibid., vol. II, p. 49. Letter to the Beyer sisters. July 31, 1837.

24. Ibid., vol. II, p. 43. Letter to Alexandra Beyer. July 20-21, 1837.

25. Ibid., vol. II, p. 167. "Hegel's Gymnasium Lectures." [April 1838].

26. Ibid., pp. 172-73.

27. Ibid., pp. 175-76.

28. Ibid., pp. 177-78.

29. Ibid., pp. 175-76.

30. Ibid., vol. I, pp. 407-8. Letter to his sisters. February 20, 1837; vol. II, pp. 41-42. Letter to Alexandra, Natalie, and Konstantine Beyer. July 19, 1837; vol. II, pp. 46-47. Letter to the Beyer sisters. July 27, 1837; vol. II, p. 165. Letter to the Beyer sisters. April 18, 1838.

31. Ibid., vol. I, pp. 407-8. Letter to his sisters. February 20, 1837.

32. Bakunin is not alone, of course, in using this scenario of cosmic alienation and return. It is one of the oldest and most frequently used of all cosmologies, especially by gnostics and kabalists of all periods. Attention has already been called to its use by Venevitinov (p. 40), and in a way quite similar to the way Bakunin uses it. Does everyone who adopts this imagery and symbolism share Bakunin's personality disorders? Many, most, or perhaps even all, of those who come to depend on the solace derived from this pattern of gnostic estrangement accompanied by assuarance of paradisiacal return may indeed share with Bakunin a sense of radical loss, betrayal, and alienation. It is obvious, however, that there are many different life experiences that can bring about this state of mind and mood, and the alienation can be more or less profound, encompass more or less of an individual's life, and last a longer or shorter time. In Bakunin's case, the causes were psychopathological and the alienation involved his entire life and lasted his entire lifetime.

33. Ibid., vol. I, p. 413. Letter to his parents. March 2, 1837; vol I, p. 421. Letter to his parents. [March 1837].

34. Ibid., vol. II, p. 65. Letter to his brothers. September-October 1837; vol. II, p. 74. Letter to N. Ketcher. [November 1837].

35. Ibid., vol. II, p. 96. Letter to his father. December 15, 1837.

36. Ibid., vol. II, p. 74. Letter to N. Ketcher. [November 1837].

37. Ibid., vol. I, p. 418. Letter to Varvara. March 27, 1837; vol. II, p. 73. "My Notes."

38. Ibid., vol. II, p. 79. Letter to his sisters. December 7, 1837.

39. Kornilov, *Molodye gody*, p. 362, note 1.

40. Steklov, *Sobranie*, vol. II, p. 153. Letter to his sisters. [March 1838].

41. Ibid., vol. II, p. 142. Letter to his sisters. [February 1838].

42. Ibid., vol. II, pp. 145–46. Letter to his sisters. [February 1838].

43. Ibid., vol. II, pp. 152–53. Letter to his sisters. March 1838.

44. Ibid., vol. II, p. 147. Letter to the Beyer sisters. March 1, 1838.

45. Ibid., vol. II, p. 162. Letter to his sisters. April 4, 1838.

46. Ibid., vol. II, p. 69. Letter to the Beyer sisters. October 30, 1837.

47. Ibid., vol. II, p. 74. Letter to N. Ketcher. [November 1837].

48. Ibid., vol. II, p. 49. Letter to the Beyer sisters. July 31, 1837.

49. Ibid.

50. Ibid., vol. II, p. 24. Letter to the Beyer sisters. June 24, 1837.

51. Ibid., vol. I, pp. 434–35. Letter to his brother Ilya. May 13, 1837.

52. See above, p. 24.

53. Steklov, *Sobranie*, vol. I, p. 420. Letter to his parents. [March 1837].

54. Ibid., vol. I, p. 431. Letter to his sisters. May 13, 1837.

55. Ibid., vol. I, p. 430. Letter to his sisters. [May 6, 1837].

56. Ibid., vol. II, pp. 99–100. Letter to his father. December 15, 1837.

57. Ibid., vol. I, p. 402. Letter to his parents. February 4, 1837; vol. I, p. 413. Letter to his parents. March 2, 1837; Kornilov, *Molodye gody*, p. 382.

58. Steklov, *Sobranie*, vol. I, p. 361. Letter to his sisters. December 8, 1836.

59. Ibid., vol. I, p. 363. Letter to his sisters. [December 1836]; vol. I, p. 364. Letter to the Beyer sisters. [December 1836]; vol. I, p. 428. Letter to his sisters. [May 1837]; vol. II, p. 23. Letter to the Beyer sisters. June 24, 1837.

60. Ibid., vol. I, p. 386. Letter to his sister Varvara. January 10, 1837.

61. Ibid., vol. I, p. 426. Letter to the Beyer sisters. [April 1837]; vol. II, pp. 29–31. Letter to the Beyer sisters. July 2, 1837; vol. II, p. 53. Letter to the Beyer sisters. July 31, 1837; vol. II, p. 55. Letter to the Beyer sisters (excerpt). [summer 1837].

62. Ibid., vol. II, pp. 41–42. Letter to Alexandra, Natalie, and Constantine Beyer. July 19, 1837.

63. Ibid., vol. II, p. 72. "My Notes."

64. Ibid., vol. II, p. 181. Letter to the Beyer sisters. [May 1838]; vol. II, p. 182. Letter to the Beyer sisters. [May 1838].

65. Ibid., vol. II, p. 191. Letter to the Beyer sisters. June 16, 1838.

66. Ibid., vol. II, p. 287. Letter to his sisters. [January 1840]. (Emphasis added.)

67. Ibid., vol. II, pp. 32–34. Letter to the Beyer sisters. July 8, 1837.

68. Ibid., vol. II, p. 44. Letter to the Beyer sisters and their brother. July 22, 1837.

69. Ibid., vol. I, p. 372. Letter to Alexandra Beyer. December 16, 1836; vol. I, pp. 374–75. Letter to his sister Varvara. December 22, 1836; vol. I, p. 377. Letter to the Beyer sisters. December 26, 1836; vol. I, p. 380. Letter to his sisters. January 4, 1837.

70. Ibid., vol. I, pp. 378–79. Letter to his sisters. December 31, 1837.

71. Ibid., vol. I, p. 382. Letter to his sisters. [January 1837]; Kornilov, *Molodye gody*, p. 308.

72. Kornilov, *Molodye gody*, pp. 330–40.

73. Steklov, *Sobranie*, vol. II, p. 88. Letter to the Beyer sisters. [December 1837].

74. Ibid., vol. II, pp. 86–87. Letter to his sisters. [December 13, 1837].

75. Kornilov, *Molodye gody*, pp. 357–62.

76. Steklov, *Sobranie*, vol. II, pp. 96–128. Letter to his father. December 15, 1837.

77. Kornilov, *Molodye gody*, pp. 363–64.

78. Steklov, *Sobranie*, vol. II, p. 128. Letter to his sisters. [December 1837].

79. Ibid., vol. II, pp. 129–30. Letter to his sisters. [December 31, 1837].

80. Ibid., vol. II, p. 133. Letter to his sisters. [February 1838].

81. Ibid., vol. II, p. 95. Letter to his sisters. [December 25, 1837].

82. Ibid., vol. I, pp. 384–85. Letter to the Beyer sisters. September 3, 1837.

83. Ibid., vol. II, p. 121. Letter to his father. December 25, 1837.

84. Ibid., vol. II, p. 72. "My Notes."

85. See, for example, Bakunin's essay-length letter to his father, December 15, 1837. Ibid., vol. II, pp. 99, 101–2, 103, 116–22.

86. Ibid., vol. II, pp. 111–12.

87. Ibid., vol. II, p. 164. Letter to the Beyer sisters. April 18, 1838.

88. Ibid., vol. II, p. 42. Letter to Alexandra, Natalie, and Constantine Beyer. July 19, 1837.

89. Ibid., vol. II, p. 103. Letter to his father. December 15, 1837; vol. II, p. 89. Letter to his sisters. December 18, 1837; vol. I, pp. 383–85. Letter to his sisters. [January 1837]; vol. I, p. 401. Letter to his sisters and brothers. February 4, 1837; vol. I, pp. 422–23. Letter to the Beyer sisters. Spring 1837; vol. II, pp. 27–28. Letter to his sisters. June 30, 1837; vol. II, p. 46. Letter to the Beyer sisters. July 27, 1837; vol. II, p. 59. Letter to the Beyer sisters. [August 1837]; vol. II, p. 67. Letter to the Beyer sisters. October 30, 1837; vol. II, p. 84. Letter to his sisters. [December 14, 1837].

90. Ibid., vol. II, p. 26. Letter to the Beyer sisters. June 30, 1837.

91. Ibid., vol. II, p. 84. Letter to his sisters. [December 14, 1837].

92. Ibid., vol. I, p. 432. Letter to his sisters. April 24, 1837.

93. Ibid., vol. I, pp. 403–5. Letter to his sisters. February 11, 1837.

94. Ibid., vol. I, p. 405.

95. Ibid., vol. II, p. 34. Letter to the Beyer sisters. July 8, 1837; vol. II, p. 44. Letter to the Beyer sisters and their brother. July 22, 1837.

96. Ibid., vol. II, pp. 48, 50. Letters to the Beyer sisters. July 27 and 31, 1837.

97. Ibid., vol. II, p. 23. Letter to the Beyer sisters. June 24, 1837; vol. II, pp. 37–38. Letter to the Beyer sisters. July 13, 1837; vol. II, p. 44. Letter to the Beyer sisters and their brother. July 22, 1837; vol. II, p. 50. Letter to the Beyer sisters. July 31, 1837.

98. Belinskii, *Sobranie*, vol. XI, pp. 160–2.

99. Steklov, *Sobranie*, vol. II, p. 82. Letter to the Beyer sisters. [December 1837].

100. Ibid., vol. II, p. 187. Letter to the Beyer sisters. [May 1838].

101. Ibid., vol. II, p. 150. Letter to his sisters. [March 1838].

102. Ibid., vol. II, pp. 164-65. Letter to the Beyer sisters. April 18, 1838.

103. Ibid., vol. II, p. 30. Letter to the Beyer sisters. July 2, 1837.

104. Ibid., vol. I, p. 221. Letter to the Beyer sisters. March 9, 1836. (Emphasis added.)

105. Ibid., vol. I, pp. 403-4. Letter to his sisters. February 11, 1837. (Emphasis added.)

106. Ibid., vol. II, p. 137. Letter to the Beyer sisters. [February 18, 1838].

107. Ibid., vol. II, p. 161. Letter to his sisters. April 4, 1838.

108. Ibid, vol. II, pp. 150-51. Letter to his sisters. [March 1838]. (Emphasis added.)

109. Ibid., vol. II, p. 147. Letter to the Beyer sisters. March 1, 1838; vol. II, p. 150. Letter to his sisters. [March 1838].

110. For the foregoing and other similar expressions of this remarkable philosophical warrant for radical (and as pathological as it is pervasive) narcissism, see Ibid., vol. II, pp. 332, 338, 341, 358, 359-60, 361, 366, 380, and excerpts from Bakunin's second and principal article on Hegel, "Concerning Philosophy," which he wrote in two parts during the second half of 1839 and early 1840. The article will be further discussed in the next chapter. (Emphasis added.)

111. Kornilov, *Molodye gody*, pp. 706-10.

112. Steklov, *Sobranie*, vol. II, p. 368. "Concerning Philosophy."

113. Ibid., vol. II, p. 165. Letter to the Beyer sisters. April 18, 1839.

114. Ibid., vol. I, p. 408. Letter to his sisters. [February 20, 1837]. (Emphasis added.)

115. Ibid, vol. II, p. 172. "Hegel's Gymnasium Lectures." [April 1838].

116. Ibid., vol. I, p. 404. Letter to his sisters. February 11, 1837.

117. Ibid., vol. II, p. 101. Letter to his father. December 15, 1838.

118. Ibid., vol. I, p. 397. Letter to his sister Varvara. January 23, 1837.

119. Ibid., vol. II, p. 175. "Hegel's Gymnasium Lectures."

120. Ibid., vol. II, p. 43. Letter to Alexandra Beyer. July 20-21, 1837.

121. Ibid., vol. II, p. 52. Letter to the Beyer sisters. July 31, 1837.

122. Ibid., vol. II, p. 31. Letter to the Beyer sisters. July 2, 1837.

123. Ibid., vol. II, p. 155. Letter to the Beyer sisters. March 13, 1838; vol. II, p. 195. Letter to the Beyer sisters. [July 1838].

CHAPTER 5. REVIVAL: SALVATION BY DEEDS

1. Steklov, *Sobranie*, vol. II, p. 196. Letter to the Beyer sisters. [July 22, 1838].

2. Ibid., vol. II, pp. 189-90. Letter to his mother. June 16, 1838.

3. Ibid., vol. II, p. 181. Letter to his sister Tatiana. May 5, 1838.

4. Ibid., vol. II, p. 196. Letter to the Beyer sisters. [July 22, 1838].

5. Ibid., vol. II, p. 147. Letter to the Beyer sisters. March 1, 1838.

6. Ibid., vol. II, p. 141. Letter to his sisters. [February 1838]; vol. II, p. 149. Letter to his sisters. [March 2, 1838]; vol. II, p. 154. Letter to the Beyer sisters. March 13, 1838; vol. II, p. 179. Letter to his brother Nicholas. April 15, 1838.

7. Ibid., vol. II, p. 182. Letter to the Beyer sisters. [May 1838]; vol. II, p. 191. Letter to the Beyer sisters. June 16, 1838; vol. II, p. 196. Letter to the Beyer sisters. [July 1838].

8. Ibid., vol. II, p. 191. Letter to the Beyer sisters. June 16, 1838.

9. Kornilov, *Molodye gody*, pp. 316-22.

10. Steklov, *Sobranie*, vol. II, pp. 189-90. Letter to his mother. June 16, 1838; vol. II, pp. 193-94. Letter to A. P. Efremov. July 9, 1838.

11. Ibid., vol. II, pp. 200-1. Letter to A. P. Efremov. August 28, 1838; vol. II, p. 200. Letter to Varvara. August 24, 1838.

12. Ibid., vol. II, pp. 202-3. Letter to his sister Varvara. [September 1838].

13. Ibid., vol. II, p. 205. Letter to his sister Varvara. [September 16, 1838].

14. Ibid.

15. Ibid., vol. II, p. 206. October 2, 1838.

16. Ibid., vol. II, p. 208. September 25, 1838.

17. Ibid., vol. II, p. 209.

18. Ibid., vol. II, p. 214. Letter to his brothers. October 11, 1838.

19. Ibid., vol. II, p. 213; vol. II, p. 222. Letter to Alexandra Beyer. November, 1838. The association between personal suffering and social apocalyptic destruction as comparable paths to rebirth is particularly apparent during this period of transition from "right" to "left" Hegelianism.

20. We should recall the character and intensity of Bakunin's reaction to Liubov's matrimonial dangers in 1833 and 1836 and also the fact that a year and a half before Liubov's death he had written his father about them at extraordinary length, expressing his revulsion toward sexuality more forcefully than he had ever done before or would do thereafter. If in fact such a sister-mother substitution did take place, then Liubov's death would understandably have had an exceptionally strong effect on Bakunin, since (through condensation and displacement) it would have meant to him the loss of the very one who had become the object of the reconciliation, the mother whom he had just that summer dared to approach as one of the innocent "children." If this conjecture is sound, then posing as a pure, submissive, powerless child would have proven even more dangerous than acting the part of a strong, virile Fichtean missionary. For, whereas the punishment for coming too close as a Fichtean missionary was his suffering "hell, hell with all its terrors," the punishment for trying to come close as one of the "children" would have appeared to be the total loss of the beloved for whom all the many strategies had been devised in the first place.

21. Belinskii, *Sobranie*, vol. XI, pp. 183-84, 186-87, 192, 201, 223.

22. Ibid., p. 204.

23. Ibid., p. 337.

24. Ibid., p. 384.

25. Ibid., p. 337.

26. Ibid., pp. 337, 389.

27. Ibid., p. 389.

28. Ibid., p. 341.

29. Ibid., p. 291.

30. Ibid., p. 289.

31. Ibid., pp. 291-92, 336.

32. Ibid., p. 334.

33. Ibid., p. 345.

34. Ibid., p. 388.

35. Ibid., pp. 239, 241, 322, 323-24.

36. Ibid., p. 344.

37. Ibid., p. 283.

38. Ibid., p. 318.

39. Ibid., pp. 318, 345.

40. Ibid., pp. 282-83.

41. Ibid., pp. 282-83, 285, 316.

42. Steklov, *Sobranie*, vol. II, pp. 203-4. Letter to V. G. Belinsky (excerpt). [September 1838]; vol. II, pp. 240-41. Letter to N. Stankevich. May 13, 1839.

43. Ibid., vol. II, pp. 226-27. Letter to his mother. January 13, 1839.

44. Ibid., vol. II, pp. 233-34. Letter to Alexandra Beyer. March 30, 1839.

45. See the preceding page.

46. Steklov, *Sobranie*, vol. II, p. 232. Letter to his sister Varvara. March 1839; Kornilov, *Molodye gody*, p. 525.

47. Ibid., vol. II, p. 244. Letter to N. Stankevich. May 13, 1839.

48. Ibid., vol. II, p. 234. Letter to Alexandra Beyer. March 30, 1839.

49. Ibid., vol. II, p. 239. Letter to N. Stankevich. May 13, 1839.

50. Ibid., vol. II, p. 246.

51. Ibid.

52. Ibid., vol. II, p. 244.

53. Ibid., vol. II, p. 237. Letter to Alexandra Beyer. April 7, 1839.

54. Ibid., vol. II, pp. 242-44. Letter to N. Stankevich. May 13, 1839.

55. Ibid., vol. II, p. 247.

56. Ibid., vol. II, p. 257. Letter to his sisters. July 22, 1839.

57. Ibid., vol. II, p. 270. Letter to his sisters. [July] 18, 1839.

58. Ibid.

59. Ibid., vol. II, p. 256. Letter to his sisters. July 22, 1839.

60. Kornilov, *Molodye gody*, p. 562.

61. Steklov, *Sobranie*, vol. II, p. 253. Letter to his sister Varvara. [June 1839].

62. Ibid., vol. II, p. 255. Letter to his sister Varvara. [July 1839].

63. Ibid., vol. II, p. 255. Letter to Natalie Beyer. [July 1839].

64. Ibid., vol. II, p. 263. Letter to his sisters. September 14, 1839.

65. Ibid., vol. II, p. 474. Notes.

66. Ibid., vol. II, p. 317. "Concerning Philosophy."

67. Ibid., vol. II, p. 319.

68. See above, p. 108.

69. See above, p. 112.

70. Steklov, *Sobranie*, vol. II, pp. 366, 371. "Concerning Philosophy." (Emphasis added.)

71. See above, p. 88.

72. Ibid., vol. II, p. 376. (Emphasis added.)

73. Ibid., vol. II, p. 380.

74. Ibid., vol. II, p. 377.

75. Ibid., vol. II, pp. 320, 321, 326, 328.

76. Ibid., vol. II, pp. 337, 384.

77. Ibid., vol. II, p. 263. Letter to his sisters. September 14, 1839.

78. Ibid., vol. II, p. 262.

79. Kornilov, *Molodye gody*, pp. 506-7.

80. Ibid., p. 618.

81. Stankevich, *Perepiska*, pp. 672-73.

82. Martin Malia, *Alexander Herzen and the Birth of Russian Socialism* (Cambridge, Mass: Harvard University Press, 1961), pp. 197 *ff.*

83. Steklov, *Sobranie*, vol. II, pp. 275-76. Letter to his sisters. [December 1838].

84. Ibid., vol. II, pp. 257-58. Letter to his sisters. July 22, 1839.

85. Ibid., vol. II, p. 279. Letter to his brother Paul. [December 24, 1839].

86. Ibid., vol. II, p. 260. Letter to his sisters. September 1839.

87. Kornilov, *Molodye gody*, p. 548.

88. Ibid., p. 553.

89. Belinskii, *Sobranie*. vol. XI, p. 464.

90. Steklov, *Sobranie*, vol. II, p. 308. Letter to Alexander Beyer. March, 1849.

91. Belinskii, *Sobranie*, vol. XI, p. 457.

92. Steklov, *Sobranie*, vol. II, p. 290. Letter to the Beyer sisters. [January 27, 1840].

93. Ibid., vol. II, p. 271. Letter to his sisters. [July] 18, 1839. Other examples of this connection Bakunin made between the marriage and his own trip to Berlin: "I crave your union for myself as well, because until it takes place a reestablishment of my relations with father, even external relations, will be impossible for me; so my trip to Berlin cannot be realized before your union with Botkin.... Both for me and for my external fate a crisis has now begun. Father must give me the means to get to Berlin.... I have reached the *ne plus ultra* separation and alienation [from father and mother]. Now I could only come closer, but that only under two conditions: first, they must quickly agree to the union of Alexander and B [Botkin], and, secondly, they must provide the money for the trip to Berlin." Ibid., vol. II, p. 271. Letter to his sisters. [July] 18, 1839; vol. II, p. 275. Letter to his sisters. December 1839. For the reference to "atamans," see Ibid., vol. II, p. 287. Letter to his sisters. [January 1840].

94. Ibid., vol. II, p. 287. Letter to his sisters. [January 1840].

95. Ibid., vol. II, p. 300. Letter to Natalie Beyer. [February 1840].

96. Ibid., vol. II, pp. 294-95. Letter to his sisters. [February 1840].

97. Belinskii, *Sobranie*, vol. XI, pp. 466, 482, 484-86, 488.

98. Ibid., p. 480. Belinsky's bitter but masterly portrait of Bakunin's financial ineptitude and general irresponsibility is worth quoting at length. "Why had he come to Petersburg? For nothing at all. What did he have with him? Nothing. When they invited him to stay with them, the Muravievs seemed pained.... When he grew bored with the Muravievs, he moved—at 12:00 midnight—to Demutov's Inn and sent back to the Muravievs for his luggage. They said, of course, that it would be better to wait until morning instead of doing this at midnight.... When he got to Demutov's, Michael had neither a kopek

with him nor any hopes of getting money from someplace or other. And this is one of the most expensive inns. One day he meets Z[aikin], and the next he asks him for money, takes it, and then again a second time, a third, and so on. Then what does he do with the money? Drinks Rhine wine, which Z[aikin] denies himself, even though he makes some 15,000 a year. And the cab fares—in Petersburg M[ichael] rushed around all over the place.... He was always going to the theater, with Zaikin always getting him tickets.... Michael more than once said that he had no place to live, but Z[aikin] said that his tongue simply could not form the words to invite him to stay with him and that he dreaded the very thought of living together with such a person." Ibid., p. 443.

99. Ibid., pp. 443, 470.
100. Ibid., p. 470.
101. Ibid., pp. 485–86.
102. Ibid., pp. 441, 443, 444.
103. Ibid., p. 484.
104. Ibid., p. 458.
105. Ibid., p. 488.
106. Ibid., p. 444.
107. Steklov, *Sobranie*, vol. II, p. 475.
108. Ibid. In his memorable description of these years, the mid and late 1830s, P. V. Annenkov presents Bakunin as *the* expert in all things Hegelian. "He was the one consulted whenever any obscure or difficult point in the master's system required elucidation.... For a while, though a very short while, Bakunin, one could say, reigned over the circle of the philosophers." As to the politically conservative implications of Bakunin's Hegelianism, Annenkov writes: "he did indeed initiate a new phase of philosophism on Russian soil with his proclamation of the doctrine that all that *really* exists is sacred.... Bakunin was responsible for the dissemination in Russia of that extreme, that very pure, but at the same time contemptuous, idealism which turned away in horror from the hubbub of ordinary life...." Most insightfully, Annenkov caught at least part of what motivated this "father of Russian idealism": "Under cover of the mathematically rigorous formulas of Hegel's logic, his romanticism superficially appeared a very austere creed, whereas it was in fact merely a matter of gratification and justification for extremely subtle and refined lusts of mentality which found its pleasures in itself." P. V. Annenkov, *The Extraordinary Decade*, trans. Irwin R. Titunic, ed. Arthur P. Mendel (Ann Arbor: University of Michigan Press, 1968), pp. 21–28. It should be noted that Annenkov did not meet Bakunin until a decade after the period he is describing and that he did not begin these memoires until the mid-1870s.

109. Steklov, *Sobranie*, vol. II, p. 304. Letter to his sisters. [February 1840].
110. Ibid., vol. II, p. 303. Letter to Alexandra Beyer. February 22, 1840.
111. Ibid, vol. II, p. 306. Letter to Alexandra Beyer. [March 1840].
112. Ibid., vol. II, p. 288. Letter to his sisters. [January 1840].
113. Ibid., vol. II, p. 293. Letter to his sisters. February 1840; vol. II, p. 304. Letter to his sisters, February 1840.
114. Ibid., vol. II, p. 295. Letter to his sisters. [February 1840].
115. Kornilov, *Molodye gody*, p. 617.
116. Steklov, *Sobranie*, vol. II, p. 295. Letter to his sisters. [February 1840].

117. Ibid., vol. II, p. 297. Letter to N. Stankevich. February 11, 1840.

118. Stankevich, *Perepiska*, pp. 673-74.

119. Steklov, *Sobranie*, vol. II, p. 270. Letter to his sisters. [December] 1839; vol. II, p. 275. Letter to his sisters. [December 1839].

120. Ibid., vol. II, pp. 392-406. Letter to his parents. [March 24, 1840].

121. Kornilov, *Molodye gody*, pp. 637-38.

122. Steklov, *Sobranie*, vol. II, p. 417. Letter to Natalie Beyer. [April 1840].

123. Ibid.

124. Ibid., vol. II, p. 421. Letter to A. I. Herzen. April 20, 1840.

125. Ibid., p. 422.

126. Malia, *Herzen*, pp. 188-96.

127. Steklov, *Sobranie*, vol. II, p. 423. Letter to his sisters. May 9, 1840; vol. II, p. 436. Letter to the Beyer sisters. June 29, 1840.

128. Ibid., vol. II, p. 434. Letter to his brothers and sisters. [June 1840].

129. Ibid., vol. II, p. 426. Letter to his brothers. [May 1840].

130. Ibid., vol. II, p. 433. Letter to his brothers and sisters. [June 1840].

131. Ibid., vol. II, p. 424. Letter to Alexandra Beyer. [May 1840].

132. Ibid., vol. II, p. 429. Letter to the Beyer sisters. June 13, 1840.

133. Ibid., vol. II, p. 432. Letter to N. Stankevich. June 18, 1840.

134. Ibid., vol. II, p. 426. Letter to his brothers. [May 1840].

135. Belinskii, *Sobranie*, vol. XI, p. 523.

136. Ibid., pp. 541-44.

137. Steklov, *Sobranie*, vol. II, p. 435. Letter to his brothers and sisters. June 29, 1840.

138. Ibid., vol. II, p. 436. Letter to the Beyer sisters. June 29, 1840.

139. Ibid.

140. Quoted in Steklov, *Sobranie*, vol. II, pp. 486-87.

141. Ibid., vol. II, pp. 408-9. Letter to his sister Tatiana. March 25, 1840.

142. Kornilov, *Molodye gody*, p. 508. See note 108, above, for Pavel Annenkov's description of Bakunin's prominence as the leading Hegelian among Russian intellectuals of the period.

143. Steklov, *Sobranie*, vol. II, pp. 302-3. Letter to Alexandra Beyer. [February 22, 1840].

144. Ibid., vol. II, p. 269. Letter to his sister Alexandra. November 1839; vol. II, p. 291. Letter to the Beyer sisters. January 27, 1840; vol. II, p. 301. Letter to his sisters. [February 21, 1840.]

CHAPTER 6. REVOLUTIONARY NOVITIATE

1. Steklov, *Sobranie*, vol. III, pp. 1-3. Letter to his relatives. July 4, 1840.

2. Ibid., vol. III, p. 2.

3. Ibid., vol. III, pp. 3-4. Letter to his sister Varvara. July 20, 1840. (Where Bakunin gives two dates, I have chosen the one following the Gregorian calendar.)

4. Ibid., vol. III, pp. 4-5.

5. Ibid., vol. III, p. 19. Letter to the Beyer sisters. September 9, 1840.

6. "Michel! We will have to study ancient languages. We will have to work, work vigorously through the winter. I hope it will go splendidly for us. The university, study, and evenings we will gather at your sister's, go to listen to good music, organize readings. Werder will visit us. Wait, let's count the months of pleasure, from October 1 to May 1—seven months, 210 days. . . . You would not believe how happy I am to be able to speak with you as 'thou.' On the title page of my *Encyclopedia* [Hegel's] I have written: Stankevich died June 24, 1840, and below: I met Bakunin the 20th of July, 1840. From all the rest of my past life I do not want to carry away another memory." (Quoted in Alexander A. Kornilov, *Gody stranstvii M. Bakunina.* Moscow: Gosudarstvennogo Izdatelstvo, 1925, pp. 51–52.)

7. Ibid., pp. 12–13.

8. Ibid., p. 14.

9. Quoted on Steklov, *Sobranie*, vol. II, pp. 484–86.

10. Ibid., vol. III, p. 9. Letter to his relatives. [August 9, 1840]. (Emphasis added)

11. Ibid., vol. III, pp. 35–36. Letter to Julie Nindel. October 29, 1840.

12. Ibid., vol. III, p. 24. Letter to the Beyer sisters. October 13, 1840.

13. Ibid., vol. III, p. 36. Letter to his parents. November 30, 1840.

14. Ibid., vol. III, p. 12. Letter to his brothers and sisters. August 30, 1840.

15. Ibid., vol. III, pp. 12–13.

16. Ibid., vol. III, pp. 15–16.

17. Ibid., vol. III, p. 18; vol. III, p. 22. Letter to the Beyer sisters. September 9, 1840.

18. Ibid., vol. III, p. 17. Letter to his brothers and sisters. August 30, 1840; vol. III, p. 25. Letter to the Beyer sisters. October 13, 1840; vol. III, pp. 32, 430. Letter to A. I. Herzen. [October 23, 1840].

19. Ibid., vol. III, pp. 31–34. Letter to A. I. Herzen. October 23, 1840.

20. Ibid., vol. III, p. 38. Letter to his sisters. [November 16, 1840].

21. Ibid., vol. III, p. 40. Letter to his sisters. December 3, 1840; vol. III, p. 43. Letter to his sisters. December 16, 1840; vol. III, p. 59. Letter to his brothers and sisters. April 15, 1840; vol. III, p. 86. Letter to his sisters. [January 1842]; Kornilov, *Gody stranstvii*, p. 43.

22. Steklov, *Sobranie*, vol. III, pp. 85–86. Letter to his sisters. [January 1842].

23. M. Dragomanov, ed., *Pisma M. A. Bakunina k A. I. Gertzenu i N. P. Ogarevu* (St. Petersburg, Brublevskii, 1906), pp. 20–21.

24. Arthur Helps, *Bettina. A Portrait* (New York: Reynal, 1957), pp. 196–97.

25. K. A. Varnhagen von Ense, *Tagebücher* (Leipzig: F. A. Brockhaus, 1863), vol. I, pp. 232, 263.

26. Kornilov, *Gody stranstvii*, p. 43.

27. Steklov, *Sobranie*, vol. III, pp. 31–32. Letter to A. I. Herzen. [October 23, 1840].

28. Henri Granjard, *Ivan Tourguenev* (Paris, 1954), p. 77. Granjard's study is the source of the biographical material on Werder summarized here.

29. Steklov, *Sobranie*, vol. III, p. 43. Letter to his sisters. December 16, 1840.

30. Ibid., vol. III, p. 47. Letter to his brother Paul. [January 1841].

31. Ibid., vol. III, p. 60. Letter to the Beyer sisters. [May 1841].

32. Ibid., vol. III, pp. 57–58, 432. Letter to A. P. Efremov. April 9, 1841.

33. Ibid., vol. III, p. 45. Letter to his brother Paul. [January 1841].

34. Ibid., vol. III, pp. 52, 54. Letter to his brother Nicholas. March 29, 1841.

35. Ibid.

36. Ibid., vol. III, pp. 53–56.

37. Ibid., vol. III, p. 55.

38. Ibid., vol. III, p. 56.

39. Ibid., vol. III, p. 54.

40. Ibid., vol. III, p. 55.

41. See below, pp. 169–175.

42. Steklov, *Sobranie,* vol. III, p. 60. Letter to his brothers and sisters. April 15, 1841.

43. Ibid., vol. III, p. 61. Letter to his relatives. September 19, 1841.

44. Ibid.

45. Hans Rosenberg, "Arnold Ruge und die 'Hallischen Jahrbücher'," *Archiv fur Kulturgeschichte,* vol. 20, book 3, p. 292.

46. Quoted in David McLellan, *The Young Hegelians and Karl Marx* (New York: Praeger, 1969), p. 1.

47. Ibid., p. 6.

48. Quoted in Nicholas Lobkowicz, *Theory and Practice* (Notre Dame, Ind.: University of Notre Dame Press, 1967), p. 186.

49. Ibid., p. 187.

50. Ibid., p. 193.

51. August von Cieszkowski, *Prolegomena zur Historiosophie* (Berlin, 1838), pp. 124, 128 ff.

52. Quoted in Lobkowicz, *Theory,* p. 235.

53. Cieszkowski, *Prolegomena,* p. 20.

54. Ibid.

55. McLellan, *Young Hegelians,* pp. 61, 63; Lobkowicz, *Theory,* p. 221; William Brazill, *The Young Hegelians* (New Haven, Conn.: Yale University Press, 1970), pp. 198, 199.

56. McLellan, *Young Hegelians,* p. 66.

57. Rosenberg, "Ruge," *Archiv,* p. 296.

58. McLellan, *Young Hegelians,* p. 29.

59. Lobkowicz, *Theory,* p. 61.

60. Steklov, *Sobranie,* vol. III, pp. 65–66. Letter to his relatives. October 22, 1841.

61. Ibid.

62. Ibid., vol. III, pp. 62–63. Letter to his sister Varvara and his brother Paul. October 27, 1841.

63. Abbe Charles Boutard, *Lamennais. Sa vie et ses doctrines* (Paris: Perrin, 1913), vol. III, pp. 183–94.

64. Steklov, *Sobranie,* vol. III, p. 63. Letter to his sister Varvara and his brother Paul. October 27, 1841.

65. Ibid., vol. III, pp. 66–67. Letter to his relatives. October 22, 1841;

vol. III, p. 75. Letter to his brother Paul and his sister Varvara. November 12, 1841; vol. III, p. 78. Letter to his sister Varvara. November 15, 1841.

66. Ibid., vol. III, p. 69. Letter to his relatives. October 22, 1841; vol. III, pp. 72-73. Letter to his brother Paul and his sister Varvara. November 4, 1841.

67. Michael Bakunin, "The Reaction in Germany," trans., Mary Barbara Zeldin, in *Russian Philosophy*, vol. I, ed., Edie, Scanlan, and Zeldin (Chicago: Quadrangle Books, 1965), pp. 389, 397, 398, 403, 406.

68. Ibid., pp. 390, 393.

69. Ibid., pp. 391, 392, 397.

70. Ibid., pp. 389, 390, 392-94, 398, 400-1, 405.

71. See above, pp. 29-30.

72. Bakunin, "Reaction," *Russian Philosophy*, vol. I, pp. 397, 398, 401, 405.

73. Recall also Paul's difficulty in getting back into the hole because his head was filled with philosophy.

74. Bakunin, "Reaction," *Russian Philosophy*, vol. I, pp. 388, 390-91, 400.

75. Ibid., p. 401.

76. Ibid., p. 388.

77. Ibid., p. 387; Steklov, *Sobranie*, vol. III, p. 113. Letter to his relatives. October 9, 1842.

78. Bakunin, "Reaction," *Russian Philosophy*, vol. I, p. 391.

79. Steklov, *Sobranie*, vol. III, p. 113. Letter to his relatives. October 9, 1842.

80. See above, pp. 28-9.

81. The Reaction in Germany is a climax and summary of the deeper unfolding as well—the awakening from a "peacefully and egotistically self-oriented state" (preoedipal); the resulting "painful contact with reality" (the failed oepidal confrontation: all the talk about "virility," "whole men," "half-men," "impotence," "paralysis," etc.); and the response to that failure both in the form of fantasies transmuting impotence into aggressive omnipotence and the identification with purity and passivity, the infantile "new heaven and new earth."

82. Steklov, *Sobranie*, vol. III, p. 86. Letter to his sisters. [January 1842].

83. Ibid., vol. III, pp. 104-5. Letter to his sister Varvara. [June 1842].

84. Ibid., vol. III, p. 105; vol. III, p. 163. Letter to his brother Paul and I. S. Turgenev. November 20, 1842.

85. Ibid., vol. III, p. 152. Letter to his relatives. November 4, 1842.

86. Ibid., vol. III, p. 81. Letter to his sister Varvara and his brother Paul. [December 1841]; vol. III, p. 113. Letter to his relatives. October 9, 1842; vol. III, pp. 115-16, 118. Letter to his relatives. October 9, 1842.

87. Ibid., vol. III, p. 164. Letter to his brother Paul and I. S. Turgenev. November 20, 1842; vol. III, pp. 168-71. Letter to his relatives. [November 20, 1842].

88. Ibid., vol. III, p. 155. Letter and instructions to his brother Paul. November 6, 1842. (For the "good soldier" expression see reference in note 95.)

89. Ibid., vol. III, p. 151. Letter to his relatives. November 4, 1842.

90. Ibid., vol. III, pp. 120-21. Letter to his brother Nicholas. October

9, 1842; vol. III, p. 163. Letter to his brother Paul and I. S. Turgenev. November 20, 1842.

91. Ibid., vol. III, p. 125. Letter to his brother Nicholas. October 10, 1842. See also vol. III, p. 159. Letter to his brother Paul and I. S. Turgenev. November 13, 1842; vol. III, p. 163. Letter to his brother Paul and I. S. Turgenev. November 20, 1842.

92. Ibid., vol. III, p. 149. Letter to his relatives. November 4, 1842.

93. Ibid. (Emphasis added.)

94. Ibid., vol. III, p. 91. Letter to Alexandra Beyer. [January 1842].

95. Ibid., vol. III, p. 102. Letter to the Beyer sisters. June 28, 1842.

96. Ibid., vol. III, p. 83. Letter to his sisters. [December 1841]; vol. III, pp. 89-90. Letter to his sisters. January 3, 1842.

97. Ibid., vol. III, p. 110. Letter to his sister Tatiana. [late summer 1842].

98. Ibid., vol. III, pp. 110–11.

99. Ibid., vol. III, pp. 89–90. Letter to his sisters. January 3, 1842.

100. Ibid., vol. III, pp. 106-7. Letter to his brother Alexi. [July 1842].

101. Ibid., vol. III, pp. 109–10. Letter to his sister Tatiana. [late summer 1842].

102. Ibid., vol. III, p. 152. Letter to his relatives. November 4, 1842.

103. Ibid., vol. III, p. 151.

104. Ibid., vol. III, p. 4. Letter to his sister Varvara. July 20, 1840.

105. Ibid., vol. III, p. 98. Letter to Alexandra Beyer. April 7, 1842.

106. Ibid., vol. III, pp. 123-24. Letter to his brother Nicholas. October 9, 1842.

107. Ibid., vol. III, p. 122.

108. Ibid.

109. Ibid., vol. III, p. 69. Letter to his relatives. October 22, 1842; vol. III, p. 73. Letter to his brother Paul and his sister Varvara. November 4, 1842.

110. Ibid., vol. III, pp. 111–12. Letter to his sister Tatiana. [late summer 1842].

111. Ibid., vol. III, pp. 14-15. Letter to his brothers and sisters. September 1, 1840.

112. Ibid., vol. II, pp. 249-50. Letter to Natalie Beyer. May 1839; vol. II, p. 263. Letter to his sisters. September 1839.

113. Ibid., vol. III, p. 98. Letter to Alexandra Beyer. April 7, 1842.

114. Ibid., vol. III, p. 110. Letter to his sister Tatiana. [late summer 1842].

115. Ibid., vol. III, p. 149. Letter to his relatives. November 4, 1842.

116. Ibid., vol. III, p. 159. Letter to his brother Paul and I. S. Turgenev. November 13, 1842.

117. Ibid., vol. III, p. 150. Letter to his relatives. November 4, 1842. (Emphasis is in the original.)

CHAPTER 7. "APOSTLE OF LIBERATION"

1. Steklov, *Sobranie*, vol. III, p. 172. Letter to Otto Weigand. January 8, 1843.

2. Ibid., vol. IV, p. 104. "Confession." July–August 1851.

3. Ibid., vol. III, p. 173. Letter to Emma Sigmund. January 15, 1843.

4. Ibid., vol. IV, pp. 104-5. "Confession."

5. Ibid., vol. III, p. 164. Letter to his brother Paul and I. S. Turgenev. November 20, 1842.

6. Ibid., vol. III, p. 181. Letter to his brother Paul. February 10, 1843; vol. III, p. 186. Letter to his sisters. February 20, 1843.

7. Ibid., vol. III, p. 183. Letter to his brother Paul. February 12, 1843; vol. III, p. 246 and March 29, 1845.

8. Ibid., vol. III, p. 149. Letter to his relatives. November 4, 1842.

9. Ibid., vol. III, pp. 181-83. Letter to his brother Paul. February 12, 1843; vol. III, pp. 185-86. Letter to his sisters. February 20, 1843; vol. III, pp. 190-92. Letter to his sisters. February 14, 1843; vol. III, p. 193. Letter to Arnold Ruge. March 11, 1843; vol. III, p. 202. Letter to his brother Paul. [April 1843]; vol. III, p. 217. Letter to his relatives. [May 1843]; vol. III, pp. 245-47. Letter to his brother Paul. March 29, 1843; vol. III, pp. 254-56. Letter to his sister Tatiana. June 29, 1843.

10. Ibid., vol. III, pp. 181-83. Letter to his brother Paul. February 12, 1843; vol. III, p. 186. Letter to his sisters. February 20, 1843.

11. Ibid., vol. III, pp. 180-81. Letter to his brother Paul. February 10, 1843; vol. III, p. 190. Letter to his sisters. February 26, 1843.

12. Ibid., vol. III, p. 180. Letter to his brother Paul. February 10, 1843.

13. Ibid., vol. III, pp. 192-96. Letter to Arnold Ruge. March 11, 1843; vol. III, pp. 206-8. Letter to his brothers. May 10, 1843; vol. III, p. 210. Letter to Arnold Ruge. May 10, 1843; vol. III, p. 217. Letter to his relatives. [May 1843]; vol. III, p. 219. Letter to his brother Paul. May 25, 1843. See also, vol. III, p. 453.

14. Ibid., vol. III, pp. 163-64. Letter to his brother Paul and I. S. Turgenev. November 20, 1842. vol. III, p. 193. Letter to Arnold Ruge. March 11, 1843.

15. Ibid., vol. III, pp. 195-96. Letter to Arnold Ruge. March 11, 1843; vol. III, p. 198. Letter to Arnold Ruge. March 19, 1843.

16. Ibid., vol. III, p. 220. Letter to his brother Paul. May 25, 1843.

17. Ibid., vol. III, p. 218. Letter to his relatives. [May 1843].

18. Ibid., vol. III, p. 187. Letter to his sisters. February 20, 1843.

19. Ibid., vol. IV, pp. 103-4. "Confession." "This morning I began reading Stein," Bakunin wrote his brother, Paul, in early November 1842. Steklov, *Sobranie,* vol. III, p. 154. See also, A Lehning, ed. *Archives Bakounine,* vol. III (Leiden: Brill, 1967), p. 432.

20. Steklov, *Sobranie,* vol. III, p. 223. "Communism."

21. Ibid., vol. III, pp. 176-77. Letter to Arnold Ruge. January 19, 1843.

22. Ibid., vol. III, p. 226. "Communism."

23. Ibid., vol. III, pp. 228-29.

24. Ibid., vol. III, p. 214. Letter to Arnold Ruge. May 1843.

25. Ibid., vol. III, p. 213.

26. Ibid., vol. III, pp. 230-31. "Communism."

27. Ibid., vol. III, p. 216. Letter to his relatives. [May 1843].

28. Ibid.

29. Ibid., vol. III, pp. 195-96. Letter to Arnold Ruge. March 11, 1843.

30. Ibid., vol. III, p. 213. Letter to Arnold Ruge. May 1843.

31. Ibid.

32. Ibid., vol. III, pp. 227, 229, 230–31. "Communism"; vol. III, p. 244. Letter to his brother Paul. March 29, 1845.

33. Ibid., vol. III, pp. 213–14. Letter to Arnold Ruge. May 1843; vol. III, p. 228. "Communism."

34. See above, p. 190.

35. A French communist organization, the League of the Just, advised Weitling, who had been a member of the group since the mid-1830s, to try and establish a "'close, intimate alliance with Frobel and Bakunin'," As quoted in N. Pirumova, *Bakunin* (Moscow: Molodaia gvardia, 1970), p. 63.

36. Steklov, *Sobranie*, vol. IV, p. 110. "Confession."

37. See above, pp. 189–190.

38. Steklov, *Sobranie*, vol. III, p. 237. Letter to Reinhold Solberg. October 14, 1844.

39. Ibid., vol. III, pp. 241, 242. Letter to the editor of *La Réforme*. [January 27, 1845].

40. Bakunin had already met some Polish émigré leaders in Brussels, Lelewel, for example. Ibid., vol. IV, pp. 110–11. "Confession."

41. Ibid., vol. IV, p. 112.

42. Ibid., vol. III, p. 161. Letter to his brother Paul and I. S. Turgenev. November 20, 1842; vol. III, p. 282. Letter to George Herweg. [December] 1847; vol. IV, pp. 108–9. "Confession."

43. Ibid., vol. IV, pp. 111, 115. "Confession."

44. Ibid., vol. III, pp. 245, 247. Letter to his brother Paul. March 29, 1845; vol. III, p. 251. Letter to his relatives. May 1, 1845.

45. Ibid., vol. III, pp. 255–56. Letter to his sister Tatiana. June 29, 1845.

46. Ibid., vol. III, p. 252. Letter to his relatives. May 1, 1845.

47. Ibid., vol. III, p. 251.

48. Ibid., vol. III, p. 247. Letter to his brother Paul. March 29, 1845. See also, vol. III, pp. 203–4. Letter to his brother Paul. [April 1843].

49. Ibid., vol. III, p. 245. (Emphasis added.)

50. Some biographers do believe that Bakunin was speaking here of his love for a woman, namely Madam Pescantini. For a brief discussion of the opposing interpretations, see Pirumova, *Bakunin*, pp. 56–57, 76–77. There is no doubt (Bakunin made it clear enough) that he sincerely wanted to "liberate" Madam Pescantini from her marriage, but there is no evidence to show that the feelings involved were any different than those motivating his earlier efforts either to break up marriages or to keep them from taking place. Moreover, even had Bakunin intended to express here his feelings about Madam Pescantini or some other woman, it is clear from the statement taken as a whole that other themes and concerns broke in and displaced any such focus—and that, for the present analysis, is the important point.

51. Steklov, *Sobranie*, vol. III, p. 245. Letter to his brother Paul. March 29, 1845.

52. Ibid., vol. III, p. 250. Letter to his relatives. May 1, 1845.

53. Ibid., vol. IV, pp. 116–17. "Confession."

54. Ibid., vol. IV, p. 117.

55. Ibid., vol. III, p. 260. Letter to *Le Constitutionnel*. February 6, 1846.

56. Ibid., vol. IV, p. 118. "Confession."

57. Ibid., vol. IV, pp. 118-19.

58. Ibid., vol. III, pp. 261, 263. Letter to Louise Focht. August 5, 1847.

59. Ibid., vol. III, pp. 264-65. Letter to George and Emma Herweg. September 6, 1847.

60. Ibid., vol. III, pp. 265-67. Letter to K. A. Varnhangen von Ense. October 12, 1847.

61. Ibid., vol. III, p. 266.

62. Ibid., vol. III, pp. 267-68. Letter to Emma Herweg. October 18, 1847.

63. Ibid., vol. III, pp. 277-78. Speech on the Anniversary of the Polish Uprising of November 29; vol. IV, p. 119. "Confession."

64. Ibid., vol. III, p. 279. Speech on the Polish Uprising.

65. See above, pp. 47, 104, 106, 108.

66. Steklov, *Sobranie,* vol. III, p. 276. Speech on the Polish Uprising.

67. Ibid., vol. III, p. 213. Letter to Arnold Ruge. May 1843.

68. Ibid., vol. III, p. 272. Speech on the Polish Uprising.

69. Ibid., vol. III, pp. 292-94; vol. III, pp. 487-89. Open letter to Count Duchâtel. February 7, 1848; vol. III, pp. 289-90. Letter to M. Lempitskii. [January 1848]; vol. IV, pp. 119-20. "Confession."

70. Ibid., vol. III, pp. 283-84. Letter to P. V. Annenkov. December 20, 1847.

71. Ibid., vol. III, p. 286. Letter to M. Lemnitskii. January 8, 1848.

72. Ibid., vol. III, p. 282. Letter to George Herweg. December 1847; vol. III, p. 287. Letter to M. Lemnitskii. January 8, 1848. Bakunin uses the words *evrei* and, more frequently, *zhid,* which I have translated as "Jew" and "yid" respectively. Although in Yiddish the term "yid" is not pejorative, it is so in English and so carries the connotations that *zhid* does in Russian. "Kike," though, might be better.

73. Ibid., vol. IV, pp. 122-23. "Confession."

74. Ibid.

75. Ibid., vol. III, pp. 294-95. Letter to *La Réforme*. March 13, 1848.

76. Ibid., vol. III, p. 284. Letter to P. V. Annenkov. December 20, 1847.

77. See above, p. 46.

78. See below, pp. 135, 189, 228, 285.

79. Steklov, *Sobranie,* vol. III, p. 265. Letter to George and Emma Herweg. September 6, 1847.

80. Ibid., vol. III, p. 347. "Appeal to the Slavs from the Russian Patriot Michael Bakunin, Member of the Slavic Congress in Prague." December, 1848. Notwithstanding those last and similar statements, it would be incorrect to ascribe Bakunin's revolutionary violence only to repressed sexuality. It is no less (and probably more) rooted in narcissistic rage and omnipotence. This will become clearer as the analysis proceeds.

81. See above, pp. 172-174.

82. See above, p. 207.

83. Steklov, *Sobranie,* vol. III, p. 276. Speech on the Polish Uprising.

84. See below, pp. 211, 224–5, 227, 281, 320, 357.

85. Steklov, *Sobranie,* vol. IV, p. 123. "Confession."

86. See above p. 199. To restate this interpretation again, Bakunin adamantly avoided any "fussy" conventional role because he identified all such roles with his father and therefore with his father's relationship with his mother. He could only conceive of such a relationship as one of "independence"; otherwise it "would be the most dangerous and repulsive thing in the world." His need for absolute "freedom" from society, his flight from conventional male roles, and his opposition to everything sexual or "animal" were all motivated by the same oedipal dread.

87. Steklov, *Sobranie,* vol. IV, p. 123. "Confession."

88. Ibid., vol. III, p. 296. Letter to *La Réformé.* March 13, 1848.

89. Ibid., vol. III, pp. 294–96.

90. Ibid., vol. III, pp. 299–300. Statement to the Berlin police. April 22, 1848.

91. Ibid., vol. IV, p. 129. "Confession."

92. Ibid., vol. IV, pp. 123–24; vol. IV, pp. 26–27. Letter to his attorney Franz Otto I. March 17, 1850.

93. Ibid., vol. IV, p. 125. "Confession."

94. Ibid., vol. IV, p. 126.

95. Ibid., vol. III, p. 297. Letter to P. V. Annenkov. April 17, 1848.

96. Ibid., vol. III, p. 297; vol. III, p. 300. Statement to the Berlin police. April 22, 1848.

97. Ibid., vol. III, pp. 499–501; vol. IV, pp. 130– 31. "Confession."

98. Ibid., vol. III, p. 503.

99. Ibid., vol. IV, pp. 131–132. "Confession."

100. Ibid., vol. III, p. 229. Letter to P. V. Annenkov. April 17, 1848.

101. Ibid., vol. IV, p. 130. "Confession."

102. Ibid., vol. IV, p. 132.

103. Ibid.

104. Ibid., vol. III, p. 301. "Foundations of a New Slavic Policy."

105. B. A. Evreinov, "Bakunin i slavianskii siezd 1848 goda v Prage," *Russki Nauchnyi Institut. Belgrad. Zapiski* (Belgrad, 1936), vol. XIII p. 153.

106. Steklov, *Sobranie,* vol. IV, pp. 140–42. "Confession."

107. This summary follows Evreinov's account.

108. Steklov, *Sobranie,* vol. IV, pp. 134, 138, 153, 157. "Confession."

109. Ibid., vol. III, pp. 301, 302–3. "Foundations of a New Slavic Policy." For the earlier Parisien expression of this centralized "federalism" see p. 200.

110. Ibid., vol. IV, pp. 153–56. "Confession."

111. See above, p. 200.

112. Steklov, *Sobranie,* vol. IV, pp. 108–9, 124, 127. "Confession."

113. Ibid., vol. IV, p. 107.

114. Ibid., vol. IV, pp. 143–44.

115. For example, Peter N. Stearns, *The Revolution of 1848* (London: Norton, 1974), p. 113.

116. Evreinov, "Bakunin i siezd," *Zapiski,* p. 158.

117. Ibid., pp. 158–160; Steklov, *Sobranie,* vol. IV, p. 158. "Confession."

118. Steklov, *Sobranie,* vol. IV, p. 162. "Confession."

119. Ibid., vol. IV, pp. 161-62.

120. Ibid.

121. Michel Bakounine, *Confession* trans. Paulette Brupbacher, notes by Max Nettlau, (Paris: Les Éditions Rieder, 1932), p. 328.

122. Steklov, *Sobranie,* vol. III, p. 315. Letter to Arnold Ruge. [August 1848].

123. Ibid., vol. III, pp. 316-17. Letter to George Herweg. August 1848.

124. Ibid., vol. III, p. 318.

125. Ibid., vol. III, p. 516. Notes.

126. Y.M. Steklov, "Bakunin i revoliutsiia 1848 g.," *Katorga i ssylka* (Moscow) 6-80 (1933): 100.

127. Steklov, *Sobranie,* vol. III, p. 528. Notes.

128. Ibid., vol. III, p. 320. Letter to L. Shtur. [September 1848].

129. Ibid., vol. III, p. 324. Letter, recipient unknown. October 2, 1848.

130. Ibid., vol. IV, p. 163. "Confession."

131. Ibid.

132. Ibid., vol. III, pp. 320-21. Letter to *La Réforme.* [September 1848].

133. Ibid., vol. IV, p. 163. "Confession."

134. Ibid., vol, IV, pp. 163-64.

135. Ibid.

136. Ibid., vol. IV, p. 165.

137. Joseph Pfitzner, *Bakuninstudien* (Prag, 1932), p. 92.

138. The following quotations are taken from two versions of the *Appeal to the Slavs,* one, an unfinished draft, written at the end of October and early November 1848, and the second, the published version, written in December 1848. Steklov, *Sobranie,* vol. III, pp. 329-44, 345-61.

139. Ibid., vol. III, pp. 335-36, 340. See also, p. 361.

140. Ibid., vol. III, p. 361.

141. Ibid., vol. III, pp. 360, 349, 362.

142. Ibid., vol. III, p. 366.

143. Ibid., vol. III, p. 346. See also, p. 335.

144. Ibid., vol. III, p. 361. The pronoun is, indeed, "her," referring as it does to the feminine noun "revolution." I am here translating the pronoun as "her" rather than "it," which would be the more conventional translation, because I believe that here, as in other instances, Bakunin unconsciously uses peculiarities of language and grammar to express hidden feelings and needs.

145. Ibid., vol. III, pp. 331-32.

146. Ibid., vol. III, pp. 346-47.

147. Ibid., vol. III, p. 347.

148. Ibid., vol. III, p. 348.

149. Ibid., vol. III, p. 347.

150. In his very first revolutionary tract, *The Reaction in Germany,* it may be recalled, he was much distressed to find that "evil passions are awakened also in us through this fight." This theme will reappear repeatedly in his later revolutionary career.

151. Steklov, *Sobranie,* vol. III, p. 533. Notes.

152. Ibid., vol. III, pp. 356-59. *Appeal to the Slavs.*

153. Ibid., vol. III, p. 358. (Compare earlier "awakenings," pp. 100, 170.)

154. Ibid., vol. III, p. 533. Notes.

155. Ibid., vol. III, pp. 367–68. Letter to George Herweg. December 8, 1848.

156. Ibid., vol. IV, p. 168. "Confession."

157. Ibid., vol. IV, p. 167.

158. Ibid., vol. IV, p. 167.

159. Ibid., vol. IV, p. 169.

160. Ibid., vol. IV, pp. 171–72.

161. Ibid., vol. IV, p. 172.

162. Ibid., vol. IV, p. 173.

163. Ibid., vol. IV, pp. 177–78.

164. Ibid., vol. IV, pp. 178–79.

165. Ibid., vol. IV, pp. 179–80.

166. Ibid., vol. IV, p. 180.

167. Ibid., vol. IV, p. 182.

168. Ibid., vol. IV, pp. 182–83.

169. Ibid., vol. IV, p. 183.

170. Ibid., vol. IV, pp. 184–87.

171. Ibid., vol. IV, pp. 188–89.

172. Ibid., vol. IV, pp. 194–95.

173. Ibid., vol. IV, p. 196.

174. Ibid., vol. IV, p. 198.

175. Ibid.

176. August Röckel, *Sachsens Erhebung und das Zuchthaus zu Waldheim* (Frankfurt a. M., 1865), pp. 144–45.

177. Steklov, *Sobranie,* vol. IV, p. 184. "Confession."

178. Röckel, *Sachsens Erhebung,* p. 144.

179. Steklov, *Sobranie,* vol. IV, p. 180. "Confession."

180. Ibid., vol. III, pp. 382–426. "Tsarism and the German Revolution" [Fall 1848–Spring 1849].

181. This second "Appeal" was published April 20, 1849 in a Dresden periodical under the title, "Die Russen in Siebenburgen. Eine Ansprache an die Czechen." Ibid. vol. III, pp. 372–79; vol. III, p. 540. Notes.

182. Ibid., vol. IV, p. 168. "Confession."

183. Ibid., vol. IV, pp. 196, 199.

184. Boris Nikolaevskii, "Bakunin epokhi evo pervoi emigratsii v vospomi-naniakh nemtsev-sovremenikov," *Katorga i ssylka* (Moscow) vols. 8–9 (1930): 95–98, 106–11; Edward Newman, *The Life of Richard Wagner* (New York; Knopf, 1937/1946), vol. II, p. 61.

185. The following account of the Dresden uprising is drawn from these sources: Veit Valentin, *Geschichte der deutschen Revolution von 1848–1849* (Berlin; Ullstein, 1931), vol. II, pp. 479–89; Max Nettlau, "Michael Bakunin in den Jahren 1848–1849," *Sozialistische Monats-Hefte. IV Jahrgang des Sozialakademiker* (Berlin) IV (1898); Tim Klein, *1848: Der Vorkampf Deutscher Einheit und Freiheit* (Munchen-Leipzig: 1914); A. von Montbé, *Der Mai-Aufstand in Dresden* (Dresden, 1850); and works by Peter Stearns, Boris Nikolaevskii, and Edward Newman cited earlier.

186. Nikolaevskii, "Bakunin epokhi evo pervoi emigratsii," p. 108.

187. Steklov, *Sobranie,* vol. IV, pp. 199–200. "Confession."

188. Ibid., vol. IV, p. 201.

189. Montbé, *Der Mai-Aufstand,* p. 121.

190. Steklov, *Sobranie,* vol. IV, pp. 199–200. "Confession."

191. Ibid., vol. III, pp. 317–18. Letter to George Herweg. [August 1848].

192. Newman, *Wagner,* vol. II, p. 95.

193. Steklov, *Sobranie,* vol. IV, p. 200. "Confession."

194. Ibid., vol. IV, p. 201; Röckel, *Sachsens Erhebung,* p. 143; Richard Wagner, *Samtliche Briefe* (Leipzig; Deutscher Verlag für Musik, 1970), vol. II, p. 674.

195. Steklov, *Sobranie,* vol. IV, p. 199. "Confession."

196. Ibid., vol. IV, p. 203. He similarly acknowledged in his "Confession" that "the fact that I was regarded as a Russian spy, moreover, drove me to some intentionally careless steps, confused everything, and landed me in trouble." See below, p. 242.

197. Ibid., vol. IV, p. 201. "Confession."

198. Ibid., vol. IV, pp. 201–2.

199. Ibid., vol. IV, pp. 203–4.

200. Newman, *Wagner,* vol. II, pp. 69, 79.

201. Valentin, *Geschichte,* vol. II, p. 484.

202. Nikolaevskii, "Bakunin epokhi evo pervoi emigratsii," p. 119.

203. Ibid., pp. 109 note 1, 110, 118; Steklov, *Sobranie,* vol. IV, p. 204. "Confession"; Valentin, *Geschichte,* vol. II, pp. 486–87.

204. See, for other examples of this important and revealing distinction, pp. 228, 294, 307, 321.

205. Steklov, *Sobranie,* vol. IV, p. 167. "Confession."

206. Ibid., vol. IV, p. 205.

207. Ibid.

208. Ibid.

CHAPTER 8. DARK NIGHT AND APOSTASY

1. Nikolaevskii, "Bakunin epokhi evo pervoi emigratsii," p. 93.

2. B.A. Evreinov, "M.A. Bakunin i Avstriiskiia vlasti v 1849–1851 godakh," *Russkii svobodnyi universitet. Prague. Nauchno-issledovatelskie obedineniie zapiski.* (Prague) IV (1931); Steklov, *Sobranie,* vol. IV, pp. 414–15. Notes.

3. Steklov, *Sobranie,* vol. IV, pp. 11–12. Letter to Arnold Ruge. October 15, 1849; vol. IV, p. 17. Letter to Adolf Reichel. December 9, 1849.

4. Ibid. vol. IV, p. 11. Letter to Arnold Ruge. October 15, 1849; vol. IV, pp. 15–17. Letters to Arnold Reichel. November 24, 1849 and December 9, 1849; vol. IV, p. 20. Letter to Matilda Reichel. January 16, 1850.

5. Ibid., vol. IV, p. 21. Letter to Matilda Reichel. January 16, 1850.

6. Ibid., vol. IV, p. 22. Letter to Matilda Reichel. February 16, 1850.

7. Ibid., vol. IV, p. 21.

8. Ibid., vol. IV, pp. 396–98, 400–1, 412. Notes.

9. Ibid., vol. IV, pp. 23–31. Letter to his attorney Frantz Otto I. March 17, 1850.

10. Ibid., vol. IV, pp. 31–94. "My Defense." [December 1849–April 1850].

11. Ibid., vol. IV, p. 68.

12. Ibid., vol. IV, pp. 22–23. Letter to Matilda Reichel. February 16, 1850.

13. Ibid., vol. IV, p. 22.

14. Ibid.

15. Ibid., vol. IV, p. 100. "Confession."

16. Ibid., vol. IV, p. 416. Notes.

17. Ibid., vol. IV, p. 366. Letter to A.I. Herzen. December 8, 1860.

18. Z. Ralli, "Mikhail Bakunin iz moikh vospominanii," *Minuvshie gody,* 10 (1908): 148.

19. V. Polonskii, ed., *Materialy dlia biographii,* vol. I, pp. 55–94.

20. Steklov, *Sobranie,* vol. IV, pp. 124, 130, 155, 180. "Confession."

21. Ibid., vol. IV, pp. 124, 145, 206. These are but a few examples of such statements.

22. Ibid., vol. IV, pp. 102, 151.

23. Ibid., vol. IV, p. 128.

24. Ibid.

25. Ibid., vol. IV, p. 149.

26. Ibid., vol. IV, p. 148.

27. Ibid., vol. IV, p. 160.

28. Ibid.

29. Ibid., vol. IV, p. 142.

30. Ibid., vol. IV, p. 152.

31. Ibid., vol. IV, p. 206. Bakunin had asked that both parents be permitted to visit him, along with his "one beloved sister." For some reason, his mother was not among the visitors, although, as we shall see, she was to visit him often after her husband's death.

32. Ibid., vol. IV, pp. 207–8. Letter to his relatives. January 4, 1852; vol. IV, pp. 216–17, 219–22, 226–8. Letter to his relatives. February 4, 1852.

33. Ibid., vol. IV, pp. 217–19.

34. Ibid., vol. IV, pp. 232–33, 238–40. Letter to his relatives. May 16, 1852.

35. Ibid. vol. IV, pp. 243–47. Letters to his relatives. [February 1854]; vol. IV, pp. 247–48. Letter to Tatiana. [February 1854]; vol. IV, pp. 248–49. Letter to Tatiana. [May 1854].

36. Ibid., vol. IV, p. 258. Letter to his mother. [fall 1855]; vol. IV, pp. 559–60. Notes.

37. Ibid., vol. IV, p. 258. Letter to his mother. fall 1855; vol. IV, p. 263. Letter to his relatives. [April 1856]. (Emphasis is added.)

38. Ibid., vol. IV, pp. 559–60. Notes.

39. Ibid., vol. IV, p. 254. Letter to E.I. Pushchina. [May 1855].

40. Ibid., vol. IV, pp. 561–62. Notes.

41. Ibid., vol. IV, p. 208. Letter to his relatives. January 4, 1852.

42. Ibid., vol. IV, p. 259. Letter to his mother. [fall 1855]; vol. IV, p. 267. Letter to his mother. August 1856. (Emphasis added); vol. IV, p. 564. Notes.

43. Ibid., vol. IV, pp. 271–72. Letter to Prince V.A. Dolgorukov. February 14, 1857.

44. Ibid., vol. IV, pp. 272–76. Petition to Alexander II. February 14, 1857.

45. The first description is recorded in Steklov, *Sobranie,* vol. IV, p. 568. Notes; the second is found in Pirumova, *Bakunin,* p. 150 and is based on the later recollections of a niece of Bakunin's who was eight years old at the time of Bakunin's visit.

46. The Decembrists were discussed in chapter 1. The Petrashevsky exiles, led by M.V. Butashevich-Petrashevsky, were in Siberia as punishment for their "conspiracy of ideas," a charge nowhere to be found in the criminal code. Their only crime was their praise for socialist ideas in their discussion circle and at a banquet in April 1849 commemorating the utopian socialist Fourier. The initial sentence was death for 15 of the members and deportation or forced labor for six others. In the final moments before the execution was to be carried out, the death sentences were commuted to exile. Among those thus spared was Fedor Dostoevsky, who was sentenced to four years of hard labor then another six years of army duty in Siberia.

47. Steklov, *Sobranie,* vol. IV, pp. 279–280. Letter to Prince V.A. Dolgorukov. March 29, 1857.

48. Ibid., vol. IV, p. 280. Letter to his mother. March 29, 1857.

49. Ibid., vol. IV, p. 282. Letter to General Y.D. Kazimirskii. August 12, 1857.

50. Ibid., vol. IV, p. 284.

51. Ibid., vol. IV, p. 569. Notes.

52. Ibid., vol. IV, p. 300. Letters to his cousins Eudoxie, Catherine, and Pachette. March 4, 1859.

53. Ibid., vol. IV, p. 570. Notes.

54. Ibid., vol. IV, p. 284. Letter to his mother. [March 28, 1858].

55. Ibid., vol. IV, pp. 286–87. Letter to General A. Ozerskii. May 14, 1858.

56. See above, pp. 185, 197.

57. Steklov, *Sobranie,* vol. IV, p. 287. Letter to General A. Ozerskii. May 14, 1858.

58. Ibid., vol. IV, p. 569. Notes.

59. Ibid.

60. Ibid., vol. IV, p. 368. Letter to A. I. Herzen. December 8, 1860.

61. Ibid., vol. IV, p. 288. Letter to Prince V.A. Dolgorukov. June 16, 1858.

62. Ibid., vol. IV, p. 570. Notes.

63. Ibid., vol. IV, pp. 290–93. Letter to M.N. Katkov. January 21, 1859.

64. Ibid., vol. IV, p. 295.

65. Ibid., vol. IV, p. 296.

66. Ibid., vol. IV, p. 374. Letter to D.E. Benardaki. January 14, 1861.

67. Ibid., vol. IV, p. 604. Notes.

68. B. Kubalov, "Strantsy iz zhizni M.A. Bakunina i evo semi v Sibiri," *Sbornik trudov professorov i prepodavatelei Gosudarstvennogo Irkutskogo universiteta,* (Irkutsk) vypusk 5 (1923): 137.

69. Steklov, *Sobrani,* vol. IV, pp. 580. The victim had tried to avoid the duel, but others, including Bakunin, insisted that the duel take place. Pirumova, *Bakunin,* p. 161.

70. Steklov, *Sobranie,* vol. IV, p. 296. Letter to M.N. Katkov. January 21, 1859; vol. IV, p. 301. Letter to P.V. Annenkov. February 25, 1860.

71. Steklov, *Sobranie,* vol. IV, pp. 303–47. Letter to A.I. Herzen. November 7, 1860; vol. IV, pp. 347–59. Reply to *Kolokol* (the *Bell).* [December 1, 1860] ; vol. IV, pp. 359–69. Letter to A.I. Herzen. December 8, 1860.

72. This is but a representative sampling of the praise that Bakunin heaps upon his new hero in these three letters to Herzen.

73. Steklov, *Sobranie,* vol. IV, p. 309. Letter to A.I. Herzen. November 7, 1860.

74. Ibid., vol. IV, p. 314.

75. Ibid., vol. IV, pp. 315–16.

76. Ibid., vol. IV, p. 310.

77. Ibid., vol. IV, p. 348. Reply to *Kolokol.* December 1, 1860.

78. Ibid., vol. IV, pp. 305, 308, 309. Letter to A.I. Herzen. November 7, 1860; vol. IV, pp. 359, 360. Letter to A.I. Herzen. December 8, 1860.

79. Ibid., vol. IV, p. 305. Letter to A.I. Herzen. November 7, 1860.

80. Ibid., vol. IV, p. 306; vol. IV, p. 360. Letter to A.I. Herzen. December 8, 1860.

81. Ibid., vol. IV, p. 306. Letter to A.I. Herzen. November 7, 1860.

82. Ibid., vol. IV, pp. 310–11.

83. Ibid., vol. IV, p. 319.

84. Ibid., vol. IV, p. 318.

85. Ibid., vol. IV, p. 327.

86. Ibid., vol. IV, p. 329.

87. Ibid., vol. IV, p. 339; vol. IV, pp. 339, 349, 351–52. Reply to *Kolokol.* December 1, 1860.

88. Ibid., vol. IV, p. 363. Letter to A.I. Herzen. December 8, 1860.

89. Ibid., vol. IV, p. 364.

90. Ibid., vol. IV, p. 361.

91. Ibid., vol. IV, pp. 364–65.

92. Ibid., vol. IV, p. 298. Letter to his cousins Ekaterina Mikhailovna and Praskove Mikhailovna Bakunin. January 1859.

93. Kubalov, "Strantsy," p. 143.

94. Steklov, *Sobranie,* vol. IV, p. 376. Letter to D.E. Benardaki. January 14, 1861.

95. Ibid., vol. IV, p. 381. Letter to his brother Nicholas. February 1, 1861.

96. Ibid., vol. IV, p. 371. Letter to M.N. Katkov. January 15, 1861. Bakunin also makes clear in this letter to Katkov just how earnest he had been in the pan-Slavist declarations and proposals he had been making over the past decade or so, that they had not been meant simply to deceive the Tsars and their servitors. What, he asks here, would happen were Austria to become a federated Slavic power? It would gradually incorporate into itself, one after another, Poland, White Russia, the Ukraine, and so on. There could not be two Slavic worlds. "That would be unnatural: one would inevitably eat the other. So, better let it be Russia eating Austria." Russia, therefore, "must become the focus of Slavic rebirth. It must break itself up into administratively autonomous parts, organically tied to each other, then be regenerated as a Russian Slavic federation." Ibid., vol. IV, pp. 371–72.

97. Ibid., vol. IV, p. 380. Letter to his brother Nicholas. February 1, 1861.

98. Kubalov, "Strantsy," p. 145.

99. B.B. Glinskii, "M.A. Bakunin i evo begstvo iz Sibiri," *Istoricheskii vestnik* 3 (1898): 1044.

CHAPTER 9. RETREAT TO ARMAGEDDON

1. *Kolokol (Bell)*. November 22, 1861, January 1, January 15, and April 8, 1862.

2. Y.M. Steklov, *Mikhail Aleksandrovich Bakunin. Evo zhizn i dieiatlenost* (Moscow: Izdatelstvo Kommunisticheskoi Akademii, 1926-1927), vol. II, pp. 18-19, 21.

3. Mikhail Lemke, "Vosemnadstat pisem M.A. Bakunina," *Byloe* 7 (July, 1906): 186, 190, 203, 205, 210.

4. Quoted in Pirumova, *Bakunin,* p. 176.

5. M.P. Dragomanov, ed., *Pisma M.A. Bakunina k A.I. Gertsenu i N.P. Ogarevu* (St. Petersburg: Brublevskii, 1906), p. 189.

6. *Kolokol* (January 15, 1862).

7. Steklov, Bakunin, vol. II, p. 35.

8. On the *Zemsky Sobor,* see p. 273.

9. For details of these encounters and associations, see E.H. Carr, *Michael Bakunin* New York: Vintage, 1961 [1937]. Chapter XX; Pirumov, *Bakunin,* Chapter V; Miklós Kun "Bakunin and Hungary (1848-1865)," *Canadian-American Slavic Studies* 10 (1976): 520-23; Alexander Herzen, *My Past and Thoughts* (New York; Knopf, 1968) vol. III, pp. 1357-371. (The pages from Herzen contain some of the most memorable, and frequently quoted, portraits of Bakunin and his frenzied activism at the time. Because Herzen's notorious penchant for colorful hyperbole makes their accuracy and value questionable, they are omitted here. See especially pp. 1357-359.) See also, Steklov, *Bakunin,* vol. II, pp. 62, 66 *ff,* 75-76, 93-94.

10. Mikhail Bakunin, "Neskolko slov iuzhnyi slavian," *Kolokol* (April 8, 1862): 1068.

11. Mikhail Bakunin, "Russkim, polskim i vsem slavianskim druziam," *Kolokol* (February 15, 1862): 1021-28. The attack in this article is directed less against the Russian state than it is against the Germans, whether in Austria and Prussia or in what Bakunin considered the Germanized Russian bureaucracy that, he argued, Peter the Great had imported and that, through the Holstein-Gottorp dynasty, had dominated Russia for a century and a half. Gradually developing through later articles, such as *The People's Cause: Romanov, Pugachev, or Pestel* which he wrote later that year, this theme was to become a virtual obsession in his last years, as we will see below. Herzen attributes this Germanophobia to Bakunin's past disillusionment: "he had paid enough for his youthful enthusiasm, for his faith in the possibility of an alliance with German democrats." Or did it still reflect the same disdain for the Germans that he had expressed over 20 years earlier when he first arrived in Berlin, the fact that in the drama he had composed for himself and spent his life repeatedly reenacting the Germans had come to personify that discipline, order, duty, social constraint, and "philistine" obedience that was always a principal target for his lance? The

still deeper source may have come through when, recalling the Prague days, he criticized Palatcky's vision of a Slavic-Austrian alliance as a form of "filthy purity, or purified filth." In any case, "to war on Germans is fine, and, what is more important, a necessary Slavic task," he wrote in *The People's Cause: Romanov, Pugachev, or Pestel?* (Among the reasons drawing him to Mazzini and Garibaldi at this time was the fact that he considered Italians and Slavs as both "natural enemies of the Germans.") *Kolokol* (January 15, 1862); "Pismo M.A. Bakunina neizvestnomu," *Byloe* 8 (August 1906): 256; Mikhail Bakunin, "Narodnoe delo: Romanov, Pugachev ili Pestel?" *Izbrannye sochineniia* (Petersburg-Moscow; Golos Truda 1920), vol. III, p. 87; Steklov, *Bakunin,* vol. II, p. 9.

12. Bakunin, "Russkim...slavianskim druziam," p. 1025.

13. Bakunin, "Narodnoe delo," pp. 88–89.

14. Bakunin, "Russkim...slavianskim druziam," p. 1028.

15. Bakunin, "Narodnoe delo," pp. 76–77, 80–82, 87. In a letter to Herzen written several years later (in 1866) Bakunin explained this appeal to Tsar Alexander II and defense of the *Zemsky Sobor* by referring to the optimism that prevailed in Russia during the first years of the Alexander II reforms. "We all spoke, wrote with the possibilities of a *Zemsky Sobor* in mind." Although, as we will see, he had by 1866 completely returned to revolutionary maximalism and looked upon all those earlier proposals as "stupid hopes," the fact remains that he acknowledged in this letter that he participated in them. (His attempt to distinguish his views from others who appealed to the Tsar to summon a *Zemsky Sobor* by saying in this letter that he had joined in the optimism only to promote the inevitable disillusionment that would follow is not convincing.) Dragomanov, *Pisma,* pp. 282–83. Further evidence to support the view that Bakunin was quite serious in this continuing hope for revolution from above (continuing, that is, from his Siberian years) is his strong attraction to the Russian peasant Martianov who had arrived in London a few months before him. Serf born, but later successful in business, Martianov urged Herzen to use the *Bell* to drum up support for the Tsar's calling a *Zemsky Sobor*. (On his return to Russia in 1863, Martianov was arrested, sentenced to five years of hard labor in Siberia, and died in exile in 1866.) Finally, Bakunin's close associations with supporters of the "red prince" Jerome Napoleon suggests the same conclusion. Carr, *Bakunin,* pp. 276–77; Kun, "Bakunin and Hungary," p. 524.

16. Bakunin, "Narodnoe delo," pp. 78, 89–90. (Here, again, one hears echoes of *The Reaction in Germany,* with its criticisms of the "evil passion" for violence arising among the revolutionaries.)

17. See index under psychology: non-violence.

18. Bakunin, "Narodnoe delo," p. 75.

19. Written by one Peter Zaichnevsky, the broadside "Young Russia" was distributed in St. Petersburg in May 1862. Among other demands, it called for the murder of the Tsar, his family, and the "royal party," their replacement by a dictatorship that would control elections to a National Assembly, and a socialist economy based on the traditional peasant commune. For a summary of the document, see Philip Pomper, *The Russian Revolutionary Intelligentsia* (New York: Crowell, 1970), pp. 82–83.

20. Lemke, "Pisem," p. 209; Bakunin, "Narodnoe delo," pp. 85–86.

21. Bakunin, "Narodnoe delo," pp. 83–85, 90–91.

22. See also chapter 10, note 154. Several years ago, while I was in Switzerland doing research and formulating these views on Bakunin, Madame Mikhailov of the International Center of Research on Anarchism (Lausanne) mentioned how much Bakunin seemed to her a woman—a most welcome confirmation coming as it did from someone so thoroughly knowledgeable about the sympathetic towards Bakunin. (See also index under psychology: feminine identification.)

23. Did the adoption of a feminine role extend beyond this sexual-revolutionary fantasy and into his relationships in real life? Was he homosexual? The helpmate role he played in relationships with strong men, his preference for being a dependent at home rather than a protective provider, his penchant for the innocent company of young ladies during his adolescence and the stimulating atmosphere of young male virile warriors in his later years, the strangely passive expressions he used in his sexual-revolutionary imagery—these and other similar hints we have seen along the way suggest, at least, the possibility. However, there is absolutely no concrete evidence whatsoever to indicate active homosexual involvements or events in his life.

24. Bakunin, "Narodnoe delo," pp. 89–90.

25. See above, note 8.

26. Herzen, *Past and Thoughts,* vol. III, p. 1357.

27. Ibid., p. 1370; Pirumova, *Bakunin,* p. 190; Jan Kucharzewski, *The Origins of Modern Russia* (New York: Polish Institute of Arts and Sciences in America, 1948), 281–87, Chapters IX and XI, passim.

28. Natalia Pirumova, "Bakunin and Herzen: An Analysis of their Ideological Disagreements at the End of the 1860s," *Canadian-American Studies* 10 (1976): 555; Herzen, *Past and Thoughts,* pp. 1363–64; Alexander Herzen, *Mikhail Bakunin i Polskoe delo* (Berlin; G. Steinitz n.d.), p. 18.

29. Steklov, *Bakunin,* vol. II, pp. 175–82.

30. "Pisma M.A. Bakunina k bratu Aleksandru i N.I. Turgenevu, "*Letopis Marksizma* (Moscow) 9–10 (1929): 97. Perhaps indicating his excited state of mind at the time, he asked his brother in another letter, "where is father living?" His father had died, it will be recalled, in 1854. Ibid., p. 96.

31. A.I. Herzen, *Sobranie sochinenii* (Moscow: Academy of Sciences, 1957), vol. XI, p. 377; Steklov, *Bakunin,* vol. II, p. 217.

32. Quoted in Pirumova, *Bakunin,* p. 200.

33. Herzen, *Past and Thoughts,* vol. III, pp. 1366, 1368. (Translation slightly changed.) Herzen, *Bakunin i Polskoe delo,* p. 30; "Pisma k bratu Aleksandru," p. 95.

34. Dragomanov, *Pisma,* p. 203.

35. Ibid., p. 210.

36. Ibid., pp. 212–16.

37. Steklov, *Bakunin,* p. 168.

38. Dragomanov, *Pisma,* pp. 300–1, 308.

39. Ibid., pp. 218, 221.

40. V. Polonskii, "M. Bakunin i ekspeditsiia 'Ward Jackson'," *Krasnii Arkhiv* 7 (1924): 113.

41. Dragomanov, *Pisma,* p. 220; Polonskii, "Ward Jackson," p. 113.

42. Unless otherwise noted, the following account is based on materials published in Polonskii, "Ward Jackson," pp. 108-45.

43. Ibid., p. 134.

44. Ibid., p. 143.

45. Dragomanov, Pisma, pp. 244-50.

46. Ibid., pp. 194-96, 226-27.

47. Ibid., pp. 228-30.

48. The feeling was reciprocated, according to Herzen: "Demontowicz, after long arguments with Bakunin, said: 'I tell you what, gentlemen, hard as it may be for us with the Russian government, our situation under it is better than what these socialist fanatics are preparing for us'." Recalling what we have already seen of Bakunin's pan-Slavist visions, his apprehension is quite understandable. (Herzen, Past and Thoughts, p. 1384, note 8.)

49. Dragomanov, Pisma, pp. 229-30.

50. Ibid., p. 242.

51. Kucharzewski, Origins, p. 401, note 5.

52. Dragomanov, Pisma, p. 227.

53. Lemke, "Pisem," pp. 196, 201; See note 10 above and Kucharzewski, Origins, p. 399 where Bakunin's plan for an Italian-Slavic alliance against the Germans is further documented.

54. Bakunin, "Russkim...slavianskim druziam," p. 1021.

55. Kolokol (January 15, 1862).

56. Kun, "Bakunin and Hungary," pp. 526-528; L.I. Menchikov, "Bakunin v Italii v 1864," Istoricheskii vestnik (March 1897): 807-34; Pirumova, Bakunin, pp. 223-28.

57. Dragomanov, Pisma, pp. 258, 264-266; "Pisma M.A. Bakunina k Grafine E.B. Salias," Letopisi Marksizma (Moscow) (1927), No. 3, pp. 90-91, 93; Kun, "Bakunin and Hungary," p. 524.

58. "Bakunin k Salias," p. 93.

59. Dragomanov, Pisma, p. 265.

60. Kun, "Bakunin and Hungary," p. 523.

61. "Pismo Bakunin neizvestnomu," Byloe 8 (August 1908), p. 264. (It is interesting to note that this design for a network of secret societies is outlined in association with a still firm and explicit dedication to pan-Slavism: "This I call pan-Slavism...faith and confidence in the great future of the Slavs," Ibid., p. 260.)

62. Arthur Lehning, "Bakunin's Conceptions of Revolutionary Organisations and their Role: A Study of His 'Secret Societies'," Essays in Honour of E.H. Carr, ed. C. Abramsky (Hamden, Conn. 1974), pp. 58-60; Steklov, Bakunin, vol. II, pp. 281-82; Pirumova, Bakunin, pp. 242-44. Bakunin was familiar with the views of Buonarroti at least from the time he began reading about him in Lorenz von Stein's Der Sozialismus und Communismus des heutigen Frankreichs. As for Pisacane, if Bakunin did not know about his views earlier, he no doubt learned all about them from Fanelli, a follower of Pisacane before he became one of Bakunin's most trusted lieutenants. Steklov, Bakunin, vol. II, pp. 281-82, note 2.

63. Kun, "Bakunin and Hungary," pp. 530-31.

64. Ibid., p. 530.

65. Ibid., pp. 530–31. M. Nettlau, *M. Bakunin. Ein Biographie* (Milan: Feltrinelli, 1971. Photocopy of the manuscript published in London, 1896–1900), vol. I, pp. 200–203.

66. "Bakunin k Salias," p. 92. For more "electricity," see above, p. 278.

67. Steklov, *Bakunin,* vol. II, pp. 302–3.

68. "Bakunin k Salias," p. 96.

69. Steklov, *Bakunin,* vol. II, p. 303 *ff.* Nettlau, *M. Bakunin,* vol. I, p. 172.

70. Lehning, Essays, p. 62.

71. Kun, "Bakunin and Hungary," pp. 531–32. Nettlau, *M. Bakunin,* vol. I, pp. 200–203.

72. Dragomanov, *Pisma,* pp. 277–78.

73. Several of these documents have been republished in Daniel Guerin, *Ni dieu ni maître* (Paris: Éditions de Delphes: n.d. pp. 197–215. Some have been available at least as far back as Nettlau published them in his manuscript biography of Bakunin (vol. I, pp. 199–235), i.e. in 1896–1900.

74. Guerin, *Nidieu,* pp. 201–3, 205.

75. Ibid., pp. 210, 213.

76. Ibid., p. 201.

77. Ibid., p. 213.

78. Ibid., p. 201.

79. Ibid., pp. 197, 198, 203, 209.

80. Ibid., pp. 199, 208, 215.

81. Ibid., pp. 202–3.

82. Quoted in Pirumova, *Bakunin,* pp. 234–5.

83. Lehning, *Essays,* pp. 63–64.

84. Michael Bakunin, *Gesammelte Werke,* ed. Max Nettlau (Berlin: Der Syndikalist, 1924), vol. III, pp. 49, 61.

85. Guerin, *Ni dieu,* pp. 207, 208.

86. Lehning, *Essays,* p. 64.

87. Bakunin, *Gesammelte Werke,* vol. III, p. 55.

88. Guerin, *Ni dieu,* p. 202; Lehning, *Essays,* p. 64.

89. Guerin, *Ni dieu,* p. 203.

90. Ibid., p. 215.

91. Bakunin, *Gesammelte Werke,* vol. III, pp. 46–47.

92. Quoted in Pirumova, *Bakunin,* pp. 235–36.

93. O.E. Cafiero, "Carlo Cafiero," *Golos minuvshevo* (May 1914): 125.

94. Menchikov, "Bakunin v Italii," p. 814.

95. Steklov, *Bakunin,* vol. II, p. 279.

96. G.N. Vyrubova, "Revoliutsionnyia vospominaniia," *Vestnik Evropy* (February, 1913): 52.

97. Dragomanov, *Pisma,* pp. 279, 282, 288–93, 315–17.

98. Ibid., p. 278.

99. Quoted in Pirumova, *Bakunin,* p. 235. This quotation, and also the one in note 82 above, are from the earliest of this series of documents concerning Bakunin's secret societies in the 1860s, a letter to August Sohlman, in Stockholm, shortly after Bakunin's return to Italy from Sweden, and from his London

meeting with Marx. See also, Lehning, *Essays*, pp. 62–64 for more details about this important document.

100. "Bakunin k Salias," p. 96.

101. E. Kornilova, "Pisma Zheny M.A. Bakunina," *Katorga i ssylka* 3 (1932): 120–121.

102. Vyrubova, "Revoliutsionnyia vospominaniia," pp. 47–48.

103. Dragomanov, *Pisma*, p. 313.

104. Quoted in Pirumova, *Bakunin*, p. 238.

105. Dragomanov, *Pisma*, p. 317.

CHAPTER 10. THE INTERNATIONAL: ZEALOTS AND PHARISEES

1. See below, pp. 315, 336.

2. Mikhail Bakunin, *Izbrannye sochinenie* (Petrograd-Moscow: Golos Truda, 1920) vol. III, pp. 100–2.

3. Michel Bakounine, *Oeuvres*, ed. James Guillaume (Paris; Stock, 1912), vol. I, p. 144.

4. James Guillaume, *L'Internationale* (Paris; Société nouvelle de librairie et d'edition: 1905), vol. I, p. 71.

5. Ibid., pp. 72–73.

6. Ibid., pp. 73–76; 75–76 (for a list of his followers, subsequent co-founders of "Alliance"); Vyrubova, "Revoliutsionnyia vospominaniia," p. 55.

7. *Marx/Bakounine: Socialism qutoritaire ou libertaire.* ed. Georges Ribeill (Paris: Union Générale D'Éditions, 1975), vol. I, pp. 73–74; Marc Vuilleumier, "Bakounine, L'Alliance Internationale de la démocratie socialiste et la première Internationale a Genève (1868-1869)," *Cahiers Vilfredo Pareto*, 4 (1964); 53–54; Max Nettlau, *La Première Internationale en Espagne (1868-1888)* (Dordrecht-Holland: D. Reidel, 1969), pp. 53–54.

8. The relevant texts on the Alliance are presented at the end of *Marx/Bakounine*, ed. Ribeill, vol. II, pp. 317–45. The foregoing quotations are from pp. 321–22, 324–25, 327, 329, 331.

9. Ibid., pp. 318, 323, 328, 331, 340–41.

10. Marc Vuilleumier, "Bakounine, L'Alliance Internationale"; Guillaume, *L'Internationale*, vol. I, pp. 92–93; Jacques Freymond, *Études et documents sur le Première Internationale en Suisse* (Genève; Librairie Droz, 1964), pp. 137–41. (For a list of Alliance members in 1869-1879, see Nettlau, *M. Bakunin*, vol. I, pp. 307–309.)

11. Guillaume, *L'Internationale*, vol. I, p. 78.

12. Ibid., p. 92.

13. Ibid.

14. Michel Bakounine. *De la guerre à la Commune (Textes de 1870-1871)*, ed. Fernand Rude (Paris: éditions anthropos, 1972), p. 434.

15. Quoted in Franz Mehring, *Karl Marx* (Ann Arbor: The University of Michigan Press, 1962), p. 410.

16. Marc Vuilleumier, "L'anarchisme et les conceptions de Bakounine sur l'organisation revolutionnaire," *Anarchiei e anarchia nel mondo contemporaneo*

(Torino) (1971); 499-500, 503-4.

17. *Marx/Bakounine,* ed. Ribeill, vol. I, pp. 74-75.

18. Bakounine, *De la guerre à la Commune,* p. 441.

19. Guillaume, *L'Internationale,* vol. I, pp. 111-13.

20. Ibid., pp. 105-7.

21. Freymond, *Études,* pp. xi, 8-9, 17.

22. Mariane Enckell, *La Fédération jurassienne* (Lausanne: La Cité, 1971), pp. 11-17; Mehring, *Marx,* pp. 413-15, 425; Nettlau, *M. Bakunin,* vol. I, pp. 317-320.

23. Freymond, *Études,* pp. 40-41.

24. Guillaume, *L'Internationale,* vol. I, pp. 107-8, 120.

25. Ibid., pp. 71, 120; Dragomanov, *Pisma,* pp. 327-31.

26. Guillaume, *L'Internationale,* vol. I, pp. 120, 125, 128, 129, 130-31, 139, 214.

27. One might recall in this context of the Marx-Bakunin dispute and its psychological dimensions something Bakunin's father said to him years before: "The hidden cause, perhaps unknown to you, of the disagreement that arose between us was a wish to rule the family." See above, p. 50. As we will see throughout this analysis of the controversy between Marx and Bakunin, with respect to the International and otherwise, there is a striking similarity between the conflict (and Bakunin's ambivalent involvement in it) and Bakunin's earlier familial battles. (Also with regard to the psychological interpretation, it is hoped that such oral imagery in association with the revolution as quoted above—"smoke," and "drink"—no longer need comment.)

28. Guillaume, *L'Internationale,* vol. I, p. 141.

29. Freymond, *Étude,* p. 154.

30. Guillaume, *L'Internationale,* vol. I, pp. 141-42.

31. Ibid., p. 147.

32. See below, pp. 277-8, 283-5, 335. Potebnia was the one who had assured Herzen and Bakunin of Russian military support for the Polish rebels and who had died in defense of that assurance. Significantly, Bakunin now, during his collaboration with Nechaev, recalled Potebnia and his martyrdom in words that graphically show the direct line running from Bakunin's youthful barrack's bravado, through his "warrior" for holy truth campaigns and the martial strategies he had worked out for his sisters and the Beyer sisters, down to the "red general," his fellow Siberian officers, Garibaldi, and Potebnia, and, now, Nechaev. See especially, *Archives Bakounine,* ed. Arthur Lehning (Leiden: Brill, 1971), vol. IV *(Michel Bakounine et ses relations avec Sergej Nečaev),* pp. 3-5. In the course of this eulogy for Potebnia, Bakunin again reveals, I believe, the deeper motivations of his own violence, those connected with the love-hate ambivalence discussed in an earlier chapter: "Potebnia hated the existing system with the same ardour and the same deep passion with which he loved the people. Both passions, love and hatred, merged into one, became the one and only motivation of all his actions and all his life. . . . His heart was passionate, but his appearance, cold." Ibid., p. 4. He is once alleged to have told his friend Reichel that he attributed "his passion for destruction to the influence of his mother." E. El, "M. A. Bakunin v Shveitsarii," *Severnii vestnik* 4 (April 1898): 179. (See also p. 198, on love/hate.)

33. Dragomanov, *Pisma,* p. 444; *Daughter of a Revolutionary: Natalie Herzen and the Bakunin-Nechaev Circle,* ed. Michael Confino (London: Alcove, 1974), pp. 292, 305, 308; Michael Confino, "Bakunin and Nechaev," *Encounter* vol. 39 (July 1972); 84, 86, 89.

34. Confino, "Bakunin and Nechaev," (July 1972): vol. 39. pp. 88–89.

35. Confino, "Bakunin and Nechaev," (July 1972): vol. 39, pp. 81, 85 and (August 1972): vol. 39, p. 91; *Daughter,* ed. Confino, pp. 293, 296; *Marx/Bakounine,* vol. II, p. 288; Fritz Brupbacher, *Michel Bakounine ou le démon de la révolte,* annoted translation by Jean Barrué (Paris: Editions du Cercle, Editions de la Tête de Feuilles, 1971), p. 229. By acting and feeling vicariously through Nechaev, Bakunin had now added still another layer of distance between himself and the role he was posing. "Always remember," he once told his follower Z. Ralli, "that revolution is made up of three-fourths fantasy and only one-fourth reality." Z. Ralli, "Iz moikh vospominanii o M.A. Bakunine," *O minuvshem* (St. Petersburg, 1909), p. 333.

36. *Michel Bakounine et ses relations slaves. Archives Bakounine,* ed. Lehning (Leiden: Brill, 1974), vol. V, pp. xxvii, 11, 14–15.

37. Ibid., pp. xxvii, 39–71.

38. For a good summary review of the debates, see Jean Barrué's commentary to his translation to Brupbacher, *Michel Bakounine,* pp. 227–51. The most recent treatment of the work, by Philip Pomper, assigns the authorship according to style and substance, attributing some of the paragraphs to Bakunin, others to Nechaev. Philip Pomper, *Sergei Nechaev* (New Brunswick, NJ: Rutgers University Press, 1979), p. 90.

39. *Daughter,* ed. Confino, pp. 224, 225, 227–29.

40. Ibid., p. 229.

41. Confino, "Bakunin and Nechaev," vol. 39 (July 1972); 83–84.

42. See below, pp. 334ff, for coverage of the later phases of the Bakunin-Nechaev collaboration. That spring (1869) another pamphlet was published that scholars often attribute to Bakunin, *The Formulation of the Revolutionary Question.* Since no author is indicated in the publication and since Nechaev seems later to have claimed it for himself, I am reluctant to analyze it here in detail as definitely Bakunin's, just as I feel constrained from any lengthy study of the *Catechism* for the same reasons. Moreover, the remarkable statements in the pamphlet—the author's defense of banditry as a revolutionary weapon and praise for the bandit as "the people's hero, defender, and avenger...the implacable foe of the state and of the whole social and civil order"—do not add to our knowledge of Bakunin's revolutionary arsenal, since we can find the same defense of the bandit in documents hearing Bakunin's name (see below, pp. 317, 346). For reviews of the pamphlet by two recent scholars who accept the work as Bakunin's, see Pirumova, *Bakunin,* pp. 295-296, her "Bakunin and Herzen," pp. 560–65, and Pomper, *Nechaev,* pp. 78–79.

In support of Pirumova, Pomper, and others who attribute the work to Bakunin, it should be said that Herzen and Ogarev, as Pirumova shows, also believed that Bakunin wrote it. It was, in fact, partially in response to this publication that Herzen wrote *Letters to an Old Comrade,* his final account of Bakunin's politics. Although the *Letters* relate more to Herzen's than to Bakunin's biography, it may be of interest at least to outline its main arguments. In mid-

March 1869 (the month Nechaev arrived), Herzen asked Ogarev to show Bakunin the manuscript of a paper he, Herzen, had begun writing that January called "Between Old Men." Then, the day after he read the *Formulation* article, which appeared May tenth and in which, he said, "Bakunin had gone completely out of control," Herzen completed the last pages of the manuscript. It was that final version that came out the following year, after Herzen's death. Essentially, *Letters* is an elaboration of Herzen's earlier criticism of Bakunin for wanting, as Herzen restates it there, "to pass directly from the first month of pregnancy to the ninth." Such are the politics, he said, of "prophets and soothsayers, of heresiarchs, fanatics and revolutionary sectarians," a form of politics based on "insane, mystical, occult elements" from which nothing but disaster could result, nothing beyond the "levelling" of Grachus Babeuf and "Cabet's system of communist corvée." "Should we really begin the new life by retaining the corps of socialist gendarmes?" "You tear along as before filled with the passion for destruction which you take for a creative passion...breaking down obstacles and respecting only the history of the future." Focusing on a phrase that Bakunin was to use more and more in the coming years, Herzen denounced those who proclaimed the "fearful words" *"déchaînement des mauvaises passions...* without taking into the least consideration how greatly they injure the cause and those who hear them." Bakunin should face facts: the bourgeois world was still strong, the new world was still weak, the peasants were conservative, the state could be of great use to the reformers, there was much of value in the existing culture, property brought with it independence and dignity, and, like it or not, a country needed an army to defend itself. But above all, Herzen stressed again and again, progress must advance gradually, as did all else in nature. The working class in the West well understood this. Now was the time, therefore, not for abstract, mystical maximalism, but for study, preparation and teaching. Words, too, were action: "eyes should be opened rather than gouged out...." A. Herzen, "Letters to an Old Comrade," *Selected Philosophical Works,* trans. L. Navrozov (Moscow: Foreign Language Publication House, 1956).

43. Freymond, *Etudes,* pp. 147–204.
44. Bakounine, *Oeuvres,* vol. V, pp. 108–9.
45. Ibid., vol. V, p. 110.
46. Ibid., vol. V, pp. 121, 122.
47. Ibid., vol. V, pp. 76–105.
48. Ibid., vol. V, pp. 210–18.
49. Ibid., vol. V, pp. 91–92.
50. Ibid., vol. V, pp. 171, 172.
51. Ibid., vol. V, pp. 181.
52. Ibid., vol. V, p. 72.
53. Ibid., vol. V, pp. 57–59.
54. Ibid., vol. V, pp. 109, 110.
55. Ibid., vol. V, pp. 209–10.
56. Ibid., pp. 199–210. In another joint revolutionary publication, this time by Bakunin and Zhukovskii, that was published in September 1869, the inheritance issue headed the list of demands for the "socioeconomic liberation of the masses." So important was this institution for Bakunin that (assuming that he was the author of this portion of the statement) he blamed the "existing politi-

cal and civic organizations" in part "on the right of hereditary property, on the familial rights of the father and husband." It was this together with "conquest" and religion, he wrote here, that comprised "the essence of the state." Consequently, "desiring the genuine and decisive liberation of the masses we seek: 1) Abolition of the right to hereditary property...." The second demand called for equalization of the rights of women and, towards that end, the "destruction of familial law and marriage." (For exerpts from this document, *Our Program,* see Pomper, *Nechaev,* pp. 53–54.) The influence in all this of Bakunin's personal life and personality difficulties, his attitude toward marriage, sexuality, "the familial rights of the father and husband," and so on seems obvious.

57. Ibid., p. 129. While the translations are my own, the foregoing quotations from the *Égalité* and *Progrès* articles were first read in an unpublished translation of these articles by Mr. Robert Cutler, who generously allowed me to read his manuscript.

58. Guillaume, *L'Internationale,* vol. I, pp. 180–81. ("'All this is utopia,' they said. 'We must concern ourselves with practical questions'." Ibid., p. 180. See also, Vuilleumier, "Bakounine, L'Alliance Internationale," pp. 81–82.)

59. Vuilleumier, "Bakounine, L'Alliance Internationale," pp. 77–79.

60. Freymond, *Études,* p. 165.

61. Guillaume, *L'Internationale,* vol. I, p. 164. When Guillaume told Bakunin that he was being too hard on Robert, Bakunin replied: "If we were interested in forming petty instruments to serve a trivial cause, then I could understand all these artificial delicacies. But since we wish to, and must, appeal to grand instincts and expansive thoughts which alone can serve us, it seems to me that we must speak expansively, grandly, frankly." Ibid., p. 167.

62. Ibid., pp. 162–63.

63. Ibid., pp. 167–68.

64. Bakounine, *De la guerre à la Commune,* p. 452.

65. Ibid., p. 453. An intriguing example of Bakunin's efforts to safeguard the influence of his secret, international Alliance within the International is his defense of his "intimate" Richard against accusations that he had forged false mandates to Third Congress of the International, meeting in Brussels, September 6–13, 1868. While quite aware that the mandate was indeed forged—"a false mandate without doubt"—Bakunin packed an investigating "jury of honor" with fellow Alliance members, kept Richard informed of the progress of his accuser's case, while repeatedly urging Richard to tell no one about those communications, and, in the end, got Richard exonerated. Bakounine, *De la guerre à la Commune,* pp. 438–40, 450.

66. Guillaume, *L'Internationale,* vol. I, p. 212.

67. Vuilleumier, "Bakounine, L'Alliance Internationale," pp. 81–83.

68. Guillaume, *L'Internationale,* vol. I, pp. 181–82.

69. Ibid., pp. 187–88.

70. On the fifth. *Archives Bakounine,* ed. Lehning, vol. IV, p. xiii.

71. Guillaume, *L'Internationale,* vol. I, p. 182, note 1.

72. Ibid., p. 198.

73. Mehring, *Marx,* p. 419.

74. Guillaume, *L'Internationale,* vol. I, pp. 200–3.
75. Mehring, *Marx,* p. 420.
76. See above, note 56.
77. Relating these facts to Bakunin's view of the International as "mother," as quoted earlier, we see a full recasting of the elemental psychodrama: the "child"—again, his term—is drawn towards and simultaneously pulls back from the "mother" (careful never to sever relations), while he conciliates and depends on the paternal authority—Marx—even as he denounces him and challenges (or, better, *pretends* to challenge) him for control of the "mother."
78. Guillaume, *L'Internationale,* vol. I, p. 208.
79. Ibid., p. 214.
80. See below, pp. 349–50.
81. Guillaume, *L'Internationale,* p. 217.
82. Ibid., pp. 217–18.
83. Ibid., pp. 223.
84. Bakounine, *Oeuvres,* vol. V, pp. 263–64.
85. Dragomanov, *Pisma,* pp. 332–33.
86. Bakounine, *Oeuvres,* vol. V, pp. 243–44.
87. Ibid., pp. 244–45, 253, 255–57, 266.
88. Dragomanov, *Pisma,* pp. 337–40.
89. Bakounine, *De la guerre à la Commune,* p. 466; Guillaume, *L'Internationale,* vol. I, p. 226.
90. Guillaume, *L'Internationale,* vol. I, pp. 225–26.
91. See above, pp. 325–6.
92. Dragomanov, *Pisma,* pp. 351–54.
93. Guillaume, *L'Internationale,* vol. I, p. 261.
94. Dragomanov, *Pisma,* p. 345.
95. Ibid., pp. 349–50.
96. Ibid., p. 349.
97. Ibid., p. 344. (This is the second time that Bakunin expressed his envy of Samson's death. The appeal is understandable, for the death was simultaneously immensely destructive and suicidal, another unity of power and punishment. See above, p. 300.
98. *Marx/Bakounine,* ed. Ribeill, vol. I, pp. 92–93.
99. Guillaume, *L'Internationale,* vol. I, pp. 242, 244.
100. Bakounine, *De la guerre à la Commune,* p. 453.
101. Ibid., p. 454.
102. Dragomanov, *Pisma,* pp. 354, 356, 360, 361.
103. *Archives Bakounine,* ed. Lehning, vol. IV, p. 3.
104. Ibid.
105. Ibid., p. 17.
106. Ibid., p. 6.
107. Ibid., pp. 7–11.
108. Ibid., p. 33.
109. Bakounine, *De la guerre à la Commune,* pp. 459. Letter to Richard. February 7, 1870.

110. Dragomanov, *Pisma,* p. 367.

111. Ibid., p. 362.

112. *Archives Bakounine,* ed. Lehning, vol. IV, pp. 43–44.

113. Ibid., vol. IV, pp. 45–46.

114. Dragomanov, *Pisma,* pp. 362–66.

115. *Marx/Bakounine,* ed. Ribeill, vol. I, pp. 147–48.

116. *Archives Bakounine,* ed. Lehning, vol. V, pp. 74–103.

117. Ibid., vol. V, pp. xx–xxi.

118. *Daughter,* ed. Confino, pp. 216, 375.

119. Ibid., pp. 163–64.

120. Ibid., pp. 164–68. The two "Natalies" are Natalie Herzen, Herzen's daughter, and Natalie Tuchkova-Ogareva, Ogarev's wife and mother of three of Alexander Herzen's children.

121. Ibid., p. 160.

122. Dragomanov, *Pisma,* p. 376.

123. *Daughter,* ed. Confino, pp. 209–10.

124. Ibid., p. 374.

125. Ibid., p. 213.

126. Ibid., p. 179.

127. Ibid., p. 180.

128. Ibid., p. 215.

129. Ibid., pp. 212, 375. However, Natalie Herzen also wrote that June, in a letter to Lopatin, another participant in the affair: "You write that 'it is hard to figure out who set up the comedy, but it is clear that Bakunin was deceived.' Unfortunately, I have to say that for *me,* even that is *not so clear.* I tell you once more that the surprise B. [Bakunin] expressed when he found out about N.'s [Nechaev's] lies seemed to me *more than* forced. Also, one cannot deny that in just this case, it would be *very advantageous* for B. to take N.'s lie on faith, for that would give him a chance to get himself, more or less deftly, out of an extremely delicate situation. Finally, I know of some *proven* instances when B. *knowingly deceived* some of his friends. If all this does not give me the right *to affirm positively* that B. is at one with N. in this affair, it gives me at least the right *to doubt* strongly B.'s sincerity in the present case." *Archives Bakounine,* ed. Lehning, vol. IV, p. lviii. (Emphasis in the original)

130. Dragomanov, *Pisma,* pp. 369, 377–78.

131. Guillaume, *L'Internationale,* vol. I, 174–75; vol. II, pp. 20–21.

132. Ibid., vol. II, p. 20. Among the victims Bakunin defended here was his old friend and financial supporter Princess Obolensky, whose estranged husband had used the Swiss authorities to have the Princess' children taken from her.

133. *Daughter,* ed. Confino, p. 215.

134. *Archives Bakounine,* ed. Lehning, vol. IV, pp. 212–13.

135. Ibid., vol. V, pp. 112–16. (The *La Marseillaise* version.) In passing, Bakunin once again revealed a preference for minimal violence, notwithstanding the apocalyptic prospects of horrendous destruction: "if one cuts off a hundred thousand heads or even more, following Marat's tally...one gains absolutely nothing; while, if one boldly and completely transforms the economic organization of society, removing, of course, with all necessary energy, the obstacles that would oppose the transformation of the present unjust society into a just one,

one will create a new world." As with all such remarks by him, one wonders, given the larger context, how the removal "with all necessary energy" will take place without Marat's violence against the "obstacles." Ibid., vol. V, p. 115.

136. Bakounine, *De la guerre à la Commune,* p. 466.

137. Guillaume, *L'Internationale,* vol. I, pp. 287–89.

138. *Marx/Bakounine,* ed. Ribeill, vol. I, pp. 115–16.

139. Bakounine, *De la guerre à la Commune,* p. 465. (Emphasis added)

140. Ibid., p. 471. (Emphasis added)

141. Enckell, *La Fédération,* pp. 28 *ff;* Mehring, *Marx,* pp. 430–32.

142. Bakounine, *De la guerre à la Commune,* p. 467. Letter to A. Richard, April 1, 1870.

143. Ibid., p. 468.

144. Enckell, *La Fédération,* pp. 34–36.

145. Guillaume, *L'Internationale,* vol. II, p. 19.

146. *Archives Bakounine,* ed. Lehning, vol. IV, pp. liv *ff,* 349–56.

147. Dragomanov, *Pisma,* p. 380.

148. Guillaume, *L'Internationale,* vol. II, p. 59.

149. Dragomanov, *Pisma,* pp. 379–84; Guillaume, *L'Internationale,* vol. II, p. 59.

150. *Archives Bakounine,* ed. Lehning, vol. IV, p. lvi. For the Liubavin affair, see above, pp. 331–2, 337.

151. Confino, "Bakunin and Nechaev," (August 1972): 90.

152. Dragomanov, *Pisma,* pp. 384–86.

153. Ibid., pp. 387–88. (In Dragomanov's collection of letters, this letter is dated May second, but its place in the sequence of letters shows that to be an error. Guillaume gives May thirtieth. Guillaume, *L'Internationale,* vol. II, p. 53.)

154. Once again we see Bakunin assuming a woman's identity. Nor was he alone in making this identification: "An old Joan of Arc," who, too, was a "maiden," Herzen said of Bakunin in 1848. Annenkov, *Decade,* p. 27. "A grown-up Liza was Martianov's name for him, according to Herzen. Herzen, *Past and Thoughts,* vol. III, p. 1378.

155. See above, p. 296.

156. Confino, "Bakunin and Nechaev," (July 1972): vol. 39, pp. 88–89. "The world of Cossacks, thieves, brigands and tramps played the role of a catalyst and unifier of separate revolts under Stenka Razin and Pugachev....Can anything be dirtier than our respectably official and civilised bourgeois and decent world, which hides under its smooth Western form the most horrible depravity of thought, feelings, relationships and deeds?...On the other hand, the people's depravity is natural, forceful, and vital....That is why I am on the side of popular brigandage and see in it one of the most essential tools for the future people's revolution in Russia." (Ibid.)

157. Ibid., (July 1972): vol. 39, p. 90; (August 1972): vol. 39, pp. 86–88.

158. Ibid., (August 1972): vol. 39, p. 85. The translation in this instance is my own, based on Confino's publication of the 1870 letter in *Cahiers du Monde Russie* 7 (1966): 658, 660.

159. Confino, "Bakunin and Nechaev," (August 1972): vol. 39, p. 91.

160. Ibid., (July 1972): vol. 39, p. 90; (August 1972): vol. 39, pp. 88, 93.

161. Ibid., (July 1972): vol. 39, p. 90.

162. Ibid., (August 1972): vol. 39, p. 88.

163. The stressed words in this stenence (which completes the quotation cited in the preceding note) were added later: According to Natalie Herzen, they do not occur in the original. Ibid., note 1.

164. Confino, "Bakunin and Nechaev," (August 1972): vol. 39, p. 88.

165. *Daughter,* ed. Confino, p. 212.

166. Confino, "Bakunin and Nechaev," (August 1972): vol. 39, p. 87.

167. Bakounine, *De la guerre à la Commune,* p. 451.

168. Ibid., p. 454.

169. Ibid., p. 461.

170. See above, p. 206.

171. Bakounine, *De la guerre à la Commune,* pp. 459–460, 462.

172. Confino, "Bakunin and Nechaev," (August 1972): vol. 39, pp. 90–92; *Daughter,* ed. Confino, pp. 305–309.

173. Confino, "Bakunin and Nechaev," (July 1972): vol. 39, pp. 85–87; (August 1972): vol. 39, pp. 89, 91; *Daughter,* ed. Confino, pp. 311, 313.

174. Confino, "Bakunin and Nechaev," (August 1972): vol. 39, pp. 92–93.

175. *Daughter,* ed. Confino, pp. 281–282, 284.

176. Ibid., pp. 290, 292, 293.

177. Ibid., pp. 295–299.

178. Ibid., p. 301.

179. Ibid., p. 311.

180. Confino, "Bakunin and Nechaev," (July 1972): vol. 39, pp. 88–89.

181. Ibid., (August 1972): vol. 39, p. 86.

182. *Daughter,* ed. Confino, p. 297.

183. Ibid., p. 225.

184. Ibid., p. 215.

185. This aspect of the quarrel is especially clear in Bakunin's letter to his "intimate" Alfred Talandier. July 24, 1870. Ibid., p. 305–9.

186. Guillaume, *L'Internationale,* vol. II, p. 64.

187. *Daughter,* ed. Confino, p. 305; Dragomanov, *Pisma,* p. 400.

188. See in particular the letter to Talandier. July 24, 1870. *Daughter,* ed. Confino, pp. 305–9.

189. Confino, "Bakunin and Nechaev," (August 1972): vol. 39, p. 91.

190. See above, pp. 222, 232, 236.

191. *Daughter,* ed. Confino, p. 313.

192. Dragomanov, *Pisma,* pp. 400–1.

193. Bakounine, *De la guerre à la Commune,* pp. 468–69. (Liebknecht was not Jewish.)

194. Ibid., p. 468.

195. Dragomanov, *Pisma,* 399.

196. Ibid., p. 401.

197. Ibid., p. 403.

198. Bakounine, *De la guerre à la Commune,* p. 510.

199. See above, p. 332.

200. Bakounine, *De la guerre à la Commune,* pp. 474–75.

201. Ibid., pp. 69–164.

202. Ibid., pp. 83–84, 92–93, 107–9, 113, 127, 139–140, 145.

203. Ibid., pp. 129, 156. (Emphasis in this and the preceding sentence added.)

204. Ibid., pp. 129-31, 149, 156, 163.

205. Ibid., pp. 71-72, 127-29, 140, 148, 157 *ff*. (As always, the imagery is startlingly revealing.)

206. Ibid., pp. 138, 140.

207. Ibid., pp. 81, 83, 151, 162-63.

208. Ibid., pp. 81, 83, 89.

209. Confino, "Bakunin and Nechaev," (July 1972): vol. 39, p. 91.

210. Bakounine, *De la guerre à la Commune,* pp. 112, 145. Significantly, even here, in this particularly extreme expression of revolutionary violence, it is by the peasants' own hands, not, as in the *Catechism of a Revolutionary,* the revolutionary's (i.e. Bakunin's) that the violence will be carried out.

211. Ibid., p. 136. (Emphasis added.)

212. Ibid., p. 117.

213. Ibid., p. 145. (Emphasis added.)

214. Ibid., pp. 146-47. (Emphasis added.)

215. Ibid., p. 109. (Emphasis added.)

216. Ibid., p. 110.

217. Ibid., pp. 134, 141, 145-46.

218. Ibid., pp. 93, 110.

219. Ibid., pp. 133, 138, 144, 145.

220. Ibid., pp. 475-77.

221. Ibid., pp. 478-79.

222. Ibid., pp. 480-82. (Emphasis added.)

223. Ibid., p. 511.

224. Unless otherwise noted, the following account of the Lyon rising is based on Maurice Moissonnier, *La Première Internationale et la commune à Lyon* (Paris: Editions Sociales, 1972); Ferdinand Rude, "Bakounine à Lyon en September, 1870," *Actes du soixante-dix-septieme Congrès des Sociétés Savantes* (Grenoble, 1952), pp. 535-51; Albert Richard, "Bakounine et L'Internationale à Lyon," *La Revue de Paris* (September 1896): 119-60; and *Documents anarchistes* (Lyon: No. 2, September 1967): 19, 27-29 and No. 7, January, 1969. For an interpretation different from mine, see Arthur Lehning, "Michel Bakounine. Theorie et Pratique du Fédéralisme ante-Etatique en 1870-1871," *International Review of Social History* 17 (1972): 455-73.

225. Dragomanov, *Pisma,* p. 408.

226. Richard, "Bakounine et L'Internationale," pp. 145 *ff;* Rude, "Bakounine à Lyon," pp. 541 *ff;* Moissonnier, *La Première Internationale*, p. 242.

227. Rude, "Bakounine à Lyon," p. 538.

228. Richard, "Bakounine et L'Internationale," pp. 150-51.

229. Ibid., p. 155.

230. Dragomanov, *Pisma*, p. 409.

231. Moissonnier, *La Première Internationale*, pp. 252-54.

232. Ibid., pp. 236-37.

233. Bakounine, *De la guerre à la Commune*, pp. 165-67.

234. Ibid., pp. 469-71.

235. Guillaume, *L'Internationale*, vol. II, p. 95.

236. Moissonnier, *La Première Internationale*, p. 256; Rude, "Bakounine à Lyon," p. 544.

237. Guillaume, *L'Internationale*, vol. II, pp. 96–97.

238. Bakunin also recalls, ten days later: "I was with our friends, telling them constantly 'Don't waste time in futile discussion: act—arrest all the reactionaries. Strike reaction at its head'." Bakounine, *De la guerre à la Commune*, p. 513.

239. *Documents anarchistes*, No. 2 (September 1967): 28.

240. Moissonnier, *La Première Internationale*, p. 263; Richard, "Bakounine et L'Internationale," p. 157.

241. Rude, "Bakounine à Lyon," pp. 547, 551; Bakounine, *De la guerre à la Commune*, p. 482; Richard, "Bakounine et L'Internationale," pp. 157–59; Guillaume, *L'Internationale*, vol. II, p. 197.

242. Bakounine, *De la guerre à la Commune*, p. 484.

243. Ibid., p. 485.

244. Ibid., pp. 498–99.

245. Ibid., pp. 486–88.

246. Ibid., pp. 513–14.

247. *Archives Bakounine*, ed. Lehning, vol. VI, pp. 213–15.

248. Bakounine, *De la guerre à la Commune*, p. 515.

CHAPTER 11. CALVARY

1. Guillaume, *L'Internationale*, vol. II, p. 132.

2. Bakounine, *De la guerre à la Commune*, p. 507.

3. Ibid., p. 508.

4. Ibid., pp. 503–4.

5. Ibid., p. 238.

6. Ibid., p. 192.

7. Ibid., p. 175. (Emphasis added.)

8. Ibid., p. 200. "Appropriate" because of Lenin's later adoption of the same title for a similarly authoritarian organizational statement.

9. Ibid. (Emphasis added.)

10. Ibid., pp. 226, 228.

11. Ibid., p. 177. (Emphasis added.)

12. Ibid., pp. 261, 267, 271.

13. Ibid., pp. 251–53.

14. Michael Bakunin, *God and State* (New York: Dover, 1970), pp. 24, 25, 28.

15. Ibid., pp. 26–27.

16. Ibid., pp. 10, 74 *ff.*

17. Ibid., pp. 12, 21.

18. Ibid., p. 27.

19. Guillaume, *L'Internationale*, vol. II, p. 151.

20. Bakounine, *Oeuvres,* vol. V, pp. 357, 358, 360.

vol. V, pp. 357, 358, 360.

21. Guillaume, *L'Internationale*, vol. II, p. 154.

22. Ibid., vol. II, p. 156.

23. Bakounine, *Oeuvres*, vol. IV, pp. 250, 253–57.

24. Ibid., vol. IV, p. 254.

25. Ibid., vol. VI, pp. 3–5; Mehring, *Marx*, p. 468.

26. Bakounine, *Oeuvres*, vol. VI, p. 5; Guillaume, *L'Internationale*, vol. II, p. 164.

27. Bakounine, *Oeuvres*, vol. VI, pp. 15–99.

28. Guillaume, *L'Internationale*, vol. II, p. 164.

29. "Michael Bakounine et L'Italie. 1871–1872," *Archive Bakounine*, ed. Arthur Lehning, vol. I, part 1, (Leiden: Brill, 1961) p. 10.

30. Mehring, *Marx*, p. 469.

31. Guillaume, *L'Internationale*, pp. 177–81; Mehring, *Marx*, p. 468.

32. Mehring, *Marx*, pp. 473–74.

33. Enckell, *La Fèdèration*, p. 58.

34. Ibid., pp. 58–66; Mehring, *Marx*, pp. 475–77.

35. Guillaume, *L'Internationale*, vol. II, pp. 229–30.

36. Dragomanov, *Pisma*, pp. 426–27.

37. Bakunin's articles and letters against Mazzini can be found in *Archives Bakounine*, ed. Lehning, vol. 1, parts 1 and 2.

38. Guillaume, *L'Internationale*, vol. II, pp. 250–51.

39. *Archives Bakounine*, ed. Lehning, vol. 1, part 2, pp. 417–18.

40. Ibid., p. 139.

41. Ibid., pp. 133–35.

42. *Marx/Bakounine*, ed. Ribeill, vol. I, p. 218.

43. Ibid.

44. Ibid., vol. I, pp. 197–98.

45. Ibid., vol. I, pp. 200, 210–12, 222.

46. Ibid., vol. I, p. 192.

47. *Archives Bakounine*, ed. Lehning, vol. I, part 2, pp. 158–59, 174–76.

48. Ibid., vol. I, part 2, p. 208.

49. Ibid., vol. I, part 2, pp. 174, 179, 224.

50. Ibid., vol. II ("Michel Bakounine et les Conflicts dans L'Internationale. 1872"), p. 3.

51. Ibid., vol. II, pp. 4–9.

52. Ibid., vol. II, pp. 19, 20, 22, 28.

53. Ibid., vol. II, pp. 72–73, 81.

54. Ibid., vol. II, p. 108.

55. Ibid., vol. II, pp. 116–17.

56. Ibid., vol. II, p. 46.

57. Ibid., vol. II, p. 47.

58. Ibid., vol. II, p. xxix.

59. Ibid., vol. III ("Michel Bakounine. Etatisme et Anarchie. 1873"), pp. xii–xiv.

60. Ibid., vol. V, p. xxxv.

61. Dragomanov, *Pisma*, pp. 430–34.

62. *Archives Bakounine*, vol. V, pp. 149–53.

63. Guillaume, *L'Internationale*, vol. II, p. 301.

64. *Archives Bakounine*, ed. Lehning, vol. III, p. xviii; vol. V, pp. xxxvii–xxxix.

65. Ibid., vol. V, p. xli.

66. Ibid., vol. II, pp. xxvii, xxx, xxxv.

67. Guillaume, *L'Internationale*, vol. II, p. 288.

68. Ibid.

69. Ibid., vol. II, p. 292.

70. *Archives Bakounine*, ed. Lehning, vol. V, p. xxxix.

71. Ibid., vol. II, p. xxxiv.

72. Ibid., vol. II, p. 133.

73. Ibid., vol. II, p. 134. (Emphasis added.)

74. Ibid., vol. II, p. liv.

75. Ibid., vol. II, p. xxx.

76. Guillaume, *L'Internationale*, vol. II, p. 312.

77. *Archives Bakounine*, ed. Lehning, vol. II, p. 135.

78. Ibid., vol. II, p. 129.

79. Guillaume, *L'Internationale*, vol. II, p. 317.

80. Ibid., vol. II, p. 316.

81. Ibid., vol. II, p. 135. (Emphasis added.)

82. Ibid.

83. See above, pp. 310, 329, 333.

84. *Marx/Bakounine,* ed. Ribeill, vol. I, pp. 307–11.

85. See above, pp. 331–32, 337.

86. *Marx/Bakounine*, ed. Ribeill, vol. I, p. 325.

87. Mehring, *Marx*, p. 489.

88. Ibid., p. 490.

89. *Marx/Bakounine*, ed. Ribeill, vol. I, p. 323.

90. In this connection, it is interesting to note Bakunin's letter to Lorenzo at the time, see above, p. 388.

91. While these debates were going on, Marx had in his possession a letter he had just received from Liubavin stating that, in Liubavin's view, "the participation of Bakunin is not at all proven," since this letter (threatening Liubavin) "could have been written by Nechaev completely without Bakunin's knowledge." *Archives Bakounine*, ed. Lehning, vol. II, pp. l, li; *Marx/Bakounine*, ed. Ribeill, vol. I, pp. 317–22.

92. Guillaume, *L'Internationale*, vol. II, p. 349. (Emphasis added.)

93. Ibid., vol. II, pp. 350–51.

94. Ibid., vol. II, p. 317; *Archives Bakounine*, ed. Lehning, vol. II, p. 134.

95. *Archives Bakounine*, ed. Lehning, vol. II, p. lvii.

96. Ibid., vol. V, pp. 182–83.

97. Ibid., vol. V, pp. 182, 184, 186.

98. Ibid., vol. V, pp. 186–90.

99. Ibid., vol. V, pp. 191–93, 196–97.

100. Ibid., vol. V, pp. 185, 188, 192, 194.

101. Ibid., vol. V, p. 185.

102. Ibid., vol. V, p. 187.

103. Ibid., vol. V, p. 184.

104. Since the focus of this biography is on what Bakunin himself said and did and not on the numerous movements and factions throughout the world that have considered themselves his followers, I have not felt it necessary to review the history of those movements and factions. Invaluable though such studies are or would be, they are not the subject of this work and, indeed, if presented here would only distract attention from the principal concern, Michael Bakunin. For a recent bibliography of at least part of the vast literature dealing with Bakunin's followers, particularly in Spain and Italy, see Arthur Lehning, *Bakounine et les Historiens*. (C.I.R.A. Supplement). Geneve: Noir, 1979. (See especially notes 9, 88, 107, 113, 114, 115.)

105. Guillaume, *L'Internationale*, vol. III, p. 10.

106. Ibid., vol. III, p. 1.

107. Ibid., vol. III, pp. 6–10.

108. Armand Ross, "Bakunin i evo Villa 'Baronata'," *Golos minuvshogo* (Moscow) vol. 5 (1914): 202.

109. Several successive diary entries in the weeks following the Saint Imier Congress graphically show the division in Bakunin's life at the time between these two "intimacies." September 22. "The Spaniards have left. — 23. Marco [Pezza], Louise [Fanelli], Armando [Cafiero], Giacomo [Nabruzzi], Malatesta have left. — 24. Smirnov and Rulev [Ralli] met with that rogue Serebrenikov. A meeting of the Russian brothers. — 25. A letter of the Russians to *La Liberté*. Telegram to Ross. In the evening, a meeting of 'purgatory' [meetings among the Russians held to judge a new candidate]. — 26. Ross has arrived. Discussions with Ross; he is becoming completely ours." Guillaume, *L'Internationale*, vol. III, pp. 10–11.

110. The decision, voted at the Hague Congress, to move the site of the General Council from London to New York, initially at least for a year, is often explained as a tactic by the Marxists to keep the Council as far away from the disruptive Bakuninists as possible. The resolution was proposed by Engels and carried by a small minority (26 to 23 with 9 abstentions).

111. Guillaume, *L'Internationale*, vol. III, p. 18 (and passim 17–51); Enckell, *La Fédération*, pp. 83–84.

112. *Archives Bakounine*, ed. Lehning, vol. III, pp. xxi–xxii.

113. Enckell, *La Fédération*, p. 93.

114. Ibid., p. 94.

115. Guillaume, *L'Internationale*, vol. III, p. 52.

116. Dragomanov, *Pisma*, pp. 443–46.

117. Guillaume, *L'Internationale*, vol. III, pp. 79–81; *Archives Bakounine*, ed. Lehning, vol. V, pp. xlii–xlvi.

118. Guilluame, *L'Internationale*, vol. III, pp. 94–96; *Archives Bakounine*, ed. Lehning, vol. V, pp. xlvi–liv.

119. *Marx/Bakounine*, ed. Ribeill, vol. I, pp. 364, 403.

120. Ibid., vol. I, pp. 367, 369, 375–76.

121. Ibid., vol. I, pp. 364–65; vol. II, p. 29.

122. Ibid., vol. I, pp. 390–91, 394–97; vol. II, pp. 19–20, 43–45. One might take that last passage, although any one of countless others would do as well, to

illustrate the way Bakunin's social and political theory (and hardly only his) performs its "dream work." The "virgin" with his repressed "passions" and "instincts" and his resulting "deprivations and miseries" seeks through violence to achieve the union, reunion, "socialism" that would gratify the "passions" and end the "deprivations." In fact, latent "dream thought," as Freud called the hidden and real desires and fears, comes through the disguise of such intellectual theory far more clearly than it does through the usual dream process and symbols.

123. Ibid., vol. II, pp. 47, 48–49.

124. See above, pp. 153, 157.

125. For example, *Marx/Bakounine,* ed. Ribeill, vol. I, p. 367 *ff;* vol. II, pp. 23, 56 *ff.*

126. *Archives Bakounine,* ed. Lehning, vol. III, p. 344.

127. Ibid., vol. III, pp. 220, 347–49.

128. Ibid., vol. III, p. 223.

129. Guillaume, *L'Internationale,* vol. III, p. 100.

130. Ibid., vol. III, p. 98.

131. Ibid., vol. III, p. 100.

132. Ibid.

133. Ibid., vol. III, p. 101.

134. Ibid., vol. III, p. 102.

135. Ibid., vol. III, p. 141.

136. Ibid., vol. III, p. 142; *Archives Bakounine,* ed. Lehning, vol. V, pp. lii–liv. (Bakunin even offered to repay what he had borrowed from them, with money he now had from Cafiero, although they refused, at first, to take it unless they were also reimbursed for what they felt they had lost when Ross had taken over the library and the Zürich Press.) Guillaume, *L'Internationale,* vol. III, p. 142.

137. Guillaume, *L'Internationale,* vol. III, pp. 143–44.

138. For the two Congresses, see above, p. 398. (Changing "established" to "confirmed" is the secret Leninist program censored by the public anarchist ideal.)

139. Guillaume, *L'Internationale,* vol. III, pp. 145–47.

140. Ibid., vol. III, pp. 181–86, 203, note 2.

141. Ibid., vol. III, pp. 198–200. The point about leaving against his will is questioned. (Ibid., vol. III, p. 201, note 1.)

142. Ibid., vol. III, pp. 200–4.

143. Ibid., vol. III, pp. 205–6, 209.

144. Ibid., vol. III, pp. 209, 235–37. (If, as Erik Erikson argues, the way one meets the last years of life is a good indication of the psychological character and quality of that life, whether or not it fulfilled one's needs, aims, and potentials, then the despondency and deep sense of waste and failure that formed Bakunin's final years make an appropriate last act to his life of fear, flight, and self-deception. In this same connection, one should recall how often Bakunin spoke of suicide: see index under suicide and death wish.

145. Ibid., vol. III, pp. 236, 238, 254.

146. Dragomanov, *Pisma,* pp. 450–52.

147. Guillaume, *L'Internationale,* vol. III, pp. 256, 283–84.

148. Ibid., vol. III, pp. 284-85.

149. Ibid., vol. III, pp. 285-86.

150. E. Kornilov, "Novye pisma M. A. Bakunina," *Byloe* (Petrograd) No. 3 (1925): 52. Much of his thoughts and feelings now seemed to dwell in the Premukhino of old. "I would so much like to see Nicholas again," he wrote home March 1, 1875, "if only for the last time, and try to arrive at some under-standing with him, both about theoretical and practical matters. And you, dear sister Sasha, I ardently desire to see you. For, indeed, we two are the last of the Mohicans from the very first, the original Premukhino world, beginning with the time that we ran around the hanging lanterns and Tatiana and I went off together to the island.... Yes, I so want to see all of you, to embrace you all with a brother's passionate joy—only do come. You could do it easily now, and it would hold no political risks, since I now live completely apart from politics...." Considering the fact that he also refers to four of his brothers in this letter, it is significant that now, at the end of his life, he should single out his childhood relationship with his sisters, and particularly Tatiana, as the "original Premukhino world." Ibid.

151. Guillaume, *L'Internationale*, vol. III, p. 286.

152. Ibid., vol. III, p. 301.

153. Ibid., vol. III, p. 313.

154. A. Bauler, "M. A. Bakunin nakanun smerti," *Byloe* 7(1907):62-87.

155. Ibid., pp. 71-72.

156. Ibid., pp. 68, 78, 83.

157. Ibid., p. 76.

158. Guillaume, *L'Internationale*, vol. I, p. 261.

159. Bauler, "Bakunin," pp. 72-74, 76.

160. Ibid., pp. 77-78.

161. Ibid., pp. 69-70, 75, 79.

162. Ibid., p. 75.

163. Ibid., pp. 79-80.

164. Guillaume, *L'Internationale*, vol. IV, pp. 26, 27-28.

165. Ibid., vol. IV, pp. 28, 31-36.

166. Or so it was in the summer of 1971.

CHAPTER 12. REQUIEM

1. Bakunin's surprising defense of social determinism is also revealing in this regard: his insistence that "man is born into society just as an ant is born into its anthill or a bee into its hive," that the individual (including even his freedom) is basically a social product, that man is a "transient and hardly perceptible link in the universal chain of past, present, and future beings." Against the background of his defiant individualism and his refusal to become just a "futile, meaningless link in the chain of humanity," this seems indeed a strange argument for Bakunin to advance. Yet, it is essentially only one more example added to the many we have already seen of Bakunin's wish to merge with one or another larger whole—nature, spirit, cosmos, people, movement, or party—and one more expression of the deeper need for the maternal reunion that psycho-

logically motivated that constant desire. Disclosing the ultimate roots of that desire still more clearly, Bakunin described both society and nature as "our mother, who forms us, brings us up, feeds us, surrounds and penetrates us to the marrow of our bones, to the intimate depths of our intellectual and moral being...." Society "is not the product but the mother of the individual." Life itself would be impossible without that social umbilical cord: "Man is in no way nor could ever be free with respect to natural laws, with respect to social laws.... No living being would be able to revolt against them without committing suicide." And again: "No one can rebel against these immutable laws without immediately... committing certain suicide." And still again: "A rebellion on his part would be... a ridiculous attempt; it would be a revolt against himself, a veritable suicide." There could hardly be a more explicit imagery for the primary fear of separation, the need to remain within the security of the "symbolic couple."

So important did Bakunin consider this analogy between society/nature and maternal feeding and nurturing that he elevated it to the level of universal law: "This is the law of nutrition.... It is general and fundamental for all living beings. It is the question of nourishment, the great problem of social economy, that constitutes the real basis of all the subsequent developments of humanity." In his age as in his youth, the central concern remained that of being "fed and nurtured"—down to that "last puff." It is no wonder that oral imagery played as great a part in Bakunin's statements as oral obsessions did in his personal life.

As in virtually every part of Bakunin's life and thought, however, these narcissistic roots beneath Bakunin's social determinism are accompanied by those reflecting the oedipal crisis and the guilt associated with it. If society and nature determined everything, he argued, the individual could not be held guilty for his failings or his crimes; he "is freed of all juridical responsibility."

> If there is no animal responsibility, there can be no human responsibility, man being subject to the absolute omnipotence of nature as much as is the most imperfect animal of this earth; so that from the absolute point of view, animals and men are equally without responsibility....
> If one has become a criminal and another has not yet developed consciousness of his humanity and human duties, the fault is neither theirs nor even their nature, but rather that of the social environment in which they were born and have developed.... The perfect specimen is the one in which all the characteristic organs of the order to which the individual belongs are harmoniously developed. *The absence or the weakness of one of those organs constitutes a defect, and when an essential organ is involved, the individual is a monster.* Monstrosity or perfection, quality or defect, all of that is given to the individual by nature and received by him at birth.

Bakounine, *Oeuvres*, vol. I, pp. 105-6, 141-42, 179, 275; vol. III, pp. 245-48, 252, 259, 266 *ff*, 272; vol. V, pp. 158-60; vol. VI, p. 88. *The Political Philosophy of Bakunin: Scientific Anarchism.* ed. G. Maximoff (Glencoe, Ill.: Free Press. 1953), pp. 144, 157-59, 263. (Emphasis added.) In general,

Maximoff's collection of quotations provides a splendid introduction to Bakunin's social theory.

2. Throughout this conceptual evolution, from Schelling to "left" Hegel, Bakunin's basic dualism is the familiar gnostic polarity, reflecting in his case, I believe, the narcissistic split between an idealized all-good image (internalized) and an all-bad image (projected), the split by which the infant protects the maternal image from his own rage against the inevitable frustrations of infancy. In normal ego development the two sides are subsequently integrated, and the child, the individualized-separated self, comes to sense then know that everything, including himself and all things and persons objective to him, are both good and bad. It was Bakunin's failure ever fully to achieve this integration and separation compounded by his subsequent (and, in part, consequent) failure to meet the oedipal challenge successfully that were ultimately responsible for this gnostic division and its later career in his life and thought. In the Schelling scenario, the first phase of the projection has already occurred: while the "good" is kept within, the "bad" is hurled outside. (For further discussion of this "object relations" process, see the references listed in Chapter 1, note 83 and the concluding chapter of this study, "Narcissus and Oedipus.")

3. Quoted in *Political Philosophy*, ed. Maximoff, p. 65. Yet, he also knew that "except by suicide, partial or total, no man can ever free himself of his natural desire" and that there was a "perpetual fear which forms the depths of all animal existence and which dominates the natural and savage individual to the point that he finds nothing within himself with which to resist and fight it." Steklov, *Sobranie,* vol. I, p. 111. Letter to his relatives. May 12, 1833; *Political Philosophy,* ed. Maximoff, p. 95.

4. See index under psychology: dissimulation.

5. Ralli, "Iz moikh vospominanii," p. 333.

6. I have reviewed this psychological interpretation in the final chapter, "Narcissus and Oedipus." See the reference listed in Chapter 1, note, 83.

7. It is difficult to date with certainty the time that Bakunin abandoned his faith in God, or at least expressions of such faith. Documents dating from the period of his Freemasonic contacts in Florence (1864–65) suggest that he was already then a convinced and militant atheist, as we saw in Chapter 9. Another indication that his atheism emerged at this time and not before, or very long before, is found in remarks Turgenev made to Herzen in March 1869. Referring to the time he had last seen Bakunin, in London before the Ward Jackson fiasco, Turgenev said that Bakunin then "still believed in a personal God,... and reproached me for my disbelief." (Quoted in I. Malinin, *Komplex edipa i sudba Mikhaila Bakinina,* Belgrade: 1934; p. 43. More important, I believe, than the question of when he ceased believing in God is the question of why he continued to focus on God and religion after he became an atheist. What was the source of this virtual obsession, this furious and incessant war against the God that had meant so much to him for so long? Who was this hated God for him? Most obviously, he was the powerful male deity, the crowning symbol of repressive power, the hypostatized father that in Bakunin's permanent drama was, indeed, experienced as the implacable, despotic force compelling Bakunin to stifle "seething" needs and desires. But why did God become the target for

this? After all, Bakunin had the state and any number of other authorities to attack. To understand the place and meaning of God in this later-life confrontation, we must recall the meaning God and religion had for Bakunin during the years in which he saw himself, and explicitly portrayed himself, as not only walking in the footsteps of Jesus, but as becoming himself another voice of God, another savior (a conviction, we should keep in mind, that he carried with him right into his revolutionary career). In that early period, God and religion were, together with the maternal "friend" within, the provider and protector of his inner world of bliss and freedom. God and the "friend" were, in fact, one and the same—a maternal God. Later, when this romantic and Idealistic way of maternal return was abandoned, first because it lacked the outlet for a display of power and then because the Tatiana crisis of late 1836 disclosed the incestual character of the romantic introversion, he adopted the love-hate dialectic. Henceforth, the return and the bond were achieved not by merging lovingly with the maternal friend within, but by passionately hating her and her surrogates, now projected outwards. Since they had shared the inner world and were essentially one, it was natural that God should suffer the same reversal as the maternal image. He worshipped his maternal God by hatred in the same dialectical way that he hated his paternal God and his "evil passions" by expressions of love (and paid for it by life-long masochistic suffering).

8. See, for example, Peter Viereck, *Metapolitics: From the Romantics to Hitler* (New York: A. A. Knopf, 1941).

9. Whereas significant segments of the "intelligentsia" seem always to be more or less susceptible to apocalyptic visions (perhaps because they share so many personality traits of the apocalyptic visionaries), larger populations become so only during periods of grave assault on life and traditional values, periods of profound and persistent loss, insecurity, and uncertainty. At such times of social and/or cultural upheaval, they temporarily experience personality disorders because of objective social conditions in the same or similar way that theorists like Bakunin suffer such disorders as a result of basic and enduring character problems. It is then that the broad "masses" swoon to the "silvery voice" of the saviors, to recall Bakunin's apt phrase. By the time some semblance of stability has returned, it is usually too late: the saviors are already firmly in control. Such has been the pattern of apocalyptic movements and their aftermath at least from the beginning of the Christian ascendancy down to the Bolshevik and Fascist revolutions of our own era.

10. W. B. Yeats, "The Man and the Echo," *The Collected Poems of W. B. Yeats* (New York: Macmillan, 1959), p. 337.

11. Bakounine, *Oeuvres*, vol. VI, pp. 343–44; *Political Philosophy*, ed. Maximoff, pp. 288, 363.

12. Bakounine, *Oeuvres*, vol. I, pp. 226–27; *Political Philosophy*, ed. Maximoff, p. 289.

13. Bakounine, *Oeuvres*, vol. II, pp. 243–44.

14. Bakounine, *Oeuvres*, vol. I, p. 274; vol. V, p. 51; *Political Philosophy*, ed. Maximoff, pp. 354–56, 367, 370–71, 384; *Archives Bakounine*, ed. Lehning, vol. III, p. 26.

15. Bakounine, *Oeuvres*, vol. V, p. 198; *Political Philosophy*, ed. Maximoff, p. 371; Bakunin, *Izbrannie sochinenie*, vol. IV, p. 219.

16. Confino, "Bakunin and Nechaev," (August, 1972): vol. 39, p. 85.

17. *Political Philosophy*, ed. Maximoff, pp. 339, 345, 380–81, 412.

18. F. Dostoevsky, *The Possessed* (New York: Modern Library, 1936), pp. 409-10.

19. Bakounine, *Oeuvres*, vol. IV, p. 400; vol. VI, p. 362.

20. In addition to this stringent party centralization and complete party commitment and submission, there were also Bakunin's support for Comintern-like subordination of the different national parties to his International "junta's" party line (i.e., his own program and regulations) and his general insistence on rigorous party orthodoxy.

21. Quoted in Moissonnier, *La Première Internationale*, pp. 97–98, note 3.

22. For example, Nettlau, *M. Bakunin,* and Vyacheslav Polonskii, "Tainyi internatsional Bakunina," *Mikhail Bakunin. Neizdannye materialy i stati* (Moscow, 1926).

23. For "Kali," see the series of quotations listed at the beginning of this book.

24. A selection of Gospel apocalyptic declarations is also included in the prefatory quotations.

25. Rabbi Tarfon, *Avot* (Chapter II, Mishna (16). *The Talmud* (Nezikin VIII.)

APPENDIX. NARCISSUS AND OEDIPUS

1. Heinz Kohut, *The Restoration of the Self* (New York: International Universities Press, 1977), pp. 5-6.

2. For a summary of this part of the interpretation see the preceding chapter, pp. 433-434.

3. A brief bibliography of works that discuss the main theories and concepts reviewed in this chapter, especially "object relations" theory, can be found in the concluding note of chapter 1.

BIBLIOGRAPHY

The bibliography contains references only to sources cited in the study. It is not intended to be a full Bakunin bibliography. In particular, it includes only a few works from the vast secondary literature that has grown up around Bakunin and his influence. Also, the focus of the biography and, consequently, the emphasis of the bibliography are on Bakunin himself and not on the numerous groups and individuals who regarded themselves as his followers.

Annenkov, P.V. *The Extraordinary Decade*. Translated by Irwin R. Titunic. Edited by Arthur P. Mendel. Ann Arbor: University of Michigan Press, 1968.

Archives Bakounine. Vols. I-VI. Edited by Arthur Lehning. Leiden: Brill, 1961–77.

Bakounine, M. *Confession*. Translated by Paulette Brupbacher. Paris: Les Éditions Rieder, 1932.

Bakounine, M. *De la querre à la Commune (Textes de 1870–1871)*. Edited by Fernand Rude. Paris: Éditions anthropos, 1972.

Bakounine, M. *Federalism, Socialisme, Antitheologisme*. Lausanne: Éditions l'Age d'Homme, 1971.

Bakounine, M. *Oeuvres*. Vols. I-VI. Edited by James Guillaume. Paris: Stock, 1907–1913.

Bakunin, M. *Gesammelte Werke*. Vols. I-III. Edited by Max Nettlau. Berlin: Der Syndikalist, 1921–1924.

Bakunin, M. *God and State*. New York: Dover, 1970.

Bakunin, M. *Izbrannye sochinenie*. Vols. I-V. Petersburg-Moscow: Golos Truda, 1920–1922.

Bakunin, M. "Neskolko slov iuzhnyi slavian." *Kolokol* (April 8, 1862)

Bakunin, M. "Pisma M.A. Bakunina k Grafine E.B. Salias." *Letopisi Marksizma* (1927), No. 3.

Bakunin, M. "Pisma M.A. Bakunina k bratu Aleksandru i N.I. Turgenevu," *Letopisi Marksizma.* 9–10 (1929).

Bakunin, M. "Pismo Bakunina neizvestnomu." *Byloe.* 8 (1906).

Bakunin, M. "Reaction in Germany." Translated by Mary Barbara Zeldin. In *Russian Philosophy.* Vol. I, edited by Edie Scanlan, and Zeldin. Chicago: Quadrangle Books, 1965.

Bakunin, M. "Russkim, polskim i vsem slavianskim druziam." *Kolokol* (February 15, 1862).

Bakunin, M. *Sobranie sochinenii i pisem, 1828-1876.* Vols. I-IV. Edited by Y. M. Steklov. Moscow: Vsesoiuznovo obshchestva politkatorzhan i ssylno-poselentsev, 1934-36.

Bauler, A. "M.A. Bakunin nakanun smerti." *Byloe* (1907). No. 7.

Belinksii, V. *Polnoe sobranie sochinenii.* Vols. I-XIII. Moscow: Academy of Sciences, 1953-59.

Belinskii, V. *Selected Philosophical Works.* Moscow: Foreign Language Publishing House, 1956.

Berezina, V. "Belinskii i Bakunin v 1830 godu." *Uchenye zapiski Leningradskogo. Gosudarstvennogo ordena Lenina Universiteta.* Seriia filologicheskii fakultet. Leningrad (1952), No. 158.

Boutard, C. *Lammenais. Sa vie et ses doctrines.* Vols. I-III. Paris: Perrin, 1905–13.

Brazill, W. *The Young Hegelians.* New Haven, Conn.: Yale University Press, 1970.

Brown, E. *Stankevich and his Moscow Circle. 1830-1840.* Stanford, Calif.: Stanford University Press, 1966.

Brupbacher, F. *Michel Bakounine ou le démon de la révolte.* Annotated translation by Jean Barrué. Paris: Editions du Cercle, Editions de la Tête de Feuilles, 1971.

Carr, E. *Michael Bakunin.* New York: Vintage, 1961; [1937]

Cafiero, O. "Carlo Cafiero," *Golos minuvshego* (May 1914).

Cieszkowski, A. *Prolegomena zur Historiosophie.* Berlin: 1838.

Confino, M., ed. *Daughter of a Revolutionary: Natalie Herzen and the Bakunin-Nechaev Circle.* London: Alcove, 1974.

Confino, M. ed. "Bakunin and Nechaev." *Encounter* 39 (July 1972 and August 1872)

Confino, M. *Violence dans la Violence.* Paris: Francois Maspero, 1973.

Documents anarchistes. 1969, No. 2, 1967 and No. 7.

Dostoevsky, F. *The Possessed.* New York: Modern Library, 1936.

Dragomanov, M., ed. *Pisma M.A. Bakunina k A.I. Gertzenu i N.P. Ogarevu.* St. Petersburg: Brublevskii, 1906.

El, E. "M. Bakunin v Shveitsarii." *Severnii vestnik* (April 1898).

Enckell, *La Fédération jurassienne.* Lausanne: La Cité, 1971.

Evreinov, B. "Bakunin i slavianskii siezd 1848 goda v Prage." *Russki Nauchnyi Institut. Belgrad. Zapiski* 13 (1936).

Evreinov, B. "M.A. Bakunin i Avstriiskia vlasti v 1849-1851 godakh." *Russkii svobodnyi universitet. Prague. Nauchno-issledovatelskie obedineniie zapiski* 4 (1931).

Fichte, J. "Einige Vorlesungen uber die Bestimmung des Gelehrten." *Johann Gottlieb Fichte's Samtliche Werke*. Vols. I-VIII. Berlin: Veit, 1845–46.
Fichte, J. "The Way towards the Blessed Life." *The Popular Works of Johann Gottlieb Fichte*. Vols. I-II. Translated by William Smith. London: Trübner, 1889.
Florinsky, M. *Russia: A History and an Interpretation*. Vols. I-II. New York: Macmillan, 1953.
Freymond, J. *Études et documents sur la Première Internationale en Suisse*. Genève: Librairie Droz, 1964.
Glinskii, B. "M.A. Bakunin i ego begstvo iz Sibiri." *Istoricheskii vestnik*, (1898), No. 3.
Granjard, H. *Ivan Tourguenev et les courants politiques et sociaux de son temps*. Paris: Institut d'études Slaves de l'Université de Paris, 1954.
Guerin, D. *Ni dieu ni maître*. Paris: Éditions de Delphes, n.d.
Guillaume, J. *L'Internationale*. Paris: Société nouvelle de librairie et d'edition, 1905, 1907 (vols. I-II) and Stock, 1909, 1910 (vols. III-IV).
Helps, A. *Bettina. A. Portrait*. New York: Reynal, 1957.
Herzen, A. *My Past and Thoughts*. Vols. I-IV. New York: Knopf, 1968.
Herzen, A. *Mikhail Bakunin i Polskoe delo*. Berlin: G. Steinitz, n.d.
Herzen, A. *Selected Philosophical Works*. Translated by L. Navrozov. Moscow: Foreign Language Publication House, 1956.
Herzen, A. *Sobranie sochinenii*. Vols. I–XXX. Moscow: Academy of Sciences, 1954–65.
Holbrook, D. *Human Hope and the Death Instinct*. Oxford, New York: Pergamon, 1971.
Jeanne-Marie, *Michel Bakounine. Une vie d'homme*. Genève: Noir, 1976.
Klein, T. *1848: Der Vorkampf Deutscher Einheit und Freiheit*. Munchen-Leipzig: W. Langeswische-Brandt, 1914.
Kohut, H. *The Restoration of the Self*. New York: International Universities Press, 1977.
Kolokol. (London). November 22, 1861; January 1, January 15, April 8, 1862.
Kornilov, A. *Gody stranstvii M. Bakunina*. Moscow: Gosudarstvennogo Izdatel-stvo, 1925.
Kornilov, A. *Molodye gody Mikhaila Bakunina*. Moscow: M. and S. Sabashnikov, 1915.
Kornilova, E. "Novye pisma M.A. Bakunina." *Byloe*. (1925), No. 3.
Kornilova, E. "Pisma Zheny M.A. Bakunina." *Katorga i ssylka*. (1932), No. 3.
Kubalov, B. "Stranitsy iz zhizni M.A. Bakunin i ego semi v Sibiri." *Sbornik trudov professorov i prepodavatelei Gosudarstvennogo Irkutskogo universiteta*. (Irkutsk, 1923), No. 5.
Kucharzewski, J. *The Origins of Modern Russia*. New York: Polish Institute of Arts and Sciences in America, 1948.
Kun, M. "Bakunin and Hungary (1848–1865)" *Canadian-American Slavic Studies*. 10 (1976).
Lehning, A. "Bakunin's Conceptions of Revolutionary Organisations and their Role: A Study of His 'Secret Societies'." In *Essays in Honour of E.H. Carr*, edited by C. Abramsky. Hamden, Conn.: Archon Books, 1974.

Lehning, A. "Michael Bakounine. Theorie et Pratique du Fédéralisme ante-Etatique en 1870-1871." *International Review of Social History* 17 (1972).

Lemke, M. "Vosemnadstat pisem M.A. Bakunina." *Byloe.* (July 1906)

Lobkowicz, N. *Theory and Practice: History of a Concept from Aristotle to Marx.* Notre Dame, Ind.: University of Notre Dame Press, 1967.

Loewald, H. "The Waning of the Oedipus Complex." *Papers on Psychoanalysis.* New Haven: Yale University Press, 1980.

Malia, M. *Alexander Herzen and the Birth of Russian Socialism.* Cambridge, Mass.: Harvard University Press, 1961.

Malinin, I. *Kompleks edipa i sudba Mikhaila Bakunina.* Belgrade: 1934.

Maximoff, G., ed. *The Political Philosophy of Bakunin: Scientific Anarchism.* Glencoe, Ill. Free Press, 1953.

Mehring, F. *Karl Marx.* Ann Arbor: University of Michigan Press, 1962.

Menchikov, L. "Bakunin v Italii v 1864." *Istoricheskii vestnik.* (March, 1897).

McLellan, D. *The Young Hegelians and Karl Marx.* New York: Praeger, 1969.

Moissonnier, M. *La Première Internationale et la Commune à Lyon.* Paris: Éditions Sociales, 1972.

Montbé, A. *Der Mai-Aufstand in Dresden.* Dresden; 1850.

Nettlau, M. *La Première Internationale en Espagne* (1868-1888). Dordrecht: Holland: D. Reidel, 1969.

Nettlau, M. *Michael Bakunin. Ein Biographie.* Vols. I-III. London, 1896-1900. Photocopy of the manuscript, Milan: Feltrinelli, 1971.

Newman, E. *The Life of Richard Wagner.* Vols. I-IV. New York: Knopf, 1933-46.

Nikolaevski, B. "Bakunin epokhi evo pervoi emigratsii v vospominaniakh nemstev-sovremenikov." *Katorga i ssylka* 8-9 (1930).

Oksman, Y.G. *Letopis zhizn i tvorchestva V.G. Belinskogo.* Moscow: Gosudarstvennogo Izdatelstvo, 1958.

Pfitzner, J. *Bakuninstudien.* Prague: Verlag der Deutschen Gesellschaft der Wissenschaften und Künste für die Tschechoslawakische Republik, 1932.

Pirumova, N. *Bakunin.* Moscow: Molodaia gvardiia, 1970.

Pirumova, N. "Bakunin and Herzen: An Analysis of their Ideological Disagreements at the End of the 1860s." *Canadian-American Slavic Studies* 10 (1976).

Polonskii, V. "M. Bakunin i ekspeditsiia 'Ward Jackson'." *Krasnii Archiv* 7 (1924).

Polonskii, V., ed. *Materialy dlia biographii M. Bakunina.* Vols. I-III. Moscow: Gosudarstvennoe Izdatelstvo, 1923-33.

Pomper, P. *Sergei Nechaev.* New Brunswick: Rutgers University Press, 1979.

Pomper, P. *The Russian Revolutionary Intelligentsia.* New York: Crowell, 1970.

Ralli, Z. "Iz moikh vospominanii o M.A. Bakunine." *O minuvshem.* (St. Petersburg) 1909.

Ralli, Z. "Mikhail Bakunin iz moikh vospominanii." *Minuvshie gody.* (1908), No. 10.

Ribeill, G., ed. *Marx/Bakounine: Socialism autoritare ou libertaire.* Vols. I-II. Paris: Union Générale D'Éditions, 1975.

Richard, A. "Bakounine et L'Internationale á Lyon." *La Revue de Paris* (September, 1896).

Röckel, A. *Sachsens Erhebung und das Zuchthaus zu Waldheim.* Frankfurt a. M.; 1865.

Rosenberg, H. "Arnold Ruge und die 'Hallischen Jahrbucher'." *Archiv für Kulturgeschichte* 20, book 3.

Rude, F. "Bakounine à Lyon en Septembre, 1870." *Actes du soixante-dix-septieme Congrès des Sociêtés Savantes.* Grenoble; 1952.

Saretsky, L., Goldman, G., and Milman, D., eds. *Integrating Ego Psychology and Object Relations Theory.* Dubuque, Iowa: Kendall-Hunt, 1979.

Schecter, D. "The Oedipus Complex: Consideration of Ego Development and Parental Interaction." *Contemporary Psychoanalysis.* (spring 1968).

Shashko, P. *Unity and Dissent Among the Russian Westerners.* Ph.D. dissertation, University of Michigan, 1969.

Simmons, E. *English Literature and Culture in Russia.* Cambridge, Mass: Harvard University Press, 1935.

Stankevich, N. *Perepiska. 1830–1840.* Moscow: Alekseia Stankevich, 1914.

Steklov, Y.M. "Bakunin i revoliutsiia 1848 g." *Katorga i ssylka.* 6–8 (1933)

Steklov, Y.M. *Mikhail Aleksandrovich Bakunin. Ego zhizn i dieiatelnost.* Moscow: Izdatelstvo Kommunisticheskoi Akademii, 1926–27.

Valentin, V. *Geschichte der deutschen Revolution von 1848–1849.* Vols. I-II. Berlin: Ullstein, 1930–31.

Varnhagen von Ense, *Tagebücher.* Leipzig: F.A. Brockhaus, 1863.

Viereck, P. *Metapolitics: From the Romantics to Hitler.* New York: A.A. Knopf, 1941.

Vuilleumier, M. "Bakounine, L'Alliance Internationale de la démocratie socialiste et la première Internationale a Genève (1868–1869)." *Cahiers Vilfredo Pareto* (1964).

Vuilleumier, M. "L'anarchisme et les conceptions de Bakounine sur l'organisation revolutionnaire." *Anarchiei e anarchia nel mondo contemporaneo.* Torino, 1971.

Wagner, Richard. *Samtliche Briefe.* Leipzig: Deutscher Verlag Für Musik, 1970.

Yeats, W. *The Collected Poems of W.B. Yeats.* New York: Macmillan, 1956.

Zenkovsky, V. *A History of Russian Philosophy.* Translated by George L. Kline. Vols. I-II. London: Routledge & Kegan Paul, 1953.

INDEX

ABOUT THE AUTHOR

ARTHUR P. MENDEL is Professor of History at the University of Michigan, where he has taught since 1962. Before that, he was on the faculties of Roosevelt University (Chicago), the State University of Iowa, and New York University.

Among Professor Mendel's principal publications are *Dilemmas of Progress in Tsarist Russia* (Harvard University Press, 1961), *The Essential Works of Marxism* (Bantam Press, 1961), *The Twentieth Century* (Colliers Press, 1964), Paul Miliukov. *Political Memoirs* and P.V. Annenkov. *The Extraordinary Decade* (edited for the University of Michigan Press) in 1967 and 1968, respectively. He was also co-translator of the *Short Stories of Tolstoy* (Bantam Press,) and has published articles in the *American Slavic and East European Review, Slavic Review, American Historical Review, History and Theory, Foreign Affairs, Ingenor, The New Republic,* the *Review of Politics* and in two collections, *Russia Under the Last Tsar* (University of Minnesota, 1969) and *Russian Thought and Politics* (Harvard University Press, 1957).

Professor Mendel received his B.A. from Roosevelt University (then College) in 1950 and his M.A. and Ph.D. from Harvard Univesrity in 1952 and 1956, respectively.